COMPARATIVE COMPANY Law

As attention moves rapidly towards comparative approaches, the research and teaching of company law has somehow lagged behind. The overall purpose of this book is therefore to fill a gap in the literature by identifying whether conceptual differences between countries exist. Rather than concentrate on whether the institutional structure of the corporation varies across jurisdictions, the objective of this book will be pursued by focusing on specific cases and how different countries might treat each of these cases. The book also has a public policy dimension because the existence or absence of differences may lead to the question of whether formal harmonisation of company law is necessary.

The book covers 12 legal systems from different legal traditions and from different parts of the world (though with a special emphasis on European countries). In alphabetical order, those countries are: Finland, France, Germany, Italy, Japan, Latvia, the Netherlands, Poland, South Africa, Spain, the UK, and the US. All of these jurisdictions are subjected to scrutiny by deploying a comparative case-based study. On the basis of these case solutions, various conclusions are reached, some of which challenge established orthodoxies in the field of comparative company law.

Comparative Company Law

A Case-Based Approach

2nd edition

Edited by
Mathias Siems
and
David Cabrelli

·HART·
OXFORD · LONDON · NEW YORK · NEW DELHI · SYDNEY

HART PUBLISHING

Bloomsbury Publishing Plc

Kemp House, Chawley Park, Cumnor Hill, Oxford, OX2 9PH, UK

HART PUBLISHING, the Hart/Stag logo, BLOOMSBURY and the Diana logo are
trademarks of Bloomsbury Publishing Plc

First published in Great Britain 2018

First edition published 2013

A catalogue record for this book is available from the British Library.

Library of Congress Cataloging-in-Publication data

Names: Siems, Mathias M., 1974- editor. | Cabrelli, David A., editor.

Title: Comparative company law : a case-based approach / edited by Mathias Siems and David Cabrelli.

Description: 2nd edition. | Oxford, United Kingdom ; Portland, Oregon : Hart Publishing,
an imprint of Bloomsbury, 2018. | Includes bibliographical references and index.

Identifiers: LCCN 2018019378 (print) | LCCN 2018021014 (ebook) | ISBN 9781509909353 (Epub) |
ISBN 9781509909360 (pbk. : alk. paper) | ISBN 9781509909346 (ePDF)

Subjects: LCSH: Corporation law.

Classification: LCC K1315 (ebook) | LCC K1315 .C663 2018 (print) | DDC 346/.066—dc23

LC record available at https://lccn.loc.gov/2018019378

ISBN: PB: 978-1-50990-936-0
        ePub: 978-1-50990-935-3

Typeset by Compuscript Ltd, Shannon
Printed and bound in Great Britain by CPI Group (UK) Ltd, Croydon CR0 4YY

To find out more about our authors and books visit www.hartpublishing.co.uk.
Here you will find extracts, author information, details of forthcoming events
and the option to sign up for our newsletters.

Preface

As attention moves rapidly towards comparative approaches, the research and teaching of company law has somehow lagged behind. Existing books on comparative company law tend to focus on the institutional structure of the corporation, but this approach risks overlooking specific cases and how the issues arising from disputes are resolved in different jurisdictions. For example, topics related to directors' duties and liability, creditor protection and shareholders' rights may best be understood by analysing how selected hypothetical cases would be solved in different countries. It is the purpose of this book to fill this gap.

The book covers 12 legal systems from different legal traditions and from different parts of the world. In alphabetical order, those countries are: Finland, France, Germany, Italy, Japan, Latvia, the Netherlands, Poland, South Africa, Spain, the UK, and the US. The strong focus on European countries aims to reflect the ongoing debate about the impact of EU harmonisation in company law. In addition, the laws of the US, Japan, and South Africa are included for the purposes of wider comparison. From a comparative perspective, the US is the most important 'exporter' of corporate governance theories and ideas, while Japan and South Africa are good examples of legal systems shaped by diverse foreign models.

This book is primarily directed at anyone interested in company law and, in particular, in its international and comparative context. Thus, the audience may be academics, researchers and students in company law from any one of the countries covered, and possibly further afield as well. Since the book provides a case-based introduction to the company laws of different countries, it may also amount to a valuable resource for legal practitioners. Furthermore, general comparative lawyers may be interested in the results of the case-based studies as they serve to shed light on whether there are clear differences between different legal families or whether functionally similar solutions are prevalent across a wide variety of jurisdictions.

We owe an immense debt of gratitude to each of the authors and country experts who so generously and effortlessly gave of their time, namely Sonja Siggberg, Jesse Collin and Lena Nordman (Finland), Pierre-Henri Conac (France), Marco Ventoruzzo and Corrado Malberti (Italy), Hisaei Ito and Hiroyuki Watanabe (Japan), Theis Klauberg (Latvia), Mieke Olaerts and Bastiaan Kemp (the Netherlands), Michał Żurek and Kamil Szmid (Poland), Irene-marié Esser and Piet Delport (South Africa) Pablo Iglesias-Rodríguez (Spain), Martin Gelter, Nemika Jha and D Gordon Smith (US). Without their sustained input, industry and patience, this project would never have come to fruition. Although each of these contributors between them can lay claim to have supplied the detailed raw material on which many of the conclusions and findings of this study were reached, they bear no responsibility for any of the shortcomings of this book.

The first edition of this book was published in 2013. We are grateful for both the positive reception of the first edition and constructive comments by friends and

colleagues. We also thank Hart Publishing for their ongoing support. The main structure of the book has remained unchanged in the second edition. However, the following
changes have been made: (i) some of the case scenarios have been modified, in particular clarifying some previous ambiguities; (ii) two jurisdictions, the Netherlands and
South Africa, have been added to all of the case studies; (iii) the general conclusion
of this book has been expanded, now with two concluding chapters adopting different methodologies; and (iv) we have sought to bring the law in our work up to date
to 1 November 2017, but some subsequent developments have been included where
possible.

Mathias Siems
David Cabrelli
Durham/Edinburgh
2 March 2018

Contents

PARTS 1 to 3
COMPARATIVE CASE STUDIES

Country reports by Sonja Siggberg, Jesse Collin and Lena Nordman (Finland), Pierre-Henri Conac (France), Mathias Siems (Germany), Marco Ventoruzzo and Corrado Malberti (Italy), Hisaei Ito and Hiroyuki Watanabe (Japan), Theis Klauberg (Latvia), Mieke Olaerts and Bastiaan Kemp (the Netherlands), Michał Żurek and Kamil Szmid (Poland), Irene-marié Esser and Piet Delport (South Africa), Pablo Iglesias-Rodríguez (Spain), David Cabrelli (UK), Martin Gelter, Nemika Jha and D Gordon Smith (US)

PART 1
DIRECTORS' DUTIES AND LIABILITY

PART 2
CREDITOR PROTECTION

PART 3
SHAREHOLDER PROTECTION

PART 4
CONCLUSION

List of Contributors

David Cabrelli (*UK, chapters 1, 10 and 12 and general editor*) is a Professor of Law at the University of Edinburgh. He is also a qualified solicitor, having practised corporate and commercial law for six years prior to taking up an academic post. He has held a visiting scholarship at St John's College, University of Oxford. His active research interests include company law, commercial law, comparative law and labour law. He is the author of various articles in these areas of law and has published a number of books on labour law and Scots commercial law.

Jesse Collin (*Finland and chapter 5 in the second edition*) currently works as an associate lawyer at Hannes Snellman Attorneys Ltd and as a doctoral candidate at the University of Helsinki. In private practice, he regularly advises on equity capital market transactions and complex corporate matters. His doctoral research focuses on traditional company law as well as the regulation of capital markets in the EU. He is a frequent lecturer at the University of Helsinki and has published in the field of capital markets, company and co-operatives law.

Pierre-Henri Conac (*France and chapter 8*) (ECGI Research associate) is a Professor of Commercial and Company Law at the University of Luxembourg. From 1999 to 2006, he was Associate Professor of Law at the University of Paris 1 (Panthéon-Sorbonne). He graduated from the University of Paris 1 (Panthéon-Sorbonne) in business law, from the HEC School of Management and from the Institute of Political Studies of Paris. He also obtained an LLM from Columbia Law School (1995). He has written numerous articles on corporate, securities and comparative law, both in French and in English. He is Managing Editor of the *Revue des sociétés*, France's oldest corporate law review, and is one of the editors of the *European Company and Financial Law Review*. He has been a member of the EU Commission-appointed Reflection Group on the Future of EU Company Law (2011) and the Informal Company Law Expert Group (2014–18). Since 2017, he has been the chair of the commission of law professors which has published the European Model Company Act (EMCA).

Piet Delport (*South Africa*) (LLB, LLD (Pret), H DipTax Law (Wits)) is a Professor in Mercantile Law at the University of Pretoria, South Africa where he teaches company law and securities law at post-graduate level. He is the author of various textbooks, such as *The New Companies Act Manual* and editor and author of *Henochsberg on the Companies Act 71 of 2008*. He has published articles in academic journals on the subjects of corporate and securities law and is a member of the Companies Tribunal.

Irene-marié Esser (*South Africa and chapter 12 in the second edition*) is a Senior Lecturer in Commercial Law at the University of Glasgow, a Professor Extraordinarius at the University of South Africa (UNISA) and a Visiting Professor at the Open University, UK. She is also an expert panel member of the EU/Africa Chamber of Commerce. She acted as an external adviser to the South African King IV Report on Corporate

Governance. In South Africa she was Professor and Co-Subject Head of Corporate Law at UNISA until March 2013, when she relocated, with her family, to Edinburgh, Scotland. She obtained her LLB at Stellenbosch University (2001), her LLM at the University of Aberdeen, Scotland (2003) and her LLD at UNISA (2008). She is also an admitted attorney of the High Court of South Africa. She has published mainly in company law, corporate governance and CSR in the UK and South Africa. She currently teaches corporate governance, corporate social responsibility and company law and supervises postgraduate research students in South Africa and the United Kingdom.

Martin Gelter (*US and chapter 3 in the second edition*) is Professor of Law at Fordham University School of Law and a Research Associate of the European Corporate Governance Institute (ECGI). He holds doctoral degrees in law from the University of Vienna (Dr. iur.) and Harvard Law School (S.J.D.) and in business administration from WU Vienna University of Economics and Business (Dr.rer.soc.oec). He was previously an assistant professor at the Department of Civil Law and Business Law at WU Vienna University of Economics and Business, an Olin Fellow and Considine Fellow in Law and Economics at Harvard Law School, a Visiting Fellow at the University of Bologna, and a Visiting Professor at the University of Paris-II (Panthéon-Assas). He is also a member of the New York Bar. His research focuses on comparative corporate governance, legal issues of accounting and auditing, corporate bankruptcy, and economic analysis of private law, and he has been published in various leading European and American journals.

Pablo Iglesias-Rodríguez (*Spain and chapter 4*) is Senior Lecturer in International Finance Law at the University of Sussex. Previously, he held academic positions at the VU University Amsterdam (Senior Researcher) and Maastricht University/Montesquieu Institute (Postdoctoral Researcher). He also held a Jean Monnet Fellowship (GGP) at the Robert Schuman Centre for Advanced Studies of the European University Institute. He is a graduate of the University of Vigo (Licenciatura en Derecho and MPhil in Applied Financial Economics) and the European University Institute (MRes and PhD in Law). He is also a qualified lawyer (Madrid Bar Association). His academic experience includes visiting engagements at various institutions, such as the University of Cambridge, Columbia University, the University of Padova, and the Warsaw University of Technology. He was also an intern at the Spanish Chamber of Commerce in France and the European Commission, DG Internal Market and Services. His main areas of research and publishing are financial law and company law.

Hisaei Chuck Ito (*Japan and chapter 6*) is a Professor at Chuo University Law School, Japan, specialising in commercial, finance and banking law. He has held visiting appointments at Georgetown Law Center, Duke University School of Law, the University of Hong Kong and the Australian National University. He is also the Director at the Institute of Comparative Law in Japan, Chuo University.

Bastiaan Kemp (*The Netherlands*) is Assistant Professor at the Faculty of Law, Maastricht University. He is also a qualified corporate lawyer at Loyens & Loeff (Amsterdam). He graduated from Maastricht University in 2013 and obtained his PhD at the same university in 2015 with a thesis on 'Shareholders' Responsibility: The Position and

Role of Shareholders and the Shareholders' Meeting'. He is a member of the editorial board of *Maandblad voor Ondernemingsrecht*, a Dutch corporate law review, and has authored publications on a wide range of corporate law and civil procedural law issues.

Theis Klauberg (*Latvia and chapter 2*) is a partner of bnt attorneys in CEE based in Riga, Latvia. He graduated from Humboldt University, Berlin, and also holds an LLM from the University of the Western Cape, South Africa, as well as an MBA from the Baltic Management Institute in Vilnius, Lithuania. He is a member of the bar associations of Hamburg, Latvia, Lithuania, and Estonia, and a board member of the German Baltic Chamber of Commerce. He has authored a number of publications on commercial law issues with a focus on the Baltic states and Central/Eastern Europe.

Corrado Malberti (*Italy and chapter 11*) has been Associate Professor of Commercial Law at the University of Trento since 2015. From 2010 to 2015 he was Associate Professor of Commercial Law at University of Luxembourg, where he was also director of the Master 1 in European Law. He graduated from the University of Milan. He completed an LLM at the University of Chicago and a PhD in Commercial Law at Bocconi University. He has published widely in the fields of company law and financial market regulation in English, Italian and French.

Nemika Jha (*US and chapter 3 in the second edition*) is an Assistant Professor at the Jindal Global Law School (India) and specialises in M&A and project finance. She is also pursuing a doctoral degree in law at Fordham University School of Law (USA). She has previously worked as an associate at Amarchand & Mangaldas & Suresh A. Shroff & Co. (India's premier law firm) and as an advocate at the Supreme Court of India where she advised clients on matters pertaining to mergers and acquisitions, commercial litigation and arbitration. She is a member of the New York Bar and has also worked at Chadbourne & Parke LLP (Washington DC) as an associate in its project finance team where she represented project developers, multilateral agencies and commercial banks in domestic and international project financings. Her research interests include M&A, corporate governance, comparative takeover regulation and project finance.

Lena Nordman (*Finland and chapter 5 in the first edition*) graduated from the University of Helsinki and has worked as a judge, arbitrator and advocate in Finland for more than 15 years, specialising in company and commercial law.

Mieke Olaerts (*The Netherlands*) is Professor of Comparative and National Company Law at the Faculty of Law, Maastricht University. She is also the Academic Director of the Maastricht Institute for Corporate Law, Governance and Innovation Policies (ICGI) and Of Counsel at a law firm in the Hague: DVDW Advocaten. Her research interests are in the area of company law with a focus, amongst others, on liability issues, company groups and corporate governance. She is member of the editorial board of European Company Law and *Tijdschrift voor Ondernemingsbestuur*, a Dutch corporate law review.

Mathias Siems (*Germany, chapters 1, 9 and 13 and general editor*) is Professor of Commercial Law at Durham University. He first studied in Munich and worked as a practising lawyer in Berlin. He also completed an LLM at the University of Edinburgh and has held visiting research positions at the European University Institute, Harvard Law School and the University of Cambridge. He has published many articles and books on comparative company law, both in English and in German.

Sonja Siggberg (*Finland and chapter 5 in the second edition*) is a partner at Hannes Snellman Attorneys Ltd specialising in private and public M&A, capital markets transactions as well as corporate governance related matters. She has advised clients on a number of equity and debt capital market transactions (both domestic and international), including IPOs, secondary share issues, public takeovers and bond issues. She also advises clients in general securities markets and corporate and law matters. She is a trusted adviser in disclosure, insider and corporate governance matters as well as other securities markets-related regulatory matters. She has been top ranked as a business lawyer by several independent market researchers. She is a graduate of the University of Helsinki.

D Gordon Smith (*US and chapter 3 in the first edition*) is Glen L Farr Professor of Law at J Reuben Clark Law School, Brigham Young University (BYU). After graduating with a JD from the University of Chicago, he was an associate in the Delaware office of the international law firm Skadden, Arps, Slate, Meagher & Flom, where he specialised in corporate and securities transactions. Prior to joining the law faculty at BYU, he taught for five years at the University of Wisconsin Law School and for six years at Lewis & Clark Law School. He has been a Visiting Professor at Vanderbilt University Law School, Arizona State University College of Law and Washington University School of Law, and he has taught courses at universities in China, Germany, Australia, Finland and France. His research interests relate to corporate and securities law, with special emphases on entrepreneurial finance and fiduciary duties.

Kamil Szmid (*Poland and chapter 7*) holds a PhD in Private Commercial Law from the Jagiellonian University, Krakow with a thesis on 'The Nature of a Joint Stock Company as a Determinant for the Application of the Principles of Freedom of Contract in Polish and American Law'. He has held visiting research positions at Yale Law School, the Max-Planck-Institut für ausländisches und internationales Privatrecht in Hamburg, Cornell Law School (Henry G Henn Memorial Prize in Corporations 2005) and the Katholieke Universiteit Leuven. He is a managing partner in KML Legal Szmid Sander Attorneys at Law, practising mainly in the fields of commercial litigation and arbitration, company and securities law, commercial contracts and real estate law. He has represented clients before arbitration tribunals, common courts, the Polish Office for Competition and Consumer Protection and the National Chamber of Appeals for public procurement. He is a member of District Bar Council of Warsaw Bar Association and has created a new practitioners programme within the structures of the Polish Bar Association.

Marco Ventoruzzo (*Italy and chapter 11*) is a Professor of Corporate Law at Bocconi University in Milan, Italy and a Professor of Law at the Dickinson School of Law, Pennsylvania State University, as well as a qualified Italian advocate. He studied economics and law in Milan, completed a PhD at the University of Brescia and an LLM at Yale. He has also held visiting posts at Louisiana State University, the

University of Hamburg and Fudan University, Shanghai. He has published widely in the fields of company and securities law, both in English and in Italian.

Hiroyuki Watanabe (*Japan and chapter 6*) is a Professor at the Faculty of Law, Waseda University, Japan, specialising in commercial and finance law. He has an LLM degree from the University of Tokyo and has held visiting appointments at the Max Planck Institute for Comparative and International Private Law etc. He has written English articles on company law, securities law and the law of trusts.

Michał Żurek (*Poland and chapter 7*) holds a PhD in Private Commercial Law from the Jagiellonian University, Krakow Poland with a thesis on 'The Reform of the Legal Capital Regulation in Private Limited Liability Companies'. He was a visiting researcher at the Max Planck Institute for Comparative and International Law in Hamburg. He is now a practising lawyer specialised in M&A transactions, corporate restructures and banking law. His contribution to the second edition of this book has been supported by the Polish National Science Center, with funding granted on the basis of decision DEC-2012/07/N/HS5/00991.

1

A Case-Based Approach to Comparative Company Law

DAVID CABRELLI AND MATHIAS SIEMS

I. Introduction

Two developments in recent years inspired the editors and country experts to come together to write this book on comparative company law. First, it reflects the extensive policy debate about the need to improve company law as well as other areas of commercial and financial law. The global financial crisis of 2008 generated a great deal of soul-searching within the wider commercial and regulatory community with regard to the effectiveness of existing laws and the general acceptability of corporate behaviour. For example, the 2015 revision of the G20/OECD Principles of Corporate Governance was justified as a 'a means to support economic efficiency, sustainable growth and financial stability'.[1] In the European Union, a 2017 consultation on 'EU Company law upgraded' followed on from various other recent initiatives that re-visited questions of company law and corporate governance,[2] and there are also examples of recent reforms and proposals in many domestic legal systems.[3]

The second driver of this project was the exponential growth in interest in comparative company law in the academic world and the community of legal practitioners. Since the early 2000s, many monographs and edited collections were published exploring this field of enquiry.[4] The burgeoning literature was mirrored by an increase in university

---

[1] See www.oecd.org/corporate/principles-corporate-governance.htm.

[2] For the consultation on 'EU Company law upgraded: Rules on digital solutions and efficient cross-border operations', see http://ec.europa.eu/newsroom/just/item-detail.cfm?item_id=58190. For previous initiatives, see http://ec.europa.eu/justice/civil/company-law/index_en.htm.

[3] eg, in Japan: Companies Act Reform 2014 (enacted on 20 June 2014). For the 2016 consultation in the UK, see www.gov.uk/government/consultations/corporate-governance-reform.

[4] The main general books published in English are (in chronological order): R Kraakman et al, *The Anatomy of Corporate Law* (3rd edn, Oxford, Oxford University Press, 2017); V Magnier, *Comparative Corporate Governance: Legal Perspectives* (Cheltenham, Edward Elgar, 2017); M Ventoruzzo et al, *Comparative Corporate Law* (St Paul, MN, West Academic, 2015); JJ du Plessis, A Hargovan, M Bagaric and J Harris,

postgraduate courses or programmes in comparative company law.[5] Moreover, the dissolution of trade barriers and mass cross-border capital flows engendered by the forces of competition and globalisation have also necessitated legal practitioners to be conversant with the company laws of jurisdictions other than their own. As corporate clients expand their interests across a broad portfolio of jurisdictions in a drive for ever greater global efficiency, their legal advisers are required to have some knowledge of each of the legal systems within which they operate.

In producing this work, the general editors and country experts intended to add to the existing academic literature, albeit by adopting a novel methodological approach to the subject. The existing academic literature on comparative company law tends to focus on the institutional structure of the corporation. For instance, discussions[6] centre around whether companies have only one board of directors ('one-tier systems') or whether there is a distinction between the management and supervisory board ('two-tier systems'), whether companies should establish committees (remuneration, appointment, audit committees etc), the identity of persons who can be appointed as a company's auditor (independence, qualification etc) and the division of powers between the board of directors and the shareholders in general meeting. Whilst this approach is important, it overlooks the dimension of specific cases in company law matters and how the issues arising from disputes are resolved in different jurisdictions. For example, topics related to directors' duties and liability, creditor protection and shareholders' rights may best be understood by analysing how carefully designed hypothetical cases would be solved in different countries. An influential case-based comparative methodology is already used by the Common Core project.[7] However, the Common Core only examines private law in a narrow sense (contract, tort etc). Therefore, the principal purpose of this book is to fill a gap in the literature by adopting a related approach in the field of company law.

Principles of Contemporary Corporate Governance (3rd edn, Cambridge, Cambridge University Press, 2015); GH Roth and P Kindler, *The Spirit of Corporate Law: Core Principles of Corporate Law in Continental Europe* (Munich, CH Beck-Hart-Nomos, 2013); AM Fleckner and KJ Hopt (eds), *Comparative Corporate Governance: A Functional and International Analysis* (Cambridge, Cambridge University Press, 2013); R Bohinc, *Comparative Company Law: An Overview on US and Some EU Countries' Company Legislation on Corporate Governance* (Saarbrücken, Müller, 2011); A Cahn and DC Donald, *Comparative Company Law* (Cambridge, Cambridge University Press, 2010); M Andenas and F Wooldridge, *European Comparative Company Law* (Cambridge, Cambridge University Press, 2009); A Dignam and M Galanis, *The Globalization of Corporate Governance* (Farnham, Ashgate, 2009); M Siems, *Convergence in Shareholder Law* (Cambridge, Cambridge University Press, 2008); P Mäntysaari, *Comparative Corporate Governance* (Berlin, Springer, 2005); KJ Hopt, E Wymeersch, H Kanda and H Baum (eds), *Corporate Governance in Context* (Oxford, Oxford University Press, 2005); JN Gordon and MJ Roe (eds), *Convergence and Persistence in Corporate Governance* (Cambridge, Cambridge University Press, 2004); JA McCahery, P Moerland, T Raaijmakers and L Renneboog (eds), *Corporate Governance Regimes – Convergence and Diversity* (Oxford, Oxford University Press, 2002).

[5] For example, in the UK, there are postgraduate modules on Comparative Corporate Law at the University of Oxford, the University of Leicester, Aston University, Queen Mary University of London, SOAS and King's College London.

[6] See eg P Davies, K Hopt, R Nowak and G van Solinge (eds), *Corporate Boards in Law and Practice: A Comparative Analysis in Europe* (Oxford, Oxford University Press, 2013); P Davies and KJ Hopt, 'Boards in Europe – Accountability and Convergence' (2013) 61 *American Journal of Comparative Law* 301.

[7] See II A, below.

More specifically, this approach may enable us to identify whether conceptual differences exist between countries in terms of the form or substance of the legal rules which comprise their company laws. Therefore, it may be possible to challenge arguments developed in the academic literature which posit that the existence of fundamental differences in the protection of shareholders across countries reduces the scope for convergence in company law systems.[8] Furthermore, this research has a public policy dimension since the existence or absence of differences matters for the question of whether formal harmonisation of company law in the EU or further afield is necessary, desirable, or at all possible.[9]

To set the scene, section II of this introductory chapter considers the method and practicalities of adopting a comparative case-based approach, including the mechanics of the process, how the relevant jurisdictions were selected and some of the difficulties encountered by the editors and country experts in designing the cases and furnishing the country solutions and comparative conclusions. Section III explains the themes of the ten hypothetical cases of this book that cover directors' duties and liability, creditor protection and shareholder protection in chapters 2 to 11 of this book. Section IV concludes with an outlook on the analysis provided in chapters 12 and 13 of this book.

II. The Method and Practicalities of a Comparative and Case-Based Approach

It is trite to claim that a comparative analysis that starts with a particular legal rule, concept or institution soon encounters difficulties if one of the legal systems under observation does not have that particular rule, concept or institution. Thus, many comparatists suggest that one should not start with a particular legal topic but with a functional question, such as a particular socio-economic problem. In the words of Ernst Rabel, it means that 'rather than comparing fixed data and isolated paragraphs, we compare the solutions produced by one state for a specific factual situation, and then we ask why they were produced and what success they had'.[10] The most striking example of such an approach is the Common Core project, though this has also had its

---

[8] See eg, LA Bebchuk and MJ Roe, 'A Theory of Path Dependence in Corporate Ownership and Governance' (1999) 52 *Stanford Law Review* 127; MJ Roe, *Political Determinants of Corporate Governance* (Oxford, Oxford University Press, 2003). See also D Cabrelli and M Siems, 'Convergence, Legal Origins and Transplants in Comparative Corporate Law: A Case-Based and Quantitative Analysis' (2015) 63 *American Journal of Comparative* Law 109.

[9] For the EU debate, see eg L Enriques, 'A Harmonized European Company Law: Are We There Already?' (2017) 66 *International and Comparative Law Quarterly* 763; M Gelter, 'EU Company Law Harmonization Between Convergence and Varieties of Capitalism' in H Wells (ed), *Research Handbook on the History of Corporate and Company Law* (Cheltenham, Edward Elgar, 2018) 323; J Mukwiri and M Siems, 'The Financial Crisis: A Reason to Improve Shareholder Protection in the EU?' (2014) 41 *Journal of Law and Society* 51.

[10] As translated in DJ Gerber, 'Sculpting the Agenda of Comparative Law: Ernst Rabel and the Façade of Language' in A Riles (ed), *Rethinking the Masters of Comparative Law* (Oxford, Hart Publishing, 2001) 190, 199. See also K Zweigert and H Kötz, *Introduction to Comparative Law* (3rd edn, Oxford, Clarendon Press, 1998) 34; Sir B Markesinis and J Fedtke, *Engaging with Foreign Law* (Oxford, Hart Publishing, 2009)

critics, who have challenged the assumptions of the functionalist method. This will be discussed in the first section below. Subsequently, we move on to address the practicalities of our own project, in particular the choice of countries and the procedure applied.

A. The Common Core Approach, its Critics and its Limitations

The term 'common core' originates from a project organised by Rudolf Schlesinger at Cornell University dealing with the formation of contracts from a comparative perspective.[11] In the mid-1990s this approach was taken up by European academics interested in contract, tort and property law (now called the 'Common Core project'). A number of comparative books deriving from this project have been published.[12] In addition, the Common Core website and further books provide explanations and reflections on the method used.[13]

The main idea behind the Common Core project is to draw up hypothetical cases and have country experts describe how these cases would be solved in their legal system. In addition, the organisers of the project explain that they are not only interested in the actual results but also (i) the manner in which different elements of statutory law, case law and scholarly writings interact with and potentially contradict each other in particular legal systems, and (ii) how policy considerations, values, economic and social factors, and the structure of legal processes may affect the solution to the case.[14] In some of the books published under the auspices of the project, these two elements appear under separate headings in the solutions.[15] However, most case solutions of the Common Core project are focused on the positive law. Thus, the overall approach of the Common Core project is fairly 'legal' and 'practical', which is apparent from the fact that the publisher promotes the series as 'assist[ing] lawyers in the journey beyond their own locality'.[16]

Short chapter conclusions and separate chapters in the final parts of the books compare the national solutions. This is done in the spirit of functionalism and universalism. The title 'Common Core' is also an overt reference to this aim. Moreover, on the project website it is stipulated that

> in very simple terms, we are seeking to unearth the common core of the bulk of European private law, i.e., of what is already common, if anything, among the different legal systems

---

37–42 (defending Rabel's method). For an interdisciplinary overview of functionalism, see R Michaels, 'The Functional Method of Comparative Law' in M Reimann and R Zimmermann (eds), *The Oxford Handbook of Comparative Law* (Oxford, Oxford University Press, 2006) 339–82.

[11] RB Schlesinger (ed), *Formation of Contracts: A Study of the Common Core of Legal Systems* (Dobbs Ferry, NY, Oceana, 1968).

[12] See the list at www.cambridge.org/core/series/common-core-of-european-private-law/9A1F0195629A3 C0607233F14029C3A25.

[13] See www.common-core.org as well as M Bussani and U Mattei (eds), *Opening Up European Law, The Common Core Project* (Bern, Staempfli, 2007).

[14] On legal formants, see also R Sacco, 'Legal Formants: A Dynamic Approach to Comparative Law' (1991) 39 *American Journal of Comparative Law* 1–34 and 343–401.

[15] See eg G Brüggemeier, A Colombi Ciacchi and P O'Callaghan (eds), *Personality Rights in European Tort Law* (Cambridge, Cambridge University Press, 2010).

[16] See the website, above n 12.

of European Union member states' and that 'common core research is a very promising hunt for analogies hidden by formal differences.[17]

The project website also states that the Common Core approach has an important policy dimension, namely that 'this kind of research should be very useful for and deserve more attention from official institutions that are encharged to draft European legislation' and that part of the Common Core's contribution entails 'building a common European legal culture'.[18]

According to David Gerber '[t]he value and importance of the Common Core project may well place it among the defining achievements in the history of comparative law'.[19] However, this enthusiasm is not shared by everyone; for example, the arch-sceptic Pierre Legrand has dismissed the Common Core publications as 'snippety compilations' that accumulate 'selected titbits extracted largely from legislative texts and appellate judicial decisions'.[20]

Moving beyond such a polemic, the main criticism of the Common Core concerns the suitability of applying the functional method of comparative law. Critics regard the assumption that all societies face the same social problems as unacceptable.[21] It is argued that human needs are not universal but are conditioned by their environments. This is obvious if one thinks about different natural environments, but it also applies more broadly. The factual situation may be identical in two countries, but this does not imply that the law-makers of both societies will necessarily feel the need to promulgate legal rules on the same issue. Thus, it is said that societies have distinct priorities and that it is unacceptable to impose an external measure on them, such as expecting them all to deal with a particular problem.[22]

Moreover, the very idea that law serves particular functions is challenged. A strict version of functionalism assumes that there is a clear sequential order: a social problem arises, courts or legislators respond to it, which in turn has the effect of solving the problem. Yet, such a view fails to consider the possibility that legal rules often arise in a complex process of historical path-dependencies, cultural preconditions and legal transplants, and that legal rules also shape the problems of society. It is also not at all untypical that law operates to serve more than one explicit function alone. Law-makers may have responded to conflicting aims or they may simply strive to offer a clear legal framework, being largely indifferent as to how it is used.[23]

---

[17] See the website, above n 13.

[18] Ibid.

[19] DJ Gerber, 'The Common Core of European Private Law: The Project and its Books' (2004) 52 *American Journal of Comparative Law* 995, 1001.

[20] P Legrand, 'Paradoxically, Derrida: For a Comparative Legal Studies' (2005) 27 *Cardozo Law Review* 631, fn 159.

[21] D Nelken, 'Comparative Law and Comparative Legal Studies' in E Örücü and D Nelken (eds), *Comparative Law: A Handbook* (Oxford, Hart Publishing, 2007) 3, 22–23; J De Coninck, 'The Functional Method of Comparative Law: Quo Vadis?' (2010) 74 *Rabels Zeitschrift für ausländisches und internationales Privatrecht* 318, 327; J Husa, 'Farewell to Functionalism or Methodological Tolerance?' (2003) 67 *Rabels Zeitschrift für ausländisches und internationales Privatrecht* 419, 438.

[22] HP Glenn, 'Com-paring' in E Örücü and D Nelken (eds), *Comparative Law: A Handbook* (Oxford, Hart Publishing, 2007) 91, 95; T Ruskola, 'Legal Orientalism' (2002) 101 *Michigan Law Review* 179, 190.

[23] J Husa, 'Comparative Law, Legal Linguistics, and Methodology of Legal Doctrine' in M Van Hoecke (ed), *Methodologies of Legal Research* (Oxford, Hart Publishing, 2011) 209, 220; M Graziadei,

Where does this leave functionalism? Some of these points raise important objections: for instance, functionalism may not work well in all areas of law or with respect to legal systems where we cannot say that the law has a well-defined purpose.[24] Nevertheless, it is also submitted that these objections do not discredit functionalism as a whole. Indeed, we hope that this book shows that using hypothetical cases offers important insights into the field of comparative company law.[25] It may also be seen as providing evidence that practical problems in company law are not so diverse across the 12 countries selected to make a case-based comparison worthless.

Nevertheless, we do not deny that the case-based approach adopted in this work possesses certain inherent limitations. For example, it is unlikely that such an approach will be useful in evaluating technical issues of company law such as the content and design of the rules on the composition of board membership, the drafting of prospectuses or the transparency of securities markets. The same applies for topics of transnational company law, such as the operations of cross-border and transnational corporations, corporate group structures and cross-border mergers and acquisitions, since a case-based approach is typically focused on the laws of a selected number of countries.

B. The Choice of Countries – and the Problems to Overcome

In accordance with one of the objectives of the project identified above, ie whether formal harmonisation of company law in the EU, or further afield, is necessary, desirable or at all possible, the main focus of this study is on the Member States of the EU. However, owing to constraints of space, it was not possible to cover the law of all Member States. Therefore, the focus is fixed on the six most populated countries (Germany, France, the UK, Spain, Italy and Poland) as well as three further Member States (Finland, Latvia and the Netherlands). In addition, the laws of the US, Japan and South Africa are included for the purposes of wider comparison. From a comparative perspective, the US is the most important 'exporter' of corporate governance theories and ideas, while Japan and South Africa are good examples of legal systems shaped by diverse foreign models. It should be clarified that the law of the US state of Delaware was used as a proxy for the US. This is attributable to the fact that Delaware corporate law is the most important and

---

'The Functionalist Heritage' in P Legrand and R Munday (eds), *Comparative Legal Studies: Traditions and Transitions* (Cambridge, Cambridge University Press, 2003) 100, 118; Michaels, 'The Functional Method of Comparative Law' (n 10) 354.

[24] For further discussion, see also M Siems, *Comparative Law* (2nd edn, Cambridge, Cambridge University Press, 2018) 38–39, 45–47, and specifically for comparative company law, see M Siems, 'The Methods of Comparative Corporate Law' in R Tomasic (ed), *The Routledge Handbook of Corporate Law* (London, Routledge, 2017) 11.

[25] We also feel encouraged by the positive reception of the first edition of this book: see the reviews by RC Nolan, (2014) 130 *Law Quarterly Review* 343; D Maltese, (2013) 72 *Cambridge Law Journal* 768; P Watts, (2013) *New Zealand Law Journal* 318, as well as L LoPucki, 'A Rule-Based Method for Comparing Corporate Laws' (2018) 94 *Notre Dame Law Review* (forthcoming).

influential in the US, with a significant number of public and private companies incorporated in that state.[26]

It would also have been interesting to include further jurisdictions from Asia, America or Africa, for instance, some of the other BRICS countries (ie Brazil, Russia, India, or China) or possibly even 'radically different legal cultures'.[27] However, apart from logistical problems, there are good reasons to focus on relatively similar countries. This is related to the feasibility of a functional approach to comparative law. Insofar as the approaches adopted by countries are relatively similar, it is likely that their law-makers regard the same socio-economic problems as legally relevant. It has also been said that a preference for similar countries has the advantage of controlling for the stage of development, ie making it easier to explore the remaining differences amongst a baseline of similarity in terms of the countries' history, society, economy and ideology.[28]

Nevertheless, some problems have to be overcome. We aimed to have some cases applicable to private limited liability companies (such as the Ltd in the UK and the GmbH in Germany) and others to public companies (such as the plc in the UK and the AG in Germany). However, we encountered the problem[29] that the form a company takes does not always correspond with the way it is used in practice. For example, on the surface, the French SARL resembles the German GmbH, and the French SA the German AG, but in France, even small to medium-sized firms and family firms often use the SA. In addition, French law offers a third legal form, the SAS, which was created to cover the area between the SA and the SARL.[30] A somewhat analogous situation exists in the US. Here, a primary distinction is made between closely and publicly held corporations, but businesses can also establish a limited liability company (LLC). The success of state LLC laws is particularly based on the fact that while LLCs have the legal form of a company, for tax purposes they are treated as a partnership. In 2005, Japan also introduced the LLC based on the US model, but without the advantage of being taxed as partnerships. By contrast, the UK law provides for a Limited Liability Partnership (LLP) which, like US LLCs, is structured similarly to a company but is taxed as a partnership.[31]

The implication of this for the case-based project was that whilst guidance was provided to country experts on the type of company that it was expected would be covered in the individual case studies, some contributors indicated possible

---

[26] See, eg, O Eldar and L Magnolfi, 'Regulatory Competition and the Market for Corporate Law', Yale Law & Economics Research Paper No 528 (2017), available at https://ssrn.com/abstract=2685969; JC Dammann and M Schündeln, 'Where Are Limited Liability Companies Formed? An Empirical Analysis' (2013) 55 *Journal of Law and Economics* 741; LA Bebchuk and A Hamdani, 'Vigorous Race or Leisurely Walk: Reconsidering the Competition Over Corporate Charters' (2002) 112 *Yale Law Journal* 553.

[27] JH Barton, J Lowell Gibbs Jr, VH Li and JH Merryman, *Law in Radically Different Cultures* (St Paul, MN, West Publishing, 1983).

[28] M Warrington and M Van Hoecke, 'Legal Cultures, Legal Paradigms and Legal Doctrine: Towards a New Model for Comparative Law' (1998) 47 *International and Comparative Law Quarterly* 495, 533; NJ Smelser, *Comparative Methods in the Social Sciences* (Englewood Cliffs, NJ, Prentice Hall, 1976) 66.

[29] For the following, see also Siems, *Convergence in Shareholder Law* (n 4) 10–14.

[30] See ch 10 at II D, below.

[31] For a comparative treatment of the LLP, see M Siems, 'Regulatory Competition in Partnership Law' (2009) 58 *International and Comparative Law Quarterly* 767–802.

alternative solutions for different types of companies.[32] On occasion, country experts also mentioned that a particular aim could not be pursued by adopting the form of company prescribed in the scenario in question, but that another form of company would be available.[33]

A more general problem may have been that the solutions received from the contributors often differed considerably in terms of structure and style. For example, some of the solutions provided a precise structure with many headings and sub-headings, whereas others provided a more discursive text. Some referred to many cases and statutory provisions in the text, whereas others only referred to them in the footnotes, often more sporadically. There were also marked variations in the extent to which contributors translated certain terms into English or in the frequency of references to international, comparative and European materials.

An attempt was made to approximate the presentation of the solutions in some instances. However, deliberately, a template was not provided as to how it was antici-pated that the solutions would be written and structured. Comparative lawyers often emphasise that it is differences in legal style, not substantive rules, which are decisive for the common/civil law divide.[34] Thus, to some extent, this book has the secondary aim of exposing these differences in legal thinking and writing. However, this point should not be stretched too far. For example, if a particular section contains many references to the academic literature, this may be an indicator of the civil law tradition, but it could also be influenced by the individual style adopted by the contributor in question.

C. The Modus Operandi of the Project

The project was coordinated by the two general editors who appointed country experts for each of the 12 jurisdictions under examination. The topics of each of the 10 hypothetical cases were selected by the two general editors, but the issues to be addressed in each case were loosely configured around the topics of directors' duties, creditor protection, shareholders' rights and the flexibility of company law and its enforcement. Each of the initial ten country experts[35] performed three tasks. First, he or she drafted one hypothetical case and a solution to that case accord-ing to the company law of his or her home jurisdiction. The decision to enable each participant to draft one of the cases was predicated on the perceived need to achieve a good mix and balance of cases, possibly reflecting different socio-economic circum-stances.[36] Second, each of the country experts then circulated their hypothetical cases and solutions amongst the other country experts and solutions were produced by

---

[32] See eg the French solutions in chs 7, 10 and 11, below.
[33] See eg the German solutions in chs 3 and 11, below.
[34] See eg Zweigert and Kötz (n 10) 63–73; Siems, *Comparative Law* (n 24) 50–83.
[35] As they were in the first edition. The Netherlands and South Africa were added in the second edition of this book.
[36] But see II pr and A, above, for functionalism and its critics.

each of the country experts to the hypothetical cases under the law of his or her home jurisdiction. Third, each country expert examined the different solutions to his or her hypothetical case and drew up a comparative conclusion. Once again, the two editors were not overly prescriptive of how the country experts should approach the task of writing the case conclusion. The comparative conclusions would identify the differences and similarities between the 12 jurisdictions and would also provide a careful comparative analysis. In particular, the following issues were addressed in the case conclusions and comparative evaluations where this was possible in light of the hypothetical case and the solutions:

1. Is it the case that formally different legal rules in the jurisdictions lead to functionally similar results? Conversely, are the rules in the jurisdictions formally similar (due to legal transplants etc) but applied differently? On a similar note, is there any evidence of increasing formal or functional convergence and is such convergence desirable bearing in mind (i) the ostensible differences in the form of company laws in jurisdictions according to whether they are grounded in the civilian or common law traditions and (ii) the differing shareholding structures in jurisdictions?

2. Is there any evidence that the legal origins theorem (from the viewpoint of the degree of shareholder protection) is relevant and/or applicable, ie is the level of shareholder or creditor protection lower in civil law countries in comparison with common law countries?

3. What are the sources of the legal rules in the jurisdictions examined, ie are they based on case law or statute law (which may or may not relate to the common law/civil law divide) and how is that significant (if at all)?

4. Whether politics or history/path-dependence matters, ie to what extent is there any evidence that politics and/or path-dependence and legal-institutional complementarities influence the form and shape of company laws in different legal systems?

5. To what extent does the nature of the shareholding structure (concentrated versus dispersed and outsider versus insider) in differing countries influence the form which the company laws take?

6. Country experts were asked to reflect on whether the solutions offer any insights into the legal transplantability of company laws, ie to what extent there was evidence of formal or functional transplants having succeeded.

7. Is there any evidence to suggest that the legal systems predominantly favour one constituency over another, eg directors, managers, shareholders, creditors, employees, etc?

8. Policy questions ought to be addressed, for instance, which solution (if any) may be superior and whether the differences may call for substantive/formal legal harmonisation or functional legal harmonisation.

9. If the case related to directors' duties and liabilities (ie a case in chapters 2 to 5 in Part 1), country experts were asked to consider the following factors and address them if they were relevant:

   a. In what circumstances does directors' liability arise?
   b. Which legal tools are used in order to prevent self-dealing transactions of directors?
   c. Does directors' liability lead to a damages or disgorgement of profits remedy? Can third parties dealing with a director in breach of duty to the company be held liable to the company?
   d. Are directors/managers/board members jointly responsible?
   e. Are there different standards of care for different members of the board? Are 'nominee' directors permitted?

    f.   Can shareholders ratify any action, decision or omission of a director and thus prevent the company from litigating against that director?

    g.   Can shareholders challenge the remuneration of directors/managers/board members and/or executives?

    h.   Is there a duty of neutrality in the case of takeovers and, if so, how and when does it arise?

10. If the case related to the relationship between creditors and the company (ie a case in chapters 6 to 7 in Part 2), country experts were asked to consider the following factors and address them if they were relevant:

    a.   Do directors owe a direct or indirect (eg via a liquidator, administrator or other insolvency practitioner) duty to the creditors of the company?

    b.   Do directors owe 'wrongful trading' obligations to creditors – ie do directors owe a duty not to continue to trade where there is no reasonable prospect of the company avoiding going into insolvent liquidation? If not, are there any circumstances in which the law will impose personal liability on directors whose companies have been dissolved or liquidated?

    c.   Is there a concept of 'piercing the corporate veil'? If so, in what circumstances will it be applicable?

    d.   Is there a subordination of shareholder loans in the case of a company in crisis?

11. If the case related to the law relating to shareholders and shareholder protection (ie a case in chapters 8 to 11 in Part 3), country experts were asked to address the following factors if relevant:

    a.   Can shareholders vote in their self-interest?

    b.   Do shareholders have to take the interests of other stakeholders into account?

    c.   Do controlling shareholders have special duties? If so, to whom?

    d.   Are shareholders' agreements – for instance, on voting rights – possible?

    e.   On what grounds (if any) can shareholders challenge a decision or resolution of the general meeting?

    f.   Is it necessary that the general meeting decides about 'de facto changes' of the company (eg the sale of substantial assets)?

    g.   Is it possible for a shareholder to take action against a director, majority shareholder or other third party to recover a loss sustained by the company? If so, in what circumstances?

    h.   Is it possible for a shareholder to sue the company or its managers or controllers where it has been conducted in a manner which is contrary to the interests of that shareholder or the shareholders generally?

    i.   Are there any limitations on the ability of shareholders to restrict the free transfer of shares?

    j.   Are there any restrictions on convertible corporate bond-holders converting their debt into equity and assuming a controlling interest in the company?

The final part of the process entailed preparing a general introduction and two concluding chapters setting out the aims, outcomes and implications of the study. These latter chapters were produced with the benefit of the comparative conclusions of each of the country experts. They were also designed to feed into some of the most important ongoing debates in the field of comparative company law and add something to them by offering a novel contribution.

III. The Hypothetical Cases

In this book we consider 10 hypothetical cases. These cases were selected in order to cover topics of directors' duties and liabilities (chapters 2 to 5), creditor protection, including the relationship between creditors and the company (chapters 6 to 7), and the law relating to shares, shareholders, shareholder protection and the flexibility of company law (chapters 8 to 11). Such an approach has the potential to reveal the extent to which the legal systems selected favour the interests of directors, majority shareholders, minority shareholders or creditors. This feeds into the higher-order abstract debates in the wider comparative company law literature on the relevance of legal origins, convergence of laws, the prevalence of the shareholder primacy norm, the significance of differing patterns of shareholder ownership and legal transplants.[37]

The view was also taken that some of these questions ought to be addressed to different types of companies.[38] Thus, the aim was to have a good mix of cases dealing with smaller, medium-sized and more substantial companies. Four of the cases asked for a solution based on the applicable law of private limited liability companies.[39] Meanwhile, the remaining six cases concerned public companies (ie joint-stock companies), some of which had their shares admitted to a stock exchange/regulated market.[40] Furthermore, the point should be made that the main focus of the cases in the project is on the company law rules of the countries selected, rather than a comparative examination of the rules of corporate governance. The connection between company law and corporate governance is particularly close.[41] Hence, although the case-based approach adopted may throw some light on certain aspects of corporate governance in the jurisdictions analysed (eg one-tier or two-tier board and the nature, structure and composition of sub-committees of the board), which is revealing or interesting from a comparative perspective, that is not the primary purpose of the project.

In detail, we deal with the following topics, structured in three parts.

A. Directors' Duties and Liability

Turning first to chapters 2 to 5 in Part 1, which address the position of the 12 jurisdictions in respect of directors' duties and liabilities, the focus of the first case in chapter two was twofold. It sought to understand the source, nature, content and

---

[37] For these topics see chs 12 and 13, below.
[38] See also II B, above.
[39] See cases in chs 2, 3, 7 and 10, below.
[40] See cases in chs 4, 5, 6, 8, 9 and 11, below. The cases on takeover law in chs 4 and 5 concern companies whose shares have been admitted to trading on a stock exchange.
[41] See also ch 13 at II B, below.

scope of a director's duties of loyalty and care, as well as to evaluate the ability of the shareholders in general meeting to authorise or ratify a breach of director's duty. It is often said that modern jurisdictions adopt the 'shareholder primacy' model, whereby directors owe legal duties to shareholders as a class and are bound to run and manage companies in their interests.[42] However, the law in the US (Delaware) amounts to an exception to this general rule and instead prioritises directors' rights and interests over those of shareholders: this is referred to as the 'director/managerial primacy' model.[43] The primary purpose of this first aspect of this case was to test these theories, in particular against the backdrop of the argument that it is most efficient to design company law with a preference for shareholders' rights and empowerment.[44]

Turning to the second aspect of the first case, namely the extent to which shareholders may *ex ante* authorise, or *ex post facto* ratify, managerial breaches of duty, there is a connection here with the aforementioned 'shareholder primacy' and 'director/managerial primacy' models. The link relates to the balance of constitutional power between the directors and the shareholders which has been struck by company law: the more power, rights and authority wielded by the directors/managers, the less influence the shareholders have over corporate decision-making and, conversely, the more rights and powers reserved to the shareholders, the more that the directors' hands are tied in administering the affairs of the company. Therefore, by enquiring as to whether shareholders have the power to absolve the directors of liability for breaches of their duties of loyalty and care, the second aspect of the first case seeks to identify whether shareholders enjoy a residual power or authority over the directors in the context of managerial wrongdoing.

The next case in chapter 3 moves away from a general consideration of directors' duties and liabilities to investigate the parameters of the legal obligations of nominee directors. Having been appointed by a third party onto the board of the company, for example by a parent company or controlling shareholder of the company, the nominee director is placed in a particularly precarious position. Although the director will be keen to ensure that the company is successful, he or she will also be mindful of the interests of his or her appointer. To that extent, the nominee director's decision-making is compromised by an inexorable division of loyalties, which will be acutely felt in the case of a decision where the interests of the company and those of his or her appointer clearly diverge. The question which arises is how the legal systems of the 12 jurisdictions under consideration strive to resolve this tension. For example, is the vote/decision of the nominee director ignored where it is taken in the interests of the appointer to the detriment of the company, or is it treated as valid as a matter

---

[42] FH Easterbrook and DR Fischel, *The Economic Structure of Corporate Law* (Cambridge, MA, Harvard University Press, 1991) 91; and SM Bainbridge, *Corporation Law and Economics* (New York, ThomsonWest, 2002) 80–81.

[43] SM Bainbridge, 'Director Primacy: The Means and Ends of Corporate Governance' (2003) 97 *Northwestern University Law Review* 547; and SM Bainbridge, 'Director Primacy and Shareholder Disempowerment' (2006) 119 *Harvard Law Review* 1735.

[44] LA Bebchuk, 'The Case for Increasing Shareholder Power' (2005) 118 *Harvard Law Review* 833. For a riposte, see WW Bratton and ML Wachter, 'The Case Against Shareholder Empowerment' (2010) 158 *University of Pennsylvania Law Review* 653.

of course, or valid subject to the satisfaction of certain conditions? These are some of the issues that the first part of this case seeks to address.

In addition, this case addresses further issues. For example, the case in chapter 3 involves an assessment of the legal recognition and validity of convertible promissory notes. Civilian jurisdictions are often portrayed as restrictive of shareholder rights and this aspect of the case seeks to test that assertion in the context of a particular security. This is particularly relevant in light of the fact that the conversion of convertible promissory notes often enables a creditor to assume a controlling interest in a company. The case scenario also asks whether there may be a breach of duty in not having selected the most qualified nominee directors. Thus, this aspect of this case relates to the more general question of whether directors and shareholders must prioritise the best interests of the company.

The case in chapter 4 also focuses on the duties of directors in a particular context where managerial loyalties may be conflicted, namely that of a takeover bid. Here, the interests of the directors of the company which is the subject of the takeover bid may deviate from the interests of the shareholders. For example, the bidder may be minded to replace the incumbent management post-takeover with its own management team in order to improve the company's commercial performance or its overall efficiency. Although the bid may be beneficial for the existing shareholders, the directors' personal and corporate loyalties diverge and they may tempted to engage in activities which are designed to protect and entrench their position as directors. One of the objectives of Directive 2004/25/EC of the European Parliament and of the Council of 21 April 2004 on takeover bids (the EU Takeover Directive)[45] was to place constraints on the power of directors to frustrate takeover bids. It does so by empowering Member States to introduce a 'duty of neutrality', namely laws regulating the ability of directors to adopt defensive tactics to a takeover bid within carefully prescribed parameters. Member States were afforded various options in the way they could implement this aspect of the EU Takeover Directive and this case enables a survey to be made of the choices made by the Member States under consideration. It also seeks to identify where the line is drawn between the powers of the directors and the shareholders to take a particular form of defensive action.

Finally, the case in chapter 5 also takes a takeover situation as its focus. It includes a cross-border dimension as the target company is listed in multiple jurisdictions. Moreover, unlike chapter 4, the principal concern is to identify the jurisdictions which apply pre-emption rights on the allotment and issue of shares by a company. In other words, the question is to what extent a company must first offer a fresh issue of shares to the existing shareholders before it is entitled to issue shares to non-shareholder third parties. This is an important issue in light of the provisions of the EU Takeover Directive, since the sanctioning of a rights issue by management is one of the means by which a takeover bid may be resisted. In addition, this case asks the country experts to reflect on the argument that a takeover defence may be justified in the interests of the company as a whole, notably due to the desire to protect the company's employees and the aim not to lose customers as a result of the takeover.

---

[45] [2004] OJ L142/12.

B. Creditor Protection

In Part 2, we move on to scrutinise the protections afforded to creditors in the company law systems of the various jurisdictions analysed in this work. The case in chapter 6 assesses the ability of a creditor of a bankrupt company to seek recourse against the shareholders or directors of that company. If the country solutions revealed that there was the potential for such liability to arise, the country experts were prompted to identify specifically the juridical basis or bases for that liability. First, the question was posed as to whether a doctrine such as 'piercing the veil of incorporation' or some other similar doctrine would permit the creditor to look behind the façade of the separate legal personality of the company to enable it to enforce against the bankrupt company's directors or shareholders. Moreover, it was intended that the qualifying criteria and conditions for that doctrine to operate be exposed. Second, country experts were asked to consider the potential for creditor recourse against the directors of the bankrupt company via the medium of directors' duties. Here, the issue was whether the law of directors' duties placed directors under an obligation to take into account the interests of creditors prior to the company entering, or once the company had entered, into a formal insolvency procedure or process. The concern was also to understand whether more heightened obligations were imposed on directors by virtue of the fact that the company had entered into bankruptcy and whether that translated into the potential for personal liability. Further, it was crucial to understand whether the creditors' rights could be enforced directly against the director or whether they would have to be enforced by a third party such as an insolvency practitioner appointed over the estate of the bankrupt company when it entered into an insolvency process. In the latter case, the absence of director recourse would mean that the creditor's position is somewhat compromised, since it will be reliant on the goodwill of the third party insolvency practitioner to vindicate and enforce its rights.

In the next case in chapter 7, the focus remains on the rights and powers of creditors instantiated through the rules and doctrines of company law. However, this case concentrates on a technical but important aspect of company law, namely the operation of the rules which together make up the capital maintenance principle. A capital maintenance principle is found in the domestic company law systems of many jurisdictions (as well as EU company law).[46] The principle strives to ensure that creditors' rights are safeguarded by prohibiting companies from returning capital to their shareholders through a variety of direct or indirect means. One of the principal rules encountered in many jurisdictions is that a company may only distribute its profits as a dividend to its shareholders on an annual basis if it has: (i) distributable profits; and/or (ii) its net assets are not less than the aggregate of its called-up share capital and undistributable

---

[46] Directive 2012/30/EU of the European Parliament and of the Council of 25 October 2012 on coordination of safeguards which, for the protection of the interests of members and others, are required by Member States of companies within the meaning of the second paragraph of Article 54 of the Treaty on the Functioning of the European Union, in respect of the formation of public limited liability companies and the maintenance and alteration of their capital, with a view to making such safeguards equivalent ([2012] OJ L315/74), previously the Second EU Company Law Directive 77/91/EEC, and now included in Directive (EU) 2017/1132 of the European Parliament and of the Council of 14 June 2017 relating to certain aspects of company law ([2017] OJ L169/46).

reserves. Not all jurisdictions require (ii) to be satisfied and there is also a degree of divergence displayed in how (i) and/or (ii) are ascertained. For example, some jurisdictions adopt accounting-based models, whereas others proceed on the basis of a solvency-based regime. In the former case, the distribution may be made out of any surplus (a) when the company's net assets (ie its aggregate assets less its aggregate liabilities) are subtracted from its legal capital as expressed in its distributable reserves or (b) in its accumulated realised profits less its accumulated realised losses. This can be contrasted with solvency-based models where the principal issue is whether the distribution will render the company insolvent in the sense that it is unable to pay its debts as they fall due over an identified sustained period of time. As such, one of the purposes of chapter 7 is to isolate which model the jurisdictions under analysis duly apply and to consider the merits and demerits of each.

Chapter 7 also goes on to address the extent to which the company laws of the jurisdictions concerned prohibit or constrain the capacity of companies to effect 'disguised distributions' of assets to the detriment of creditors, for example by transferring assets to a third party or particular shareholder or shareholders at undervalue or by acquiring assets from a third party or particular shareholder or shareholders in excess of the market value. Once again, country experts were asked to ascertain the doctrinal bases for the imposition or non-imposition of such liability and whether disguised transfers were directly or indirectly precluded or restricted, or whether other legal doctrines operated as functional equivalents and achieved the same result.

C. Shareholder Protection

In Part 3, the cases concentrate on the general rights and protections of shareholders and the flexibility of company law. In particular, chapters 8 and 9 are designed to expose the breadth and limits of shareholders' rights enshrined in law. For example, the case in chapter 8 seeks to establish whether shareholders have an entitlement to challenge the decisions of majority shareholders where the latter have failed consistently to vote in favour of the distribution of an annual dividend over a period of time. If the directors and majority shareholders decide to retain profits in the company, the question is whether there are any legal mechanisms enabling the minority shareholders to overturn that decision. The second matter addressed by the case in chapter 8 is whether the vote of an interested shareholder in favour of merging the company with another company is somehow tainted and can be ignored on the ground that it is null and void. Alternatively, one may consider whether that vote is valid, whilst leaving the shareholder open to liability under some other legal doctrine.

Meanwhile, the case in chapter 9 looks to understand the circumstances in which shareholders have a right to ask questions of management at a general meeting. Whilst this is an area which has been harmonised in the EU by virtue of Article 9 of the Shareholder Rights Directive,[47] a measure of discretion is afforded to Member

---

[47] Directive 2007/36/EC of 11 July 2007 on the exercise of certain rights of shareholders in listed companies ([2007] OJ L184/17) (as amended).

States to shape the limits of that right, for instance by imposing restrictions in order to protect commercial confidentiality and the circumstances in which the shareholder will be deemed to be abusing his or her right to ask questions. Furthermore, this case addresses the legal effect of a purported breach of shareholder rights and whether this operates to invalidate any resolutions passed at a general meeting. In this case, the resolution in question was passed to enable the merger between the company and a third party corporation to proceed. The issue is whether a disgruntled shareholder alleging a procedural violation of company law or the corporation's constitution has the power to prevent such a merger from proceeding by attaining an order from the court that the merger resolution was null and void.

Unlike chapters 8 and 9, which focus on the rights of shareholders, chapter 10 seeks to highlight the legal processes recognised in the various jurisdictions which enable shareholders to enforce those rights. Here, the protections of shareholders, particularly minority shareholders, come to the fore. One of the key issues addressed is whether it is possible for an aggrieved minority shareholder to challenge a breach of directors' duties or the actions of a controlling shareholder through the medium of a derivative action. A derivative action allows a shareholder to attain relief from a director or majority shareholder for the benefit of the company where a corporate decision taken by those directors or the majority shareholders is tainted by self-interest or impropriety, or breaches the company's constitution or mandatory provisions of national company law. Thus, a successful legal challenge does not give rise to a personal remedy in favour of the shareholder. Country experts were asked to identify the restrictions on the power of shareholders to raise derivative actions, for example whether there were any minimum share capital ownership requirements or whether the genuineness of the shareholder in raising the claim would be considered in advance of a full hearing. This particular case provides the opportunity to consider the theory that civilian jurisdictions prioritise the elimination of horizontal agency costs over vertical agency costs and that common law jurisdictions with widely dispersed ownership seek to achieve the opposite.[48] Chapter 10 also seeks to examine the flexibility of the company law regimes of the 12 jurisdictions analysed. Country experts were asked to consider whether it was possible for a decision to be taken informally by the shareholders with unanimous consent where company law rules or the terms of the company's constitution specifically required a formal vote to be taken at a properly convened general meeting.

Finally, we turn to the case in chapter 11 whose purpose is to consider whether any legal constraints are placed on the ability of shareholders to restrict the free transfer of shares in the company's constitution. The possibility of the company conferring pre-emption rights on the transfer of shares in favour of existing shareholders is considered, as well as the ability of the company to restrict a third party from inheriting shares on the occurrence of the death of a shareholder. These two aspects of the case in chapter 11 enable us to address the contention that common law jurisdictions are more flexible than the civil law as regards the structuring and configuration of shareholder rights. Moreover, as this final case includes draft articles of a company,

---

[48] See the discussion in ch 12, II B and III C.

it provides a practically important – though in academic research often neglected – element of addressing issues of corporate governance.

IV. Conclusion

In this introductory chapter, we explained the method associated with a case-based approach to comparative company law and the practical problems it must overcome. We also outlined the principal topics of the subsequent case studies in chapters 2 to 11. We aim to cover representative themes that are relevant for the company laws of the countries under investigation. However, the case studies of this book can also be used separately and it will also be clarified at the outset of the chapters how they relate to other topics addressed elsewhere in this book.

The structure of the country solutions in the chapters is as follows: in order to achieve consistency, the first solution is always from the contributor who produced the case in question. This is followed by the other countries of the same legal family, starting with the jurisdictions, such as France, Germany and the UK, that may have borne an influence on this.[49] Subsequently, the solutions of the countries of the other legal family are presented. Japan follows as the final solution, since its company law has been both influenced by the civil and common law legal families. Of course, this order does pre-empt the view that there are telling differences between civil and common law jurisdictions in the field of company law; indeed, the chapter conclusions often highlight, and try to explain, unexpected similarities and differences.

Following on from these 10 case studies in chapters 2 to 11, the two concluding chapters provide a general analysis of differences and similarities between legal systems in company law. This will be based, on the one hand, on a ruled-based and conceptual comparative analysis in chapter 12, and on the other, on a quantitative analysis in chapter 13. In substance, chapter 12 uses four prominent claims of the comparative company law literature as a conceptual framework: the 'legal origins claim', the 'shareholder primacy claim', the 'patterns of shareholder ownership claim' and the 'convergence claim'. By contrast, in the quantitative chapter 13 the three levels of analysis are the nature and content of the respective legal rules of company law (the 'form'), the sources of those rules (the 'style') and the results reached on the application of such rules (the 'substance').

These two concluding chapters will challenge some of the established orthodoxies in the field of comparative company law, such as the relevance of 'legal origins' and the alleged superiority of certain models of corporate governance. This is not to deny that our analysis, as well as the prior selection of cases and countries, includes degrees of subjectivity. Nevertheless, we hope that this book will be of interest for readers in this field whether they agree or disagree with some of our choices and findings.

---

[49] Thus, the default order of countries is France, Germany, Italy, Spain, the Netherlands, Finland, Poland, Latvia (for the civil law countries) and the UK, South Africa and the US (for the common law countries).

Part 1

Directors' Duties and Liability

2

General Case on Directors' Duties

THEIS KLAUBERG (EDITOR)

Main topics: directors' duties (objective or subjective test); business judgment rule; directors' liability; ratification of breach of directors' duties.

Related topics: duties of nominee directors (see chapter 3, below); duties of directors in the context of a takeover bid (see chapters 4 and 5, below); directors' duties in insolvency (see chapter 6, below); enforcement of directors' duties (see chapter 10, below).

I. Scenario

The shares of a Latvian private limited liability company KOKS SIA (hereinafter 'the Company'), which produces chipboards used mostly for furniture production, are owned 95 per cent by Mr A1 and 5 per cent by Ms A2. Management is carried out by the director Mr B. After a period of five years of economic growth, Latvia experiences a severe economic crisis. Since the furniture industry is cutting production, for three months, the Company's sales have gradually dropped, and customers cancel orders, demand discounts and extensions of payment terms, or simply delay payment. The Company's bankers have indicated that further credit will not be extended in subsequent months.

Mr B estimates that the available cash reserves are sufficient to meet creditors' claims for another two to three weeks. In order to raise additional cash, he decides to sell 25 per cent of the existing assets of the Company to an international wholesaler with a 50 per cent discount to the current market price. Unfortunately, sales figures do not improve, and one month later the Company is unable to pay its suppliers. In order to be able to continue production, Mr B decides to take on a loan from a private individual. However, one of the conditions of the loan is that the Company pays interest at a rate which is 150 per cent above the current average annual interest rate offered by commercial banks. Mr B obtained the consent of the 95 per cent shareholder Mr A1 immediately prior to entering into the loan transaction.

After four weeks, several debtors default and the Company cannot pay for the goods supplied to it. Mr B requests a legal opinion on what his duties are as a director and whether any of his actions or omissions may constitute a breach of his duties as a director. He is also concerned that he may be exposed to the imposition of criminal liabilities and would like to know whether that might be true.

II. Case Studies

A. Latvia

i. Directors of a Latvian Private Limited Liability Company

A private limited liability company incorporated in accordance with Latvian law (*sabiedrība ar ierobežotu atbildību* (SIA))[1] is a commercial company based on a fixed amount of share capital owned by a fixed number of shareholders. It is the most relevant commercial legal entity in Latvia, where approximately 85 per cent of the registered commercial enterprises choose this legal form.

With regard to the commercial activities of the company, the liability of the shareholders is limited to the share capital assigned to them as documented in the register of shareholders. The register of shareholders, annual balance sheets, statutes and other company documents are filed with the Latvian Register of Enterprises (Latvijas Republikas uzņēmumu reģistrs (LRL)),[2] which is a public register. The minimum share capital of the company is €2,800. However, the 2010 reforms introduced a new type of company, whereby the share capital may be less than the regular SIA if certain conditions are met (Commercial Code, section 185). Latvian company law follows a continental European legal tradition or, more precisely, a company law model also found in Germany[3] and Switzerland.[4] The statutory rules on companies are spelt out in the comprehensive act on commercial subjects and activities, namely the Commercial Code. It is complemented by the regulation on civil partnerships (Civil Code, sections 2241–2280)[5] and other principles of contract law which are laid down in the principal codification of civil law in Latvia, namely the Civil Code.[6] The Latvian

---

[1] For more detail on the Latvian SIA, see T Klauberg, 'Länderbericht Lettland' in R Süß and T Wachter (eds), *Handbuch des internationalen GmbH-Rechts* (2nd edn, Angelbachtal, Zerb, 2011) 1003; P Dalderis and L Zubulis, 'Latvia' in K Van Hulle and H Gesell (eds), *European Corporate Law* (Baden-Baden, Nomos, 2006) 221; T Klauberg, *Gesellschaftsrecht in Estland, Lettland und Litauen* (Heidelberg, Hüthig-Jehle-Rehm, 2004) 23.

[2] The Latvian Register of Enterprises publishes information in English and Latvian at www.ur.gov.lv.

[3] A Lošmanis, 'Jaunais Latvijas Komerclikums' in *Tiesību transformācijas problēmas sakarā ar integrāciju Europas Savienībā [Problems of Transformation of Law in Connection with European Integration]* (Riga, University of Latvia Press, 2002) 297.

[4] A Loeber, 'Die Gesellschaft (G) nach dem lettländischen Zivilgesetzbuch vom Jahre 1937 (ZGB)' 1937/1938 *Rigasche Zeitschrift für Rechtswissenschaft* 67 (2002 facsimile reprint 2789).

[5] K Torgāns, *Saistību tiesības II. daļa* (Riga, TNA, 2008) 178.

[6] On the background to the Civil Code, see DA Loeber, 'Vorwort' in T Klauberg (ed), *1937.gada Latvijas Republikas Civillikums – Lettlands Zivilgesetzbuch von 1937* (Riga, Latvijas Vestnesis, 2006) 39.

private limited liability company features an optional two-tier system of corporate governance, and thus while its shareholders are required to appoint a board of directors, they may also appoint a supervisory board. If a supervisory board is formed, its role is to appoint the directors to the board of directors and oversee their activities (Commercial Code, sections 220 and 291). However, in the present case, as in the vast majority of private limited liability companies in Latvia, a supervisory board has not been created.

The management of a Latvian limited liability company is carried out by the members of the board of directors,[7] which may consist of one or more natural persons. The size of the board of directors is laid down in the company's articles of association. If several directors are appointed, they exercise management jointly (Commercial Code, sections 221 and 222). Persons appointed as members of the board of directors are registered in the public and internet-based database kept by the LRL, and each member of the board of directors so registered has full rights to represent the company, which cannot be limited vis-a-vis dealings with third parties (Commercial Code, section 223(3)). The directors may conclude contracts in the name of the company and exercise other powers belonging to the company as its representatives (Civil Code, section 1410). Thus, the board of directors as an entity is a body whose decisions and activities are deemed to have been exercised by the company directly.[8] In certain circumstances, the management of the company and the right of representation may be delegated to or taken over by other persons, such as a liquidator, an administrator in insolvency or bankruptcy, by members of the supervisory board or by shareholders.[9] A director may resign at any time by serving notice upon the company to that effect. After such resignation, however, the director may be held liable for decisions he or she made whilst he or she was a director. In the event that a supervisory board is formed, one of its tasks is to appoint the board of directors. Otherwise, this is done by a resolution of the meeting of shareholders (Commercial Code, sections 210(1)(no 4) and 224(1)).

ii. Duties of the Directors

The director Mr B is the only member of the board of directors, the governing body of the Company. In this role, his duties comprise the management of the Company's administration and business affairs as well as acting as the representative of the Company towards third parties.[10] As a minimum, the legal duties of directors impose an obligation on Mr B to take or refrain from activities which may result in the insolvency of the Company. The deterioration of the economic situation in Latvia has had a significant impact on the Company's financial position. On account of section 221(6) of the Commercial Code, directors are also obliged to inform the supervisory

---

[7] For more detail on the board of directors, see A Strupišs, 'Valde kā kapitālsabiedrības pārstāve' (2002) 39 *Likums un Tiesības* 342; and on the management and representation functions in Latvian companies, see A Loeber, *Tirdzniecības tiesību pārskats* (Riga, Valters un Rapa, 1926) 96, and 143 in particular on capital companies.

[8] K Balodis, *Ievads Civiltiesībās* (Riga, Zvaigzne ABC, 2007) 93.

[9] Strupišs, 'Valde kā kapitālsabiedrības pārstāve' (n 7) 343.

[10] Commercial Code, s 221(1).

board immediately of the Company's worsening financial condition or of any other conditions, which are relevant to the commercial dealings of the Company. Since a supervisory board has not been created in the Company's case, this obligation is owed towards the shareholders Mr A1 and Ms A2 in the general meeting. Mr B has taken a number of measures which require further analysis, but it is already doubtful whether the obligation to inform has been fulfilled. Although the shareholders can be expected to be aware of the generally poor economic situation, the director is obliged to provide the shareholders with a more detailed account of the likely effect of the situation on the commercial activities of the Company. The situation in the furniture market has been declining for more than six months; therefore, the obligation to inform shareholders immediately has clearly not been complied with.

The commercial and management decisions taken by Mr B have to be analysed according to the due diligence general principle laid down in section 169(1) of the Commercial Code. This provision directs that the directors are under an obligation to act diligently or, more precisely, to carry out their duties as *able and careful managers* in respect of all activities concerning the management of the Company. Examples of able and careful management are not set out in the Commercial Code. Therefore, a director's conduct has to be evaluated individually on the basis of this test[11] and any commercial decisions which fall outside its scope will be deemed to result in a breach of duty. In the context of the management of the Company, the diligence test therefore imposes an obligation on directors to act carefully when taking decisions in connection with the administration, representation and commercial dealings of the Company. This includes making the necessary inquiries and the collection of economic data to provide a basis for an informed decision, a meaningful assessment of the available options and timely action. Management decisions must therefore be aimed at avoiding losses for the Company and generally be in its interests. This general duty to act in the interests of the Company complements the due diligence principle. It originates from the general obligation of partners not to act against the interests of the partnership (Civil Code, section 2251(1)) and is expressed in specific statutory obligations pertaining to commercial companies, such as the prohibition against competition applicable to directors (non-competition clause in the Commercial Code, section 171(1)).

The duty to act as an able and careful manager must be assessed according to an objective standard: any conduct must be objectively necessary to avoid financial losses and so it is of no consequence that the director acts or would have acted with a lesser degree of care and diligence in relation to his own personal property. This assessment must be made in accordance with a proper interpretation of the diligence test, taking into account the relevant provisions of the Civil Code[12] which regulate specific contractual relationships, and by taking into account the general principle which applies a common objective standard governing all relations regulated by civil contract.[13]

---

[11] See also Judgment of the Latvian Supreme Court in case no SKC-102/2014 of 27 May 2014.

[12] Civil Code, s 2250(1) for a partnership. For other references, see L Abramoviča, 'Krietna saimnieka rūpības nozīme Komerclikumā' *Jurista Vārds* 07.11.2006, 44 (447) 1.1.

[13] K Torgāns, *Civillikuma komentāri* (Riga, Mans ipasums, 2000) § 1645, no 2: 'in civil law relations, any person may expect from others the required understanding, knowledge and diligence, to perform his obligations' (own translation).

Since directors have been appointed in order to take commercial decisions in a business sphere amongst other professionals,[14] the relevant standard against which their activities are measured is high.[15]

Therefore, in the event of a sale of 25 per cent of the Company's existing stock to an international wholesaler with a 50 per cent discount to the current market price, Mr B would be deemed to have fulfilled his duties as a director only if his conduct met the diligence test according to an objective standard; in other words, the standard of another manager possessing the requisite skills and acting with such care as can be expected from such a person under the same circumstances in the sphere of professional businesspeople. Taking into account the market conditions and more specifically the circumstances whereby sales drop and payment terms are prolonged, selling part of the Company's stock is certainly not contrary to this standard. However, granting a 50 per cent discount may constitute a breach of the director's duties if this transaction results in a loss for the Company, for example, because the price is below the costs of production or if the market conditions were such that a sale to another customer with a substantially smaller discount would have been possible. The director is under a duty to analyse in sufficient detail both the production costs and the market conditions in order to prevent the Company from sustaining financial losses on conclusion of the sale.

Furthermore, by borrowing from a private individual on credit terms which are 150 per cent above the current average annual interest rate offered by commercial banks, Mr B will be deemed to have fulfilled his duties as a director provided that it is demonstrable that an able and careful manager would have taken this decision. In order to be able to continue production, and bearing in mind the refusal of the Company's bankers to provide further credit, Mr B had no option but to find other sources of cash. The conditions attached to the loan are such that they may damage the financial position of the Company. Mr B's decision will be deemed to have passed the diligence test, thus fulfilling his duties as a director, if he can show that he has conducted a reasonably detailed analysis of the credit market and was unable to receive more favourable conditions. Although directors are not liable towards the Company for decisions made in good faith which have been endorsed by the meeting of shareholders (according to the Commercial Code, section 169(4)),[16] even if his decision may have required further analysis to pass the diligence test, Mr B can still be held liable, even though his conduct was approved by the shareholders, by way of an action brought by creditors of the company for the benefit of the company (pursuant to Commercial Code, section 170(2)(3)).

---

[14] A Lošmanis, 'Par topošo Latvijas komerctiesību aktuālajiem mezglu punktiem' *Jurista Vārds* 12.05.2009, 20 (127).

[15] A Strupišs, *Komerclikuma komentāri I, A daļa Komercdarbības vispārīgie noteikumi (1.-73. panti)* (Riga, A Strupiša juridiskais birojs 2003) 195, § 496, with regard to the similar case of commercial agents appointed as professional participants in the business sphere and who are thus under the statutory obligation to act diligently.

[16] For more detail on the board of directors, see E Novicāne, 'Valdes locekļa atbrīvošana no atbildības' *Jurista Vārds* 21.02.2017, 8 (962).

In the event that claims are made against Mr B and the Company is able to prove (i) that it has suffered loss, (ii) as a result of the performance or non-performance of Mr B and (iii) a causal link between the loss and the performance or non-performance,[17] the onus of proof to establish that he has acted diligently and has fulfilled his duties shifts over to him (Commercial Code, section 169(3)).[18] Hence, for both decisions analysed here, Mr B would need to be able to provide evidence which explains the background to his decision and the analysis which he applied in order to show that he acted as an honest and careful manager and in good faith. Otherwise, it is presumed that Mr B is liable to the Company for any losses caused by his conduct.

If the Company is unable to satisfy its commitments towards its creditors owing to a lack of funds where the due date for payment of such debts has passed and the debt commitments of the Company exceed its assets (Insolvency Act, sections 57(5) and 57(6); Commercial Code, section 209), Mr B is also under an obligation to file an insolvency petition with the competent court. At the point in time where the Company is unable to pay for goods it has received, the application must be filed immediately (Insolvency Act, section 60(3)). The statutory duty to lodge an insolvency petition arises at the moment the terms for payment provide that payment is due. Therefore, imminent illiquidity by itself does not trigger such a duty. However, when it was established one month earlier that the company's cash reserves would last for only another two to three weeks, it was the duty of Mr B to provide immediate notice of that fact to the Company's shareholders (Commercial Code, section 219). Therefore, the lack of timely intimation of the potential insolvency of the Company to the shareholders constitutes a breach of Mr B's duties as a director.

iii. Personal Liability of Directors

According to the general rules on liability (Civil Code, sections 1770–92), a director must compensate a company in respect of any losses which it has incurred as a direct result of his or her actions as a director.[19] Where more than one director acts, they are jointly liable for losses to the company (Commercial Code, section 169(2)). As mentioned above, the onus of proof that the director has acted diligently and is therefore without fault falls on the director him-/herself. If the director can establish that he or she has acted as an able and careful manager in any proceedings raised for compensation for losses, liability is excluded (Commercial Code, section 169(3)).

For a personal liability claim to be brought in the competent court, a shareholders' resolution passed by a simple majority of the votes present is required (Commercial Code, section 172(1)). Moreover, a minority of shareholders representing 5 per cent of the issued share capital of the Company[20] may also demand that the company instigate

---

[17] On the development of the respective court practice, see A Strupišs, 'Komerctiesību attīstība piemērošanas praksē' *Jurista Vārds* 05.12.2017, 9.

[18] Judgment of the Latvian Supreme Court in case no SKC-25/2012 of 25 January 2012.

[19] On the issue of liability of directors of a Latvian private limited liability company, see also J Bērziņš, 'Komercsabiedrības amatpersonu civiltiesiskās atbildības aspekti' *Jurista Vārds* 12.05.2009, 19 (20).

[20] In addition, shareholders representing €71,100 or more of the issued share capital are entitled to demand that proceedings be instigated against a director.

proceedings. With regard to the inactivity of Mr B and his decision to sell stock on the basis of a discount, the 95 per cent shareholder Mr A1 and/or the 5 per cent shareholder Ms A2 would therefore be required to take a formal resolution to sue the director for personal liability and appoint one or more representatives of the Company in the court proceedings.[21] However, the decision to enter into a loan transaction with very unfavourable conditions was approved by Mr A1 and therefore by a majority of the shareholders of the Company. Nevertheless, minority shareholder Ms A2 may raise an additional personal liability claim against Mr B to challenge the loan transaction. Such a challenge would be based on the rule that the approval of management decisions by a meeting of the shareholders does not extinguish the right of minority shareholders to raise personal liability claims (Commercial Code, section 173(2)). In the event that claims are raised by the minority which are manifestly unfounded, however, the relevant minority shareholders are obliged to compensate the Company in respect of any related costs it may incur (Commercial Code, section 172(7)). In the event that neither shareholder decides to instigate proceedings, the creditors of the Company are entitled to bring a claim on behalf of the Company against the director (Commercial Code, section 170(1)). Where such a claim is raised by the creditor on behalf of the Company, the director may not raise any objection to the effect that the shareholders in fact endorsed his or her decision, or that potential claims between the Company and the director have already been settled.

In addition, if it can be established that Mr B intentionally or as a result of his negligent conduct drove the Company into insolvency, thereby causing substantial harm to the rights and interests of other parties (Criminal Act, section 213), he may be subject to criminal liability. Any failure to file an insolvency application within the time limits set by law may also result in criminal liability on the part of Mr B (Criminal Act, section 215). However, so far, the courts have merely allowed for civil liability where there has been late submission of insolvency applications.[22]

Despite the relatively large number of cases brought before the Supreme Court of Latvia, it is difficult to determine whether and to what extent the (in)activity of Mr B in the present case would lead to civil or criminal liability in Latvian legal practice.[23] During the years of economic growth, which coincided with the introduction of the

---

[21] If a supervisory board is formed, its board members represent the company in court: Commercial Code, s 172(3).

[22] Judgment of the Latvian Supreme Court in case no PAC-0400 of 24 November 2011.

[23] The court practice is seen as becoming increasingly strict in the interpretation of what constitutes a breach of duty; for an overview of recent cases, see A Strupišs, 'Komerctiesību attīstība piemērošanas praksē' *Jurista Vārds* 05.12.2017, 9 (10); earlier, the courts were more lenient: in Case C-2089/12 of 22 March 2007, the Riga Court of Second Instance ruled that a breach of the accounting rules and resulting losses were *not* deemed to have arisen as a result of a lack of diligent management, while it is an accepted principle that to ensure that proper accounts of the company are kept is a core part of the director's duties: K Čakste, *Tirdzniecības tiesības. Ievads un 1.daļa* (Riga, Publisher unknown, 1939) 117. Meanwhile, in the decision of the Latvian Supreme Court in case no SKC-25/2012 of 25 January 2012, it was held that where a company has demonstrated that it has (i) suffered loss (ii) as a result of the performance or non-performance of the director and (iii) there is a causal link between (i) and (ii), the burden shifts to the director to prove that he acted as an honest and careful manager in the particular circumstances and that he has not committed even the most minor of oversights. If the director's conduct is in pursuance of a direction by the shareholders, it was also held that the directors will not be liable for a breach of their duty of care.

current company law framework, there were few opportunities for the Latvian courts to determine the scope and effect of the rules on the duties and liabilities of directors of distressed companies. The recent severe economic crisis, which has affected the Latvian economy and most Latvian companies, has had an effect on the number of legal cases dealing with the duties and activities of directors in distressed companies. However, given the time taken for legal proceedings to be brought to their conclusion, it took several years before the courts of the third and highest instance delivered relevant judgments. Nonetheless, each and every judgment issued by the Supreme Court on issues related to directors' duties was heavily influenced by the unique facts of the case; thus, it is difficult to draw general conclusions. On account of the proximity of the regulatory framework of Latvian and German company and commercial law, it is submitted that German legal doctrine developed with regard to directors in a German private limited liability company (*Gesellschaft mit beschränkter Haftung* (GmbH))[24] may assist in determining in more detail the exact duties of directors in (distressed) Latvian companies.

B. France

i. Introduction

KOKS SIA (hereinafter 'the Company') is a limited liability company. Under French law, it would be a *Société à responsabilité limitée* (SARL). There are no directors in a SARL, only managers (*gérants*). The duties of managers in a SARL are approached in the same way as the duties of directors and managers of a public limited liability company (*Société anonyme* (SA)) or of a simplified public limited liability company (*Société par actions simplifiée* (SAS)). The principles applicable to the civil liability of managers in an SARL, an SA and an SAS have been developed by the French courts and are identical.

Managers and directors are held to a duty of care in the case of the SARL,[25] the SA and the SAS.[26] In general, the Commercial Code provides that the directors are individually or jointly and severally liable to the company or third parties either for infringements of the laws or regulations applicable to the company, or for breaches of the articles of association, or for tortious or negligent acts of management.

French courts have a wide discretion to decide what amounts to a breach of the duty of care. The manager or director is held to an objective standard, thus comparing him or her to what a reasonable manager or director would have done in the same situation. The burden of proof is on the plaintiff to establish that the duty of care was breached.

---

[24] Overviews can be found in R Jula, *Der GmbH-Geschäftsführer* (Berlin, Springer 2007) 67 and U Schneider, 'Organpflichten und Haftung in der GmbH und GmbH & Co. KG' in G Krieger and U Schneider (eds), *Handbuch Managerhaftung* (Cologne, Otto Schmidt, 2007); see also ch 9, below.
[25] Commercial Code, Art L 223-22.
[26] Commercial Code, Art L 225-251.

ii. Breach of a Duty of Care where the Company Remains Solvent

In general, the French courts tend not to second-guess the decisions of the board of directors or the management of a company, as long as the company remains solvent (or *in bonis*). Therefore, in substance, the result is broadly equivalent in effect to the 'business judgment rule'.

In the case of Mr B, given the very difficult conditions being experienced by the Company, which could only meet its creditors' claims for the next two or three weeks, the solution would depend on whether the Company is continuing to make a profit on the sale of the assets or not too large a loss on it. Given the steep discount, this is highly improbable. The sale is probably made at a loss, but this might not be enough to constitute a breach of a duty of care given the difficult circumstances.

Turning to the issues raised by the level of the interest rate, which is 150 per cent above the current average annual interest rate offered by commercial banks, it is clear that this is very high indeed. Therefore, it is more straightforward to conclude that there was a breach of the duty of care here.

As long as a company remains solvent, the French courts generally do not tend to second-guess decisions taken by the directors. In the case of Mr B, if the Company was able to avoid bankruptcy, a court would probably find that there was no breach of his duty of care.

The fact that Mr B's decision to enter into the loan transaction was approved by shareholder Mr A1 (who holds 95 per cent of the Company's share capital) does not protect him from liability. Under French company law, no decision of the shareholders in general meeting can have the effect of extinguishing or preventing the raising of a suit.[27] This principle is explicitly stated to apply in the case of the SA, but it also applies to the SARL and the SAS. However, a court might take into account the fact that the transaction was approved by the majority of the Company's shareholders in determining whether or not (and, if so, to what extent) there was a breach of the duty of care.

Mr B should not be subject to criminal sanctions on the basis of an abuse of corporate assets (*abus de biens sociaux*) since he had no personal interest in the transaction.

iii. Breach of a Duty of Care where the Company Files for Bankruptcy

When a company files for bankruptcy, the French courts are much more willing to find a breach of duty of care. In addition, there are specific provisions which target directors. However, in such a case, the duties are owed to the creditors, not the shareholders.

In the Company's case, given the circumstances, it has had to file for bankruptcy because it is no longer able to pay its debts. The behaviour of Mr B would therefore subject him to several specific provisions of the Commercial Code which apply when a company has filed for bankruptcy.

---

[27] Commercial Code, Art L 225-253.

First, the Commercial Code allows a judge to hold a director or manager (*dirigeant de droit*) personally liable for part or the whole of the debts of a company when a managerial error (*faute de gestion*) or errors contributed to the existence of irretrievable debts (*action en responsabilité pour insuffisance d'actif, which replaced the action en comblement de passif in 2005*).[28] Simple negligence used to be enough to incur liability. However, the law was changed in 2016 and now simple negligence cannot give rise to an *action en responsabilité pour insuffisance d'actif.* The burden of proof is on the plaintiff. If it can be established that Mr B's managerial errors contributed to the existence of irretrievable debts, he could be held liable on this ground. This is the case here since the sale of 25 per cent of the Company's stock at a 50 per cent discount and taking a loan at a high interest rate significantly reduced the Company's assets and increased the amount of its irretrievable debt.

Second, a court has the power to apply a civil sanction of individual insolvency (*faillite personnelle*)[29] and a criminal sanction of individual bankruptcy (*banqueroute*)[30] against a director who has abusively continued a business which is losing money when the situation could only realistically lead to insolvency. In the case of individual insolvency, a director may be disqualified from acting as a director or manager of a company and is subject to a number of potential sanctions. In the case of individual bankruptcy, a director is liable to receive a custodial sentence and a fine. Given the very difficult situation experienced by the Company in the two months preceding its insolvency and the lack of any realistic prospect of a general economic turnaround, a French court would probably consider that he should have filed for bankruptcy sooner.

Finally, a court can also apply a civil sanction of individual insolvency (*faillite personnelle*)[31] and a criminal sanction of bankruptcy (*banqueroute*)[32] to the director who has used ruinous means in order to gain funds and tried to avoid or delay the filing of a bankruptcy petition. In the case of Mr B, a French court is bound to hold that the sale of corporate assets at a deep discount and the loan transaction with the high interest rate constitute ruinous means.

iv. Summary and Conclusions

It is difficult to say with any certainty whether Mr B would be liable for a breach of his duty of care where the Company remains solvent, given the wide discretion afforded to, and the restraint exercised by, the French courts in this area and the very difficult circumstances experienced by the Company at the time the sale was made and the loan transaction was concluded. However, if the Company files for bankruptcy, Mr B would very probably be considered to have breached his duty of care.

---

[28] Commercial Code, Art L 651-2.
[29] Commercial Code, Art L 653-3.
[30] Commercial Code, Art L 626-2.
[31] Commercial Code, Art L 653-5.
[32] Commercial Code, Art L 654-2.

C. Germany[33]

i. Introduction

The structure and registration of companies is similar in Latvia and in Germany. The *Aktiengesellschaft* (AG) is the German public company and the GmbH is the German private limited company. There are about 21,000 AGs and 1,320,000 GmbHs in Germany.[34] In contrast to Latvia, these two companies are regulated in different Acts (the AktG and GmbHG).

The incorporation of a GmbH requires a minimum capital of €25,000 (GmbHG, § 5). However, the 2008 'MoMiG reform' of the GmbHG[35] has also introduced a new type of limited company (*Unternehmergesellschaft*), which can be started with a minimum capital of €1 but which has to allocate one-quarter of its annual profits to its capital reserve until the €25,000 level is achieved. GmbHs usually have just one board of directors unless they choose to have a separate supervisory board (GmbHG, § 52). The GmbH is represented by the directors (GmbHG, § 35(1)).

ii. Directors' Duties

Directors' duties are addressed in general terms in § 43(1), (2) of the GmbHG, which states that 'the directors shall conduct the company's affairs with the due diligence of a prudent businessman ...; directors who breach the duties incumbent upon them shall be severally and jointly liable to the company for any damage arising'.[36] On the one hand, one could call these obligations objective (as in Latvia) because personal attributes of the director, such as inexperience or inability, are irrelevant.[37] On the other hand, directors enjoy the benefits of a business judgment rule, which has been developed by case law.[38] Furthermore, if the directors have acted on instructions received by the general meeting, they are usually not liable.[39] However, it is insufficient that the shareholders merely consent to the conduct of the directors. The burden of proof is divided between the company and its directors. The company has to show that the conduct of the directors has caused damage to it, whereas the directors have to show that they acted competently and diligently.[40] It may be possible that Mr B could avoid liability under these general rules. He would have to prove that there were good reasons

---

[33] Abbreviated statutes: AktG = Law on Public Companies; GmbHG = Law on Private Limited Companies; InsO = Insolvency Code; StGB = Criminal Code.

[34] Search with Orbis (https://orbis.bvdinfo.com) on 12 May 2018.

[35] Gesetz zur Modernisierung des GmbH-Rechts und zur Bekämpfung von Missbräuchen (MoMiG) of 23 October 2008, BGBl I 2008, 2026.

[36] Translation available at www.gesetze-im-internet.de/englisch_gmbhg/index.html. On enforcement, see ch 10 at II E, below.

[37] See U Noack and W Zöllner in *Baumbach & Hueck's GmbHG* (21st edn, Munich, Beck, 2017) § 43, para 11.

[38] Confirmed in BGH (German Federal Supreme Court), NJW 2008, 3361; Noack and Zöllner, ibid, § 43, para 22.

[39] BGH (German Federal Supreme Court), NJW 2000, 1571; Noack and Zöllner, ibid, § 43, para 33.

[40] See Noack and Zöllner, ibid, § 43, para 36. A similar procedure is expressly provided for in AktG, § 93(2) (s 2) for the AG.

why the sale at a discount and the loan were *ex ante* an acceptable response to the risk of insolvency.

Further duties are specifically imposed on directors of companies that are close to insolvency. The directors have to call a shareholders' meeting immediately if the annual balance sheet or a balance sheet drawn up in the course of the company's financial year shows a loss of half of the share capital (GmbHG, § 49(3)). Possibly, this has occurred in the present case. Moreover, the directors have to file for insolvency if the company is unable to pay its debts or if the assets of the company do not cover its liabilities (InsO, § 15(1)). If the directors do not file for insolvency, they have to indemnify the company for any payments made after that date (GmbHG, § 64). However, here it does not appear to be the case that the company was insolvent at that time.

The case also asks whether any omission may constitute a breach of Mr B's duties. Directors of a GmbH (or an AG) have the duty to organise the running of the Company in a way that information on the financial situation is readily available.[41] This may also include a system of risk evaluation.[42] Furthermore, inactivity may lead to liability in the case of multiple directors (which is not relevant here) since directors have a duty to cooperate with, and to supervise, their fellow directors.

iii. Criminal Sanctions

With respect to criminal sanctions, the most relevant provisions are those that criminalise the duty to notify the loss of half of the capital and the obligation to file for insolvency (§ 84 GmbHG; § 15a InsO). The maximum sentence is three years for intent; it is one year for negligence, which it can be argued is applicable here. While, as such, breaches of directors' duties do not lead to criminal sanctions, a controversial judgment of the German Federal Supreme Court held that directors could be culpable of criminal breach of trust (§ 266 StGB) because they approved large payments in a takeover battle.[43] However, this would require intent; thus, it is unlikely that Mr B would face this sanction in the present scenario.

D. Italy

In Italy the two most common types of incorporated companies are the *Società per azioni* (Spa) and the *Società a responsabilità limitata* (Srl). Both these entities are regulated by the Civil Code (CC) as amended by the 2003 Corporate Law Reform. The Spa is the Italian public company, while the Srl is the Italian version of the private limited liability company.

In order to establish an Srl, the law in principle requires a minimum share capital of €10,000 (CC, Article 2463, paragraph 2, no 4); however this provision should now be read in combination with the recently introduced Article 2463, paragraph 4, of the

---

[41] BGH NZG 2012, 940 (confirming previous case law).
[42] Explicitly in AktG, § 91(2), but also extended to the GmbH: Noack and Zöllner (n 37) § 35, para 33.
[43] BGH, NJW 2006, 522.

CC which, under certain conditions, allows the incorporation of Srls with a minimum share capital 'lower than €10,000' and 'at least equal to €1'.

Italian Srls are managed by a board of directors or by a single director, even if strong decision-making powers are provided to the shareholders by the law or the articles of association. The audit function is performed by a single internal auditor or by an internal board of auditors; furthermore, an external auditor may also be appointed. However, it should also be stressed that the establishment of an audit function is not always mandatory. In particular, the appointment of an audit function is necessary when the company should prepare consolidated accounts or when it should be subject to the review of an external auditor (see CC, Article 2477).

The duties and the powers of the directors of an Srl are set out in the Civil Code (Articles 2475, 2475-*bis*, 2475-*ter* and 2476). In contrast to the provisions applicable in the context of the board of directors of an Spa, no specific provision addresses the issue of the standard of conduct of the directors of an Srl. In particular, the statute governing the Srl does not contain a provision similar to Article 2392 of the CC, which states that 'the directors [of an Spa] must perform the duties required of them by law and the by-laws with the diligence required being governed by the nature of the appointment and their specified tasks and duties'. In light of the absence of a specific criterion governing the standard of conduct of the directors of an Srl, it has been argued that reference should be made to the general rules on the performance of obligations and, in particular, to Article 1176, paragraph 2 of the CC, which states that, in performing their duties, directors must exercise the due diligence which is required by the nature of their appointment.[44] In performing their duties, however, the directors are also protected by legal principles that are functionally similar to the business judgment rule.[45]

With regard to the standard of review imposed on the directors of an Srl, Article 2476 of the CC states that 'the directors are jointly and severally liable towards the company for damage caused by their failure to comply with the duties imposed on them by the law and by the articles of association in relation to the management of the company'. Italian scholars debate the extent of the liability of directors where they have acted in accordance with the instructions of the shareholders[46] and the position remains unresolved. The difficulty is created by the relationship between the general principle which requires – and imposes on – the directors the duty to manage the company, and Article 2476, paragraph 7 of the CC, which states that the shareholders who have intentionally undertaken or have authorised the carrying out of acts detrimental to the company, to the shareholders or to third parties are jointly and severally liable with the directors.[47]

---

[44] G Bartalini, 'La responsabilità dei soci e degli amministratori' in M Sarale (ed), *Le nuove s.r.l.* (Bologna, Zanichelli, 2008) 617 ff, 653 ff; A Angelillis and G Sandrelli, 'Commento *sub* art. 2476' in P Marchetti, LA Bianchi, F Ghezzi and M Notari (eds), *Commentario alla Riforma delle società, Società a responsabilità limitata* (Milan, Giuffrè-Egea, 2008) 665 ff, 678 ff.

[45] See eg Bartalini, 'La responsabilità dei soci e degli amministratori' (n 44) 657 ff.

[46] *Cf* Bartalini (n 44) 669 ff; Angelillis and Sandrelli, 'Commento *sub* art. 2476' (n 44) 791 ff.

[47] In particular on this problem, see V Meli, 'La responsabilità dei soci nelle s.r.l.' in P Abbadessa and GB Portale (eds), *Il nuovo diritto delle società, Liber amicorum Gian Franco Campobasso*, vol 3 (Turin, Utet, 2007) 667 ff.

In addition to these duties, if an Srl faces challenging economic circumstances and more than one-third of its share capital is lost, Article 2482-*bis* of the CC provides that the directors are under a specific duty to call a general meeting in order to take the necessary measures. Moreover, Article 2482-*ter* of the CC states that if both (a) more than one-third of the share capital is lost and (b) the share capital is below the minimum share capital as indicated in Article 2463, paragraph 2, no 4 of the CC (ie €10,000), the directors must (i) call a general meeting to reduce the share capital and contemporaneously increase it to an amount not lower than that legal minimum[48] or, alternatively, (ii) convert the company into another form. If, in a situation like this, the directors fail to call the general meeting, they are in breach of duty and can be held liable under Article 2485, paragraph 1 of the CC, which states that 'directors without delay shall ascertain the occurrence of a cause of dissolution' and adds that '[t]he directors, in the case of delay or an omission, are personally liable on a joint and several basis for damage caused to the company, to the shareholders, to the company creditors and to third parties'. In addition, according to Article 2486, paragraph 2 of the CC, 'the directors are personally and jointly liable for damage caused to the company, to the shareholders, to the company's creditors and to third parties, by actions or omissions committed' after the occurrence of a cause of liquidation.[49] A delay in the filing imposed by Article 2485, paragraph 1 of the CC may also result in an administrative sanction under Article 2630, paragraph 1 of the CC on the directors for an amount up to €1,032, not excluding the possibility of other criminal sanctions.

In the instant case, if Mr B acted after the loss of more than one-third of the Company's share capital, this arguably falls within the scope of Articles 2485 and 2486 of the CC. Thus, Mr B is probably liable for the damage caused to the Company, to the shareholders, to the Company's creditors and to third parties and could also be sanctioned under Article 2630, paragraph 1 of the CC. In this specific situation the business judgment rule would not be applicable, because Mr B violated his specific duty to call the general meeting of the shareholders in order to preserve the integrity and the value of the corporate assets after the occurrence of a cause of liquidation.

E. Spain

i. Introduction

The *Sociedad Anonima* (SA) is the Spanish public company and the *Sociedad de Responsabilidad Limitada* (SL) is the Spanish private limited company. There are about

[48] Prior to October 2011, both the Italian courts and legal practitioners were of the view that it was necessary to reduce a company's capital and contemporaneously increase its share capital, ie a two-stage process. However, in October 2011, the notaries of Milan issued a new guideline that approved the possibility of simply increasing the share capital without a prior capital reduction. Therefore, it is now debated whether a prior reduction is necessary. As a result, it is difficult to be sure whether an Italian court would permit a straightforward increase in the share capital. The matter is complicated by the fact that the wording of Art 2482-*ter* – which is set out above – has not changed.

[49] For a detailed analysis of this matter, cf F Bonelli, *Gli amministratori di s.p.a. dopo la riforma delle società* (Milan, Giuffrè, 2004) 164 ff.

89,392 SAs and 1,146,131 SLs in Spain.[50] Since July 2010, these two corporate forms are now regulated in the same Act, the Ley de Sociedades de Capital (LSC) – Corporate Enterprises Act.[51]

The incorporation of an SL generally requires a minimum capital of €3,000 (LSC, Article 4.1). An SL's management can be entrusted to a director, to a group of them or to a board of directors (LSC, Article 210.1) and, in the latter case, the number of directors should be between three and 12 (LSC, Article 242.1–2). The SL is represented by the directors (LSC, Articles 209 and 233.1).

ii. Directors' Duties

The directors' duty of care is generally addressed by Article 225 of the LSC, and comprises three main obligations. First, the essence of the duty of care is reflected in the very general requirement of directors to conduct themselves as 'ordered businessmen'; this general standard is, however, to be interpreted on a case-by-case basis, in light of the specific role and functions attributed to each of them (LSC, Article 225.1). Second, directors must dedicate themselves sufficiently to the good management of the company (LSC, Article 225.2). Third, directors must request and collect from the company relevant information to enable them to comply with their duties (LSC, Article 225.3).[52] Furthermore, directors in Spain are subject to a business judgment rule that has long been recognised by case law and according to which a court may specifically hold the conduct to be in compliance with directors' duties.[53] The business judgment rule was incorporated into statute in 2014[54] and covers directors' discretionary strategic or business decisions which are adopted: (i) in good faith; (ii) without having a personal interest in the decision; (iii) with sufficient information; and (iv) following an adequate decision-making procedure (LSC, Article 226.1).

Spanish company law directs that Mr B would be held liable for any damages that are attributable to malicious or negligent actions or omissions which are against the law, the by-laws of the Company or the duties inherent in his office (LSC, Article 236.1). Moreover, all of the directors that adopted/performed the damaging

[50] INE, *Anuario Estadístico de España*, 2016, p 271, available at www.ine.es/prodyser/pubweb/anuario16/anu16_09finan.pdf.
[51] Real Decreto Legislativo 1/2010, de 2 de julio, por el que se aprueba el texto refundido de la Ley de Sociedades de Capital (LSC). Before the passing of the LSC, both types of companies were regulated in separate Acts – the Real Decreto Legislativo 1564/1989, de 22 de diciembre, por el que se aprueba el texto refundido de la Ley de Sociedades Anónimas (for SAs) and the Ley 2/1995, de 23 de marzo, de Sociedades de Responsabilidad Limitada (for SLs).
[52] For an application of this requirement by the Spanish courts see, eg, STS (Sentencia Tribunal Supremo), of 10 November 2010.
[53] With regard to this issue, the SAP Madrid (Sentencia Audiencia Provincial de Madrid) of 24 September 2009, recognises that it is not the task of the court to determine whether a corporate decision is appropriate from a business perspective. On the issue of the business judgment rule in Spain, see C Paz-Ares, 'La responsabilidad de los administradores como instrumento de gobierno corporativo' (2003) *Indret: Revista para el Análisis del Derecho* 31. The extent of the director's discretion in adopting business decisions is limited, inter alia, by the principle of 'reasonable prudence' according to which corporate decisions must be founded on rational criteria which avoid exposing the assets of the company to unjustified risks; see V Ribas Ferrer, *El deber de lealtad del administrador de sociedades* (Madrid, La Ley, 2010) 197–99.
[54] Ley 31/2014, de 3 de diciembre, por la que se modifica la Ley de Sociedades de Capital para la mejora del gobierno corporativo.

agreement/action are jointly liable to the Company, the shareholders and the creditors (LSC, Articles 236.1 and 237). There are, however, cases in which directors may be able to avoid such liability. This would apply to those directors who are able to prove that they were not involved in the adoption or performance of the agreement or the action which constituted a breach and that they did not know about that agreement/action, or that, even if they knew about it, they took all adequate measures to avoid the harm, or at least voiced their explicit opposition against such agreement/action (LSC, Article 237). None of this, however, applies to Mr B, who is acting as sole director.

The fact that Mr B's decision to enter into the loan transaction was approved by shareholder Mr A1 does not operate to relieve him of liability in terms of Article 236.2 of the LSC. This provision directs that any damaging action or agreement which has been adopted, authorised or ratified by the shareholders of the Company in general meeting will, in no case, exonerate a director from liability.

Therefore, the Spanish courts would be required to evaluate whether the business judgment rule would apply to this case or not and whether there was a violation of the duty of care. The burden of proof is divided between the Company and Mr B.[55] Hence, in the instant case, the Company would have to show that Mr B's decisions resulted in the Company suffering loss and Mr B would have to demonstrate that he acted in a diligent manner when deciding that there were good reasons for selling the assets at a discounted price and for entering into the loan transaction at an interest rate above the current average interest rate offered by commercial banks.

iii. Rules of Insolvency and Criminal Law

Spanish law imposes specific duties upon directors in the context of corporate insolvency. Corporate insolvency is regulated in a separate piece of legislation, namely the Ley Concursal (LCon) – Insolvency Act.[56] Directors must file for insolvency within a period of two months after they have known or should have been aware that the company was insolvent (LCon, Articles 3.1 and 5.1).[57] Insolvency is defined by the LCon as a situation where the debtor 'cannot regularly perform its obligations' (LCon, Article 2.2). It would appear, however, that this stage has not been reached in our case study. If directors fail to file for insolvency when required, they may be disqualified from acting as a director, obliged to compensate creditors in respect of loss suffered or ordered to pay part of the amount of the debts owed to the creditors. (LCon, Articles 165.1, 172 and 172 (bis)). In addition, where the Company's net worth (ie the value of its current assets less its current liabilities) goes below half of its share capital value – and there is no obligation to file for insolvency – directors have a period of two months to call a general meeting of the shareholders in order to decide on the dissolution of the Company (LSC, Articles 363.1(e) and 365.1); if this is the case here,

---

[55] In this regard, see V Cortés Domínguez, 'Apuntes sobre la carga de la prueba en el proceso sobre responsabilidad de los administradores por ejercicio de la acción social de responsabilidad por la sociedad' (2002) 6 *Revista Jurídica de la Universidad Autónoma de Madrid* 41.

[56] Ley 22/2003, de 9 de Julio, Concursal.

[57] See Á Rojo and E Beltrán, 'El Concurso de Acreedores' in A Menéndez and Á Rojo (eds) *Lecciones de Derecho Mercantil*, vol II (12th edn, Cizur Menor (Navarra), Civitas-Thomson Reuters, 2014) 512.

Mr B could be held liable towards the Company's creditors for a failure to call the meeting (LSC, Article 367). This liability would include liabilities of the Company – legal, contractual or extra-contractual – which arise subsequent to the statutory cause of dissolution of the Company.[58]

When it comes to potential criminal liability, the Código Penal (CP) – Criminal Code – addresses the criminal offence of punishable insolvency. Amongst other matters, this provision covers actions or omissions that constitute a serious breach of the duty of care in the management of the company's finances and which result in a reduction of the company's assets, or are used to hide the company's real economic situation (CP, Article 259.9). In our case, some of Mr B's actions diminish the assets of the company; therefore, if a court were to hold that those actions by Mr B constituted a serious breach of the duty of diligence, then Mr B could be subject to criminal liability, specifically imprisonment of one to four years and a fine of eight to twenty-four months (CP, Article 259.1).

F. The Netherlands[59]

i. Introduction

Dutch law distinguishes between two types of companies: the *Naamloze vennootschap* (NV) which is the Dutch public limited liability company and the *Besloten vennootschap* (BV), the Dutch private limited liability company. Both company forms are regulated by Book 2 of the Dutch Civil Code (DCC). In 2012 the laws applicable to the BV were substantially reformed and made more flexible. Since 2012 a Dutch private company can be set up without minimum capital. A public limited liability company requires a minimum capital of €45,000.[60]

Both the NV and the BV have a board of directors which can either be a one-tier or a two-tier board. The two-tier board is the traditional board model in the Netherlands. However, companies are free to opt for a one-tier board model if they wish.[61] A supervisory board becomes mandatory once the company meets the requirements of being a so-called *structuurvennootschap* which is, in short, a large company with a certain minimum number or employees.[62] This regime applies to both Dutch public as well as private limited liability companies which qualify as so called 'large' (*structuurvennootschap*) companies.[63] However, a one-tier board system is also possible within

---

[58] See, eg, J Bataller, 'Artículo 363. Causas de disolución' in Á Rojo and E Beltrán (eds), *Comentario de la Ley de Sociedades de Capital* (Cizur Menor (Navarra), Civitas-Thomson Reuters, 2011) 2575–78.

[59] Abbreviations: DCC=Dutch Civil Code; HR = Hoge Raad = Dutch Supreme Court; OK = Ondernemingskamer = Enterprise Chamber; Rb = rechtbank = District Court. An unofficial translation of Dutch company law as incorporated in bk 2 of the Dutch Civil Code can be found on www.dutchcivillaw.com/civilcodebook022.htm.

[60] DCC, Art 2:45.

[61] DCC, Art 2:129a/239a.

[62] DCC, Art 2:153/263. A so-called *structuurvennootschap* is a company which meets the following requirements for 3 consecutive years: issues capital and reserves of a minimum of €16m, a mandatory works council, and at least 100 employees working in the Netherlands.

[63] DCC, Art 2:153 for the public limited liability company; DCC, Art 2:263 for the private limited liability company.

a so-called 'structure regime company'. Therefore, instead of opting for a separate supervisory board, the company can choose to appoint non-executives onto the board of directors, and in doing so fulfil its obligations on the basis of the regime applicable to large companies (*structuurregime*).[64]

ii. Duties of Directors

Directors' duties are largely the same for private and public limited liability companies. KOKS is a private limited liability company so it would be a BV under Dutch law. Therefore, in the remainder of this section, we will primarily refer to the rules applicable to the Dutch private limited liability company.

The general expectations regarding the obligations of directors are set out in Article 2:129/239-5 DCC. Directors of both public and private limited liability companies must, in the performance of their duties, act in the interest of the company and the enterprise connected with it. Dutch law contains various legal bases for claims concerning directors' liability. In this respect, a distinction can be made between internal liability, ie directors' liability towards the company itself on the one hand and external liability on the other, ie liability towards third parties. With regard to internal liability, the main basis for liability can be found in Article 2:9-2 DCC. This liability concerns the liability of the directors towards the company and is applicable to both private and public limited liability companies alike. External liability concerns the liability of directors towards third parties such as creditors. These liability claims are often based on a tort (*onrechtmatige daad*). Another form of external liability concerns liability in the case of bankruptcy, which will be discussed below.[65]

iii. Duties and Liability Towards the Company

With regard to the (internal) liability towards the company, Article 2:9 DCC provides that every director is responsible towards the company for the proper performance of his or her duties. The task of every director includes responsibility for the general conduct of the company's affairs. The potential liability incorporated in Article 2:9 DCC is a collective liability of all directors jointly. In order to hold its directors liable, the company will have to establish that (i) there was improper management/fulfilment of duties for which (ii) the directors can be seriously blamed (*ernstig verwijt*). Once this is established, individual directors may be exculpated from liability depending on the circumstances of the case. In order to be exculpated, the individual director will have to prove that, given the specific tasks awarded to him/her, he/she is not seriously to be blamed for the improper management (*onbehoorlijk bestuur*) of the company and that he/she was not negligent in taking measures to avert the negative consequences of the improper management.

---

[64] DCC, Art 2:164a/274a jo 2:129a/239a.
[65] DCC, bk 2 also provides various other more specific grounds for liability, eg, liability for misleading annual accounts in DCC, Art 2:139/249.

The threshold of serious blame (*ernstig verwijt*) has been codified in recent years but stems originally from case law.[66] It constitutes a high threshold which will be difficult to satisfy. Much will depend on the circumstances of the case. In case law, many circumstances have been established that are important to take into account. These relevant circumstances include amongst others: the type of activities of the company and the risks that may result from those activities, the division of tasks within the board, potential guidelines for directors, the information available to the board, as well as the knowledge and diligence that can be expected of a responsible and diligent director.[67] The fact that the director of a company in financial difficulties sells parts of the company's assets at a discount in order to weather the financial storm, does not necessarily mean that the director acted against the interest of the company and therefore breached his or her duties. For instance, it may be possible to establish that a responsible and diligent director would have believed that this could be a successful restructuring measure enabling the company to overcome its financial difficulties.[68] With regard to the loan agreement, it is clear that the interest rate is very high, namely 150 per cent above the current average annual interest rate offered by commercial banks. It may therefore be clearer that there is an improper performance of directors' duties with regard to the loan transaction than with regard to the sale of assets. After all, it seems more obvious that such a high interest rate would be against the interest of the Company and the enterprise connected with it. However, whether or not entering into the loan is sufficient to constitute serious blame on behalf of the directors, is difficult to assess. A lot will depend on the circumstances of the case such as whether or not the Company would be able to obtain the loan from somewhere else against more favourable conditions or whether it can be established that the loan was necessary for the Company's survival or a planned/necessary reorganisation.

It is stated in the case that the director obtained the consent of the 95 per cent shareholder prior to entering into the loan agreement. The mere fact that shareholders have agreed to the transaction does not mean that the director is exempted from his or her duty to act in the interest of the company and is therefore exempted from a potential breach of his duties. Dutch law, since the 2012 reforms, provides for the possibility for shareholders of a private limited liability company to give specific instructions to the board provided that this possibility is stipulated in the articles of association.[69] However, regardless of the instructions received, directors remain responsible for safeguarding the interest of the company and the enterprise connected with it. Article 2:239-4 DCC provides that, if an instruction right is incorporated in the articles of association, directors are obliged to follow the instructions unless these

---

[66] HR 10 January 1997, *NJ* 1997, 360, with a note by JMM Maeijer (*Staleman/Van der Ven*).

[67] Ibid.

[68] See in this respect with regard to restructuring measures in company groups Hof Den Haag 12 November 2013, *JOR* 2014/32, with a note by Verboom (*Rosenberg Polak q.q./ Van Ommen c.s.*); Hof Den Haag 18 August 2015, *JIN* 2015/199, with a note by Wolf (*Culi d'or*). See on directors' liability near insolvency: M Olaerts, *Vennootschappelijke beleidsbepaling in geval van financiële moeilijkheden (diss.)* (Antwerp, Intersentia, 2007); TPJ Hanssen, 'De taak, verantwoordelijkheid en persoonlijke aansprakelijkheid van een bestuurder van een kapitaalvennootschap in financieel zwaar weer jegens een crediteur' (2015–16) *TvOB* 186–98.

[69] DCC, Art 2:239-4.

instructions are contrary to the interest of the company and the enterprise connected with it. Therefore, the fact that the director acted upon an instruction does not exempt the director from his or her duty to act in the best interest of the company and the enterprise connected with it.

iv.   Duties Towards Third Parties and Liability in the Case of Insolvency

Directors of a public limited liability company are obliged to call a general meeting when the company is faced with financial difficulties in order to discuss the measures to be taken.[70] Such a general meeting should be held within three months of it having become plausible to the board that the equity (*eigen vermogen*) of the company has decreased to an amount equal to or less than half of the paid and called up capital. Such a duty is, however, not codified for directors of a private limited liability company. Dutch law does not contain a codified duty for directors of a private or public limited liability company to file for bankruptcy. Directors who continue trading on behalf of an insolvent company will, however, face liability risks as will be explained below. It is worth noting that in order to be able to file for bankruptcy, the board of a private as well as a public limited liability company will need the consent of the shareholders unless stipulated otherwise in the articles of association.[71] The main duties of directors in the vicinity of insolvency have developed over the years in case law. According to Dutch case law directors can be held liable on the basis of a tort by third parties such as creditors if they, at the time of entering into the contract, knew or ought to have known that the company would not within reasonable time be able to fulfil its obligations or would not be able to provide relief for potential damages resulting from non-performance (the so called *Beklamel* rule).[72] This is a form of secondary liability as it is a liability of the director alongside the liability of the company itself.[73] Therefore, in the hypothetical case under discussion the unpaid creditors who entered into a contract with the company at a time where it was or ought to have been clear to the director that the company would not be able to fulfil its obligations, can initiate a tort claim against the director. In addition, directors can also be held liable if the plaintiff can establish that the director has caused or has permitted the company not to fulfil its obligations towards third parties. However, here too, serious blame on behalf of the director is required and much will depend on the circumstances of the case.[74] Liability towards third parties may be imposed if it can be established that the director, upon entering into the loan transaction and/or the sale transaction, knew or ought to have known that this would lead to non-performance by the company of its obligations.

---

[70] DCC, Art 2:108a.

[71] DCC, Art 2:136 for the public limited liability company and DCC, Art 2:246 for the private limited liability company.

[72] HR 6 October 1989, *NJ* 1990/286, with a note by JMM Maeijer (*Beklamel*).

[73] See Annex to the Study on Directors' Duties and Liability in the EU prepared for the European Commission DG Markt 2013, Country report: Netherlands, at p A 624, available at http://ec.europa.eu/justice/civil/company-law/corporate-governance/index_en.htm.

[74] HR 8 December 2006, JOR 2007/38 (*Ontvanger/Roelofsen*); HR 23 May 2014, *NJ* 2014/325, with a note by Van Schilfgaarde.

Furthermore, Dutch bankruptcy law includes a specific provision in terms of which the receiver/liquidator can raise a liability action against the board of directors.[75] This action can be initiated against directors of a private as well as a public limited liability company and the provisions for both types of company are largely similar. Article 2:248 DCC specifically provides that in the case of a private limited liability company in the state of insolvency, every director is jointly and severally liable against the insolvent estate for the amount of debt which cannot be paid after the assets of the company have been liquidated, if it can be established that the board has performed its duties in a manifestly improper manner (*manifestly improper conduct*[76] *or kennelijk onbehoorlijk bestuur*) and if it is likely that this has been the major cause of the bankruptcy. The improper performance should have taken place within three years prior to bankruptcy.[77] The liquidator will have a stronger claim in cases where the annual accounts have not been published on time or in cases where the board did not fulfil its duty to maintain a proper administration. In those two cases it will be established that the board has not properly performed its duties and it will be presumed that this improper performance was the main cause of insolvency.[78] The latter presumption can be rebutted by the board. The untimely publication of the annual accounts or the improper administration on the other hand lead directly to the establishment of improper management which cannot be rebutted. If the liquidator cannot make use of these legal presumptions, ie if there is a proper administration and timely publication of the annual accounts, the directors can still be held liable. In that case the court will have to assess whether the board acted in accordance with what can be expected of a reasonable director.[79] This liability is also a collective liability of the board for which individual directors can exculpate themselves depending on the circumstances of the case.

Since 2016[80] the public prosecutor or the receiver in the case of bankruptcy can also request the court to bar the director from directorship in the future.[81] This can, for example, be applied to a director who has been held liable on the basis of Article 2:138/248 DCC or who has willingly allowed the company to enter into legal transactions leading to serious disadvantages to creditors.

v. Criminal Sanctions

Directors of companies can be subjected to criminal sanctions.[82] Criminal sanctions may, for example, be imposed in cases where the directors have deliberately published

---

[75] DCC, Art 2:138 for the public limited liability company and Art 2:248 for the private limited liability company.

[76] See Country report Netherlands (n 73).

[77] DCC, Art 2:248-6.

[78] DCC, Art 2:138/248-2.

[79] HR 8 June 2001, *NJ* 2001/454 (*Panmo*).

[80] *Stb.* 2016, 153.

[81] Bankruptcy Code, Art 106a.

[82] JB Huizink, Groene Serie Rechtspersonen, art. 2:9 aant. 16.1. See also DR Doorenbosch, 'Bestuurdersaansprakelijkheid in het strafrecht' in M Holtzer, AFJA Leijten, and DJ Oranje (eds), *Geschriften vanwege de Vereniging Corporate Litigation 2014–2015, dl. 128 Van der Heijden-reeks* (Deventer, Kluwer 2014–15) 305–21.

annual accounts that deceive.[83] Criminal liability may furthermore arise if the director or supervisor has excessively used or abused corporate funds or has allowed corporate funds to be used in such a manner that has led to a severe disadvantage to the company threatening its existence.[84] General liability under criminal law can be found in Article 51 of the penal code. This imposes criminal sanctions on those who have commissioned the corporation to enter into the criminal act where the corporation has committed a criminal act.[85]

G. Finland

i. Introduction

The Limited Liability Companies Act 2006[86] (CA) regulates both private and public companies in Finland. A limited liability company is called *osakeyhtiö* (abbreviated as 'Oy' for private companies and 'Oyj' for public companies) in Finnish and *aktiebolag* ('Ab' and 'Abp', respectively) in Swedish.

The incorporation of a private company requires a minimum share capital of €2,500 and the incorporation of a public company requires a minimum share capital of €80,000.[87]

A limited liability company is managed by the board of directors. The board consists of between one and five persons unless the company's articles of association provide otherwise. If the board consists of three persons or fewer, a deputy member of the board is mandatory.[88]

The company may also have a managing director. The managing director is appointed by the board and is in charge of the daily management of the company. A company may also have a supervisory board, in which case its composition and duties must be provided for in the company's articles of association.

ii. Directors' Duties

The CA includes both explicit provisions on the exact duties of the company's management as well as certain general principles, the most relevant being the principles of equal treatment of the shareholders, fulfilling the objective operational purpose of the company and the duty of care. Pursuant to the general principles of the CA, the management (the board of directors, the managing director and the supervisory board) is under the duty to act with due care (duty of care) and to act in the best interests of

---

[83] Dutch Penal Code, Art 336.

[84] Dutch Penal Code, Arts 342 and 347.

[85] See with regard to this provision more specifically Doorenbosch, 'Bestuurdersaansprakelijkheid in het strafrecht' (n 82). See further with regard to criminal sanctions: Country report Netherlands (n 73).

[86] Osakeyhtiölaki 624/2006 is the main body of legislation regulating company law aspects of limited liability companies. There are also separate statutory Acts regulating eg insurance companies and financial institutions, which are limited liability companies. These Acts apply in addition to the CA.

[87] CA, c 1, s 3

[88] CA, c 6, ss 1 and 8.

the company (duty of loyalty).[89] The best interests of the company are influenced by its purpose. By virtue of chapter 1, section 5 of the CA, the purpose of a company is to generate profit for its shareholders, unless otherwise provided in the articles of association. Whether the directors have acted with due care is assessed on an objective basis and the standard of care is how a prudent person would act in the same situation.[90]

The CA provides for remedies when a director has failed to fulfil his or her duties or tasks, including the general duty of care. The basis for liability is more extensive when it comes to damage caused to the company itself. Firstly, a director is liable for damages for the loss that he or she has negligently caused to the company in violation of the general duty of care. Secondly, a director is also liable to the company, a shareholder or a third party for damage caused either deliberately or negligently in violation of the provisions of the CA (other than just the duty of care) or the company's articles of association.[91] Consequently, directors may be held liable not only for their acts but also for neglecting their duties. However, the directors may enjoy the benefit of the business judgment rule, similar to the business judgment rule in Delaware that protects directors from liability.[92] The burden of proof lies as a general rule with the person claiming a breach and loss. However, a presumption of negligence exists in the case of a violation of an explicit provision of the CA (ie, other than the general principles) or of the articles of association, or in the case of an act to the benefit of a related party, in which cases the director in question must prove that he or she has acted with due care.

The duty of care obliges the directors to keep themselves informed on an ongoing basis of all aspects that are of relevance to the company's business. Proper accounting records and financial statements are essential, but are not sufficient in and of themselves. High-risk situations, such as the scenario in the case study, clearly call for an enhanced duty of care. The assessment of a company's solvency would need to be based on a comprehensive evaluation.[93]

The CA also contains the so-called *corporate benefit* test. This means that any transaction, such as the sale of the company's assets or engaging in the loan agreement as in the present case study, must be based on eligible commercial grounds, support the company's business activities and be in the best commercial interests of the company. The corporate benefit test is linked to the provisions on permitted distribution of assets according to which 'any transaction which reduces the assets or increases the liabilities of a company without having sound business reasons is regarded as an illegal

---

[89] CA, c 1, s 8.

[90] Explanatory notes of the CA, Hallituksen esitys 109/2005, 195. See also J Mähönen and S Villa, *Osakeyhtiö I* (Helsinki, Talentum, 2015) 349. On the fiduciary duties of the board of directors, see W Lindholm and T Holmström, 'Innebörden av aktiebolags styrelsemedlems s.k. fiduciary duty enligt finsk rätt – särskilt med hänsyn till offentliga köpeanbud' (2005) *Tidskrift utgiven av Juridiska Föreningen i Finland* 278–94.

[91] CA, c 22, s 1(1).

[92] The business judgment rule is not included in the CA as a specific provision, but the rule is mentioned in the CA's preparatory works. Based on Finnish legal literature and case law, such a rule seems to be applicable also in Finland. Explanatory notes of the CA, Hallituksen esitys 109/2005, 194–5. For the US see J, below.

[93] A Kaarenoja and S Suontausta, 'Maksukyvyttömyys ja osakeyhtiön varojenjako' (2007) *Defensor Legis* 239, 255–56; SA Villa, 'Maksukykyisyys ja tasetesti osakeyhtiölain ja Uuden Seelannin yhtiölain mukaan' in A Saarnilehto (ed), *Yhtiöoikeudellisia kirjoituksia VI* (Turku, Turun Yliopisto, 2007) 137–69.

distribution of assets'. If the sale of assets or the loan agreement are not based on sound business reasons, it could be argued that they would constitute an unlawful distribution of assets.[94] The line between lawful and unlawful acts must be drawn on a case-by-case basis and it is therefore possible that Mr B has fulfilled his duty to act with due care.

Further pursuant to the CA, assets may not be distributed if it is known (based on proper financial monitoring) that the company is insolvent or that the distribution will cause the company to become insolvent.[95] Since the purpose of these provisions is also to protect the other stakeholders in addition to the shareholders, shareholder Mr A1's consent to the loan does not free Mr B from liability in damages to the creditors if he has failed to apply the solvency test and is unable to establish that he has acted with due care.[96] It is also possible that shareholder Mr A1 might be found liable for damages to the creditors of the company.[97]

It should also be noted that directors have certain duties where insolvency is possible such as a duty to register notification of the loss of share capital if the company's equity becomes negative. This duty is discussed in further detail in Chapter 6 at II G below.

iii. Criminal Sanctions

The main rule in the CA is that the criminal sanctions are for serious breaches of the CA and the primary remedy is liability for damages.[98] With regard to criminal sanctions, the most relevant provision is the one that criminalises the unlawful distribution of assets.[99] Pursuant to this provision, a person who intentionally violates the protection of the shareholders or the creditors by distributing the assets of the company in contravention of the provisions of the CA may be convicted of a criminal offence. The sanction is a fine or imprisonment of up to one year. However, such sanction would require intent from Mr B.

H. Poland

The limited liability company (*spółka z ograniczoąodpowiedzialnością*) is the most popular form of corporate vehicle in Poland. The originating power of the company is vested in the shareholders in general meeting. The shareholders are not and may not be rendered liable for the debts of the company. The company's assets are available to meet its debts. If a shareholder is also a director, the shareholder will be liable under the rules applicable to directors.

---

[94] The sale of assets clearly below current market prices is an example of an unlawful distribution of assets, which is referred to in the Explanatory notes of the CA, Hallituksen esitys 109/2005, 124, CA, c 13,s 1(3).
[95] CA, c 13, s 2.
[96] CA, c 22, s 1(2) and (3).
[97] CA, c 22, s 2.
[98] Explanatory notes of the CA, Hallituksen esitys 109/2005, 209 and explanatory notes of the previous CA, Hallituksen esitys 27/1977, 11 and 117.
[99] CA, c 25, s 1.

As regards the commercial activity of the company, the basic corporate documenta-
tion, for example, its articles (company deed), register of shareholders, annual balance
sheets et al, must be filed with the public National Court Register (*Krajowy Rejestr
Sądowy*). The minimum share capital of the company is PLN 5,000 (approximately
€1,200).[100] Polish company law regulation follows EU regulations. The statutory rules
on companies are spelt out in the comprehensive act on commercial subjects and
activities, namely the Commercial Companies Code (CCC). It is supplemented by the
regulation on civil partnerships and other principles of contract law which are laid
down in the principal codification of civil law in Poland, namely the Civil Code (CC).
Poland has a two-tier system of corporate governance. Corporate decision-making is
divided between the shareholders' meeting and the board of directors, and the latter
may be divided between a management board and a supervisory board. The company
may appoint a supervisory board and/or an audit commission.[101] Appointments to the
management board may be made from amongst the shareholders or from outsiders.
Pursuant to Article 201 of the CCC, directors are appointed and removed by resolution of the supervisory board, unless stated otherwise in the company deed.

In Poland, the liability of directors is regulated by numerous legal provisions: the
CCC and CC set out the principal rules on the liability of the directors, whilst the
Penal Code, the Fiscal Penal Code, the Bankruptcy Act and the Tax Ordinance prom-
ulgate specific offences and penalise breaches of duties.

The management board has the right to 'represent the company and manage its
business'. The management board's members are entitled to manage the affairs of
the company and to represent it in respect of all court and out-of-court acts of the
company. Members of the management board are obliged to conduct themselves with
the 'highest level of diligence required of a professional' – this is the duty of care and
diligence. According to Article 293 of the CCC, a management board member will
be liable to the company for losses occasioned to the latter as a result of any action
or omission which is contrary to the law or the provisions of the company's articles,
unless he or she is able to show that he or she is not at fault. Therefore, in order for a
director to be liable under Article 293 of the CCC, the damage inflicted must arise as
a result of unlawful actions or actions contrary to the company's articles. There is a
presumption in favour of a breach of duty and so the director must prove that he or
she is not guilty. The typical breaches are, inter alia: mismanagement (acting to the
company's detriment), lack of managerial care, failure to oversee the company's affairs
and/or a failure to report. Our case falls within the last example, for instance when
the losses on the balance sheet exceed the sum of the supplementary capital, reserve
capital and a half of the share capital of the company. According to Article 233 of
the CCC, in this situation, the management board must summon a meeting of the
shareholders forthwith with the purpose of adopting a resolution on the continued
existence of the company. Since Mr B is the only member of the management board,
he exercises all of the rights and obligations attached to it. There is no suggestion that

---

[100] But see also ch 6, n 81, below, for recent reform proposals.
[101] However, according to Art 213.2 of the CCC, in companies with an initial capital in excess of PLN
500,000 and 25 shareholders, it is compulsory to have a supervisory board and an audit commission.

Mr B has fulfilled his obligation and convened a general meeting of the shareholders of the company. Thus, we can assume that he has failed to do so. The omission to do so subjects him to a fine of up to PLN 20,000 as well as imposing liability on him to the company for any damage caused by the failure to convene the meeting.

Furthermore, Mr B's conduct should also be assessed in light of the provisions of Polish Bankruptcy Law. Article 11.2 of the Bankruptcy Law provides that a company is insolvent when it fails to pay its debts as they fall due and its liabilities exceed its assets, notwithstanding that it is able to meet its due obligations on time. Directors are obliged to file a bankruptcy application within two weeks of the satisfaction of either of these grounds for bankruptcy. The hypothetical case states that after four weeks, several debtors default and the Company is unable to pay for goods it has received. Mr B ought to have filed a bankruptcy application when its sales figures did not improve subsequent to the sale of 25 per cent of the Company's stock at the very latest. In the event of late filing or a failure to file such a bankruptcy application, Mr B will be liable for any losses suffered by the Company that arise as a result of the failure to file the petition in due time. Directors may also be deprived of the right to undertake commercial activities on their own account and certain other functions, eg a supervisory board membership for a period of 3–10 years. If enforcement against the Company proves to be ineffective, the directors are jointly and severally liable for the Company's obligations, which will not be the case if they file the bankruptcy petition on time. The failure to file the bankruptcy application with the court on time may also subject the directors to tax and social security liabilities as well as penal liability under the Polish Penal Code (this imposes penal sanctions for a failure to file a bankruptcy application within the relevant time upon pain of a fine, restriction of liberty or a term of imprisonment of up to one year).

Mr B's conduct should also be analysed in light of the legal requirement to exercise the 'highest level of diligence required from a professional' in terms of his duty of care and diligence as a director. Pursuant to Article 483 of the CCC (mentioned above), Mr B is required to act diligently and with due care in respect of all activities concerning the management of the Company. In the light of Article 293.2 of the CCC, Mr B must discharge his duties with a degree of diligence which is proper for the professional nature of his activities. The CCC does not define the term 'diligence [which is] proper for the professional nature of activities'. Therefore, Mr B's conduct should be evaluated taking into account all the circumstances which were relevant to Mr B in the process of taking the business decisions for the Company. Mr B may be held liable to the Company for losses arising as a result of his decisions which were taken without due diligence. Mr B has taken two significant decisions on behalf of the Company, namely the sale of 25 per cent of the Company's stock at a 50 per cent discount and thereafter committing the Company to a loan under credit conditions which are 150 per cent above the current average annual interest rate offered by commercial banks. Certainly, both transactions could be assessed as prejudicial to the Company's interests. However, taking into account the fact that the Company is experiencing a crisis and its financial position is deteriorating, assuming that (i) Mr B carefully analysed the market situation, (ii) there was no opportunity for the Company to secure financial aid from other sources under more favourable conditions, and (iii) the hypothetical director acting with due care would have taken the same or a similar decision in the same circumstances, then one could treat these two decisions as having been made with the due managerial care of a professional, in good faith, in compliance with law, in reliance upon professional advice (legal, tax and accountancy) and not contrary to the interests of the Company. Nevertheless, notwithstanding what conclusion one reaches in respect of the lawfulness of Mr B's decisions (ie whether he acted with a degree of diligence proper for the professional nature of decisions made), it is extremely unlikely that he would be held liable to the Company in respect of the loan transaction, since we are told that the majority shareholder Mr A1, who holds 95 per cent of the Company's shares, approved it. The only possibility that Mr B might be liable to the Company would arise if a shareholder filed a complaint in order to seek redress for any losses inflicted upon the Company. However, taking into account the fact that the majority shareholder Mr A1 approved the loan transaction, the only threat to Mr B is that the minority shareholder Ms A2 might bring an action, as she did not express her approval of the loan transaction prior to its conclusion.

Directors may also be held criminally liable. The most common grounds for the imposition of such liability are: abuse of trust (Penal Code, Article 296), acting to the detriment of the company, failure to make a bankruptcy filing (CCC, Article 586), acting on unfair competition, etc. According to Article 296 of the Penal Code, anyone who is obliged to take care of the financial affairs or commercial activities of another person and who causes material damage by abusing the power vested in him/her is subject to liability. This kind of abuse applies to directors. This offence may even be committed unintentionally.

I. The UK[102]

i. Introduction

The CA 2006 is the main Act of Parliament which regulates companies in the UK. In addition to the CA 2006, companies are also regulated by other domestic UK legislation,[103] common law rules, European legislation and European law generally (for example, the partial harmonisation directives on company law)[104] and certain

---

[102] Abbreviations: CA 2006 (the Companies Act 2006); IA 1986 (the Insolvency Act 1986); FSMA 2000 (the Financial Services and Markets Act 2000); FCA (the Financial Conduct Authority); Model Articles (Model articles of association of private companies limited by shares (in reg 2 of and sch 1 to the Companies (Model Articles) Regulations 2008, SI 2008/3229), private companies limited by guarantee (in reg 3 of and sch 2 to the Companies (Model Articles) Regulations 2008, SI 2008/3229) and public limited companies (in reg 4 of and sch 3 to the Companies (Model Articles) Regulations 2008, SI 2008/3229)) (the 'Model Articles '); Listing Rules (the Listing Rules of the FCA (https://www.handbook.fca.org.uk/handbook)); City Code (the City Code on Takeovers and Mergers (www.thetakeoverpanel.org.uk/wp-content/uploads/2008/11/code.pdf)); UK Corporate Governance Code (the UK Corporate Governance Code (www.frc.org.uk/getattachment/b0832de2-5c94-48c0-b771-ebb249fe1fec/The-UK-Corporate-Governance-Code.aspx)).

[103] eg, the IA 1986 and the FSMA 2000, including statutes which apply generally to 'legal persons', such as the Sale of Goods Act 1979.

[104] At the time of writing, the UK was negotiating its exit from the European Union, but the formal withdrawal is unlikely to take place until some time in 2019. For that reason, the UK national reports in this book presume that the UK is a member of the EU.

other special rules (for example, the FCA's Listing Rules, the City Code and the UK Corporate Governance Code). A limited company by shares in the UK may be private or public (plc). The CA 2006 defines 'private' and 'public' companies in the following terms: a 'private company' is any company that is not a plc; and a plc is a company limited by shares or limited by guarantee with a certificate of incorporation that states it is a plc and which has complied with all the necessary provisions of the CA 2006 with regard to registration or re-registration as a public company.[105] Like Latvian and Spanish law, private companies and plcs are regulated by the same Act of Parliament (the CA 2006).

There is no minimum capital requirement for private companies limited by shares in the UK. A plc must have a nominal value of allotted share capital which is not less than the statutory 'authorised minimum' amount fixed by section 763 of the CA 2006. At present, the minimum capital requirement for a plc is £50,000 or the prescribed euro equivalent.[106] At least one-quarter of this figure, ie £12,500, must be paid up when the shares of the plc are allotted.[107] Private companies limited by shares are prohibited from offering their shares to the public for investment,[108] whereas plcs are entitled to do so. However, plcs are subject to a greater degree of regulation by the legal system.

The management of the private company limited by shares and the plc is conducted by a unitary board of directors and the board is responsible for the management of the company's business, for which purpose it may exercise all the powers of the company in terms of the provisions of the articles of association. The articles of association of a private company limited by shares or a plc are based on the Model Articles to the extent that the articles of association are modified or disapplied by the company. The powers of the management are subject to instruction and initiation rights vested in the shareholders of the private company or the plc which arise where such members pass a special resolution[109] in general meeting or by written resolution procedure[110] enjoining the directors to take, or refrain from taking, certain specified courses of action.[111] The size, proceedings and deliberations of the board of directors are governed by the articles of association of the private company limited by shares or the plc.[112] However,

---

[105] CA 2006, s 4(1) and (2).

[106] CA 2006, s 763(1).

[107] CA 2006, s 586(1).

[108] CA 2006, s 755(1).

[109] A special resolution is a resolution passed by a majority of not less than 75% of the shareholders of the company: CA 2006, s 283.

[110] This is a procedure which enables private companies to pass shareholder resolutions without holding a general meeting in terms of the CA 2006, ss 281(1) and 288–300.

[111] See eg Model Articles of association of a private company limited by shares, the Companies (Model Articles) Regulations 2008, SI 2008/3229, reg 4 of sch 1, Model Articles for a private company limited by guarantee, the Companies (Model Articles) Regulations 2008, SI 2008/3229, reg 4 of sch 2, and Model Articles for public limited companies, the Companies (Model Articles) Regulations 2008, SI 2008/3229, reg 4 of sch 3.

[112] Model Articles of association of a private company limited by shares, the Companies (Model Articles) Regulations 2008, SI 2008/3229, regs 3, 5, 6, 7, 16 and 17 of sch 1, Model Articles for a private company limited by guarantee, the Companies (Model Articles) Regulations 2008, SI 2008/3229, regs 3, 5, 6, 7, 16 and 17 of sch 2 and Model Articles for public limited companies, the Companies (Model Articles) Regulations 2008, SI 2008/3229, regs 3, 5, 6, 7 and 20 of sch 3.

the CA 2006 dictates that a plc must have at least two directors and a private company must have at least one.[113]

ii. Sale at a Discount

Since Mr B is the sole director of the Company, the responsibility for the management of the Company and the administration of its business affairs is vested in him alone.[114] In terms of section 174 of the CA 2006, the directors of a company are under a duty to exercise reasonable care, skill and diligence. This duty is owed to the Company in terms of section 170(1) of the CA 2006 and so the Company has the right to sue Mr B for any losses which it sustains as a result of a breach of this duty. This statutory duty is not automatically breached simply because the director has been incompetent and his or her actions have resulted in the company sustaining a loss. Instead, whether a director has complied with the duty in any particular case requires his or her conduct to be assessed on both an objective and a subjective basis. The assessment is objective to the extent that the director's conduct will be compared with the general knowledge, skill and experience that may reasonably be expected of a person carrying out the functions which are performed by the director in relation to the company. In this regard, evidence of what is normal in the field of commerce in which the company operates is of considerable relevance.[115] Thus, the objective standard operates to draw a minimum standard of care, skill and diligence, and if the particular director falls below it, he or she will be in breach of duty. Nevertheless, the particular director will not necessarily be treated as having complied with the section 174 duty simply because he or she has satisfied the objective standard. Instead, a higher standard of conduct may be expected of the particular director over and above the objective standard, since the subjective strand of the duty of care, skill and diligence may well function to 'raise the bar' by comparing the particular director's actions or omissions with the standard of general knowledge, skill, care and diligence that the particular director actually possesses or has. For example, if a finance director has 20 years' experience as a qualified chartered accountant, he or she will be judged against the higher standard of someone who has such experience. The effect of the subjective component is that if the particular director falls below the higher standard (which is to be expected from someone of his or her higher level of knowledge, skill and experience), he or she will be in breach of his or her duty, notwithstanding the fact that he or she has satisfied the lower objective standard. In certain circumstances, a director may breach both the objective and subjective standards.[116]

The duty of skill, care and diligence under section 174 of the CA 2006 imposes continuing obligations (like Latvian law) on (i) a director to take positive steps to keep

---

[113] CA 2006, s 154(1) and (2).

[114] Subject to the shareholders' reserve powers specified in the articles of association whereby they may resolve to pass a special resolution instructing or precluding Mr B from taking certain action, on which, see Model Articles (n 112), reg 4 of sch 1.

[115] *Abbey Forwarding Ltd. v Hone* [2010] EWHC 2029 (Ch) at [198] per Lewison J.

[116] See, eg, the director in *Re D'Jan of London Ltd* [1994] 1 BCLC 561 (Ch), who signed an insurance proposal form without reading it.

himself or herself informed about the Company's affairs and to join with his or her co-directors in supervising and controlling them[117] and (ii) the directors, collectively and individually, to acquire and maintain a sufficient knowledge and understanding of the Company's business to enable them properly to discharge their duties as directors.[118] It is essential for the officers of a company to ensure that the company maintains proper accounting records so that the Company's commercial decisions are made on the basis of reliable information and so that if the business fails, the liquidator's administration of the winding-up is facilitated.[119]

The principal issue to be determined is whether Mr B breached the mixed objective/ subjective standard in section 174 of the CA 2006 by selling 25 per cent of the Company's stock at a 50 per cent discount to the market price. Whilst we know that Mr B has run the company for five years, the hypothetical case does not specifically reveal his background, for example, the degree of skill, experience and knowledge which he possesses as an individual. For this reason, it is assumed that it is unlikely that there will be a differential between the objective and subjective levels of knowledge, skill, care and diligence reasonably to be expected of Mr B in the instant case, and so it is suggested that it is perfectly reasonable to proceed on the basis of the objective standard. On the basis of the objective test comprised within section 174 of the CA 2006 duty, it is submitted that absent special circumstances articulated below, it is most likely that Mr B will be deemed not to have breached his duty of care, skill and diligence. Therefore, in terms of the facts of the hypothetical case, there is nothing to suggest that Mr B has failed to discharge these obligations and so it is submitted that there are no grounds for finding that he has breached the section 174 duty on this particular basis.

iii. Loan Transaction

No view is articulated here as to whether the actions of Mr B in concluding the loan transaction on behalf of the Company are sufficient to establish a breach of his duty to exercise reasonable care, skill and diligence under section 174 of the CA 2006. The basis for adopting such an approach is that Mr B will not be liable for a breach of the section 174 duty since his conduct in obtaining the loan was ratified by the shareholders of the company.[120] Section 239(1) of the CA 2006 directs that the members have the power to relieve a director of liability in respect of conduct which amounts to negligence, default, breach of duty or breach of trust in relation to the company.

---

[117] Secretary of State for Trade and Industry v Baker (No 6) [1999] 1 BCLC 433 (Ch) 489a–d (Parker J), approved by the Court of Appeal in Baker v Secretary of State for Trade and Industry [2001] BCC 273 (CA) 283 (Morritt LJ). See also Lexi Holdings (In Administration) v Luqman [2009] EWCA Civ 117, [2009] 2 BCLC 1.

[118] Re Westmid Packing Services Ltd [1998] 2 All ER 124 (CA) 130a–b (Lord Woolf MR) and ARB International Ltd. v Baillie [2013] EWHC 2060 (Comm), [2013] 2 CLC 255.

[119] Secretary of State for Trade and Industry v Arif [1997] 1 BCLC 34 (Ch); Re Firedart Ltd, Official Receiver v Fairall [1994] 2 BCLC 340 (Ch).

[120] For an example of the unanimous voting approval of the shareholders relieving a director of any potential liability for breach of the s 174 duty, see Madoff Securities International v Raven [2013] EWHC 3147 (Comm) at [288] per Popplewell J.

The decision of the Company to ratify such conduct must be made by ordinary resolution[121] of its members.[122] Therefore, since the facts of the hypothetical case narrate that Mr B obtained the prior approval of the 95 per cent shareholder Mr A1, it is assumed that such consent was obtained by shareholder Mr A1 passing an ordinary resolution.[123] Since this means that the loan transaction has been ratified by shareholder Mr A1, Mr B cannot be sued for breach of duty under section 174 of the CA 2006 – whether the loan transaction represents a breach of duty on the part of Mr B or not (on which no concrete view has been expressed). In adopting this position, it is presumed that (i) the relevant circumstances surrounding the loan transaction were fully and frankly disclosed and explained to shareholder Mr A1 when he was asked to vote to ratify Mr B's conduct pursuant to the resolution;[124] (ii) shareholder Mr A1 was not a person connected to Mr B[125] and (iii) if the loan transaction amounted to a breach of Mr B's duty to exercise reasonable care, skill and diligence under section 174 of the CA 2006 (on which no concrete view is expressed), it fell within the class of wrongs recognised by the common law as ratifiable by the shareholders.[126]

The courts have also developed the law to the extent that directors owe duties such as the duty to exercise reasonable care, skill and diligence under section 174 of the CA 2006 to the company to take into account the interests of the company's creditors where the company is insolvent or nearing insolvency.[127] It has been held that the duty of reasonable care in section 174 of the CA 2006 in this context obliges a director not to act in a way that would prefer one creditor over another[128] or to leave the creditors

---

[121] In terms of the CA 2006, s 282(1), an ordinary resolution is a resolution that is passed by a simple majority of the members of the company.

[122] CA 2006, s 239(2).

[123] If this assumption is misplaced, the effect would be that Mr B's breach would not have been ratified, since the Company would be unable to avail itself of the common law 'member's unanimous consent' rule in *Re Duomatic Ltd* [1969] 2 Ch 365 (Ch). The unanimous consent rule only applies if *all* of the members of the Company consent without passing a shareholder resolution and since shareholder Mr A1 owns only 95% of the shares of the Company, this would be insufficient for the rule to be engaged: see ch 10 at II A, below.

[124] This is necessary in terms of *Kaye v Croydon Tramway Co* [1898] 1 Ch 358 (CA); *Tiessen v Henderson* [1899] 1 Ch 861 (Ch); *Baillie v Oriental Telephone and Electric Co Ltd* [1915] 1 Ch 503 (CA) 514; *New Zealand Netherlands Society 'Oranje' Inc v Kuys* [1973] 1 WLR 1126 (PC); *Knight v Frost* [1999] 1 BCLC 364 (Ch); *Re RAC Motoring Services Ltd* [2000] 1 BCLC 307 (Ch).

[125] CA 2006, s 252(2) sets out a list of the persons deemed to be connected with the director, eg members of the director's family and companies, trusts, partners and partnerships in which the director has an interest.

[126] The common law rules on the ratifiability of breaches of director's duties are preserved by the CA 2006, s 239(7) (see *Franbar Holdings Ltd v Patel* [2008] EWHC 1534 (Ch), [2009] 1 BCLC 1, 16 at [47] (William Trower QC)), ie a breach of duty by a director will not be ratifiable where the director's conduct was 'of fraudulent character or beyond the powers of the company' (*Burland v Earle* [1902] AC 83 (PC) 93 (Lord Davey)). Davies and Worthington have suggested that the common law confines non-ratifiable wrongs to the decisions of directors which involve the misappropriation of the company's property: PL Davies and S Worthington, *Gower's Principles of Modern Company Law* (10th edn, London, Sweet & Maxwell, 2016) para 16–124 at 574–76, contrasting *Cook v Deeks* [1916] 1 AC 554 (PC) and *Menier v Hooper's Telegraph Works* (1874) LR 9 Ch App 350 (CA) with *Regal (Hastings) Ltd v Gulliver* [1967] 2 AC 134 (HL), *NW Transportation Co v Beatty* (1887) 12 App Cas 589 (PC) and *Burland v Earle* [1902] AC 83 (PC). See also C Riley, 'Derivative Claims and Ratification: Time to Ditch Some Baggage' (2014) 34 *Legal Studies* 582. On the basis that the loan transaction entered into by the company at the instigation of Mr B does not fall into such a category, it is submitted that Mr B's conduct is not an unratifiable wrong.

[127] *West Mercia Safetywear Ltd v Dodd* [1987] BCLC 250 (CA).

[128] *Re HLC Environmental Projects Ltd* [2013] EWHC 2876 (Ch), [2014] BCC 337.

generally in a worse position than on liquidation.[129] Since the duty is owed to the company, a creditor has no free-standing right to sue the director for a breach of duty and proceedings must be raised by the company's liquidator against the director once the company has entered into insolvent liquidation. Whether a company is insolvent or on the verge of insolvency is an issue for objective assessment and directors must take independent financial and legal advice to confirm the position.[130] As the courts have noted, the exact point in time when the risk to creditors' interests becomes real for these purposes will ultimately have to be judged on a case-by-case basis.[131] Indeed, some guidance is provided by section 123 of the IA 1986. In terms of section 123(1)(e) and (2) of the IA 1986, a company is deemed to be insolvent where it is it is proved to the satisfaction of the court that the company is unable to pay its debts as they fall due or its assets exceed its liabilities, taking into account its contingent and prospective liabilities. In the case of *BNY Corporate Trustee Services Ltd v Eurosail-UK 2007-3BL plc (BNY)*,[132] the Court of Appeal decided that the latter test is designed for the purpose of assisting the court in addressing the former test,[133] ie that the former is the true, single test.[134] It went on to direct that whether a company is unable to pay its debts is to be assessed in two timeframes on a balance of probabilities: the company's inability to pay its current debts as they fall due and its inability to pay a contingent or prospective liability when it becomes due in the future.[135] Where a company is insolvent, the members have no power to ratify a director's breach of duty under section 174 of the CA 2006 if that would adversely affect the interests of the company's creditors.[136] Applying the test in *BNY*, it is submitted that there is sufficient evidence from the facts of the hypothetical case to suggest that the Company was in a position to pay its current debts as they fell due when Mr B committed the Company to the sale transaction. However, it would appear that the Company was unable to pay its current debts as they fell due and its contingent or prospective liabilities when they became due in the future when shareholder Mr A1 ratified Mr B's conduct in causing the Company to enter into the loan transaction. Therefore, the section 174 duty of care to take into account the interests of the Company's creditors is engaged and the question is whether Mr B breached the mixed objective/subjective standard by entering into the loan transaction. Once again, since the hypothetical case does not specifically reveal Mr B's skill-set – the degree of skill, experience and knowledge which he possesses as an individual – we must proceed on the basis of the objective standard.

---

[129] *Re Welfab Engineers Ltd* [1990] BCC 600 (Ch).

[130] *Colin Gwyer & Associates v London Wharf (Limehouse) Ltd* [2002] EWHC 2748 (Ch), [2003] 2 BCLC 153.

[131] *Re HLC Environmental Projects Ltd* [2013] EWHC 2876 (Ch), [2014] BCC 337, 362 per John Randall QC and *Dickinson v NAL (Realisations) Staffordshire Ltd* [2017] EWHC 28 (Ch) at [113] per HHJ David Cooke.

[132] *BNY Corporate Trustee Services Ltd v Eurosail-UK 2007-3BL plc* [2011] EWCA Civ 227, [2011] 3 All ER 470 (CA).

[133] Ibid, 496a–d (Neuberger MR).

[134] Ibid, 496g–j and 497f (Neuberger MR).

[135] Ibid, 498b–d (Neuberger MR).

[136] B Leahy, 'Directors' Liabilities: Exemption, Indemnification and Ratification' in S Mortimore (ed), *Company Directors: Duties, Liabilities and Remedies* (2nd edn, Oxford, Oxford University Press, 2013) 470 at para 20.51.

On the basis of the objective test comprised within the section 174 of the CA 2006 duty and the rule that a director must not act in a way that would leave the creditors in a worse position than on liquidation,[137] it is submitted that it is not wholly obvious that Mr B has failed to meet that standard by entering into the loan transaction. As has been noted by the UK courts, in the absence of 20/20 hindsight, it is difficult to draw the line between 'acceptable risk[-taking] that an entrepreneur may properly take and an unacceptable risk the taking of which constitutes'[138] a breach of the duty to creditors in the lead-up to insolvency. Therefore, at the stage reached in the hypothetical case, it is not clear that Mr B would be liable for breach of duty and there is a powerful argument that entering into the loan transaction was for the benefit of the creditors (since it would support a continuation of profitable trading) rather than a cessation of trading followed by the sale of the Company's assets on a distressed sale basis which would lead to heavy losses for the creditors. Moreover, the fact that Mr B took professional advice is 'an important factor in determining if he was in breach of his duty to exercise reasonable care' and will generally work in his favour.[139]

iv. Wrongful Trading

If the Company subsequently enters into insolvent liquidation, there is the possibility that section 214 of the IA 1986, which proscribes 'wrongful trading', may be invoked by the liquidator of the Company to sue the director. Wrongful trading is a statutory concept which is separate from directors' duties.[140] A director will be deemed to have engaged in wrongful trading if at some time before the commencement of the winding-up of the company, he or she knew or ought to have concluded that there was no reasonable prospect that the company would avoid insolvent liquidation.[141] The test for determining the point in time at which the director knew or ought to have known that the company should have ceased trading is assessed on the basis of a mixed objective and subjective measure of scrutiny.[142] If the director is held to be guilty of such wrongful trading, the court may declare that the director is liable to make such contribution (if any) to the company's assets as it thinks proper, ie the director may be found personally liable.

By instructing the Company's lawyers to provide a legal opinion, Mr B is obviously keen to obtain advice on whether his (i) conduct generally and (ii) failure to cease trading to date represents a breach of section 214 of the IA 1986. In each case, the point

---

[137] Re Welfab Engineers Ltd (n 129).

[138] Facia Footwear Ltd (In Administration) v Hinchcliffe [1998] 1 BCLC 218 (Ch) 228 (Sir Richard Scott VC). See also Re Pro4Sport Ltd (In Liquidation) [2015] EWHC 2540 (Ch), [2016] BCC 390, 399 per HHJ Behrens.

[139] Re Pro4Sport Ltd (In Liquidation) [2015] EWHC 2540 (Ch), [2016] BCC 390, 399 per HHJ Behrens.

[140] For the difference between the UK law on 'wrongful trading' and the counterpart in German law, see T Bachner, 'Wrongful Trading – A New European Model for Creditor Protection?' (2004) 5 European Business Organization Law Review 293.

[141] IA 1986, s 214(2).

[142] IA 1986, s 214(4). Therefore, the test is more or less the same as that applied in the case of the director's duty to exercise reasonable care, skill and diligence under the CA 2006, s 174: Gregson v HAE Truxtees Ltd [2009] 1 All ER (Comm) 457, 462g per Robert Miles QC and Re D'Jan of London Ltd [1994] 1 BCLC 561.

in time at which the director ought to have ceased trading will be highly fact-sensitive. On balance, provided that Mr B has routinely monitored the financial and accounting position of the Company, for the same reasons advanced above in connection with the duty under section 174 of the CA 2006, it is submitted that it is unlikely that he will be deemed to have breached the wrongful trading provisions of section 214 of the IA 1986.[143] Generally, since the courts are anxious to avoid the application of hindsight bias[144] and are keenly aware that (i) they are not best equipped to second-guess the commercial judgement of directors and (ii) the cessation of trade by a company may be premature, they are generally reluctant to hold a director to be in breach of the wrongful trading provisions.[145] Furthermore, the fact that Mr B has taken legal advice on his personal position is a factor which will be applied in his favour by a court, since this will provide some evidence that he had taken every step with a view to minimising the potential loss to the Company's creditors in conformity with his obligation in section 214(3) of the IA 1986.[146] Finally, the case reveals that it was four weeks subsequent to the loan transaction that several debtors defaulted and the Company was unable to pay for goods it had received. This provides additional grounds to suggest that Mr B ought not to have caused the Company to cease trading prior to that point in time.

v. Liability for Omissions

As stated above, the duty of skill, care and diligence under section 174 of the CA 2006 imposes certain continuing obligations (like Latvian law) on a director to take certain courses of action.[147] Likewise, in terms of the wrongful trading provisions in section 214 of the IA 1986, there is the potential for a director to be found personally liable where he or she fails to cease trading at a particular point in time. However, on balance, there would appear to be nothing in the hypothetical case to indicate that Mr B failed to act in a particular fashion. Suffice to say that it is unlikely that he would be held liable for a breach of section 174 of the CA 2006 or section 214 of the IA 1986 if he is deemed to have kept himself informed about the Company's affairs and acquired and maintained a sufficient knowledge and understanding of the Company's business.[148]

---

[143] eg, in *Re Produce Marketing Consortium Ltd (No 2)* [1989] BCLC 520 (Ch) 550 (Knox J), it was stated that a director will be expected, at the very least, to have kept accounting records which are such as to disclose with reasonable accuracy at any time the financial position of the company.

[144] See *Re Hawkes Hill Publishing Co Ltd (in liquidation)* [2007] BCC 937, 952 (Lewison J) and *Re Ralls Builders Ltd (in liquidation)* [2016] BCC 293 at 330 and 339 (Snowden J).

[145] In particular, see *Re Continental Assurance Co of London plc (In Liquidation) (No 4)* [2007] 2 BCLC 287 (Ch) 409 at [281] (Park J) and *Abbey Forwarding Ltd. v Hone* [2010] EWHC 2029 (Ch) at [196]–[207] (Lewison J).

[146] *Re Hawkes Hill Publishing Co Ltd (in liquidation)* [2007] BCC 937; *Re Continental Assurance Co of London Plc* [2007] 2 BCLC 287 and *Re Ralls Builders Ltd (in liquidation)* [2016] BCC 293 at 331–32 and 337 per Snowden J. See also R Goode, *Principles of Corporate Insolvency Law* student edn (London, Sweet & Maxwell, 2011) 675 at para 14-46 and B Hannigan, *Company Law* (4th edn, Oxford, Oxford University Press, 2016) 358 at para 15-28.

[147] *Secretary of State for Trade and Industry v Baker (No 6)* (n 117) (Parker J), approved by the Court of Appeal in *Baker v Secretary of State for Trade and Industry* (n 117) (Morritt LJ); *Re Westmid Packing Services Ltd* (n 118) (Lord Woolf MR).

[148] *Lagunas Nitrate Company v Lagunas Syndicate* [1899] 2 Ch 392 (CA) 435 (Lindley MR).

vi. Miscellaneous Issues, Including Potential for Other Forms of Civil Liability or Criminal Liability

In terms of UK company law, it is only where a plc suffers a serious loss of capital (ie the net assets of the plc are half or less of its called up share capital) that there is an obligation on the directors to call a general meeting to consider whether any, and if so what, steps should be taken to deal with the situation.[149] No such obligation would be imposed on Mr B, since he is a director of a private limited company. In theory, Mr B may be liable for misfeasance under section 212 of the IA 1986. Misfeasance occurs where in the course of a winding-up it appears that a director has misapplied or retained or become accountable for any money or property of the Company or been guilty of any misfeasance or breach of any fiduciary or other duty in relation to the Company. In such circumstances, the liquidator or any creditor may apply to the court for the conduct of such director to be examined. The court has the power to order the director to repay, restore, or account for any such money or property of the Company, or to make a contribution to the Company's assets by way of compensation for such misfeasance or breach of fiduciary or other duty. Mr B may also be liable for fraudulent trading under section 213 of the IA 1986, but this would be difficult to prove, since a liquidator (assuming that the Company subsequently entered into insolvent liquidation) would have to convince a court that Mr B intended to deceive and defraud the Company's creditors. This involves a high standard of proof inasmuch as there would have to be evidence of a clear intention on the part of Mr B to engage in fraud and it is submitted that the facts of this case make this unlikely. Finally, it would be unlikely that Mr B would be held criminally liable for fraud on the basis that there would appear to be an absence of any fraudulent intent.

vii. Conclusion

In summary, it is unlikely that Mr B's conduct in respect of the sale and loan transactions would be treated as a breach of (i) section 174 of the CA 2006 or (ii) the wrongful trading provisions in section 214 of the IA 1986. Furthermore, there is an absence of evidence to indicate that Mr B ought to have procured the Company to cease trading prior to the point in time at which he sought legal advice. Finally, there are insufficient grounds to conclude that Mr B's failure to take positive action amounted to a breach of duty under section 174 of the CA 2006 or section 214 of the IA 1986.

---

[149] CA 2006, s 656. This was based on Art 17 of the Second Council Directive 77/91/EEC on the coordination of safeguards which, for the protection of the interests of members and others, are required by Member States of companies within the meaning of the second paragraph of Article 58 of the Treaty, in respect of the formation of public limited liability companies and the maintenance and alteration of their capital, with a view to making such safeguards equivalent ([1977] OJ L026/1), on which, see also ch 6, below. This Directive was subsequently replaced by Directive 2012/30/EU (OJ L315/74) and its provisions are now included in Directive (EU) 2017/1132 of the European Parliament and of the Council of 14 June 2017 relating to certain aspects of company law ([2017] OJ L169/46).

J. The US[150]

Two distinct forms can be used to create a privately held, limited liability entity in the US. One form, the limited liability company (LLC), is created through the formal filing of the 'certification of organisation' (sometimes called the 'articles of organisation').[151] LLCs are quickly becoming the most popular form for small businesses in the US due to the absence of corporate formalities and taxation advantages over the traditional corporate form. In the situation described in the hypothetical case, individuals holding ownership interests would be called 'members' of the LLC, while the director would be called the 'manager'.

The other form, the traditional corporation, is created through the formal filing of the 'certification of incorporation' (often called the 'articles of incorporation' or 'charter').[152] In a similar fashion to the Latvian private limited liability company, individuals holding ownership interests would be called 'shareholders', while the individual with management responsibilities would be the 'director'. With rare exceptions, the daily affairs of a corporation are managed by or under the direction of a board of directors, comprised of at least one person. The shareholders of a corporation do not directly manage the business and affairs of the corporation, but they are entitled to vote on various corporate actions, including the election and removal of directors,[153] amendment of the corporation's charter,[154] approval of a merger or consolidation,[155] and other fundamental transactions,[156] as well as the ratification of conflict-of-interest transactions.[157] With the exception of the election and removal of directors and amendment of by-laws, all of these votes must be initiated by the board of directors. Most corporations, even closely held corporations like the one described in the case, also vest 'officers' with managerial responsibilities. Officers are employees of the corporation and, generally speaking, they exercise the authority granted to them by the board of directors.

Neither the LLC nor the corporation has a minimum capital requirement. The personal liability of the members (LLC) or shareholders (corporation) of the company is limited to the amount of capital actually invested in the company.

The decision to sell 25 per cent of the existing stock of the Company to an international wholesaler with a 50 per cent discount to the current market price is an ordinary

---

[150] As there is no general corporate law covering the entire US, the solutions presented for the US will focus primarily on the Delaware Limited Liability Company Act (DLLCA) and the Delaware General Corporation Law (DGCL). Although Delaware law is not necessarily representative of the entire US, the DGCL has long been recognised as the most sophisticated and developed corporation law within the US. To date, Delaware remains the 'most popular state of incorporation for public corporations'. See DG Smith and CA Williams, *Business Organizations: Cases, Problems, and Case Studies* (New York, Aspen, 2008) 224. More recently, Delaware has become a popular domicile for limited liability companies and the DLLCA has become an influential source of law relating to this form of business entity.

[151] See generally Revised Uniform Limited Liability Act, § 201(a).

[152] See generally DGCL, § 102(a).

[153] DGCL, § 211(b).

[154] DGCL, § 242(b).

[155] DGCL, § 251(c).

[156] Other fundamental transactions include approving the sale of assets not in the ordinary course of business (DGCL, § 271) and approving the dissolution of the company (DGCL, § 275(b)).

[157] DGCL, § 144(a)(2).

business decision that would be made by the manager of an LLC or the officers or directors of a corporation. If the Company sold all or substantially all of its property and assets, some LLC statutes (but not the DLLCA) would require the consent of the members,[158] and corporation statutes require approval of both the board of directors and the shareholders.[159]

The decision by the director to take on a loan with credit conditions 150 per cent above the current average annual interest rate offered by commercial banks also falls within the discretion of the board of directors, again subject to the common law duties described below. While approval from a majority or controlling shareholder is not required, such approval may serve to insulate the director from liability for breaching one or more of these duties. Likewise, the manager of an LLC has the discretion to enter into a loan agreement, unless that discretion has been circumscribed by the LLC agreement or the manager's common law duties.

As a manager of a corporation or an LLC, the director described in the case would have two primary duties to the Company and its shareholders or members – the duty of care and the duty of loyalty – with various doctrines within each of these large categories. Unlike in Latvia, however, the directors' duties are not specifically set out in the Delaware statutes.[160] Instead, such duties have been developed by courts as a matter of common law.

The duty of care, in its simplest terms, requires the director to carry out his or her corporate duties with appropriate care so as to avoid injuring the corporation. This duty, however, is rarely used by courts to impose liability upon directors. Delaware courts have held in the corporate context that:

> [I]n the absence of facts showing self-dealing or improper motive, a corporate officer or director is not legally responsible to the corporation for losses that may be suffered as a result of a decision that an officer made or that directors authorised in good faith ... no matter how foolish the investment may appear in retrospect.[161]

This doctrine, commonly referred to as the 'business judgment rule', also applies to LLCs. Because of the business judgment rule, directors and managers are almost never liable for decisions made within the scope of their assigned responsibilities. The case offers no facts implying that the director acted outside of his assigned responsibilities, so the director's actions would likely fall within the business judgment rule. Consequently, in the absence of proof of self-dealing or other actions taken in bad faith, the director will not be held liable for breach of the duty of care.

Even if a court were to find that the director breached his or her duty of care, Delaware law allows companies to exculpate directors from personal liability for breach of the duty of care in their certificate of incorporation (corporations).[162] LLC law tends to be less restrictive than corporate law in this respect. While some statutes

---

[158] See the Revised Uniform Limited Liability Act, § 407(c).

[159] DGCL, § 271(a).

[160] The statutes of some other states describe these duties using language that draws on the common law of managers' duties.

[161] *Gagliardi v Trifoods International, Inc*, 683 A 2d 1049, 1051–52 (Del Supr 1996).

[162] DGCL, § 102(b)(7).

provide that fiduciary law has a mandatory core that cannot be waived or avoided by contract, the Delaware LLC statute provides that: 'It is the policy of this chapter to give the maximum effect to the principle of freedom of contract and to the enforceability of limited liability company agreements'. Moreover, the statute allows a member's or manager's fiduciary duties to be 'expanded or restricted or eliminated by provisions in the limited liability company agreement; provided, that the limited liability company agreement may not eliminate the implied contractual covenant of good faith and fair dealing'.[163]

Most corporations and many LLCs include exculpatory clauses in their organisational documents to protect their directors and managers from personal liability and to entice such directors or managers to remain with the company. Consequently, if the Company were a typical Delaware company, an exculpatory provision would likely be included in its certificate of incorporation, which would remove or limit any finding of personal liability for breach of the duty of care.

The duty of loyalty is also not engaged by the present scenario. The duty of loyalty is generally mandatory in the case of corporations, but it can be eliminated in Delaware LLCs under the statute cited above. It usually encompasses situations where the director has placed his or her personal interests before those of the corporation, such as taking for himself or herself a business opportunity which rightfully belonged to the company.[164] None of the circumstances presented here suggest that the director acted in such a manner.

One branch of the duty of loyalty holds that a director acts in bad faith by committing an 'intentional dereliction of duty, a conscious disregard for one's responsibilities'.[165] Here, the director appears to recognise his duty to ensure the financial stability of the Company and is taking appropriate steps to fulfil those responsibilities. While it is possible that the adverse terms of the two transactions could be viewed as bad faith on the part of the director, the Delaware courts have not evinced a desire to second-guess the substantive terms of business transactions, absent evidence of self-dealing by directors or managers. In recent years, much attention has been paid to the possibility of waiving fiduciary duties in the LLC context. Interpreting the provision cited above,[166] the Delaware Court of Chancery has consistently held that participants in an LLC can limit or eliminate fiduciary duties.[167] For a time, it was even disputed whether managers of Delaware LLCs had fiduciary duties by default.[168] A 2013 amendment to the Delaware LLC statute clarified that they do if the agreement is silent, stating that 'the rules of law and equity, including the rules of law and equity relating to fiduciary duties and the law merchant, shall govern'.[169]

A breach of fiduciary duty under corporate law does not ordinarily give rise to criminal liability. For the most part, criminal penalties are imposed for violations of

[163] DLLCA, §18-1101.
[164] See eg *Hollinger International, Inc v Black*, 844 A 2d 1022 (Del Supr 2004).
[165] *In Re The Walt Disney Company Derivative litigation*, 906 A 2d 27, 64 (Del Supr 2006).
[166] DLLCA, §18-1101(c); see also § 18-1101(e).
[167] See eg *Gerber v Enter Prods Holdings, LLC*, 2012 WL 34442, at *13 (Del Ch, 6 January 2012).
[168] *Cf Auriga Capital Corp v Gatz Properties*, 40 A.3d 839, 849–856 (Del Ch 2012) with *Gatz Properties, LLC v Auriga Capital Corp*, 59 A.3d 1206, 1218–20 (Del 2012).
[169] DLLCA, §18-1104.

federal securities laws (such as the Securities Exchange Act of 1934 and the Sarbanes Oxley Act of 2002) in connection with issues such as insider trading and accounting fraud.[170] Given that there is no breach of fiduciary duty in this case coupled with the fact that the Company is a private limited liability company, imposition of criminal liability on Mr B is highly unlikely.

K. South Africa

i. Introduction

South Africa follows a hybrid system of corporate governance. It is partly legislated and partly voluntary.[171] Directors' duties and the principles of good governance are not only regulated in terms of legislation[172] and the common law but important recommendations are also contained in codes of best practice such as the *King IV Report on Corporate Governance*.[173] The Companies Act 2008 came into operation on 1 May 2011. The Act is intended to be appropriate regulation in respect of the legal, economic and social context of South Africa as a constitutional democracy and open economy and to retain existing law that meets these objectives as part of company law.[174] The Companies Act 2008 replaced the Companies Act 61 of 1973, with the exception of the provisions relating to the winding-up of insolvent companies.

In terms of the Companies Act 2008 a 'director' is defined in section 1 as 'a member of the board of a company, as contemplated in section 66, or an alternate director of a company and includes any person occupying the position of a director or alternate director, by whatever name designated'. The rights and duties of the directors, in addition to those in the common law, are determined by the Companies Act 2008. Section 66 of the Companies Act 2008 states that the business and affairs of the company must be managed by or under the direction of the board. It therefore seems as if this section now places a positive duty to manage on directors. This differs from the position under the Companies Act 1973, where directors were organs or functionaries

---

[170] See, eg, Securities Exchange Act, §32; Sarbanes-Oxley Act, §906.

[171] See, in general, I Esser and MK Havenga (eds) *Corporate Governance Annual Review* (South Africa, LexisNexis, 2012) and in general on corporate governance *Mthimunye-Bakoro v Petroleum Oil and Gas Corporation of South Africa (SOC) Limited* [2015] JOL 33744 (WCC) and cases cited there.

[172] In the context of corporate law the Companies Act 71 of 2008 (hereafter 'the Companies Act 2008') is the relevant Act. The Act came into operation on 1 May 2011. In February 2007 a draft Companies Bill was published. During September 2008 Parliament's Trade and Industry Portfolio Committee approved the Companies Bill of 2008. In December 2008 the Portfolio Committee amended the Bill. The Companies Act 2008 was assented to on 8 April 2009. Draft Regulations to the Companies Act were published for comment on 22 December 2009 and again on 29 November 2010. See N 1664, *GG* 32832 of 22 December 2009 and *GG* 33695 of 27 October 2010 for the Regulations and the Amendment Bill. The Companies Amendment Bill B40-2010 was approved by the Portfolio Committee on Trade and Industry on 10 March 2011. The Companies Amendment Act 3 of 2011 was signed into law on 20 April 2011; see *GG* 34243 of 20 April 2011.

[173] Available at www.iodsa.co.za. The *King IV Report on Corporate Governance* was issued on 1 November 2016. Disclosure on the application of *King IV* is effective in respect of financial years starting on or after 1 April 2017 but immediate transition is encouraged. *King IV* replaces the *King Report on Governance, 2009* with its *Code of Corporate Governance (King III)* in its entirety.

[174] MK Havenga (ed), *Company Secretarial Practice* (Cape Town, Juta 2016) para 7.1.2.1.

of the company and the source of their management powers was a delegation from the shareholders.[175]

Section 66 provides for four different types of directors. These are:[176]

- a director appointed in terms of the Memorandum of Incorporation;
- an *ex officio* director;
- an alternate director; and
- a director elected by shareholders.[177]

A director must provide the company with written consent before being entitled to serve as a director (section 66(7)).

The Companies Act 2008 also partially codifies directors' duties.[178] It is not a complete codification however, and the common law principles relating to directors' duties are preserved to the extent that those have not been amended, expressly or by implication, by the Companies Act 2008. Directors therefore have to comply with both the statutory and common law duties.[179]

Section 76 of the Companies Act 2008 deals with the standard of conduct expected from directors. In this section, 'director' includes an alternate director, a prescribed officer,[180] a person who is a member of a committee of a board of a company, or of the audit committee of a company, irrespective of whether or not the person is also a member of the company's board.

ii. Ratification

Ultimate (indirect) control of a company is usually in the hands of the shareholders as they have the power to appoint and remove directors.[181] As discussed above, the level of protection that shareholders receive in terms of the Companies Act 2008 is, however, different compared to the Companies Act 1973 as shareholders no longer have an original decision-making power that is delegated to the directors. This is attributable to the enactment of section 66. Section 66(1) apparently creates a positive duty on the board of directors to manage the company as it provides that the business and affairs of the company *must be managed* by or under the direction of its board.[182] Owing to

---

[175] See PA Delport, 'The Division of Powers in a Company' in C Visser, JT Pretorius and MM Koekemoer (eds), *Essays in Honour of Frans Malan* (Durban, LexisNexis South Africa 2014) 81–92.

[176] See Companies Act 2008, ss 66(4)(a)(i), 66(4)(a)(iii), 66(4)(b) and 68(1). The Memorandum of Incorporation (MoI) is the constituent document of the company: Companies Act 2008, s 15.

[177] See also Havenga, *Company Secretarial Practice* (n 174) para 8.2.

[178] See Companies Act, ss 75 and 76 and Havenga (n 174) para 8.11.

[179] PA Delport (ed), *Henochsberg on the Companies Act 71 of 2008* (Durban, LexisNexis, South Africa, Service issue November 2016) 290(5) and FHI Cassim (ed), *Contemporary Company Law* (Cape Town, Juta, 2012) 403.

[180] A 'prescribed officer' is defined as 'the holder of an office, within a company, that has been designated by the minister in terms of section 66(11)' and performs the (management) functions as described in reg 38 in terms of the Companies Act.

[181] See, generally, J Armour, L Enriques, H Hansmann and R Kraakman 'The Basic Governance Structure: The Interests of Shareholders as a Class' in R Kraakman et al, *The Anatomy of Corporate Law* (3rd edn, Oxford, Oxford University Press 2017) 51.

[182] In terms of the Companies Act 1973 the directors acted as functionaries (organs or agents) of the company. See Delport, *Henochsberg* (n 179) 250(2) and Cassim, *Contemporary Company Law* (n 179) 403.

the use of the words 'business and affairs', it also means that the ultimate power is no longer with the shareholders in general meeting, unless otherwise stated in the Act or the Memorandum of Incorporation (MOI). The powers of the directors are now given by statute and not delegated or derived from an agreement between the shareholders and the directors.[183] The ultimate responsibility for good corporate governance thus lies with the board of directors.[184]

The significance of the power to manage the business and affairs in terms of section 66 is twofold.[185] The power is now original and no longer delegated from the shareholders. This means, inter alia, that the shareholders no longer have the inherent residual power to take a decision in case of, for example, a deadlock.[186] The second implication of this is especially relevant in the context of this case study. Unless the qualifications of section 66 are complied with, the board of directors is now the ultimate organ of the company.[187] The significance of this is that the share-holders, as erstwhile ultimate holders of authority and power,[188] cannot at common law ratify any actions by the directors beyond their authority or in transgression of their duties in acting on authority of the shareholders, except to the extent that the Act or the MOI expressly provides otherwise.[189] The ratification by the 95 per cent shareholder, as explained in the case study, is thus irrelevant due to the enactment of section 66.

iii. Directors' Duties

The two actions of Mr B, namely the sale of 25 per cent of the assets at a 50 per cent discount and the loan that was taken at an average annual interest rate that is 150 per cent above the rate of the commercial bank, have the potential to result in a breach of his duties as a director and subsequent liability in terms of sections 77 and/or 218(2).

In the instant case, the relevant duties are the duty to act with the necessary care, skill and diligence as well as the fiduciary duty to act in the best interests of the

---

[183] Delport, 'The Division of Powers in a Company' (n 175) 81–92.

[184] MK Esser and I Havenga (eds), *Corporate Governance Annual Review 2012* (Durban, LexisNexis South Africa 2012) 30. See I Esser and PA Delport, 'Shareholder Protection Philosophy in Terms of the Companies Act 71 of 2008' (2016) 79 *Journal for Contemporary Roman-Dutch Law* 1, 9.

[185] Delport, *Henochsberg* (n 179) 250(3).

[186] This principle was, however, not applied consistently in the Act, and s 81(1)(d) refers to the deadlock ground as a ground for the winding-up of a solvent company. In Delport, *Henochsberg* (n 179) 250(3) it is stated that 'if the directors are in deadlock, the power to take over the powers of the directors does not transfer to the shareholders as the 'highest authority in the company'. The same principle applies if the MoI or Act does not provide who must exercise the power.

[187] In terms of s 66(1) of the Companies Act 2008, the board is the highest authority. Thus, if the board acts, the company acts. The board can thus sign such a contract without any authority from the company (or any other organ like the shareholders).

[188] See, eg, *John Shaw & Sons (Salford) Ltd v Shaw* [1935] 2 KB 113 (CA); *Scott v Scott* [1943] 1 All ER 582 (Ch) 584–85; HS Cilliers et al, *Cilliers and Benade Corporate Law* (Durban, Butterworths 2000) 21.

[189] See, eg, s 20(2) of the Companies Act 2008 for express authority to ratify certain ultra vires or unauthorised acts. Whether the MoI can give that authority is doubted as it would be in conflict with s 78, which states that any provision in the MoI that relieves a director from the duties as in ss 75 or 76 or from liability for non-compliance (s 77) is void.

company. Both these duties have been codified in the Companies Act. Section 76(3)(b) partially codifies the fiduciary duty to act in the best interests of the company and section 76(3)(c) the duty of care, skill and diligence.

As stated before, the common law is still applicable and thus relevant when considering whether a duty has been breached or not. With regard to the duty to act in the best interests of the company the issue is whether or not the director, subjectively, and based on objective facts, believed that he/she acted in the best interests of the company. As such, this engages the state of mind of the relevant director. Directors must thus exercise their powers in what they consider, and not what the courts consider, is in the best interests of the company.[190] But this subjective test is not without limits.[191] The absence of a reasonable ground may be the basis for a finding that a director did not act in the best interests of the company.[192] It has been held that the test is to determine whether the reasonable person would regard the actions of the director in question as reasonable.[193] There must be reasonable grounds for the belief of the directors that they were acting in the best interests of the company.

When testing whether the duty of care, skill and diligence has been breached a dual test will be applied. The test is both objective and subjective.[194] Objectively, it is required that the director exercises the degree of care, skill and diligence that may reasonably be expected form a person in that position carrying out the same functions. Subjectively, the size of the company, the nature of the company, the responsibilities, knowledge and experience of the relevant director will also be taken into account. The scope of the director's duty will thus vary in accordance with his/her knowledge, skills and experience. The subjective test can therefore be higher than that as determined objectively, but the objective standard will always be the minimum level.

Section 76(4) introduced a safe harbour provision into South African company law stating that a director is presumed or deemed to have acted in accordance with sections 76(3)(b) and (c), referred to above, that is in the best interests of the company and with the necessary care, skill and diligence, if the director has taken reasonably diligent steps to become informed about the matter and the director made a decision, or supported a decision of a committee or the board, with regard to that matter, and the director had a rational basis for believing, and did believe, that the decision was in the best interest of the company. There should have been no self-dealing or proper disclosure, in terms of section 75, if necessary. On compliance with these requirements the courts will not review the decision that was taken by the director.[195] This business judgment rule is thus applicable in the context of the fiduciary duty to act in the best interests of the company as well as the duty to act with the necessary care, skill and diligence. In *Visser Sitrus (Pty) Ltd v Goede Hoop Sitrus Ltd and others*,[196] the Court

[190] *Re Smith & Fawcett Ltd* [1942] Ch 304, 306. See also *Hogg v Cramphorn Ltd* [1967] Ch 254, 268.
[191] See Cassim (n 179) 524.
[192] *Gethning v Kilner* [1972] 1 WLR 337, 342. This is discussed in Cassim (n 179) 524.
[193] See *Shuttleworth v Cox Brothers & Co (Maidenhead) Ltd* [1927] 2 KB 9; *Teck Corp Ltd v Millar* (1972) 33 DLR (3d) 288 (BCSC); *Charterbridge Corporation Ltd v Lloyds Bank Ltd* [1970] Ch 62.
[194] See Companies Act 2008, s 76(3). See Cassim (n 179) 558–61.
[195] See Cassim (n 179) 563–64 on the business judgment rule.
[196] 2014 (5) SA 179 (WCC).

made it clear that, based on section 76(4), the duty to act in the best interests of the company is not an objective one in the sense that the courts can review the actions of the directors and determine what is, objectively speaking, in the best interests of the company. What is required is that the directors, having taken reasonable diligent steps to become informed, should subjectively have believed that their decision was in the best interests of the company and this belief must have had a 'rational basis'.[197] The rationality criterion is based on an objective test (ie what is in the best interests of the company), but is more easily satisfied than a test as to whether a decision is objectively in the best interests of the company.[198] This evaluation, if the directors take a particular decision, can also be done on the basis of (an adaptation of) the rationality principle as applied in the exercise of a public power, ie the exercise of the power must be rationally related to the purpose for which the power was given.[199]

If a breach of a duty occurs the relevant director will be liable based on section 77. Section 77 is also supplemented with section 218(2) stating that any person who contravenes any provision of the Act will be liable to any other person for any loss or damage suffered by that person as a result of the contravention.[200] Section 77(2)(a) deals with liability based on a breach of a fiduciary duty and section 77(2)(b) determines that a director will be liable in accordance with the principles of the common law relating to delict for any loss, damages or costs sustained by the company as a consequence of a breach of section 76(3)(c).

In view of the above it would be difficult to establish that Mr B was not in breach of his fiduciary duty to act in the best interests of the company. To sell 25 per cent of the company's assets at a 50 per cent discount is probably not in the best interests of the company, even if it will raise additional cash. As iterated before, directors should subjectively have believed that their decision was in the best interests of the company and this belief must have had a 'rational basis', which is determined objectively. This does not seem to be the case *in casu*. When determining whether the director breached the duty of care, skill and diligence the dual test must be applied. In this case it can be argued that selling assets at such a substantial discount is not in line with the degree of care, skill and diligence that may reasonably be expected from a person in the position of the director, carrying out the same functions. No factors are provided in the set of facts to indicate a higher degree of care, skill and diligence to be expected from the director. The director will, however, have the protection offered by the business judgment rule and if he complies with the requirements, the court will not review his decision. But based on the facts, *in casu*, it seems that this will not be successful.

---

[197] *Visser Sitrus (Pty) Ltd v Goede Hoop Sitrus Ltd and others* 2014 (5) SA 179 (WCC), para 74, with reference to the *In re Smith & Fawcett Ltd* case (n 190).

[198] See N Locke and I Esser 'Corporate Law (Including Stock Exchanges)' in *Annual Survey of South African Law* (Cape Town, Juta, 2014) for a discussion of this case.

[199] Delport, *Henochsberg* (n 179) 298 and *Visser Sitrus (Pty) Ltd v Goede Hoop Sitrus Ltd and others* (n 197), para 75. See also *Pharmaceutical Manufacturers Association of South Africa and Another: In re Ex Parte President of the Republic of South Africa and Others* 2000 (2) SA 674 (CC) para 85. This test for rationality is purely objective: *Minister of Defence and Military Veterans v Motau and Others* 2014 (5) SA 69 (CC) para 69. Lack of rationality would, however, require gross negligence or recklessness, not mere negligence: See R Stevens and P de Beer, 'The Duty of Care and Skill, and Reckless Trading: Remedies in Flux?' (2016) 29 *SA Mercantile Law Journal* 250, 284.

[200] See Delport, *Henochsberg* (n 179) 640 as to the s 218(2) liability in addition to that in s 77 of the Companies Act 2008.

The position of Mr B and whether or not he committed a breach of one of his duties, as a director, might be more problematic in the context of the loan that he has taken out. Section 22(1) determines that the company must not carry on its business recklessly, with gross negligence, with intent to defraud any person or for any fraudulent purpose. Section 22 is not confined to the winding-up of a company. It will also apply to a company that is a going concern. Section 77(3)(b) states that a director of a company will be liable for any loss, damages or costs sustained by the company as a direct or indirect consequence of the director having 'acquiesced in the carrying on of the company's business despite knowing that it was being conducted in a manner prohibited by section 22(1)'. The important question is thus when a director's conduct will fall under the scope of section 22(1). The definition of 'recklessness' is especially relevant here. Recklessness is not a mere error of judgment, but rather a disregard for the consequences of one's actions.[201] To determine whether the business was conducted in a reckless manner the court will have regard to the scope of the operations of the company, functions and powers of the company, the amount of the debts involved, the extent of the company's financial difficulties and the prospects, if any, of recovery.[202] In *Ozinsky NO v Lloyd*,[203] it was found that if the director continues to carry on business when it is clear, in the opinion of a reasonable businessman, that there will be no reasonable prospect of creditors receiving payment when due, it will usually amount to recklessness.[204] Section 22(2) goes further stating that if section 22(1) has been breached, ie the business was carried on recklessly, then the Commission may issue a notice to the company to show cause why the company should be permitted to continue carrying on its business.[205]

Based on the facts and the interpretation of 'recklessness' under section 22(1) it seems that Mr B did conduct the affairs of the company in a reckless manner when taking out the loan from an individual at a very high interest rate at a time when it was clear that the company's sales figures were not improving. He did this while the company was already not in a position to pay its suppliers. Based on this, Mr B will be liable to the company in terms of section 77(3)(b) or to third parties in terms of section 218(2).

Finally, Mr B can also be held criminally liable based on section 214(1)(c) of the Companies Act where it is held that a party will be guilty of an offence if knowingly a party to conduct prohibited by section 22(1).

---

[201] Cassim (n 179) 591.

[202] *Fisheries Development Corporation of SA Ltd v Jorgensen; Fisheries Development Corporation of SA v AWJ Investments (Pty) Ltd* 1980 (4) SA 156 (W). See also *Philotex v Snyman* 1998 (2) SA 138 (SCA).

[203] 1992 (3) SA 396 (C) at 414G.

[204] If a company is commercially insolvent, ie cannot pay its debts as they fall due, continued operations will usually be reckless.

[205] The Commission could also issue a compliance notice (s 171), and if the company fails to comply, the result could be criminal liability (s 214(3)) and an application for an order of delinquency in respect of the director/s (s 162).

L. Japan

i. Director's Duty to the Company

Under Article 330 of the Companies Act 2005 (CA) in Japan, the relationship between a director and the company is governed by the provisions on mandate in the Civil Code.[206] Article 644 of the Civil Code provides that a mandatory shall assume a duty to administer the mandated business with the care of a good manager in compliance with the main objectives of the mandate (duty of due care). Therefore, a director owes a duty of due care to the company and must comply with that duty when he or she conducts its business affairs as a director to the extent that the company mandates him or her to do so. Furthermore, Article 355 of the CA provides that directors must undertake their duties in a loyal manner to the company in compliance with laws and regulations, the articles of incorporation, and resolutions of shareholders' general meetings (duty of loyalty). Some commentators argue that the duty of loyalty is different from the duty of due care. Analogous to the characterisation of a director as a fiduciary of the company and its shareholders under US case law, they argue that the director owes a strict duty to avoid a conflict-of-interest situation, which proscribes him or her from pursuing benefits in favour of himself or herself or a third party.[207] However, case law in Japan has held that the duty of loyalty is designed to clarify and amplify the duty of due care under the provisions of the Civil Code which govern the mandatory obligations applied with equal force to the director's duty.[208] Therefore, case law and prevailing theory suggests that there is no difference in a legal sense between the duty of due care and the duty of loyalty.[209]

ii. Standard of the Duty of Due Care

If a director breaches the duty of due care and causes harm to the company, he or she is liable for the losses suffered by the Company as a result thereof. Whether a director has complied with his or her duty of due care in connection with a particular decision he or she has taken depends on the facts of the case. Before undertaking a review of a director's decision or conduct, the Japanese judiciary sometimes declares certain general propositions which are formulated within the rubric of the standard of the duty of due care. A director will often be compelled to take a decision urgently in difficult circumstances under which uncertainty will persist. Therefore, in order to determine whether there has been a breach of duty by a director, one has to consider whether the director (i) rationally collected material information, (ii) examined the relevant issues in light thereof and discussed the matter with his or her colleagues with a view to coming to a rational decision, and (iii) the decision and performance of the director must be compared to that of the ordinary standard of management in the

---

[206] As for the English translation to the code text of the Companies Act 2005 and other statutes, see www.japaneselawtranslation.go.jp.

[207] K Egashira, *Kabushikigaisha-hô* [*Laws of Stock Corporations*] (7th edn, Tokyo, Yuhikaku, 2017) 434–35.

[208] Supreme Court, 24 June 1970, *Minshu* (Private Law Report) vol 24, no 6, p 625.

[209] Egashira, *Kabushikigaisha-hô* (n 207) 435.

commercial environment.[210] If a plaintiff is unable to establish the director's negligence in connection with any losses suffered by the Company as a result thereof, the director will not be liable for the loss. This is the so-called 'business judgment rule' which case law in Japan has established is analogous to that in the US case law.

iii. Sale of the Company's Assets

The decision of Mr B to sell the Company's assets at a cheap price must be considered in light of the business judgment rule referred to above. Indeed, a particular case decided by the courts in Japan is of particular relevance. In that case, a director sold the assets of the company at one-fifth or one-tenth less than its current market price before it was near-insolvent. The director argued that the purpose of the sale was to enable the company to save tax and that the cash which he expected would be generated would benefit the company's cashflow position. It became difficult for the company to dispose of its inventory in the ordinary course of business owing to its reputation for conflict with its customers. Therefore, the director subsequently consulted with a business partner as a buyer to provide a large discount for the price of the inventory, and made an arrangement for the sale of the goods. Finally, the company became insolvent and the receiver appointed by the court pursued the director for a breach of his duty of care in selling assets at a high rate of discount and causing serious harm to the company.[211] The Yokohama District Court held that a director has the power to decide how to sell the company's assets to a third party. Even if the price and manner of the sales are not in the ordinary course of business, a director is entitled to decide how to reach a price and make an appropriate arrangement for the sales insofar as the objective of the transaction complies with economic rationality. However, one must recall that the court will decide whether there has been a breach of duty on a case-by-case basis.

iv. The Loan Transaction

Article 362 of the CA provides that where a director seeks to borrow money or other resources from a bank and it represents a significant amount to the company, a director must obtain the approval of the board of directors before entering into such an arrangement (CA, Article 362(4)(iii)). In general, Article 362 of the CA requires a company to attain such approval in respect of any decision to (i) dispose of important assets, (ii) borrow a significant amount, (iii) appoint or dismiss an important employee including any manager, (iv) establish, change or abolish any important structures, including branch offices, or (v) exercise any other 'important' business affairs. Therefore, these important matters must be tabled before a meeting of the board and the company is not entitled to delegate such decision-making to any individual chief executive officer (CEO) or other executive director.

The standard as to what is 'important' or 'significant' is discussed in the case law. The Supreme Court has held that whether or not the asset to be disposed of is

---

[210] Ibid, 328.
[211] Yokohama District Court, 3 March 2005, HanreiJiho, no 1934 at 121.

'important' could be determined by taking into consideration the price of the asset, the value of the asset expressed as a percentage of the total assets of the company, the purpose of the asset, the method of its alienation, the past treatment of such an asset by the company etc.[212] Following this decision of the Supreme Court, the Tokyo Local District Court has also addressed the circumstances in which a company's borrowing will be considered 'significant.' The Court held that the significance of the borrowing could be determined by taking into consideration the amount of the loan, the value of the loan expressed as a percentage of the total assets or current earnings of the company, the purpose of the borrowing, the past treatment of such borrowing by the company etc.[213]

Although the hypothetical case does not indicate the amount of the loan, the interest rate seems particularly unusual and it would appear to be urgently necessary to revive the cashflow situation of the Company's business. If the amount of the borrowing is deemed to be 'significant', Mr B would be required to disclose material information about the borrowing and obtain the approval of the board of directors of the Company. However, since Mr B is the only director of the Company, in reality, the Company has no board of directors for decision-making purposes. In that case, the general meeting of the shareholders of the Company has the authority to decide any matter relating to the organisation, operations and administration of the Company.[214] The hypothetical case suggests that the Company did not hold a general meeting to obtain the consent of the shareholders to the borrowing, but Mr B has secured informal consent from shareholder Mr A1 who has a 95 per cent shareholding. It is true that the CA enables a company to skip the process of calling a general meeting, but this is only possible if all of the shareholders with voting rights agree to forgo the holding of the general meeting.[215]

If a director fails to secure the approval of the Company (board decision or general meeting decision) to such significant borrowing, the question is whether the loan contract between the Company and the lender is rendered invalid. Case law has held that the loan agreement would be valid because Mr B committed the Company to the contract and the directors have the authority to decide any of the business affairs of the Company. However, if the lender had knowledge of the fact that Mr B entered into the loan agreement without the approval of the Company or was grossly negligent, the Company can challenge the validity of the loan agreement by proving that the lender had such knowledge or was grossly negligent.[216]

v. Criminal Penalties Pursuant to the Bankruptcy Act

Under the Bankruptcy Act 2004, where a person inflicts harm on a creditor by disposing of the debtor's property in a manner which is disadvantageous to creditors, that person is liable to a sentence of imprisonment for a period of up to no more than

---

[212] Supreme Court, 1 June 1994, *Minshu*, vol 48, no 1, at 1.
[213] Tokyo District Court, 17 March 1997, HanreiJiho, no 1605, at 141.
[214] CA, Art 295.
[215] Egashira (n 207) 328.
[216] Supreme Court, 22 September 1965, *Minshu*, vol 19, no 6, at 1656.

10 years or a fine of up to no more than 10 million yen, or both (Bankruptcy Act 2004, Article 265). Such actions are treated as being fraudulent if the director knowingly sold the company's assets at a price which is commercially irrational or there is no rational economic purpose for the transaction. Mr B has been simply passive in the face of the Company's suppliers' default, so his conduct is unlikely to constitute a crime of fraudulent bankruptcy.[217]

III. Conclusion

A. Introduction

All of the legal systems examined require directors of a company with limited liability to act with due care in their dealings on behalf of the company. In order to comply with this duty, in general, conduct corresponding to that of a reasonable businessman will be sufficient, but there are differences in the standard applied and its definition. The conduct expected of a director is spelt out in more detail in statutory law and court decisions. Whether the activities in question in this case, namely selling assets at a discount or taking out an expensive loan, result in a breach of duties and impose liability on Mr B, depends on how much leeway directors are granted or, in other words, how a business judgment rule is established.

Different approaches exist with regard to the issue of proof of damage and the requirements for meeting the due care test, although in essence, in all jurisdictions except France, the onus is on the director to show that his or her actions satisfied that test (and in France too, in practice, the director will try to prove that he fulfilled his duty of care in order to fend off the suit). Fewer similarities exist between the jurisdictions studied when it comes to the requirements for shareholder approval of the director's actions. Whereas shareholders' approval relieves the director of liability to the Company in Poland, the UK and the US, in contrast, in Latvia, France, Spain, Germany, South Africa, the Netherlands and Finland, such approval does not relieve the director of liability, and in Italy this issue is unresolved and continues to be debated.

B. Duties of Directors

All of the jurisdictions reviewed require the directors of limited liability companies to comply with a due care principle. However, no common definition of this concept exists. For example, it is described as acting with due care (France), with diligence (Italy), by exercising reasonable care (the UK) and with skill and diligence (the US). Similar to the Latvian standard, which imposes an obligation on directors to carry out their duties as able and careful managers, in Germany and Spain directors are required to act with the care of a competent (Germany) or ordered (Spain) businessman.

---

[217] M Ito, *Bankruptcy Act: Civil Rehabilitation* (3th edn, Tokyo, Yuhikaku, 2014) 744.

Meanwhile, Polish law requires directors to act with the 'highest level of diligence required of a professional' and South Africa has introduced a dual test, which takes into account both subjective and objective criteria. In South Africa, the statutory rules spell out in detail which circumstances are to be taken into account in determining whether the director has acted in the interests of the company and if his actions were justified by a rationally based analysis. The German and Latvian approaches are similar, which is perhaps unsurprising, as many German company law principles have been received into Latvian company law. The due care standard in all jurisdictions is an objective one, ie reasonable and appropriate knowledge, skills and experience can be expected from a director of the company in question, whereas individual shortfalls such as inexperience are not accepted as justifications in the event that a director has not properly carried out his or her duties. Some jurisdictions expressly address the question whether a higher standard applies to those directors who possess additional specialist skills, such as in the UK, where such a higher standard is expected. During the operation of a company, and of distressed companies in particular, the due care principle would thus oblige directors to gather relevant information and conduct a meaningful analysis and risk evaluation. This information has to be supplied to the shareholders, in terms of which the formal calling of a meeting of the shareholders may be required (Germany, Italy, Poland, the Netherlands and Spain).[218]

C. Breach of Directors' Duties

The level of importance which the different jurisdictions accord to the due care principle varies. All jurisdictions apply a standard to evaluate the conduct of directors, whereby the actions or omissions of directors in their dealings on behalf of the company are in principle evaluated as to their merits only where the company suffers losses. Although such a test allows directors a certain leeway as regards their business decisions, in the event of losses borne by the company, some jurisdictions require a higher level of justification for the actions or inactions of the director than others. In Germany, Finland and Latvia, directors are obliged to show that their actions were justified to minimise losses. In the US (Delaware), on the other hand, in line with the 'director primacy' model, a violation of the due care principle would only be invoked by the courts where the facts reveal self-dealing or improper motives on the part of the directors (therefore, directors are almost never held liable for their actions). In France, the conduct of the director will in practice in most cases only be evaluated in the event that the company actually becomes insolvent. The other jurisdictions, however, evaluate the actions of the director in terms of the due care principle if losses occur, and the director is under an obligation to demonstrate that his or her actions were required and acceptable, to a higher or lesser degree, depending on the jurisdiction concerned. Consequently, the application of the due care test in relation to the actions of the director in the case at hand does not produce identical results in every jurisdiction considered.

---

[218] See ch 6, below.

Generally, if the director can prove that he or she took measures which were an acceptable response to the circumstances at hand, under German, Latvian, Finnish, Spanish, UK, Dutch, South African or Polish law, the due care standard would be met. This would require the director's decision-making to be based on sound business reasons which had been established following a meaningful analysis of the facts. In all of the jurisdictions surveyed, this would in principle be possible with regard to both the loan and the sale transactions. With regard to the loan transaction, however, the application of Finnish and French law would more likely result in a finding that the director was in breach of duty on the ground that the particularly high interest rate casts serious doubt on the sufficiency and rigour of the director's analysis of the Company's circumstances. The onus of proving that the director acted diligently lies with the director. In France, on the other hand, the onus of proof would lie with the plaintiff. However, the courts would most probably in any event find a breach only as long as the actions of the directors led to the actual insolvency of the company. In the US (Delaware), a breach of the due care duty requires facts which show self-dealing or improper motives; therefore, both of the actions of the director in the case at hand would pass the test. In the event that the distressed company is close to insolvency, additional duties apply in all jurisdictions, and a breach would thus be established more easily based on a failure to comply, for example, with the duty to report to the shareholders on time.[219]

One of the objectives in this case was to test the theory that the 'shareholder primacy' model was in the ascendancy in most jurisdictions. This is the theory that directors' duties are owed to the shareholders of the company as a class, so that directors must manage companies in their interests. Meanwhile, it has been argued that the corporate law of Delaware amounts to one of the exceptions to this general rule whereby a 'director primacy' model is adopted which serves to subordinate the interests of the shareholders to those of the directors by shielding the latter from liability for a breach of duty in the lion's share of circumstances. The findings in relation to the director's duty of loyalty and care in this case do not provide support for that theory, since there does not appear to be any material distinction between the law of Delaware and many of the other 11 jurisdictions examined. Although the business judgment rule is clearly applied strongly in the law of Delaware to deny liability, the same result would be reached under German, Latvian, Finnish, Spanish, UK, Dutch, South African and Polish law on other grounds.

D. Shareholder Approval of the Activities of the Director

Finally, the approval of the actions of the director by the majority of shareholders is evaluated differently in the jurisdictions. If the shareholders have approved the actions of the director, he or she cannot be held liable in Poland, Japan and the US (Delaware), whereas in the UK this would be the case only if the action in question is deemed to be ratifiable by case law. In Latvia, South Africa, the Netherlands, Spain and France,

---

[219] See ch 6, below, for a full discussion of the issues arising where a company is nearing insolvency.

on the other hand, such shareholder approval does not release the director from liability. In Germany, the courts differentiate between circumstances in which the directors acted in accordance with the instructions of the shareholders (which prevents liability) or merely with their consent (which does not prevent liability). Once again, there is insufficient evidence furnished by the rules on the *ex ante* or *ex post* approval of ratification of a director's breach of duty to demonstrate that the law of Delaware functions to protect directors more than the other eleven jurisdictions examined. Indeed, the law of Poland, Japan and the UK (under certain circumstances) would also enable shareholders to relieve directors of their liability.

E. Conclusion

Directors' duties are defined in general terms by all jurisdictions and in a similar way. However, when specific conduct on the part of the directors is evaluated by the duties, the results differ. The result depends notably on the scope of discretion accorded to directors by the courts in the application of the business judgment rule and also on whether courts require certain consequences (eg resulting insolvency) or (improper) motives. In addition, the interrelation between the actions of the directors and the shareholders' approval or instructions differs to some extent. Directors should thus be able to show that their conduct, as well as their reasons for this conduct, pass the due care test, but they will have to accept that the result of the application of the test will differ. Directors who act in more than one jurisdiction will have to expect that their conduct may be considered a breach of their duties in one jurisdiction, whereas in others, that same conduct would pass without consequences. This will put additional burdens on those companies that are active in several jurisdictions through subsidiaries or with branches or representative offices, and it is suggested that a closer alignment of the applicable legal standards and practice with regard to directors' duties and their satisfaction would be beneficial to the activities of the directors of such companies, and thus the companies themselves.

3

Duties of Nominee Directors

MARTIN GELTER, NEMIKA JHA AND D GORDON SMITH (EDITORS)*

Main topics: directors' duties in case of nominee directors; conflict of interests and duty; transactions between directors and the company; directors' liability; promissory notes.

Related topics: general case on directors' duties (see chapter 2, above); duties of directors in context of takeover bid (see chapters 4 and 5, below); directors' duties in insolvency (see chapter 6, below); enforcement of directors' duties (see chapter 10, below).

I. Scenario

Venture Capitalist (VC) invested substantial funds in exchange for a 20 per cent share in Startup Company (SC), an internet company created by Founder. In connection with this investment, VC, Founder and other investors in SC entered into a shareholders' agreement that entitled VC to nominate two of SC's seven directors. All of the shareholders who were parties to the shareholders' agreement were required to vote their shares in favour of VC's nominees, thus ensuring their election.

Over the first year after VC's investment, SC experienced persistent financial problems due to its ongoing need for capital. SC's board of directors considered various financing options and ultimately decided to pursue a loan from VC. The loan would be evidenced by a promissory note that was convertible into common shares of SC. VC's nominee directors – both of whom are shareholders, directors and officers of VC – participated in the examination of financing options and approved the loan transaction.

Within just a few months, SC defaulted under the express terms of the loan agreement, thus triggering the conversion of the loan into common shares. Following

---

* Martin Gelter and Nemika Jha are responsible for the current edition of this chapter; Gordon Smith was responsible for the first edition.

the conversion, VC owned approximately 35 per cent of SC's outstanding equity. By contrast, Founder's share of SC declined from nearly 60 per cent to approximately 30 per cent. Founder would like to challenge the validity of the loan transaction on the ground that VC's nominee directors were subject to a conflict of interest at the time they approved the loan transaction.

In addition, Founder finds out that VC's nominee directors for SC's board were not their first choice. The nominee directors who VC initially wanted to appoint to the board would have been significantly more experienced; yet, VC decided to put forward more junior nominee directors who it instructed to pursue VC's interests and to implement VC's instructions to the greatest possible extent. Founder takes the view that both directors and shareholders must prioritise the best interests of the company.

He asks a lawyer of your country about advice on the following two issues: (i) Is the loan transaction between SC and its existing investors valid? (ii) Did VC breach any duties towards SC in not selecting the most qualified nominee directors?

Note: the scenario assumes that SC is established in the form of a private company. If a convertible promissory note cannot be provided by a private company in your jurisdiction, please indicate whether it could have been provided by a public company.

II. Case Studies

A. The US

i. Introduction

In the US, the incumbent board of directors typically nominates the directors to be voted on by shareholders. As a practical matter, therefore, the shareholders of large, publicly traded companies traditionally have had little opportunity to determine the composition of the board of directors, short of a proxy contest or hostile takeover. With effect from 1 August 2009, the Delaware General Corporation Law (DGCL) expressly permits the adoption of a by-law providing shareholder access to the corporation's proxy statement for the purposes of director elections. In addition, in 2010 the Securities and Exchange Commission (SEC) adopted amendments to the federal proxy rules to allow for shareholder nominations of directors, but the most important of these amendments was struck down by a federal court in 2011.[1] These legal innovations are likely to increase shareholder involvement in director elections and it is possible that they could result in further development of the law relating to nominee directors. As it stands, that law is largely confined to closely held corporations, such as SC in the hypothetical case. The shareholders in closely held corporations often allocate director seats amongst themselves, either by creating separate classes of shares, each with unique voting rights, or by entering into a shareholders' agreement like the one in the hypothetical case. Both of these strategies are permitted under Delaware corporate law, and the directors elected under either strategy are expected

---

[1] *Business Roundtable v SEC*, 647 F 3d 1144 (DC Cir 2011).

to serve the interests of the corporation generally. Issues are most likely to arise when a director is viewed as serving the interests of the nominating shareholders at the expense of the other shareholders, and these issues typically would be analysed as conflict-of-interest transactions. This is the scenario posed by the hypothetical case.

ii. Conflict-of-Interest Transactions

Conflict-of-interest transactions were considered void or voidable under the common law of Delaware.[2] In 1967, Delaware adopted section 144 of the DGCL to provide a safe harbour against such results.[3] Section 144 provides that a conflict-of-interest transaction is neither void nor voidable solely by reason of the conflict if the transaction was approved, after full disclosure, either by (i) a majority of the disinterested directors or (ii) a good faith vote of the (disinterested) stockholders. Section 144 offers the same protection to a transaction that is 'fair as to the corporation as of the time it is authorised, approved or ratified'.[4]

The hypothetical problem contemplates a conflict-of-interest transaction under section 144, which covers a 'transaction ... between a corporation [SC] and any other corporation, partnership, association, or other organisation [VC] in which 1 or more of its directors or officers [the VC nominees] are directors or officers, or have a financial interest'.[5] Based on the facts in the hypothetical problem, VC's nominee directors were 'interested' in the loan transaction. If even one of the other directors on the board were disinterested, however, and that director approved the transaction in good faith with an understanding of the material facts relating to the conflict and the transaction, the transaction would be neither void nor voidable solely by reason of the conflict.[6]

Even if SC's board of directors complied with section 144, the transaction could be invalid if the directors of SC breached their fiduciary duty of loyalty in approving the transaction.[7] Under Delaware law, directors are given the benefit of the business judgment rule: 'a presumption that in making a business decision the directors of a corporation acted on an informed basis, in good faith and in the honest belief that the action taken was in the best interests of the company'.[8]

Whilst the Delaware courts have held that compliance with section 144 is a 'minimum requirement to retain the protection of the business judgment rule',[9] complying with

---

[2] See B Rohrbacher et al, 'Finding Safe Harbor: Clarifying the Limited Application of Section 144' (2008) 33 *Delaware Journal of Corporate Law* 719, 722–23.

[3] See eg EL Folk, III, *The Delaware General Corporation Law: A Commentary and Analysis* (Boston, MA, Little Brown, 1972) 82: 'Section 144(a) is negative in effect. A contract or transaction covered by the statute is not void or voidable solely because those approving a transaction have a conflict of interest ... The validating effect does not go beyond removing the spectre of voidability'.

[4] DGCL, § 144(a)(3).

[5] DGCL, § 144(a).

[6] Rohrbacher et al, 'Finding Safe Harbor' (n 2) 737: 'Under the section 144 statutory analysis, so long as there is one informed, disinterested director on the board, and so long as he or she approves the transaction in good faith, the transaction will not be presumptively voidable due to the offending interest. In other words, a nine-member board with a single disinterested director may approve a covered transaction and reap the benefits of the section 144 safe harbor'.

[7] *In re Cox Communications, Inc Shareholders Litigation*, 879 A 2d 604, 615 (Del Ch 2005).

[8] *Aronson v Lewis*, 473 A 2d 805, 812 (Del 1984).

[9] *HMG/Courtland Properties, Inc v Gray*, 749 A 2d 94, 113 (Del Ch 1999).

section 144 does not ensure the protection of the business judgment rule. A plaintiff may rebut the presumption of the business judgment rule at the pleading stage by pleading 'facts that support a reasonable inference that in making the challenged decision, the board of directors breached either its duty of loyalty or its duty of care'.[10] As a practical matter, this typically requires allegations that a majority of the directors were interested in the transaction or 'beholden' to the interested directors. A director is 'beholden' to another director when the first director is so under the second director's influence that the first director's discretion would be sterilised.[11] At the trial stage, a plaintiff would attempt to rebut the presumption of the business judgment rule by proving these allegations.

The hypothetical case contemplates a board of seven directors, two of whom (the VC nominees) were interested in the challenged transaction. If a plaintiff could demonstrate that two other directors were 'beholden' to the VC nominees, the presumption of the business judgment rule would be successfully rebutted. In that instance, the court would turn to the so-called 'entire fairness' analysis.[12] Under this standard, the courts evaluate transactions for 'fair dealing' (embracing 'questions of when the transaction was timed, how it was initiated, structured, negotiated and disclosed to the directors, and how the approvals of the directors and the stockholders were obtained')[13] and 'fair price' (which 'relates to the economic and financial considerations of the proposed' transaction).

The result in this case would depend on the outcome of this entire fairness analysis, which is exceedingly fact-dependent. If the parties in the hypothetical case entered into the transaction with complete information – and there is no information in the hypothetical facts to suggest otherwise – then the transaction would likely be approved by a Delaware court. While one could imagine facts in which the substance of the transaction would be so egregious that a Delaware court would be reluctant to enforce the deal, the Delaware courts usually defer to the parties to craft their own terms.[14]

iii. Selection of Nominee Directors

State corporate law generally does not establish formal requirements for directors beyond that they must be natural persons.[15] In publicly traded corporations, § 407 of the Sarbanes-Oxley Act requires disclosure as to whether at least one member of the audit committee qualifies as a 'financial expert.' This provision does not apply in a privately held firm such as SC. Thus, whether VC breached any duties towards SC in not selecting the most qualified nominee directors will primarily be a question

---

[10] *Gantler v Stephens*, 965 A 2d 695, 706 (Del 2009).

[11] See *Rales v Blasband*, 634 A 2d 927, 936 (Del 1993).

[12] *Weinberger v UOP, Inc*, 457 A 2d 701, 711 (Del 1983).

[13] Ibid. See also *In re Trados Inc. Shareholders Litigation*, 73 A.3d. 17 (Del Ch 2013); *In re Nine Sys. Corp. Shareholders Litigation*, 2014 Del Ch LEXIS 17 (Del Ch, Sep 4, 2014) (stating that 'directors owe fiduciary duties to all stockholders, not just a particular subset of stockholders ... To prove that a corporate director has confronted the dual fiduciary problem, a plaintiff must establish: (i) that the interests of the second beneficiary diverged from those of the common stockholders; and (ii) that the director faced a conflict of interest because of his or her competing duties'), *Carsanaro v Bloodhound Technologies, Inc.*, 65 A.3d 618 (Del Ch 2013).

[14] The analysis would not change if one of the directors was also an executive officer of SC because both s 144 and corporate fiduciary duties apply to officers and directors.

[15] DGCL, §141(b).

of contract. Meticulously drafted shareholder agreements may expressly provide for minimum qualifications that nominee directors must satisfy. A remedy in contract law will be available in the event of a breach. If the shareholders' agreement does not provide for any criteria, a fiduciary duty claim under the state's corporate law may still be available.

Traditionally, courts have not held shareholders to a fiduciary duty standard in deciding the selection of directors and officers. However, with respect to closely held corporations, some states like Massachusetts adopt the view that shareholders owe one another fiduciary duties akin to those in a partnership.[16] In the context of actions resulting in a 'squeeze-out' of a minority shareholder, the Massachusetts courts have required a majority shareholder to establish a legitimate business purpose in removing a minority shareholder from a directorship.[17] It is unlikely that this case law would apply in the hypothetical case, given that VC was neither a controlling shareholder nor attempting to squeeze out the Founder.

In Delaware, only a controlling shareholder in certain situations owes a fiduciary duty to the corporation and the minority shareholders.[18] Usually, a controlling shareholder will own a majority interest in the corporation or exercise control over the business affairs of the corporation.[19] Even if a shareholder owns less than 50 per cent of the outstanding shares, if that shareholder exercises domination through actual control of corporate conduct, the shareholder may qualify as a controlling shareholder.[20] The shareholder's power must be 'so potent that independent directors … cannot freely exercise their judgment, fearing retribution' from the controlling minority shareholder.[21] In the present hypothetical, VC does not own a majority position in the corporation and will not ordinarily owe a fiduciary duty to the corporation.

B. The UK[22]

i. Introduction

In terms of UK company law, the articles of association[23] of a private limited company govern the appointment of directors. The Model Articles direct that the shareholders

---

[16] See Donahue v Rodd Electrotype Co. of New England, Inc., 367 Mass 578, 328 N.E. 2d 505 (1975).

[17] See Wilkes v Springside Nursing Home, Inc., 353 N.E.2d 657 (Mass 1976).

[18] See Hollinger International, Inc. v Black 844 A. 2d 1022 (Del 2004).

[19] See Ivanhoe Partners v Newmont Min. Corp. 535 A.2d 1334 (Del 1987).

[20] See Citron v Fairchild Camera & Instrument Corp. 569 A.2d 53 (Del. 1989); Ivanhoe Partners v Newmont Mining Corp. 535 A.2d 1334 (Del 1987); In re KKR Financial Holdings LLC Shareholder Litigation, 101 A.3d 980 (Del Ch 2015).

[21] See In re Morton's Restaurant Group, Inc. Shareholders Litigation, 74 A.3d 656 (Del Ch 2013).

[22] Abbreviations: CA 2006 (the Companies Act 2006); FSMA 2000 (the Financial Services and Markets Act 2000); FCA (the Financial Conduct Authority); Model Articles (Model articles of association of private companies limited by shares (in reg 2 of and sch 1 to the Companies (Model Articles) Regulations 2008, SI 2008/3229), private companies limited by guarantee (in reg 3 of and sch 2 to the Companies (Model Articles) Regulations 2008, SI 2008/3229) and public limited companies (in reg 4 of and sch 3 to the Companies (Model Articles) Regulations 2008, SI 2008/3229); Listing Rules (the Listing Rules of the FCA (www.handbook.fca.org.uk/handbook/LR.pdf)).

[23] This solution proceeds on the basis of an assumption that SC has adopted the Model Articles applicable to private limited companies by shares as its articles of association in terms of sch 1 to the Companies (Model Articles) Regulations 2008, SI 2008/3229.

are entitled to appoint the directors[24] by ordinary resolution. However, the directors can also co-opt a person onto the board as a director.[25] In the UK, shareholders' agreements are legally binding in contract law[26] and they may validly oblige shareholders to vote in a particular manner, for example, by voting in favour of a candidate as a director who was proposed by a shareholder.

ii. Conflict of Interests and Duty

The first issue to be addressed in the hypothetical case concerns the fact that VC's nominee directors (who are also directors of VC) faced a conflict of interest and duty insofar as they approved SC's loan transaction with VC as board members of SC. There is nothing in UK company law which prohibits directors from holding multiple directorships or even from directly or indirectly (eg through another company) engaging in business that competes with the company[27] of which they are a director, provided that the requisite approvals under the CA 2006 are secured beforehand from the board of directors or shareholders.[28] According to section 175(1) of the CA 2006, a director of a company must avoid a situation in which he or she has, or can have, a direct or indirect interest that conflicts, or possibly may conflict, with the interests of the company. This duty to avoid a conflict of interests is owed by VC's two nominee directors to SC in terms of section 175(1) of the CA 2006. Thus, SC is entitled to sue VC's two nominee directors for any losses (inter alia) which it sustains as a result of breach of this duty. This statutory rule is based upon the equitable principle that any person owing fiduciary duties must not put himself or herself in a position in which he or she has or can have conflicting interests or duties[29] and is enforced strictly by the courts.[30]

In the cases of *Central Bank of Ecuador v Conticorp SA*[31] and *Hawkes v Cuddy*,[32] the Judicial Committee of the Privy Council and the Court of Appeal have both held that the fact that a director of a company has been nominated to that office by a shareholder does not, of itself, impose any duty on the director to his or her nominator.[33] On the face of the facts of the hypothetical case, the nominee directors

---

[24] See the Model Articles, reg 17(1)(a) of sch 1 to the Companies (Model Articles) Regulations 2008, SI 2008/3229.

[25] Model Articles, reg 17(1)(b) of sch 1 to the Companies (Model Articles) Regulations 2008, SI 2008/3229.

[26] See, eg, *Russell v Northern Bank Development Corp Ltd* [1992] 1 WLR 588 (HL).

[27] However, in Scots law, there would appear to a general duty which prohibits a director from competing with the company; see the obiter dicta of Lord President Hamilton in *Commonwealth Oil & Gas Company Ltd v Baxter* [2009] CSIH 75, 2009 SLT 1123, 1126 [5].

[28] For a comprehensive analysis of the legal position of nominee directors, see D Ahern, 'Nominee Directors' Duty to Promote the Success of the Company: Commercial Pragmatism and Legal Orthodoxy' (2011) 127 *Law Quarterly Review* 118.

[29] *Aberdeen Railway Co v Blaikie Bros* (1854) 1 Macq 461 (HL Sc).

[30] *Regal (Hastings) Ltd v Gulliver* [1967] AC 134 (HL); *O'Donnell v Shanahan* [2009] EWCA Civ 751, [2009] 2 BCLC 666; and *Towers v Premier Waste Management Ltd* [2011] EWCA Civ 923.

[31] [2015] UKPC 11; [2016] 1 BCLC 26.

[32] *Hawkes v Cuddy* [2009] EWCA Civ 291, [2010] 2 BCC 597.

[33] The director may owe duties to his or her nominator if he or she is an employee or officer of the nominator, or by reason of a formal or informal agreement with his or her nominator, but such duties do not arise out of his or her nomination, but out of a separate agreement or office. Such duties cannot, however, detract from his duty to the company of which he or she is a director when he or she is acting as such, see *Hawkes v Cuddy* [2009] EWCA Civ 291, [2010] 2 BCC 597, 605 [32], (Stanley Burnton LJ).

of VC appear to have infringed their duty to avoid a conflict of interests in terms of section 175(1) of the CA 2006 and it is no defence for them to argue that they were acting in the best interests of VC, their nominator.[34] However, section 175(4) of the CA 2006 stipulates that the conflict of interest duty is not breached if (a) the situation cannot reasonably be regarded as likely to give rise to a conflict of interest or (b) the matter has been authorised by the directors. With regard to section 175(4)(b), on the facts of the case, there is nothing to suggest that (i) the nominee directors of VC disclosed the existence of their conflict of interests to the board of SC and/or that (ii) the board of SC authorised their conflict in advance of passing the resolution of SC's board of directors to approve the loan transaction. Since authorisation cannot be retrospective, the nominee directors of VC would be unable to take advantage of the exception in section 175(4)(b) of the CA 2006.[35] It should be noted that if VC's two nominee directors had voted on any board resolution, like German law (see E, below), their votes would not be counted.[36]

Turning to section 175(4)(a) of the CA 2006, at present, there is no case law interpreting what is meant by the words 'the situation cannot reasonably be regarded as likely to give rise to a conflict of interest'. Thus, it is difficult to form a concrete view on whether this defence would be available to the nominee directors of VC in the case at hand. Having said that, during the period when the Companies Bill was progressing through, and being debated in, the UK Parliament, Lord Goldsmith, the then Attorney-General, provided guidance to the effect that 'the expression "if the situation cannot reasonably be regarded as likely to give rise to a conflict of interest" introduces the concept of reasonableness which makes the situation easier from the point of view of a director and avoids a very harsh test'[37] and '[i]f the matter falls outside the ambit of the company's business, a real conflict of interest is unlikely'.[38] The courts in the UK are entitled to refer to ministerial statements in the UK Parliament on a bill as an aid to statutory interpretation.[39] Moreover, in terms of the common law rules which governed the duties of directors to avoid conflicts of interest before the entry into force of section 175 of the CA 2006 on 1 October 2008,[40] the courts routinely emphasised the

---

[34] See *Central Bank of Ecuador v Conticorp SA* [2015] UKPC 11; [2016] 1 BCLC 26, 49–50 per Lord Mance.

[35] It should be noted that there has recently been a suggestion that Scots law entitles a Scottish court to hold that the company's actions show that it conferred implicit consent in favour of a conflicted director's breach of duty, thus relieving that director from liability. See *Commonwealth Oil & Gas Company Ltd v Baxter* (n 27) 1126–27, [10] (Lord President Hamilton). However, contrast the approach of Lord President Hamilton with Lord Drummond Young's application of the traditional restrictive approach to informed consent in *Park's of Hamilton (Holdings) Ltd v Campbell* [2014] CSIH 34; 2014 GWD 18-338 at [38]–[42]. Consideration will not be given to this notion of implicit consent here, since it is unclear to what extent this rule represents (i) the position in English law (although it may form part of the 'unanimous consent' rule, eg in *Re Duomatic Ltd* [1969] 2 Ch 365 (Ch)) or (ii) Scots law generally for that matter.

[36] CA 2006, s 175(6).

[37] Hansard HL 6 February 2006, vol 678, col GC293 (Lord Goldsmith).

[38] Hansard HL 9 May 2006, vol 681, col 864 (Lord Goldsmith). Author's annotations in square brackets.

[39] *Pepper v Hart* [1993] AC 593 (HL) 634C–E and 640C (Lord Browne-Wilkinson).

[40] CA 2006, s 170(4) directs that the 'general duties [of directors, including the section 175 duty to avoid conflicts] shall be interpreted and applied in the same way as common law rules or equitable principles, and regard shall be had to the corresponding common law rules and equitable principles in interpreting and applying the general duties'. Author's annotations in square brackets.

strictness of the obligation not to allow a conflict to arise between duty and interest.[41] On the basis of such non-statutory guidance and taking into account the common law position, it is submitted that it is unlikely that an argument by the nominee directors of VC that SC's conclusion of the loan transaction did not amount to a breach of duty under section 175(4)(a) of the CA 2006 would be successful. Further, it is reasonably clear that the loan transaction does not 'fall outside the ambit of' SC's or VC's business. Therefore, the conclusion must be drawn that VC's two nominee directors have breached section 175 of the CA 2006.

iii. Transactions or Arrangements between Directors and the Company

Where a director of a company is in any way, directly or indirectly, interested in a proposed transaction or arrangement with the company, he or she must declare the nature and extent of that interest to the other directors prior to the company entering into the transaction or arrangement.[42] This duty to declare is owed by VC's two nominee directors to SC in terms of section 170(1) of the CA 2006. Therefore, it would appear that VC's nominee directors ought to have declared the nature and extent of their interest in the loan from VC to SC to the other directors of SC, since they are indirectly interested in that transaction by virtue of their directorships of VC.[43]

However, there is an argument that the nominee directors of VC can take advantage of the exception set out in section 177(6)(b) of the CA 2006. Here it is provided that the directors are not liable:

> [I]f, or to the extent that, the other directors are already aware of [the directors' interest in the proposed transaction or arrangement, ie the loan with SC] (and for this purpose the other directors are treated as aware of anything of which they ought reasonably to be aware).[44]

In the instant case, it is abundantly clear that the directors and shareholders of SC are fully aware of the fact that two of their directors are the nominee directors of VC and of the existence of the loan transaction between SC and VC. For this reason, it is submitted that the exception applies to relieve the two nominee directors of liability for the prima facie breach of section 177 of the CA 2006.

Further, unlike the German solution and the provisions of the CA 2006 considered above, which apply where the conflict of interest does not involve a transaction or arrangement between the company and a director,[45] if the two nominee directors of

---

[41] *Aberdeen Railway Co v Blaikie Bros* (n 29); *Bhullar v Bhullar* [2003] EWCA Civ 424, [2003] BCC 711, 720–23 (Jonathan Parker LJ); and *O'Donnell v Shanahan* (n 30) 690–91 at [70]–[71] (Rimer LJ).

[42] CA 2006, s 177(1) and (4).

[43] In the event that the nominee directors of VC fail to comply with the provisions of s 177 of the CA 2006, this failure will render the loan contract voidable at the instance of SC against any party thereto who has notice of the breach of duty and any profit which the directors derived from the contract is recoverable from them by SC. See, eg, *Transvaal Lands Co v New Belgium (Transvaal) Land and Development Co* [1914] 2 Ch 488 (CA); *Re Marini Ltd* [2003] EWHC 334 (Ch), [2004] BCC 172, 195–96 at [62]–[66] (Seymour J, QC).

[44] Author's annotations in square brackets.

[45] CA 2006, s 175(6).

VC voted[46] in favour of the loan transaction, these votes would not be invalid, unless the articles of association provided otherwise.[47]

iv. Status of the Promissory Note

It is perfectly lawful in the UK for plcs or private companies to issue promissory notes which are convertible into common stock, ie debt-to-equity instruments are permissible and not uncommon.[48]

v. Selection of Nominee Directors

UK company law prescribes certain restrictions on persons who are not eligible to be appointed as a director, for example persons under the age of 16 by virtue of section 157 of the CA 2006, and undischarged bankrupts in terms of section 11 of the Company Directors Disqualification Act 1986. However, a lack of previous experience as a director or inexperience generally is not one of the applicable criteria and there is no impediment to the appointment of such directors. Further, as a shareholder, VC owes no duties to SC or Founder: UK company law does not recognise a concept such as shareholder fiduciary or general duties. Moreover, it is unlikely that VC would be treated as a shadow director in terms of section 251 of the CA 2006. The end result is that it would not be possible for Founder or SC to challenge VC for the appointment of two inexperienced and junior individuals as directors of SC.

vi. Summary and Conclusion

The board's approval of the loan transaction between SC and VC is likely to result in a finding that VC's two nominee directors have breached their duty to avoid a conflict of interest and duty in terms of section 175 of the CA 2006. The effect of such a breach of duty is that SC will be entitled to (i) sue the two nominee directors for any losses which it has sustained as a result of their breach of duty or (ii) rescind the loan transaction concluded with VC.[49] However, the effect of section 177(6)(b) of the CA 2006 is that

---

[46] There is no evidence in the hypothetical case that any such votes have been passed.

[47] The Model Articles enable the directors to vote on resolutions concerning an actual or proposed transaction or arrangement with the company provided that certain conditions are met: see, eg, the Model Articles, reg 14(2), (3) and (4) of and sch 1 to the Companies (Model Articles) Regulations 2008, SI 2008/3229. See, eg, PL Davies and S Worthington, *Gower's Principles of Modern Company Law* (10th edn, London, Sweet & Maxwell, 2016) para 16-58 at 519.

[48] If SC had been a listed plc, it would have been required to comply with the Listing Rules drawn up by the FCA as the 'competent authority' in terms of the FSMA 2000, s 73A. Since the promissory note is entered into by SC and VC and VC is a 'substantial shareholder' of SC (as VC is entitled to exercise or to control the exercise of 10% or more of the votes at general meetings of SC), it would amount to a 'related party transaction' in terms of Listing Rule 11 and would require prior shareholder approval in terms of Listing Rule 11.1.7(3).

[49] CA 2006, s 178; Davies and Worthington, *Gower's Principles of Modern Company Law* (n 47) para 16-111 at 563; *Lagunas Nitrate Company v Lagunas Syndicate* [1899] 2 Ch 392 (CA); and *Transvaal Lands Co v New Belgium (Transvaal) Land and Development Co* (n 43).

VC's two nominee directors will not be in breach of their duty under section 177(1) of the CA 2006 to declare to the other directors the nature and extent of their indirect interest (as directors of VC) in the loan transaction between SC and VC.[50]

C. South Africa

i. Introduction

A nominee director is a de jure director who 'owes' his nomination to a shareholder or another third party like a bank. A large shareholder may, for example, agree to purchase shares in the company subject to representation on the board. Or a shareholder may not be able to sit on the board owing to time constraints or lack of expertise. Nominee directors are useful in these circumstances. It must be emphasised that although such directors can be referred to as 'nominees', they owe their duties to the company and not the shareholder who nominated them.[51]

In terms of section 66(4)(b) of the Companies Act 2008, at least 50 per cent of the directors have to be elected by shareholders. As long as at least 50 per cent of the directors of a profit company are elected by the shareholders, then the remainder may be appointed by third parties. The appointment of the nominee directors in this case is thus valid.

ii. Conflict of Interests

The presence of nominee directors can lead to a possible conflict of interest should the interests of the company not coincide with those of the nominator.[52] The legal position is, however, that the nominee must serve the interests of the company (SC) and not the interests of the nominator (VC).[53] Nominee directors may take their nominators' wishes into account, but in so doing they may not act as mere puppets and must still consider the best interests of the company.[54] It is stated that:

> A director must not act primarily in the interests of those who may have been influential in securing his appointment. For example, if a large shareholder secures the appointment of that director in order to protect the wishes of that shareholder, the director, in acting in the best interests of that shareholder and not of the company would clearly be acting in

---

[50] Section 200 of the CA 2006, which operates to prohibit a company from entering into a loan transaction with a person connected with one of its directors without the advance approval of its members, is not considered here since it only applies to plcs or companies associated with a plc and it is assumed that SC is a private company.

[51] FHI Cassim (ed), *Contemporary Company Law* (Cape Town, Juta 2012) 406. See also *S v Shaban* 1965 (4) SA 646 (W), 651; *Fisheries Development Corporation of SA Ltd v Jorgensen; Fisheries Development Corporation of SA Ltd v AWJ Investments (Pty) Ltd* 1980 (4) SA 156 (W), 163 and *Boulting v Association of Cinematograph, Television and Allied Technicians* [1963] 2 QB 606, 626.

[52] *Scottish Co-operative Wholesale Society Ltd v Meyer* [1959] AC 324, 366–67.

[53] *Fisheries Development Corporation of SA Ltd v Jorgensen; Fisheries Development Corporation of SA Ltd v AWJ Investments (Pty) Ltd* 1980 (4) SA 156 (W), 163

[54] MK Havenga (ed), *Company Secretarial Practice* (Cape Town, Juta, 2016) para 8.11.2.2 and *Fisheries Development Corporation of SA Ltd v Jorgensen; Fisheries Development Corporation of SA Ltd v AWJ Investments (Pty) Ltd* 1980 (4) SA 156 (W), 163.

bad faith and illegally. From a practical perspective, this is often one of the most difficult boardroom conflicts for the company secretary to handle, as often such 'nominee directors' (especially inexperienced ones) confuse their shareholder rights with their duties and responsibilities as directors.[55]

Nominee directors are also subject to directors' duties. The nominee directors, in the case study, should thus act in accordance with directors' duties and, *in casu*, specifically in line with section 75. In this case the nominee directors are also directors of VC (the nominator). Generally, the director may owe duties to his or her nominator if he or she is an employee or officer of the nominator, or by reason of a formal or informal agreement with his or her nominator, but such duties do not arise out of his or her nomination, but out of a separate agreement or office. Such duties cannot, however, detract from his duty to the company of which he or she is a director when he or she is acting as such.[56] The fact that the directors of SC, as appointed by VC, are also directors of VC makes them 'related parties'[57] for the purposes of section 75. Section 75 determines that it is the duty of a director who is interested in a contract or a proposed contract with the company to declare the nature of his or her interest at a meeting of the directors of the company. Disclosure of any 'personal financial interests' that the director or a related party has should be disclosed. A director's personal interests should thus not conflict with the interests of the company. A 'personal financial interest' is defined in section 1 as:

(*a*) ... a direct material interest of that person, of a financial, monetary or economic nature, or to which a monetary value may be attributed; but

(*b*) does not include any interest held by a person in a unit trust or collective investment scheme in terms of the Collective Investment Schemes Act, 2002 (Act No. 45 of 2002), unless that person has direct control over the investment decisions of that fund or investment;

In view of the above it seems that the nominee directors were 'related parties' and had to disclose their 'personal financial interest' as required by section 75. They are thus in breach of section 75 by not disclosing as required. The consequence is that the loan agreement is void.[58] Ratification by the shareholders is, however, possible by way of an ordinary resolution following disclosure.[59]

iii. Duty to Select Most Qualified Directors

Any person, including a foreigner, may be a director of a company registered in South Africa. There are no specific qualifications required of directors in terms of company

---

[55] Havenga, *Company Secretarial Practice* (n 54) para 8.11.2.2.

[56] See ch 2, above. See also *Hawkes v Cuddy* [2009] EWCA Civ 291, [2010] 2 BCC 597, 605 [32].

[57] For the purposes of s 75, 'related person', when used in reference to a director, has the meaning set out in s 1, but also includes a second company of which the director or a related person is also a director, or a close corporation of which the director or a related person is a member. In s 1 'related', when used in respect of 2 persons, means persons who are connected to one another in any manner contemplated in s 2(1)(a) to (c).

[58] *Omar v Inhouse Venue Technical Management (Pty) Limited and Others* 2015 (3) SA 146 (WCC), para 64.

[59] See s Companies Act 2008, s 75(7)(b).

legislation, subject to section 69.[60] Shareholders also have no fiduciary duties towards the company so they can appoint and elect directors as they please.[61] It has been specifically held that where the authority to appoint a director is placed in a third party, there is no obligation on that party to appoint the most suitable person.[62]

Shareholders may, however, agree expressly or tacitly, that there is a personal relationship of confidence and trust, and in this relationship the shareholders may owe a duty of good faith to the other shareholders.[63] In *Hulett & others v Hulett*,[64] it was held, with reference to the decision of the House of Lords in *Ebrahimi*,[65] that '[i]t is true that "there is room in company law for recognition of the fact that behind it, or amongst it, there are individuals, with rights, expectations and obligations inter se which are not necessarily submerged in the company structure"'.

If this is the case, then it could be argued that VC had a duty to act in the best interests of the company and the other shareholders to appoint competent and qualified directors. The remedies in this case would, however, be winding-up in terms of section 81 on the basis of the deadlock principle. Deadlock can be 'complete deadlock' situations (formal deadlock such as inability to pass resolutions due to a lack of a majority vote) and the 'deadlock principle' (substantive deadlock) which will be cases where there is a deadlock based on internal factors, eg the principles such as in the *Ebrahimi* case.[66]

D. France

The solution, as to the loan transaction, would be the same whether SC is a public company (*Société anonyme* (SA)) or a simplified public limited company (*Société par actions simplifiée* (SAS)) or a limited company (*Société à responsabilité limitée* (SARL)). In France, SC would probably not be a limited company because it would offer less flexibility, especially in relation to financing. The most likely company form which would have been used in this case would have been an SAS.

---

[60] Section 69 defines persons who are ineligible to become directors and those who are eligible, but disqualified.

[61] Cassim, *Contemporary Company Law* (n 51) 381. The right to vote on the shares is a personal right and it is the property of the shareholder: *Pender v Lushington* (1877) 6 ChD 70, 75; *Sammel v President Brand Gold Mining Co Ltd* 1969 (3) SA 629 (A), 680 where the principle is stated that 'for the rule is well established that a vote, being a proprietary right of shareholding, may be exercised by the shareholder in his own interests'. See PA Delport (ed), *Henochsberg on the Companies Act 71 of 2008* (Durban, LexisNexis, South Africa, Service issue November 2016) 171. See also *Living Hands (Pty) Ltd and Another v Ditz and Others* 2013 (2) SA 368 (GSJ), para 21; *Amdocs SA Joint Enterprise (Pty) Ltd v Kwezi Technologies (Pty) Ltd* 2014 (5) SA 532 (GJ), para 23.

[62] *Kuwait Asia Bank EC v National Mutual Life Nominees Ltd* [1991] AC 187 (PC), 220. See Cassim (n 51) 423.

[63] Delport, *Henochsberg* (n 61) 171 and *Amdocs SA Joint Enterprise (Pty) Ltd v Kwezi Technologies (Pty) Ltd* (n 61) para 23.

[64] 1992 (4) SA 291 (A), 307GI.

[65] *Ebrahimi v Westbourne Galleries Ltd & another* [1973] AC 360 (HL), 379b–c, per Lord Wilberforce.

[66] *Erasmus v Pentamed Investments (Pty) Ltd* 1982 (1) SA 178 (W); *Apco Africa Incorporated v Apco Worldwide (Pty) Ltd* [2008] 4 All SA 1 (SCA), 10; *Msizi v Watt Energy (RF) (Pty) Limited (Mark Scheepers Intervening Party)* 2015 JDR 2035 (ECG), para 49.

The shareholders' agreement which entitles VC to appoint two of SC's seven directors is very common in practice and is a valid agreement under French company law.

However, under French company law, it is not possible to issue a promissory note (*billet à ordre*) convertible into shares/stocks. The reason is that only securities (*valeurs mobilières*), such as bonds (*obligations*), can be converted into shares and promissory notes are not securities. This rule applies to an SA, an SAS and an SARL. If the loan was not convertible into shares in the case of an SA, the board of directors would have had the capacity to approve it. In such a case, the approval of the loan would be a related party transaction because the loan is concluded with a shareholder who owns more than 10 per cent of the shares and two directors of SC have a 'direct interest' in the transaction since they represent VC.[67] Since the two directors voted, the transaction would be voidable if it had detrimental consequences for SC. Therefore, in this hypothetical the two directors would have been precluded from voting and the transaction would have been voidable if it had detrimental consequences for SC. However, this does not seem to be the case here. In addition, the shareholders can ratify a resolution which was not properly approved by the board of directors, with a special vote being taken after a report of the statutory auditors has been drawn up.[68]

In the case of an SAS, it is not compulsory to have a board of directors. Therefore, there is no scope for *ex ante* authorisation – but only *ex post* approval – by the shareholders in the case of a transaction with a shareholder who owns more than 10 per cent of the shares.[69] The loan would have been signed by the President of the SAS. The same rule applies for an SARL, except that the loan would have been signed by the manager (*gérant*) and that a loan with a single shareholder would also be covered.[70] The articles of association could provide for a board of directors, and an *ex ante* authorisation, in the case of both the SAS and the SARL.[71] However, the French Cour de cassation has held that a violation of a provision of the articles of association, which would be the case here because VC's nominee directors approved the transaction, cannot result in the nullification or invalidation of the decision taken.[72] Therefore, minority shareholders can only sue for damages in respect of such a breach.

If we assume that convertible bonds would have been issued instead of a promissory note, the solution would have been different. Convertible bonds can only be issued by a decision of the shareholders in an extraordinary general meeting.[73] First, in the case of an SA, there must be a decision of the board of directors. The power to decide upon an increase in share capital or an issuance of convertible bonds can be delegated to the board of directors. However, in the case of SC, the share increase is

---

[67] Commercial Code, Art L 225-38.

[68] Commercial Code, Art L 225-42 al 3. Cass com (Cour de cassation, Commercial Chambre), 18 October 1994, Bull Civ IV, n° 304.

[69] Commercial Code, Art L 227-10.

[70] Commercial Code, Art L 223-19.

[71] In the case of an SARL, each member of the 'board' of managers is entitled to bind the company. The 'board' of an SARL is not a collective organ.

[72] Cass Civ 3e (Cour de cassation, Third Civil Chamber), 19 July 2000, n° 98-17.258, *RJDA* 12/00, n° 1122; *Bull Joly* 2001 70, with a note by L Grosclaude; *Dr sociétés* 2000, comm n° 170, with a note by Th Bonneau; Cass Com (Cour de cassation, Commercial Chamber), 14 June 2005, n° 02-18.864, *RJDA* 10/05, n° 1123; *Bull Joly* 2005 1412, with a note by P Le Cannu; D 2005 AJ 1777.

[73] Commercial Code, Art L 228-92.

allocated to one person only, which is VC. In the case of a share increase allocated to one person only (*augmentation de capital à personne dénommée*), the shareholders in extraordinary general meeting cannot delegate the power to decide a share increase to the board of directors.[74] The solution is the same in the case of convertible bonds since the Commercial Code provides that the general rules for an increase in share capital apply by reference.[75]

This decision of the board of directors to put the issue of convertible bonds to a vote of the shareholders' meeting would not be treated as a related party transaction because it is subject to a decision of the shareholders' meeting. Therefore, the only issue is whether VC can vote at the extraordinary shareholders' meeting which will decide on the share issuance. In such a case, Article L 225-138 of the Commercial Code directs that the parties who are the beneficiaries of the decision cannot take part in the vote. If the beneficiaries took part in the vote, the decision to issue the bonds would be void.[76] A minority shareholder such as Founder would have the capacity to seek the nullification of the issuance of the convertible bonds in court.[77]

The same prohibition on taking part in the vote would also apply if SC had been an SAS.[78] Meanwhile, despite the lack of explicit provisions, on the satisfaction of certain conditions, an SARL can also issue convertible bonds.[79] In such a case, although there are no provisions or case law on the issue, the regime which regulates capital increases in respect of an SARL should apply. No provision explicitly bars VC from voting, and therefore, the issuance could not be avoided or nullified on this ground.

In general, under French company law, unless a legal provision prevents a shareholder or a director from voting, he or she is entitled to vote. In the absence of a legal provision, the French courts will refuse to invalidate the exercise of a shareholder's voting rights on the basis of a conflict of interest. This applies irrespective of whether the company is an SA, an SAS or an SARL. A recent case provides an illustration of the reluctance of the French courts to deprive a shareholder of his or her voting rights, except where there is a legal provision to the contrary.[80] Here, a minority shareholder claimed that the majority shareholder should have been deprived of the right to vote on a decision to convert all of the founder's shares (*parts de fondateurs*) into ordinary shares, which diluted his shareholding. The majority shareholder was the main holder of the founder's shares and stood to benefit from an overvaluation of the founder's shares. This case concerned the shareholders' meeting, but also can be applied to votes at the level of the board of directors. Therefore, the outcome is heavily dependent on whether a transaction can be treated as a related party transaction where the director has a direct or indirect (subject to judicial interpretation) interest. If this is not the case, and there is no specific prohibition in the Commercial Code, the courts refuse to disregard the voting rights of a shareholder or a director.

---

[74] Commercial Code, Art L 225-138.
[75] Commercial Code, Art L 228-92.
[76] Commercial Code, Art L 225-149-3 al 3.
[77] Commercial Code, Art L 235-1.
[78] Commercial Code, Art L 227-1.
[79] *Mémento Francis Lefebvre Sociétés commerciales*, 2012, n° 73140.
[80] Cass Com (Cour de cassation, Commercial Chamber), 19 September 2006, *Revue des sociétés*, 2007, 540 with a note by D Schmidt.

Under French company law, VC is free to appoint any director. There is no duty that he chooses the most qualified directors. The only issue VC could face would be if the directors were unqualified. However, he would most probably not face any liability for choosing directors who are not qualified enough for the job. There are no requirements for directors to be especially qualified in non-listed companies. The directors must act in the best interests of the company and not in the best interests of the shareholder who appointed them. However, in practice, directors do represent special interests who appointed them. As long as their decision can also be considered to be in the best interests of the company, they are not subject to a breach of the duty of care.

The directors appointed by VC follow his instructions to the greatest extent possible. Under French law, directors cannot be subject to binding instructions of shareholders or some shareholders. Such instructions could turn VC into a shadow director (*administrateur de fait*) making him liable for any breach of duty of care. However, the threshold applied by courts to consider that a shareholder is a shadow director is very high. This would not be the case simply because VC provides instructions to two directors to protect his interests.

E. Germany[81]

Directors are usually appointed by the shareholders' general meeting (GmbHG, § 46(5)). It is also possible for the articles of association to provide that a shareholder has the right to appoint a certain number of directors (*Entsenderecht*).[82] Moreover, as in the hypothetical case under consideration, a shareholders' agreement can oblige shareholders to vote in a particular way (*Stimmbindungsvertrag*),[83] for example, by approving candidates proposed by another shareholder or other shareholders.

In the hypothetical case VC's nominee directors faced a conflict of interest because they took a decision on the loan transaction with VC in their capacity as board members of SC. German law solves such a problem by a general provision of the German Civil Code on 'contracting with oneself'. It states that 'an agent may not, unless otherwise permitted, enter into a legal transaction in the name of the principal with himself in his own name or as an agent of a third party, unless the legal transaction consists solely in the performance of an obligation' (BGB, § 181).[84] Thus, the votes of the two nominee directors are invalid and it was for the remaining disinterested directors to take the decision on the loan transaction.[85] However, they also approved it. Thus, § 181 of the BGB does not make the transaction itself invalid.

---

[81] Abbreviated statutes: AktG = Law on Public Companies; BGB = Civil Code; GmbHG = Law on Private Limited Companies.

[82] U Noack and W Zöllner in *Baumbach & Hueck's GmbHG* (21st edn, Munich, Beck, 2017) § 35, para 7.

[83] BGH (German Federal Supreme Court), BGHZ 48, 163; W Zöllner in *Baumbach & Hueck's GmbHG* (21st edn, Munich, Beck, 2017) § 47, para 113.

[84] For an English translation of the German Civil Code, see www.gesetze-im-internet.de/englisch_bgb/index.html.

[85] BGH (German Federal Supreme Court), BB 1994, 165; Noack and Zöllner in *Baumbach & Hueck's GmbHG* (n 82) § 35, para 131.

Directors are also obliged to comply with general fiduciary duties.[86] In particular, in Germany there is also a duty of loyalty. Thus, directors must act in the interests of the company and not solely in their own private interest.[87] In the present case, the two interested votes are already invalid owing to § 181 of the BGB. Thus, as in the US, the courts would presumably examine whether the other directors were 'beholden' to the two nominee directors.

With respect to a possible breach of duty in not having selected the most qualified nominee directors, the German literature mainly discusses the corresponding problem of the appointment of a nominee supervisory board director of a public company. Here it is suggested that, while in principle the nominating shareholder is free to select any nominee director, the shareholder is also under the obligation to consider the interests of the company.[88] Thus, here we have the situation that a shareholder does not only have a right vis-a-vis the company but faces a corresponding duty. In particular, it is said that the shareholder should not choose a director who is evidently unsuitable.[89] Nominee directors also have to preserve the interests of the company and must not be bound to act upon instructions of the shareholder.[90] Thus, applying these principles to the current scenario, it is likely that VC committed such a breach in failing to consider the interests of the company (SC).

Finally, it needs to be noted that, until recently, it used to be impossible for German private companies (GmbHs) to issue a promissory note convertible into common stock.[91] This kind of convertible security (in Germany called *Wandelschuldverschreibung*) is explicitly allowed under the law of public companies (AktG, § 221).[92] For private companies the 'MoMiG reform'[93] inserted the provision that the articles of association can authorise the managers to increase capital within at most 5 years (§ 55a GmbH). Some authors therefore suggest that it is now also feasible for private companies to issue a *Wandelschuldverschreibung* though the precise design is still a matter of debate.[94]

F. Italy[95]

As a general rule, the directors of an Italian Srl are appointed by the shareholders (Article 2479, paragraph 2, no 2 of the CC). However, according to Article 2468,

---

[86] See ch 2 at II C, above.

[87] Noack and Zöllner (n 82) § 35, para 39.

[88] M Habersack in *Münchener Kommentar zum Aktiengesetz* (4th edn, Munich, Beck 2014) § 101 para 45.

[89] Ibid, § 101 para 45.

[90] Ibid, § 101 para 51.

[91] See J Mandl, 'Die Wandelschuldverschreibung bei der GmbH' (2006) *Neue Zeitschrift für Gesellschaftsrecht* 778.

[92] However, other shareholders (such as Founder) would have a pre-emptive right to buy these convertible instruments (AktG, § 221(4)).

[93] See ch 2 at II C, above.

[94] See, eg, H Wicke, *GmbHG* (3rd edn, Munich, Beck 2016) § 55 para 2; K Helmreich, 'Wandelschuldverschreibungen bei der GmbH als Brücke bei Bewertungsdifferenzen im Rahmen von M&ATransaktionen' (2011) *Gesellschafts- und Wirtschaftsrecht* 561.

[95] Abbreviations: CC = Italian Civil Code (codice civile); Spa = public company (*Società per azioni*); Srl = private limited company (*Società a responsabilità limitata*).

paragraph 3 of the CC, the articles of association may grant 'the shareholders, individual special rights regarding the administration of the company or the distribution of its profits'. It is usual for one of these individual special rights to be the right to appoint one or more directors.[96] In addition, shareholders may also conclude shareholders' agreements which include special rights for the appointment of the directors. These agreements, however, have no legal effect as against the company.

In order to put the instant case properly within its context, it is also important to highlight that an Srl is not allowed to issue promissory notes convertible into shares under Italian company law. Securities of this type, however, may be issued by an Spa where, as a default rule, the general meeting of the shareholders rather than the board of directors will take any decision on this matter.

Starting with the question of whether VC breached any duties towards SC in not selecting the most qualified nominee directors, it should be said that, traditionally, fiduciary duties are not imposed on shareholders, who, with regard to the appointment of directors, are allowed to appoint the persons who, in their perspective, are more suitable to become directors.

With regards to the decisions and actions taken by the board, an examination of the provisions of Italian law which regulate the conduct of the directors of an Srl reveals that the problem presented in the case would be addressed by Article 2475-*ter* of the CC. According to the second paragraph of this provision, 'a decision taken by the board of directors with the decisive vote of a director in a conflict-of-interest situation with the company can be challenged within ninety days by the other directors, if it causes economic damage to the company'. In addition, it is provided that 'any rights acquired by a third party in good faith on the basis of any action performed in pursuance of the [invalid] decision, shall not be prejudiced'.[97] On the other hand, the first paragraph of this provision states that

> any contract which is entered into by the directors on behalf of the company (having the legal representation of the company) in a conflict of interest situation with a third party or on its behalf, is voidable at the company's request, if the conflict was known or ought to have been known by the third party'[98]

In brief, examining only the issue of breach of the fiduciary duties, the VC nominees can be treated as interested directors. Thus, it would be necessary to investigate whether their votes were decisive in the board resolution that approved the loan. In addition, Article 2475-*ter*, paragraph 1 of the CC may also play a role if the individual director who executed the loan on behalf of the company is in a conflict-of-interest situation.[99]

These conclusions, however, are highly speculative since an Srl is not allowed to issue promissory notes convertible into shares and, in the case of an Spa, these

[96] M Cavanna, 'Partecipazione e "diritti particolari" dei soci' in M Sarale (ed), *Le nuove s.r.l.* (Bologna, Zanichelli, 2008) 101 ff, 117 ff.
[97] Author's annotations are shown in square brackets.
[98] On the conflict of interest of directors in the case of an Srl generally, see M Ventoruzzo, 'Commento *sub* art. 2475-*ter*' in P Marchetti, LA Bianchi, F Ghezzi and M Notari (eds), *Commentario alla Riforma delle società. Società a responsabilità limitata* (Milan, Giuffrè-Egea, 2008) 599 ff.
[99] Ibid, 606 ff and 656 ff.

securities are generally issued upon a resolution of the general meeting. Therefore, it is unlikely that the board of directors of an Srl would ever find itself in a situation similar to that indicated in the hypothetical case.

G. Spain

In Spain, the appointment of the directors of the *Sociedad de Responsabilidad Limitada* (SL) falls within the competence of the shareholders' general meeting (Ley de Sociedades de Capital (LSC) – Corporate Enterprises Act, Article 160(b)).[100] Moreover, this competence is exclusive, meaning that only the general meeting can appoint them (LSC, Article 214.1). An exception to this rule applies when the company is created, and the initial directors are thus nominated by the founding members (LSC, Article 22.1(e)) and not by the general meeting.[101] A shareholders' agreement – which is possible according to the principle of freedom of contract enshrined in Article 1255 of the Código Civil (CC) – Civil Code[102] – could establish that SC's shareholders who are part of such agreement should vote in a particular way.[103] However, it is worth noting that shareholders' agreements do not have any legal effect vis-a-vis the company (LSC, Article 29).[104]

Turning to the loan transaction approved by the board of SC, where VC's nominee directors – who were nominated by VC and are shareholders, directors and officers of the latter – are in a position of a conflict of interest, this could be dealt with on the basis of the prohibitions set out in the CC in relation to self-contracting. Article 1459.2 of the CC provides that where an agent is entrusted with the management of goods on another person's behalf, he or she cannot acquire them. This general provision could be applied by analogy to situations of conflict of interest between directors and their company.[105]

Self-dealing by directors may also constitute a breach of the duty of loyalty which is found in general company law (LSC, Article 227). According to the duty of loyalty, directors must exercise their functions as loyal representatives, in good faith, and in the best interests of the company (LSC, Article 227.1). This duty imposes on directors an obligation to subordinate their own interests to the interests of the company in those cases in which there is a conflict of interest.[106] In addition, Spanish company law

---

[100] Real Decreto Legislativo 1/2010, de 2 de julio, por el que se aprueba el texto refundido de la Ley de Sociedades de Capital (LSC).

[101] See JL Iglesias Prada and J García de Enterría, 'La Fundación de las Sociedades de Capital' in A Menéndez and Á Rojo (eds) *Lecciones de Derecho Mercantil*, vol II (12th edn, Cizur Menor (Navarra), Civitas-Thomson Reuters, 2014) 437.

[102] Real Decreto de 24 de julio de 1889 por el que se publica el Código Civil.

[103] See A Vaquerizo, 'Artículo 29. Pactos reservados' in Á Rojo and E Beltrán (eds), *Comentario de la Ley de Sociedades de Capital* (Cizur Menor (Navarra), Civitas-Thomson Reuters, 2011) 399–400.

[104] This is a consequence of the general principle of relativity of contract (CC, Art 1257.1). See Vaquerizo, 'Artículo 29. Pactos reservados' (n 103) 400–03.

[105] See V Ribas Ferrer, *El deber de lealtad del administrador de sociedades* (Madrid, La Ley, 2010) 700.

[106] Excluding those cases where the company, after disclosure of the conflict by the concerned director, authorises the director's conduct. See V Ribas Ferrer, 'Artículo 226. Deber de lealtad' in Á Rojo and E Beltrán (eds), *Comentario de la Ley de Sociedades de Capital* (Cizur Menor (Navarra), Civitas-Thomson Reuters, 2011) 1620. See, also, Art 230.2 of the LSC.

imposes a duty on directors to avoid conflicts of interest, for example, by abstaining from transacting with the company (LSC, Article 229.1(a)). Moreover, directors who find themselves in a direct or indirect conflict situation must not participate in deliberations about and/or cast votes on matters to which the conflict of interest relates (LSC, Article 228(c)). The duties of directors in conflict-of-interest scenarios also apply whenever such conflicts affect persons that are related[107] to the directors concerned (LSC, Articles 228(c) and 229.2) – as is the case of VC. In the instant case, despite the fact that VC's nominee directors were clearly in a conflict situation, they did not refrain from participating in the decision regarding the loan by VC. Therefore, one can assume that they breached the duties which they owed towards SC. The law provides that any votes cast by a director in a conflict-of-interest situation are invalid (CC, Article 6.3).[108] The validity of the decision regarding the loan agreement would very much depend on whether the two votes cast by VC's nominee directors were necessary to reach the majority required to adopt it or not; in this regard, if their votes were determinative, then the decision would be void since it would have been adopted without complying with the requirements for a majority vote and hence it would be in breach of company law.[109] The participation of VC's nominee directors in the vote on the loan transaction could also affect the validity of the decision regarding the loan agreement on the basis that it damaged the company's interests for the benefit of one of its shareholders[110] – in the instant case, VC (LSC, Articles 204.1 and 251.2).

Shareholders with at least 1 per cent of the issued share capital of the company have the right to challenge decisions of the board of directors which are against the law, the by-laws of the company, the regulations of the general meeting of the company, the regulations of the board of directors of the company, or which damage the interests of the company to the benefit of one or more shareholders or a third party (LSC, Articles 204.1 and 251.1–2). As such, Founder would be entitled to challenge the decision regarding the loan agreement to the extent that he owns more than the minimum share capital required to initiate legal proceedings – and, also, because such decision is challengeable. According to Spanish company law, the deadline to initiate the proceedings is within 30 days after the shareholders who wish to challenge the decision knew about the latter, with an additional overall time limit of one year after the decision was adopted by the board of directors (LSC, Article 251.1). In the instant case it is unclear when Founder first found about the decision on the loan transaction and, hence, whether the time constraints are such that he would be entitled to challenge it.

---

[107] The concept of 'persons related to the directors' of the LSC (LSC, Art 231) includes companies that are able to appoint and/or remove, or that have actually designated, a majority of the directors of another company (LSC, Art 231.1(d); and Código de Comercio – Code of Commerce, Art 42.1(d)). This is not the case of VC, which only had 20% of the share capital of SC and nominated 2 out of 7 directors of the latter. However, some commentators propose a more flexible interpretation of the concept of 'persons related to the directors' of Art 231 of the LSC which would also embrace the persons that appoint nominee directors – in this respect see the SJM (Sentencia del Juzgado de lo Mercantil) No 3 de Madrid of 30 October 2013.

[108] See Ribas Ferrer, *El deber de lealtad del administrador de sociedades* (n 105) 642.

[109] Ibid, 644–45.

[110] See JR Salelles, 'Artículo 251. Impugnación de acuerdos del consejo de administración' in Á Rojo and E Beltrán (eds), *Comentario de la Ley de Sociedades de Capital* (Cizur Menor (Navarra), Civitas-Thomson Reuters, 2011) 1814.

As regards the loan agreement itself, Founder may challenge its validity on the grounds that it does not comply with the consent requirements of Article 1261 of the CC. Founder could also argue that the directors entered into the loan agreement in breach of their duties of loyalty, and challenge its validity on this basis (LSC, Article 232).

Whereas Spanish legal scholarship generally recognises the existence of a duty of loyalty of shareholders towards the company,[111] the nomination of directors who were less experienced than those originally intended for the position, does not *per se* constitute a breach of the duties of VC towards SC. Spanish company law acknowledges the fact that shareholders may be in a position of conflict of interest when they cast votes regarding the appointment of directors, but it does not prohibit them from doing so (LSC, Article 190.3).

Finally, it should be noted that SLs are not allowed to issue convertible promissory notes under Spanish company law (LSC, Article 401.2), although public companies (SAs) are entitled to do so (LSC, Articles 401.1 and 414).

H. The Netherlands[112]

Under Dutch law directors are generally appointed by the general meeting of shareholders.[113] The articles of association can, however, provide that the directors are appointed by a meeting of the holders of certain types of shares. This can even be a meeting of holders of shares without voting rights in the case of a private limited liability company. Every holder of shares with voting rights should, however, be able to participate in the election of at least one director.[114] The articles of association can furthermore provide that the general meeting has to appoint the directors on the basis of a binding list of nominees. However, the general meeting can always disregard the list of nominees provided this is decided with a two-thirds majority.[115]

The hypothetical case mentions a shareholder agreement to vote in a certain way. Shareholder agreements are possible under Dutch law. Nevertheless, despite the shareholder agreement, the shareholder can still vote differently from this agreement. A deviation from the agreement can, however, lead to a breach of the shareholder agreement.[116] It is accepted in the literature that a shareholder agreement requiring

---

[111] For a review of literature on this issue, see M Sáez Lacave, 'Reconsiderando los deberes de lealtad de los socios: el caso particular de los socios de control de las sociedades cotizadas' (2016) 1 *InDret* 10, 10–13.

[112] Abbreviations: DCC=Dutch Civil Code; HR = Hoge Raad = Dutch Supreme Court; OK = Ondernemingskamer = Enterprise Chamber; Rb = rechtbank = District Court. An unofficial translation of Dutch company law as incorporated in bk 2 of the Dutch Civil Code can be found on www.dutchcivillaw.com/civilcodebook022.htm.

[113] DCC, Art 2:132/2:242. This is not the case in large companies, so-called *structuurvennootschappen*. These are, however, left outside the scope of this answer to the hypothetical case under consideration.

[114] DCC, Art 2:242-1.

[115] DCC, Art 2:243-1 and 2.

[116] G van Solinge and MP Nieuwe Weme, *Mr. C. Assers Handleiding tot de beoefening van het Nederlands Burgerlijk Recht. 2. Vertegenwoordiging en rechtspersoon. Deel II. De rechtspersoon* (Deventer, Kluwer, 2009) nr 387; PJ Dortmond, *Mr E.J.J. van der Heijden Mr W.C.L van der Grinten Handboek voor de naamloze en de besloten vennootschap* (Deventer, WEJ Tjeenk Willink, 2013) nr 217.1.

shareholders to vote in such a way that they each have a representative on the board is valid.[117] The shareholder agreement should, however, not frustrate mandatory legal provisions or provisions of the articles of association.[118]

The hypothetical case seems to refer to a conflict of interest on the part of VC's nominee directors in signing the loan agreement. Conflicts of interests in private limited liability companies are regulated by Article 239-6 of Book 2 of the DCC. This section prescribes that directors with a conflict of interest should not take part in the discussion and decision-making. If this means that no board resolution can be taken, the decision-making power will be shifted to the supervisory board. In the absence of a supervisory board, the decision can be taken by the general meeting unless the articles of association provide otherwise. The question is, however, whether the situation in the hypothetical case would qualify as a conflict-of-interest situation under Dutch law. There is not enough information available in order to determine whether the nominee directors actually have a direct or indirect 'personal' interest that is in conflict with the interest of the company. Having a direct or indirect personal conflict of interest is required to trigger the aforementioned conflict-of-interest rule.[119] Under Dutch law a potential conflict of interest is in itself not enough, as there have to be actual circumstances that can affect the way the involved members of the board are influenced in their behaviour, as a result of which they would not be able to act objectively and with integrity.[120] The mere fact that the director acts in various capacities is not sufficient for a conflict-of-interest situation to arise.[121] Even if we assume that the nominee directors would have a conflict of interest, this would in principle not affect the validity of the transaction.[122] It can, however, lead to the annulment of the board decision[123] as well as to the liability of the director towards the company on the basis of Article 2:9 DCC if the director participated in the decision-making without disclosing his or her conflict of interest.[124]

Nominee directors are, just as every other director in the company, under the duty to act in the best interests of the company and the enterprise connected with it.[125] What constitutes this best interest depends on the circumstances of the case. It has, however, been established in case law that within private limited liability companies this corporate interest cannot necessarily be equated to the interests of the shareholders.[126] If the company carries on an enterprise, the interests of the company will generally concern the promotion of the lasting success of that enterprise. The Dutch Supreme Court has established in the Cancun case concerning a joint venture that the collaboration of nominee directors in a dilution of the stake of one of the shareholders by

---

[117] Dortmond, *Mr E.J.J. van der Heijden Mr W.C.L van der Grinten Handboek voor de naamloze en de besloten vennootschap* (n 116) nr 217.1.

[118] Ibid, 217.1.

[119] Ibid, 233.1.

[120] HR 29 June 2007, *NJ* 2007, 420.

[121] Dortmond (n 116) nr 233.1.

[122] Ibid, nr 233.1.

[123] Such a decision can be avoided under DCC, Art 2:15-1 sub a. Ibid, nr 233.1.

[124] See Dortmond (n 116) nr 233.1.

[125] DCC, Art 2:239-5.

[126] Hof Amsterdam (OK), 12 October 2016, *RO* 2017/3 (*Highfields Capital/Delta Lloyd*).

the other shareholder can constitute mismanagement (*wanbeleid*) in an inquiry proce- dure. In the Cancun case there was, in short, a shareholder agreement on the basis of which shareholders had agreed to collaborate in the joint venture on the basis of equality. The shareholding of one of the shareholders was eventually diluted due to various share transactions. The Supreme Court (Hoge Raad) ruled that this dilution constituted mismanagement (*wanbeleid*) of the company. The Court emphasised that nominee directors also have to serve the interests of the company. What constitutes this interest depends on the circumstances of the case. As mentioned above, if the company carries on an enterprise, the interests of the company will generally be served by promoting the lasting success of that enterprise. The Court furthermore ruled that in a joint venture the corporate interest is also determined by the type and content of the agreed collaboration between shareholders which can entail that the interests of the company are served by providing for a balanced and stable relationship between the shareholders.[127]

It follows that in the hypothetical case under consideration it is unclear whether under Dutch law this would lead to a conflict-of-interest situation. Even if it could be established that the VC nominee directors had a conflict of interest, this would still not affect the validity of the transaction. The directors may, however, be in breach of their duty to serve the best interests of the company and the enterprise connected with it as this interest may be served by a good relationship between the shareholders and the avoidance of the dilution. There is therefore a risk that the dilution of the Founder's stake could lead to mismanagement (*wanbeleid*) on the part of the directors. There is also a possibility that it would lead to the liability of directors towards the company. However, all of this would depend, among other matters, on what the shareholders have agreed regarding their cooperation. The hypothetical case does not concern a joint venture and it is therefore uncertain whether or not the aforementioned case law would be directly applicable to the case under consideration.

With regard to the question whether there is a breach of duty because the share- holders have not selected the most qualified nominee directors, it should be mentioned that, in general, shareholders are allowed to serve their own interests and vote in a way that serves best their own interests.[128] Nevertheless, shareholders will always have to take into account the standards of reasonableness and fairness towards the company and their fellow shareholders.[129] This can mean that under specific circum- stances shareholders might be in breach of this duty. However, it is unclear whether this would be the case here. It could perhaps be argued that the shareholder has acted against what might be expected to be standards of reasonableness and fairness when it knowingly appoints directors that are unsuitable for the job. It has been suggested

---

[127] HR 4 April 2014, *NJ* 2014/286, with a note by Van Schilfgaarde.

[128] HR 30 June 1944, *NJ* 1944/465 (*Wennex*); HR 13 November 1959, *NJ* 1960/472 (*Distileerderij Melchers*) and HR 19 February 1960, *NJ* 1960/473 (*Aurora*). See in this respect Dortmond (n 116) nr 172.4; BF Assink and WJ Slagter, *Compendium Ondernemingsrecht, Deel 1* (Deventer, Kluwer, 2013) § 46; MJ Kroeze, *Mr. C. Assers Handleiding tot de beoefening van het Nederlands Burgerlijk Recht. 2. Rechtspersonenrecht. Deel I*. De rechtspersoon* (Deventer, Kluwer 2015) nr 228; JW Winter and JB Wezeman, *Mr P van Schilfgaarde Van de BV en de NV* (Deventer, Kluwer, 2013) nr 67.2.

[129] DCC, Art 2:8.

in the literature that a shareholder agreement to appoint a manifestly incompetent candidate as a director, would be invalid because it would go against reasonableness and fairness.[130]

Dutch private limited liability companies are, in principle, allowed to issue a promissory note convertible into stock. However, the board has to consider the interests of the company which can also mean that it has to take into account the importance of a good relationship among its shareholders which can include, depending on the circumstances, preventing a dilution of shareholder positions as described above. Generally, shareholders have to decide on the issuance of new shares. However, this power can be delegated to the board.[131]

I. Finland

i. Introduction

The shareholders' general meeting appoints the board of directors unless the articles of association stipulate that the supervisory board has the power to appoint the board of directors. A minority of the directors may be appointed in accordance with some other procedure set out in the articles of association.[132] A shareholders' agreement, which obliges the parties to it to vote or act in a prescribed way is valid between the contracting parties. It is common in Finland for directors to hold multiple directorships.

ii. Conflicts of Interest

By the virtue of chapter 6, section 4 of the Companies Act 2006 (CA), a director has a conflict of interest in respect of contracts entered into (i) between the director and the company ('self-contracting; contracting with oneself') and (ii) between the company and a third party, where the director will receive a significant benefit therefrom and that benefit may be contrary to the interests of the company (ie disqualification). A disqualified director may not take part in the decision making of the matter in question.[133]

Pursuant to the CA and the legal literature, it is unlikely that nominee directors would be held to be disqualified based on (i), unless VC were wholly owned by the nominee directors, since the nominee directors themselves are not the direct counterparties to the loan transaction. However, the nominee directors, being shareholders, directors and officers of VC, could be held disqualified under (ii) should they receive a significant benefit from the transaction. In addition, the duty of care and loyalty requires directors to act unconstrained by undue influences in the decision-making

---

[130] van Solinge and Nieuwe Weme, *Mr. C. Assers Handleiding tot de beoefening van het Nederlands Burgerlijk Recht. 2. Vertegenwoordiging en rechtspersoon. Deel II. De rechtspersoon* (n 116) nr 386.

[131] DCC, Art 2:206.

[132] Limited Liability Companies Act (CA, 624/2006), c 6, s 9.

[133] J Mähönen and S Villa, *Osakeyhtiö III – Corporate Governance* (Helsinki, Talentum, 2012) 242–47.

process. Acting as the director of both counterparties of a transaction may create an assumption that the director in question is not unconstrained by undue influences to participate in the consideration of the transaction in question although he or she would not be strictly disqualified from participating pursuant to the CA.[134]

Should the nominee directors be considered disqualified based on (i) or (ii) above, the decision of the board of SC would be invalid. However, there are no explicit provisions in the CA governing how board decisions may be invalidated and the consequences for such breaches are yet to be clarified by case law. Shareholders are not generally entitled to argue that decisions of the board are invalid. However, based on the legal literature a shareholder may be able to argue that the decision is invalid in relation to the said shareholder, where the rights of the said shareholder are directly affected by the decision. Therefore, Founder could, at least in theory, be able to take action on the grounds that the board's decision was invalid due to the existence of a conflict of interest. Founder would also be entitled to sue the two nominee directors for losses Founder might have sustained as a result of their violation of the provisions of the CA.[135]

Under Finnish law, the loan transaction would also be evaluated in light of the fiduciary duties and the principle of equal treatment.[136] A loan transaction that benefits the company as a whole (SC and its shareholder collective) is not contrary to the principle of equal treatment even if the loan conditions might result in a weakened position of another shareholder (Founder). The principal criterion applicable is that VC should not receive any undue benefit at the Founder's expense. In the present case, the board of SC has considered various financing options. The outcome of the assessment as to whether the loan transaction confers an undue benefit in favour of VC is dependent on whether this option is in the best interests of SC. If the loan transaction is in the best interests of SC, the decision would be valid. The case scenario does not reveal any grounds for concluding that the directors would have breached their fiduciary duties. The loan transaction would thus be valid.

Contrary to the directors' duties, the prevailing opinion in the legal literature is that the shareholders have a right to be selfish and they may promote their own self-interest. Thus, the shareholders do not have a specific duty to promote the benefit of the other shareholders.[137] In general, a shareholder is free to select any nominee director to the company. However, the nominee directors are obliged to preserve the interests of the company and must not be bound to act upon the instructions of the shareholder.[138] Despite the right to follow their own interests, the shareholders may not breach or contribute to a breach of the CA. A shareholder may be held liable for damages for the loss that a shareholder, by contributing to a violation of the CA, has deliberately or negligently caused to the company, another shareholder or a third party.[139] According to the legal literature and preparatory works of the CA, shareholder liability for

---

[134] M Airaksinen, P Pulkkinen and V Rasinaho, *Osakeyhtiölaki I* (Helsinki, Talentum, 2010) 435–36 and Mähönen and Villa, *Osakeyhtiö III – Corporate Governance* (n 133) 244.

[135] Explanatory notes of the CA, Hallituksen esitys 109/2005, 81; Mähönen and Villa (n 133) 307; c 22, s 1(2).

[136] Mähönen and Villa (n 133) 244–45.

[137] Ibid, 466.

[138] Ibid, 466–67.

[139] CA, c 22, s 2.

damages may arise, for example, when a shareholder persuades the directors to breach the CA.[140] More detailed information is needed to assess the shareholder's liability in the matter at hand. However, in this case it is likely that appointment of the nominee directors did not conflict with the CA.

iii. Status of Convertible Promissory Notes

Option rights and other special rights, which entitle the holder to receive shares, such as convertible promissory notes, can be issued only if there is a pressing financial reason for the company to do so.[141] The decision is taken by the shareholders' general meeting (or by the board if so authorised by the shareholders' general meeting in terms of CA, chapter 10, section 2). The decision must be supported by at least two-thirds of the votes cast by the shareholders represented at such meeting.

J. Poland

The hypothetical case will be solved in the light of provisions of the Commercial Companies Code (CCC) relating to public companies. It should be stressed that terms such as 'privately held corporation' or 'closely held corporation' are not defined in Polish law. Both public companies (*Spółka akcyjna*) and limited liability companies (*Spółka z ograniczoną odpowiedzialnością*) can be created as 'private', but only a public company can go public. A public company is a company in which at least one share is dematerialised within the meaning of the Act on trading in financial instruments. There are many structural differences between the Polish public company and limited liability company, but of significance in the given scenario is that in accordance with Article 174, section 6 of the CCC, neither bearer documents, nor registered documents, nor documents to order may be issued in respect of rights to shares or rights to the profits of the limited liability company – whereas a public company may issue documents for registered or bearer shares. This means that a shareholder's rights to receive shares in the limited liability company may not be embodied in paper. Equity rights can be transferred only on the general principles of civil law, not as securities.[142] At the request of shareholders, the management board may issue a certificate confirming the status and number of shares of a shareholder in the limited liability company. However, the certificate cannot be regarded as a security (equity paper).[143] The above reflects one of

---

[140] Explanatory notes of the CA, Hallituksen esitys 109/2005, 196; Mähönen and Villa (n 133) 466–67.

[141] CA, c 10, s 1.

[142] See M Rodzynkiewicz, *Kodeks spółek handlowych. Komentarz* (Warsaw, LexisNexis, 2009) 293 note 9. However, there is one exception to this rule of thumb. In accordance with Art 19, s 1 of the Act on Bonds, a limited liability company may issue participation bonds, granting rights to profits of the company.

[143] See Rodzynkiewicz, *Kodeks spółek handlowych. Komentarz* (n 142) 293 note 9; W Pyzioł in W Popiołek, W Pyzioł, J Frąckowiak, A Witosz and A Kidyba (eds), *Kodeks spółek handlowych. Komentarz* (Warsaw, LexisNexis, 2008) notes 8–9 to Art 174, §6 of the Commercial Companies Code; T Siemiątkowski and R Potrzeszcz in R Potrzeszcz, T Siemiątkowski, JP Naworski and K Strzelczyk (eds), *Komentarz do kodeksu spółek handlowych, t. II* (Warsaw, LexisNexis, 2011) note 10 to Art 174, § 6 of the Commercial Companies Code; A Kidyba, *Kodeks spółek handlowych. Komentarz, t. I* (Krakow, Kantor Wydawniczy Zakamycze, 2005) 757–58.

the most important differences between a Polish limited liability company and public company.[144] In the context of the given scenario, this means that a 'promissory note that was convertible into common shares of SC' could not be issued by a limited liability company since the convertible promissory note would entail conferring rights to shares. However, such an instrument might be issued by a public company. Moreover, the above conclusion is supported by the current wording of Article 20 of the Act on Bonds and the principle of *numerus clausus* of securities. In accordance with Article 20 of the Act on Bonds, convertible bonds may only be issued by a public company, provided that such a possibility is stipulated in the articles of association (*statut*). Article 448, sections 1–4 of the Polish Civil Code imposes additional conditions by stipulating that the persons to whom the right to take up shares has been granted must exercise that right on the terms laid out in a resolution of the shareholders' meeting, ie convertible bond holders in the given scenario. In addition, the *numerus clausus* of securities is a reference to the idea that it is only the legislature that is entitled to link the execution and disposal of a right with the possession of a document incorporating the right. Some commentators object that it is not directly stipulated that securities can only be issued on the basis of existing laws and in the manner indicated therein.[145] However, in accordance with the orthodox view, the *numerus clausus* principle applies to the present case since securities are not merely contractual obligations but are also pieces of property with effect *erga omnes*.[146]

Turning away from the issue of the validity of the convertible promissory note, the answers to this case would be the same in both the cases of the limited liability company and the public company. Thus, the following discussion will cover both the law of the limited liability and the public company. Under Polish law, a conflict-of-interest situation arises when a person's private interests interferes in any way with the interests of the company. A conflict situation can occur when an officer or director enters into a transaction or has an interest that may make it difficult to perform his or her obligations objectively and effectively. Conflicts of interest may also arise when an officer or director receives a personal benefit from a third party as a result of his or her position in the company. For example, under Polish law, loans, or guarantees of obligations of loans, to a company's board of directors may create conflicts of interest.

As two of SC's directors who participated in the assessment of the financing options and approved the loan transaction are simultaneously owners, directors and officers of VC, the issues arising should be analysed in terms of three relationships: (i) the relationship between the directors and SC, (ii) the relationship between the directors and the shareholders of SC and (iii) the relationship between SC and VC.

According to Articles 209 and 377 of the CCC, in the event of a conflict of interest between the company and a management board member, the management board member must abstain from participating in the determination of such matters and he

---

[144] See, eg, Pyzioł in *Kodeks spółek handlowych. Komentarz* (n 143), note 8 to Art 174, § 6 of the Commercial Companies Code.

[145] See, eg, P Machnikowski, 'Numerus clausus papierów wartościowych inkorporujących wierzytelności' (2000) 8 *Państwo i Prawo* 53–65.

[146] See, eg, M Romanowski in A Szumański (ed), *System Prawa Prywatnego, t. 18, Prawo papierów wartościowych. Suplement* (Warsaw, CH Beck, 2006) 34.

or she may request that an entry be made in the minutes of the board meetings to that effect. These articles in the CCC give expression to the duty of loyalty of the management board members to the company, but not in relation to the shareholders of the company: in Polish company law, there is no scope for management board members to be civilly liable towards the company's shareholders.[147] Polish law does not provide *expressis verbis* for fiduciary duties known in some jurisdictions which arise between management board members of a company and its shareholders.

As a result of an absence of rules on the direct liability of management board members of a company towards the shareholders of the company, the management board members may only be indirectly liable to such shareholders to make good damage caused to the company by the shareholders bringing an action against such a member of the management board for his or her wrongful conduct. Thus, in the light of current court rulings, it will be difficult to render management board members directly liable towards shareholders. However, certain doctrinal arguments have been presented recently which may impose such liability. Most of them refer to the concept of limited liability and its roots. First, it is argued that the notion of the interests of the company must be construed in the light of the interests of all shareholders, taking into account the proportionality principle of rights and contributions.[148] Second, it has been argued that the company should be treated as a web of legal relationships, which consists of relations between shareholders themselves, between shareholders and the company and between shareholders and management and supervisory board members. This relationship is contractual in nature. A contract between the management board members and the company's shareholders may be implied from the nature of the membership of the management board and the existence of strong shareholder rights to remove managers of the company from office (see CCC, Article 368, section 4).[149] Moreover, the concept of a direct relationship between the shareholders and managers of the company was addressed in the Supreme Court ruling dated 21 December 2005, where the Court referred to the cumulative rights of shareholders to appoint members of the supervisory board in a public company.[150] The Court ruled that supervisory board members serve as representatives of all shareholders if they were elected by the general shareholders' meeting.

A breach of Articles 209 and 377 of the CCC may result in the liability of the management board member, including but not limited to removal from his or her post. Some authors[151] also claim that there is a breach of these articles where the management board members are in a conflict-of-interest situation on the basis that this can also be treated as a legal act which is inconsistent with the principles of community life.

---

[147] See, eg, A Szumański in *Odpowiedzialność cywilna. Księga pamiątkowa ku czci Profesora Adama Szpunara pod red. Małgorzaty Pyziak – Szafnickiej* (Krakow, Kantor Wydawniczy Zakamycze, 2004) 601.

[148] See, eg, A Opalski, 'O pojęciu interesu spółki handlowej' (2008) 11 *Przegląd Prawa Handlowego* 21.

[149] Some authors claim that the right to remove the management board members of the public company may not be excluded in the articles of association.

[150] See, eg, IV CK 311/05, unpublished.

[151] See, eg, Rodzynkiewicz, *Kodeks spółek handlowych. Komentarz* (n 142) 380–81; A Szumański in S Sołtysiński, A Szajkowski, A Szumański and J Szwaja (eds), *Kodeks spółek handlowych. Komentarz, t. II* (Warsaw, CH Beck, 2002) 414.

On this ground, it is argued that the conduct of a member of the management board in a conflict-of-interest situation will be null and void (Polish Civil Code, Article 58, item 2). However, it is not wholly clear whether the transaction would be treated as null and void under Polish law and there is a debate as to what is the correct doctrine. However, there is no direct provision corresponding to that which exists in US (Delaware) law and therefore both standpoints may be possible.

Notwithstanding the above, in light of Articles 293 and 483 of the CCC, a management board member must exercise a degree of diligence in the discharge of his or her duties which is proper for the professional nature of his or her actions. Thus, if a management board member fails to act with the proper degree of diligence and in non-compliance with law or the company's constitution and his or her actions cause wilful damage to the company, then he or she will be held liable. However, the director will have a defence if he or she can demonstrate that the damage would have been caused regardless of his or her fault. Nevertheless, there are some commentators who claim that a management board member will be liable for damage caused to the company even if he or she did not participate in the decision which caused such damage or voted against that decision on the ground that a director's role is to prevent any action being taken which would be detrimental to the company.[152]

Finally, it should be noted that the CCC does not provide for any rules for conflict-of-interest liability between a parent company and its subsidiary, with the exception of certain information obligations.

With respect to a possible breach of duty in not having selected the most qualified nominee directors, the problem may be analysed in the light of Articles 249 (limited liability company) or 422 (public company) of the CCC. A general meeting resolution that is contrary to the company's articles or good practice and prejudicial to the interests of the company or intended to wrong a shareholder may be appealed by an action to revoke the resolution brought against the company (ie the resolution concerning the selection of said two less qualified directors). However, the right to bring such an action to revoke is vested in any shareholder who votes against the resolution and, upon the resolution being adopted, who demanded that his objection be put on record. The voting requirement does not apply to a shareholder with a non-voting share (Article 422, section 2, sub-section 2), a shareholder who was unduly prevented from participating in the general meeting, or a shareholder who was absent from the general meeting in circumstances where the general meeting had been improperly summoned or the resolution was adopted on a matter not included in the agenda. Since all shareholders voted in favour of VC's nominee, there are no grounds for questioning the resolution concerning the selection of directors.

We also believe that, despite the above, the conduct is unlikely to amount to an infringement of 'good practice' or 'interests of the company', considering that all other minority shareholders had approved the nomination of VC's directors before. Article 422 of the CCC regulates some aspects of the duty of loyalty of the shareholder

---

[152] See M Rodzynkiewicz, *Comercial Companies Code – Commentary* (Warsaw, LexisNexis, 2009) 543; M Allerhand, *Kodeks handlowy. Komentarz* (Lviv, 'Kodeks' Spółka Wydawnicza z ograniczoną odpowiedzialnością, 1935) 463 (note 8 to Art 292 of the Commercial Code).

in the public company. Legal doctrine raises the argument that the right to appeal against the resolutions of shareholders' meeting is one of the absolute instruments for the protection of minority shareholders. In particular, it introduces the loyal duty to exercise voting rights, which prohibits the use of rights at the general meeting of shareholders in a manner inconsistent with good practices and to the victimisation of other shareholders.[153] However, there is no obligation to elect directors with the greatest possible experience, and, generally speaking, the shareholder is free to choose any person as a director, which corresponds with his/her right to appoint the directors. On the other hand, the shareholders must act with good faith, in the interest of the company and not to the detriment of other shareholders. However, unless the selection is not manifestly detrimental to the company (the person is evidently unsuitable), it would be hard to prove that there is such a negative effect upon the interests of the company.

K. Latvia

In the case of Latvian private limited liability companies, directors are appointed by the general meeting of the shareholders (*sabiedrība ar ierobežotu atbildību*: Commercial Code, section 210(1)4)) or by the supervisory board in the case of a public limited liability companies (*akciju sabiedrība*: Commercial Code, section 292(1)1)). Company shareholders may conclude civil agreements between one another,[154] therefore the shareholders' agreement whereby VC is entitled to appoint two directors, is valid.

It is unclear whether the loan transaction between SC and its existing investors is either void or voidable under Latvian law. First of all, Latvian law does not explicitly prohibit directors from concluding contracts between themselves and the company they represent. A number of provisions exist which regulate the conduct of agents, including directors, for example, the general duty to act with diligence and care (Civil Code, section 2295; Commercial Code, section 169(1)) and the duty to 'complete the matter in the most advantageous way' for the appointer in the case of a nominee (Civil Code, section 2301).[155,156] Thus, agents and directors are under an obligation to act in the interests of the appointing company SC only,[157] and as a result of the duty to act as a loyal director, the interests of the appointer (VC) are secondary to those of the company.[158] Therefore, although acting for both parties in the loan transaction may result in a breach of these duties, such a violation does not result in the concluded transaction itself being void or voidable; instead, it merely triggers potential liability

---

[153] See K Szmid, *Natura spółki akcyjnej jako delimitacja swobody umów w prawie polskim i amerykańskim* (Warsaw, CH Beck, 2015), 381–84.

[154] Law on the Enterprise Register of the Republic of Latvia, s 14(2). See also A Strupišs, 'Komerctiesību attīstība: problēmas un perspektīvas' *Jurista Vārds* 07.11.2017, 107.

[155] Judgment of the Latvian Supreme Court in case no SKC-16/2011 of 12 January 2011.

[156] Judgment of the Latvian Supreme Court in case no SKC-139/2016 of 30 May 2016.

[157] K Balodis, *Civillikuma komentāri* (Riga, Lietas Valdījums, 2000) § 2295 no 2. For public limited liability companies, see also Commercial Code, s 309(3)(2).

[158] A Strupišs, *Komerclikuma komentāri III, B daļa. Komersanti XI sadaļa. Kapitālsabiedrības (134–184. panti)* (Riga, A Steupiša juridiskais birojs, 2003) 145, § 343.4.

on the part of the directors towards the company (Commercial Code, section 169(2); Civil Code, section 2295).

Likewise, one cannot judge the conduct of VC's nominee directors as violating the general prohibition against impermissible conduct, rendering the resulting transaction void (Civil Code, section 1415). Latvian commentaries refer to § 138 of the German Civil Code (BGB) in this context, which states that a legal transaction that is contrary to public policy is void. However, § 138 of the BGB does not deal specifically with the issue of 'contracting with oneself'.[159] The Latvian provision which sets out a general prohibition only covers conduct which objectively violates existing law.[160] However, as already noted, Latvian law does not deal with the issue of self-contracting expressly.

As a result, having acted for both parties to the loan agreement in the present case does not render the respective agreement invalid or voidable. Such conduct may, however, give rise to a claim for liability against VC's nominee directors.

With regard to a possible violation of duties on the part of VC in the process of selecting 'their' directors, Latvian law does not create an obligation upon shareholders to select the most qualified nominee directors. In the present case, the choice of an unsuitable director therefore does not have any consequences.

Finally, it should be noted that notes convertible into common stock are permitted for public limited liability companies only (Commercial Code, section 244). Consequently, convertible obligations may not be issued by private limited liability companies.

L. Japan

i. Shareholder Agreement and Qualification of the Nominee Director

In general, a shareholders' agreement is effective as a contract under private law. However, if the agreement includes provisions which conflict with the terms of the Companies Act 2005 (CA), the agreement is rendered ineffective and the provisions of the CA will prevail.

Moreover, in principle, the nominating shareholder is free to select any nominee director. However, if the nominee director made an irregular transaction which was detrimental to the company under the pressure of a controlling shareholder (VC) and harmed the company's interests, the nominee director will be liable to the company for damages arising as a result thereof in terms of the CA, Article 423(1).[161]

ii. Convertible Promissory Note

Regarding such a 'convertible promissory note' as the present case shows, there is no definite provision in the CA. Under the CA, a stock company can issue a 'convertible

---

[159] See the solution to this case under German law at II E, above (reference to BGB, § 181).
[160] Balodis, *Civillikuma komentāri* (n 157) 214.
[161] K Egashira, *Kabushikigaisha-hô [Laws of Stock Corporations]* (7th edn, Tokyo, Yuhikaku, 2017) 449.

bond (a bond with share options)', but the said promissory note is a 'note' and does not meet the requirement for a 'bond' under the CA.

In this way, the said promissory note can be regarded as an illustration of 'Properties Contributed in Kind' under the CA as a kind of so-called 'Debt Equity Swap' (with a contingent condition). The issue of shares for subscription in exchange for the properties contributed in kind requires a resolution of the company's board of directors.[162] In addition, the stock company must appoint an inspector to investigate the value of the properties contributed in kind where the properties contributed in kind consist of a money claim to the stock company, and the value with respect to such money claim exceeds the book value of the debt representing such monetary claim.[163]

iii. Conflict-of-Interest Transaction

If a director intends to enter into a transaction in a personal capacity or on behalf of a third party with the company, the director will be in a conflict-of-interest situation, and the CA requires the director to disclose the existence of the relevant transactions at a shareholders' general meeting or at a board meeting and obtain the approval of the shareholders' general meeting or the board meeting. The same rules apply where the company proposes to guarantee the debts of a director or carry out any transaction with a person other than the director that results in a conflict of interest between the company and such director.

Any transaction with a person other than the director that results in a conflict of interest between the company and such director is referred to as an 'indirect transaction'. Prior to the enactment of the CA and the amendments made to the Commercial Code 1981, there was no explicit provision regulating such indirect transactions which constituted a potential conflict of interest between the director and the company where the director was not a party to the transaction, for example, a loan or guarantee by the company for the benefit of the director. The Supreme Court has held that if a director enters into a loan agreement with a third party other than the company in an individual capacity and the company guarantees the director's debt to the third party, such a transaction operates to confer a benefit on the director as an individual. Therefore, the company would be in a conflict-of-interest situation. The transaction between SC and VC would be regulated under the same provisions on conflict-of-interest transactions, ie as an indirect transaction between the director and SC.[164]

The aforementioned decision of the Supreme Court also ruled that a conflict-of-interest transaction would be invalid if a director failed to secure the approval of the company through a shareholders' general meeting or a board meeting. However, the company will not be able to challenge the validity of the transaction unless it is able to prove that the counterparty to the transaction entered into it with the knowledge that there was an unapproved conflict situation or had no such knowledge, but was

---

[162] CA, Art 199(1)(i), 200(1), 201(1).
[163] CA, Art 207.
[164] Supreme Court, 25 December 1968, *Minshu*, vol 22, no 13, at 3511.

grossly negligent.[165] This interpretation will apply to the transaction entered into between SC and VC in the hypothetical case.

iv. Approval by General Meeting or Board Meeting

If SC is a 'company with a board of directors',[166] a director who finds himself or herself in a conflict-of-interest transaction vis-a-vis SC or a third party other than SC is required to disclose the relevant transaction at a board meeting and obtain its approval.[167] Where no such approval is attained, but all the shareholders agree that the director may enter into such a transaction, the Supreme Court has ruled that it is not necessary for the director to secure board approval in such circumstances. The reason for that decision is based on the fact that the conflict of interest provisions in the CA are designed to protect the company and since the shareholders have reached a consensus on the matter, these provisions are treated as satisfied.[168] This interpretation will apply to the case in terms of Article 356 of the CA (a shareholders' general meeting required for approval).

If SC does not have a board of directors, a director who finds himself or herself in an indirect conflict-of interest transaction is required to secure the approval of a shareholders' general meeting of the Company. However, as noted above, if all of the shareholders of SC reached a consensus in favour of the transaction in question, it is unnecessary for SC to call a general meeting to seek such approval.

III. Conclusion

A. Introduction

The legal systems examined would reach different conclusions as to whether the loan transaction between SC and its existing investors was valid. The outcomes vary not only across the common law/civil law divide, but also within each of these two legal traditions. Part B below briefly addresses two threshold questions to determine whether the scenario would arise in the jurisdictions examined: the validity of a shareholders' agreement granting two SC board member positions to VC nominees and the validity of the promissory note convertible into common shares of stock. Part C addresses the conflict of interest that is the central focus of the case and the implications of that conflict for the validity of the loan transaction between SC and its existing investors. Part D discusses whether VC is subject to any duties in selecting directors. Finally, part E addresses relevant policy issues and comparative theory.

---

[165] Ibid.
[166] CA, Art 2(7).
[167] CA, Arts 356 and 365.
[168] Supreme Court, 26 September 1974, *Minshu*, vol 28, no 6, at 1306.

B. Shareholders' Agreements and Convertible Promissory Notes

In each of the countries examined, the shareholders' agreement between VC, Founder and the other investors in SC would probably be valid. The general rule in all countries is that shareholders elect directors at a shareholder meeting. The shareholders may commit themselves in advance to vote for certain nominees in a shareholders' agreement, which appear to be widely used and universally enforceable.

Promissory notes that are convertible into common stock are enforceable in the US, the UK and South Africa. However, civil law countries place various restrictions on this form of security. In Italy, Spain, Poland and Latvia, the promissory note described in the case would be invalid, as only public limited companies are allowed to issue convertible promissory notes, but not private limited companies. In Germany, a 2005 reform seems to allow them in the case of private companies as well, but the issue is not entirely clear. France does not allow promissory notes convertible into stock, but does permit convertible bonds. By contrast, Japan allows a convertible note in the case of a stock company, but not a security that qualifies as a bond. The Netherlands allows promissory notes in principle, but the possibility of dilution may create limitations. In Finland, convertible promissory notes are allowed only if the company has a pressing financial reason to issue the notes. Therefore, we find evidence here of the argument that civilian jurisdictions place greater hurdles than the common law in front of companies who wish to issue particular security instruments. This provides support for the contention that the company laws of common law jurisdictions are more flexible inasmuch as they more freely enable companies to create more elaborate packages of rights in favour of shareholders. Moreover, civilian jurisdictions typically require shareholders to approve the issuance.

C. Conflict of Interests

By participating in the decisions regarding the loan, the VC nominee directors placed themselves on both sides of the transaction. Nevertheless, a conflict of interest does not automatically invalidate the loan transaction in any of the countries examined. The transaction would be invalid only if the directors failed to follow the procedures specified for conflict-of-interest transactions.

All countries examined recognise that directors have a duty (which most countries label 'fiduciary') not to act in a self-serving manner, and they limit the ability of interested directors to participate in conflict-of-interest transactions. Directors must not prioritise the interests of VC (by whom they were nominated) over the interests of SC, ie the companies on whose boards they serve.[169] Most of the countries examined would require the interested directors to abstain from voting. The US, the UK, South Africa and Japan, on the other hand, would allow the interested directors to participate in the

---

[169] For a comparative analysis of the duties of 'constituency directors', see M Gelter and G Helleringer, 'Lift not the Painted Veil! To whom are Directors' Duties really Owed?' (2015) *University of Illinois Law Review* 1069.

transaction as long as the conflict of interest was disclosed to and approved by disinterested shareholders or directors before the transaction was consummated.

If the directors failed to observe the procedural rules described above – either by failing to abstain from voting on the interested transaction or by failing to disclose the conflict of interest – various outcomes are possible in the countries examined. In many of the countries, the transaction would be void or voidable. In France, for example, if the interested directors voted on the loan, the transaction would be voidable if it had detrimental consequences for the company. While in the UK, retrospective approval is not possible, in South Africa, the loan is void unless the directors obtain ratification from shareholders. In Japan and Italy, by contrast, the transaction would be voidable by SC, but only if VC knew about the conflict of interest, which it surely did in this instance, and the board or shareholders did not approve the transaction after full disclosure of the conflict. US and UK law would allow SC to rescind the loan if VC's nominee directors had breached their duty of loyalty.

Other countries simply invalidate the votes of the interested directors. In Germany, for example, the votes of VC's nominee directors would be invalid, and the validity of the transaction would turn on whether VC's nominee directors influenced the non-interested directors. Similarly, Spanish law would invalidate the votes of VC's nominee directors if those directors breached their duty of loyalty to the company.

In a few countries, the remedy would not be the invalidation of the loan transaction or the votes of the interested directors, but liability against the directors. Among these countries, in Finland there is a theoretical argument in favour of a finding that the loan transaction would be invalid under Finnish law. Finland, however, appears to be the only country where direct liability towards the Founder is contemplated. Polish and Latvian law do not provide for the direct liability of board members for a breach of duty, but board members may be indirectly liable for SC's losses. Similarly, in the Netherlands the loan would be valid, but the board's decision could be invalidated and the board members could be liable to the company. In both the US and the UK, in the event of a breach of duty, not only can the loan be rescinded, but SC would also be entitled to sue VC for any losses.

The loan transaction would likely be valid in the US, the Netherlands, and in some situations in Finland, Germany, Japan, Spain and the UK. US law often defers to the actions of companies and would find the transaction valid. In Finland, if the loan transaction benefited the company as a whole, it would be held valid. In Germany, if the non-interested directors had not been swayed by the interested directors and approved the loan transaction, the transaction would be valid. Similarly, in Spain, the loan transaction would be valid if the non-interested directors' votes were enough to sustain the transaction. In Japan, SC would be able to challenge the validity of the transaction if proven that the interested directors' actions were without company approval. In the UK, the loan transaction would be valid because SC is a private company and not a public company.

D. Selection of Directors

Generally, few countries impose duties on shareholders in the election or nomination of directors. All countries report that shareholders are in principle free in how they make the choice. In publicly traded firms, securities law may impose certain require-ments, such as the Sarbanes-Oxley Act in the US, but these do not apply here. In a number of countries, the shareholders' duty of loyalty might in theory play a role, for example, in Spain. In the US, only controlling shareholders are subject to a duty of loyalty, and some states (but not Delaware) establish additional fiduciary duties in closely held corporations, which will most likely not impose restrictions in the selection of directors. In the UK, South Africa and Italy, shareholders are generally not subject to a fiduciary duty.

Even where fiduciary duties do apply to shareholders, they would likely not play a role in this case. Generally, all jurisdictions report that shareholders can in princi-ple further their own interests when voting and may freely decide for whom to vote. However, at least in France, Germany, the Netherlands and Poland shareholders are under a duty not to select a manifestly unqualified or unsuitable director. In this particular case, however, in Poland, Founder would not be able to sue to invalidate the election of the directors because all shareholders voted in favour. In Finland, VC might be liable to shareholders or third parties if it deliberately or negligently inflicted damages on them. Ultimately, at least in the US and South Africa, the selection of unsuitable directors by VC might be a contract law issue under the terms of the share-holder agreement between VC and Founder.

E. Conclusion

The foregoing results illustrate both formal and functional differences among the juris-dictions reviewed. Each country recognises a conflict of interest, but the countries display great variation in the mechanisms used to deal with the conflict and in the degree to which conflict is tolerated. As to the latter point, comparing the outcomes in countries that rely heavily on case law and countries that rely heavily on codes suggests some functional differences. In jurisdictions that are heavily dependent on judicial decisions rather than codes, such as the US, more deference appears to be shown to interested transactions than in code-based jurisdictions. This result seems inevitable, as codes are unable to provide the same nuanced consideration of context as adjudication.

The experience in France, though anecdotal, seems to support the notion that when courts are allowed to consider all of the facts and circumstances, conflict-of-interest transactions are more likely to be approved than they would be under a strict enforcement of codes. Under the Commercial Code in France, the loan transaction would be invalid if the interested directors voted and the transaction had detrimental consequences for the company, but a recent French case confirms that the courts will exercise some restraint when interested directors vote, provided the transaction cannot be considered to be a related party transaction where directors have a clear indirect interest.[170]

---

[170] Transparency and approval of related party transactions is now also addressed in Art 9c Directive (EU) 2017/828 of 17 May 2017 amending Directive 2007/36/EC as regards the encouragement of long-term share-holder engagement ([2017] OJ L132/1), which has to be transposed by the Member States by 10 June 2019.

If this pattern is maintained across jurisdictions, it could provide some support for the legal origins theorem.[171] The connection between a tolerance of interested trans-actions and economic development is straightforward: many start-up firms rely on interested transactions because arm's-length transactions are not readily available to unproven firms. Thus, a jurisdiction that is more tolerant of interested transactions is more encouraging of start-up firms. Such jurisdictions seem willing to accept the social costs of interested transactions in exchange for the social benefits of start-ups.

[171] See also ch 12, below.

4

Obligations of Directors in Takeovers

PABLO IGLESIAS-RODRÍGUEZ (EDITOR)

Main topics: directors' duties in the context of a takeover bid; board neutrality rule; legality of directors' defensive tactics; whether approval by general meeting is needed for the sale of substantial assets; conflict of interests and duty; duty of skill, care and diligence; directors' liability.

Related topics: further duties of directors in the context of a takeover bid (see chapter 5, below); directors' duty of loyalty (see chapter 3, above); enforcement of directors' duties (see chapter 10, below).

I. Scenario

Corporation A is incorporated as a public listed company in your country. Its shares are traded on the main stock exchange of your jurisdiction. Corporation A operates in the real estate sector through a large network of sales agencies located throughout the country. Its most recent financial results show a decrease in the company's profits, principally attributable to the decisions of the board, which, although falling into the category of the business judgment rule, have led to substantial losses being borne by the firm.

During the past few months, Corporation B has been considering whether to acquire 100 per cent of the shares of Corporation A at a price 'P' with a premium of 40 per cent in relation to the average share price of Corporation A during the previous financial year. One of Corporation B's directors, Mr q, is also a director of Corporation A and has informed Corporation A's board about Corporation B's intentions to buy Corporation A's shares.

A week later, Corporation B makes public its offer to acquire the shares of Corporation A. Within a matter of three hours of Corporation B's bid going public, the board of Corporation A convenes a meeting at which it decides to sell 30 per cent of its real estate agencies at a price below their average market value on the pretexts that (i) the productivity of the agencies was low and (ii) Corporation A needed to generate cash for future investments. The real estate agencies were sold to Corporation C, a bank whose aim is to establish its own agencies in the sold properties. One of the directors of Corporation A, Ms r, is also a member of the board of Corporation C and has voted in favour of the transaction at the board meetings of both Corporations A and C. The sale of these assets is conducted in secret and without informing the shareholders of Corporation A.

At a general meeting of the shareholders which was called to discuss the terms of the offer, the board of Corporation A attempts to convince the shareholders of Corporation A that the price of Corporation B's offer is not adequate and does not reflect the real value of Corporation A; however, the shareholders decide not to grant the directors any special means of mounting a defence against Corporation B's takeover bid.

A week later, the board of Corporation A makes public the sale of its assets to Corporation C. Having learnt of the decision of the board of Corporation A to sell 30 per cent of its real estate agencies, the board of Corporation B states that the takeover would not make economic sense any more. Many shareholders of Corporation A are now also concerned and the majority of shareholders reject the takeover bid. Thus, whilst the directors of Corporation A have satisfied the objective of warding off the takeover, Corporation B has incurred a large amount of expenditure in formulating the offer (legal costs, publicity, etc) and Corporation A's shareholders have lost a unique opportunity to sell their shares at a premium over the prevailing market price.

In terms of the law of your jurisdiction, are the directors of Corporation A permitted to sell a significant proportion of Corporation A's assets after (i) they have become aware of Corporation B's offer, or (ii) Corporation B's bid has been made public? Do they bear any liability for that transaction? If so, what is their liability towards Corporation A, its shareholders and Corporation B? Are q and r liable in terms of the fiduciary duties they owe to Corporation A or its shareholders?

II. Case Studies

A. Spain

i. The Relationship between Company and Securities Law

First, in order to understand whether this transaction complies with Spanish law, it is important to analyse the takeover provisions of the relevant securities laws and regulations which will determine (i) whether the neutrality/passivity rules apply to the board of directors of Corporation A, prohibiting them from taking any action that may frustrate the offer and (ii) whether the directors of Corporation A are liable to the parties who suffered losses as a result of the measures which were taken.

If the neutrality/passivity rule applies and the directors breach it, they may be held liable on the basis of the regime established by general Spanish company law.

ii. The Duty of Neutrality

The main issue is whether the directors of Corporation A breached Spanish securities and takeover laws by selling the assets of Corporation A. More specifically, the content and scope of any neutrality/passivity rule will determine whether the directors of Corporation A were allowed to proceed with the sale of the assets to Corporation C after Corporation B made its offer public.

The objective of a neutrality/passivity rule is to prevent the directors of a target company from taking any action which would frustrate a takeover offer without first attaining shareholder approval.[1] The proscribed actions include, but are not limited to, the target company issuing new shares, selling its assets or, in general, adopting any measures which would reduce the attractiveness of the target company to the offeror.[2]

The European Directive on Takeover Bids (hereinafter the EU Takeover Directive)[3] amounted to a minimum harmonisation measure. Therefore, different Member States were given various options within certain parameters with regard to the actual design and content of the neutrality rule which they could adopt. As a result, the content of the neutrality rules adopted by the Member States was crafted in different terms. In Spain, the principle of the neutrality of the directors of a target company in the case of a takeover existed in law long before it was developed in the EU Takeover Directive. The neutrality rule was first introduced into Spanish securities law by the Real Decreto 1197/1991 (hereinafter the 1991 Royal Decree on Takeovers),[4] which was the first proper regulatory attempt to regulate takeovers in Spain. With regard to the

---

[1] The scope and content of the neutrality/passivity rule has been the subject of academic debate. For example, whereas Easterbrook and Fischel advocate a very strict regime in which all defensive measures are prohibited (FH Easterbrook and DR Fischel, 'The Proper Role of a Target's Management in Responding to a Tender Offer' (1981) 94 *Harvard Law Review* 1161), Gilson argues for a more flexible regime in which defensive measures are prohibited but management is permitted to solicit alternative competitive bids (R Gilson, 'Seeking Competitive Bids versus Pure Passivity in Tender Offer Defense' (1982) 35 *Stanford Law Review* 51).

[2] A good review of the different defensive actions, both *ex ante* measures requiring shareholder approval and *ex post* actions that would not require it, is provided by GA Jarrell, JA Brickley and JM Netter, 'The Market for Corporate Control: The Empirical Evidence since 1980' (1988) 2 *Journal of Economic Perspectives* 49.

[3] Directive 2004/25/EC of the European Parliament and of the Council of 21 April 2004 on takeover bids ([2004] OJ L142/12). The European regime follows a very different scheme from that in the US. As stated by M Ventoruzzo in 'Europe's Thirteenth Directive and U.S. Takeover Regulation: Regulatory Means and Political and Economic Ends' (2006) 41 *Texas International Law Journal* 171 at 194:

> The US system addresses this conflict of interest (between directors and shareholders) mainly through the fiduciary duties owed by the directors to the shareholders, holding them liable in cases of breach of their duties of loyalty or of care, as developed in takeover case law. On the contrary, the European approach freezes directors' powers once a public offer has been launched and requires any action that might adversely affect the outcome of the takeover to be approved by the shareholders.

[4] Real Decreto 1197/1991, de 26 de julio, sobre régimen de las ofertas públicas de adquisición de valores.

obligations of the board of a target company in a takeover, Article 14.1 of the Decree stipulated that:

> From the publication of the suspension of trading of shares of the target company until the publication of the result of the takeover offer, the board of directors of the target company shall not conduct any operations, acting alone or in concert, whose main purpose is to frustrate the offer or which are not in the ordinary course of business of the target company.

Moreover, the same provision stipulated that directors 'shall ensure that the interests of shareholders prevail over their own interests' (1991 Royal Decree on Takeovers, Article 14.1). In particular, the Decree specified activities which the board was not allowed to engage in, such as 'the sale ... of real estate or other company's assets when this may frustrate or damage the offer' (1991 Royal Decree on Takeovers, Article 14.1). Since this rule only applied in circumstances where the shares of the target company had been suspended from trading, the effect would be that Corporation A's directors would not be prevented, under the 1991 Royal Decree on Takeovers, from selling the company's assets after they had become aware of the takeover offer but before the publication of the suspension of the trading of the shares.

The 1991 regime remained as above until Spain implemented the EU Takeover Directive. The EU Takeover Directive, which came into force in 2004, applied the neutrality principle at the European level. In Article 9.2 of the EU Takeover Directive, it is provided that:

> During the period referred to in the second sub paragraph, the board of the offeree company shall obtain the prior authorisation of the general meeting of shareholders given for this purpose before taking any action, other than seeking alternative bids, which may result in the frustration of the bid and in particular before issuing any shares which may result in a lasting impediment to the offeror's acquiring control of the offeree company.

If we apply the law to the instant case, the question is whether the board of Corporation A would be permitted to sell the assets after the offer was made public. To that extent, it is necessary to revert to the text of the EU Takeover Directive, which provides Member States with two possible ways of implementing the neutrality rule. On the one hand, Member States may prohibit the board of a target firm from adopting defensive measures – such as the sale of the assets – without shareholder approval as soon as the bid is made public. On the other hand, Member States may adopt a more restrictive regulatory framework with regard to the period during which the neutrality/passivity rule operates. In this respect, Member States may require such shareholder authorisation to be obtained at an earlier stage – for example, as soon as the board of the target company becomes aware that the bid is imminent. The first scenario would allow the board of Corporation A to proceed with the sale of the assets after it became aware of the offer but before the offer was made public, whereas the second scenario would preclude Corporation A's board from acting in that way by imposing the requirement that it must not proceed with the sale of the assets as soon as it has knowledge of the bid.[5] Thus, the

---

[5] Art 9(2) of the EU Takeover Directive directs that:

> Such authorisation shall be mandatory at least from the time the board of the offeree company receives the information referred to in the first sentence of Article 6(1) concerning the bid and until the result of

European regime provides discretion to Member States as to the point in time at which the prohibition on the sale of assets by the board of a target corporation, without shareholder approval, should begin.

The EU Takeover Directive was implemented in Spain in 2007 by the Ley 6/2007 – the 2007 Act on Takeovers[6] –, which amended several provisions of the Ley del Mercado de Valores (LMV) – the Securities Markets Act,[7] subsequently incorporated into the Texto Refundido de la Ley del Mercado de Valores (TRLMV)[8] –, and its implementing regulation, the Real Decreto 1066/2007, namely the 2007 Royal Decree on Takeovers.[9] The TRLMV delegates the determination of the period during which the neutrality/passivity rule operates to the 2007 Royal Decree on Takeovers.[10] Article 28.1 of the 2007 Royal Decree on Takeovers opted for the first, and less strict, regulatory scheme offered by the EU Takeover Directive, by stipulating that the board must obtain shareholder authorisation from the moment the bid is made public:

> From the public announcement of the public offering … until the publication of the result of the offer, the board … shall obtain the prior authorisation of the general shareholders' meeting … before proceeding with any action which may impede the success of the bid, subject to the exception that the board may examine the possibility of competing bids … In particular it shall not … c) Proceed with the sale … of real estate or other assets of the company, where such actions may frustrate the success of the bid.

Hence, in the instant case, the board of Corporation A could proceed lawfully – in terms of the provisions of Article 134 of the TRLMV and of Article 28 of the 2007 Royal Decree on Takeovers – to sell the real estate agencies at any point in time between the moment it became aware of the offer until the offer was made public, without being required to attain the approval of the shareholders of Corporation A; such action would not, in principle, constitute a breach of Spanish securities/takeover law. However, in the instant case, the board of Corporation A sold the assets after the bid by Corporation B was made public. This is therefore a violation of Spanish securities and takeover law. According to Article 236 of the Ley de Sociedades de Capital (LSC) – Corporate Enterprises Act –[11] directors will be liable to the company, its shareholders and creditors for damage suffered resulting from negligent or intentional conduct or omissions which are contrary to the law, the company's by-laws or in breach of the duties inherent in their office. Claims against directors for damages to the company

---

the bid is made public or the bid lapses. Member States may require that such authorisation be obtained at an earlier stage, for example as soon as the board of the offeree company becomes aware that the bid is imminent.

[6] Ley 6/2007, de 12 de abril, de reforma de la Ley 24/1988, de 28 de julio, del Mercado de Valores, para la modificación del régimen de las ofertas públicas de adquisición y de la transparencia de los emisores.

[7] Ley 24/1988, de 28 de julio, del Mercado de Valores.

[8] Real Decreto Legislativo 4/2015, de 23 de octubre, por el que se aprueba el texto refundido de la Ley del Mercado de Valores.

[9] Real Decreto 1066/2007, de 27 de julio, sobre el régimen de las ofertas públicas de adquisición de valores.

[10] Art 134.1 of the TRLMV stipulates that: 'During the time period and in the terms to be determined by regulation, the board of directors of the target firm … shall obtain the prior authorisation of the general shareholders' meeting … before proceeding with any action which may impede the success of the bid'.

[11] Real Decreto Legislativo 1/2010, de 2 de julio, por el que se aprueba el texto refundido de la Ley de Sociedades de Capital (LSC).

are, as a general rule, brought by the company (LSC, Article 238) although, under certain circumstances, they may be brought by shareholders with certain percentages of the company's share capital – at least 3 per cent for listed companies and a minimum of 5 per cent for non-listed companies (LSC, Articles 239, 168 and 495.2(a)) – or by the company's creditors (LSC, Article 240). One of the instances where minority shareholders can bring an action for damages to the company is when such action is grounded on a breach of the duty of loyalty by the directors (LSC, Article 239.1). The decision regarding the sale of the real estate agencies below market value by the board of directors of Corporation A, would not necessarily qualify, *per se*, as a breach of the directors' duty of loyalty. The hypothetical case suggests that there may have been good commercial reasons for the adoption of such a course of action, and, therefore, this decision might be protected by the business judgment rule.[12] However, the hypothetical scenario also indicates that this decision was taken within a matter of three hours of the offer being made public by Corporation B and, moreover, the board of Corporation A seemed to use some 'pretexts' to justify the sale. These elements could indicate that the main purpose of the board of Corporation A was to frustrate Corporation B's offer. This line of reasoning would, in turn, allow shareholders such as Corporation B, with at least 3 per cent of the share capital of Corporation A, to bring a suit against the directors of Corporation A for damages caused to the latter.

Moreover, shareholders and third parties who are able to show that the actions of directors caused them a direct damage may bring an individual claim for damages against the directors (LSC, Article 241). Therefore, Corporation B – both as a third party and/or a shareholder – and other shareholders could bring individual claims if they were able to show such a direct damage resulting from the decision of the directors of Corporation A.[13]

According to the TRLMV, the breach of the neutrality/passivity rule constitutes a serious infraction of the securities regulatory framework, which may lead to the directors of a target company – such as Corporation A – being subject to various forms of administrative liability; for example, they may be fined, suspended from office, disqualified from office or publicly reprimanded (TRLMV, Articles 280.2 and 306).

In addition, Corporation A may have not complied with the rules on market abuse adumbrated in the TRLMV. In this regard, issuers such as Corporation A are obliged to make public and to communicate to the Comisión Nacional del Mercado de Valores (CNMV) – the Spanish Securities Markets Commission – material information (TRLMV, Articles 228.1-2). Such information must be disclosed as soon as the relevant decision is adopted or the contract is signed with third parties – in the hypothetical case, Corporation C (TRLMV, Article 228.3). Corporation A did not disclose such information and thus acted in breach of the TRLMV. This constitutes a

---

[12] On the business judgment rule, see ch 2 at II E, above.

[13] Academic opinion has expressed scepticism concerning the possibility of directors of the target company being liable to the offering company. These concerns are based mainly on the opinion that, first, it would be difficult to establish a direct nexus between the behaviour of the directors and the damage suffered by the offeror and, second, that the purpose of the neutrality rule is not to protect the offeror but instead to safeguard the interests of the shareholders of the target company; on this point, see G Pomar and S Lacave, 'La eficacia del deber de pasividad de los administradores sociales en presencia de una OPA: mecanismos privados frente a públicos' (2007) 1 *Indret: Revista para el Análisis del Derecho* 1.

serious infraction of the securities regulatory framework (TRLMV, Article 282.7) and may lead to the forms of administrative liability referred to in the previous paragraph.

iii. Directors' Duties

It is possible to identify two individuals, namely q and r, who might be liable on the basis of the general rules of Spanish company law and, in particular, in terms of a breach of their duties as directors. In 2003, by virtue of the introduction of the Ley de Transparencia – the Transparency Act[14] – the regulation of directors' duties underwent dramatic changes in Spain. The Spanish law of directors' duties was changed from a very generic legal regime – with no detailed specification or definition of the different standards which directors were expected to discharge in terms of the duties – to a more developed legal framework. The regime concerning the duties of directors was further developed by the LSC and a reform of the latter adopted in 2014.[15]

With regard to q, it is evident from the case that he is contemporaneously a director of both Corporation A and Corporation B. Having informed Corporation A's board of Corporation B's board's intentions to acquire Corporation A, q has potentially committed a breach of his duty of loyalty. First, turning to Article 227 of the LSC, a general breach on the part of q can be identified: 'Directors shall exercise their functions as loyal representatives, in good faith, and in the best interests of the company'.[16] Insofar as q revealed Corporation B's takeover plans, he provided Corporation A's board with information which could potentially be used by the latter to adopt actions opposed to the interests of Corporation B or of its shareholders, such as defensive measures against the takeover. Q's behaviour would hence likely constitute a breach of Article 227 of the LSC in relation to the duties he owes as a director to Corporation B.

In particular, q's behaviour would constitute a violation of the duty of confidentiality set out in Article 228(b) of the LSC, according to which directors must keep confidential any information that they receive in the exercise of their functions. Q's situation falls within the scope of this provision; first, he is a director who is in possession of confidential information, namely the plans of Corporation B to acquire Corporation A; second, the information was obtained as a result of his position as a director of Corporation B. The extent of the liability of q towards Corporation B on

---

[14] Ley 26/2003, de 17 de julio, por la que se modifican la Ley 24/1988, de 28 de julio, del Mercado de Valores, y el texto refundido de la Ley de Sociedades Anónimas, aprobado por el Real Decreto Legislativo 1564/1989, de 22 de diciembre, con el fin de reforzar la transparencia de las sociedades anónimas cotizadas. The Transparency Act was introduced as a result of a corporate governance reform process that started in 1998 with the publication of the Olivencia Report, and which was subsequently complemented in 2003 by the Aldama Report, both containing corporate governance recommendations for public limited companies.

[15] Ley 31/2014, de 3 de diciembre, por la que se modifica la Ley de Sociedades de Capital para la mejora del gobierno corporativo.

[16] The law uses a very vague and generic term, namely the 'best interest of the company'. A comprehensive study on the interpretation of the concept of 'company's interests' is provided by J Sánchez-Calero Guilarte in 'El interés social y los varios intereses presentes en la sociedad anónima cotizada' (2002) 246 Revista de Derecho Mercantil 1653. Case law in the field suggests that this is to be understood as 'the addition of the particular interests of shareholders'. See. eg. STS (Sentencia Tribunal Supremo) of 4 March 2000.

this basis would very much depend on whether it is possible to show a link between q's behaviour and the damage sustained by Corporation B.

Q's behaviour may also be considered an unfairly competitive act in terms of Article 13.1 of the Ley de Competencia Desleal – Unfair Competition Act[17] – according to which the disclosure of trade or business secrets is considered unfair. The prosecution of such behaviour would require that the person disclosing the trade secrets acted with the purpose of obtaining a benefit – for himself, herself or for a third party – or with the intention of damaging the holder of the trade secrets (Ley de Competencia Desleal, Article 13.3). In the instant case, it is possible that q disclosed the confidential information with the intention of benefiting Corporation A, and thus prosecution under the Unfair Competition Act would likely be applicable.

Q's action may also consist of a violation of the Código Penal (CP) – Criminal Code[18] – according to which persons who reveal another's secrets that they have knowledge of because of their job, will be punished with a custodial sentence and a fine (CP, Article 199.1).

In terms of the market abuse regulatory regime, the disclosure of information by q could also amount to a breach of rules concerning inside information. 'Inside information' is defined by the TRLMV to include any concrete information directly or indirectly referred to issuers of securities which is not public and that, if made public, could influence the price of those securities (TRLMV, Article 226.1). Under the TRLMV, the holders of inside information are bound to abstain from communicating it to third parties (TRLMV, Article 227.1(b)). In the instant case, q's disclosure of Corporation B's intentions to Corporation A's board may also be treated as a breach of the inside information rules. Such behaviour would constitute a serious infraction of the securities regulatory framework and be subject to administrative sanctions (TRLMV, Article 282.6) and, under certain circumstances, to criminal law sanctions (CP, Article 285.1).

Turning now to r, who is a director of both Corporation A and Corporation C, the effect of her involvement in the sale transaction is that she may be in breach of her duty of loyalty. The LSC is instructive in respect of the actions of r. On the one hand, Article 229.3 of the LSC stipulates that directors must communicate to the board any direct or indirect conflicts they might have with the interests of the company. On the other hand, according to Article 228(c) of the LSC, directors in a situation of conflict of interest must not participate in deliberations or voting procedures relating to decisions to which such conflict refers.[19]

In the case under consideration, there is potentially a direct conflict arising from the position of r as director of both Corporation A and Corporation C. Moreover, r has taken part and not abstained from involvement in the decision of Corporation A to sell the real estate assets to Corporation C. This might be detrimental to the interests of Corporation A. For example, r may vote in favour of the sale transaction, not on the grounds that it is for the commercial benefit of Corporation A but, rather, that it

---

[17] Ley 3/1991, de 10 de enero, de Competencia Desleal.
[18] Ley Orgánica 10/1995, de 23 de noviembre, del Código Penal.
[19] See also the solution ch 3 at II G, above.

is to her own personal advantage, whereby she will expect to receive a direct or indirect benefit from Corporation C when the transaction is approved by Corporation A. Whereas the participation of an individual as a director in two boards of directors of different companies is not, in itself, a breach of Spanish company law, the involvement of a director in a decision in which she has a conflicting interest does indeed constitute an infringement of Article 228 of the LSC and, as such, r might be subject to liability on the grounds of the rules regarding directors' liability set out in the LSC. R's liability may not only include the obligation to compensate for damages but also to reverse the unjust enrichment (LSC, Article 227.2). As in the Spanish solution to chapter 3 above, the validity of the agreement by the board of Corporation A to sell the assets to Corporation C would very much depend on whether the vote by r was essential or not for the decision to be adopted.

The liability on an individual basis of q and r towards the shareholders of Corporation B and Corporation A, respectively, for a breach of their fiduciary duties is generally problematic. This is because fiduciary duties are devised to provide protection to the company, not to its shareholders as such. Hence, the potential for Corporation B and Corporation A's shareholders to secure damages from q and r, respectively – assuming that all the requirements for the individual liability claim applied – would be limited.[20]

With regard to the liability of q towards Corporation B and of r towards Corporation A for the damages resulting from violations of their fiduciary duties, this would be a more realistic option. However, in such a case, there would be additional problems that could limit the scope to claim damages, which are caused by the feasibility of identifying a causal nexus between the actions and behaviour of q and/or r and the losses experienced by Corporation B and by Corporation A.

iv. Summary

The case first asked whether the decision of the board of Corporation A to sell the assets amounted to a breach of the neutrality/passivity rule. Spain implemented the neutrality rule regarding the behaviour of directors in takeovers within the parameters set by the EU Takeover Directive. The neutrality rule applies from the moment the offer is made public rather than from the moment the board of Corporation A becomes aware of the intentions of Corporation B to make a takeover offer. As such, under Spanish law, the decision by the board of Corporation A would be in breach of the neutrality/passivity rule. Moreover, the fact that the decision on the sale of assets was adopted immediately after the offer was announced by Corporation B, and justified with some pretexts, suggests that the directors of Corporation A may have also breached their duty of loyalty towards Corporation A. These breaches may result in both civil and administrative liability of the directors of Corporation A. In addition, by not disclosing the decision concerning the sale of the assets, Corporation A infringed market abuse rules.

---

[20] In this regard, see V Ribas Ferrer, *El deber de lealtad del administrador de sociedades* (Madrid, La Ley, 2010) 657–58.

As regards the position of q and r, their behaviour may also lead to various forms of liability. Concerning q, the disclosure of Corporation B's intentions to the board of Corporation A does constitute a breach of his fiduciary duties towards Corporation B and, more specifically, of the duty of confidentiality. Moreover, this may also consist of a breach of insider trading rules and result in criminal liability. When it comes to r, by voting for the sale transaction as a director of both Corporation C and Corporation A, she acted in a situation of conflict of interest and breached her duty of loyalty towards Corporation A. This may have consequences for the validity of the decision of the board of Corporation A. Regarding the liability of q and r for damages to the shareholders of Corporation B and Corporation A, respectively, on the basis of their breaches of fiduciary duties, such an option might be complicated, among other reasons, because fiduciary duties are owed to companies and not individually to their shareholders. The liability of q and r for damages caused to Corporation B and Corporation A, respectively, due to lack of compliance with their duties, might be possible, but, in such a case, the complexities would arise from the difficulty in establishing a link between the behaviour of the directors and the damage to the companies.

B. France

The French Commercial Code provides that the directors are:

> [I]ndividually or jointly and severally liable to the company or third parties either for infringements of the laws or regulations applicable to public limited companies, for breaches of the memorandum and articles of association, or for tortious or negligent acts of management.[21]

This article includes a general duty of care (*devoir de diligence*). Moreover, all acts of the directors have to be in accordance with the company's social interest (*intérêt social*). Since the law is quite general, the courts have fleshed out the content of this duty. In addition, in 1996, the French Supreme Court formally recognised a duty of loyalty (*devoir de loyauté*) in a case which concerned the chairman of the board.[22] This decision can be extended to any member of the board since the chairman of the board is a director. The beneficiaries of this duty are the shareholders taken individually.

i. *Right of Directors to Sell a Significant Portion of the Company's Assets*

France implemented the European Directive on Takeover Bids (hereinafter the EU Takeover Directive)[23] in 2006[24] in the Monetary and Financial Code[25] and the Commercial Code.[26] At the time, France introduced the 'board neutrality rule' as well

---

[21] Commercial Code, Art L 225-251.

[22] Cass Com (Cour de cassation, Commercial Chamber), 27 February 1996 (Vilgrain), *Bull civ IV*, n° 65; *RTD civ* 1997 114 with a note by J Mestre; *JCP* 1996 II, n° 22665 with a note by J Ghestin; *JCP E* 1996. II. 838 with a note by D Schmidt and N Dion; *Bull Joly* 1996 485, with a note by A Couret.

[23] Directive 2004/25/EC (n 3).

[24] Loi n° 2006-387 du 31 mars 2006 *relative aux offres publiques d'acquisition*, JO n° 78 1 avril 2006, p 4882.

[25] Monetary and Financial Code, Art L 433-1 and L 433-3.

[26] Commercial Code, Art L 233-32 ff.

as the 'reciprocity rule'. However, in 2014, France removed the 'board neutrality' principle in order to help protect French companies ('Florange Act').[27] Therefore, there is
no obligation to obtain the prior authorisation of the general meeting of shareholders
before taking any action which may result in the frustration of the bid, including seeking alternative bids.[28] However, the extraordinary shareholders' meeting can modify
the articles of associations to opt in to the board neutrality rule.[29] This modification
of the articles of association can also be subject to the reciprocity rule.[30]

The offer period (*période d'offre*) starts when the securities regulator, the Autorité
des marchés financiers (AMF), publicises the main elements of the bid.[31] However,
since the board is no longer subject to the neutrality rule, the starting point of the offer
period has no impact on the validity of the defences implemented.

The board of directors and the management of Corporation B can adopt anti-
takeover measures without first requesting the authorisation of the shareholders,
provided that these decisions fall within their powers of management. In the case of
Corporation B, the sale of a substantial portion of the assets of the company is within
the powers of the board and is therefore valid. There have been calls, however, to
reform the position and to provide a voting right to the shareholders in case of sale of
the main assets of the company.

However, the sale was concluded below market value and for dubious business
reasons. The fact that the sale was approved would reduce the likelihood of liability
for the board of directors and the management, but would not eliminate it. Indeed,
the right to sue the directors is protected against any contrary decision of the general
shareholders' meeting. No decision of the general shareholders' meeting, such as the
approval of the sale, can have the effect of extinguishing or preventing a suit.[32] Under
French company law, such sale would probably be considered to be a breach of the
social interest of the company. Therefore, the risk that the directors of Corporation A
who approved the sale might be sued is high.

ii. Duties of Directors

a. Liability of Director q

Director q is subject to a duty of confidentiality which he owes to Corporation A and
Corporation B.[33] When Director q disclosed to Corporation A that Corporation B
intended to launch a takeover of Corporation A, he violated his duty of confidentiality. Therefore, he can be held liable for damages to Corporation B for having disclosed
the fact that it was about to launch an offer for the shares of Corporation A.

In addition, q is also in breach of his duty of loyalty vis-a-vis Corporation B. By
informing Corporation A of the impending offer, he allowed Corporation A to organise

---

[27] Loi n°2014-384 of 29 mars 2014 *visant à reconquérir l'économie réelle*, JO 1st April p.6227.
[28] Commercial Code, Art L 233-32.
[29] Commercial Code, Art L 233-33-I.
[30] For the reciprocity rule of EU takeover law, see also ch 5 at III, below.
[31] AMF General Regulation, Art 231-2 6°.
[32] Commercial Code, Art L 225-253.
[33] Commercial Code, Art L 225-37 al 5.

an effective defence which led to the failure of the bid. It could be argued that since q also owed a duty of loyalty to Corporation A, he had a duty to inform Corporation A of the impending offer. However, the duty of loyalty of q towards Corporation A does not imply or allow him to violate his duty of loyalty towards Corporation B. Therefore, under French company law, q could probably be sued for damages for breach of his duty of loyalty towards Corporation B.

The final point to mention is that q's conduct also constitutes prohibited insider communication under insider dealing law.[34]

b. Liability of Director r

Under French company law, contracts, such as a contract for the sale of assets, entered into between two companies who have a common director (and in certain other circumstances) are subject to a requirement that there be a prior authorisation of the contract by the board of directors.[35] Agreements authorised by the board of directors are then subject to *ex post* approval by the shareholders' general meeting[36] where the interested director and the interested shareholder cannot vote.[37] These provisions do not apply to agreements relating to current operations which are entered into under normal terms and conditions.[38]

In the case of the sale by Corporation A of 30 per cent of its real estate agencies for a price below the average market value, Corporation B is subject to an obligation to obtain the prior authorisation of the board since the contract is concluded between two companies that have common directors. The exemption for current operations entered into under normal terms and conditions is not applicable since the sale of 30 per cent of the assets of the company is not a current operation of the company, ie it is outside the normal course of its business. In addition, the price was below market value, which means that the terms and conditions were not normal.

The interested director is not entitled to vote on the resolution of the board of directors to approve the sale.[39] In the case of Corporation A, Director r participated in the vote. The position under French case law is that contracts entered into with the prior authorisation of the board of directors, but which include the vote of an interested director, may be cancelled if they have prejudicial consequences for the company, irrespective of whether the vote of the interested director was essential to approve the contract or not.[40] Since the sale has been entered into below market value, the contract is detrimental to the interests of the company. Therefore, one might assume that the vote is null and void.

However, before such a conclusion can be drawn, a provision of the Commercial Code must first be considered. Article L 225-42 al 3 of the Commercial Code provides

---

[34] Monetary and Financial Code, Art L 465-1.
[35] Commercial Code, Art L 225-38.
[36] Commercial Code, Art L 225-41.
[37] Commercial Code, Art L 225-40.
[38] Commercial Code, Art L 225-39.
[39] Commercial Code, Art L 225-40.
[40] CA Aix (Court of Appeal of Aix-en-Provence) 15 May 1990, *Dr sociétés* 1991, n° 379; Cass Com (Cour de cassation, Commercial Chamber) 18 October 1994, *RJDA* 12/94 n° 1307.

that the shareholders can ratify the resolution which was not approved or irregularly approved by the board of directors, with a special vote after a report of the statutory auditors has been drawn up.[41] However, in the case of Corporation A, it seems that there was a general meeting and no special report of the shareholders explaining why Director r participated in the vote of the board of directors of Corporation A. As an interested shareholder, Director r would have been prohibited from voting.[42]

Although a French court has discretion whether to annul a detrimental contract or not,[43] the end result is that it would probably declare the contract void. In addition, Director r could be held liable for a breach of her duty of care.

iii. Summary and Conclusion

The type of defence used by Corporation A would probably lead to the directors being sued for damages by minority shareholders acting in the name of Corporation A. The available defences against a takeover in France are legion, but are all subject to the legal requirement to respect the social interests of the company, which generally leads boards of directors in France to be very cautious.

C. Germany[44]

i. Duty of Neutrality

The European Directive on Takeover Bids (hereinafter 'the EU Takeover Directive')[45] was implemented in Germany by the German Takeover Act (WpÜG). There are two versions of the duty of neutrality of the management board of the target company (WpÜG, §§ 33, 33a): the first (WpÜG, § 33) is the default rule which also allows the general meeting to authorise the board to take defensive measures even before the bid has been announced. The second (WpÜG, §§ 33a) applies if the articles of association of the company 'opt in' to this rule, with the main difference being that the general meeting can only authorise the board to take defensive measures after the bid has been announced.[46] Apart from this point of difference, both provisions apply 'in the period from publication of the decision to make an offer to the publication of the results',[47] which is the case in the present scenario. In substance, it seems likely that there would be a violation of these provisions as the management is not allowed to sell a material part of the company (such as the real estate agencies),[48] at least where this was done without the explicit approval of the general meeting.

---

[41] Commercial Code, Art L 225-42 al 3.

[42] Commercial Code, Art L 225-40 al 4.

[43] Cass Com (Cour de cassation, Commercial Chamber), 22 November 1977, *Bull civ IV*, n° 276.

[44] Abbreviated statutes: AktG = Law on Public Companies; BGB = Civil Code; GmbHG = Law on Private Limited Companies; WpHG = Securities Trading Act; WpÜG = Takeover Act.

[45] Directive 2004/25/EC (n 3).

[46] Thus, it is only this second option that strictly follows the EU Takeover Directive.

[47] See ch 5 at II C, below, for further discussion.

[48] See M Schlitt and C Riess, *Münchener Kommentar zum Aktiengesetz, Band 6* (3rd edn, Munich, Beck, 2011) § 33 WpÜG, paras 97–100 (for the term 'material', refer to r 21.1 of the City Code).

A violation of the duty of neutrality would not impact on the validity of the sale as such. It would also not enable the bidder to have its expenses reimbursed. The duty of neutrality is not regarded as a legal rule that directly protects the bidder.[49] It is also debated whether shareholders can have a direct claim against the company.[50] Even if this is the case, a bidder who already holds some shares of the target cannot demand reimbursement of expenses, since these costs are treated merely as collateral damage (*Reflexschaden*).[51]

Directors in breach of the duty of neutrality have to compensate their company for any losses which it sustains (AktG, § 93(2)). In the present case, the undervalue transaction can also be a breach of the general directors' duties, depending on further details as well as the business judgment rule (AktG, § 93(1)).[52] This too would lead to the imposition of an obligation on the directors of the management board to compensate the company (AktG, § 93(2)). Generally, the supervisory board is intended to enforce claims against the management board.[53] The general meeting can compel the supervisory board to assert a claim against the management board (AktG, § 147(1)). Moreover, a minority shareholder with a 1 per cent share of the registered capital or a stock-exchange value of €100,000 has the right to bring an action in its own name (AktG, § 147a).[54]

ii. Further Duties

With respect to Director r, the situation is similar to that in the German law solution to chapter 3. Thus, in accordance with § 181 of the BGB, her vote on the board resolution is treated as invalid.[55] It is also possible that this will translate into a breach of the fiduciary duties by the entire board.[56] In addition, as in Spanish law, there is a separate breach of fiduciary duties on the part of r herself if she did not disclose her conflict of interests to her fellow board members. Thus, she would have to compensate the company for any losses it sustains (AktG, § 93(2)) – which would be relevant if her (invalid) vote was decisive for the sale of the real estate agencies.

More detail is required in order to answer the question of whether the decision of the board of directors to sell the real estate agencies has violated the participation

---

[49] Schlitt and Riess, ibid, § 33 WpÜG, para 248 (no tortious liability based on BGB, § 823(2)).

[50] Schlitt and Riess, ibid, § 33 WpÜG, para 239.

[51] Schlitt and Riess ibid, § 33 WpÜG, para 240.

[52] See ch 2 at II C, above. This case concerned a private company; however, the principles of directors' duties are similar for GmbHs and AGs.

[53] *Cf* BGH (German Federal Supreme Court), BGHZ 135, 244, 253-4 (*ARAG/Garmenbeck*) (applying AktG, § 112).

[54] However, preliminary judicial oversight of the suit is provided for in order to prevent the abusive exercise of the right. Therefore, the court can only permit an action to continue if the minority have previously called on the company to file a suit, damage appears to have done to the company owing to dishonesty or a gross breach of law and there are no reasons which are not in the interests of the company that it ought not to be permitted to continue. If the application for admission is unsuccessful, the minority shareholder(s) must bear the costs. If, instead, the action is permitted but then it is subsequently dismissed, the minority shareholder(s) is/are in principle entitled to a claim for reimbursement of costs (AktG, § 147a(6)).

[55] See also U Hüffer and J Koch, *Aktiengesetz* (12th edn, Munich, Beck, 2016) § 78, para 6 (for the AG, whereas ch 3 at II E, above, concerned a GmbH).

[56] See the solution to ch 3 at II E, above.

rights of the general meeting. The general meeting is vested with the power of sale of the whole assets of the company (AktG, § 179a). Additionally, according to case law, the management board is obliged to refer issues relating to the conduct of business to the general meeting if serious interference with shareholders' rights and interests is likely.[57] This is presumed, particularly on the spinning off of an operation constituting the most valuable part of a company's assets.

Director q has breached the duty of confidentiality imposed on members of the management and supervisory board (AktG, §§ 93(1)(s3), 116). Director q's conduct also constitutes unlawful disclosure of inside information.[58] Moreover, there is a breach of contract on the ground that board members have a contractual relationship with their company. Such breaches of the duty of confidentiality and of insider dealing rules lead to criminal sanctions (AktG, § 404; WpHG, § 119). The predominant view is that the criminal sanction of the breach of a duty of confidentiality (but not the breach of insider dealing law) also constitutes a breach of general tort law (BGB, § 823(2) with AktG, § 404).[59] Damages in tort law do not cover the expenses of formulating the offer since these expenses would also have occurred if the offer had been success-ful. However, the company can use tort law in order to receive compensation for the lost profits of the failed takeover (which may be difficult to establish). The situation is more straightforward in the case of the breach of contract, because here there is a choice between compensation for damages (BGB, § 280) and reimbursement of futile expenses (BGB, § 284).

D. Italy[60]

According to Article 104, paragraph 1 of the Consolidated Law on Finance (CLF), as amended by Legislative Decree no 146/2009, which entered into force on 1 July 2010, the default rule is that if the by-laws of a company do not opt out of the neutrality rule:

> Unless approved by the ordinary or extraordinary shareholders' meeting, depending on the attributable level of decision-making powers, Italian listed companies whose securities are involved in the offering shall abstain from action or transactions that could counteract the achievement of the aims of the offering.

This provision goes on to provide that this abstention obligation applies from the date on which the notice of the bidder's decision to pursue the bid is disclosed to the public and notified to the Italian supervisory authority (Consob). The moment when the

---

[57] BGH (German Federal Supreme Court), BGHZ 83, 122 (Holzmüller).

[58] Arts 14(c), 10 of Regulation (EU) No 596/2014 of the European Parliament and of the Council of 16 April 2014 on market abuse (market abuse regulation) and repealing Directive 2003/6/EC of the European Parliament and of the Council and Commission Directives 2003/124/EC, 2003/125/EC and 2004/72/EC Text with EEA relevance (OJ L173 12/6/2014).

[59] H Schaal, *Münchener Kommentar zum Aktiengesetz, Band 6* (3rd edn, Munich, Beck, 2011) § 404, para 4.

[60] Abbreviations: CC = Italian Civil Code (codice civile); CLF = Consolidated Law on Finance; Spa = public company (*Società per azioni*).

bid has to be disclosed to the public and notified to the Italian supervisory authority is indicated in Article 102, paragraph 1 of the CLF, which states that, as soon as it has been taken, the decision to pursue the takeover has to be notified to Consob and disclosed to the public without delay.[61]

As such, if the sale of the real estate agencies qualifies as a contract that may 'counteract the achievement of the aims of the offering', the directors have concluded a transaction in violation of Article 104 of the CLF and they may be held liable in terms of the usual actions provided by Italian law under Articles 2393 ff of the CC. In particular, in the instant case, the directors may be sued by the company after a resolution of the general meeting or a resolution of at least two-thirds of the members of the board of auditors (CC, Article 2393), by the shareholders representing at least 2.5 per cent of the share capital (CC, Article 2393-*bis*) or by the company's creditors (CC, Article 2394).[62]

Director q probably violated the last paragraph of Article 2391 of the CC, which is a provision generally considered to be the Italian equivalent of the corporate opportunity doctrine. According to this provision, a director is liable to pay damages where the company has suffered loss and that is attributable to the fact that the director has used data, information or business opportunities obtained in connection with his or her office, for his or her own benefit or for that of third parties.[63] In addition, criminal (CLF, Article 184) and administrative sanctions (CLF, Article 187-*bis*) may apply,[64] since the information disclosed to Corporation A falls into the definition of inside information under Article 181 of the CLF, ie:

> [I]nformation of a precise nature which has not been made public relating, directly or indirectly, to one or more issuers of financial instruments or one or more financial instruments and which if it were made public would be likely to have a significant effect on the prices of those financial instruments.

With regard to the position of Director r, who is sitting on both the boards of Corporation A and Corporation C, Article 2391 of the CC will apply.[65] According to this provision, which addresses the problem of the 'interests of directors' in the case of an Spa, directors must inform the board of any personal interest they have in any specific company transaction or any interest in respect of third parties. In addition, in these circumstances, the board resolution must adequately justify the reasons and the suitability of the transaction for the company. If these provisions are violated or if the resolution of the board of directors is adopted with the decisive vote of an interested director, the resolution may be challenged if it is harmful to the company. Finally, pursuant to Article 2391, paragraph 4 of the CC, the director is liable for

---

[61] F Annunziata, *La disciplina del mercato mobiliare* (8th edn, Turin, Giappichelli, 2015) 388 ff.

[62] *Cf* C Mosca, 'Commento *sub* art. 104' in P Marchetti and LA Bianchi (eds), *La disciplina delle società quotate nel testo unico della finanza I* (Milan, Giuffrè, 1999) 259 ff, 305 ff.

[63] M Ventoruzzo, 'Commento *sub* art. 2391' in P Marchetti, LA Bianchi, F Ghezzi and M Notari (eds), *Commentario alla Riforma delle società. Amministratori* (Milan, Giuffrè-Egea, 2005) 423 ff, 490 ff.

[64] Annunziata, *La disciplina del mercato mobiliare* (n 61) 447 ff.

[65] On the conflict of interest of the directors in the Spa, see generally Ventoruzzo, 'Commento *sub* art. 2391' (n 63) 483 ff.

any losses caused to the company attributable to his or her actions in violation of Article 2391 of the CC.[66]

E. The Netherlands[67]

i. Sale of Assets as a Defence Mechanism

The board neutrality rule which stems from the European Takeover Directive[68] was never implemented in Dutch law. The main rules regarding the permissibility of defensive measures against takeovers in the Netherlands have developed over the years in case law. When it comes to defensive measures in general, it is accepted that the board of directors can in principle defend the company against a hostile takeover.[69] Defensive measures are permissible if they are necessary in order to safeguard the continuity of the company and the interests of its stakeholders. Whether or not this is the case will depend on the specific circumstances of the case. Of importance in this respect is whether or not the board could reasonably expect the defence to be necessary in order to maintain the status quo while awaiting the outcome of the negotiations. Furthermore, defensive measures should generally be of a temporary nature. Finally, in order to answer the question whether a defence is justified, it is important that the measures taken are necessary and proportionate to the threat posed.[70]

A situation comparable to that posed in the hypothetical case occurred in the Netherlands in 2007 in the ABN AMRO case.[71] Here, a consortium of three banks was interested in acquiring the Dutch bank ABN AMRO. The board of ABN AMRO strived to protect the company against the takeover by, amongst other matters, entering into a merger with a third party: Barclays. The board of ABN AMRO also decided, after the consortium had announced its intention to acquire the shares in ABN AMRO, to sell off an important part of its assets, namely La Salle, to Bank of America. It was suggested at the time that La Salle constituted an important part of the company from the point of view of the potential acquirers (ie the consortium of three banks).[72] The shareholders of ABN AMRO initiated a legal action against ABN AMRO with regard to the sale of assets by starting an inquiry procedure at the Enterprise Chamber of the Court of Amsterdam.

The role of shareholders in the case of a sale of important assets of a public limited liability company (NV) is regulated by Article 2:107a DCC. This article contains a

---

[66] On damages in case of a violation of Art 2391 of the CC, see generally Ventoruzzo (n 63) 483 ff.

[67] Abbreviations: DCC = Dutch Civil Code; HR = Hoge Raad = Dutch Supreme Court; OK = Ondernemingskamer = Enterprise Chamber; Rb= rechtbank = District Court. An unofficial translation of Dutch company law as incorporated in bk 2 of the Dutch Civil Code can be found at www.dutchcivillaw.com/civilcodebook022.htm.

[68] Art 9 of Directive 2004/25/EC (n 3).

[69] See BF Assink and WJ Slagter, *Compendium Ondernemingsrecht, Deel 1* (Deventer, Kluwer 2013) § 76.5.

[70] HR 18 April 2003, *NJ* 2003/286, with a note by JMM Maeijer (*Rodamco North America, Rodamco North America/VEB*).

[71] See about the ABN AMRO case in English: D Quinn, 'Dutch treat: Netherlands Judiciary only Goes Halfway towards Adopting Delaware Trilogy in Takeover Context' (2008) 41 *Vanderbilt Journal of Translational Law* 1211.

[72] Quinn, ibid.

non-exhaustive list of board decisions that require the approval of the general meeting. According to this article, shareholder approval is required for, amongst other matters, the sale to a third party of the entire enterprise of the company, or most of the enterprise of the company, or the acquisition or disposal of a participating stake in the capital of another legal person to the value of at least one-third of the amount of the assets according to the balance sheet. In the ABN AMRO case the Court concluded that the sale of La Salle could not be classified as a defensive measure to preclude a bid by the consortium. Furthermore, the Supreme Court (Hoge Raad) interpreted Article 2:107 a DCC in a restrictive manner in accordance with the view expressed in the parliamentary history. According to this interpretation, in terms of its size, the sale of La Salle did not fall within the ambit of the decisions requiring shareholder approval as defined in Article 2:107a DCC because it did not meet the required thresholds. In conclusion, the Supreme Court refused to give a broad interpretation to Article 2:107a DCC and therefore ruled that the sale of La Salle fell within the scope of the power conferred in favour of the board.[73]

ii. Liability and Potential Consequences of the Sale Transaction

In Dutch law, there is no general prohibition on a director taking defensive measures after he/she has become aware of an offer or after a public bid has been made. It is however possible that the board must ask for shareholder approval before selling important parts of a company, as discussed in the previous section. Whether or not this is the case in the hypothetical case is difficult to establish and the fact that this question has been subject to court proceedings in the Netherlands demonstrates that it is not easy to determine from the outset. It should be mentioned that even if prior shareholder approval was not requested in a situation where this would have been required, the lack of consent does not affect the power of representation of the directors to legally bind the company vis-a-vis third parties and therefore the validity of the transaction.[74]

If, however, it can be established that the board of directors acted contrary to Article 2:107a DCC and should have asked the shareholders for their consent, this can lead to a breach of directors' duties and therefore impose liability on the directors towards the company on the basis of Article 2:9 DCC and/or to a finding of mismanagement (*wanbeleid*) pursuant to an inquiry procedure. An additional point is that since the sale of the company's assets was below market value, this can mean that the directors acted against the interests of the company which can increase their risk of liability. If the loss sustained by the shareholders simply reflects the loss in the company's share value, the shareholders will generally not be able to raise a direct suit against the directors.[75] The lawsuit would primarily have to be initiated by the company itself as the directors owe their duty to the company and Dutch law does not allow a derivative action. Shareholders can however initiate direct action against the directors on

---

[73] HR 13 July 2007, *JOR* 2007/178 with a note by Nieuwe Weme.
[74] DCC, Art 2:107a-2.
[75] HR 2 December 1994, *NJ* 1995, 288 (*Poot/ABP*); Assink and Slagter, *Compendium Ondernemingsrecht, Deel I* (n 69) § 14.

the basis of tort law if it can be established that those directors have directly violated a specific duty of care (*specifieke zorgvuldigheidsnorm*) owed to those shareholders. However, the mere loss in share value of itself is insufficient.

In principle there will most likely be no scope for liability towards the bidder unless there were prior negotiations between the bidder and the target which had entered such a stage that aborting those negotiations would become unlawful under general rules of contract law.[76] This could lead to pre-contractual liability. However, there is nothing in the hypothetical scenario suggesting that this would be the case.

iii. Position of Mr Q and Ms R

Mr Q has a duty to act in the best interest of the companies to which he has been appointed as a board member. In the event that Mr Q was not delegated by Corporation B to discuss the potential bid with Corporation A, it could be argued that he did not act in the best interests of the latter. A violation of his duties towards the company could lead to directors' liability on the basis of either Article 2:9 DCC or tort law.[77] In both cases, however, serious blame on the part of Mr Q would be required. Mr Q's actions can also qualify as unlawful disclosure of inside information.[78]

With regard to Ms R, if it can be established that she has an actual direct or indirect conflict of interest, she should have abstained from participating in the decision making of the board according to Article 2:129-6 DCC.[79] The fact that she did take part in the decision-making process despite having a conflict of interest, could lead to internal liability towards the company on the basis of either Article 2:9 DCC or tort law.[80] Here too, however, this would require serious blame on the part of the directors.

F. Finland

i. Introduction

Takeover regulation and market practice in Finland have evolved over the past few years. The European Directive on Takeover Bids (hereinafter 'the EU Takeover Directive')[81] was implemented in Finland as of 2006 along with detailed self-regulation on the procedures to be applied in takeover situations. In 2013, significant changes were introduced to Finnish securities laws (including the new Securities Markets Act (the SMA, 746/2012) which was enacted together with related regulations) that also affected takeovers and in 2014 a new takeover code was introduced (the Helsinki Takeover Code). The Helsinki Takeover Code provides for recommended procedures based

---

[76] AS Hartkamp and CH Sieburgh, *Mr. C. Assers Handleiding tot de beoefening van het Nederlands Burgerlijk Recht. 6. Verbintenissenrecht. Deel III. Algemeen overeenkomstenrecht* (Deventer, Kluwer 2014) 197.

[77] DCC, Art 6:162.

[78] Arts 14(c), 10 of Regulation (EU) No 596/2014 on market abuse (n 58).

[79] For the rules on conflicts of interest, see ch 3 at II H, above.

[80] DCC, Art 6:162.

[81] Directive 2004/25/EC (n 3).

on prudent market practice and is largely derived from the application of company and securities law in takeover situations. Pursuant to the SMA, if a bidder chooses not to comply with the code, an explanation must be provided pursuant to the 'comply or explain' formula.

ii. Duty of Neutrality

The duty of neutrality set out in Article 9(2) of the EU Takeover Directive was implemented by chapter 11, section 14 of the SMA. This stipulates that if the board of the target company intends to authorise a share issue or decide on actions and arrangements falling within the board's general competence after a disclosed takeover bid has come to its knowledge, the board is obliged to transfer the matter to the general meeting for a decision.[82] It is noteworthy that most measures falling within the scope of this provision are not typically matters to be resolved at the general meeting. For example, without an existing takeover bid, the asset sale would in many situations fall under the general competence of the board. The rationale for this provision is to transfer the authority for deciding on possible takeover defence measures to the shareholders.[83]

However, the matter need not be transferred to the general meeting if the procedure complies with the general principles of the Companies Act 2006 (CA) and Article 3 of the EU Takeover Directive, in which case, the board is obliged to disclose, without delay, the reason for the non-transfer. Pursuant to the preparatory works of the SMA, the matter may not need to be transferred to the general meeting if there is a weighty reason not to do so. A weighty reason could be, for example, that the takeover bid is not in line with the interests of the shareholders, the tendered consideration is lower than the current market value of the company's shares or the takeover bid is clearly hostile and intended to harm the business activities of the company.[84]

It seems that the takeover bid in question was not particularly hostile and the tendered consideration was slightly above the Finnish market average. It also seems that Corporation A's board had no grounds for the non-transfer after the bid was published. In addition, Corporation A failed to disclose the reasons for the non-transfer as required pursuant to the SMA. Therefore, it seems likely that the directors acted in violation of the aforementioned provisions when resolving on the sale of a significant proportion of Corporation A's assets after Corporation B's bid was made public. Chapter 11, section 14 of the SMA only applies to situations where the bid has been made public and the possible sale of the assets before the bid had been made public should be evaluated on the basis of the general principles of the CA.

The directors may be held liable to the company, a shareholder or a third party, such as the bidder, for damage caused either deliberately or negligently in violation of the provisions of the CA (other than simply the duty of care) or the company's articles

---

[82] SMA, c 11, s 14 and CA, c 6, s 7(2).

[83] Explanatory notes of the CA, Hallituksen esitys 32/2012 vp 143–44 and J Parkkonen and M Knuts, *Arvopaperimarkkinalaki* (Helsinki, Talentum, 2015) 596–99.

[84] Explanatory notes of the CA, Hallituksen esitys 32/2012 vp 143.

of association as discussed in more detail in Chapter 2 at II G above. Further, the directors may also be held liable for damages caused pursuant to the SMA.[85]

iii. Further Duties

The CA does not contain specific provisions relating to the position and duties of the board of the target company in a takeover bid situation. The role of the board must be evaluated in light of the general principles of the CA, setting the interests of the company and its shareholders as the basis for the assessment. However, pursuant to the Helsinki Takeover Code and preparatory works to the CA, when the board of the target company has received information about an intention relating to a public take-over bid that is of a serious nature, its task is to seek the best possible outcome for the shareholders. In order to fulfil its duties, the board should take active steps to ensure that the best possible outcome is achieved for the shareholders. The board should also compare the value of the offer with other potential strategic alternatives available to the company to assess how to maximise shareholder value. Similarly, the board should not reject proposals that could provide value to shareholders. Examining and evaluating these alternatives forms part of the evaluation of the bid.[86]

The sale of Corporation A's assets and, therefore, prematurely disrupting a serious takeover bid may be deemed a breach of the directors' duties. As stated above, in a takeover situation the board is obliged to seek the best possible outcome for the shareholders. It is unlikely that the under-priced asset deal would constitute the best possible outcome given Corporation B's offer of price P with a 40 per cent premium over Corporation A's shares.

It is possible that both Mr q and Ms r breached the provisions on conflicts of interest because they participated in the decision-making process in terms of both of the counterparties to the transactions. As discussed in Chapter 3 at II I above, by virtue of chapter 6, section 4 of the CA, a director is in a conflict-of-interest situation where contracts are entered into (i) between the director and the company and (ii) between the company and a third party, where the director will receive a significant benefit therefrom and that benefit may be contrary to the interests of the company (disqualification). A disqualified director may not take part in the decision-making surrounding the matter in question. Moreover, from the shareholders' point of view it is important in a takeover bid situation that the directors can, unconstrained by undue influences, further the interests of the shareholder collective. As also noted in the explanatory notes to the Helsinki Takeover Code, the duty of care and loyalty requires directors to act in a way that is unconstrained by undue influence in the decision-making process. Acting as the director of both counterparties to a takeover bid may create an assumption that the director in question is not unconstrained by undue influence to participate in the consideration of the transaction in question. In order to comply with the duty of care and loyalty the director may have to consider whether he or she should refrain

---

[85] CA, c 22, s 1.
[86] Explanatory notes of the CA, Hallituksen esitys 41, Helsinki Takeover Code 14 and in legal literature, eg, J Mähönen and S Villa, *Osakeyhtiö I – Yleiset periaatteet* (Helsinki, Talentum, 2015) 384–85.

in any case from participating in the decision-making procedure owing to potential for undue influences.[87] As discussed above, a breach of the explicit provisions of the CA or SMA may lead to directors' liability in damages.

Corporation A's board decided to sell off substantial assets (30 per cent of the real estate agencies) below market value within a week of becoming aware of Corporation B's acquisition plans. Whether that decision has a sound business reason depends on the facts of the case. The reasons of Corporation A's board would be referred to as 'pretexts' under Finnish law. The timing of this sale at undervalue also indicates that it is designed to make a possible takeover less attractive to Corporation B. A sale of assets at undervalue without any sound business rationale is unlawful.[88] Directors q and r can both be held liable for damages arising from the loss.

It is noteworthy that Director q has disclosed confidential information. There are no explicit provisions on confidentiality in the CA and the duty of confidentiality is approached from the viewpoint that directors act as fiduciaries of the company and disclosure of confidential information may constitute a breach of the director's duty of loyalty pursuant to the CA.[89] It is also noteworthy that Mr q's conduct may constitute unlawful disclosure of insider information.[90]

G. Poland

In order to analyse the hypothetical case, one must refer to Polish securities law as well as the Polish Commercial Companies Code (CCC). Moreover, the EU Takeover Directive[91] will be applicable where there is only partial implementation.

i. Duty of Neutrality

Poland makes use of the opt-out from the duty of neutrality rule which is offered by the EU Takeover Directive by granting companies governed by Polish law an option to implement the duty of neutrality into their articles. According to Article 80a, section 1 of the Act of 29 July 2005 on Public Offering, Conditions Governing the Introduction of Financial Instruments to Organised Trading, and the Public Companies (hereinafter 'the Public Offering Act'), the articles of association of a public company may provide that during the tender offer for the sale or exchange of all the remaining shares of the company, the management board and the supervisory board of such company are obliged to obtain the prior consent of the general shareholders' meeting where they propose to take measures whose aim is to thwart the announced tender offer. According to Article 80, section 2 of the Public Offering Act, the obligation referred to in paragraph 1 does not apply to conduct which might lead to the announcement

---

[87] The Helsinki Takeover Code, Recommendation 4; Mähönen and Villa, *Osakeyhtiö I – Yleiset periaatteet* (n 86) 242–47.
[88] CA, c 13, s 1(3).
[89] Mähönen and Villa (n 86) 382–83.
[90] Arts 14(c), 10 of Regulation (EU) No 596/2014 on market abuse (n 58).
[91] Directive 2004/25/EC (n 3).

of a tender offer by another entity in relation to the same shares (the so-called 'white knight' strategy). In the circumstances referred to in section 1, a company's articles of association or an agreement concluded by the company and shareholders must provide that the following are disallowed:

1. limitations on exercising voting rights, defined in the articles of association of the company or any agreement concluded between the company whose shares are subject to the tender offer and shareholders of that company, or in an agreement concluded between such shareholders, provided that the agreement became effective after 21 April 2004; and
2. preference shares as to voting rights.

Polish law applies a subjective test in evaluating whether there has been frustrating action in respect of a takeover bid, in the sense that there is a requirement to prove that the management board was motivated by a desire to take action aimed at warding off the announced tender offer. In other words, it does not suffice to show that a given action may lead to the cancellation of the tender offer, but, instead, real evidence of such a purpose is required. Thus, Poland makes use of the opt-out of the Directive's duty of neutrality rule by granting the companies governed by Polish law the option to implement the duty of neutrality into their articles. There is no information in the hypothetical case as to whether such a neutrality rule has been provided in the articles of association of Corporation A. Therefore, *de lege lata* under Polish law, the directors of Corporation A would not have been prevented from committing the company to the sale of a significant portion of Corporation's A assets simply because they had become aware of Corporation's B takeover offer. However, one must also examine the respective provisions of the CCC in order to examine other regulatory controls on the behaviour of the directors.

ii. Ratification by Shareholders' General Meeting

The transaction covers the sale of 30 per cent of Corporation A's real estate agencies at a price below the average market value. In accordance with Article 393, sections 3 and 4 of CCC, a resolution of the shareholders' general meeting is required for the transfer or lease of an enterprise or an organised part thereof and the establishment of a limited right *in rem* thereon and for an acquisition and transfer of an immovable property, perpetual usufruct or a share in immovable property, except where the company's articles provide otherwise. In accordance with Article 17, section 1 of the CCC, it is provided that where the CCC requires a resolution to be passed by the shareholders' general meeting, or the supervisory board of a company in order for a company to perform such an act in law (eg a resolution), any act in law performed in the absence of the requisite resolution will be treated as null and void. Consent may be granted before a company performs such an act or after such an act has been performed. However, in the case of the latter, the requisite approval must be given no later than two months from the date when the company performed the relevant act. Any consent given after the action is taken operates retroactively from the date of performance of the act in law. Thus, under Polish law, the sale of 30 per cent of the real estate agencies can be treated as the sale of an organised part of the business of

Corporation A, falling under the coverage of Article 393, section 3 of CCC. These provisions significantly limit the scope of freedom of the management board to commit Corporation A to a sale of its assets – the so-called 'crown jewels strategy' – irrespective of the purposes attributed to the transaction in the hypothetical case (ie that the productivity of the agencies was low and Corporation A needed to generate cash for further investments). Since the real estate agencies were sold to one entity in one transaction, this transaction clearly falls within the scope of a 'sale of an organised part of the enterprise' and would require the consent of the shareholders' general meeting, failing which the transaction will be null and void. In addition to the above ground for treating the transaction as a nullity, it could also be considered null and void under Article 393, section 4 of CCC when considered in conjunction with the provisions of Article 17, section 1 of the CCC. Since the transaction covers the sale of real estate agencies, it will involve questions relating to the title to the real estate agencies. Therefore, if Corporation A is the owner of the properties from which the real estate agencies operate – although there is no information in the hypothetical case in this regard – the sale of the properties may be performed only with the consent of the shareholders' general meeting.

iii. Directors' Liability to the Company

The next issue to be addressed is whether the directors of Corporation A bear any liability for the transaction concluded in contravention of such provisions. The answer is that they will be so liable, since in terms of Article 483, section 1 of the CCC, the directors of Corporation A are liable to the company for losses caused which are attributable to their negligence or conduct which is undertaken in contravention of the law or the provisions of the company's articles, unless they can demonstrate that they are not at fault. Since the transaction was in contravention of the law, ie it was taken without the consent of the shareholders in general meeting, the directors can be held liable to Corporation A.

In the light of the facts provided in the hypothetical case, it is highly improbable that the shareholders of Corporation A would have approved the decision of the directors, since we are told that they 'have lost a unique opportunity to sell their shares at a price which they had approved'. Moreover, since a presumption of directors' fault operates, the onus falls on the director to prove an absence of fault. Pursuant to Article 486, section 1 of the CCC, where the company has failed to bring action for relief within one year of the disclosure of the harmful act, any shareholder or person otherwise entitled to participate in the company's profit or in the distribution of assets may file a complaint to make good the damage done to the company.

Moreover, the liability of the directors is unlimited, which means that they will be personally liable for both damages and lost profits. Theoretically, this indicates that the directors' liability to indemnify could cover the actual damage caused to Corporation A, ie the sale of the real estate agencies below the average market value at a discount, as well as any lost profits that these agencies could have generated based upon binding agreements with third parties and lost profits that could have resulted from the takeover, ie profits attributable to the generation of synergies, consolidation etc. However, the final head of claim is particularly controversial, since these profits could be classified by the court as 'hypothetical damages'. The Polish courts usually exclude hypothetical damages from the 'lost profits' category. The main difference is that, whereas there is a probability approaching certainty that the loss would have been sustained in the case of lost profits, with respect to 'hypothetical damage', the probability is definitely smaller to the point that it may be a mere possibility of loss. In other words, it is only some chance of profit.[92] However, before reaching a final conclusion on this matter, one must analyse matters more deeply in the light of all the circumstances of the hypothetical case. For example, notwithstanding the above, the directors of Corporation A may be obliged to restore Corporation A to its previous state, meaning that it may be enjoined to procure the repurchase of the real estate agencies.[93]

One ought to stress that directors may be released from all claims which Corporation A could have against them in respect of the transaction for the sale of the real estate agencies, provided that they obtain an acknowledgement from the shareholders of Corporation A that they have complied with their duties. However, this is unlikely to be applicable in our case for two reasons: first, the shareholders voted in favour of the takeover; and, second, in accordance with Article 487 of the CCC, where an action has been brought by shareholders pursuant to Article 486 of the CCC, those liable to make good the damage caused may not invoke a resolution of the shareholders in general meeting whereby they were granted an acknowledgement from the shareholders that they have fulfilled their duties. Thus, even if the directors somehow obtained the shareholders' approval or acknowledgement, they could not invoke it in proceedings initiated by a shareholder of Corporation A.

iv. Directors' Liability towards the Shareholders of the Company; Fiduciary Duties

The liability of the directors under Article 483, sections 1 and 2 of the CCC constitutes a liability to the company. Another question is the scope of the directors' liability towards the shareholders of the company. One question is whether a shareholder of Corporation A could initiate proceedings against the directors of Corporation A claiming for lost profits, ie the difference between the price that he would have obtained if the takeover had proceeded and the price he actually obtained on the free market for his shares. First, one must examine the concept of the duty of loyalty of directors in Polish legal doctrine.

The duty of loyalty is not *expressis verbis* specified in the Polish CCC: a principle to the effect that directors should run the company in conformity with its interests is not

---

[92] See the ruling of Polish Supreme Court, 24 August 2007 (V CSK 174/07) and the ruling of Court of Appeals in Katowice, 17 January 2001 (I ACa 1094/00). See also Z Radwański in *System prawa cywilnego. Prawo zobowiązań — część ogólna pod red. Z. Radwańskiego, t. III, cz. I* (Wrocław, Zakład Narodowy im Ossolińskich, 1981) 280; W Czachórski, *Zobowiązania, Zarys wykładu* (Warsaw, LexisNexis, 2009) 78.

[93] See under Art 474 of the Commercial Code (the predecessor of Art 483 of the Commercial Companies Code): A Szajkowski in S Sołtysiński, A Szajkowski and J Szwaja, *Kodeks handlowy, Komentarzt. t. II*, wyd. 2 (Warsaw, CH Beck, 1998) 1228; and J Frąckowiak in J Frąckowiak, A Kidyba, K Kruczalak, W Pyzioł and I Weiss, *Kodeks handlowy, Komentarz* (Warsaw, Wydawnictwo Prawnicze PWN, 1998), note 2 to Art 474 of the Commercial Code.

specifically provided for in Polish law. Nevertheless, it is argued that such a principle exists and can be implied from various provisions of the CCC.[94] Moreover, in order to justify the existence of a duty of loyalty in Polish jurisprudence, numerous commentators invoke Article 10(a)2 and 21q(2) of the draft Fifth European Directive, which provides that all members of the management board should perform their duties in the best interests of the company as an example of appropriate corporate governance standards.[95] However, the question arises as to how the concept of 'interests of the company' should be understood. There is no definition of this notion in legislation. However, some explanation of this notion can be found in the Code of Best Practice for Public Companies dated 2005 (hereinafter 'the 2005 Code of Best Practice').[96] According to sections 32 and 33 of the 2005 Code of Best Practice:

> bearing in mind the interests of the company, the management board sets forth the strategy and the main objectives of the company's operations, and submits them to the supervisory board ... The management board is liable for the implementation and performance of the same in accordance with legal regulations and best practice. In the determination of the interests of the company, one should keep in mind the justifiable long-term perspective and interests of the shareholders, creditors, employees of the company and other entities and persons cooperating with the company, as well as the interests of the local community.

It seems that unless the directors of Corporation A prove that they acted in the interests of the company, ie the interests of one of the above-mentioned group of stakeholders, a presumption operates to the effect that they failed to advance the interests of the company on the ground that they acted against the interests of its shareholders. The directors of Corporation A blocked the takeover which would have brought premiums to the shareholders. Therefore, it can be argued that a director cannot simply block the takeover and instead, in order to justify the adoption of

---

[94] The duty of loyalty principle is usually implied from the CCC, Arts 377, 379, s 1 and 380, s 1. Art 377 of the CCC states that:

> 'in the event of a conflict of interest between the company and a management board member, or the member's spouse, relations and in-laws within the second degree and persons with whom the member has a personal relationship, the management board member shall abstain from participating in deciding such matters and he may request that this be recorded in the minutes.

Meanwhile, Art 379, s 1 of the CCC stipulates that:

> in a contract between the company and a management board member, including a dispute with a management board member, the company shall be represented by the supervisory board or by an attorney appointed under a resolution of the general meeting.

Finally, Art 380, s 1 of the CCC directs that:

> the management board member shall not, without the consent of the company, involve himself in a competitive business or participate in a competitive partnership or company, whether as partner in such partnership or as member of a body of such company, nor shall he be involved with another competitive legal person by sitting on its body. This prohibition shall apply equally to having interests in a competitive company, in the event that the management board member should hold 10 per cent or more shares in it or have the right to appoint at least one member of the management board.

[95] Although the draft Fifth European Directive was never adopted as a part of the *acquis communautaire* owing to disputes about employee co-determination, some commentators apply a functional approach and believe that the duty to act in the best interests of the company results from the nature of the company itself and that the draft of the Fifth European Directive serves as an example of this.

[96] Available at www.ecgi.org/codes/code.php?code_id=165.

anti-takeover tactics, they must show that they had reasonable grounds to think that the takeover amounted to a real threat to the interests of the company by virtue of the fact that a given shareholder would lose out therefrom, and their reaction must be commensurate to the threat posed.[97] However, there is insufficient information in the hypothetical case to suggest that Corporation B had any negative intent with regard to Corporation A. As such, the likelihood that the directors of Corporation A would be able to justify their actions in terms of the aforementioned provisions is particularly slim.

In Polish doctrine, the concept of the idea of the 'interests of the company' has been explicitly expressed in the Code of Best Practice for Stock Exchange (WSE) Listed Companies 2016 (hereinafter 'the 2016 Code of Best Practice'),[98] which replaced the ambiguous versions of 2010 and 2012. According to the 2016 Code of Best Practice:

> a listed company is managed by its management board, whose members act in the interest of the company and are responsible for its activity. The management board is responsible among others for the company's leadership, engagement in setting and implementing its strategic objectives, and ensuring the company's efficiency and safety. A company is supervised by an effective and competent supervisory board. Supervisory board members act in the interest of the company and follow their independent opinion and judgement. The supervisory board in particular issues opinions on the company's strategy, verifies the work of the management board in pursuit of defined strategic objectives and monitors the company's performance. However, it has to be pointed out that the above 'definition' does not explain 'to whom' the duty of loyalty or the duty of care are owned.

The detailed provisions of the Best Practice follow the 'comply or explain' approach. Consistent non-compliance with a principle or an incidental breach require the company to immediately report pursuant to § 29.3 of the Exchange Rules. It should be noted that the company's explanations of the reasons and circumstances of non-compliance should be sufficiently exhaustive to provide genuine information on the reasons for the non-compliance and to allow for an assessment of the company's position on compliance with the principles of the Best Practice[99]

We have established that the directors of Corporation A owed contractual obligations towards Corporation A, resulting from the nature of the corporation itself. However, a remaining question concerns the obligations which they owe to

---

[97] Comparative argument from famous case of *Unocal Corp v Mesa Petroleum Co*, 493 A 2d 946 (Del 1985) 947.

[98] Available at www.ecgi.org/codes/documents/poland_best_practice_for_GPW_listed_companies_2016.pdf.

[99] Ibid, 2–3. See, eg, the announcement of Orlen, an oil company listed on the Warsaw Stock Exchange, as follows:

> As a public company, listed on the Warsaw Stock Exchange, we comply with the 2016 Code of Best Practice for WSE Listed Companies … If any rule from the code of the 2016 Code of Best Practice for WSE Listed Companies is breached by us, we will publish a regulatory announcement regarding that issue. Moreover, in accordance with the Polish regulations on capital markets and the Rules of the Warsaw Stock Exchange, every year we will publish a report on PKN ORLEN compliance with corporate governance rules. This report is an appendix to the Management Board report on the operations of the Company for the certain financial year, ie it is a part of the annual financial statement.

Corporation A's shareholders. One ought to mention at this juncture that all relations between stakeholders in the company can be characterised as a 'nexus of contracts' as Easterbrook and Fischel described in their landmark book *The Economic Structure of Corporate Law*.[100] One can question whether this theory is reflective of the position in the case of the Polish regulation of corporations. At first glance, the thesis is very attractive. One could argue that it is indeed the case that within a public company, different contractual relations are established between stakeholders, which have the act of incorporation of the company as their source. However, there is no well-established doctrine in Poland which governs such relationships. Thus, the likelihood that any lawsuit raised on the basis of such a theory would be successful is particularly low. Moreover, even in circumstances where supervisory board members are elected by different interest groups, it is argued that such members still remain representatives of the company rather than representatives of the constituency that voted for their election.[101] In Poland, there is a strong tradition of characterising the duties of managers as the relationship between managers and the company, with an obligation imposed on the managers to act in best interests of the company.

It seems, however, that there are grounds for constructing the contractual relationship directly between the members of the management board and supervisory board and the same shareholders. This is so because of a need to fill the notion of the 'interests of the company' with specific content, which will usually be treated as the interests of shareholders.[102] It should be acknowledged that even if the management board or the supervisory board of the company is appointed by a third party or shareholder entitled personally, it must be assumed that this does not change the parties to the fiduciary contract. In addition, in this case, the parties to such an agreement are all shareholders. As a result of the delegation provided for in the articles of association shareholders agree to conclude an agreement with a member of the management board or supervisory board by a representative (eg a third party or a particular shareholder individually authorised). Thus, a third person or shareholder individually authorised may not recommend the member of the management board (or supervisory board) to act solely in the interests of that person/shareholder.[103]

---

[100] FH Easterbrook and DR Fischel, *The Economic Structure of Corporate Law* (Cambridge, MA, Harvard University Press, 1991). See further K Szmid, *Natura spółki akcyjnej jako delimitacja zasady swobody umów w prawie polskim i amerykańskim* (Warsaw, CH Beck, 2015).

[101] According to Art 385, s 3 of the CCC, at the request of shareholders who represent no less than one-fifth of the company's initial capital, the supervisory board must be elected at the next shareholders' general meeting by a vote held by the separate groups, even if the company's articles provide for a different mechanism for appointing the supervisory board.

[102] The Supreme Court (see judgment dated 21 December 2015, IV CK 311/05, unpublished) has expressed the view that members of the supervisory board appointed following the implementation of individual rights of the shareholder (Art 354, s 1 of the CCC) or following the selection by separate groups (Art 385, s 3 of the CCC) are direct representatives of the electors. If, however, they are elected by the general assembly following the standard procedure provided for in Art 385, s 1 of the CCC, members of the supervisory board must perform their functions on behalf of all shareholders. The aforementioned decision of the Supreme Court can be read as an attempt to construct a corporate fiduciary duty directly between the shareholders and members of the supervisory board.

[103] See further Szmid, *Natura spółki akcyjnej jako delimitacja zasady swobody umów w prawie polskim i amerykańskim* (n 100) 285–90.

v. Liability of q and r

They could also raise an *ex delicto* lawsuit based on Article 415 of the Polish Civil Code, which states that any person who has caused damage to another is obliged to redress it. The shareholders will have to prove the illegality of the directors' action, that they are in contravention of binding rules of law and that they are at fault. In the case of liability based on Article 415 of the Polish Civil Code, there is no presumption of guilt as in Article 483 of the CCC.

The final issue to address is the liability of q and r in terms of the fiduciary duties which they owe to Corporations A and B or their shareholders. As described above, directors are fiduciaries of the company and they must act in the best interests of the company. According to Article 377 of the CCC, in the event of a conflict of interest between the company and a management board member, or the member's spouse, relations and in-laws within the second degree and persons with whom the member has a personal relationship, the management board member must abstain from participating in a vote on a resolution in relation to such matters and he or she may request that this be recorded in the minutes. With regard to r, it is evident from the case that she is contemporaneously a director of both Corporations A and C. She had an obvious conflict of interest and should have abstained from participating in a vote on a resolution in relation to such anti-takeover action, namely the sale of real estate agencies at a price below the average market value. Notwithstanding the fact that she breached her obligation based on Article 377 of the CCC, which will result in the imposition of liability under Article 483 of the CCC, she also breached the duty of loyalty which she owes to Corporation A. She did not act in the best interests of Corporation A since the sale was below the average market value and she would find it difficult to show that she acted in such a way in order to protect the other interests of the company as was discussed previously. One must recall that the directors of Corporation A would not have reasonable grounds to believe that Corporation B would act to the detriment of Corporation A.

With regard to q, it is evident from the case that he is contemporaneously a director of both Corporation A and Corporation B. He undoubtedly breached his duties to Corporation B by informing Corporation A's board about Corporation B's intentions to buy Corporation A's shares and by taking part in the decision to sell the real estate agencies of Corporation A in order to block the takeover, both of which might suffice to impose liability under Article 483 of the CCC. The behaviour of q caused damage to Corporation B, resulting in it incurring a large amount of expenditure in formulating the offer (legal costs, publicity etc).

Directors q's conduct also constitutes an unlawful act of unfair competition under the Unfair Competition Act 1993 (UCA). An act of unfair competition is to transfer, disclose or use someone else's secret information, or purchase them from an unauthorised person, if it threatens or violates the interests of the entrepreneur. The company's secret is understood to be any technical, technological, organisational, business or other information undisclosed to the public and having a commercial value, which an entrepreneur has taken the necessary steps to maintain its confidentiality (Article 11 of the UCA). Under Article 18 of the UCA in connection with Article 415 of the CC, Corporation B will be entitled to sue q for damages for the lost profits of the failed takeover (which, however may be difficult to establish as the German solution to this scenario explains). Director q will be also subject to penal responsibility either under Article 22 of the UCA,[104] Article 266 of the Polish Penal Code or Article 180 of the Act on Trading in Financial Instruments dated 2005.[105] Director q's behaviour also constitutes unlawful disclosure of inside information under EU law (as discussed for the other Member States in this chapter).

H. Latvia

i. The Sale of the Agencies

The European Directive on Takeover Bids (hereinafter 'the EU Takeover Directive')[106] is implemented in Latvia by Chapter V, Sections 65 to 83 of the Financial Instrument Market Law.[107] Accordingly, takeover offers for the acquisition of shares in public limited liability companies which are traded on a regulated market may be either compulsory or voluntary. Section 66 of the Financial Instrument Market Law provides for compulsory offers, which may only be exercised by the limited class of persons described therein.

Voluntary takeover offers are regulated by section 67 of the Financial Instruments Market Law and may be used by anyone. The person offering the agencies for sale in the present case is Corporation A. As a public limited liability company, Corporation A may be represented by the board of directors (Commercial Code, section 303(1)). However, the board of directors of Corporation A consists of several directors. The directors may only jointly represent the company (Commercial Code, section 303(1)), unless the company's articles/by-laws prescribe separate rights of representation. In the hypothetical case, it is not clear whether such single representation rights are provided for in the company's articles/by-laws.

On the one hand, according to the Commercial Code, a board of directors has the right to take decisions if more than one-half of the members of the board of directors take part in the meeting of the board of directors (Commercial Code, section 310(1)). If the board of directors has fewer members than provided for in the company's articles, the quorum is determined according to the number of members of the board of directors specified in the company's articles (Commercial Code, section 310(1)). Therefore, if the entire board of directors of Corporation A has voted in favour of the sale and purchase transaction, all members of the board are jointly liable for losses that

---

[104] Whoever, contrary to its duty in relation to the entrepreneur, reveals another person or uses in his own business a trade secret if it causes serious harm to the entrepreneur, is subject to a fine, or imprisonment for up to 2 years.

[105] Whoever, contrary to the prohibition referred to in Art 156, para 2 of point 1 of the Act on Trading in Financial Instruments, reveals confidential information, is subject to a fine of 2,000,000 zł and/or imprisonment up to 3 years.

[106] Directive 2004/25/EC (n 3).

[107] Latvijas Vēstnesis 175 (2490), 11 December 2003. An English translation of the Act is available at www.fktk.lv/en/law/financial-instruments-market/laws.html.

they have caused to Corporation A (Commercial Code, sections 169(2), 310(1), (2)). On the other hand, there is a general prohibition of competition in relation to members of the board of directors of a company stated in the Commercial Code: section 171(1) provides that a member of the board of directors may not, without the approval of the general meeting of shareholders:

(1) be a general partner in a partnership, or a shareholder with supplementary liability in a limited liability or public company which is engaged in the same field of commercial activities as the company;

(2) conclude transactions in the same field of commercial activities as the company in his or her own name or in the name of a third person; and

(3) be a member of the board of directors of another company which is engaged in the same field of commercial activities as the company, except in cases when the company and the other company are part of the same group of companies.

If a member of the board of directors violates the provisions of section 171(1) of the Commercial Code, the company is entitled to request compensation for losses.

Therefore, if the entire board of directors of Corporations A and C voted in favour of this sale and purchase transaction, but r violated the prohibition on competition and the other board members acted as honest and careful managers (Commercial Code, section 169(3)), only r can be held liable.

One must also consider whether the takeover offer was discussed by the general meeting of Corporation A, since section 77(5) of the Financial Instrument Market Law provides that:

[F]rom the moment when the offeror notifies the board of directors and the supervisory board of a target company about its intention to make a voluntary share buy-back offer until the expiration date of the offer, the executive board and the council shall obtain the prior authorisation of the shareholders' meeting in order to carry out activities that may frustrate the success of the buyout offer. Such authorisation is not necessary, where alternative share buyout offers are sought.

The question of whether the sale of the agencies has been carried out in accordance with the above provision requires additional information as to whether both the executive board of directors and the supervisory board of Corporation A were provided with the takeover offer.

The subsequent section 77(6) of the Financial Instrument Market Law addresses the period that precedes the knowledge of the target's boards about the takeover offer. It provides that the approval of the shareholders' meeting is necessary 'in respect of any decision that is not intrinsic to the normal course of the target company's business and whose implementation may frustrate the share buy-back offer'. It is submitted that it is doubtful whether the sale of the agencies constitutes a transaction outside the scope of Corporation A's ordinary course of business. It concerned only 30 per cent of the agencies and thus did not constitute the main part of the company's assets. Such business is unlikely to qualify as the restructuring or reorganisation of the company or its line of trade. The sale of assets is part of the business of most public limited liability companies. Decisions in connection with such transactions are therefore not outside the scope of management required for the pursuit of the normal course of the business of the company. However, if the transaction was classified as constituting business outside the normal course of the company's trade, this would have required the approval of the shareholders' meeting. Nonetheless the breach of this requirement would not render the transaction invalid. It may, however, result in liability for damages.

ii. Liability for Damages

a. Liability towards Corporation A

Liability could arise in respect of a violation of a contractual or statutory obligation owed towards Corporation A if such breach resulted in Corporation A incurring losses. According to Latvian commercial law, the members of the board of directors are liable for losses that they have caused to the company. In particular, three standard criteria must be satisfied by Corporation A in order to claim compensation (or security): losses, whether already arisen or anticipated; performance or non-performance of the member of the board; and a causal link between the loss and performance or non-performance of the member of the board.

The duty to obtain the consent of the meeting of shareholders exists solely to protect the interests of the shareholders. This is also in line with the purpose of this provision, which is designed to protect the economic interests of the shareholders in the event of a conflict of interests. The directors are under an obligation to inform of such conflicts of interests (Commercial Code, section 309(3)). Since r was acting for both parties in the transaction, this constitutes a conflict of interest and results in a violation of her duties as a director (see chapter 3, above). A claim for liability, however, also requires losses resulting from such violation of duties to be demonstrated on the part of Corporation A. Since no information on such damage or loss exists, a claim for liability cannot be raised.

b. Liability towards the Shareholders of Corporation A

With regard to the shareholders, a liability claim may be based on section 1772 of the Civil Code, which regulates the criteria for a claim for lost profits or a decrease in their anticipated profits. However, it is doubtful whether the requisite causal link between the breach of a contractual or statutory duty and losses is shown in the present case. The shareholders' losses have not been caused by the violation of the requirement to obtain the approval of the meeting of shareholders, but arise as a result of the sale of the agencies, because in theory such sale could have taken place even if shareholder approval would have been attained. In this case, the takeover would likewise not have taken place. For a valid liability claim, it would on the contrary have to be established that approval would with certainty have been refused.

c. Liability towards Corporation B

The criteria for a claim for liability (Civil Code, section 1784) are not met. No violation of the contractual or statutory obligations owed towards Corporation B on the part of the directors can be established in the present case. Their conduct is acceptable in terms of ordinary business standards.

d. Liability of r and q towards Corporation A and its Shareholders Based on a Violation of Fiduciary Duties

As the case in chapter 3 above, r's conduct constitutes a violation of the duties of loyalty and to avoid a conflict of interests which she owes as a director to Corporation A. However, it is doubtful whether any resulting losses can be established to justify a liability claim (on which, see above).

e. Liability of q towards Corporation A and its Shareholders Based on a Violation of Insider Trading Rules

Q may be liable towards Corporation A and B for a violation of the prohibition on the use of inside information in terms of section 193(2) of the Criminal Law and section 84(1) of the Financial Instrument Market Law and section 1784 of the Civil Code. However, as noted above, one would be required to establish losses on the part of Corporation A and B, which arise as a direct result of such misuse of information.

I. The UK[108]

i. General Introduction

The EU Takeover Directive[109] was implemented by Part 28 (sections 942–92 of the CA 2006) of the CA 2006. In terms of sections 942(1) and 943(1) of the CA 2006, the Panel on Takeovers and Mergers (hereinafter the Panel) has the power to make rules which give effect to certain articles of the EU Takeover Directive.[110] The Panel does so by promulgating, modifying and enforcing the City Code, which sets out general principles and specific rules.[111] The scope of application of the City Code is wider

---

[108] Abbreviations: CA 2006 (the Companies Act 2006); FSMA 2000 (the Financial Services and Markets Act 2000); FCA (the Financial Conduct Authority); Model Articles (Model articles of association of private companies limited by shares (in reg 2 of and sch 1 to the Companies (Model Articles) Regulations 2008, SI 2008/3229), private companies limited by guarantee (in reg 3 of and sch 2 to the Companies (Model Articles) Regulations 2008, SI 2008/3229) and public limited companies (in reg 4 of and sch 3 to the Companies (Model Articles) Regulations 2008, SI 2008/3229)); Listing Rules (the Listing Rules of the FCA (https://www.handbook.fca.org.uk/handbook/LR/)); City Code (the Takeover Code issued by the Panel on Takeovers and Mergers (www.thetakeoverpanel.org.uk/wp-content/uploads/2008/11/code.pdf?v=2May2017)).

[109] Directive 2004/25/EC (n 3).

[110] In particular, Arts 3(1) (general principles regarding takeovers), 4(2) (establishment of supervisory authority), 5 (protection of minority shareholders, the mandatory bid and the equitable price), 6(1)–(3) (information concerning bids), 7–9 (time for acceptance, disclosure of all information and documents and neutrality rule) and 13 (rules governing the conduct of takeover bids). The City Code predates the coming into force of the EU Takeover Directive and was adapted in May 2006 to comply with it.

[111] Twelfth edition from September 2016, available at www.thetakeoverpanel.org.uk/wp-content/uploads/2008/11/code.pdf?v=2May2017.

than the EU Takeover Directive. Article 1(1) of the EU Takeover Directive applies to takeover bids for the securities of companies governed by the laws of Member States, where all or some of those securities are admitted to trading on a regulated market in one or more Member States. However, the City Code's application is not restricted to companies whose securities are traded on a regulated market. It also covers private companies whose securities have been traded on exchanges such as the London Stock Exchange (eg, where the private company's shares were admitted to the Official List)[112] or multilateral trading facilities in the UK at any time during the 10 years prior to the date of announcement of the proposed takeover bid, a possible offer, or the point in time at which the directors of the target company have reason to believe that a bona fide offer from a bidder might be imminent.[113]

The law and regulation of takeovers in the UK straddles both company law and securities law. Takeovers are specifically regulated by UK company law in Part 28 of the CA 2006. Moreover, takeovers are regulated on the basis of the self-regulatory system administered by the Panel within a formal regulatory structure set out in sections 942–65 of the CA 2006. The City Code supplements the terms of Part 28 of the CA 2006 and both must be read together in order to appreciate the full extent of the regulatory landscape in the UK.

Article 9(2) of the EU Takeover Directive stipulates when the board of an offeree company becomes subject to the duty of neutrality. As articulated in the Spanish solution above,[114] the Takeover Directive provides Member States with two possible means of implementing the neutrality rule.[115] By virtue of Rule 21 of the City Code, in the UK, the duty of neutrality applies with effect from the moment that the directors of the target company have reason to believe that a bona fide offer from a bidder 'might be imminent'. Thus, the embargo on defensive tactics without prior shareholder approval begins before the takeover offer of the bidder is made public.[116]

ii. Director q's Liability

a. Breach of the Neutrality Rule in the City Code

Rule 21 of the City Code provides that the board of an offeree company must not engage in any of the following activities without the prior approval of the offeree company's shareholders in general meeting:

> (a) ... any action which may result in any offer or bona fide possible offer being frustrated or in shareholders being denied the opportunity to decide on its merits; or (b) ... (iv) sell, dispose of or acquire, or agree to sell, dispose of or acquire, assets of a material amount ...

---

[112] The FCA maintains the 'Official List', which is a list of shares and securities listed on the London Stock Exchange (LSE). In this capacity, the FCA is referred to as the UK Listing Authority (UKLA).

[113] See A3–A4 of the City Code for further details of the types of private company to which the City Code applies.

[114] See II A, above.

[115] Member States may prohibit the board of a target firm from adopting defensive measures without prior shareholder approval (i) as soon as the bidder's bid is made public or (ii) at an earlier stage, namely as soon as the board of the offeree company becomes aware that the bid is imminent.

[116] This can be contrasted with Spain, Germany and Italy, where the neutrality rule applies from the moment the bid is made public. See III, below.

Guidance Note 2 to Rule 21 of the City Code directs that 'the Panel will normally consider relative values of 10 per cent or more as being of a material amount'. Since Corporation A's line of business is real estate and it has decided to sell 30 per cent of its real estate agencies to Corporation C without obtaining prior shareholder approval after the directors had become aware of the impending takeover bid albeit before the takeover bid was publicised, it is assumed that this is very likely to represent the sale of a 'material amount' of its assets. In terms of Rule 21 of the City Code, this is unlawful. By virtue of paragraph A14 of the City Code,[117] the Panel has the power to order 'a person' to pay compensation to the shareholders or former shareholders of the offeree company for a breach of the neutrality rule in Rule 21 of the City Code.[118] However, any aggrieved shareholder or company (such as Corporation B) will not be entitled to sue the offeree company or the directors of the offeree company for a breach of Rule 21 of the City Code.[119] Thus, as a director of Corporation A, q is unlikely to be civilly liable to the shareholders of Corporation A, Corporation A itself or Corporation B for a breach of Rule 21 of the City Code.

b. Breach of the Listing Rules

Corporation A is a listed plc and so must comply with the Listing Rules drawn up by the FCA in terms of sections 73A and 74 of the FSMA 2000. The FCA maintains the 'Official List', which is a list of shares and securities listed on the LSE. Listing Rule 10.5.1 requires a listed company to (i) send an explanatory circular to its shareholders and obtain their prior approval in general meeting[120] for a Class 1 transaction and (ii) ensure that any agreement which captures a Class 1 transaction is made conditional on prior shareholder approval being obtained. It is submitted that the sale of the real estate agencies to Corporation C amounts to a Class 1 transaction in terms of the tests set out in Listing Rule 10.2 and the Gross Assets Test 2R and 3G in Listing

---

[117] See the City Code at section '10 (c) Compensation rulings'.

[118] This is notwithstanding the provisions of s 954 of the CA 2006. The most that the Panel may do is to (a) take enforcement action against the offeree company or board of directors of the offeree company by levying penalties where it has, or they have, breached the City Code (CA 2006, s 952(1) and see A14 of the City Code at section '10(b) Compliance Rulings') or (b) make an application to the court where a person (ie the offeree company or the directors of the offeree company) has contravened a requirement imposed by or under the City Code duly enjoining the court to make such order as it thinks fit to secure compliance with the relevant provision of the City Code (CA 2006, s 955(1) and see A14 of the City Code at section '10(d) Enforcement by the Courts'). However, as noted in PL Davies and S Worthington, *Gower's Principles of Modern Company Law* (10th edn, London, Sweet & Maxwell, 2016) para 28–9 at pp 927–28, resort to the aforementioned (a) and (b) on the part of the Panel is likely to be rare indeed.

[119] Section 956(1) of the CA 2006 directs that a breach of the City Code does not give rise to civil liability for breach of statutory duty. It is also worth noting that the shareholders of the offeree company or Corporation B have no power to challenge the sale of the real estate agencies to Corporation C, since s 956(2) of the CA 2006 stipulates that any breach of the City Code 'does not make any transaction void or unenforceable or (subject to any provision made by rules) affect the validity of any other thing'.

[120] The general rule in UK law is that the sale of the entire (or any) assets and undertaking of a company does not need to be approved by the shareholders in advance as the power to take such a decision is within the remit of the board of directors in terms of the Model Articles of a public limited company (see para 3 of and sch 3 to the Companies (Model Articles) Regulations 2008, SI 2008/3229).

Rule 10 Annex 1.[121] The hypothetical case is clear to the effect that the shareholders of Corporation A did not pass a resolution approving the sale of the agencies and so Corporation A has breached Listing Rule 10.5.1.

In terms of section 91 of the FSMA 2000, the FSA has no power to impose a penalty upon a director such as q for a breach of the Listing Rules unless he was knowingly concerned in the contravention. From the information provided in the hypothetical case, it is difficult to say whether q was 'knowingly concerned' in Corporation A's failure to comply with Listing Rule 10.5.1. Nevertheless, a contravention by Corporation A of the Listing Rules or the imposition of a penalty by the FCA upon q would be insufficient in itself to make q civilly liable to Corporation A, the shareholders of Corporation A or Corporation B. Further, as noted in the case of *Hall v Cable and Wireless plc*,[122] if the shareholders of Corporation A raise a civil claim against Corporation A for breach of the Listing Rules, this will be unsuccessful.

c. Breach of Duty of Care, Skill and Diligence

As mentioned in the UK solution to chapter 2, above,[123] as a director of Corporation A, q is under a duty to exercise reasonable care, skill and diligence in terms of section 174 of the CA 2006. Whether q's (i) breach of the duty of neutrality or (ii) failure to ensure that Corporation A complied with Listing Rule 10 amount to a failure on the part of q to comply with the section 174 duty requires a mixed objective and subjective assessment to be made of his conduct.[124] By selling the real estate agencies and breaching the Rule 21 duty of neutrality and Listing Rule 10, it is submitted that a court would rule that q's conduct fell below the standard of general knowledge, skill and experience that may reasonably be expected of a person carrying out the functions carried out by q in relation to Corporation A, ie the minimum standard that would be reasonably expected from a director of a listed plc such as Corporation A in the UK on the basis of an objective assessment. Since the section 174 duty to exercise reasonable care, skill and diligence is owed to Corporation A in terms of section 170(1) of the CA 2006, Corporation A will be entitled to sue q for losses which it sustains as a result of q's breach of duty which fall within the scope of the director's duty of care.[125] However, it is unlikely that Corporation A will be minded to take such legal action against q. In   the absence of special circumstances,[126] the shareholders of Corporation A or

---

[121] That is to say, that since it is stipulated that the real estate agencies of Corporation A sold to Corporation C represent 30% of the total of its estate agencies, it is assumed that this amounts to a sale of assets in excess of 25% of the total non-current assets, plus the total current assets, of Corporation A.

[122] *Hall v Cable and Wireless plc* [2009] EWHC 1793 (Comm), [2011] BCC 543 (QB) 548–49 (Teare J) and *Brown v Innovatorone plc* [2012] EWHC 1321 (Comm) at [1268]–[1276] (Hamblen J).

[123] See ch 2 at II I, above.

[124] For references, see ibid.

[125] *South Australian Asset Management Corporation v York Montague Ltd* [1997] AC 191 (HL) 214 (Lord Hoffmann).

[126] See, eg, *Heron International Ltd v Lord Grade* [1983] BCLC 244 (CA) and *Dawson International plc v Coats Paton plc* [1988] 4 BCC 305.

Corporation B will have no general right of action against q since q's duties are not owed to them individually.[127]

d. Breach of Fiduciary Duties

Section 171(1) of the CA 2006 stipulates that a director must only exercise powers for the purposes for which they are conferred. It is well established that directors may not use their powers for improper purposes and this may include using them as a means of initiating defensive tactics to thwart a takeover bid. For example, in the case of *Hogg v Cramphorn Ltd*,[128] where the directors of a target company issued shares in order to frustrate a bid, it was held that they were in breach of duty since they had exercised the power to issue shares for the purpose of maintaining their control over the affairs of the company. The decision of the Supreme Court in *Eclairs Group Ltd. v JKX Oil & Gas Plc*[129] is a similar case, where the directors restricted the voting and alienation rights of certain shareholders because they were fearful of those shareholders launching a 'corporate raid'. In the case of *Howard Smith Ltd v Ampol Petroleum Ltd*,[130] Lord Wilberforce held that it is necessary to assess the nature of the power exercised in order to discover whether it was exercised for an improper purpose. His Lordship also clarified that whether the power was exercised for a proper purpose is to be determined objectively by the court.[131] Here, the directors of Corporation A exercised the power to sell the assets of Corporation A, which is vested in them on a general basis by virtue of Regulation 3 of the Model Articles.[132] In light of *Hogg v Cramphorn Ltd* and *Howard Smith Ltd v Ampol Petroleum Ltd*, the key issue is whether the directors exercised the power of sale with the primary purpose of warding off Corporation B's takeover bid. From the facts of the hypothetical case, it would appear that the frustration of the takeover bid was the most obvious cause of the sale of the real estate agencies, since it is stated in the hypothetical case that the reasons articulated[133] for the sale were in fact pretexts. For that reason, it is submitted that director q is in breach of the section 171(1) duty which is owed to Corporation A,[134] but again, it is doubtful whether Corporation A will seek to take legal action against director q for breach of the section 171 duty. However, the duty is not owed to the

[127] However, the shareholders of Corporation A or Corporation B (if Corporation B is a shareholder of Corporation A) may have rights as shareholders to challenge q's breach of duty in terms of a derivative claim or proceedings, albeit that such a form of legal action is unlikely to be successful in the case of a public limited company such as Corporation A. See ch 10 at II A, below for further details on this issue.
[128] *Hogg v Cramphorn Ltd* [1967] Ch 254 (Ch).
[129] [2015] UKSC 71; [2016] 1 BCLC 1.
[130] *Howard Smith Ltd v Ampol Petroleum Ltd* [1974] AC 821 (PC) 835F–H (Lord Wilberforce).
[131] Ibid, 832F–H (Lord Wilberforce). See also *Cayne v Global Natural Resources plc* (unreported, Chancery Division, 12 August 1982) (Sir Robert Megarry VC). However, *cf* this with the opinion of Lord Sumption in *Eclairs Group Ltd. v JKX Oil & Gas Plc* [2015] UKSC 71; [2016] 1 BCLC 1, 9f.
[132] Companies (Model Articles) Regulations 2008, SI 2008/3229, sch 1.
[133] That the real estate agencies were sold on the grounds that (i) their productivity was low and (ii) Corporation A needed to generate cash for future investments.
[134] CA 2006, s 170(1).

shareholders of Corporation A or Corporation B and as such, they will have no locus to sue.[135]

In addition, since q is also a director of Corporation B, there is the possibility that he is in breach of his section 175 of the CA 2006 duty to avoid a conflict of interest and duty. By voting on the resolution to approve the sale of the real estate agencies, q may have breached this duty to Corporation A. Further, by disclosing Corporation B's intention to submit a takeover for Corporation A's shares and by voting in favour of the board resolution of Corporation A to sell the real estate agencies, q may also have breached the section 175 duty which he owes to Corporation B as a director of Corporation B.

Turning first to the potential breach of section 175 vis-a-vis Corporation A, section 175(4) of the CA 2006 directs that the duty to avoid a conflict of interest and duty is not breached if (a) the situation cannot reasonably be regarded as likely to give rise to a conflict of interest or (b) the matter has been authorised by the directors of Corporation A.[136] With regard to section 175(4)(b), on the facts of the hypothetical case, there is nothing to suggest that the directors of Corporation A approved q's conflict in advance of the sale transaction.[137] Moreover, like the UK solution to chapter 3, above, there is little traction in favour of the view that the sale transaction can reasonably be considered to 'fall outside the ambit of' Corporation A's business. For that reason, it is submitted that q is in breach of his section 175 duty which is owed to Corporation A in terms of section 170(1) of the CA 2006. However, it is unlikely that Corporation A will be minded to take such legal action against q. In the absence of special circumstances,[138] the shareholders of Corporation A or Corporation B as bidder will have no right of action since q's duties are not owed to them individually.[139]

Turning to q's potential breach of the section 175 duty which he owes to Corporation B, it is submitted that q is also in breach.[140] The section 175 duty is owed to Corporation B in terms of section 170(1) of the CA 2006 and, as such, Corporation B

---

[135] However, the shareholders of Corporation A or Corporation B (if Corporation B is a shareholder of Corporation A) may have rights as shareholders to challenge q's breach of duty by raising a derivative claim or proceedings. See ch 10 at II A, below for further details.

[136] For details, see ch 3 at II B, above.

[137] Section 175(5)(b) of the CA 2006 also stipulates that a plc such as Corporation A must have a provision in its constitution before such prior authorisation may be tendered and the hypothetical case does not confirm the existence of such a provision.

[138] See, eg, *Heron International Ltd v Lord Grade* (n 126) and *Dawson International plc v Coats Paton plc* (n 126).

[139] However, the shareholders of Corporation A or Corporation B (if Corporation B is a shareholder of Corporation A) may have rights as shareholders to challenge q's breach of duty. See ch 10 at II A, below for further details.

[140] Again, there is no information in the hypothetical case to the effect that the directors of Corporation B authorised q's conflict of interest (that is to say, the disclosure of Corporation B's intentions to submit a takeover bid for Corporation A's shares and his vote in favour of the board resolution of Corporation A to sell the real estate agencies) in advance. Since Corporation B is a plc, again, the constitution must contain a provision which permits such prior authorisation in advance under s 175(5)(b) of the CA 2006 and the hypothetical case fails to say whether such a provision exists. Thus, it is assumed that there is no such provision. Moreover, it appears to be reasonably clear that q's disclosure of Corporation B's intention to submit a takeover bid and his approval of the sale transaction fell within the scope of Corporation B's business.

has the right to sue q for any losses which it sustains as a result of his breach of duty. Moreover, in terms of section 178 of the CA 2006, it will be entitled to an account of any profits which q has obtained as a result of his breach of duty.[141]

e. Duty of Confidentiality and Insider Dealing

By disclosing confidential information to Corporation A about Corporation B's impending takeover bid, q is in breach of the obligation of confidence which he owes to Corporation B. This obligation is owed by q to Corporation B in his capacity as a fiduciary rather than by virtue of an implied term of his contract of employment.[142] Q is also in breach of his obligation to disclose his own misconduct to Corporation B.[143] Thus, Corporation B will have a remedy against q in respect of such breaches.

It is also submitted that q is guilty of the criminal offence of 'insider dealing' in terms of section 52(2)(b) of the Criminal Justice Act 1993, even though the hypothetical case suggests that there has been no dealing in the securities[144] of Corporation A, B or C. Since q as a director is an 'insider' who has disclosed 'insider information' to 'another person' 'otherwise than in the proper performance of the functions of his employment, office or profession', this is sufficient for the commission of the 'tipping off' offence. However, no civil liability attaches for a breach of the Criminal Justice Act 1993. Nevertheless, such conduct on the part of q also amounts to 'market abuse' in accordance with the market abuse regulation[145] and section 122A–122I of the FSMA 2000 for the same reasons that the requirements of section 52(2)(b) of the Criminal Justice Act 1993 have been satisfied. The FCA may impose a penalty on q of such amount as it considers appropriate[146] or publish a statement to the effect that he has engaged in market abuse.[147] The FCA (and the Secretary of State) is also able to apply for injunctions and restitution orders.[148] Whilst civil liability would attach if q is an 'authorised person' for the purposes of the FSMA 2000,[149] this is unlikely on the facts of the hypothetical case, since there is no need for q to be authorised to act as a director of Corporation A or Corporation B. For that reason, it is unlikely that private persons such as the shareholders of Corporation A or Corporation B would have a right of action against q even though they may have suffered loss as a result of the commission of the 'tipping off' offence or the market abuse.

---

[141] *Cook v Deeks* [1916] 1 AC 554 (PC) 565 (Lord Buckmaster LC); *Regal (Hastings) Ltd v Gulliver* [1967] 2 AC 134 (HL) 143 (Lord Russell).

[142] S Deakin and G Morris, *Labour Law* (6th edn, Oxford, Hart Publishing, 2012) paras 4.110–4.113 at 370–77.

[143] *Item Software (UK) Ltd v Fassihi* [2004] EWCA Civ 1244, [2004] BCC 994.

[144] Sch 2 to the Criminal Justice Act 1993 defines 'securities' as shares, debentures and other debt securities, options contracts, warrants, futures contracts, depositary receipts and contracts for differences.

[145] Regulation (EU) No 596/2014 on market abuse (n 58).

[146] FSMA 2000, s 123(1).

[147] FSMA 2000, s 123(3).

[148] FSMA 2000, ss 380–83.

[149] FSMA 2000, s 138D(2).

iii. Director R's Liability

a. Breach of the Neutrality Rule, the Listing Rules and the Duty of Care, Skill and Diligence

As with Director q and for the same reasoning, it is submitted that the breach of the Listing Rules and the neutrality rule in Rule 21 of the City Code will render Director r in breach of the duty of care, skill and diligence which she owes to Corporation A on the basis that her conduct fell below the standard of general knowledge, skill and experience that may reasonably be expected of a person carrying out the functions carried out by r in relation to Corporation A. Since the section 174 duty to exercise reasonable care, skill and diligence is owed to Corporation A in terms of section 170(1) of the CA 2006, Corporation A will be entitled to sue r for losses which it sustains as a result of r's breach of duty which fall within the scope of the director's duty of care.[150] However, it is unlikely that Corporation A will be minded to take such legal action against r. In the absence of special circumstances,[151] the shareholders of Corporation A or Corporation B as bidder will have no such right of action since r's duties are not owed to them individually.[152]

b. Breach of Fiduciary Duties

For the same reasons articulated above in relation to Director q, it is submitted that Director r is in breach of the section 171(1) duty to exercise powers only for the purposes for which they are conferred. Since r and the other directors are in breach of duty, the contract of sale of the real estate agencies between Corporation A and Corporation C is voidable; in other words, Corporation A can elect to set the contract aside[153] since the duty is owed to Corporation A.[154] For obvious reasons, it is doubtful whether Corporation A would seek to sue r for breach of this duty. Corporation B or the shareholders of Corporation A have no such power of suit.[155]

In addition, in the same vein as chapter 3, above, since the sale of the real estate agencies by Corporation A to Corporation C represents an indirect interest on the part of r (in her capacity as a director of Corporation A) in a proposed transaction with Corporation C, in order to comply with section 177 of the CA 2006, she must declare the nature and extent of that interest to the other directors of Corporation A prior to Corporation A entering into the transaction with Corporation C.[156] Director r

---

[150] *South Australian Asset Management Corporation v York Montague Ltd* [1997] AC 191 (HL) 214 (Lord Hoffmann).

[151] See, eg, *Heron International Ltd v Lord Grade* (n 126) and *Dawson International plc v Coats Paton plc* (n 126).

[152] However, the shareholders of Corporation A or Corporation B (if Corporation B is a shareholder of Corporation A) may have rights as shareholders to challenge r's breach of duty. See ch 10 at II A, below for further details.

[153] *Howard Smith Ltd v Ampol Petroleum Ltd* (n 106) 838C (Lord Wilberforce).

[154] CA 2006, s 170(1).

[155] Once again, the shareholders of Corporation A or Corporation B (if Corporation B is a shareholder of Corporation A) may have rights as shareholders to challenge r's breach of duty. See ch 10 at II A, below for further details.

[156] CA 2006, s 177(1) and (4).

is indirectly interested in the proposed sale transaction since she is also a director of Corporation C. This duty to declare is owed by r to Corporation A in terms of section 170(1) of the CA 2006. However, r may be able to avail herself of the exception set out in section 177(6)(b) of the CA 2006. Here it is provided that r will not be liable

> if, or to the extent that, the other directors are already aware of [r's interest in the proposed transaction or arrangement, ie the sale of the real estate agencies] to [Corporation C] (and for this purpose the other directors are treated as aware of anything of which they ought reasonably to be aware).[157]

In the instant case, it is abundantly clear that the directors and shareholders of Corporation A ought to have been aware of the fact that r was also a director of Corporation C. For this reason, it is submitted that the exception applies to relieve r of liability for the prima facie breach of section 177 of the CA 2006 in not declaring the nature and extent of her indirect interest in the sale transaction to the other directors of Corporation A. It is also worth mentioning that r's vote in favour of the sale transaction would not be invalid, unless the articles of association provided otherwise.[158]

c. Breach of 'Substantial Property Transactions' Provisions in Sections 190–96 of the CA 2006

Section 190 of the CA 2006 prohibits a director (or a person connected with such a director) from directly or indirectly acquiring a substantial non-cash asset from the company without first obtaining the approval of the members of the company by ordinary resolution. Since Director r is also a director of Corporation C, it would appear to be the case that r has indirectly (as a director of Corporation C) acquired the real estate agencies from Corporation A. An asset is a 'substantial non-cash asset' if its value represents in excess of 10 per cent of Corporation A's asset value and is more than £5,000. From the facts of the hypothetical case, it is submitted that this test is satisfied on the basis that the real estate agencies amount to 30 per cent of Corporation A's total estate agencies. Therefore, they are likely to be of considerable value. Since the members of Corporation A have not passed an ordinary resolution approving the sale in advance, section 190 of the CA 2006 has been breached and Corporation A will be entitled to a remedy against r. However, the shareholders of Corporation A or Corporation B as bidder will have no such right of action against r and it is unlikely that Corporation A will have sufficient motivation or incentive to take legal action against r for a breach of section 190 of the CA 2006.

iv. Summary and Conclusion

Corporation B will be entitled to sue q for a breach of (i) section 175 of the CA 2006, (ii) his fiduciary duty of confidentiality and (iii) his fiduciary duty to disclose

---

[157] Author's annotations in square brackets.

[158] The Model Articles enable r to vote on resolutions concerning an actual or proposed transaction or arrangement with the company provided that certain conditions are met; see, eg, Davies and Worthington, *Gower's Principles of Modern Company Law* (n 118) para 16–58 at 519.

his own misconduct. As a result, Corporation B will be able to recover any losses it has sustained, or any gains enjoyed by q, as a result of those breaches. Subject to those three exceptions, the general position is that whether any personal liability is owed by Directors q and r to Corporation B or the shareholders of Corporation A will depend on the establishment of a special factual relationship between the parties. For example, Directors q and r may come into close personal contact with Corporation B or particular shareholders of Corporation A and the facts may be sufficient to establish liability in the law of agency or tort/delict.[159] However, from the facts of the hypothetical case, there is nothing to suggest any special relationship or assumption of responsibility on the part of Directors q and r to Corporation B or the shareholders of Corporation A. Nor is there anything in the facts which is indicative of reliance on the part of Corporation B or the shareholders of Corporation A on the actions of Directors q and r. Thus, the end result is that it is only Corporation A itself which has a right to claim against Directors q and r for a breach of sections 171(1), 174, 175 and 190 of the CA 2006, and such directors will only be liable to Corporation A. For self-explanatory reasons, it is unlikely that Corporation A will have sufficient incentive to sue q and/or r.

J. The US

i. Introduction

As regards the scenario, under SEC Rule 13d-1(a), Corporation B would be required to file a statement with the SEC within 10 days after acquiring a beneficial ownership of more than 5 per cent of Corporation A's shares, which would put Corporation A's board on notice about Corporation B's plans at an early stage. The sale of assets by Corporation A would be required to be disclosed on a Form 8-K within four business days of the sale.[160] Thus, Corporation B would not find itself in the position of being surprised by the transaction after the stockholders of Corporation A agreed to accept the offer. Despite these differences in the possible facts, this solution will address more generally the actions of the board of directors of Corporation A to fend off the advances of Corporation B.

ii. The Authority of Corporation A's Directors to sell Corporation A's Assets to Ward off a Takeover Bid

Under Delaware law, the directors of Corporation A may be permitted to sell a significant portion of Corporation A's assets to ward off Corporation B's takeover bid.

---

[159] *Peskin v Anderson* [2001] 1 BCC 874 (CA) 880 at [33]–[34] (Mummery LJ) and *Sharp v Blank* [2015] EWHC 3220 (Ch); see also *Allen v Hyatt* (1914) 30 TLR 444 (PC), where it was held that the directors had held themselves out to the shareholders as agents on their behalf and that they were liable to account to the shareholders for the profit they had made: *Coleman v Myers* [1977] 2 NZLR 225; *Heron International Ltd v Lord Grade* (n 126); *Dawson International plc v Coats Paton plc* (n 126).

[160] Note that in the EU too there is a disclosure requirement for the acquisition of major shareholdings as well as a duty of 'ad hoc' disclosure: art 9 of Directive 2004/109/EC of the European Parliament and

Typically, decisions of the directors are afforded deference under the business judgment rule. Under the business judgment rule, directors who act in good faith and with sufficient information are shielded from personal liability if the court concludes that the decision can be 'attributed to any rational business purpose'.[161]

However, since a takeover bid presents a unique threat to directors' potential individual self-interest to remain in power, the courts will engage in an enhanced judicial review of anti-takeover decisions.[162] This enhanced judicial review has two prongs. First, the court enquires as to whether the directors reasonably perceived a threat to the corporation and its stockholders. The court places the burden of proof on the defendant directors to show the existence of this threat, and the directors satisfy this burden by showing good faith and reasonable investigation.[163] The 'proof is materially enhanced … by the approval of a board comprised of a majority of outside independent directors who have acted in accordance with the foregoing standards'.[164] In this case, two of the directors of Corporation A have some issues regarding whether they have independent status (see below), but as long as a majority of the directors are independent, the judgment of the board of directors regarding the perception of a threat will likely be respected.

If the directors satisfy this first enquiry, which they are almost always capable of doing, the court then asks whether the action taken in response to the threat is 'reasonable in relation to the threat posed'.[165] In the present case, the directors sold 30 per cent of Corporation A's real estate agencies on the 'pretexts' of low productivity and a need for cash. Generally speaking, courts in the US hold that the '[t]he sale of an asset which has the result of making a company less attractive to a tender offeror can be a proper exercise of a board of directors' business judgment'.[166] The Delaware Supreme Court has stated, however, that '[the] powers [to protect the corporation from an outside threat] are not absolute. A corporation does not have unbridled discretion to defeat any perceived threat by any Draconian means available'.[167] Ultimately, the judgment of the court will be highly fact-intensive and will involve an evaluation of the reasonableness of the sale. The Delaware courts rarely find defensive actions unreasonable under these standards.

iii. Directors q and r's Fiduciary Duties to Corporation A

Two primary duties constrain corporate directors in the US: the duty of care and the duty of loyalty. The duty of care requires directors to make decisions in a careful

---

of the Council of 15 December 2004 on the harmonisation of transparency requirements in relation to information about issuers whose securities are admitted to trading on a regulated market and amending Directive 2001/34/EC (OJ L 390 31/12/2004) (as amended) and art 17 of the Regulation (EU) No 596/2014 on market abuse (n 58).

[161] *Unitrin, Inc v Am Gen Corp (in Re Unitrin, Inc)*, 651 A 2d 1361, 1374 (Del 1995).
[162] *Unocal Corp v Mesa Petroleum Co*, 493 A 2d 946, 955 (Del 1985).
[163] *Cheff v Mathes*, 199 A 2d 548, 555 (1964).
[164] *Unocal* (n 162) 955.
[165] Ibid.
[166] *Whittaker Corp v Edgar*, 535 F Supp 933 (ND Ill 1982).
[167] *Unocal* (n 162) 955.

and well- informed manner.[168] An analysis of a purported violation of a duty of care focuses primarily on the directors' decision-making process. Thus, a decision that ultimately harms the company, even severely, will not be found to violate the duty of care as long as the directors have taken the time to carefully consider all the relevant factors. The case does not raise any concerns regarding the duty of care.

The duty of loyalty requires directors to refrain from engaging in self-interested transactions. Such transactions can take many forms, including the use of confidential information for personal gain, appropriating corporate opportunities for personal use or treating the corporation to which one owes a fiduciary duty unfairly. The Delaware General Corporation Law (DGCL) provides that a self-interested transaction is not void or voidable if the interested party discloses all material facts relating to the conflict of interest and the transaction is subsequently approved by disinterested directors or stockholders.[169]

The case involves two directors of Corporation A who may have issues with regard to the duty of loyalty. q is a director of both Corporation A and Corporation B, thus placing him in the uncomfortable position of being privy to Corporation B's plans before an offer was made to Corporation A. q dealt with this awkward situation by informing Corporation A's board of directors about Corporation B's intentions to buy Corporation A's shares, thus enabling Corporation A to take the pre-emptive step of selling some of its assets. While q may have disclosed confidential information belonging to Corporation B, this disclosure does not engage any of the fiduciary duties q owes to Corporation A or its stockholders. Presumably, A's shareholders can only have been benefited by the disclosure or, if they were harmed, they were harmed by reason of A's board's decision to ward off the takeover bid.

In contrast, r's position as a director on the board of directors of both Corporation A and Corporation C does suggest that r may have breached her duty of loyalty to Corporation A. The case does not indicate that r disclosed her interest in Corporation C. In these circumstances, a Delaware court would engage in an 'entire fairness' review of the transaction in question. The entire fairness test has two components: fair dealing and fair price.[170] The fair dealing aspect enquires into 'when the transaction was timed, how it was initiated, structured, disclosed to the directors, and how the approvals of the directors … were obtained'.[171] The fair price aspect relates to the 'economic and financial considerations' of the transaction.[172]

In the present case, it is unclear how the transaction between Corporations A and C was initiated and how the approvals of the other members of the board of directors were obtained. If r was the person who suggested selling the agencies to Corporation C, if r advocated that a below-market value price was necessary to expedite the sale or if r pressured the other directors to agree to the transaction, then a court may conclude that r's dealings were unfair to the corporation. If there were alternative buyers for

---

[168] *Smith v Van Gorkom*, 488 A 2d 858, 873 (Del 1985).
[169] DGCL, § 144(a)(3).
[170] *Weinberger v Uop*, 457 A 2d 701, 711 (Del 1983).
[171] Ibid.
[172] Ibid.

Corporation A's agencies who could have paid a higher price whilst still purchasing the agencies in sufficient time to ward off the takeover attempt, a court may conclude that the price paid by Corporation C was unfair and r may be held liable for the lost value.

It is possible that the directors in question may have breached their duty of loyalty to the stockholders of Corporation A in connection with the offer from Corporation B. Assuming that this offer took the form of a hostile tender offer rather than a negotiated merger, the board of directors of Corporation A would be obliged under Rule 14e-2 of the Securities Exchange Act of 1934:

> [N]o later than 10 business days from the date the tender offer is first published or sent or given, [to] publish, send or give to security holders a statement disclosing that the subject company:
>
> 1.   Recommends acceptance or rejection of the bidder's tender offer;
> 2.   Expresses no opinion and is remaining neutral toward the bidder's tender offer; or
> 3.   Is unable to take a position with respect to the bidder's tender offer. Such statement must include the reason(s) for the position (including the inability to take a position) disclosed therein.

In issuing this statement, the board of directors may have been influenced by the conflicts of interests discussed above (and, most specifically, the conflict involving r), and r's actions in connection with the statement would be evaluated under the same 'entire fairness' standard previously discussed.

K. South Africa

The law relating to takeovers and offers is contained in Parts B and C of the Companies Act 2008 as well as the Takeover Regulations,[173] giving effect to these Parts of the Act. Takeover provisions apply to regulated companies in respect of affected transactions and in respect of these transactions, a person making an offer must comply with the Companies Act and the Regulations as above, and must not give effect to the affected transaction unless the Takeover Regulation Panel (Panel)[174] has issued a compliance certificate or has granted an exemption.[175] A regulated company is, inter alia, a public company,[176] and an affected transaction[177] includes an offer to acquire more than 35 per cent of the voting securities of a regulated company. An offer is defined as a proposal of any sort which, if accepted, would result in an affected transaction.[178] The Takeover Regulations will thus apply *in casu*. Section 126 is specifically relevant as it deals with the frustration of an offer being made.

---

[173] These Regulations are prescribed by the Minister in consultation with the Takeovers Regulations Panel.
[174] Established in terms of the Companies Act 2008, s 196.
[175] Companies Act 2008, s 121.
[176] Companies Act 2008, s 118(2).
[177] Companies Act 2008, s 117(1)(c).
[178] Companies Act 2008, s 117(1)(f).

Section 126 provides that:

Restrictions on frustrating action.—(1) If the board of a regulated company believes that a *bona fide* offer might be imminent, or has received such an offer, the board must not—

(*a*) take any action in relation to the affairs of the company that could effectively result in—

    (i) a *bona fide* offer being frustrated; or

    (ii) the holders of relevant securities being denied an opportunity to decide on its merits;

(*b*) issue any authorised but unissued securities;

(*c*) issue or grant options in respect of any unissued securities;

(*d*) authorise or issue, or permit the authorisation or issue of, any securities carrying rights of conversion into or subscription for other securities;

(*e*) *sell, dispose of or acquire, or agree to sell, dispose of or acquire, assets of a material amount except in the ordinary course of business;*

(*f*) enter into contracts otherwise than in the ordinary course of business; or

(*g*) make a distribution that is abnormal as to timing and amount.

The board of Corporation A is thus not allowed to take any action to frustrate the offer. The sale to Corporation C will frustrate the offer. The sale is in contravention of section 126(1)(e) if the board of Corporation A believes that a bona fide offer might be imminent or if it has received an offer.[179] In this case the offer made by Corporation B to Corporation A has been made public. Regulation 99 refers to an offer or an approach to an offer being made. Contravention of this provision will be a breach of the fiduciary duties towards Corporation A.

The sale of the assets to Corporation C probably falls within the ambit of section 112 which provides that the sale of all or a greater part of the assets or undertaking[180] needs a special resolution. The shareholders thus have to approve the sale; this did not happen *in casu*.

The directors of Corporation A will thus be liable to Corporation A on the basis that they breached their fiduciary duty as well as the duty to act with the necessary degree of care, skill and diligence. This is based on the fact that they contravened section 126. Furthermore, if one takes the view that the sale to Corporation C did not have to comply with section 112, as it only relates to 30 per cent and not 50 per cent, then it will still be a breach of the duties of the directors of Corporation A if they continue with the sale. Firstly, the fact that they sell 30 per cent of its real estate agencies at a price below the average market value will result in a breach of the duty of care, skill and diligence. Furthermore, the directors are not allowed to ward off a takeover as that is a breach of their fiduciary duty to act for a proper purpose.[181] Directors must thus exercise their powers for the objective purpose for which the power was given to

---

[179] As defined in s 117(1)(f) of the Companies Act 2008.

[180] All or greater part is defined in s 1 of the Companies Act 2008 as, in the case of a company's undertaking, more than 50% of the value of its entire undertaking, fairly valued. In this case it can be argued that 30% of real estate agencies at below market price could be 50% of its undertaking and this within the ambit of s 112.

[181] *Hogg v Cramphorn* [1967] Ch 254; *Howard Smith Ltd v Ampol Petroleum Ltd* [1974] AC 821 (PC).

them and not for a collateral or ulterior purpose. *In casu*, the purpose of the sale to Corporation C was to prevent the takeover from Corporation A.

In terms of Regulation 108, a person who is on the board of both the offeror and offeree companies is conflicted and non-independent, cannot vote on the board of the offeree company, and must withdraw from any deliberations. In this case, Mr q is a director of both Corporations A and B and hence, should not be involved in any deliberations.

The director of Corporation B, Mr q, will also be liable to Corporation B owing to various breaches of his duties owed towards Corporation B. By disclosing confidential information Mr q did not comply with his fiduciary duties towards Corporation B. He can also be guilty of insider trading. Section 78(4)(a) of the Financial Markets Act[182] provides that an 'insider' who knows that he or she has 'inside information' and who discloses the 'inside information' to another person, commits an offence. Mr q will qualify as an 'insider' and the information will also qualify as 'inside information' in terms of the definitions provided in section 77.[183]

If a breach of a duty occurs, as explained above, the relevant director will be liable based on section 77 of the Companies Act 2008. Section 77 is also supplemented by section 218(2) which states that any person who contravenes any provision of the Act will be liable to any other person for any loss or damage suffered by that person as a result of the contravention.[184] Section 77(2)(a) deals with liability based on a breach of a fiduciary duty and section 77(2)(b) determines that a director will be liable in accordance with the principles of the common law relating to delict for any loss, damages or costs sustained by the company as a consequence of a breach of section 76(3)(c). Corporation B acquired an 18 per cent shareholding stake in Corporation A, but it is not stated in the facts when Corporation B began these acquisitions. Two issues may be important here. In the first instance it should be noted, as stated above, that Part B of the Companies Act 2008 as well as the Takeover Regulations apply to an affected transaction in respect of a regulated company. The acquisition of a beneficial interest of a regulated company in the circumstances as contemplated in section 122(1)

---

[182] Act 19 of 2012.

[183] Section 77 states that:

'inside information' means specific or precise information, which has not been made public and which-

(a) is obtained or learned as an insider; and
(b) if it were made public, would be likely to have a material effect on the price or value of any security listed on a regulated market;

'insider' means a person who has inside information-

(a) through-

  (i) being a director, employee or shareholder of an issuer of securities listed on a regulated market to which the inside information relates; or
  (ii) having access to such information by virtue of employment, office or profession; or

(b) where such person knows that the direct or indirect source of the information was a person contemplated in paragraph (a).

[184] See PA Delport (ed), *Henochsberg on the Companies Act 71 of 2008* (Durban, LexisNexis, South Africa, Service issue November 2016) 640 as to the s 218(2) liability in addition to that in s 77 of the Companies Act 2008.

is an affected transaction.[185] Section 122 provides that a person must notify a regulated company in the prescribed manner and form within three business days after that person acquires (or disposes of) a beneficial interest in sufficient securities of a class issued by that company such that, as a result of the acquisition, the person holds a beneficial interest in securities amounting to 5, 10, or 15 per cent, or any further whole multiple of 5 per cent, of the issued securities of that class. Although this is a fundamental transaction, section 121(b)(i) of the Companies Act will not apply, owing to the exemption granted.[186] The acquiring person must notify the particular regulated company and the company must file a copy with the Panel and report the (acquisition) information to the holders of the relevant securities. Secondly, Regulation 98 provides that during an offer period, any (allowable) dealings in securities must be disclosed to the Panel. Corporation B would appear to have also failed to comply with this requirement.

Any issuer considering a transaction must also comply with the requirements of the JSE Ltd Listings Requirements.[187] The requirements will depend on the transaction size relative to that of the issuer proposing to make it. The different categories of transactions are:

1. Category 2—a transaction where any percentage ratio is 5 per cent or more but each is less than 30 per cent;
2. Category 1—a transaction where any percentage ratio is 30 per cent or more or if the total consideration is not subject to any maximum.[188]

The percentage ratios are the percentages resulting from each of the following calculations:

1. consideration to market capitalisation being the consideration divided by the aggregate market value of all the listed equity securities, excluding treasury shares of the listed company; or
2. dilution, being the number of listed equity securities issued by a listed company as consideration for an acquisition compared to those in issue, excluding treasury shares prior to the transaction.

If the transaction is partly in cash and partly in shares the category size for such transaction is to be calculated by first assessing the cash to market capitalisation percentage and then adding this percentage to the dilution percentage.[189] A category 2 transaction requires the publication of certain prescribed information (to the public), while a category 1 transaction requires, in addition, that the company informs the shareholders of a general meeting to approve the transaction.[190] The facts do not indicate the market

---

[185] Companies Act 2008, s 117(1)(c)(iv).
[186] TRP Guideline 4/2011 in terms of s 201(2)(b) of the Companies Act 2008 provides a blanket exemption from the provisions of s 121(b)(i).
[187] The JSE Ltd is an exchange, with various trading boards, licensed in terms of the Financial Markets Act which is administered by the Financial Services Board in terms of the Financial Services Board Act 97 of 1990.
[188] JSE Ltd Listings Requirements, para 9.5.
[189] JSE Ltd Listings Requirements, para 9.6.
[190] JSE Ltd Listings Requirements, paras 9.15 and 9.20.

capitalisation of Corporation A, and it is therefore not possible to determine the percentage ratio of the transaction with Corporation C. However, if the board did not comply with the Listings Requirements, if it was required to do so, the shareholder/s do not have a direct claim against directors/board. Subject to the provisions of the Financial Markets Act,[191] the enabling Act in respect of the JSE Ltd, the JSE Ltd has the power to suspend or remove the securities from listing, if it is in the public interest to do so,[192] and it can also censure the directors, which could include a private or public censure, disqualifying the director/s from acting as director/s of a listed company for any period of time and/or impose a fine not exceeding the amount as stipulated in the Financial Markets Act.[193] Non-compliance with the Listings Requirements will, it is submitted, be a breach of fiduciary duties towards the company as provided for under the common law and the Companies Act 2008, and will, also, be a breach of the duties to act with care, skill and diligence under the common law and the Companies Act 2008 as discussed above.

L. Japan

i. Sale of 'Crown Jewels' of the Target

There is no 'board neutrality rule' concerning takeover bids in Japan. However, the conduct of the directors of a target company is subject to fiduciary duties. The disposal of a material part of the company's assets (crown jewels) requires the approval of an extraordinary resolution of the shareholders in general meeting on the basis that it amounts to a business transfer (Companies Act (CA), Articles 467(1)(i)(ii) and 309(2)(xi)), and gives rise to legal issues in relation to the director's duty of loyalty (CA, Article 355).[194] In the present case, it is submitted that the sale of the real estate agencies would not constitute a breach of a director's fiduciary duty if these agencies are not a material part of the company.

   In the present case, the bid failed due to the lack of support from the shareholders of the target company. In Japanese law, there is also a special provision that would allow the withdrawal of a takeover bid in such a scenario. In principle, the bidder cannot withdraw the takeover bid after having made public the notice to commence the takeover bid (Financial Instruments and Exchange Law, Article 27-11(1)). However, if the target company disposed of or transferred its material property during the offer period of the takeover bid, the bidder may withdraw the takeover bid. So, if these agencies which company A sold are a material part of the Corporation A, Corporation B can withdraw its takeover bid legally (Enforcement Ordinance of the Financial Instruments and Exchange Law, Article 14(1)(i).)

---

[191] See Financial Markets Act, s 12.
[192] JSE Ltd Listings Requirements, paras 1.6 and 1.11.
[193] JSE Ltd Listings Requirements, para 1.20; Financial Markets Act, s 71.
[194] If that is not the case, the extraordinary shareholders' meeting must decide about a sale of the whole assets of the company (CA, Arts 467(1) and 309(2)).

ii. Undervalue Transaction in Relation to a Related Party

A director owes a duty of loyalty to the company (CA, Article 355). Therefore, when a director's decision results in the company being committed to an undervalue transaction with a related party, the director in breach is liable to compensate the company for the losses which the company sustains (CA, Article 423(1)). In the present case, the undervalue transaction may constitute a breach of the director's duty of loyalty. A shareholder has the right to file an action against the director (derivative suit) in order to establish liability on the part of the director. A shareholder owning the shares of the company consecutively for the preceding six months or more is also entitled to demand that the company file an action to pursue the liability of a director (CA, Article 847(1)). If the company fails to file such an action within 60 days from the date of the shareholders' demand, the shareholder(s) who made such a demand may file an action on behalf of the company to pursue the liability of the director (CA, Article 847(3)).

In addition, the shareholder(s) may immediately file an action to pursue the liability of a director on behalf of the company in circumstances where the company is likely to suffer irreparable harm if the said period is permitted to elapse without any action being taken (CA, Article 847(5)).

iii. Director q's Vote and Conflict of Interests

In the present case, Director q was also a director of Corporation A. Directors who have a special interest in a resolution to be voted on at the board of directors' meeting are not permitted to participate in the vote (CA, Article 369(2)).

iv. Restriction on Competition etc.

If a director intends to carry out, for himself or herself or for a third party, any transaction in the line of business of the company, he or she is obliged to disclose the material facts on the relevant transactions at a meeting of the board of directors and obtain its approval (CA, Article 365(1)). If the relevant transaction does not satisfy this requirement ('competition'), the director may be liable for the losses which the company sustains if he or she utilised the trade secrets of the company.[195] If a director neglects his or her duties, he or she is liable to the company for losses arising as a result therefrom (CA, Article 423(1)). Furthermore, if a director engages in such a transaction in violation of the provisions of Article 356(1), the amount of profit obtained by the director as a result of such transaction is presumed to be the amount of the losses suffered by the company (CA, Article 423(2)). Relief from such liability may not be given without the consent of all shareholders (CA, Article 424).

In the present case, Director r may be liable for losses[196] which the company suffers as a result of the sale of the real estate agencies to Corporation C. Director q's conduct

---

[195] Osaka District Court, 31 January 2002, in *Kinyû Shôji Hanrei* 1339, 44.
[196] It includes the amount of the profits obtained by the director as a result of such transaction (CA, Art 423(2)).

may also constitute 'tipping' under insider dealing rules (Financial Instruments and Exchange Law, Article 166(3)). The breach of insider dealing rules leads to criminal sanctions (Financial Instruments and Exchange Law, Article 197(2)).

III. Conclusion

A. Introduction

The results of the analysis reveal a substantial degree of heterogeneity as to how different legal systems address the obligations of directors of target companies during a takeover. With regard to general fiduciary duties, whilst there are some differences in the specific approaches, the jurisdictions examined generally acknowledge the behaviour of both directors Mr q and Ms r as constitutive of breaches of the duties of care and/or loyalty which could serve as the basis of their potential liability.

B. Board Neutrality Rules

Neutrality/passivity rules preclude directors of a company targeted by a takeover to engage in certain conducts that may result in the frustration of the offer by the bidder – such as the sale of assets of the company – without obtaining the previous consent of the shareholders. The main purpose of board neutrality rules is to protect the shareholders of the target companies from such defensive measures by their own directors. The solutions show that board neutrality rules are not applied by all of the jurisdictions under scrutiny. Notably, the legal systems of the US (Delaware) and Japan do not set neutrality rules applicable to the boards of directors of public companies. This does not mean that in those jurisdictions directors face no constraints in the adoption of defensive measures against takeovers, but, instead of neutrality rules, the legal systems of Delaware and Japan address the lawfulness of directors' behaviours during takeovers by way of fiduciary duties; for example, Delaware courts may need to determine whether the sale was based on rational business objectives. In contrast with Delaware and Japan, in the EU, the EU Takeover Directive[197] introduced a board neutrality rule.[198] However, the EU Takeover Directive grants EU Member States considerable flexibility in deciding whether and how to implement board neutrality.[199]

---

[197] Directive 2004/25/EC (n 3).

[198] For a comprehensive evaluation of the jurisdictional transposition of the EU Takeover Directive, see the Takeover Bids Directive Assessment Report from 2013, available at https://publications.europa.eu/en/publication-detail/-/publication/67501b75-7583-4b0d-a551-33051d8e27c1/language-en.

[199] For an analysis of the position of different EU Member States before and after the implementation of the EU Takeover Directive as regards the board neutrality rule, see PL Davies, E-P Schuster and E van de Walle de Ghelcke, 'The Takeover Directive as a Protectionist Tool?' in U Bernitz and W-G Ringe (eds), *Company Law and Economic Protectionism: New Challenges to European Integration* (Oxford, Oxford University Press, 2010) 105–60.

First, the EU Takeover Directive gives discretion to EU Member States regarding the decision about whether to implement neutrality obligations or not. Nevertheless, those EU Member States that decide to opt out from the neutrality regime must confer upon companies the right to implement board neutrality provisions in their articles/by-laws.[200] Of the EU Member States examined in this study, France, Germany, Italy, the Netherlands and Poland have opted out of the neutrality system, with the result that its implementation would ultimately be decided by the shareholders of Corporation A and incorporated into its articles/by-laws. Among the Member States which have opted out from the neutrality rule, Italy is an interesting example because, under Italian law, the board neutrality applies unless the concerned company decides to opt out through a modification of its articles/by-laws; hence, in Italy, the board neutrality rule is the default rule. The other EU Member States analysed in this study – Finland, Latvia, Spain and the UK – have decided not to opt out of the neutrality regime, and, consequently, in those jurisdictions, board neutrality is mandatory for companies such as Corporation A.

Secondly, apart from the possibility of opting out from the board neutrality rule, the EU Takeover Directive also grants EU Member States discretion in deciding when the neutrality obligations for directors of a company become applicable. The 'trigger point' can be either the moment when the bid is made public or an earlier time, such as when the board of the target company becomes aware that the bid will be submitted imminently. EU Member States also display variation in this regard. The UK, one of the four EU jurisdictions analysed where neutrality is mandatory, makes neutrality obligations applicable from the moment when the directors of the target company have grounds to believe about an imminent takeover offer (a similar approach is also followed by South African Law). However, in most of the EU jurisdictions examined – Finland, France, Germany, Italy, Latvia, Poland and Spain – the law prescribes the moment when the bid is made public, with certain variations therein,[201] as the relevant time (see Table 4.1).

Table 4.1 The board neutrality rule in perspective

		Mandatory neutrality rule	**Neutrality rule trigger point**
EU	Finland	Yes	Bid public + directors' knowledge
	France	Opt-out	Bid public
	Germany	Opt-out	Bid public
	Italy	Opt-out	Bid public
	Latvia	Yes	Bid public + notification to directors
	The Netherlands	Opt-out	Na

(Continued)

[200] Directive 2004/25/EC (n 3), art 12(1) and (2).
[201] eg in Finland there is an additional express requirement whereby neutrality applies from the moment when the directors of the target company have knowledge that the bid has been made public.

Table 4.1 *(Continued)*

		Mandatory neutrality rule	**Neutrality rule trigger point**
	Poland	Opt-out	Bid public
	Spain	Yes	Bid public
	The UK	Yes	Directors become aware of imminent bid
Non-EU	Japan	No neutrality rule	Na
	South Africa	Yes	Directors become aware of imminent bid
	The US	No neutrality rule	Na

When it comes to the liability of directors for eventual damages caused by a breach of the neutrality rule, the consequences would be different across countries; in some jurisdictions – eg Finland and Spain – such a breach could result in liability towards Corporation A, the shareholders of Corporation A as well as Corporation B; however, in the majority of jurisdictions analysed, liability could only be established towards Corporation A but not in relation to its shareholders or Corporation B as a bidder. In the UK, the breach of the neutrality provisions set in the City Code would not render the directors of Corporation A liable to Corporation A, the shareholders of Corporation A or Corporation B.

Rather than promoting a uniform regime, the board neutrality provisions of the EU Takeover Directive have led to a substantially diverse framework in which different EU Member States have accommodated their regulatory choices to their own preferences.[202]

C. The Sale of Corporation A's Assets

Another issue which has been analysed in the different jurisdictions is whether the decision adopted by the board of directors concerning the sale of important assets of Corporation A should be subject to the approval of its shareholders. Such authorisation would probably be required in Finland, Germany, Italy, Poland, South Africa, Spain and the UK. On the one hand, this includes all the jurisdictions in which neutrality is mandatory with the exception of Latvia, where the neutrality rule's trigger point was not reached when the decision to sell the assets was adopted by the board of Corporation A. On the other hand, shareholder approval would also be required in some of the countries where neutrality is not mandatory; for example, although Poland opted out of the EU's board neutrality regime, according to Polish company law, the sale of

---

[202] Whether Member States should be granted freedom as regards the implementation of a board neutrality rule has been the subject of debate; for an argument against the elimination of opt-out provisions, see JA McCahery and EPM Vermeulen, 'The Case Against Reform of the Takeover Bids Directive' (2011) 22 *European Business Law Review* 541.

30 per cent of Corporation A's real estate agencies would consist of a 'sale of an organised part of the enterprise' and require shareholder approval. In other legal systems, such as Japan (and possibly the Netherlands), whilst the board of directors has no absolute discretion to decide on the sale of the company's assets, the specific conditions which would require shareholder approval do not apply in the context of the decision by the board of Corporation A.

D. Directors' Duties

In addition to neutrality obligations, the general fiduciary duties applicable to directors of Corporation A, Corporation B and Corporation C were very relevant to determining whether there was potential liability on the part of directors such as Mr q and Ms r as a result of their respective behaviour. Whilst the applicable regime differs among jurisdictions, all of them have developed – through statute and/or case law – a catalogue of directors' duties that covers the diverse range of misconduct addressed in the case.

The main potential breaches identified relate to the duties of care and of loyalty. First, concerning Mr q's behaviour, this consists of a breach of fiduciary duties – eg the duty of loyalty – and/or confidentiality obligations in most legal systems. Moreover, in most regimes, the disclosure of information to Corporation A by Mr q would constitute a breach of market abuse rules concerning the use of inside information and would have criminal sanctions attached. Turning to Ms r, the vote in a conflict-of-interest situation would generally constitute a violation of her duties as director; however, as explained in chapter 3, the consequences of such a vote for the validity of the agreement by the board of Corporation A would vary across jurisdictions.

E. Conclusion

The main issue addressed in this case was whether the directors of Corporation A committed a breach of their duties during the takeover bid launched by Corporation B. In the majority of the legal systems examined, directors are subject to specific duties applicable in takeover processes, which set limits on the scope of their behaviour, actions and decisions. The EU Takeover Directive establishes a board neutrality rule which precludes directors from adopting defensive measures during a takeover process without prior shareholder approval. The EU Takeover Directive has not, however, led to a uniform regime. Some EU Member States have opted out of the system of mandatory neutrality, giving companies discretion as regards whether they want to opt in and apply board neutrality. Other EU Member States apply the system of mandatory neutrality. In one of the EU jurisdictions examined, board neutrality is the default rule and companies are given the right to opt out of such system. The EU Takeover Directive also gives Member States some flexibility in deciding the moment when the neutrality rule is engaged; whereas in most of the EU jurisdictions assessed the neutrality rule's trigger point is the moment when the bid is made public, others have chosen a stricter approach, requiring board neutrality from the moment when the directors become aware of an imminent bid. Outside the EU, South Africa also embraces the stricter version of mandatory board neutrality. In contrast with the EU and South African regimes, in the US (Delaware) and Japan there is no board neutrality rule.

The sale of Corporation A's real estate agencies would constitute a breach of the neutrality rule in a majority of the analysed jurisdictions where board neutrality is mandatory; however, in some countries that do not apply mandatory board neutrality, such a sale would also require the approval of Corporation A's shareholders.

When it comes to the liability of the directors of Corporation A for a failure to comply with the neutrality rule, the legal systems examined generally embrace, when applicable, their liability towards Corporation A; however, the liability of directors of Corporation A towards its shareholders or Corporation B – as the bidder – is rarely contemplated.

With regard to other general directors' duties, in most of the legal systems addressed, the behaviour of Mr q and Ms r would qualify as breaches of their duties, notably of the duties of care, and of loyalty, and could lead to liability for damages towards Corporation A and/or Corporation B.

5

Cross-Border Takeovers and Takeover Defences

SONJA SIGGBERG, JESSE COLLIN AND LENA NORDMAN (EDITORS)*

Main topics: directors' duties in the context of a takeover bid; stakeholder protection; the reciprocity rule; the board neutrality rule; the legality of directors' defensive tactics; pre-emption rights on an allotment and issue of shares; directors' liability.

Related topics: further duties of directors in the context of a takeover bid (see chapter 4, above); directors' duty of loyalty (see chapter 3, above); enforcement of directors' duties (see chapter 10, below).

I. Scenario

Target plc ('the Target') has its registered office and headquarters in jurisdiction A ('Home Jurisdiction'). It is also listed in the Home Jurisdiction; recently, it also got listed on two foreign stock exchanges. Bidder plc ('the Bidder') has its registered office and headquarters and is listed in a foreign jurisdiction B ('Foreign Jurisdiction'). For a long period of time, the Bidder had been looking for an opportunity to expand its business into markets in the Home Jurisdiction. After a period of prolonged research and analysis, the Bidder makes it known to the chairman of the board of directors of the Target that it intends to make a bid for 100 per cent of the shares of the Target.

The board of the Target discusses the bid at some length and holds several meetings with its professional advisers. Although the terms of the tender offer are not completely inadequate, the takeover bid is not, as a whole, favourable to the Target and

* Sonja Siggberg and Jesse Collin are responsible for the current edition of this chapter; Lena Nordman was responsible for the first edition.

the desirability of foreign ownership is particularly doubtful. The board of directors of the Target resolves to accept the chairman's proposal to protect the Target's independence. This will be achieved by virtue of the Target implementing a 'shareholders' rights plan'. The Target's shareholders' rights plan is a 'flip-in' plan. In other words, in terms of the articles of association of the Target, the existing shareholders (excluding the Bidder) will be given the right to subscribe for additional shares in the Target at 50 per cent of their market value as soon as an outside acquirer achieves a threshold stake of 20 per cent of the shares of the Target. The main motivation behind this plan was to protect the company's employees since Target has many employee shareholders who fear that they may face redundancies in the event of a takeover.

Furthermore, having anticipated that the Bidder is likely to publicise the takeover bid without a recommendation in favour of the bid by the board of the Target, the Target also puts in place a 'customer assurance programme'. The purpose of this programme is to ensure that the Target will not lose clients during the bid process if it ultimately develops into a prolonged takeover battle. The customer assurance programme compensates the Target's clients for any disruption of services and deliveries which they might experience if the Bidder's takeover bid succeeds.

The Bidder announces its takeover bid, addressing the shareholders of the Target directly without the cooperation of the board of the Target. A shareholders' rights plan is not lawful in the Foreign Jurisdiction. The Bidder intends to challenge the shareholders' rights plan in the court, if necessary, in order to obtain a declaration that it is invalid. The Bidder will also seek an order from the court setting aside the customer assurance programme on the basis that it unreasonably increases the financial exposure of the Bidder. How would the courts assess the legality of the Target's shareholders' rights plan and the customer assurance programme? Moreover, to what extent could the Bidder and the shareholders of the Target challenge the conduct of the board of directors of the Target?

II. Case Studies

A. Finland

i. Regulatory Introduction

Since 2013, the main rules of Finnish takeover law are found in the Securities Markets Act ((SMA, 746/2012)), which is supplemented by the Helsinki Takeover Code operating on a 'comply or explain' basis;[1] takeovers also need to comply with the rules of the Finnish Companies Act 2006 (CA).

The SMA is applicable to public takeover bids launched to acquire shares admitted to trading on a regulated market in Finland. The SMA is also applied when the target

---

[1] See ch 4 at II F, above.

company's corporate seat (referring to the company law registered office) is in Finland and the shares or securities are listed on a regulated market in an EEA Member State other than Finland.[2] Further, the SMA is applied to the target company whose shares are listed in several jurisdictions if the corporate seat is in Finland as in this case. Certain states within the European Economic Area apply a reciprocity rule to provisions which restrict defensive takeover action. If a company becomes the target of a bid from a company which is not subject to equivalent restrictions, the target can disapply the restrictions and take frustrating action against the bid.[3] However, reciprocity provisions are not applicable in Finland.

ii. The Shareholders' Rights Plan

As discussed in Chapter 2 at II G above, the Finnish corporate governance framework is guided by certain general principles and the corporate benefit test. In general, the board needs to analyse carefully to what extent it may engage in defensive conduct. Owing to the principle of equal treatment of shareholders, the board must take a neutral role in relation to the shareholders and intra-shareholder relationships and the board may not make resolutions or take other measures that are conducive to conferring an undue benefit to a shareholder or another person at the expense of the company or another shareholder.

As discussed in Chapter 4 at II F above, the board's main duty in a takeover situation is to seek the best possible outcome for all shareholders. The board may not favour certain shareholders or defer a proposed takeover without justification or reasons. It seems that the main motivation behind the 'shareholders' rights plan' is to favour a certain group of shareholders, ie employee shareholders. Therefore, the shareholders' rights plan is likely to constitute a breach of the principle of equal treatment and be deemed unlawful under the CA.

Turning to the question of the decision-making process, it should be noted that the CA requires the general meeting to (i) decide on share issues or (ii) authorise the board to pass a resolution on such share issues. It is highly unlikely that the board of a Finnish company would have an existing share issue authorisation to the extent described in the case. Even if the board had a pre-existing authorisation, the board would be obliged to transfer the matter to the general meeting for resolution. As discussed in Chapter 4 at II F above, if the board of the target company intends to exercise a share issue authorisation or decide on actions and arrangements belonging within the board's general competence, after a disclosed takeover bid has come to its knowledge, the board is obliged to transfer the matter to the general meeting to be decided.[4] The general meeting of the Target would need to resolve or authorise the board to resolve the 'shareholders' right plan'. Even if the general meeting accepted the plan, the board may not implement a resolution passed by general meeting that conflicts with the principle of equal treatment.

---

[2] Chapter 14, ss 1 and 2 of the SMA.
[3] See generally III, below.
[4] SMA, c 11, s 14.

iii. The Customer Assurance Programme

A customer assurance programme is a strategy, which a company pursues that is generally recognised as consistent with normal business practices in certain situations (depending on the product and the market) and the need to establish ongoing business relationships or minimise customers' or industry analysts' concerns about the company's future. However, the customer assurance programme in this particular scenario is triggered by a takeover bid and its terms (implemented in legally binding contracts) only come into force if the takeover succeeds. It seems that the programme is designed to make the takeover considerably more difficult and expensive for the Bidder. On the other hand, the programme aims to secure the Target's client base.

It may be argued that the programme contains an element of defensive measure in this case. Structural defensive takeover actions are not generally prohibited as long as they are in line with the benefit of the company and the principle of equal treatment of shareholders is complied with. As discussed above and in Chapter 4 at II F, the board may have to transfer the resolution on the implementation of such programme to the general meeting for decision if it may prevent or result in the frustration of, or materially impede implementation of, the takeover bid or its material terms.[5]

The directors may be held liable to the company, a shareholder or a third party, such as the Bidder, for damage caused either deliberately or negligently in violation of the provisions of the CA (other than merely the duty of care) or the company's articles of association as discussed in Chapter 2 at II G above. Further, the directors may also be held liable for damages caused pursuant to the SMA.

B. France

i. Introduction

France implemented the EU Takeover Directive[6] in 2006[7] by virtue of the Monetary and Financial Code[8] and by modifying the Commercial Code.[9] The implementation of the EU Takeover Directive did not significantly alter the situation in France. Takeovers have been strictly regulated since the 1970s in France and French law was already compatible with the principles and rules included in the EU Takeover Directive, particularly with regard to the 'board neutrality rule' and 'breakthrough' rules, which both already existed in France, although with some differences. However, in 2014, France removed the 'board neutrality' rule in order to help protect French companies ('Florange Act').[10] Therefore, there is no obligation, when the offer period (période d'offre) has already begun, to obtain the prior authorisation of the general meeting of

---

[5] Ibid.

[6] Directive 2004/25/EC of the European Parliament and of the Council of 21 April 2004 on takeover bids ([2004] OJ L142/12).

[7] Loi n°2006-387 du 31 mars 2006 relative aux offres publiques d'acquisition, JO n° 78, 1 avril 2006, p 4882.

[8] Monetary and Financial Code, Art L 433-1 and L 433-3.

[9] Commercial Code, Arts L 233-32 ff.

[10] Loi n°2014-384 of 29 mars 2014 visant à reconquérir l'économie réelle, JO 1 April p 6227.

shareholders before taking any action which may result in the frustration of the bid, including seeking alternative bids.[11]

Under French law, the validity of a takeover defence is evaluated according to the law and regulations of the country (*lex societatis*) where the target company is incorporated. In this case, the Target has its legal seat in France. Therefore, the validity of takeover defences adopted by the Target's board of directors or the shareholders in general meeting is to be evaluated according to French company and securities law, and more particularly according to the rules of the Commercial Code.

France allows listed companies to opt into the 'board neutrality' and 'reciprocity' rules.[12] Where the company has opted for the board neutrality rule, if the Bidder also applies the 'board neutrality rule' and the company has also opted in, its board of directors, supervisory board, chief executive officer or any senior executive officer (*directeur général délégué*) is obliged to obtain the prior authorisation of the general meeting of shareholders for this purpose before taking any action, other than seeking alternative bids, which may result in the frustration of the bid.[13] However, the board neutrality rule is only applicable during the offer period. The offer period starts when the securities regulator, the *Autorité des marchés financiers* (AMF), discloses the main elements of the bid.[14] Therefore, the board neutrality rule is not triggered by the Bidder's announcement of the bid or by the fact, such as in the case of the Target, that both the Bidder and the Target know privately that a bid is about to be made.

Therefore, whether Target has opted for the board neutrality rule or not, the board of directors and the management of Target can adopt anti-takeover measures without obtaining the prior authorisation of the shareholders as long as these decisions are within their powers and, if the board neutrality rule has been implemented, can be fully implemented before the offer is officially filed.

Under French company law, the freedom of management of a company and its board of directors – even in circumstances where they are not obliged to obtain the prior authorisation of the shareholders – is limited by the general principles and rules of company and securities law. Turning first to company law, all defences have to be in accordance with the 'company's social interest' (*intérêt social*). According to one approach, promoted by the two most important business organisations,[15] the social interest of the corporation should be construed broadly. It should include the interest of the company, the shareholders, the employees, the clients and third parties: a stakeholder approach. This can be contrasted with the second, more restrictive, conception, whereby the social interests of the corporation equate solely with the interests of the shareholders. This latter conception closely follows Articles 1832 and 1833 of the French Civil Code, but is not predominant in France. Whilst the definition of the social interest is quite broad, it clearly operates as a limitation on the actions of the directors and management. Another important company law principle is the principle

---

[11] Commercial Code, Art L 233-32.

[12] Commercial Code, Art L 233-33 I. See also ch 4 at II B, above. For the reciprocity rule see also III, below.

[13] Commercial Code, Art L 233-32.

[14] AMF General Regulation, Art 231-2 6°.

[15] AFEP/MEDEF, *The Corporate Governance of Listed Corporations*, December 2008, available at www.code-afep-medef.com.

of equality amongst shareholders. Therefore, all shareholders, including the Bidder, must be treated equally.

As to securities law, it should be stressed that all takeover defences have to comply with the securities law principles applicable to takeovers and included in the Monetary and Financial Code and in the AMF general regulation. Such principles were already recognised by French law before the implementation of the EU Takeover Directive in 2006. Some of these principles directly concern takeover defences. For instance, the AMF general regulation states that:

> In order to enable an offer to be conducted in an orderly fashion in the best interests of investors and the market, the parties concerned shall respect the principles of free interplay of offers and counter-offers, equal treatment and information for all holders of the securities of the persons concerned by the offer, market transparency and integrity, and fairness of transactions and competition.[16]

These principles are binding and limit, for instance, the freedom of the board of directors to adopt defences which would only hamper one offeror but not another. This rule also applies to potential offers. The rationale for this approach is that the adoption of such a defence would interfere with the free interplay of offers and counter-offers. These approaches were left unchanged by the 2014 Florange Act which removed the board neutrality rule.

The fact that the main motivation behind the plan was to protect the company's employees would probably not lead to any challenge to the validity of the plan. The reason for this proposition is that the social interests of the company can take into account the interests of the employees. However, it should not be the only reason for the plan, which would not be the case here. In addition, the Florange Act of 2014 reinforces the view that the social interests of the company are to be interpreted from a stakeholder perspective rather than from a shareholder approach.

ii. The Legality of the Shareholders' Right Plan

In the case of a public company (*Société anonyme* or SA) such as the Target, the decision to issue shares is a power which is vested in the extraordinary shareholders' meeting.[17] However, such power can be delegated to the board of directors, both as to the principle that shares can be issued generally (*délégation de compétence*) or as to the implementation of the decision to issue shares in a specific case (*délégation de pouvoirs*).[18] There are certain limits as to the amount and duration of the delegation.[19]

---

[16] AMF General Regulation, Art 231-3.
[17] Commercial Code, Art L 225-96.
[18] Commercial Code, Art L 225-129-2.
[19] These provisions reflect the terms of the previous Art 29 of Directive 2012/30/EU of the European Parliament and of the Council of 25 October 2012 on coordination of safeguards which, for the protection of the interests of members and others, are required by Member States of companies within the meaning of the second paragraph of Article 54 of the Treaty on the Functioning of the European Union, in respect of the formation of public limited liability companies and the maintenance and alteration of their capital, with a view to making such safeguards equivalent (OJ L315/74 14/11/2012) which became Art 68 of Directive (EU) 2017/1132 of the European Parliament and of the Council of 14 June 2017 relating to certain aspects of company law ([2017] OJ L169/46).

In companies whose shares are admitted to trading on a regulated market, such as the Target, the board of directors can sub-delegate to the chief executive officer (CEO) or, with the agreement of the former, to senior executives.[20]

The 'flip-in' plan would probably be implemented through a decision of the general shareholders' meeting delegating the authority to the directors to issue shares in circumstances where the Bidder launches a takeover bid. However, under French company law, the issuance of shares is subject to pre-emption rights (*droits préférentiels de souscription*).[21] These pre-emption rights can only be excluded if the beneficiaries are identified,[22] which is not the case here, or if the company is listed when the increase in capital is conducted through a private placement arrangement, which would not be the case here either.[23] As a consequence, the board of directors of the Target cannot exclude the pre-emption rights for specifically one shareholder.

Even if the increase in capital would not have excluded the Bidder, if the company applies the board neutrality rule, any delegation of authority which might function to frustrate the offer is suspended during the offer period.[24] Therefore, where the company applies the board neutrality rule, since this defensive measure would not have been fully implemented once the takeover is launched or when the Bidder crosses the 20 per cent capital threshold (unless it does so before launching the takeover), the implementation of the 'flip-in' plan would need to be confirmed by a shareholders' meeting. If the company does not apply the board neutrality rule, the delegation of authority to increase the capital, which might function to frustrate the offer, is suspended during the offer period.

Whether the company applies the board neutrality rule or not, the French legislature explicitly allowed a type of 'flip-in' plan, while also stipulating that the Bidder could not be excluded. Indeed, in 2006, the French legislature created a new anti-takeover system, which took its inspiration from Delaware law, called the 'rights offer' (*bons d'offre*). According to this system, an extraordinary shareholders' meeting, voting with the lower quorum and majority requirements applicable in the case of an ordinary meeting (to facilitate approval), can authorise the issuance of rights which give all of the shareholders the right to purchase shares at a discount.[25] The Bidder cannot be excluded because of the principle of equality of shareholders. These rights become void as soon as the bid is cancelled or withdrawn, which demonstrates that they are designed to act as a deterrent or as a means of forcing an increase in the price.

A 'flip-in' plan, such as the one envisaged in the case of the Target, would only be valid under French law if it includes the Bidder. Where the board of directors of the Target proceeds with a 'flip-in' plan that excludes the Bidder, the latter can sue the directors for damages on the basis of a derivative action (ie on behalf of the Target, since the Bidder is a shareholder of the Target). In addition, if the Bidder was excluded from participation in a 'flip-in' plan allowed by the Commercial Code, it could be nullified.

---

[20] Commercial Code, Art L 225-129-4.
[21] Commercial Code, Art L 225-132.
[22] Commercial Code, Art L 225-138, I al 1.
[23] Commercial Code, Art L 225-136.
[24] Commercial Code, Art L 233-32.
[25] Commercial Code, Art L 225-32 II.

iii. The Legality of the Customer Assistance Programme

The programme is designed to make the offer more costly for the Bidder. This type of defence is unusual in France. Since the programme is not targeted specifically at one bidder but is of equal application to all potential bidders, it would probably be considered valid under the principle that no defence should interfere with the free interplay of offers and counter-offers. The situation is different from a case (the Aventis case) which occurred in France in 2004 where a target company (Aventis), during the offer period, decided to issue rights to all shareholders which applied in the case where the bidder (Sanofi) was successful, but the bidder lost a contested patent on an important drug (Plavix) prior to the expiry of a certain period. Since the Aventis case involved a share for share exchange offer, the motive for issuing the rights was to protect the shareholders of the target in case the shares they received lost significant value if the bidder later lost its patent. In the Aventis case, the AMF ruled that a rights plan was contrary to the general principles applicable to takeovers because this defence could only apply to one bidder and not to all potential bidders, and therefore created inequality amongst the bidders.[26] The solution in the Aventis case was adopted prior to the implementation of the Transparency Directive 2004/109/EC of 15 December 2004[27] and was not tested in court. However, the prohibition on the targeting of one bidder is certainly still valid. Therefore, since the 'customer assistance programme' in the hypothetical case is not directed at the Bidder but applies with equal force to all bidders, it is not in violation of the principle of equal treatment.

However, any takeover defence, such as a customer assistance programme, has to be in accordance with the company's social interests. Even if the operation of the programme was authorised by the shareholders, directors can be sued for damages if it appears that there was no valid business reason – apart from attempting to prevent the takeover – for the implementation of the programme. Such a kind of defence has not been tested in the courts. However, in the case of the Target, it is uncertain whether such a defence would be deemed to conform to the social interest, because companies subject to a takeover do not usually undergo any disruption. In addition, contrary to the US (see J, below), which is the source of this type of defence, a prolonged takeover battle is not permitted in France, further weakening the rationale for the customer assistance programme.

iv. Summary and Conclusion

Takeover defences are subjected to close scrutiny under French law and directors can be held liable in damages for taking action that a court deems contrary to the company's social interests. Such action is possible even if the shareholders approved a particular type of defence. However, since 2006, a new type of 'poison pill' has been established in the Commercial Code in order to allow French companies to better

---

[26] PH Conac, 'Les bons de souscriptions "Plavix" et les principes généraux des offres publiques' (2005) *Revue des Sociétés* 321.
[27] [2004] OJ L390/38.

protect themselves. Since the legal regime is carefully prescribed, the risks of liability for the directors where this instrument is used are reduced.

C. Germany[28]

i. Introduction

German takeover law is based on the Takeover Act (WpÜG) and the general company law. In contrast to Finland or the UK, there is no takeover code supplementing the codified law.[29]

The Takeover Act is applicable to offers for the acquisition of shares issued by a target company which are admitted to trading on an organised market (WpÜG, § 1(1)). This is straightforward if the target company is a company with its seat in Germany whose securities are admitted onto a stock exchange in Germany. In such a scenario involving a dual connection to Germany, it is irrelevant that the company is also admitted to a stock exchange in another country.[30] There are some discussions as to whether the term 'seat' should be understood as the registered office or the real seat of the company; the prevailing view now interprets the Act as referring to the registered office, in line with the English-language version of the Takeover Directive.[31]

In contrast to Finnish law, German takeover law enables companies to provide a reciprocity of takeover defences in their articles (WpÜG, § 33c), which is relevant if a foreign company does not follow a strict duty of board neutrality.

According to the wording of the Takeover Act, the provisions dealing with takeover defences apply 'after publication of the decision to make an offer and until publication of the result' (WpÜG, §§ 33(1), 33a(2)).[32] However, it has been suggested in the literature that consideration of the objectives of the law supports an interpretation that focuses on the moment from which the bidder learns about the takeover bid.[33] In the present case, the Target and the Bidder were in negotiations about a friendly takeover bid. This should not be equated with an announcement of the bid because it is still uncertain whether the Bidder was really prepared to make a bid without the consent of the Target's board.

ii. The Shareholders' Rights Plan

Even under general German company law, the shareholders' rights plan is, however, unlawful. German public companies can increase their capital by way of (i) a regular

---

[28] Abbreviated statutes: AktG = Law on Public Companies; WpÜG = Takeover Act.

[29] A voluntary code (Übernahmekodex) was in place from 1995 to 2001, prior to the enactment of the WpÜG.

[30] For the complicated overlap of laws in other cases, see WpÜG, § 1(2)–(5).

[31] See M Lehmann in *Münchener Kommentar zum BGB* (6th edn, Munich, Beck, 2015), Internationales Finanzmarktrecht, paras 420–22.

[32] For an English translation of the WpÜG, see www.bafin.de/SharedDocs/Veroeffentlichungen/EN/Aufsichtsrecht/Gesetz/WpUEG_en.html.

[33] M Schlitt and C Riess, *Münchener Kommentar zum Aktiengesetz, Band 6* (3rd edn, Munich, Beck, 2011) § 33 WpÜG, para 69.

decision of the general meeting, (ii) a conditional capital increase, or (iii) authorised capital (AktG, §§ 182–206). Since a conditional capital increase is only allowed for a narrow list of purposes (AktG, § 192), the present case is interpreted as a change of the articles of association authorising the management board of Target plc to issue new shares (AktG, § 202). Since shareholders of German companies have pre-emption rights (AktG, §§ 186(1), 203(1)), it would have been necessary that the authorisation provided an explicit exclusion of such rights.[34]

Moreover, the exclusion of pre-emption rights must be based on well-founded reasons (*sachliche Gründe*) and must also comply with the principle of equal treatment of shareholders (AktG, § 53a; WpÜG, § 3(1)). Potentially, the interests of employees (and employee shareholders) could be relevant here. It is commonly held that German public companies have to consider the interests not only of the shareholders but the entire enterprise, including its employees and other stakeholders.[35] However, in the present case, the exclusion of the pre-emption right not only favours employees (and employee shareholders) but distinguishes between the Bidder and other non-employee shareholders. There is no case law on such a distinction, but the literature suggests that the authorised capital cannot be used by the management board in order to exclude the pre-emption rights of one specific shareholder (ie here the Bidder).[36]

The Bidder has no right to challenge this violation of the law in its capacity as a bidder. However, it can do so as a shareholder. In the case of an unlawful exclusion of pre-emption rights, disadvantaged shareholders can successfully file actions for an injunction and declaratory judgments, and as part of these actions, they can also obtain interim court orders.[37] If the shares have already been issued to the other shareholders, they can claim for personal damages.

iii. The Customer Assurance Programme

The customer assurance programme could be challenged on two grounds. First, shareholders can successfully file an action for injunction if the directors were obliged to ask for shareholder approval because of a 'serious interference with shareholders' rights and interests'[38] and failed to do so. It is doubtful, however, whether the customer assurance programme would be regarded as significant enough to deviate from the general division of powers between management and shareholders in the case of such a transaction with the former.

---

[34] A different (and disputed) question is whether this authorisation also has to specify in detail the means by which the pre-emption rights are excluded.

[35] See, eg, M Gelter, 'Taming or Protecting the Modern Corporation? Shareholder-Stakeholder Debates in a Comparative Light' (2011) 7 *New York University Journal of Law and Business* 641 at 678–703. A corresponding statement is found in the non-binding German Corporate Governance Code, available at www.dcgk.de/en/code.html, Section 4.1.1.

[36] This may have been different if the shareholders themselves had decided to do so by taking a regular decision to increase the capital; see W Bayer, *Münchener Kommentar zum Aktiengesetz, Band 4* (4th edn, Munich, Beck, 2016) § 202, para 75 and § 203, para 133 with reference to WpÜG, § 33(2).

[37] U Hüffer and J Koch, *Aktiengesetz* (12th edn, Munich, Beck, 2016) § 203, paras 38–39.

[38] See ch 4 at II C, above.

Second, the programme may breach substantive rules. Since it was effected before the bid was announced, the specific duty of board neutrality was not yet applicable (as above). Nevertheless, the general principles of the Takeover Act apply. According to § 3(3) of the WpÜG, the management board of the target is bound to 'act in the best interests of the target company'. The legislative materials approach the 'interests of the company' in the sense of a stakeholder position, embracing inter alia the interests of shareholders and of employees,[39] whereas others focus on the interests of the shareholders only.[40] Additionally, general fiduciary duties impose restrictions on the management board.[41] Overall, it is not entirely clear how this would translate into the evaluation of the customer assurance programme. In favour of its validity, one can argue that it is within the business judgment of the management board to plan for the situation if the takeover is unsuccessful.

If the customer assurance programme were found to be unlawful, the Bidder could not challenge it directly. Even as a shareholder, it would have no direct right to an injunction or compensation in respect of any diminution in its share value.[42] However, under certain conditions, it could bring an action against the management board to pay compensation to the company.[43]

D. Italy[44]

The sources of regulation of takeovers in Italian law are: (i) Articles 101-*bis* ff of the CLF; (ii) regulations issued by Consob (the Italian supervisory authority); and, in part, (iii) the general company law. Thus, in contrast to Finland, the rules on takeovers are legally binding and are not based on best practices.

According to Article 101-*ter*, paragraph 3 of the CLF, Consob supervises takeovers involving securities issued by a company with its registered office in an EU Member State which are admitted to trading on an Italian regulated market. Where Consob is the competent supervisory authority, matters concerning the price and the procedure of the offer are governed by Italian law, whereas, for matters relating to company law, such as the conditions under which the board of the target may undertake any action which might result in the frustration of the bid, the applicable rules and the competent authority are those of the EU Member State in which the target has its registered office.[45] Assuming for the purposes of this solution that the registered office of the

---

[39] *Regierungsentwurf zum WpÜG*, BT-Drucks 14/7034 35, at 52.

[40] U Wackerbarth in *Münchener Kommentar zum Aktiengesetz, Band 6* (3rd edn, Munich, Beck, 2011) § 3 WpÜG, para 19 (*Gesellschaftsinteresse* not *Unternehmensinteresse*).

[41] For these points, see ch 2 at II C and ch 4 at II C, above.

[42] G Spindler in *Münchener Kommentar zum Aktiengesetz, Band 2* (4th edn, Munich, Beck 2014) § 93 para 302.

[43] See ch 4 at II C, above.

[44] Abbreviations: CC = Italian Civil Code (codice civile); CLF = Consolidated Law on Finance; Spa = public company (*Società per azioni*).

[45] In addition, according to Art 101-*ter*, para 5 of the CLF, when the takeover bid involves securities issued by a company with its registered office in Italy and admitted to trading solely on one or more regulated markets of other EU Member States, the matters relating to company law are governed by the Italian law and Consob is the relevant supervisory authority.

Target is in Italy, we can conclude that in this case the applicable law to the takeover is Italian law.

After the amendments to takeover regulation provided for by Legislative Decree no 146/2009, as a default rule the CLF requires the boards of Italian target companies not to implement measures that may frustrate the success of a takeover bid, unless these measures are authorised by the general meeting of the target. The new wording of the Italian regulation on takeovers also enables companies to implement the breakthrough rule provided for in the EU Takeover Directive.[46] In addition, Italian law has also implemented the reciprocity clause of the EU Takeover Directive. In particular, according to Article 104-*ter* of the CLF, the neutrality/passivity and breakthrough rules are not applicable to takeover bids made by 'entities not subject to such provisions or equivalent provisions, or by a company or entity controlled by such entities'. Consob decides whether the provisions applicable to the bidder and to the target are similar or equivalent. However, in Article 104-*ter*, paragraph 4 of the CLF, the Italian reciprocity clause also requires that:

> Any measure adopted by the issuer that could frustrate the bid [according to the reciprocity clause] must be expressly authorised by the shareholders' meeting, with regard to a possible takeover bid, in the eighteen months prior to disclosure of the decision to implement a takeover bid.[47]

Since this provision would appear to require the authorisation of the general meeting in order to apply the reciprocity clause,[48] some legal commentators consider the implementation of this provision to be highly problematic.[49]

The neutrality rule applies only after the communications are made to the public and to Consob pursuant to Article 102 of the CLF. However, Article 102, paragraph 8 of the CLF also provides that when rumours of a possible takeover offer spread to the public and there are irregularities in the market performance of a company's security or securities, some general disclosure obligations of listed companies are imposed upon potential offerors, and Consob may request information from any person who appears to be informed of such a potential takeover offer.

With regard to the shareholders' rights plan, Italian shareholders are entitled to exercise a pre-emption right which, inter alia, can be excluded where there is a special interest of the company ascertained by a specific resolution of the general meeting (CC, Article 2441). Thus, in Italian company law, the proposed shareholders' rights plan would not be permitted even if the main motivation behind this plan was to protect the company's employees.

The consequences of an unjustified exclusion of pre-emption rights, however, are not clear. In particular, the opinions of scholars[50] vary as to whether the resolution is void or voidable. The difference between these two approaches is relevant, since if the

---

[46] Directive 2004/25/EC (n 6).

[47] Author's annotations in square brackets.

[48] *Cf* R Costi, *Il mercato mobiliare* 10th edn (Turin, Giappichelli, 2016) 89.

[49] F Annunziata, *La disciplina del mercato mobiliare* (8th edn, Turin, Giappichelli, 2015) 395.

[50] R Benassi, 'Commento *sub* art. 2441' in A Maffei Alberti (ed), *Commentario breve al diritto delle società* (3rd edn, Padua, CEDAM, 2015) 1160 ff, 1164.

resolution was considered to be void, any person would be allowed to challenge the exclusion of the pre-emption right within a three-year period. However, if the resolution was treated as voidable, the class of persons entitled to challenge the resolution within 90 days of it being passed would be restricted to the members of the other corporate bodies[51] and the shareholders that did not vote in favour of the exclusion.[52]

Finally, since the decision to adopt the customer assurance programme was taken before the disclosure of the bid, this probably falls outside the scope of application of the neutrality/passivity rule applicable in Italian law. However, one must also stress that even where the approval of the general meeting be already secured, according to Article 104, paragraph 1-*bis* of the CLF, the board may not implement any decision taken before the disclosure of the bid that has not been yet implemented wholly or in part and that does not fall within the normal business practices of the company, if such a decision could frustrate the success of the bid. Thus, additional information is required in order to investigate whether this part of Article 104 of the CLF has been violated.

E. Spain

As explained in the Spanish solution to the previous case,[53] takeovers in Spain are essentially regulated by the Texto Refundido de la Ley del Mercado de Valores (TRLMV) – Securities Markets Act[54] – as well as the 2007 Royal Decree on Takeovers. General Spanish company law also prescribes rules that are applicable to takeovers. Although there is no Takeover Code in Spain, some provisions of the Good Governance Code of Listed Companies do address the issue.[55] Takeover regulations are generally applicable in the case of the acquisition of a company whose shares are wholly or partially admitted to trading on an official Spanish secondary market and, at the same time, have their registered office in Spain (TRLMV, Article 129; and 2007 Royal Decree on Takeovers, Article 1.1). The hypothetical case clearly falls within the scope of aforementioned provision.[56]

The TRLMV allows companies such as the Target to disapply the provisions concerning board neutrality where the Bidder is foreign and it does not follow similar neutrality rules (TRLMV, Article 134.3). However, such a decision requires the general

---

[51] In this context, 'the members of the other corporate bodies' is a reference to the directors and the internal auditors in the traditional Italian board structure, the directors in the one-tier board structure, and the members of the supervisory board and the members of the management board in the two-tier board structure.

[52] *Cf* ch 9 at II C, below.

[53] See ch 4 at II A, above.

[54] Real Decreto Legislativo 4/2015, de 23 de octubre, por el que se aprueba el texto refundido de la Ley del Mercado de Valores.

[55] eg, Principle 1 of the Good Governance Code of Listed Companies reads: 'In general, companies should avoid bylaw clauses whose underlying purpose is to hinder possible takeover bids'.

[56] It is possible for the Spanish rules on takeovers to be applied to cases where the target firm does not have its registered office in Spain, provided certain requirements are met (2007 Royal Decree on Takeovers, Art 1.2).

meeting of shareholders to have provided their authorisation within the 18 months preceding the publication of the bid (TRLMV, Article 134.3).

In the instant case, there would likely be no breach of the duty of neutrality by the board of directors of the Target owing to the fact that both the shareholders' rights plan and the customer assurance programme were adopted before the bid was publicly announced by the Bidder. As such, the decisions to adopt the plan and the programme both fall outside the scope of the protection provided by Article 28 of the 2007 Royal Decree on Takeovers. Nevertheless, according to Spanish takeover regulations, the general shareholders' meeting of the Target must approve or confirm any measures – not yet implemented/applied – that have been adopted by the board of directors of the Target prior to the moment when the application of the duty of neutrality is triggered, where those measures fall outside the normal activities of the Target and their application may frustrate the takeover bid (2007 Royal Decree on Takeovers, Article 28.2). These requirements are very general[57] and have not been developed further. Therefore, it is not clear how the courts would interpret them. If the shareholders' rights plan and the customer assurance programme were to be treated as falling within this category, they would, however, require the approval of the Target's shareholders, even if the plan or programme were adopted before the public announcement of the bid.

The shareholders' rights plan would be unlawful because it does not comply with the provisions on pre-emption rights in Spanish company law (Ley de Sociedades de Capital (LSC) – Corporate Enterprises Act, Article 304).[58] In this regard, under Spanish law, it is possible for the general shareholders' meeting of public limited companies – such as the Target – to delegate the power to issue new shares to the board of directors (LSC, Article 297.1(b)). Moreover, in those instances, and, whenever the company is listed – as is the case of the Target – the general shareholders' meeting may also delegate to the board of directors the power to exclude, wholly or partially, the pre-emption rights in relation to those new shares, where this is deemed to be in the company's best interests (LSC, Article 506.1). The main motivation behind the shareholders' rights plan seems to be the protection of the employees and, notably, of the employee shareholders. According to Spanish company law, directors must act in the 'company's best interests' (LSC, Article 227.1). The case law of the Spanish Supreme Court tends to interpret such interests as the common interests of the shareholders – rather than the interests of a particular category of shareholder or stakeholder;[59] therefore, in this case, it may be difficult to justify a case that the shareholders' rights plan is being pursued in the best interests of the Target. Moreover, it could also be argued that the shareholders' rights plan is in breach of the principle of equal treatment of shareholders (LSC, Articles 97 and 514).[60]

---

[57] On the problematic interpretation of Art 28.2 of the 2007 Royal Decree on Takeovers, see J García de Enterría, 'El deber de pasividad de los administradores de una sociedad afectada por una OPA' (2008) 2 *Revista de derecho del mercado de valores* 89.

[58] Real Decreto Legislativo 1/2010, de 2 de julio, por el que se aprueba el texto refundido de la Ley de Sociedades de Capital (LSC).

[59] See, eg, the STS (Sentencia Tribunal Supremo) of 18 November 2002.

[60] For a complete examination of the principle of equal treatment of shareholders developed by the LSC, see A Martínez Flórez, 'Artículo 97. Igualdad de trato' in Á Rojo and E Beltrán (eds), *Comentario de la Ley de Sociedades de Capital* (Cizur Menor (Navarra), Civitas-Thomson Reuters, 2011) 820–44.

The Bidder would face difficulties in challenging the decision by the board of directors of the Target in court. However, shareholders of the Target with at least 0.1 per cent of the share ownership could challenge the relevant decision entered into by the board of directors of the Target (LSC, Articles 251.1 and 495.2(b)).[61] According to the Ley de Enjuiciamiento Civil (LEC) – Civil Procedure Act – the legal action would be raised in the civil courts (LEC, Article 249.1.3). Moreover, shareholders could also attain interim measures in order to suspend the execution of the shareholders' rights plan (LEC, Article 727.10). Hence, in the instant case, the Bidder could ultimately challenge the resolution as a shareholder of the Target but not as a party in the takeover transaction.

Turning to the customer assurance programme, for the reasons explained above, the duty of neutrality of directors in takeovers would not apply to its adoption. It is unclear whether it could be challenged on the basis of the failure to obtain shareholder approval. In this regard, the board is required to call a shareholders' general meeting when it considers it necessary or convenient for the company's interests (LSC, Article 167); such necessity or convenience is arguably present in this case. Moreover, general company law prescribes a number of decisions which require shareholder approval (LSC, Article 160), but the customer assurance programme would not fit within any of them. If it could be demonstrated that the customer assurance programme is contrary to the law, the by-laws of the Target, or, more generally, that it benefits a given category of shareholders, such as employee-shareholders, but is detrimental to the interests of the Target, then it could be challenged by the shareholders of the Target – including the Bidder – who represent at least 0.1 per cent of the share capital (LSC, Articles 251.1 and 495.2(b)). As part of the process, the Target's shareholders could ask for precautionary measures to be taken (LEC, Article 727.10).

As a third party, the Bidder would face limitations in bringing a claim for damages against the directors of the Target. However, shareholders – including the Bidder – with at least 3 per cent of the share capital of the Target could file, subject to the fulfilment of certain requirements, a claim for damages (LSC, Articles 239, 168 and 495.2(a)) if they were able to demonstrate that the behaviour of the directors – for instance, the adoption of the shareholders' rights plan and/or the customer assurance programme – had inflicted loss upon the Target. Another possibility for shareholders and third parties would be to file an individual claim, if they are able to show that the directors' actions caused them direct loss (LSC, Article 241).

F. The Netherlands[62]

i. Introduction

The hypothetical case study concerns a cross-border takeover in the sense that the Bidder has its registered office in a different jurisdiction from the Target. The Target

---

[61] The shareholders would have a period of 30 days from the moment they became aware of the agreement to challenge (LSC, Art 251.1).

[62] Abbreviations: DCC=Dutch Civil Code; HR = Hoge Raad = Dutch Supreme Court; OK = Ondernemingskamer = Enterprise Chamber; Rb= rechtbank = District Court. An unofficial translation of

has its registered office and headquarters in the home jurisdiction and is also listed in the home jurisdiction as well as on two foreign stock exchanges. Since the Target is a Dutch company, Dutch law will apply to the role and actions of its board. Dutch law applies the incorporation theory.[63] Assuming that the Bidder is already a shareholder of the Target, this shareholder would be able to challenge the actions of the board in a Dutch court. Since we have no background information on the rules of the foreign stock exchanges, this hypothetical case will be solved on the basis of Dutch law.

ii. Position of the Board of the Target Company

As discussed in the case study concerning the duties of the board in takeovers in chapter 4, the Netherlands has not implemented the so-called 'board neutrality' rule.[64] The main rules regarding the permissibility of defensive measures against takeovers have developed in the case law. Dutch law does, however, allow companies to voluntarily apply the board neutrality rule. If this rule is applied on a voluntary basis, the Target can also make use of the so-called 'reciprocity rule' in a case where the Bidder does not apply the same rules. This is codified in Article 2:359 b DCC. However, this is not relevant to the hypothetical case study under discussion.

As mentioned above, it is accepted under Dutch law that the board of directors can in principle defend the Target against a hostile takeover.[65] Defensive measures are permissible if they are necessary in order to safeguard the continuity of the Target and the interests of its stakeholders. Whether or not this is the case will depend on the specific circumstances. Of importance in this respect is whether the board could reasonably expect the defence to be necessary in order to maintain the status quo while awaiting the outcome of the negotiations. Furthermore, defensive measures should generally be of a temporary nature. Finally, in order to answer the question whether a defence is justified, it is important that the measures taken are necessary and proportionate in relation to the threat posed.[66]

Shareholders, such as the Bidder, who do not agree with the actions taken by the board can start an inquiry procedure with the Enterprise Chamber of the Court of Appeal of Amsterdam.[67] This court will examine whether there are sound reasons to doubt the appropriateness of the conduct of business of the Target (*gegronde redenen om aan een juist beleid of juiste gang van zaken te twijfelen*).[68] If this is the case, the Enterprise Chamber can appoint investigators who will look further into the matter. The court can also take measures, such as, for example, dismissing the board once it

Dutch company law as incorporated in bk 2 of the Dutch Civil Code can be found at www.dutchcivillaw. com/civilcodebook022.htm.

[63] DCC, Art 10:118.

[64] See ch 4 at II E, above.

[65] See BF Assink and WJ Slagter, *Compendium Ondernemingsrecht, Deel 1* (Deventer, Kluwer, 2013) § 76.5.

[66] HR 18 April 2003, *NJ* 2003/286, with a note by JMM Maeijer (*Rodamco North America, Rodamco North America/VEB*). See Assink and Slagter, *Compendium Ondernemingsrecht, Deel 1* (n 65) §76.5.

[67] DCC, Art 2:344.

[68] DCC, Art 2:350. See for the translation and further elaboration of the procedure in the Annex to the Study on Directors' Duties and Liability in the EU prepared for the European Commission DG Markt 2013, Country report: Netherlands, at p A 624, available at http://ec.europa.eu/justice/civil/company-law/ corporate-governance/index_en.htm.

has been established that the Target has been mismanaged (*wanbeleid*).[69] In addition, the Enterprise Chamber can enact all interim measures it deems necessary in the course of the procedure.[70] This inquiry procedure has often been used in cases concerning takeovers such, as for example, in the ABN AMRO takeover, discussed in the previous chapter.[71] Where it concerns the strategy of the Target, the board is generally given wide discretion to take the measures which it deems necessary. It is, however, possible that a defensive measure is regarded as contrary to standards of reasonableness or fairness which in turn can be a ground for mismanagement (*wanbeleid*).[72] However, the inquiry procedure cannot be used to claim damages from a director of the Target.[73]

iii. The Shareholders' Rights Plan

The shareholders' rights plan requires shares to be issued to the existing shareholders with the exception of the Bidder. The decision to issue new shares in a Dutch public limited liability company (NV) rests, in principle, with the shareholders. However, this right can be delegated for a maximum of five years to the board of directors after which period, the delegation can be renewed.[74] Assuming that the right to issue new shares has been delegated to the board, it can be said that the board would be able to issue a shareholders' rights plan. However, it would be difficult to exclude the Bidder from such a plan in circumstances where the Bidder is already a shareholder of the Target. After all, all shareholders have pre-emptive rights.[75] These pre-emptive rights can only be set aside by a two-thirds majority of the shareholders.[76] It can also be set aside by another organ or body of the Target provided that the power to do so has been delegated to that organ or body for a maximum of five years.[77] It is unlikely that in the hypothetical case such a majority can be achieved. Pre-emptive rights are also applicable to call options.[78] Pre-emptive rights do not apply if shares are issued to employees.[79] In the Gucci case this technique was used in an attempt to defend the company against a hostile takeover.[80]

iv. The Customer Assurance Programme

Putting in place a customer assurance programme is in principle something which falls within the power of the board of directors. After all, satisfying customers is related

---

[69] DCC, Art 2:357.
[70] DCC, Art 2:349a.
[71] See ch 4 at II E, above, and HR 13 July 2007, *JOR* 2007/178, with a note by Nieuwe Weme. See for other inquiry procedures related to takeovers HR 18-April 2003, *NJ* 2003/286, with a note by JMM Maeijer (*Rodamco North America, Rodamco North America/VEB*); OK 3 March 1999, *JOR* 1999/87 (*Gucci*).
[72] Hof Amsterdam 27 May 1999, *NJ* 1999/487 (*Gucci*).
[73] See Country report Netherlands (n 68).
[74] DCC, Art 2:96-1.
[75] DCC, Art 2:96a.
[76] DCC, Art 2:96a-7.
[77] DCC, Art 2:96a-6.
[78] DCC, Art 2:96a-8.
[79] DCC, Art 2:96a-1.
[80] Hof Amsterdam 27 May 1999, *NJ* 1999/487 (*Gucci*).

to the daily management and operations of the Target. However, in the hypothetical case it can be argued that the programme was put in place to fight off the potential bid/hostile takeover. If shareholders feel this is the case, they can start, as mentioned above, an inquiry procedure at the Court of Appeal in Amsterdam requesting it to appoint investigators to scrutinise the way the Target has been managed. However, on various occasions the court has decided that the strategy of a company is the prerogative of the board under the supervision of the supervisory board.[81] Shareholders can make their opinion known by making use of the rights and powers awarded to them by the law and the articles of association. However, the board is in principle not obliged to consult the shareholders prior to taking a decision which falls within the ambit of the power awarded to the board.[82] The customer assurance programme will therefore most likely be allowed under Dutch law.

G. Poland

In Poland, there is no special regulation or code on takeovers as in UK or German law. However, provisions which have a bearing on the hypothetical case can be found in both the Commercial Companies Code (CCC) and the Act of 29 July 2005 on Public Offering, Conditions Governing the Introduction of Financial Instruments to Organised Trading, and the Public Companies (hereinafter 'the Public Offering Act'). Moreover, the EU Takeover Directive[83] will be applicable in those areas where there is only partial implementation. Under Polish law, the hypothetical case should be analysed from at least three perspectives: (i) duties of the management board in the event of a takeover bid, in particular, the neutrality principle provided for in the EU Takeover Directive and its implementation in Polish law; (ii) provisions regulating authorised share capital; and (iii) the equal treatment rule applicable to all shareholders. The hypothetical case concerns a public limited company (plc), the Polish equivalent being a public company (*spółka akcyjna*).

Poland makes use of the opt-out in the EU Takeover Directive in relation to the duty of neutrality rule. It does so by granting companies governed by Polish law the option to incorporate the duty of neutrality into their articles. According to Article 80a, section 1 of the Public Offering Act, the articles of association of a public company may provide that during the tender offer for sales or exchange of all the remaining shares of the company, the management board and the supervisory board of such company are obliged to obtain the prior consent of the shareholders' general meeting in order to take measures which are aimed at *cancelling* the announced tender offer. According to Article 80, section 2 of the Public Offering Act, the aforementioned obligation will not apply to actions leading to an announcement of a tender offer regarding the same shares by another entity (the so-called 'white knight' strategy). In the situation referred to in section 1 of Article 80, the company's articles of association must

---

[81] HR 13 July 2007, NJ 2007/434 (*ABN AMRO*).
[82] HR 13 July2007, NJ 2007/434 (*ABN AMRO*). See in this respect Assink and Slagter (n 65) §76.5.
[83] Directive 2004/25/EC (n 6).

provide that any of the following shall have no effect: (i) limitations on the exercise of voting rights, defined in the articles of association of the company or any agreement between the company whose shares are covered by the tender offer and shareholders of that company, or in an agreement between such shareholders, provided the agreement has entered into effect subsequent to 21 April 2004; and (ii) preference shares as to voting rights. This also applies to those shares that have the advantage of multiple voting rights (but only non-public companies). Polish law applies a subjective test in the evaluation of the directors' conduct. Therefore, there is a requirement to prove that the management board has taken action aimed at cancelling the announced tender offer. In other words, it is not enough to show that a particular decision or activity may lead to the cancellation of the tender offer; a real evidence of purpose is required.

Polish law on the regulation of takeovers is somewhat fragmented. It covers some aspects of the takeover, but not all. *De lege lata*, there is no general ban on the management board of a public company adopting takeover defences. However, whilst the Polish regulatory provisions do not ban the management board from taking decisions or action designed to frustrate a takeover bid in the absence of the prior consent of the shareholders' general meeting – this can be attributed to Poland's decision to opt out of the board neutrality rule in Article 9 of the EU Takeover Directive – an analysis of the potential structural mechanisms available to the management board in order to frustrate a hostile bid reveal that either they would be treated as null and void or weak and ineffective. In other words, although there is general freedom on the part of the management board to apply anti-takeover defences, these measures appear to be weak. This is attributable to the fact that Polish law will operate to prohibit some of these structures. For example, raising the amount of shareholder capital in order to frustrate a bid causes difficulties for the management board, since this power falls within the competence of the shareholders' general meeting. Thus, the management board has no capacity to raise the share capital without first attaining shareholder approval.

In Polish law, the 'poison pill' mechanism is usually analysed in light of the provisions concerning the increase in share capital of a company.[84] There is the possibility of entrusting the management board with the a priori power to raise the capital of the company up to a certain level (target capital). However, this power may be used only where such right in favour of the management board has been conferred in the articles of association of the company. Its utility is limited for the purpose of this hypothetical case, since the case refers only to the *ex post* situation. Nevertheless, it ought to be stressed that the legal option of conferring a power in favour of the directors to increase the share capital is usually provided for in most statutes of public companies: according to Article 444, section 1 of the CCC, the company's articles may authorise the management board, for a period of no more than three years, to

---

[84] See, eg, C Podsadlik, *Wrogie przejęcie spółki* (Warsaw, LexisNexis, 2003); K Oplustil and M Bobrzyński, 'Europejskie prawo przejęć spółek publicznych. Trzynasta Dyrektywa UE z zakresu prawa spółek i jej implikacje dla prawa polskiego' (2004) 1 *Studia Prawnicze* 47 ff.; K Oplustil and M Bobrzyński, 'przejęcie po europejsku', *Rzeczpospolita* dated 5.08.2004; A Sobol, 'Wrogie przejęcie w świetle postanowień XIII dyrektywy w sprawie publicznych ofert nabycia akcji' (2005) 7 *Monitor Prawniczy* 336 ff.; K Oplustil, 'Obrona przed wrogim przejęciem publicznej spółki akcyjnej w prawie europejskim i polskim – uwagi de lege lata i de lega ferenda (cz. II)' (2006) 6 *Prawo spółek* 2 ff.

increase the initial share capital of the company in accordance with the terms of that article. The management board may exercise the authority vested in it by making one or more consecutive initial share capital increases within the limits set in Article 444, section 3 of the CCC (target capital). Pursuant to Article 444, section 2, the authority to increase the initial share capital may be given to the management board for consecutive periods which must not exceed three years. For this authorisation to be effective, however, the company's articles must be amended. The management board must issue these shares exclusively for cash consideration, save where the authorisation to increase the initial share capital allows for shares to be taken up for non-cash consideration. However, there are some further limitations concerning how far the management board can go, namely: (i) the management board's authority to increase the initial share capital must not extend to the power to make increases out of the company's own means;[85] (ii) the management board must not issue preference shares or other special rights; and (iii) resolutions of the management board which fix the issue price and the nature and extent of the non-cash consideration payable for the shares require the approval of the supervisory board, save where the company's articles provide otherwise. Further, according to Article 446, section 1 of the CCC, a resolution of the management board adopted within the parameters of the authorisation contained in the company's articles will amount to a valid substitution for a resolution of the shareholders' general meeting on increasing the initial share capital. The management board is obliged to decide on all matters relating to the increase in the initial share capital, unless the provisions of the CCC or the authority conferred upon the management board provide otherwise. Article 444, section 7 of the CCC specifically provides that the scope of the authorisation in favour of the management board to increase the initial share capital of the company may provide for the issue of subscription warrants referred to in Article 453, section 2 of the CCC with the time limit for the exercise of the subscription rights elapsing no later than the period for which the authorisation was given. In turn, Article 453 provides that a company may, for the purposes of increasing its initial share capital in accordance with the provisions of the CCC, issue registered securities or bearer securities that entitle the holder to subscribe for or take up shares which exclude the pre-emption rights of shareholders (subscription warrants). However, Article 453 requires – as a principle – the exclusion of pre-emption rights for all shareholders.

However, Polish legal doctrine permits the derogation from the principle of equal treatment of shareholders, if it is objectively justified. The circumstances which justify the unequal treatment of shareholders should be assessed primarily from the point of view of the interests of the company.[86] On 13 May 2004, the Polish Supreme Court

---

[85] An initial capital increase out of the company's means is regulated by ch 4, Division 3 of the CCC. In accordance with Art 442, s 1 of the CCC, the general meeting may increase the initial capital by allocating to this purpose: (i) amounts held in reserve capital created from profit, if they may be employed to this end; (ii) reserves created in the case of a reduction of initial capital (CCC, Art 457, s 2); (iii) reserve capital created from undistributable profits in terms of the company's articles; and (iv) the supplementary capital.

[86] See, eg, S Sołtysiński in *Kodeks spółek handlowych, vol. I, Komentarz do artykułów 1-150* (Warsaw, CH Beck, 2001) 306; JA Strzępka and E Zielińska in *Kodeks Spółek Handlowych. Komentarz pod red. J.A. Strzępki* (Warsaw, CH Beck-Legalis, 2009), note to Art 20 of the Polish Commercial Companies Code; A Szumański, *Przymusowy wykup akcji drobnych akcjonariuszy*, PPH no 11 (2001) 1–10; A Kidyba,

issued a ruling (V CK 452/03) which stated that the effectiveness of the inclusion of an authorisation in the statute of the company to the effect that the management board can exclude or limit the pre-emption rights of certain shareholders – by increasing the share capital from within the authorised capital – should be assessed primarily from the point of view of the interests of the company. The Supreme Court decided that the CCC permits the introduction of restrictions on the pre-emptive right of shareholders, if their limitation or exclusion is introduced with a view to the furtherance of important interests of the target company. The principle of equal treatment of shareholders is not treated as a counter-argument to this position, as it allows for the differentiation of shareholders in different situations. The CCC also enacts a number of far-reaching exceptions to this principle, such as the ability to issue preference shares or personal rights. Special rights or privileges granted to a particular shareholder, however, have their justification in the particular role or importance of a shareholder for the company, eg, in case of a strategic investor. The same should be evaluated with respect to the behaviour of the board towards 'attacking' shareholders. Selective exclusion of subscription rights will be unacceptable only if management violates the duty of loyalty.[87] The management could justify their actions in such a way that the 'attacker' in fact heading for liquidation or dissolution of the company or control of the company would jeopardise the long-term policy of the board. The possibility of exclusion of subscription rights for only some of the shareholders cannot be ruled out. Article 433 § 2 of the CCC restricts the principle expressed in § 1 of this provision and the requirement of equal treatment of shareholders of Article 20 of the CCC is not absolute. In the interests of the company the general meeting may therefore – pursuant to Article 433 § 2 of the CCC – exclude or limit pre-emption rights, also with regard to certain shareholders.[88]

Taking into account the above-mentioned arguments, it must be stressed that the Target's shareholders' rights plan to subscribe for additional shares in the Target at 50 per cent of their market value as soon as an outside acquirer achieves a threshold stake of 20 per cent of the shares of the Target will be null and void under Polish law, unless clearly justified in its best interests: it would constitute a preference which is not allowed in relation to authorised share capital that can be issued pursuant to authorisation vested in the management board. Such a resolution of the management board would be null and void and can be challenged before the court in accordance

---

Kodeks Spółek Handlowych. Komentarz do art. 1-300, vol I, issue 3 (Kraków, Zakamycze, 2005) 138; A Koch and J Napierała, *Prawo handlowe. Spółki handlowe, umowy gospodarcze* (Kraków, Zakamycze, 2002) 120–21.

[87] See further K Szmid, *Natura spółki akcyjnej jako delimitacja zasady swobody umów w prawie polskim i amerykański* (Warsaw, CH Beck, 2015).

[88] See, eg. A Radwan, *Prawo poboru w spółce akcyjnej* (Warsaw, CH Beck, 2004) 296–97; S Sołtysiński in S Sołtysiński A Szajkowski, A Szumański and J Szwaja, *Kodeks spółek handlowych, t III. Komentarz do artykułów 301-458* (Warsaw, CH Beck, 2008) 1452–53, S Pawelec, *Podmiotowe ograniczenia prawa poboru w spółce akcyjnej,* PPH 2007, No 4; *idem, Realizacja prawa poboru przy emisji akcji róznychy rodzajów,* PPH 2007, No 9; A Radwan, *Wybrane aspekty podmiotowej strony prawa poboru akcji,* Pr. Sp. 2003, No 3. Against selective pre-emptive right, see M Rodzynkiewicz, *Kodeks spółek handlowych. Komentarz* (Warsaw, Lexis Nexis 2009) 932; W Popiołek in JA Strzępka, *Kodeks* (Warsaw, CH Beck, 2003) 1259; R Czerniawski, *Kodeks spółek handlowych, Przepisy o spół- ce akcyjnej, Komentarz* (Warsaw, Dom Wydawniczy ABC 2004) 478; K Osajda, 'Kodeks spółek handlowych w orzecznictwie Sądu Najwyższego w I półroczu 2004' Glosa 2005 no 2, p 11.

with Article 189 of the Polish Civil Procedure Code. The Bidder will have to prove that the management board resolution was passed against the interests of the Bidder. If the only purpose of the 'flip-in' plan was to 'water down' the existing shareholders' share capital, such a plan is clearly contradictory to the principle of equal treatment of shareholders found in Article 20 of the CCC, which provides that all shareholders of the company should be treated equally in the same circumstances. However, the conclusion may be different if the plan is to protect employees, who may face redundancies in the event of a takeover.

Turning to the customer assurance programme, the relevant issues impacting upon it are less straightforward. It is a well-established legal doctrine in Europe that a 'scorched earth policy' is not allowed.[89] It is argued that such action is absolutely contrary to the interests of the company. It is questionable, however, to what extent the customer assurance programme can be treated as imposing additional obligations on the Target with the aim of threatening the Bidder's takeover bid or the extent to which it is simply a continuation of the Target's ordinary course of business. It must be stated that the CCC[90] confers a fairly broad discretion on the management board in relation to the management of the company. However, this can be contrasted with the discretion given to the management board pursuant to the 'flip-in' plan. Whereas the competence to increase the share capital remains in the hands of the general meeting of the shareholders, the general authority to manage the business rests upon the management board, save for those areas where the supervisory board and the general meeting have competence. There is insufficient information in the hypothetical case concerning the amount of the customer assurance programme and its value vis-a-vis the assets of the Target, which could assist in assessing the case. Nevertheless, generally speaking, it seems that the tactic of deploying the customer assurance programme could be sustained in court, given the fact that its purpose is to protect the Target's clients. The main obligation of the management board is to act in the interests of the company, which can be understood as the aggregate interests of the stakeholders. The Target's clients are undoubtedly one of those stakeholders. However, it should be noted that in Poland, there is no case law concerning the validity of such anti-takeover defence and therefore it is difficult to predict how the court would resolve the issues arising in such a situation.

---

[89] KJ Hopt, 'The Duties of the Directors of the Target Company in Hostile Takeovers – German and European Perspectives' in G Ferrarini, KJ Hopt and E Wymeersch (eds), *Capital Markets in the Age of Euro: Cross-border Transactions, Listed Companies and Regulation* (The Hague, Kluwer Law International, 2002) 416–17.

[90] According to Art 368, s 1 of the CCC, the management board must manage the affairs of the company and represent the company. There is a general recognition that the management board has the competence to increase the share capital within the limits of the company's authorised capital and that this is an example of the board's prerogative to manage the company. See S Sołtysiński in S Sołtysiński, A Szajkowski, J Szwaja and A Szumański, *Kodeks spółek handlowych, t III* (Warsaw, CH Beck, 2008) 1526. However, how far this competence extends is debatable since the Polish CCC lacks a provision similar in effect to s 157(a) of the DGCL, which confers upon the board of directors general authority to issue rights and options which entitle the holders thereof to acquire share capital.

H. Latvia

As in the previous case,[91] the scope of the duties of the management of a target company in Latvian law depends on when the takeover bid was announced to the board of directors and the supervisory board: section 77(5) of the Law on the Financial Instrument Market.[92] Although the Bidder holds negotiations and subsequently announces the bid to the shareholders of the Target, the bid is never formally announced to the management board and the supervisory board of the Target. Therefore, the scope of the duties of the management of the Target is set out in section 77(6) of the Financial Instrument Market Act, which provides that the approval of the shareholders meeting is necessary 'in respect of any decision that is not intrinsic to the normal course of the target company's business and whose implementation may frustrate the share buyout offer'.

Whether the implementation of the shareholders' rights plan and the customer assurance programme fall outside the scope of the normal course of the Target's business is doubtful. It could, however, be argued in favour of such an interpretation that both measures have been implemented specifically because of the takeover bid and not in the normal course of business. In that case, the approval of the meeting of the shareholders would have been required for their implementation, failing which both could be declared invalid.

In addition, the shareholders' rights plan itself contravenes Latvian law. In the event of an issue of new shares, all shareholders have a statutory right of pre-emption to acquire the new shares in proportion to their existing holding (Commercial Code, section 251(1)). Share issues may also not be divided during a share buyout offer, and board decisions sanctioning the same are illegal (Financial Instruments Market Law, sections 78(3) and 69(3)). The pre-emption right may not be removed by resolution of the meeting of shareholders or as a result of a modification of the company's statutes or articles (Commercial Code, section 253) as long as the respective shareholder exercises his or her right in the given timeframe (Commercial Code, section 251(3)). It is of no consequence that the bid may have a detrimental effect on the interests of employee shareholders, even if this may go against the interest of the company, for example where employees have been sought to be motivated by the board to become shareholders as a means of an employee ownership and participation plan.[93] Therefore, the right of pre-emption may not exclude the new outside acquirer from exercising it, and based on the principle of equal treatment of shareholders (Financial Instrument Market Law, Section 54(1)),[94] the conditions for the exercise of the pre-emption rights must

---

[91] See ch 4 at II H, above.

[92] Finanšu instrumentu tirgus likums, Latvijas Vēstnesis 175 (2490) 11 December 2003. An English translation of the Act is available at www.fktk.lv/en/law/financial-instruments-market/laws.html.

[93] For a description of such Employee Share Ownership plans and their legal framework in Latvia and other EU states, see T Muravska and T Klauberg in J Lowitzsch et al, 'The Promotion of Employee Ownership and Participation' Study prepared by the Inter-University Centre for European Commission's DG Markt, 2014, available at http://ec.europa.eu/internal_market/company/docs/modern/141028-study-for-dg-markt_en.pdf.

[94] See also Directive 2012/30/EU (n 19), art 46 and now Directive (EU) 2017/1132 (n 19), art 85.

not differ. The end result is that the takeover offer to acquire newly issued shares for 50 per cent of their market value must not exclude the Bidder.

If the customer assurance programme is indeed considered to be part of the normal course of the Target's business and thus does not require the approval of the share-holders' general meeting, it may nevertheless be in breach of the general prohibition on interference with share buyout offers (Financial Instrument Market Law, section 78(1)) or the fiduciary duties of the directors towards the company.[95] However, the decisions of the director may be viewed as satisfying the business judgment rule test,[96] where the directors are taking measures to protect the company not (only) against the bid, but in order to avoid negative consequences for the Target's business.

I. The UK[97]

i. General Introduction to Cross-border Takeovers and the Applicable Law

As noted in the UK solution in chapter 4, above, the EU Takeover Directive[98] is implemented by Part 28 of the CA 2006 and the City Code. In terms of Article 12(3) of the EU Takeover Directive, Member States may apply a reciprocity rule to provisions which restrict takeover action. In other words, if a company based in Member State A is the target of a bid from a company located in another Member State B which is not subject to equivalent restrictions, the target can disapply the restrictions and take frustrating action against the bid. However, reciprocity provisions are inapplicable in the UK.[99]

The UK solution to the hypothetical case in chapter 4, above[100] highlighted that the law and regulation of takeovers in the UK straddle both company law and securities law. It is important to establish whether the legal issues fall within the categories of company law or securities law. Since this case concerns the actions of the Target in a hostile takeover bid situation, it is clear that it is a company law matter. In ascertaining the applicable law which governs the cross-border takeover bid in this hypothetical case, it is assumed that the Target's securities have been admitted to trading on a regulated market in the Home Jurisdiction and the two other stock exchanges where its shares are listed are not located in the EU. Therefore, since the Target's registered

---

[95] See also ch 2 at II A, above.

[96] For more detail on the business judgment rule, see E Novicāne and Z Kļaviņa, 'Valdes locekļu atbildība par biznesa lēmumiem: Vai Komerclikumā jāievieš business judgment rule?' *Jurista Vārds* 18.09.2012, 38(737).

[97] Abbreviations: CA 2006 (the Companies Act 2006); Model Articles (Model articles of association of private companies limited by shares (in reg 2 of and sch 1 to the Companies (Model Articles) Regulations 2008, SI 2008/3229), private companies limited by guarantee (in reg 3 of and sch 2 to the Companies (Model Articles) Regulations 2008, SI 2008/3229) and public limited companies (in reg 4 of and sch 3 to the Companies (Model Articles) Regulations 2008, SI 2008/3229)); City Code (the Takeover Code (www.thetakeoverpanel.org.uk/wp-content/uploads/2008/11/code.pdf?v=2May2017)).

[98] Directive 2004/25/EC (n 6).

[99] See the UK government's reasoning for this approach in *Company Law Implementation of the European Directive on Takeover Bids: A Consultative Document*, January 2006 (available at http://webarchive.national-archives.gov.uk/20060715205232/http://www.dti.gov.uk/files/file10384.pdf) 28–29 at paras 3.11–3.13.

[100] See ch 4 at II I, above.

office is located in the Home Jurisdiction, on the basis of the provisions in the City Code, the end result is that (i) the Panel on Takeovers and Mergers (the Panel) will have sole jurisdiction;[101] (ii) the City Code will apply to regulate the takeover and (iii) the divided jurisdiction provisions of Article 4 of the EU Takeover Directive will not apply. Thus, for the purposes of this solution, we are assuming that the registered office of the Target is in the UK (ie the Home Jurisdiction is the UK) and that the proper law which regulates the takeover is UK law, as set out in the City Code.

ii. The Legality of the Shareholders' Rights Plan

The implementation of the shareholders' rights plan contained in the articles of association will (i) involve putting in place a directed share issue on a non pre-emptive basis which excludes the Bidder from participation (it is assumed that the Bidder is a shareholder of the Target) and (ii) amount to the directors engaging in frustrating action subsequent to the directors of the Target having reason to believe that a bona fide offer from the Bidder 'might be imminent' and so will be contrary to Rule 21 of the City Code (as in the UK solution in chapter 4, above).

a. The Company Law Rules Governing Directed Share Issues

In terms of UK company law, the power to allot shares resides in the shareholders of a company. Since the Target is a public company, the directors have no power to allot shares unless authorisation to do so is conferred upon them by way of authorisation in the articles or by way of authorisation by the shareholders passing an ordinary resolution.[102] Such devolution of the authority to allot may be generally conferred on the directors for a period not exceeding five years[103] or granted for a specific exercise of the power only. Since the shareholders' rights plan is found in the articles of association of the Target, it is assumed that the articles also confer power upon the directors to allot the shares in implementation of the plan. However, even if the allotment of shares pursuant to the shareholders' rights plan is not authorised in terms of the articles or an ordinary resolution passed by the shareholders, it will nevertheless be valid and cannot be legally challenged on the basis that it is void or voidable.[104]

Section 561(1) of the CA 2006 directs that all existing shareholders of the Target are entitled to pre-emption rights on a fresh issue of shares.[105] The effect of section 563(2)

---

[101] See A3(a)(i) of the City Code.

[102] CA 2006, ss 549(1) and 551(1).

[103] However, a listed plc such as the Target will be expected to comply with the guidelines of the Investment Management Association, which recommend that companies have shareholders annually renew general authorities to allot (see www.ivis.co.uk/media/9665/Share-Capital-Management-Guidelines-July-2014-.pdf) at the company's annual general meeting. These guidelines do not possess the force of law. However, listed plcs routinely follow them owing to the extensive 'soft' power and influence wielded by institutional shareholders.

[104] CA 2006, s 549(6).

[105] CA 2006, s 551(3). It is also noteworthy that a listed plc such as the Target will be expected to comply with the guidelines of the Investment Management Association. These guidelines provide that a listed plc should not allot more than two-thirds of its existing issued ordinary share capital in any one fresh issue of shares (see https://www.ivis.co.uk/media/9665/Share-Capital-Management-Guidelines-July-2014-.pdf).

of the CA 2006 is that if the Target or the directors of the Target knowingly authorise or permit the implementation of the directed share issue in terms of the shareholders' rights plan, the Target and those directors will be jointly and severally liable to compensate any person to whom an offer should have been made in accordance with those provisions for any loss, damage, costs or expenses which that person has sustained or incurred by reason of it. Thus, the Bidder would be successful if it sued the Target or the Target's directors in respect of the losses which it had incurred, provided that it was able to show that the Target or the directors knowingly authorised or permitted the directed share issue and the claim was made within two years of the date of the delivery to the registrar of companies of the return of allotment in terms of section 555 of the CA 2006.[106] The Target and/or its directors will be deemed to have 'knowingly authorised or permitted' the directed share issue if it can be shown that it or they contravened section 563(2) of the CA 2006 with knowledge of the facts upon which the contravention depends.[107] In the hypothetical case, it appears to be clear that the directors of the Target were aware that the implementation of the shareholders' rights plan would defeat the Bidder's pre-emption rights and so contravene the provisions on the allotment of shares in the CA 2006.

The losses which the Bidder may recover in terms of section 563(2) of the CA 2006 are as follows:

1. financial losses, including any devaluation in the market price of the Bidder's shares caused by the directed share issue;

2. damage, including liquidated harm sustained but not limited to financial loss, subject to the existence of a causative link between the damage and the directed share issue; and

3. costs and expenses, including professional fees.[108]

However, there are a number of exceptions where section 561 of the CA 2006 is inapplicable. In the case of a plc such as the Target, the most important exceptions are stipulated in sections 570 and 571 of the CA 2006. Sections 570 and 571 enable the directors of a plc who are generally or specifically authorised to allot shares for the purposes of section 551 to allot such shares as if section 561 did not apply to the allotment, provided that such disapplication has been sanctioned by the articles or by a special resolution of the shareholders of the plc. In the UK, there does not need to be any legitimate reason for the shareholders of a company to disapply the pre-emption rights. However, since the Target is a listed plc, in practice, it must be stressed that it is extremely unlikely that it would be able to persuade its institutional investors that the implementation of the non-pre-emptive directed share issue should proceed. Institutional investors are extremely reluctant to approve any requests for the disapplication of their pre-emption rights and would only sanction the Target's directed share issue proposal in very limited circumstances as set out in the guidelines of the Pre-Emption Group, for example, where it is proposed that pre-emption rights in respect of no more than 5 per cent of the issued share capital of the company are to be disapplied, there is

---

[106] CA 2006, s 563(3).

[107] *Burton v Bevan* [1908] 2 Ch 240 (Ch) 247 (Neville J).

[108] G Morse (ed), *Palmer's Company Law: Annotated Guide to the Companies Act 2006* (2nd edn, London, Sweet & Maxwell, 2009) para 5.931.

a good business case and it can be shown that the directed share issue will not lead to any shareholder sustaining a dilution in value or power.[109] It is submitted that no such business case pertains here and it is clear that the Bidder's position will be prejudiced by the share issue.

However, even in the unlikely event that the Target's institutional investors were prepared to approve the implementation of the shareholders' rights plan, the Target would still have to persuade its shareholders to pass a special resolution excluding the section 561 pre-emption rights or rely on a provision in the Target's articles which sanctions the disapplication. Since the shareholders' rights plan is included in the articles of association, it can perhaps be assumed that the articles also provide for the exclusion of the pre-emption rights of all of the existing shareholders in compliance with section 570 of the CA 2006. If that is the case, then section 563(2) of the CA 2006 will not be engaged to enable the Bidder to recover any damage, financial losses or costs and expenses which it has incurred, sustained or suffered from the Target or the directors of the Target. However, if the articles do not disapply the members' pre-emption rights, there will have been no compliance with section 570 or 571 of the Act. Therefore, section 563(2) of the CA 2006 will be applicable and will empower the Bidder to seek compensation in respect of its losses.

The Bidder might be well advised to apply to the court for the Target's statutory register of members[110] to be rectified in terms of section 125 of the CA 2006. Section 125 of the CA 2006 provides that any 'person aggrieved, or any member of [a] company' (such as the Bidder) may apply to the court for an order rectifying the Target's register of members if the name of any person is, without sufficient cause, entered in the Target's register of members. In the case of Re Thundercrest Ltd,[111] on the application of an aggrieved existing shareholder who had been marginalised by the directors of the company from participation in a share allotment and issue, the Court made an order to remove the names of the directors from the register of members when shares had been allotted to them in breach of the statutory pre-emption rights. The Court held that the directors had committed wrongdoing and should not be able to take advantage of it. If the Bidder was successful in its application to the court to rectify the statutory register of members by removing the name of the allottees pursuant to the directed share issue, the effect would be more or less the same as if the directed share issue had been invalidated. However, it should be stressed that Re Thundercrest will only apply where the directors have committed some wrongdoing and in such a case, the register of members will only be rectified to remove the names of those directors, rather than third parties. It is submitted that although there may be such wrongdoing on the part of the directors in the present hypothetical case, a court order sanctioning the rectification of the register of members which is restricted to the removal of the names of the directors will not be of great practical utility to the Bidder.

---

[109] See Pre-Emption Group, *Disapplying Pre-emption Rights – A Statement of Principles 2015*, pp 4 and 5, available at www.pre-emptiongroup.org.uk/getmedia/655a6ec5-fecc-47e4-80a0-7aea04433421/Revised-PEG-Statement-of-Principles-2015.pdf.aspx.
[110] The statutory register of members must be maintained by every public limited company registered in the UK and is commonly kept at its registered office in terms of ss 113 and 114 of the CA 2006.
[111] *Re Thundercrest Ltd* [1994] BCC 857 (Ch).

If the directors of the Target resolve to implement the directed share issue in terms of the shareholders' rights plan, this will not afford equivalent treatment to all shareholders. This will be contrary to the principle of equal treatment of shareholders and a breach of General Principle 1 of the City Code.[112] As noted in the UK solution to the case in chapter 4, above, by virtue of paragraph A14 of the City Code,[113] the Panel has a general power to order 'a person' to pay compensation to the shareholders or former shareholders of the Target (including the Bidder) for a breach of the General Principles or the rules of the City Code.[114] However, any aggrieved shareholder or company (such as the Bidder) will not be entitled to sue the Target or its directors for breach of General Principle 1 of the City Code.[115] Furthermore, the shareholders of the Target (ie the Bidder) have no power to challenge the validity of the implementation of the shareholders' rights plan on the ground that it breached General Principle 1.[116]

The end result is that it would be extremely unlikely that the directed share issue would be implemented in terms of the shareholders' rights plan, since the institutional investors of the Target would reject any request from the Target for it to proceed. However, in the unlikely event that the Target's institutional investors did sanction the directed share issue, its implementation would be legally valid and beyond legal challenge. Moreover, the Bidder is unlikely to be successful if it applied to the court to rectify the Target's register of members under section 125 of the CA 2006 by removing the names of all of the allottees. However, depending on the existence of a provision in the articles of association excluding the pre-emption rights of all of the existing shareholders in compliance with section 570 or 571 of the CA 2006, the Bidder may be entitled to recover from the Target or its directors on a joint and several basis in respect of any damage, financial losses and/or costs and expenses which it incurred, suffered or sustained as a result of the directed share issue. The fact that the implementation of the shareholders' rights plan was designed to protect the Target's employees is irrelevant to the legal position.

b. Breach of the Neutrality Rule in the City Code

Rule 21.1(b)(ii) of the City Code directs that as soon as the board of the Target has reason to believe that a bona fide offer might be imminent, the board must not, without the approval of the shareholders in general meeting, issue or grant options in respect of any unissued shares. Since there is no suggestion in the hypothetical case that the shareholders of the Target passed an ordinary resolution approving the issue of shares and the purpose of the shareholders' rights plan is specifically designed to give the existing shareholders (excluding the Bidder) the right to subscribe for additional shares in the Target at 50 per cent of their market value as soon as an outside acquirer achieves

---

[112] See B1 of the City Code.

[113] See the City Code at A14, section '10 (c) Compensation rulings'.

[114] This gives substance to the provisions of the CA 2006, s 954. For further details, see the UK solution to the case in ch 4 at II I (ii) (a), above.

[115] Section 956(1) of the CA 2006 provides that a breach of the City Code does not give rise to civil liability for breach of statutory duty.

[116] Section 956(2) of the CA 2006 directs that any breach of the City Code 'does not make any transaction void or unenforceable or (subject to any provision made by rules) affect the validity of any other thing'.

a threshold stake of 20 per cent of the shares of the Target, it is clear that Rule 21 of the City Code, which proscribes post-bid defensive measures, has been breached. However, for the same reasons explored above and in the UK solution to the case in chapter 4, above, a breach of Rule 21 will not affect the validity of the implementation of the shareholders' rights plan or entitle the Bidder to compensation from the Target or its directors. The one exception is if the Panel decides to invoke its power under paragraph A14 of the City Code to call on 'a person' to pay a sum of money in compensation to the Bidder. Once again, the reason for the implementation of the shareholders' rights plan will have no bearing on the legal position, ie the fact that it was motivated by a desire to protect the Target's employees.

iii. The Legality of the Customer Assurance Programme

The implementation of the customer assurance programme falls within the general powers of the directors in terms of Regulation 3 of the Model Articles.[117] Thus, there would appear to be no general obligation on the directors of the Target to obtain the approval of the shareholders prior to its implementation or to call a general meeting of the shareholders to approve it in advance. However, in terms of Rule 21 of the City Code, its implementation will indeed require an ordinary resolution of the shareholders of the Target to be passed, since the customer assurance programme was put in place subsequent to the board of the Target having reason to believe that a bona fide offer might be imminent. Nevertheless, for the same reasons explored above,[118] the breach of Rule 21 will not affect the validity of the customer assurance programme or its implementation and so the Bidder will have no entitlement to compensation from the Target or its directors in respect of such a breach. Again, the one exception is if the Panel decides to invoke its power under paragraph A14 of the City Code to call on 'a person' to pay a sum of money in compensation to the Bidder.

iv. The Conduct of the Directors of the Target

Did the directors of the Target breach their duties by implementing the shareholders' rights plan and/or the customer assurance programme? As articulated in the previous solution,[119] since it has been submitted that the implementation of the shareholders' rights plan and/or the customer assurance programme both amount to a breach of the neutrality rule in Rule 21 of the City Code, it is likely that the directors of the Target are in breach of the duty of care, skill and diligence which they owe to the Target on the basis that their conduct fell below the objective minimum standard of general knowledge, skill and experience that may reasonably be expected of a person carrying out the functions performed by a director in relation to the Target. Since the section 174 duty to exercise reasonable care, skill and diligence is owed to the Target in terms

[117] Model Articles of association of a plc, reg 3 of sch 3 to the Companies (Model Articles) Regulations 2008, SI 2008/3229.
[118] See also ch 4 at II I, above.
[119] See ch 4 at II I, above.

of section 170(1) of the CA 2006, the Target will be entitled to recover from the directors the losses which it sustains as a result of their breach of duty which falls within the
scope of the director's duty of care.[120]

There is also the possibility that the implementation of the shareholders' rights
plan amounts to a breach of the directors' duty to only exercise their powers for the
purposes they were conferred in terms of section 171(b) of the CA 2006. For example,
in the case of *Hogg v Cramphorn Ltd*,[121] the directors of a target company, acting in
good faith, had issued shares with special voting rights to the trustees of a scheme
set up for the benefit of the target company's employees, in an attempt (which proved
successful) to ward off a third party's takeover bid. The Court held that issuing shares
as a means of forestalling a takeover bid was an improper use of the director's power
to issue shares and that it would be an actionable wrong at the instance of the target
company (unless the breach was ratified by the shareholders of the target company in
general meeting in terms of section 239 of the CA 2006).[122] The fact that the scheme
might protect the interests of the Target's employees is irrelevant to the legal position.
As for the implementation of the customer assurance programme, there is an argument that it amounts to a breach of the duty of the directors of the Target in terms
of section 172 of the CA 2006 to act in the way they consider, in good faith, would
be most likely to promote the success of the Target for the benefit of its members as a
whole.

However, it must be stressed that the duties of the directors in sections 174, 171(b)
and 172 of the CA 2006 are owed to the Target only. On the facts of the hypothetical case, it is unlikely that the Target will be minded to take legal action against its
directors for breach of duty under section 174, 171(b) or 172 of the CA 2006, unless
the Bidder's takeover bid was successful and post-takeover proceedings were raised.
However, assuming that the Bidder's takeover bid is unsuccessful, in the absence of
special circumstances,[123] the shareholders of the Target, including the Bidder, will have
no right of action against the directors of the Target for breach of duty since the directors' duties are not owed to them individually.[124]

v. Summary and Conclusion

The shareholders of the Target, including the Bidder, have no right to set aside the
shareholders' rights plan or the customer assurance programme on the basis that it
is void or invalid. Likewise, insofar as the implementation of the shareholders' rights
plan or the customer assurance programme might amount to a breach of the duties
of the directors of the Target, the shareholders of the Target, including the Bidder,

---

[120] *South Australia Asset Management Corporation v York Montague Ltd* [1997] AC 191 (HL) 214
(Lord Hoffmann).
[121] *Hogg v Cramphorn Ltd* [1967] Ch 254 (Ch).
[122] *Howard Smith Ltd v Ampol Petroleum Ltd* [1974] AC 821 (PC) and *Eclairs Group Ltd v JKX Oil & Gas
Plc* [2015] UKSC 71, [2016] 1 BCLC 1 are 2 similar cases.
[123] See, eg, *Heron International Ltd v Lord Grade* [1983] BCLC 244 (CA) and *Dawson International plc
v Coats Paton plc* [1988] 4 BCC 305.
[124] However, the shareholders of the Target, including the Bidder, may have rights (in their capacity as
shareholders) to challenge the directors' breaches of duty. See ch 10 at II A, below for further details.

will have no power to invalidate them or seek compensation for breach of duty.[125] However, if the shareholders' rights plan is implemented in the absence of compliance with section 570 or 571 of the CA 2006, section 563(2) of the CA 2006 will apply and empower the Bidder to seek compensation and recover any damage, financial losses or costs and expenses which it has incurred or sustained from the Target or the directors of the Target as a result of the plan's implementation.

J. The US

i. Introduction

The subject case posits a cross-border takeover, with the Target in the home jurisdiction (Delaware). In this situation, Delaware law would apply to the actions of Target's board of directors. The Target's shareholders would have standing to challenge those actions, as would the Bidder, assuming that it owns some shares in Target.[126] The cross-border nature of the transaction is irrelevant in evaluating the validity of the shareholders' rights plan and the customer assurance programme.

ii. The Legality of the Target's Shareholders' Rights Plan

The Delaware courts have developed an extensive jurisprudence to evaluate the adoption of various shareholders' rights plans (poison pills), dating to the mid-1980s.[127] Because poison pills 'fundamentally are defensive devices',[128] the courts employ an enhanced level of judicial scrutiny under the *Unocal* standard,[129] which requires directors to demonstrate two things before their adoption of the poison pill will be allowed: (i) the board must show that the bidder's offer presents a 'danger to corporate policy and effectiveness';[130] and (ii) the board must show that its 'defensive response was reasonable in relation to the threat posed'.[131]

The first prong of the *Unocal* standard is rarely used as a basis to invalidate a poison pill, but the Delaware Court of Chancery recently focused on that portion of the standard in evaluating a poison pill adopted by a closely held corporation having only three shareholders. In this unusual context,[132] the defendants argued that the adoption of a flip-in pill was justified by a threat to the company's corporate culture,

---

[125] Again, this is subject to the point that the Bidder may have rights as a shareholder of the Target to challenge, and seek compensation in respect of, the directors' breach of duty. See ch 10 at II A, below.

[126] See especially *City Capital Assocs v Interco, Inc*, 551 A 2d 787, 800 (Del Ch 1988).

[127] The seminal case on poison pills in Delaware was *Moran v Household Int'l, Inc*, 500 A 2d 1346 (Del 1985), which involved a 'flip-over' poison pill.

[128] *eBay Domestic Holdings, Inc v Newmark*, 16 A.3d 1, 28 (Del Ch 2010).

[129] *Unocal Corp v Mesa Petroleum Co*, 493 A 2d 946, 954 (Del 1985). See also *Air Products and Chemicals, Inc. v. Airgas, Inc.*, 16 A.3d 48 (Del Ch 2011) and *Third Point LLC v Ruprecht*, C.A. No 9469-VCP (Del Ch 2 May 2014).

[130] Ibid at 955.

[131] Ibid.

[132] *eBay Domestic Holdings, Inc v Newmark* (n 128) at *30 ('this case involves a unique set of facts heretofore not seen in the context of a challenge to a rights plan. To my knowledge, no decision under Delaware law has addressed a challenge to a rights plan adopted by a privately held company with so few stockholders').

thus harkening back to the well-known case of *Paramount Communications, Inc v Time Inc.*[133] The Court rejected the argument, finding that the 'defendants failed to prove, as a factual matter, the existence of a distinctly protectable … culture and further failed to prove, both factually and legally, that they actually decided to deploy the Rights Plan because of [that] culture'.[134] The subject case as such would normally pose a more traditional context for the adoption of a poison pill, and the Delaware courts would almost certainly recognise the existence of a 'danger to corporate policy and effectiveness'. However, the explicitly stated motivation to protect employees from redundancy could be a problem under this prong. As stated by the Delaware Court of Chancery in *eBay*,

> [h]aving chosen a for-profit corporate form, […] directors are bound by the fiduciary duties and standards that accompany that form. Those standards include acting to promote the value of the corporation for the benefit of its stockholders. […] Thus, I cannot accept as valid for the purposes of implementing the Rights Plan a corporate policy that specifically, clearly, and admittedly seeks not to maximize the economic value of a for-profit Delaware corporation for the benefit of its stockholders […].'[135]

Very likely directors would have to establish that the objective of protecting employees is rationally related to benefits for stockholders, which in practice is often only a matter of how the argument is framed.

The second prong of the *Unocal* standard is the focus of attention in most poison pill cases. While flip-in poison pills, such as the one described in the case study, are routinely upheld by the Delaware courts under this standard – even when such poison pills are quite restrictive[136] – the courts have invalidated more aggressive forms of poison pills that are found to be 'show stoppers'.[137] The rationale for these decisions is found in an elaboration of the *Unocal* standard in *Unitrin, Inc v Am Gen Corp*,[138] which held that a defensive measure is not 'reasonable in relation to the threat posed' if the measure is either 'preclusive' or 'coercive'.[139] If the court determines that a defensive measure is neither preclusive nor coercive, it then enquires whether the response falls within a 'range of reasonableness'.[140]

A defensive measure is preclusive if it makes it 'mathematically impossible or realistically unattainable' for the bidder to wage a proxy fight or acquire the target.[141] However, a defensive measure does *not* make it mathematically impossible or realistically unattainable merely because it 'inhibits' the bidder's ability to institute a merger or wage a proxy fight.[142] Stated another way, '[t]he fact that a combination of defensive

---

[133] *Paramount Communications, Inc v Time Inc*, 571 A 2d 1140 (Del 1990).

[134] *eBay Domestic Holdings, Inc v Newmark* (n 128) at *34.

[135] Ibid.

[136] See *Versata Enterprises, Inc v Selectica, Inc*, 2010 WL 3839786 (Del 2010) (approving a poison pill with a 5% trigger on the ground that it was a reasonable way to protect the target company's net operating loss carryovers).

[137] See *Carmody v Toll Bros*, 723 A 2d 1180, 1187 (Del Ch 1998) ('dead hand' poison pill). See also *Quickturn Design Sys, Inc v Shapiro*, 721 A 2d 1281, 1283 (Del 1998) ('no hands' poison pill).

[138] *Unitrin, Inc v Am Gen Corp*, 651 A 2d 1361 (Del 1995).

[139] Ibid at 1387.

[140] Ibid at 1387–88.

[141] Ibid at 1389.

[142] Ibid.

measures makes it more difficult for an acquirer to obtain control of a board does not make such measures realistically unattainable, ie preclusive'.[143] In the instant case, the court would evaluate whether the Bidder could gain control of the Target board, thus positioning itself to redeem the poison pill. Only if the Bidder is prevented from gaining control would the poison pill be considered 'preclusive'.

A defensive measure is coercive if it effectively removes a shareholder's choice between a bidder's proposal and a management-sponsored alternative. Stated another way, a defensive action is coercive if it is 'aimed at "cramming down" on its shareholders a management-sponsored alternative'.[144] Nothing in the instant case suggests that the poison pill would have this effect.

If the court decided that a defensive measure was neither preclusive nor coercive, it would then enquire whether the response fell within a 'range of reasonableness'.[145] The *Unitrin* Court described this enquiry in a manner that encouraged courts to be very deferential to the defensive action:

> [t]he ratio decidendi for the 'range of reasonableness' standard is a need of the board of directors for latitude in discharging its fiduciary duties to the corporation and its shareholders when defending against perceived threats ... [t]he concomitant requirement is for judicial restraint.[146]

While the Delaware courts have recently evinced a willingness to intervene if the poison pill is not redeemed in a timely fashion,[147] the adoption of the poison pill in the subject case would almost certainly be reasonable.

iii. The Legality of the Customer Assurance Programme

The Delaware courts have not had an opportunity to evaluate a 'customer assurance programme' like the one described in the subject case, but such programmes have been described by commentators as 'embedded defences', which refers to 'a term embedded in a contract with a non-shareholder counterparty that has an antitakeover effect'.[148]

While defensive actions are typically evaluated under the *Unocal* standard discussed above, the Delaware courts have from time to time invalidated conduct of the board on other grounds. For example, in *Quickturn Design Systems, Inc v Shapiro*,[149] the Delaware Supreme Court held that a 'no hands' poison pill 'violated fundamental Delaware law' by taking an action that would deprive a future board of directors of the power to discharge its statutory duties.

Similarly, in *Unisuper Ltd v News Corp*,[150] Chancellor Chandler evaluated a board's alleged contract with stockholders regarding the term of a poison pill by reference

---

[143] *Versata Enterprises, Inc v Selectica, Inc* (n 136) at *16.
[144] *Unitrin, Inc v Am Gen Corp* (n 138) at 1387.
[145] Ibid at 1387–88.
[146] Ibid at 1388.
[147] See *Versata Enterprises, Inc v Selectica, Inc* (n 136) at *18.
[148] See eg G Subramanian, 'The Emerging Problem of Embedded Defenses: Lessons From *Air Line Pilots Ass'n, International V. Ual Corp.*' (2007) 120 *Harvard Law Review* 1239, 1242.
[149] *Quickturn Design Systems, Inc v Shapiro* (n 137).
[150] *Unisuper Ltd v News Corp*, 2005 WL 3529317 (Del Ch 2005).

to the statutory charge placing directors in charge of the business and affairs of the corporation.[151] While this statutory grant of authority 'precludes a board of directors from ceding that power to outside groups or individuals',[152] the alleged contract at issue in *Unisuper* would be valid because it gave power to shareholders. As stated by Chancellor Chandler, 'when shareholders exercise their right to vote in order to assert control over the business and affairs of the corporation the board must give way'.[153]

The customer assurance programme could be viewed as an attempt to deprive a future board of directors of the power to discharge its statutory duties. However, it is difficult to distinguish this sort of contract from other contracts. In *Unisuper*, Chancellor Chandler rightly observed that '[b]y definition, any contract a board could enter into binds the board and thereby limits its power … [s]ection 141(a) does not say the board cannot enter into contracts'.[154] Thus, one suspects that the customer assurance programme would be evaluated under the *Unocal* standard, and the outcome of that evaluation is uncertain.

K. South Africa

i. Relationship between Shareholders of the Target Company, the Bidder and the Board of the Target Company

As mentioned in chapter 4, takeovers are regulated by sections 117–127 of the Companies Act 2008 and the Takeover Regulations. Takeover provisions will apply when a regulated company enters into an affected transaction. In the present case, the Target is a regulated company and the transaction is an affected transaction.[155] In such a case the Bidder's offer must be issued to the board of the Target and not to the shareholders directly.[156] In terms of South African law, the chairman of the board is not an executive position and the only entity that is in control of a company is the board of directors.[157] It is therefore accepted that the notice to the chairman is not a notification to the board of the company. In this case it was therefore not made to the board but to the shareholders directly. The effect of this is that the Takeover Regulation Panel will not issue a compliance certificate in terms of section 121 of the Companies Act 2008.[158]

ii. The 'Flip-in' Plan and Customer Assurance Programme

The Memorandum of Incorporation (MoI) of the Target will, presumably, be amended to make provision for the 'flip-in' plan. A special resolution is required and the notice

---

[151] DGCL, § 141(a).
[152] *Unisuper Ltd v News Corp* (n 150) at *6.
[153] Ibid.
[154] Ibid.
[155] See the discussion in ch 4 at II K, above. See also Companies Act 2008, ss 117 and 118.
[156] See reg 99. Any communication to the shareholders must therefore be through the board of the Target.
[157] See Companies Act, s 66(1) and discussion under ch 3 at II C, above.
[158] See the discussion in ch 4 at II K, above.

of the amendment[159] must include a reference to the rights of a shareholder under section 164 of the Companies Act 2008. Section 164 deals with the appraisal rights of dissenting shareholders.

Section 37(8) of the Companies Act 2008 provides that:

> If the Memorandum of Incorporation of a company has been amended to materially and adversely alter the preferences, rights, limitations or other terms of a class of shares, any holder of those shares is entitled to seek relief in terms of section 164 if that shareholder—
>
> (a)   notified the company in advance of the intention to oppose the resolution to amend the Memorandum of Incorporation; and
>
> (b)   was present at the meeting, and voted against that resolution.

If the 'flip-in' is implemented, the consideration paid for the shares must be adequate. If it is not, it will be a breach of the fiduciary duties of the directors, although the share issue will not be void.[160] An issue at a discount of 50 per cent, as is the case *in casu*, does not seem to be an adequate consideration for the shares. If the share issue is equal to or more than 30 per cent of the voting rights before the issue, the issue must be approved by a special resolution of shareholders.[161]

The power to issue shares rests with the board, unless the MoI provides otherwise. The board must use this power subject to their fiduciary duties, ie they must act bona fide in the interests of the Target and for a proper purpose. An issue of shares under these circumstances would not be for a proper purpose.[162]

In South Africa there is no obligation, under the common law or in terms of the Companies Act 2008 for the issue of shares in a public company to be pro rata to existing shareholdings.[163] However, if the Target is listed on any of the Boards of the JSE Ltd, it must also comply with the Listings Requirements.[164] In terms of the Listings Requirements, an issuer must ensure that all holders of any class of its securities that are in the same position, receive fair and equal treatment.[165] Subject to a

---

[159] See s 169(1)(c) of the Companies Act 2008 regarding amendments to the MoI.

[160] See s 40 of the Companies Act 2008. See PA Delport (ed), *Henochsberg on the Companies Act 71 of 2008* (Durban, LexisNexis, South Africa, Service issue November 2016) 178(3) for a discussion of this section.

[161] Companies Act 2008, s 41(3).

[162] See the discussion of the duty to act for a proper purpose in ch 4 at II K, above. The application of the business judgment rule (s 76(4) of the Companies Act 2008) (see in ch 2 at II K, above) may, however, change this position. In terms of the business judgment rule, a director is deemed to have exercised its powers or performed its functions as a director if (i) he/she took reasonably diligent steps to become informed about the matter, (ii) either (a) the director had no material financial interest in the subject matter of the decision and had no reasonable basis to know that any related person had a personal financial interest in the matter, or (b) the director complied with the requirements of s 75 of the Companies Act 2008 with respect to any relevant financial interest, and (iii) the director made a decision, or supported the decision of a committee or the board, with regard to that matter and the director had a reasonable basis for believing, and did believe, that the decision was in the best interests of the company.

[163] See also discussion in ch 11 at II K, below. If the shares, or options to subscribe for shares, are not issued pro rata to existing shareholdings, and they are issued (also) to a director or related or inter-related party as defined in s 2 of the Companies Act 2008, the issue must be approved by a special resolution: s 41(1) of the Companies Act 2008. If the shares that are issued are 30% or more of the existing pre-issue voting rights, a special resolution is required to authorise the issue, irrespective of whether it was pro rata or not: s 41(3).

[164] See discussion in ch 4 at II K, above in respect of the JSE Ltd and the Listings Requirements.

[165] Para 3.27 of the Listings Requirements.

waiver to that effect by ordinary resolution of the shareholders,[166] an issuer proposing to issue equity securities for cash must first offer those securities (unless the issue
is an acquisition issue) effected by way of a rights offer, to existing holders of equity
securities[167] in proportion to their existing holdings. Only to the extent that such securities are not taken up by holders of equity securities under the offer may they then
be issued for cash to other persons or otherwise than in the proportion mentioned
above.[168] The exclusion of the Bidder, if it owns shares in the Target, will therefore be
a contravention of the Listings Requirements.[169]

In addition, section 126 of the Companies Act 2008 also restricts the powers of the
board as they are not allowed to frustrate the operation of an offer.

In respect of the customer assurance programme the issue will be whether or not it is
in line with the fiduciary duties of the board of directors. The aim of the programme is
clearly to protect the interests of the Target. However, the relevant question is whether
or not it was entered into otherwise than in the ordinary course of business as in terms
of section 126(f).[170] It does not seem, objectively, that this was the case.

L. Japan

i. Relevant Legislation on Takeover Bids

The Financial Instruments and Exchange Law (FIEL), which came into effect in
September 2007, regulates tender offers and certain disclosure requirements. Stock
purchases and issues of shares for subscription and assignments of businesses are
regulated by the Companies Act (CA), which came into effect in May 2006.

ii. Special Rules for Foreign Buyers

When a foreign company acquires in excess of 10 per cent of the shares of a listed
company, it must, in principle, notify the Ministry of Finance and the minister in
charge of the relevant industry within 15 days under Article 21 of the Foreign Exchange
and Foreign Trade Law (FEFTL). However, in the case of certain regulated industries
which are deemed to be critical to national security, it must provide for prior notification to the Ministry of Finance and the minister in charge of the relevant industry, and
the foreign company cannot obtain such shares until 30 days after such notification is
made. With respect to such prior notification, the Ministry of Finance and the minister

---

[166] Para 3.32 of the Listings Requirements.
[167] 'Equity share capital' is defined in the Listings Requirements as a company's issued share capital, but
excluding convertible securities or securities which are regarded as debt instruments.
[168] Para 3.30 of the Listings Requirements.
[169] See discussion in ch 4 at II K, above as to the effect of this contravention.
[170] This section provides that:

> Restrictions on frustrating action.—(1) If the board of a regulated company believes that a bona fide
> offer might be imminent, or has received such an offer, the board must not—
>
> (f) enter into contracts otherwise than in the ordinary course of business

in charge of the relevant industry can block or modify the plan under certain situations as prescribed in the FEFTL.[171]

iii. The Target Board's Response to a Hostile Takeover Bid

Under the FIEL, with respect to a tender offer, the target company must file a position statement report within 10 business days of the first date of the tender offer period (FIEL, Article 27, no 10(1)), and its position is generally decided by a board resolution. However, stock purchases and tender offers can be made without the approval of the target board. Some companies institute guidelines against hostile takeovers, and such guidelines generally stipulate that if a target board receives a proposal, the target board will decide whether such proposal will maximise shareholder value and will announce the terms of the offer and the position of the target board.

iv. Permitted Defensive Measures

Unlike the position in the EU, there is no specific 'board-neutrality rule' concerning takeover bids in Japan.[172] The Companies Act does not prohibit a target company from taking the following action, albeit that such takeover defensive measures have increasingly become an object of criticism:[173]

1. institute a rights plan using share purchase warrants with discriminatory conditions, such that only certain shareholders can execute the warrants;
2. amend its articles of incorporation to alter the requirements for resolutions on the removal of directors;
3. grant an issue of shares or share purchase warrants with a call option exercisable by the target company and/or a put option exercisable by the shareholders with discriminatory conditions;
4. issue new shares or classified shares with veto rights concerning certain transactions with a friendly third party; and
5. enter into a merger, share exchange or formation of a joint holding company by stock transfer, with a friendly company.

The disposal of the 'crown jewel' assets of a target company requires the approval of an extraordinary resolution at an extraordinary shareholders' meeting as a business transfer (CA, Articles 467(1)(i)(ii), 309(2)(xi)) and gives rise to legal concerns regarding the application of the director's duty of loyalty (CA, Article 355).

---

[171] The Children's Investment Master Fund (TCI), a British investment fund with a 9.9% stake in Electric Power Development Co, Ltd (J-Power), an electricity wholesaler, had reported to the Ministry of Finance and the Ministry of Economy, Trade and Industry its plan to boost its stake in J-Power to 20% in accordance with the FEFTL. However, in April 2008, both ministers advised TCI to drop or change its plan, as they could not approve the proposal, and issued a formal withdrawal order for TCI in May 2008. See M Iwakura and N Ishikawa, *The International Comparative Legal Guide to Mergers & Acquisitions 2012* (London, Global Legal Group Ltd, 2012) 150.

[172] However, recently, the EU-style takeover law has been matters of concern in Japan, on which, see H Watanabe, 'Designing a New Takeover Regime for Japan: Suggestions from the European Takeover Rules' (2010) 30 *Zeitschrift für Japanisches Recht* 89.

[173] Generally, the target board, with the benefit of outside advice, will decide whether a proposed takeover will maximise shareholder value.

v. The Shareholders' Rights Plan and the Customer Assurance Programme

In principle, the issue of shares for subscription only requires a resolution of the Target's board of directors (CA, Articles 238–40). However, if the issue price is for free or is especially favourable to the subscribers, it is necessary for the issuer to obtain the approval of its shareholders in general meeting (CA, Articles 238(2), 239(1), 240(1) and 309(2)(vi)). The main motivation for this plan was to protect the Target's employees and potentially, therefore, the interests of employees (and employee shareholders) could be relevant here. However, in the present case, the exclusion of the pre-emption right not only favours employees (and employee shareholders) but differentiates between the Bidder and other non-employee shareholders.[174]

The customer assurance programme in the present case is triggered by a takeover bid and its terms (implemented in legally binding contracts) come into force only if the takeover succeeds. The programme is designed to make the takeover considerably more costly for the Bidder and it is also a defensive measure in the nature of a 'poison pill' device.

Hence, in the present case, both the shareholders' rights plan and the customer assurance programme should be adopted at the Target's shareholders' general meeting in order to comply with the provisions of Japanese Companies Act.

vi. The Shareholders' Rights Plan, 'Poison Pills' and the Tender Offer System in Japan

In the *Bull-Dog Sauce* case, the general meeting of shareholders of the company approved the proposal to issue without compensation, to all shareholders, share options subject to the discriminatory terms of exercise. The Supreme Court denied an injunction sought by the takeover bidder, Steel Partners.[175] However, it is doubtful whether the Supreme Court's decision in this case is an authority for the proposition that 'invoking a defensive plan based on a resolution of the general meeting of shareholders' is permitted in every case. In the *Livedoor-Nippon Broad* casting case, with respect to the issuance of share purchase warrants, the Tokyo High Court ruled that such issuance must be suspended if the company's primary purpose is to: (i) lower the shareholding ratio of a particular shareholder who is seeking to attain control of the company through a hostile takeover; and (ii) maintain and ensure the existing management's control of the target company.[176] In Japan, it could be said that introducing a shareholders' rights plan is currently permitted owing to insufficient confidence in the tender offer system. An influential scholar has opined that if no rights plan were to be permitted under the existing law of Japan, management might engage in conduct to introduce even more powerful defensive measures against hostile takeovers through legislation; this was why rights plans were construed to be legal.[177]

---

[174] See also German Solution at C (ii), above.
[175] Supreme Court, 7 August 2007, in *Minshu* vol 61, no 5, at 2215. Both the District Court and the High Court reached the same conclusion.
[176] Tokyo High Court, 23 March 2005, in *Kinyû Shôji Hanrei* 1214, 6.
[177] K Egashira, 'Jizen no Baishû Bôeisaku: Hatsudôji no Mondai' ['Takeover Defensive Measures Introduced in Advance: Problems Occurring upon Launch'] (2007) 145 *Hô-no-Shihai* 28. See also Watanabe,

III. Conclusion

The present case follows up from the discussion on takeovers in chapter 4. The conclusion of that chapter already provided an overview of the legal differences in terms of the duty of board neutrality and whether this duty will only be triggered by the publication of the takeover bid. These topics are also relevant in the present case. Yet, in addition, it addresses three further topics, namely, the cross-border dimension of takeovers, the use of a 'shareholders' rights plan' and a 'customer assurance programme' as possible 'poison pills'.

A. The Cross-border Dimension

Complex questions of conflict of laws can arise in the context of a cross-border takeover bid.[178] For instance, if a company's securities are listed only on a foreign stock exchange, it may be necessary to distinguish between the disclosure provisions of (i) takeover law and securities regulation, and (ii) directors' duties and shareholder involvement belonging to company law. There are also some countries, in particular the US, that even apply some provisions of domestic takeover law when a significant proportion of the shareholders of the target company are resident in its jurisdiction.

In the present case, such complications do not arise since the Target is also listed in its home jurisdiction. Moreover, it has both its registered seat and its headquarters in this country: thus, the distinction between countries of the 'incorporation theory' and the 'real seat theory'[179] is not relevant in the present case. As a result, all solutions agree that the company and takeover law of country A is applicable (*lex societatis*).

The solutions from the EU Member States also show that many of them provide for the 'reciprocity' of takeover defences according to the EU Takeover Directive.[180] This is complicated by the fact that Member States can 'opt out' of the Directive's restrictions on takeover defences (Article 12(1)), but then companies can subsequently decide to 'opt in' (Article 12(2)) and other Member States can adopt the 'reciprocity rule' (Article 12(3)). Table 5.1 illustrates this point with company A being registered in country A, and company B in country B. It should be noted that the default options of Article 12 are that countries do not 'opt out' and provide reciprocity, and companies do not 'opt in' (as such, these elements are shown in square brackets in the table below where it was deemed useful for the purpose of clarification).

'Designing a New Takeover Regime for Japan (n 172) 92, suggesting that this may change in the future if shareholder participation rights become more effective.

[178] For an overview of the following points, see M Siems, 'The Rules on Conflict of Laws in the European Takeover Directive' (2004) 1 *European Company and Financial Law Review* 458.

[179] This topic has been particularly relevant in the EU and its Member States. For a comprehensive comparison, see C Gerner-Beuerle, F Mucciarelli, E Schuster and M Siems, *Study on the Law Applicable to Companies* (Final Report for European Commission, DG Justice, 2016).

[180] Directive 2004/25/EC (n 6). For the countries of this book, see ch 4 at III, above. For all Member States, see Commission Staff Working Document, *Report on the Implementation of the Directive on Takeover Bids of 21 February 2007*, SEC(2007) 268.

Table 5.1: Defence mechanisms in cross-border takeovers in the EU

	Company A **cannot** use defence mechanisms when …	Company A **can** use defence mechanisms when …
Company B **cannot** use defence mechanisms when …	— [neither country 'opts out'] — both countries 'opt out', but both companies 'opt in' [regardless of reciprocity] — country A 'opts out' but company A 'opts in' [regardless of reciprocity] — country B 'opts out' but company B 'opts in' [regardless of reciprocity]	— both countries 'opt out' and only company B 'opts in' [and country B does not provide reciprocity] — country A 'opts out' [company A does not 'opt in'; country B does not provide reciprocity]
Company B **can** use defence mechanisms when …	— both countries 'opt out' and only company A 'opts in' [and country A does not provide reciprocity] — country B 'opts out' [company B does not 'opt in' and country A does not provide reciprocity]	— both countries 'opt out' [and neither company 'opts in'] — both countries 'opt out', company A 'opts in' and country A provides reciprocity [or company B 'opts in' and country B provides reciprocity] — country A 'opts out' and country B provides reciprocity — country B 'opts out' and country A provides reciprocity

In the present case, we are told that the shareholders' rights plan would not be lawful in the Foreign Jurisdiction. Thus, one may think that this country (assuming it is in the EU) may not have opted out of the Takeover Directive. However, it will become clear that it is not actually the Takeover Directive which is the main benchmark for the takeover defences in the current scenario.

B. The Shareholders' Rights Plan

To start with, it is worth noting that the Takeover Directive does not provide a reason why the shareholders' rights plan ('flip-in plan') should be invalid. Since the decision of the board of directors to adopt this plan[181] preceded the takeover bid, the principle of board neutrality in Article 9 of the Directive is not yet applicable.[182] Rather, whilst the plan can be regarded as a pre-bid defence, the relevant provision of the Directive (Article 11) only addresses topics such as the restrictions of voting rights and the

---

[181] This decision is the moment that is decisive for the purposes of the application of the board neutrality principle (ie not the authorisation of the general meeting to increase the company's share capital): see, eg, T Papadopoulos, *EU Law and the Harmonization of Takeovers in the Internal Market* (The Hague, Kluwer, 2010) 121.

[182] However, Member States are free to impose the board neutrality principle in this case as well. See ch 4 at III, above.

transferability of shares, but does not include the regulation of a pre-bid shareholders' rights plan.

However, EU company law restricts the potential for such a plan to be adopted. Since issuing new shares requires an increase in capital in the majority of the Member States examined in this book, first, it matters that, in general, any such increase and the issuance of new shares must be decided upon by the general meeting; however, the general meeting can also authorise the board of directors to increase the capital or to issue new shares for a period not exceeding five years.[183] Second, since the plan excludes shareholders that hold more than 20 per cent of the shares, the provision on pre-emptive rights may be violated: in general, shares must be offered to all shareholders in proportion to the capital represented by their shares.[184] However, the general meeting can restrict this right on the condition that the board of directors provides a written report indicating the reasons for the restriction or withdrawal of the right of pre-emption. The Member States also have the power to sanction the general meeting to authorise the board of directors to take this decision.[185] Thus, for the present case this means that there has been a failure to involve the general meeting. Even if it is assumed that the general meeting authorised the board to raise the share capital, there is no indication that it also authorised an exemption from the pre-emptive rights (noting that, for instance, the UK case study indicates that this would only happen very rarely; also noting that under Spanish law there may even be a requirement for shareholder participation based on takeover law before a bid has been made).

In addition, some of the European case studies advance substantive reasons why the shareholders' rights plan is unlawful. According to German law, there have to be good reasons to exclude pre-emptive rights, while the Italian solution refers to the requirement for a 'special interest' to exclude particular shareholders, and the Spanish solution points towards a possible violation of the duty to act in the interests of the company. A number of European solutions also refer to the principle of the equal treatment of general company law (Finland, France, Germany, Italy, Latvia; in substance also Poland).[186] The UK seems to be the exception: here; it is said that only if the implementation of the plan extended to the phase after the bid had been made would the equal treatment provision of takeover law be applicable.[187] In South Africa, rather than the general provisions of company law, listing requirements seem to require an issuer to ensure that all shareholders are in the same position and receive fair and equal treatment.

The US and Japan differ from the European countries considerably. Here, the starting point is that primary competence for capital measures lies with the board of directors. In general, there are also no pre-emption rights. However, the Japanese solution reaches the result that approval of the general meeting is necessary in the present

---

[183] Previously Directive 2012/30/EU (n 19), art 29 and now Directive (EU) 2017/1132 (n19), art 68.

[184] Previously Directive 2012/30/EU (n 19), art 33(1) and now Directive (EU) 2017/1132 (n19), art 72(1).

[185] Previously Directive 2012/30/EU (n 19), art 33(4) and (5) and now Directive (EU) 2017/1132 (n 19), art 72(4) and (5).

[186] See also Directive 2012/30/EU (n19), art 46 and now Directive (EU) 2017/1132 (n 19), art 85.

[187] Similarly, the French solution refers to the fact that takeover law may apply in the implementation phase, in particular, the principle of board neutrality.

case since the shares are issued at a discount value. In addition, if shareholder approval were obtained, there is some ambiguity in the recent Japanese case law on whether an injunction may be granted owing to reasons of discrimination.

The fact that one of the goals of the plan was to protect the Target's employees leads us to question whether a country's corporate governance model leans towards shareholder or stakeholder primacy. For example, in France it seems that protecting shareholders at the expense of other stakeholders would be an acceptable goal in some situations and the Target is required to operate in accordance with its 'social interests', which is derived from a stakeholder rather than shareholder approach. Moreover, German public companies have to consider the interests not only of the shareholders but the entire enterprise, including its employees and other stakeholders. On the other hand, the corporate governance model in, for example, the UK is clearly based on shareholder primacy, since the fact that the implementation of the plan was designed to protect the Target's employees is irrelevant to the legal position.

The only solution that is entirely based on case law is the US one. The Delaware courts have developed a number of substantive standards in response to different types of 'poison pills'; yet, in the end, it seems likely that the US courts would not object to the current shareholders' right plan. Thus, the result is that in the present situation, the US is different from the other legal systems, both in the relevant sources of law and the result.

C. The Customer Assurance Programme

None of the courts of 12 countries has had the opportunity to deal with a customer assurance programme as described in the hypothetical case. There was a similar case in the US, but it was settled without requiring a formal resolution in a court judgment.[188] The French case study only mentions a somewhat similar case where the competent supervisory authority (the AMF) decided that it mattered whether such a measure was specifically aimed at one particular bidder.

Thus, in all of the 12 countries considered, there is some uncertainty as to how a customer assurance programme would be addressed. Some of the case studies consider the potential requirement to attain the approval of the general meeting, but most of them reach the conclusion that the customer assurance programme would fall within the general competence of the directors.

Furthermore, it is considered relevant whether directors have the duty to act primarily in the interests of the shareholders or whether stakeholder interests can also be taken into account. The French, German and Polish solutions indicate that stakeholder interests may be taken into account; as such, this would speak in favour of the customer assurance programme. The company's 'social interests' seem to play an important role in France in particular. By contrast, the Finnish solution states that only the interests of shareholders are decisive in the context of takeovers. The 'shareholder

---

[188] See D Millstone and G Subramanian, 'Oracle v. PeopleSoft: A Case Study' (2007) 12 *Harvard Negotiation Law Review* 1.

primacy' approach is also usually seen as prevalent in the US and the UK, though there are also some indicators that stakeholder interests are relevant here.[189]

In the end, most of the case studies adopt the position that the customer assurance programme would presumably not be unlawful, possibly also considering the business judgment rule (explicitly mentioned in the German and Latvian solutions). However, especially the solutions from the US and Japan are slightly more unclear, with the US solution referring to recent case law which dealt with related questions.

D. Conclusion

The overall result is that the shareholders' rights plan but not the customer assurance programme violates the general rules of company or securities markets law and regulations in most of the countries reviewed in this case study. Insofar as that is the case, the case studies agree, however, that the Bidder would have no means of enforcement qua bidder. However, the Bidder is also a shareholder of the target company. This may provide some mechanism of enforcement, depending on the clarification of further details, such as the proportion of shares held and the precise remedy sought (avoidance, damages etc.).[190]

There are also some notable differences and similarities between countries (with some of those related to those already discussed in chapter 4, above). They can be summarised as follows. First, it may be desirable to talk about Europe and South Africa on the one hand, with their board neutrality rule and the provisions on share capital,[191] and the US and Japan on the other hand. Second, however, the case studies also reveal a degree of variation within the European countries: for example, the UK and Finland may be different from the others since both countries have a takeover code and both seem to be more focused on shareholder (as opposed to stakeholder) interests. Third, this is not to deny the fact that there are some similarities between the US, the UK and South Africa: for instance, in these three jurisdictions, it is their case studies which most frequently refer to case law (though there is more specific case law on takeover defences in the US). Fourth, one can also take the view that the main result of the present case is 'US exceptionalism' inasmuch as it confers considerable discretion on management as regards the use of 'poison pills'.

A final point worth highlighting is that takeover law appears to be a topic that is extensively discussed in all of the legal systems covered in this book. However, it is interesting to note that hostile public takeovers are relatively rare in most countries, with the exception of the US.[192] Thus, it does not seem to be the case that the legal discussion necessarily follows the economic one, but it may also anticipate certain events that may or may not occur in the near future.

---

[189] See generally M Siems, *Convergence in Shareholder Law* (Cambridge, Cambridge University Press, 2008) 175–82.

[190] These topics are also addressed in other chapters of this book. See, eg, ch 2, above, and ch 10, below.

[191] Namely, Directive 2004/25/EC (n 6) and Directive (EU) 2017/1132 (n 19), previously Directive 2012/30/EU (n19).

[192] For empirical data, see M Becht, P Bolton and A Roell, 'Corporate Governance and Control', National Bureau of Economic Research Working Paper 9371, Cambridge, MA, NBER, 2002, at Table 2.

Part 2

Creditor Protection

6

Piercing the Corporate Veil

HISAEI ITO AND HIROYUKI WATANABE (EDITORS)

Main topics: application of the 'piercing the corporate veil' doctrine; directors' duties in the context of insolvency; directors' liability.

Related topics: directors' duties in general (see chapter 2 above); other forms of creditor protection (see chapter 7, below); enforcement of directors' duties (see chapter 10, below).

I. Scenario

Y owns 95 per cent of the shares of a non-listed public limited liability company (Company A). His wife, B, and father, C, own the other five per cent nominally. When Y asks B and C to appoint him as the CEO of Company A, Y assures both of them verbally that neither of them would need to be involved in Company A's business, nor would Y cause B and C any difficulties in managing and running the business. Y takes all business decisions by himself without consulting B, C and/or Company A's board of directors (which the law requires a company to hold when it decides its business). Y has neither called a meeting of the board nor a general meeting. B is subsequently formally appointed as a director of Company A, but C is not, although his advice is afforded great weight by Y.

When Company A is approaching insolvency, Y commits Company A to a contract with X whereby Company A will purchase the products of X. Y expects the transaction to deliver great benefits to Company A. However, not long after the formation of the contract, it becomes clear to Y that Company A is experiencing severe financial difficulties and that it is likely that Company A will be unable to pay X the price for the products. Company A enters into bankruptcy before the time for payment of the price in terms of the transaction.

Can X claim that Y is personally liable in his capacity as a shareholder and/or director of Company A for the debts owed by Company A to X (pursuant to the contract entered into between Company A and X)? If so, will the court hold that Y's personal liability is based on (i) a breach of his duties as a director to X as a creditor, (ii) the so-called 'piercing the corporate veil' doctrine or (3) some other rule of law? Can X claim that B and C are also personally liable for the debts owed by Company A to X (pursuant to the contract entered into between Company A and X)? If so, will the court base such liability on a finding that (i) B and C have breached a duty to monitor Y's behaviour as CEO of Company A, and if so, on what legal basis, (ii) B, as a director, has breached her legal duties as a director, or (3) C is deemed to be a 'de facto' or 'shadow' director and so, is liable because he has breached his duties as a director?

II. Case Studies

A. Japan

i. Piercing the Corporate Veil

A company has a juridical personality separate from its members and directors.[1] If a company is a closely held corporation, for example where a shareholder owns 100 per cent of the issued shares of the company, it may be that the strict separation of the personalities between the member and the company will lead to unjust or unequal treatment in a particular case. Therefore, case law has developed the so-called 'piercing the corporate veil' doctrine to resolve disputes which arise in the case of closely held corporations.

In general, the application of the doctrine of separate legal personality means that a transaction entered into by a representative director or officer on behalf of a company is validly formed as between the company and the third party. A representative director of the company has the authority to handle and manage the company's assets. However, if the application of this principle leads to an inadequate or unjust result in a particular case, it is possible to apply the 'piercing the corporate veil' doctrine to set aside the separation of legal personality between the company and its members or a controlling shareholder or director. Since the 'piercing the corporate veil' doctrine is a matter of last resort for a judge, we must analyse the applicability of this doctrine in a careful manner.

ii. Case Law

The Supreme Court has held that two requirements must be fulfilled in order to apply the 'piercing the corporate veil' doctrine: the first is the 'abuse of juridical personality' requirement and the second is the 'straw man' requirement.[2] The first requirement is satisfied where the corporate personality of the company is used as an instrument by a

---

[1] Companies Act 2005 (CA), Art 3.
[2] Supreme Court, 27 February 1969, *Minshu*, vol 23, no 2 at 511.

controlling shareholder in order to achieve an illegal or unjust purpose.[3] For example, where a company near insolvency sets up a new company to hide assets and discharge the company's debts, the Supreme Court ruled that the separation of the company and the new company should be denied, and creditors of the company were allowed to claim against the new company.[4]

The 'straw man' case indicates that a company is substantially owned and managed by an individual controlling shareholder and a party to a transaction is doubtful whether the transaction is made with the company or with the individual. The mere fact that the shareholder controls the company does not lead to the conclusion that the 'straw man' category has been satisfied. The case law requires other criteria to be met, such as that no general meeting or board meeting was held, that it was not possible to identify whether the transaction was entered into on behalf of the company or the individual concerned, or whether the assets of the company were being used for the benefit of the individual shareholder.[5]

The effect of the application of the doctrine is to deny the separation of juridical personality of the two entities. It can lead to the denial of the limited liability of a shareholder and allow a creditor of the old company to challenge a new company, or to deny the priority of a shareholder's loan to the company which is undercapitalised.[6]

Turning to the hypothetical case, if Y is in control of Company A and X misunderstands the position because the contract is substantially initiated by Y and believes the debtor could be Y because the management of Company A and Y's personal affairs are run in the same manner, X can argue that Y should be liable for Company A's debt to X.

iii. Director's Duty to a Third Party

In terms of Article 429 of the CA, if a director is grossly negligent in the performance of his or her duties, such director will be liable to a third party for any damages arising as a result thereof. Although the CA does not impose any duty on a director to a third party (see Articles 330 and 355), the director is liable in respect of any damage or loss sustained by a third party that is caused by a violation of his or her duty to the company. This idea was incorporated into the Amendment of the Commercial Code in 1966, which governed all forms of companies. Before the amendment, there were many smaller business associations in the form of *Kabusiki Kaisha* (Company Limited by Shares). Although the Commercial Code was designed for only publicly held corporations, it was also applied to small and closely held corporations. These small companies experienced serious difficulties in complying with the rules for a publicly held corporation. For example, it was uncommon for small companies to issue share certificates required for the free transfer of the shares or to call shareholders' or board meetings. Therefore, Parliament decided to legislate for special provisions for small

---

[3] Supreme Court, 26 October 1973, *Minshu*, vol 27, no 9 at 1240.
[4] Ibid.
[5] Tokyo High Court, 9 August 1978, *HanreiJiho*, no 904 at 65; Osaka High Court, 27 February 1981, *HanreiJiho*, no 1015 at 121 etc.
[6] K Egashira, *Kabushikigaisha-hô [Laws of Stock Corporations]* (7th edn, Tokyo, Yuhikaku, 2017) 42.

and close companies under which it provided that the articles of incorporation of a company may require a shareholder to attain the approval of the company prior to the assignation of his or her shares to a third party other than another shareholder. It has been said that almost one million companies amended their articles of incorporation to include such restrictions on the transferability of shares. At the same time, Parliament also introduced a provision which imposed directors' liability to a third party in certain circumstances. Even if a creditor's claim is not met by the company, it can claim against the director who violated his or her duty to the company and caused the creditor loss as a result.

As for the legal nature of the liability of the director to the third party, two different theories potentially apply. The first theory provides that the nature of the director's liability is based on the law of tort, in terms of which a director is liable to a third party only if the requirements of tort law are satisfied. However, Article 709 of the Civil Code directs that the director is not liable for damages caused by his or her simple negligence and case law provides that this is a special kind of statutory liability imposed on directors because they play an important role in the management of the business of small companies. In order to protect a third party contracting with such a company, the law imposes a special kind of liability on the director who breaches his or her duty to the company and, as a result, causes damage to the third party, insofar as there is a causal relationship between the director's misconduct and such damage.[7]

Since the liability of directors under Article 429 is a special rather than tortious liability, it has been held that the period of limitation for the extinction of such liability is 10 years under Article 167 of the Civil Code, rather than three years for torts under Article 724 of the Civil Code.[8]

iv. Legal Issues Relating to Article 429 of the CA

a. Knowledge or Gross Negligence

The courts have held that a director is liable where the director committed the company to a sales contract notwithstanding that he or she should have realised that the company would be unable to meet the debt.[9] However, the cases do not explain the reason why such misconduct constitutes a breach of duty to the company. Some commentators argue that, in an insolvent or near-insolvent situation, directors tend to take higher risks in order to achieve higher returns. The director continues the company's business even if doing so would make the company's financial position worse. However, the director is under a duty to consider the possibility of bankruptcy or rehabilitation of the company under the duty of due care which he or she owes to the company. If the director is successful in avoiding the damage, that may result in the protection of the company's creditor.[10]

---

[7] Supreme Court, 26 November 1969, *Minshu*, vol 23, no 11 at 2150.

[8] Supreme Court, 17 December 1974, *Minshu*, vol 28, no 10 at 2059. However, the Court ruled that Art 722 of the Civil Code relating to contributory negligence could be considered in a case relating to Art 429 of the CA case (Supreme Court, 4 October 1984, *HanreiJiho*, no 1143 at 143).

[9] Supreme Court, 15 April 1966, *Minshu*, vol 20, no 4 at 660; Tokyo High Court, 30 June 1980, *HanreiJiho*, no 973 at 120.

[10] Egashira, *Kabushikigaisha-hô* (n 6) 505–06.

b. Damage

If a director's misconduct causes damage to a third party as well as the company, such damage is referred to as 'indirect damage', for example, where a company becomes insolvent by virtue of the directors' mismanagement or conflict-of-interest transactions.[11] A shareholder may also suffer such indirect damage by virtue of the directors' misconduct, and the Supreme Court has held that the director will be liable under Article 429 of the CA[12] in such circumstances. However, this ruling has been criticised on the ground that such indirect damage of the shareholder could be remedied by a shareholder derivative suit (CA, Article 847).[13]

Even if a director's misconduct does not cause any harm to the company, a creditor may suffer damage as a result of the misconduct. This is called 'direct damage', for example, when a company is nearing insolvency and a director commits the company to entering into a loan even where the director anticipated that the company would not be in a position to repay the loan. This sort of dispute comprises a mixture of a director's liability to a third party and a director's tortious liability. However, unresolved questions remain regarding how to treat the dispute from a procedural point of view.

c. Nominal Director

A question for resolution is whether a director will be relieved of liability to a third party because he or she is a nominal director, never participated in the management of the corporation and was assured by the CEO that he or she would not need to be involved in the running of the company – such as B in the present scenario. In the case of small companies, it is common for a CEO to have provided a personal guarantee in respect of the company's debts when the company obtains a loan from a bank. If the company subsequently enters into bankruptcy, an unsecured creditor cannot collect his or her debt from the personal assets of the CEO. Owing to the fact that a creditor will look to recover its debts from parties with a 'deep pocket', he or she may initiate litigation against those nominal directors other than the CEO or executive directors.

The Supreme Court has held that the board of directors is obliged to monitor a director's commercial conduct. Therefore, a director as a member of the board is under a duty to monitor all the business conduct of the representative directors of the company. If the director discovers wrongdoing on the part of a representative director, he or she would have to call a board meeting to consider such misconduct.[14] On the other hand, some recent decisions of lower courts have refused to hold such a nominal director liable on the grounds that (i) the director had never received any remuneration or compensation from the company and (ii) the director lived far away from the premises of the company and had been omitted from board meetings for a long period of time.[15]

---

[11] Tokyo High Court, 29 March 1983, *HanreiJiho*, no 1079 at 92; ibid, 8 May 1984, *HanreiJiho*, no 1147 at 147.
[12] Supreme Court, 9 September 1997, *HanreiJiho*, no 1618 at 138.
[13] Tokyo High Court, 18 January 2005, *Kinyu Shoji Hanrei*, no 1209 at 10.
[14] Supreme Court, 22 May 1972, *Minshu*, vol 27, no 5 at 655.
[15] Sendai High Court, 26 May 1988, *HanreiJiho*, no 1286 at 143; Tokyo District Court, 31 January 1990, *Kinyu Shoji Hanrei*, no 858 at 28.

d. De Facto Director

In small companies, it is not unusual for some of the directors not to have been elected in accordance with the law – which could be relevant for C in the present case. Nevertheless, on occasion, persons such as controlling shareholders, directors of the parent company or statutory auditors step up to take the initiative of informally managing the company. The lower courts have held such persons liable to third parties, referring to them as a 'de facto organiser' or 'de facto director'. However, the basis for such a cause of action is not wholly clear and so it is uncertain how the theory of de facto director and the doctrine of piercing the corporate veil operate in conjunction to resolve disputes.

B. France

i. Introduction

Company A has only three shareholders. Under French company law, there must be at least seven shareholders and three directors[16] in the case of a public company (*Société anonyme* (SA)).[17] In the case of a simplified public limited company (*Société par actions simplifiée* (SAS)), there is no minimum number of shareholders.[18] This is also the case for a limited liability company (*Société à responsabilité limitée* (SARL)).[19] However, whatever the legal form adopted by Company A, the concept of fictitious company (*Société fictive*) and bankruptcy laws would equally apply in the same way.

Under French company law, there are several tools that can be used in order to pierce the corporate veil and hold a director or a shareholder liable for the debts of a company.

ii. Liability of the CEO (Y) of Company A to a Creditor (X)

A director or a shareholder can be held liable for the debts of a company if the company is deemed to have been fictitious (*société fictive*). This is a case law concept established by the Cour de cassation as early as the beginning of the twentieth century.[20]

There are several possible grounds for a judge to treat a company as fictitious. The most common ground is where there is a lack of willingness on the part of the shareholders to form a company and to behave as shareholders (*affectio societatis*). Since it is difficult to identify such a lack of willingness to form a company, the French Cour de cassation admits that judges can invoke the *ex post* behaviour of shareholders in order to assess whether they lacked the requisite *affectio societatis* from the start.[21] It should

---

[16] Commercial Code, Art L 225-17.
[17] Commercial Code, Art L 225-1.
[18] Commercial Code, Art L 227-1.
[19] Commercial Code, Art L 223-1.
[20] Cass req (Cour de cassation, Chamber for Petitions), 29 June 1908, *DP* 1910.1.233, with a note by M Percerou.
[21] Cass Com (Cour de cassation, Commercial Chamber), 12 October 1993, *Bull Joly* 1993 1265, with a note by M Jeantin, D 1993, IR 262, *Rev sociétés* 1994 283, with a note by F Bénac-Schmidt, *Dr sociétés* 1994, n° 1, with a note by T Bonneau.

be stressed that the mere fact that the shareholders are members of the same family is not enough to create a presumption that the company is fictitious.[22]

In the case of Company A, the wife and the father of the founder Y hold only 5 per cent of the shares nominally. This seems to imply that they do not really want to get involved in the running of Company A. In addition, they were told by founder Y that they would not be involved in the running of Company A. Y has also behaved as if there were no other shareholders and directors. According to French case law, these elements would probably be sufficient to justify treating Company A as a 'fictitious' company at the time it was formed.[23] Indeed, if shareholders B and C did not make any contribution in cash or in kind, the probability of a French court declaring the company to be fictitious would be even higher.[24] The fact that B was appointed as a director would not change this conclusion.

The 'fictitiousness' of a company can be invoked by a creditor even if the company is solvent. In the case of the bankruptcy of a company, because of its collective nature, only specific organs of the bankruptcy proceedings, including the judge himself or herself, can invoke the 'fictitiousness' of the company.[25] The consequence of a judicial finding that a company is 'fictitious' is that the bankruptcy proceedings will be extended to the majority shareholder, ie the latter will also be made bankrupt. Therefore, in the case of Company A, a French judge would probably hold, given the facts, that the company is fictitious and that the bankruptcy proceedings should be extended to shareholder Y. In such a case, there would only be one bankruptcy proceeding.

iii. Liability of Directors of Company A to a Creditor (X)

Apart from the notion of the fictitious company, French bankruptcy laws also allow the judge to hold a de jure director or manager (*dirigeant de droit*), or a de facto director or manager (*dirigeant de fait*), personally liable for a part or the whole of the debts of a company when a managerial error (*faute de gestion*) or errors contributed to the existence of irretrievable debts (*action en responsabilité pour insuffisance d'actif*, or before 2005 *action en comblement de passif*).[26] Simple negligence used to be sufficient for a director to incur liability under this provision. However, the law was changed in 2016 and simple negligence cannot give rise to an *action en responsabilité pour insuffisance d'actif.*

If it can be established that Y's management errors contributed to the existence of irretrievable debts, which indeed seems to be the case, he or she could also be held liable on this ground. However, since a French court would probably hold the company to be fictitious in the first place, there probably would not be any necessity for such an *action en comblement de passif* to be raised against Y. A finding that the company is

---

[22] Cass Com (Cour de cassation, Commercial Chamber), 21 December 1982, *BRDA* 1983, n° 12, p 21, *Bull. Joly* 1983. 194, *RTD com* 1983. 476, with a note by P Merle.

[23] See, eg, Cass Com (Cour de cassation, Commercial Chamber), 5 January 1983, *Bull Joly* 1983. 183; CA Paris (Court of Appeal of Paris), 28 January 1999, *Dr sociétés* 1999, no 90, with an observation by T Bonneau.

[24] CA Paris (Court of Appeal of Paris), 26 February 1981, *Gaz Pal* 1981 2 669, with a note by APS.

[25] Commercial Code, Art L 621-2 al 2.

[26] Commercial Code, Art L 651-2.

'fictitious' is more efficient from the viewpoint of creditor protection, since Y would then be held liable for all of the debts of Company A.

Directors, such as shareholder B can be subject to the *action en responsabilité pour insuffisance d'actif*, but not members of the supervisory board since they only control the managers and do not take management decisions themselves.[27] Even if B does not act as a director, since no meeting of the board is held, she is subject to her duties as a director.

As to C, who is not a director but whose advice is afforded great weight by Y, this is not enough to make him a de facto director under French case law.

Notwithstanding the fact that the directors of a company may have accepted their directorship position for personal reasons such as family or friendship ties, the French courts approach the lack of supervision of the chief executive officer (CEO) by the directors as a managerial error which can subject them to an *action en comblement de passif*. There are numerous cases which have adopted this position.[28] Therefore, in the case of Company A, Directors B and C would certainly be held to have breached their duty to monitor the CEO and could be held liable to cover part or all (to be shared with the CEO) of the irretrievable debts owed to creditor X through an *action en responsabilité pour insuffisance d'actif*.

iv. Liability of Shareholders of Company A to a Creditor (X)

Since shareholder C is not a director of Company A, he would not incur any liability in the case of bankruptcy/insolvency. The reason is that shareholders are under no duty to supervise the management and they did not act as 'shadow directors' (*dirigeants de fait*).

v. Summary and Conclusion

The French courts have several tools at their disposal in order to pierce the corporate veil. Most cases of piercing the corporate veil occur when the company is in bankruptcy, but its application is not limited to this situation.

C. Germany[29]

i. Possible Liability of Y

A company that is unable to pay its debts must file for insolvency.[30] If this is not done, creditors have a direct claim against the directors based on tort law (BGB, § 823(2) with

---

[27] Cass Com (Cour de cassation, Commercial Chamber), 12 July 2005, n° 1238, *RJDA* 2/06 n° 169.

[28] Decisions of the Cour de cassation, Commercial Chamber: Cass Com, 30 October 2000, n° 1786, *RJDA* 2/01 n° 210; Cass Com, 25 June 2006, n° 1285, *RJDA* 12/02, n° 1305; Cass Com, 31 January 1995, *Rev sociétés* 1995, p 763, with a note by Y Guyon; Cass Com, 7 July 1992, *Bull Joly* 1992 1192; 14 December 1993, *Bull civ* IV, n° 473, p 345; CA Aix-en-Provence (Court of Appeal of Aix-en-Provence), 3 February 1966, *Rev sociétés* 1966.437, with a note by Plaisant; *JCP* 1966 II 14861, with a note by Percerou.

[29] Abbreviated statutes: AktG = Law on Public Companies; BGB = Civil Code; GmbHG = Law on Private Limited Companies; InsO = Insolvency Code.

[30] See ch 2 at II C, above.

InsO, § 15a).[31] Other breaches of the directors' duties of care can only be enforced by the creditors if recourse against the company proved ineffective and if there is a gross violation of directors' duties (AktG, § 93(5) for management board; AktG, § 116 for supervisory board). In the present case, there is no indication that Y did not file for insolvency, and the mere fact that Y commits Company A to a contract at a time when the company is approaching insolvency cannot, as such, be seen as a gross violation of the duty of care.

As regards the position of Y as a shareholder, in Germany too, the concept of 'piercing the corporate veil' is a possible starting point. It has, in principle, been accepted by the German courts,[32] but it is rarely applied. Four situations are discussed: first, some commentators support veil piercing in the case of acute undercapitalisation of the company, ie a severe imbalance between debt and equity; second, the intermingling of the capital of the company and the shareholder can justify the imposition of personal liability; third, in some cases of groups of companies, the parent company may be directly liable. However, usually, the codified German law of groups of companies (AktG, §§ 291–331) operates to provide relief; fourth, where funds are withdrawn which destroys the economic basis of a company (*existenzvernichtender Eingriff*), the German courts will pierce the corporate veil. In the present case, it is unlikely that any of these four exceptions are fulfilled.

The academic literature discusses further legal grounds for direct claims, but, again, these are rare exceptions.[33] There is usually no claim based on 'pre-contractual liability' (BGB, § 311) because this would require the director to have created an atmosphere in negotiations such that the other party trusted the individual more than the company. Tort law can only apply in special situations, such as where a director commits a traffic accident or if a provision of criminal law is infringed that is intended to protect a third party. Tortious liability also applies in the case of 'intentional damage contrary to public policy' (*Verstoß gegen die guten Sitten*), for instance, in extreme cases of securities fraud.[34] None of this is relevant in the present case.

ii. Possible Liability of B and C

There are no reasons why B and C should be liable as shareholders. We have already seen that none of the rare cases of veil piercing are applicable. Furthermore, no duty is imposed on minority shareholders to monitor the management of a company. Shareholders have no duty to vote in a particular way unless the general fiduciary duty among shareholders requires a particular decision to be taken.[35] In the present case,

---

[31] See JU Haas in *Baumbach & Hueck's GmbHG* (21st edn, Munich, Beck, 2017) § 64, para 145.

[32] See, eg, BGH (German Federal Supreme Court), NJW 1956, 785; NJW 1970, 2015; NJW 1974, 134, 492; NJW 1977, 1449 (insufficient capital as such does not lead to the piercing of the corporate veil); NJW 1981, 522; NJW 1994, 1801; NJW 2002, 3024 (a case where courts previously used an analogy with the law on groups of companies; see also BGH, NJW 2001, 3622); *cf* also overview in U Hüffer and J Koch, *Aktiengesetz* (12th edn, Munich, Beck, 2016) § 1, paras 15–33.

[33] G Spindler in *Münchener Kommentar zum Aktiengesetz, Band 2* (4th edn, Munich, Beck 2014) § 93, paras 302–20.

[34] BGH, BGHZ 160, 149; NJW 2004, 2668; BGHZ 160, 134; NJW 2005, 2450.

[35] BGH, NZG 2016, 781. See also ch 7 at II C and ch 10 at II E, below.

there is no violation of such a general fiduciary duty because the only other shareholder is Y, the CEO of Company A. Moreover, a breach of this duty would not lead
to a direct claim by the creditors against the shareholders, but merely to an obligation
to compensate the company.[36]

As regards their possible duties as directors, in the present scenario it may be alleged
that B and C did not adequately supervise the actions of Y. With respect to B, the
informal understanding that she should not be involved in the running of the business
may constitute an illustration of wilful ignorance that can, in some circumstances, lead
to a breach of duty.[37] However, this omission is unlikely to lead to a gross violation of
duty, which is necessary for a direct claim by a creditor (see (i) above).

With respect to C, the problem is that he has not been appointed as a director. In
the law of private companies (GmbHs), it is suggested that someone who acts as the
manager of the firm without having been appointed to the position can be regarded as
its de facto manager (*faktischer Geschäftsführer*). This person will then be subject to
the same liability rules as the firm's legally appointed manager.[38] For public companies
(AktG), commentary has focused on whether a void appointment may be treated as
temporarily valid (*fehlerhafte Bestellung*).[39] For reasons of legal certainty, however,
there must always be an explicit appointment decision.[40] Hence, any de facto behaviour could, at best, justify the treatment of the relevant individual as an 'apparent
agent' (*Anscheinsvertreter*) under general commercial law.[41] However, in the present
scenario, there is no indication that C created the impression that he was an agent of
Company A.

D. Italy[42]

The piercing of the corporate veil is not generally allowed in Italian company law.
However, several remedies have been developed to address the problems created by the
possible abuses of limited liability.

Examining the position of Y, an Italian court would probably consider the facts
presented in the hypothetical case to be a violation of Articles 2394 and 2394-*bis* of
the CC, which are two provisions governing the liability of directors in Spas. It should
also be assumed that Y is a director of the company, since CEOs in Italy normally
are 'delegated directors' appointed to the general management of the company. It is

[36] See Hüffer and Koch, *Aktiengesetz* (n 32) § 53a, para 27.
[37] See M Habersack, in *Münchener Kommentar zum Aktiengesetz, Band 2* (4th edn, Munich, Beck 2014)
§ 116 paras 30–37 (eg duties to create a functional organisation; to take part in management; to exercise own
judgement; to intervene if necessary; to mutually supervise).
[38] See, eg, U Haas and H Ziemons in *Beck'scher Online-Kommentar GmbHG* (27th edn, Munich, Beck,
2016) § 43, paras 17–21.
[39] See Hüffer and Koch (n 32) § 84, paras 12–13.
[40] Ibid, § 108, para 4.
[41] See K Hopt in A Baumbach & K Hopt (eds), *Handelsgesetzbuch* (37th edn, Munich, Beck, 2016)
Einleitung vor § 48, para 6.
[42] Abbreviations: CC = Italian Civil Code (codice civile); Spa = public company (*Società per azioni*);
Srl = private limited company (*Società a responsabilità limitata*).

also possible that a CEO does not sit on the board of directors and that he is simply appointed 'general manager'. However, if this is the case, according to Article 2396 of the CC, the same rules concerning the liability of directors would apply to him, as a 'general manager', if he has been appointed to that position by the general meeting or according to a provision of the by-laws.

The first paragraph of Article 2394 of the CC provides that the directors are liable to the creditors of the company if they fail to comply with their duties to preserve the integrity of the company's assets. In the second paragraph of this provision, it is also made clear that creditors may directly sue directors only when the assets of the company are insufficient to satisfy their claims. Article 2394-*bis* of the CC, on the other hand, clarifies that this action can also be undertaken during bankruptcy procedures, and it grants standing to the bankruptcy receiver to raise such an action.

It is a matter of debate whether a direct action similar to that provided by Article 2394 of the CC is available in the case of the Srl. In fact, there is no reference in Article 2476 of the CC – which governs the liability of the directors of an Srl – to an action raised by the creditors against the directors.[43] In any case, in the case of an Srl, legal scholars adopt the view that creditors are at least allowed to file an indirect action against the directors.[44]

With regard to B, since she was arguably appointed as a director or 'general manager', she could face the same liability which would be imposed on Y as provided under Articles 2394 and 2394-*bis* of the CC. A distinction should be drawn, however, between the situation where Y is appointed as a 'delegated director' and the case where the appointment is as a 'general manager'. In the former case, according to Article 2381, paragraph 6 of the CC, directors, like B, should simply act on an informed basis, and ask the 'delegated directors' to provide the board with information on the current affairs of the company. In the latter case, ie when, according to Article 2396 CC, a 'general manager' is appointed, in the absence of 'delegated directors', all directors, including B, that are the persons to whom the management of the company is entrusted, may be held liable under Article 2392 of the CC.[45]

Turning to the position of C, the Italian courts recognise the concept of 'de facto directors'.[46] However, given the facts presented, since C was not involved in the management of the company, it is unlikely that an action based on this doctrine would succeed. Another important principle that may justify an action against C can be found in Article 2476, paragraph 7 of the CC, which stipulates that the shareholders of an Srl 'who have intentionally decided or authorised the carrying out of acts detrimental to the company' are jointly and severally liable with the directors for these decisions. The scope of application of this provision is subject to debate, and according to one

---

[43] *Cf* R Guidotti, 'Commento *sub* art. 2476' in A Maffei Alberti (ed), *Commentario breve al diritto delle società* (3rd edn, Padua, CEDAM, 2015) 1379 ff, 1396 ff.

[44] See, eg, ibid, 1397.

[45] According to this provision 'the directors [of an Spa] must perform the duties required of them by law and the bylaws with the standard of diligence required being governed by the nature of the appointment and their specified tasks and duties'.

[46] See, eg, A De Nicola, 'Commento *sub* art. 2380-*bis*' in P Marchetti, LA Bianchi, F Ghezzi and M Notari (eds), *Commentario alla Riforma delle società, Amministratori* (Milan, Giuffrè-Egea, 2005) 79 ff, 86 ff.

reading, the reach of the liability extends to the shareholders of an Spa.[47] However, since the hypothetical case does not mention the fact that C authorised or carried out acts detrimental to the company, he is outside the scope of Article 2476, paragraph 7 of the CC. Nor would C be liable for a violation of the duty to monitor, which cannot be imposed on shareholders, but only on directors.

As an alternative to any legal action based on the liability of the directors of the company – or of the shareholders who have intentionally decided or authorised the carrying out of acts detrimental to the company – the piercing the corporate veil doctrine is applied extremely rarely in Italian law. Indeed, both Articles 2325 and 2462 of the CC (which apply respectively to the Spa and the Srl) provide that only the company is liable for corporate obligations. A few provisions, however, perform a function similar to the veil piercing doctrine, such as the following:

1. In both the Spa and the Srl, when the shares of a company are owned by a single shareholder, that person can be held liable where the company enters into insolvency, if the contributions are not fully paid or if there has been a failure to publicise the fact that the company is owned by a single shareholder.

2. Article 2467 of the CC is a provision that postpones the reimbursement of loans made by the shareholders to an Srl when 'there is an excessive imbalance of debt compared to net capital'. This article addresses the problem of undercapitalisation, which is common among Srls owing to their low minimum capital requirement. It is a matter of debate whether this provision may be extended to Spas.[48]

3. A third rule applies when the company is subject to the 'direction and coordination' of other entities. In this case, Article 2497 of the CC provides that where companies and entities which are carrying out the direction and coordination of a company act in their own interests or in the interests of other parties, they are directly liable for the damages suffered by the shareholders of the companies subject to such direction and coordination. In addition, Article 2497-*quinquies* of the CC prescribes that the principles of Article 2467 of the CC on loans made by the shareholders of an Srl also apply to financing made in favour of the company.

In conclusion, Director Y will probably be sued directly by Company A's creditors under Article 2394 of the CC, and it will not be necessary to invoke more elaborate theories. B could be held liable either for a violation of the duty to act on an informed basis or, more in general, for having violated her duties as director. With regard to C, he will probably not be subject to any liability under the law, since he was neither appointed a director, nor was he acting as 'de facto director' or authorised to act, nor in fact had he carried out any act.

---

[47] For a description of the different theories, see A Angelillis and G Sandrelli 'Commento *sub* art. 2476' in P Marchetti, LA Bianchi, F Ghezzi and M Notari (eds), *Commentario alla Riforma delle società, Società a responsabilità limitata* (Milan, Giuffrè-Egea, 2008) 665 ff, 796 ff.
[48] G Balp, 'Commento *sub* art. 2467' in Marchetti et al, *Commentario alla Riforma delle società, Società a responsabilità limitata* (n 47) 227 ff, 266 ff.

E. Spain

When a company is unable to pay its debts, its directors are obliged to file for insolvency (Ley Concursal (LCon) – Insolvency Act, Articles 3.1 and 5.1).[49] If the directors fail to do so, they may be held liable to compensate for damages or to pay part of the amount of the debts owed to the creditors (LCon, Articles 165.1, 172, and 172 (bis)). In the instant case, it is not evident, however, that Y did not file for insolvency as required.

Turning to the potential breach of directors' duties as the basis for X's claim, it is unclear that Y's decision to commit Company A to a contract with X at a point at which Company A was nearing insolvency consisted of a breach of his duties, since Y would appear to have taken such measures with the expectation of resolving Company A's difficult situation. Of course, it is assumed that Y adopted that decision in an informed and diligent way.[50] Nevertheless, if X was of the view that Y was culpable of a breach of his duties, it could raise a claim against Y for damages caused to Company A, based on Article 240 of the Ley de Sociedades de Capital (LSC) – Corporate Enterprises Act.[51] However, for X to proceed under Article 240 of the LSC, it is a requirement that such action has not been first brought by Company A or its shareholders, and, also, that Company A's assets are insufficient to cover its debts. Otherwise, if X was able to show that it suffered loss that was directly caused by the actions of Y in breach of his duties as director, then X could file an individual claim (LSC, Article 241). Opinion amongst Spanish scholars is divided between those who consider that the individual claim exercised by creditors against directors is a self-contained regime and others who see Article 241 of the LSC as an instance of the application of the general rules prescribed by Article 1902 of the Civil Code on extra-contractual liability.[52]

Turning to the doctrine of piercing the corporate veil, this has been accepted by the Spanish courts, notably since the 1980s.[53] The application of this concept would, however, be justified only on the occurrence of certain circumstances such as abuse of law, confusion and intermingling of capital, and effective external control/management or undercapitalisation, which do not seem to apply in this hypothetical case.[54]

Shareholders are subject to a duty of loyalty according to which they are obliged to abstain from conduct which is contrary to the interests of the company.[55] However,

---

[49] See ch 2 at II E, above.

[50] eg, STS (Sentencia Tribunal Supremo) of 20 November 2008 provides for the exoneration of directors from liability for unpaid promissory notes on the basis that, although those directors decided to issue promissory notes in a moment of economic difficulty for their company, close to compulsory liquidation, they took logical and reasonable measures to avoid that situation.

[51] Real Decreto Legislativo 1/2010, de 2 de julio, por el que se aprueba el texto refundido de la Ley de Sociedades de Capital (LSC).

[52] A comprehensive analysis of this discussion is provided by J Alfaro Águila-Real, 'La llamada acción individual de responsabilidad contra los administradores sociales' (2002) 18 *Revista de Derecho de Sociedades* 45, 48–53.

[53] A landmark case is STS (Sentencia Tribunal Supremo) of 28 May 1984.

[54] On the application of the concept of 'piercing the corporate veil' in the US, Spain and Mexico, see R Obando Pérez, 'Una visión dual de la doctrina del levantamiento del velo de la persona jurídica' (2003) 25 *Revista del Instituto de la Judicatura Federal* 159.

[55] See V Ribas Ferrer, *El deber de lealtad del administrador de sociedades* (Madrid, La Ley, 2010) 325–28.

B and C have not engaged in behaviour of that kind. In the instant case it could nevertheless be argued that, by being director but at the same time refraining from participating in the affairs of the board and taking care of company matters, B could be committing a breach of the duty of care (LSC, Article 225). The duty of care requires directors to be diligently informed about the business of the company and also to monitor other directors,[56] something that does not seem to have happened in this case. As regards whether C may be acting as a de facto director, Spanish company law is likely to answer this question in the negative. It defines de facto directors as: (a) those who actually perform the functions of directors – regardless of their formal appointment as such; or, (b) those upon whose instructions the directors act (LSC, Article 236.3). However, C seems largely unengaged when it comes to the day-to-day business of Company A. In this respect, the fact that C's advice is afforded great weight by Y does not necessarily indicate the fulfilment of any of the abovementioned conditions. However, if C was considered a de facto director, he may be liable for breach of duty under Article 236.3 of the LSC, which explicitly recognises the liability of de facto directors.

Spanish company law determines that directors are jointly and severally liable (LSC, Article 237).[57] X could file an individual claim against all the directors of A, or against one or some of them; in the latter case, if one or some directors were held liable, they would have a right of recourse against the other directors of A (Código Civil (CC) – Civil Code,[58] Article 1145).[59]

F. The Netherlands[60]

i. Possible Liability of Y

Under Dutch law X would be able to hold Y liable in his role of director. The basis for the liability of Y as a director towards X as a creditor of Company A would be a tort claim.[61] In order to establish the liability of Y, X as a plaintiff would have to prove that Y can be seriously and personally blamed for the tortious act (*ernstig verwijt*). The question of what constitutes such serious blame has been further developed in case law. Most importantly in this case, is the so-called Beklamel rule which was developed by the Supreme Court (Hoge Raad) in the Beklamel case. According to this Beklamel rule, directors can be held liable to third parties such as creditors on the basis of a tort (*onrechtmatige daad*) if they, at the time of entering into the transaction, knew or

---

[56] See eg V Ribas Ferrer, 'Artículo 226. Deber de lealtad' in Á Rojo and E Beltrán (eds), *Comentario de la Ley de Sociedades de Capital* (Cizur Menor (Navarra), Civitas-Thomson Reuters, 2011) 1613–20.

[57] See ch 2 at II E, above.

[58] Real Decreto de 24 de julio de 1889 por el que se publica el Código Civil.

[59] See, eg, M Valmaña Ochaita, *La Responsabilidad Civil Derivada del Folleto Informativo en las Ofertas Públicas de Suscripción y Venta de Acciones* (Las Rozas (Madrid), La Ley, 2006) 537.

[60] Abbreviations: DCC=Dutch Civil Code; HR = Hoge Raad = Dutch Supreme Court; OK = Ondernemingskamer = Enterprise Chamber; Rb= rechtbank = District Court. An unofficial translation of Dutch company law as incorporated in bk 2 of the Dutch Civil Code can be found on www.dutchcivillaw.com/civilcodebook022.htm.

[61] DCC, Art 6:162.

ought to have known that Company A would not within a reasonable period of time be able to fulfil its obligations or would not be able to provide relief for potential damages resulting from non-performance.[62] If X can establish that this was the case, he will most likely be able to hold Y liable for entering into the contract in the name and on behalf of Company A. This liability is not a collective board liability which rests upon all members of the board jointly. It is rather an individual liability of the director who caused the company to enter into the contract. Since Y is a director of Company A, it will be most logical to base a claim on the Beklamel rule. Liability as a shareholder is also possible. However, this would be more difficult to establish as it is only accepted in exceptional cases. Dutch case law does recognise the concept of veil piercing. However, direct veil piercing (*vereenzelviging*) is rarely recognised. Dutch case law has also developed various rules concerning the so-called indirect liability of shareholders (*indirect doorbraak*). This is a liability based on a tort (*onrechtmatige daad*) committed by shareholders or shadow directors.[63]

ii. Possible Liability of B and C

The abovementioned liability on the basis of tort law (*onrechtmatige daad*) is a form of personal liability which means that the plaintiff will have to establish for each and every director individually that serious culpability rests upon him or her. B is appointed as a director of company A. However, B did not enter into the contract in the name and on behalf of Company A and therefore the Beklamel rule described above cannot be used against B. B can, however, also be held liable to X on the basis of a tort (*onrechtmatige daad*). This will be the case if X can establish that B as a director has caused or has permitted Company A not to fulfil its obligations towards third parties. However, the additional criterion of serious blame on behalf of the director is also imposed and, here, much will depend on the circumstances of the case.[64] The test applied to determine directors' liability in such a case is whether the acts or omissions of the director concerned against the creditor are, given the circumstances, so negligent that it can be said that he or she can be seriously and personally blamed. According to the rules established in case law the latter can be the case if it can be established that the directors knew or reasonably should have known that the consequences of the actions of the company – which the director has permitted or caused – would result in non-performance by the company of its obligations or that the company would not be able to provide relief for potential damages resulting from these actions.[65]

Whether or not this is the case here, will depend on the knowledge that B as a director had or should have had at the relevant time and therefore the weighing of the circumstances by the court. There have been cases in which the lower court was less strict towards a director who was not really involved in the running of the company

---

[62] HR 6 October 1989, *NJ* 1990/286, with a note by JMM Maeijer (*Beklamel*).

[63] See with regard to veil piercing in company groups SM Bartman, AF Dorresteijn and M Olaerts, *Van Het Concern* (Deventer, Kluwer, 2016) c VIII.

[64] HR 8 December 2006, *JOR* 2007/38 (*Ontvanger/Roelofsen*); HR 23 May 2014, *NJ* 2014/325, with a note by Van Schilfgaarde.

[65] Ibid.

as seems to be the case here for B.[66] However, it has been contested in the literature whether or not this is the right approach and this issue has not yet been resolved by the case law.[67] As far as the monitoring duty of B as a director is concerned, the Dutch Supreme Court (Hoge Raad) has acknowledged that a director who did not cause the company to enter into an agreement can nevertheless be held liable if it can be established that he or she was closely involved with the company entering into the agreement (*anderszins nauw bij de desbetreffende overeenkomst is betrokken geweest*). Here too, serious blame on behalf of the fellow directors is required. This will require more than the mere fact that the fellow director did not ensure that the company fulfilled its obligations under the contract.[68]

On the basis of the information provided in the hypothetical case under discussion, it is unlikely that C will be held liable. C is not appointed as a director of Company A and he only holds a small amount of the shares. Dutch law recognises the concept of de facto or shadow directorship. However, it does not distinguish between these two terms. The only codification of the concept of shadow/de facto directorship can be found in Article 2:138/248-7 DCC which concerns directors' liability in the case of insolvency.[69] This provision stipulates that the rules concerning the liability of directors in the case of bankruptcy are equally applicable to de facto/shadow directors. Third parties can also bring a claim against a de facto/shadow director on the basis of a tort.[70] However, it is not clear whether C could qualify as a shadow/de facto director. The hypothetical case under discussion only mentions that C's advice is afforded great weight by Y. This is not sufficient to establish C's liability as a shadow/de facto director as this would require direct interference in the management of the company at the very least.[71]

G. Finland

i. Introduction

As a general rule, shareholders have no personal liability for the obligations of a limited liability company under Finnish company law. Nevertheless, in exceptional circumstances, personal liability for the obligations of a limited liability company may arise. For example, shareholders could be held liable against creditors in their capacity as directors for damages they have caused by violating the provisions of the Companies

---

[66] Hof Arnhem 23 January 2007, *JOR* 2007/215, with a note by Kortmann.

[67] See for an overview M Olaerts, 'De beperkte bestuurder' (2012) 2 *TvOB* 45.

[68] HR 8 January 1999, *NJ* 1999/318 (*Pelco/Sturkenboom*): for a situation where the district court did hold a fellow director liable, see Rb Midden-Nederland 12 October 2016, *RO* 2017/8.

[69] See Annex to the Study on Directors' Duties and Liability in the EU prepared for the European Commission DG Markt 2013, Country report: Netherlands, at A 615, available at http://ec.europa.eu/justice/civil/company-law/corporate-governance/index_en.htm.

[70] Ibid, A 622.

[71] There is discussion in the literature regarding what is required in order to qualify as a shadow/de facto directorship. Two requirements are often suggested: direct interference and setting aside the actual board (*feitelijke terzijde stelling*); the latter requirement would seem to have become less relevant in recent case law. See in this respect Bartman et al, *Van Het Concern* (n 63) 274–77.

Act 2006 (CA). Moreover, shareholders may be liable for damages in some cases of a negligent breach of the CA.

There is no explicit rule in the CA for piercing the corporate veil. However, it should be noted that in a recent ruling, the Supreme Court ruled that the corporate veil may be pierced in some situations. In said ruling, a company used a wholly owned subsidiary to avoid certain administrative fees. The subsidiary's board was identical to the parent company's board and, according to the ruling, the subsidiary did not have any independent operations and the only perceptible purpose of the subsidiary was to avoid those administrative fees. Therefore, it was ruled that the veil of limited liability may be pierced if it is apparent that the purpose of the arrangement is to misuse limited liability.[72] However, it is unlikely that this Supreme Court ruling would apply as such in this situation.

ii. Possible Director's Liability of Y and B

Directors have certain duties in the vicinity of insolvency, such as a duty to notify the register at once on the loss of share capital when the board of directors notices that the company has negative equity.[73] In practice, failing to file a timely register notification may lead to personal liability of the directors to the creditors of the company. In addition, the board of directors of a public company, such as in the present case, must without delay draw up financial statements and an annual report in order to ascertain the financial position of the company in the event that the board of directors notices that the equity of the company is less than one half of the share capital. The board of directors would also be obliged to convene a general meeting without delay to consider measures to remedy the financial position of the company (CA, chapter 20, sections 23(1) and 23(3)).

A failure to fulfil the abovementioned obligations may lead to the liability of Y and B as the directors of Company A. However, the case does not clearly indicate the exact financial position of Company A or the timeline of the events. The key issue to examine is therefore the point at which Company A lost its share capital. If the contract between Company A and X was concluded before the loss of share capital (negative equity), Y would generally not be held liable towards X by virtue of the CA. Members of the board of the directors and the managing director are liable in damages for the loss that they, in violation of the duty of care, have deliberately or negligently caused to the company. They are held liable in damages for the loss towards a shareholder or a third party if directors have caused the loss deliberately or negligently by violating the articles of association or the provisions of the CA other than the duty of care.[74] However, if Company A has failed to fulfil its abovementioned duties pursuant to chapter 20, section 23 of the CA, Y was aware thereof, and X can establish that it would not have concluded the contract with Company A had it known about the loss

---

[72] Supreme Court of Finland, KKO 2015:17.

[73] The criterion is objective, meaning what the reasonable board of directors should notice based on ongoing financial monitoring.

[74] CA, c 22, s 1; see also ch 2 at II G above.

of share capital, or concluded the contract on other conditions, Y could be held liable for damages for the part of the loss sustained by X that is attributable to Y's omission.

One of the key duties of the board of directors is monitoring the operative management, including the managing director, of the company. The board of directors must oversee the administration of the company and the appropriate organisation of its operations. The board of directors is also responsible for the appropriate arrangement of the control of the company accounts and finances.[75] Therefore B has, as the director of Company A, a duty to monitor Company A's management, including the actions of the managing director Y. Y's assurances as a shareholder do not exempt B from this obligation. The failure to fulfil this duty may constitute a breach of the duty of care and the explicit provision of the CA and therefore lead to liability in damages as discussed in more detail in Chapter 2 at II G, above.

iii. Possible Shareholder Liability of B and C

B and C are minority shareholders. As shareholders they are generally not liable towards the company, another shareholder or a third party, such as X. However, shareholders that contribute to a violation of the CA or the articles of association and, thus, deliberately or negligently cause a loss to a creditor, are liable for damages related to a loss.[76] Moreover, if C is de facto director and uses the powers granted to directors by virtue of chapter 6, section 2(1) of the CA, he may be held liable for damages without formally being a director.[77] Likewise, shareholders that in practice control the behaviour of the directors might be held liable as if they were directors.[78]

H. Poland

i. Personal Liability of a Director to X as a Creditor Based on Breach of Fiduciary Duties

Under Polish law, directors of a limited liability company may be held liable for a breach of fiduciary duties to creditors in accordance with Article 299 of the Polish Commercial Companies Code (CCC). According to section 1 of this article, the members of the management board are jointly and severally liable for the obligations of the company where a claim against the company has proved fruitless. A member of the management board may be relieved of the liability referred to in section 1 of Article 299 of the CCC by showing that a petition for a declaration of the bankruptcy of the company was filed, that proceedings to arrange for such a petition were instituted in due time, that the failure to file a petition for declaration of the bankruptcy of the company or make arrangements for the same were not attributable to his or her fault, or that the creditor suffered no damage, notwithstanding that no petition for

---

[75] CA, c 6, s 2.
[76] CA, c 22, s 2.
[77] J Mähönen and S Villa, *Osakeyhtiö III – Corporate Governance* (Helsinki, Talentum, 2012) 452–55.
[78] Ibid, 312.

declaration of the bankruptcy of the company was filed or no arrangements were made for the same. This claim can be treated as the equivalent to the American doctrine of 'piercing the corporate veil', which implies that in the case of approaching insolvency, the director should give priority to the creditors of the company. Although the above claim under Article 299 of the CCC is not specifically formulated as being a part of the fiduciary duties of directors to creditors, it undoubtedly can be treated as such. In our hypothetical case, if the company was a limited liability company, Creditor X would be entitled to sue Director Y and the latter would be liable to the former, provided that X had sought to enforce directly against Company A and that had been ineffective.

There is no equivalent to Article 299 of the CCC in the law of public companies. Thus, the hypothetical case would have to be solved differently. To start with, in a public company there is no general fiduciary duty of management or supervisory board members to creditors. However, board members are obliged to file for bankruptcy within two weeks of the company's insolvency. Pursuant to Article 11, section 2 of the Bankruptcy Act, a corporation is insolvent when the company does not pay its debts as they fall due and when its liabilities exceed its assets, notwithstanding that it may be able to fulfil its due obligations on time. A violation of the duty to file for insolvency can lead to a criminal penalty (CCC, Article 586). However, the CCC does not provide creditors with a direct action against those who violate these obligations.

Thus, any attempt to construct a right of action in favour of a creditor would have to be based on tort law and the general provisions in the regulations of the Civil Code. Under Article 490 of the CCC in conjunction with Article 415 of the Civil Code, the creditor would have to prove: (1) fault on the part of the director; (2) the illegality of the director's conduct, both with regard to binding legal provisions and/or the 'principle of social coexistence'; (3) a causative link between the conduct of the director and the loss/damage caused to the creditor; and (4) loss/damage.

It could be argued that the complete disregard of corporate formalities goes against this 'principle of social coexistence'. Nevertheless, the chance of success of a claim on such a basis is relatively low. It would be difficult to prove that disregarding formalities by not holding a general meeting of shareholders and the management board could of itself cause damage to a creditor, irrespective of other circumstances. Even in Delaware, where the doctrine of piercing of corporate veil is well established, it is understood that several requirements have to be met:[79] the disregarding of corporate formalities must be accompanied by the undercapitalisation of the company, the commingling of assets, fraud or control. Moreover, it would be difficult to prove in a Polish court that a failure to hold an appropriate amount of capital in relation to the scope of the company's business breaches the 'principle of social coexistence'. The Polish CCC only provides for minimal capital requirements and shareholders enjoy limited liability insofar as they meet these requirements and their company has been properly registered. One could also argue that no-one can claim that the capital was

---

[79] See, eg, *Van Dorn Co v Future Chemical and Oil Corp*, 753 F 2d 565 (7th Cir 1985): '[the] corporate entity will be disregarded and the veil of limited liability pierced when two requirements are met: First, there must be such unity of interest and ownership that the separate personalities of the corporation and the individual [or other corporation] no longer exist; and second, circumstances must be such that adherence to the fiction of separate corporate existence would sanction a fraud or promote injustice'. But see also K, below.

insufficient on the ground that the law provides for minimum capital requirements. In addition, the exercise of control over the company may be deemed to constitute the normal prerogative of the dominating shareholder as long as it is in accordance with the proportionality principle of rights and contributions. Finally, it is doubtful whether a creditor could invoke the infringement of 'the principle of social coexistence', since the principle of *caveat emptor* may be used to argue that creditors should secure their own interests by other means than those provided for by company law.

Some authors also invoke the *actio pauliana* ('*skarga pauliańska*') as regulated in Articles 527 ff of the Civil Code as the Polish example of 'piercing the corporate veil'. In accordance with this article, if a third party has obtained a financial benefit as a result of legal action which is to the detriment of the creditors, each creditor may seek recognition that this conduct was ineffective if the debtor was aware of the resultant harm to the creditors and the third party knew or ought to have been aware of such harm. The legal action is detrimental to creditors if the debtor as a result of this activity has become insolvent or became insolvent in a higher degree than it was before the conduct. The suit should in principle be directed against a third party that has obtained a financial benefit thanks to a transaction with the debtor. However, Article 527 of the Civil Code will not be helpful in the hypothetical case. Y does not transact with Company A (it is a transaction between Company A and X); thus, there is no transaction (legal action) between Y and Company A to invalidate, and the application of Article 527 of the Civil Code could not result in the liability of Y. Moreover, there are other substantial differences between Article 527 of the Civil Code and the concept of 'piercing the corporate veil'. First of all, Article 527 of the Civil Code only applies to the situation where the company has become insolvent as a result of a particular 'legal action' (usually a deal between a company and a third party), whereas 'piercing the corporate veil' is a much broader concept, which includes disregarding corporate formalities, parent-subsidiary situations, commingling of assets etc. In addition, the court decree granted on the basis of the *actio pauliana* (Civil Code, Article 527) is enforceable only against part of the assets of a third party (Civil Code, Article 532). Thus, the liability of the third party is limited in this case. By contrast, in the case of a 'piercing the corporate veil' claim, the creditor can enforce against the entire property of the shareholder (third party), not only the part of the property which he or she received from the company. Furthermore, where Article 527 of the Civil Code applies, the plaintiff must prove the insolvency of the debtor company.[80]

To sum up, as regards the so-called 'piercing the corporate veil' doctrine, the Polish courts have failed to develop such a doctrine. The Polish law tradition is different from the Anglo-American common law system. The protection of creditors is realised by virtue of the institution of minimum share capital. In the case of a limited liability company, the minimal share capital is quite low, ie at least PLN 5,000, whereas in the case of a public company, it is at least PLN 100,000.[81]

---

[80] See the judgment of the Appeal Court in Lublin, 19 March 1997, I ACa 27/97 LexPolonica, no 1605788. However, it is said that the creditor may also establish the insolvency of the company by other means.

[81] However, it should be noted that in 2010 the Panel on Company Law of Civil Law Codification Commission to the Minister of Justice prepared the draft reform of the structure of a limited liability company (*Spółka z ograniczoną odpowiedzialnością*). The draft provides for the removal of the minimum

ii. Liability of B and C for the Debts Owed by Company A

As regards the legal duties of B as a formally appointed director, the solution would be different depending on whether the company is a limited liability company (*spółka z ograniczoną odpowiedzialnością*) or a public company (*spółka akcyjna*). Concerning the first possibility, the liability of B will be the same as indicated in (i). However B may be relieved of the liability referred to in section 1 of Article 299 of the CCC by showing that a petition for a declaration of bankruptcy of the company was filed, that proceedings to arrange for such a petition were instituted in due time, that the failure to file a petition for declaration of bankruptcy of the company or make arrangements for the same were not attributable to his or her fault, or that the creditor suffered no damage, notwithstanding that no petition for declaration of the bankruptcy of the company was filed or no arrangements were made for the same. Concerning the latter, the liability of B will be hard to prove, since it would have to be based on tort law.

C does not hold any formal position in the company as a director or manager. The notion of 'de facto' or 'shadow' directors has not been accepted in Poland. Under Article 299 of the CCC, it is necessary to prove that a person held a position as member of the management board. Thus, it adopts a rather formal approach. Article 299 of the CCC cannot be applied by analogy to other persons.

According to Article 151, section 4 of the CCC for a limited liability company and Article 301, section 5 of the CCC for a public company, shareholders are not liable for the obligations of the company. The rule is deemed to be mandatory (*ius cogens*). The piercing of the corporate veil as mentioned above will not be applicable because (i) it is not binding in Poland and (ii) even if it were, A and B were only minority shareholders without any involvement in the management of Company A. In accordance with Article 7 of the CCC, a shareholder can only be liable for the liabilities of a company if the former is a dominant company which has entered into a contract with the latter foreseeing the management of the dependent company or the transfer of its profit. But such liability requires an explicit contract, whereas a de facto holding is not regarded as sufficient.

Moreover, as mentioned previously, the concept of piercing the corporate veil operates wholly independently of the mechanisms of tort liability, which could ultimately be applied in the given scenario. First, tort liability is associated with the need

---

initial share capital requirement and refers to the UK Companies Act 2006. The team consisted of: Associate Professor Adam Opalski, Dr Krzysztof Oplustil, Associate Professor Tomasz Siemiątkowski, Associate Professor Stanisław Sołtysiński, Associate Professor Andrew Szumański and Dr Iur Joanna Warchoł. The team responsible for preparing the project were Associate Professor A Opalski and Dr K Oplustil. The project was evaluated during a conference with the participation of specialists in corporate law, which took place at the Polish Ministry of Justice on 18 October 2010. The project was subsequently adopted by the plenary KKPC on 28 October 2010. For more details, see *The Draft Reform of the Structure of a Limited Liability Company Property* (2000) 12, Przegląd Prawa Handlowego 12/2010, available on the Company Law Forum (http://forumprawaspolek.pl). The general assumptions of the project were also described in the articles by A Opalski, K Oplustil and S Sołtysiński, 'Sp z o.o.: Reforma kapitału zakładowego' *Rzeczpospolita*, 15 January 2011 and 'Reforma kapitału zakładowego spółki z o.o.' *Rzeczpospolita*, 18 January 2011; critically, M Tofel and M Szumbarski, 'Reforma struktury majątkowej spółki z o.o.' *Rzeczpospolita*, 24 February 2011; A Kidyba, 'Krytycznie o reformie kapitału zakładowego w spółce z o.o.' *Rzeczypospolita*, 2 December 2011.

to demonstrate a causal link between the damage to the creditor and the shareholder's fault, in which an important element would be the influence of the shareholder on the company and the damage that this causes to the creditor. By contrast, the liability of shareholders under the concept of piercing the veil is not dependent on damage, but rather has the nature of a guarantee, where the shareholder is directly liable towards the creditor irrespective of damage but based upon certain conditions.

I. Latvia

If Director Y had duly filed for the insolvency of Company A, liability would only be imposed upon him as a result of a breach of the duty to act as an able and careful manager in terms of section 169(1) of the Commercial Code (CC).[82] If the company has a board of directors, which is made up of several directors, they manage the company jointly (CC, section 302). However, rights to represent the company may be conferred on one director by virtue of a provision in the company's articles/by-laws/statutes (CC, section 303(1)). It is suggested that Y has been provided with rights to act as the sole representative of Company A and that contracts signed by him on behalf of the company are thus valid. It is submitted that Y's conduct will comply with the business judgment test and that he will not be liable based on a violation of the duty to act as an able and careful manager.

Any liability on the part of Y, B or C as shareholders of Company A is generally excluded by virtue of section 137(3) of the Commercial Law, which prescribes that shareholders are not liable for the obligations of their companies. Liability claims may therefore be directed towards the company, but not towards individual shareholders.[83] An exception to this rule applies in the case of shareholders of limited liability companies, who have voted in favour of resolutions at the general meeting of shareholders which have implemented decisions resulting in losses to the company (Commercial Law, section 210(2)). Moreover, in groups of companies, a parent company may in some cases be liable directly for the obligations of a subsidiary company by virtue of sections 20, 21, 29 and 33 of the Law on Concerns.[84] Thus far, the Latvian courts have not accepted any arguments based on the 'piercing the corporate veil' doctrine.[85] However, it has been suggested that in certain extreme cases, liability should attach to the shareholders under Latvian company law. Owing to the proximity of the Latvian commercial law system to that of Germany, it would be possible to apply the principles of German law. Therefore, such extreme cases could include cases of acute undercapitalisation, the intermingling of the capital of the company and the shareholder or a withdrawal of funds destroying the economic basis of the company.[86]

[82] Likums 'Komerclikums', Latvijas Vēstnesis 158/160 (2069/2071), 13 April 2000. See also ch 2 at II A, above.

[83] A Strupišs, *Komerclikuma komentāri III* (Riga, A Strupiša juridiskais birojs, 2003) § 41.

[84] Likums 'Koncernu likums', Latvijas Vēstnesis 131/132 (2042/2043), 23 March 2000.

[85] For more detail on the 'piercing the corporate veil' doctrine, see A Alliks, 'Korporatīvā plīvura pacelšanas krimināltiesiskie aspekti' *Jurista Vārds* 09.07.2013, 27/28 (778/779).

[86] See the solution to German law at C, above.

It can, nonetheless, be argued that B, acting as the director of Company A, has failed to act as an honest and careful manager (Commercial Law, section 169(1)).[87] Subsequently, her actions as the director could give rise to a liability claim should a certain threshold be met following the assessment of relevant objective criteria. The court's reasoning as regards C being the 'de facto' or 'shadow' director, however, cannot be predicted with any certainty owing to a lack of relevant case law on this matter; rather, it is likely that, here too, German legal doctrine may provide some guidance.

J. The UK[88]

i. Introduction

In terms of UK company law, there is only scope for Y, B and C to be held personally liable to creditors (such as X) or liquidators of Company A in their capacity as directors. Shareholders are generally under no liability to companies, creditors, shareholders or third parties for the purposes of UK company law.[89] Where shareholders are held liable, such liability arises by virtue of the operation of rules of other branches of the law such as agency law, trust law or contract law, or owing to the shareholder being treated as a de facto or shadow director in terms of the common law or section 251 of the CA 2006.

ii. Director Y's Liability

a. Breach of Fiduciary Duties

According to section 172 of the CA 2006, Director Y is under a duty to promote the success of Company A. Section 172(1) of the CA 2006 directs that Director Y must act in the way he considers, in good faith, would be most likely to promote the success of Company A for the benefit of its members as a whole, and in doing so have regard (amongst other matters) to the likely consequences of any decision in the long term, the interests of Company A's employees, the need to foster Company A's business relationships with suppliers, customers and others, the impact of Company A's operations on the community and the environment, the desirability of Company A maintaining a reputation for high standards of business conduct and the need to act fairly as between members of Company A. During the UK parliamentary debates, Lord Goldsmith, the Attorney-General, described the duty to 'promote the success' of the company as imposing a duty on directors to secure or achieve a 'long-term increase in the value' of a company.[90] The section 172 duty is owed to Company A in terms of section 170(1) of the CA 2006.

However, rather intriguingly, section 172(3) states that the section 172(1) duty to 'promote success' has effect subject to any enactment or rule of law requiring directors,

---

[87] See also ch 2 at II A, above.
[88] Abbreviations: CA 2006 (the Companies Act 2006); IA 1986 (the Insolvency Act 1986).
[89] However, challenges can be made to limited classes of resolution passed by shareholders.
[90] Hansard HL 6 February 2006, vol 678, col GC256 (Lord Goldsmith).

in certain circumstances, to consider or act in the interests of creditors of the company. The significance of this provision rests in the fact that prior to the enactment of section 172, the common law developed a line of authority to the effect that directors owed duties indirectly to creditors.[91] Thus, the effect of section 172(3) of the CA 2006 is to preserve, rather than repeal, those common law rules. The common law courts have adopted the position that the duty to take account of creditors' interests is owed by directors to the company – rather than directly to the creditors[92] – when a company is insolvent or nearing insolvency. Whether a company is on the verge of insolvency is an issue for objective assessment and directors must take independent financial and legal advice to confirm the position.[93] In such circumstances, the duty to have regard to the interests of the company's creditors arises because it is the creditor's position in the company's liquidation which will be affected by the director's actions. Since the director's duty to take into account the interests of creditors when the company is insolvent or nearing insolvency is owed to the company rather than directly to the creditors, it is only indirectly through a liquidator acting on behalf of the company that the creditors' interests are represented. The end result is that a creditor such as X is denied standing to sue Y for breach and only a future liquidator of Company A would have title to sue Director Y.[94]

b. Wrongful Trading

The standing to sue Director Y for a purported breach of the 'wrongful trading'[95] provisions vests in the liquidator appointed to liquidate and wind up Company A. For this reason, section 214 of the IA 1986 is no longer considered here.

c. Piercing the Corporate Veil

The common law courts in the UK have developed a line of authority which enables a creditor of a company to seek redress against a shareholder or director of that company. The doctrine is commonly applied to remove the separate legal personality of the company and the 'limited liability' feature of the modern company in order to enable creditors or other third parties to seize the assets of shareholders (or beneficial shareholders) or directors (including de facto or shadow directors) of the company.[96] However, it performs a marginal role in UK law and the courts are reluctant to

---

[91] See, eg, the dictum of Lord Templeman in *Winkworth v Edward Baron Development Co Ltd* [1986] 1 WLR 1512 (HL) 1516E–G; D Prentice, 'Creditor's Interests and Director's Duties' (1990) 10 *Oxford Journal of Legal Studies* 265.

[92] *Yukong Line Ltd of Korea v Rendsburg Investments Corp of Liberia* [1998] 1 WLR 294 (QB); *West Mercia Safetywear Ltd v Dodd* (1988) 4 BCC 30 (CA); *Re Halt Garage (1964) Ltd* [1982] 3 All ER 1016 (Ch); *Kuwait Asia Bank EC v National Mutual Life Nominees Ltd* [1991] 1 AC 187 (PC); *BTI 2014 LLC v Sequana SA* [2016] EWHC 1686 (Ch) at [477]–[478] per Rose J.

[93] *Colin Gwyer & Associates v London Wharf (Limehouse) Ltd* [2002] EWHC 2748 (Ch), [2003] BCC 885.

[94] *Yukong Line Ltd of Korea v Rendsburg Investments* (n 92) 311–12 (Toulson J).

[95] See ch 2 at II I, above, for further details.

[96] See *Adams v Cape Industries plc* [1990] Ch 433; *Trustor AB v Smallbone (No 2)* [2001] 1 WLR 1177 (Ch); *Yukong Lines Ltd of Korea v Rendsburg Investments* (n 92); and *Ord v Belhaven Pubs Ltd* [1998] BCC 607 (CA).

invoke it. The doctrine will be applied in two circumstances, (i) first, where the court is satisfied that the corporate veil is such that it is a 'mere façade concealing the true facts'[97] and the company is incorporated to conceal the true actors lying behind it, ie the 'concealment principle',[98] or (ii) the company has been incorporated with the specific objective of facilitating fraud or enabling the persons controlling the company to evade their existing legal obligations or liabilities, ie the 'evasion principle'.[99] As such, in the absence of fraud, where a company is formed to harbour potential future liabilities or legal obligations, this is perfectly valid in terms of UK company law. In the present hypothetical case, there is no evidence that Company A is a 'facade' or 'sham' or 'device', nor is there any suggestion that it was engaged in any fraud or impropriety or that it was formed for the specific purpose of enabling its shareholders, directors or controllers to dodge their legal obligations or any liabilities.[100] For that reason, it is clear that the doctrine will have no application in this case.

iii. Director B's and C's Liability

a. The Status of B and C

From the hypothetical case, it would appear that B and C are shareholders of Company A and B is also a director of Company A. Since shareholders owe no duties to the company absent special circumstances (see the UK solution to the case in chapter 4, above), B and C will not be liable to X in their capacity as shareholders. However, as a director, B will owe a duty to monitor Y and his failure to do so as a director may amount to a breach of duty. In the case of *Re Westmid Packing Services Ltd,*[101] Lord Woolf MR stipulated that each individual director owes a duty to the company to inform himself or herself about its affairs and to join with his or her co-directors in supervising and controlling them. However, in the case of *Lexi Holdings (In Administration) v Luqman,*[102] the Court of Appeal slightly refined its earlier decision in *Re Westmid*. In *Lexi Holdings*, it ruled that non-executive directors would be liable for a breach of the section 174 duty of care, skill and diligence if they failed to actively monitor, and report to the company's professional directors and auditors, the criminal actions of a rogue executive director who had dishonestly misapplied the funds of the company, causing resulting loss to the company. In order to establish liability on the part of directors for a failure or omission to monitor and review the actions of a fellow rogue director, Sir Andrew Morritt C in the Court of Appeal suggested that it was necessary to show that the former knew of the prior criminal activity of the latter

---

[97] *Woolfson v Strathclyde RC* 1978 SC (HL) 90, 96 (Lord Keith of Kinkel); *Adams v Cape Industries plc* [1990] Ch 433, 539–41 (Slade LJ); *Trustor AB v Smallbone (No 2)* [2001] 3 All ER 987 (Ch) 995f–h (Sir Andrew Morritt VC).

[98] *Prest v Petrodel Resources Ltd.* [2013] 2 AC 415.

[99] Ibid, 484 per Lord Sumption. For an example of the 'evasion' principle in action, see *Wood v Baker* [2015] EWHC 2536 (Ch).

[100] See *R v Powell* [2016] EWCA Crim 1043 for a decision where the Court of Appeal refused to pierce the veil of incorporation because it could not be established that the controllers of the company had set up the company to avoid their environmental obligations.

[101] *Re Westmid Packing Services Ltd* [1998] 2 All ER 124 (CA) 130 (Lord Woolf MR) and *Secretary of State for Trade and Industry v Baker (No 5)* [1999] 1 BCLC 433 (Ch) 486 (Parker J).

[102] *Lexi Holdings (In Administration) v Luqman* [2009] EWCA Civ 117, [2009] BCC 716.

and failed to do anything about it.[103] Since there is no evidence in the hypothetical case of any criminal activity on the part of Director Y, it is submitted that B and any other directors on the board of Company A will not be liable to Company A or X for a breach of their section 174 duties as directors.

However, if we assume that B has breached his duty to monitor Y, this duty is owed to the creditors of Company A on the basis that Company A is insolvent or nearing insolvency, and can only be enforced by a liquidator of Company A for the same reasons described above in the case of Y. As such, once again, a creditor such as X will have no standing to make a direct claim against B in respect of B's breach of duty, even if it is established that B has breached his section 174 CA 2006 duty to monitor Y (which is unlikely).

b. De Facto or Shadow Directorships

If C is treated in law as a de facto or shadow director, he may owe duties to Company A and be liable to it or a liquidator for a breach of section 172 of the CA 2006 or section 214 of the IA 1986 in terms of (ii) a. and/or b. above.[104] First, a director is deemed to be a de facto director if he or she undertakes the functions of a director, although not formally appointed.[105] Moreover, the individual must purport to act as a director, may require to be held out as such and must have real influence over the decision-making process of the company.[106] It is submitted that C does not satisfy these basic requirements and, for that reason, it is clear that he is not a de facto director. Second, section 251(1) of the CA 2006 directs that a shadow director is a person in accordance with whose directions or instructions the directors of the company are accustomed to act.[107] The individual must have a real influence in the corporate affairs of the company,[108] but unlike a de facto director, a shadow director does not purport to act as a director. Again, there is insufficient evidence to demonstrate that C had a real influence over the board of directors of Company A. For that reason, there is no basis for X or Company A to establish liability against C.

c. Piercing the Corporate Veil

For the same reasons advanced above, there are no grounds for the veil of incorporation to be pierced to render B and C liable to X.

iv. Summary and Conclusion

In terms of UK law, there are no legal routes available which would enable X to sue Y or others directly to personally recover any of its losses. X would need to rely on a

---

[103] *Lexi Holdings (In Administration) v Luqman* [2009] BCC 716, 727–28.

[104] In the case of *Ultraframe (UK) Ltd v Fielding* [2005] EWHC 1638 (Ch), it was held that the mere fact that a person fell within the statutory definition of 'shadow director' was not enough to impose upon him the same fiduciary duties to the relevant company as were owed by a de jure or de facto director.

[105] *Re Hydrodam (Corby) Ltd* [1994] BCC 161 (Ch).

[106] *Gemma Ltd (In Liquidation) v Davies* [2008] EWHC 546; BCC 812 (Ch).

[107] CA 2006, s 251(1).

[108] *Secretary of State for Trade and Industry v Deverell* [2001] Ch 340 (CA), 350G–55E (Morritt LJ).

liquidator of Company A to raise a claim against Y and/or B for a breach of (i) the common law duty owed to Company A's creditors or (ii) the wrongful trading provisions in section 214 of the IA 1986. If the liquidator was minded to sue, it is submitted that both claims would have no more than a reasonable prospect of success.

K. The US

In the US, a shareholder of a corporation is typically liable only to the extent of his or her investment in the corporation. Notwithstanding this general rule of limited liability, in certain circumstances the courts will go beyond the protections of the corporation and require a shareholder to pay the amount for which the corporation is liable for under the contract.

The traditional justifications for limiting the shareholder's liability is that it facilitates and encourages the free exchange of shares in the public markets and reduces the need of shareholders to monitor managers. In closely held corporations such as Company A, however, traditional justifications are less pronounced. In a typical closely held corporation, those supplying capital and those who manage the firm are the same people. Company A is no exception. Commentators have argued, and empirical studies have demonstrated, that courts are willing to 'pierce the corporate veil' in the context of a closely held corporation, but not in dealing with a large corporation with publicly traded shares.

Knowing exactly what factors will entice a court to pierce the corporate veil remains somewhat elusive in the US. In deciding whether to hold a shareholder personally liable, the general inquiry is whether the corporation is effectively the 'alter-ego' of the dominant shareholder.[109] Although this rule can be simply stated, the potential factors considered by the court muddy the analysis:

> [A]n alter ego analysis must start with an examination of factors which reveal how the corporation operates and the particular defendant's relationship to that operation. These factors include whether the corporation was adequately capitalized for the corporate undertaking; whether the corporation was solvent; whether dividends were paid, corporate records kept, officers and directors functioned properly, and other corporate formalities were observed; whether the dominant shareholder siphoned corporate funds; and whether, in general, the corporation simply functioned as a facade for the dominant shareholder.[110]

The difficulty in applying this standard lies in evaluating the appropriate weight given to each factor. In our present hypothetical case, Shareholder Y has clearly disregarded corporate formalities by, for example, not holding meetings of the board of directors. Although the courts often cite such actions as justification for piercing the corporate veil, they are generally reluctant to hold a shareholder personally liable without proving that 'some "fraud or injustice" would be perpetuated through misuse of the corporate form.'[111] Generally, the mere fact that a contracting partner is not going to be paid is

---

[109] See, eg, *Maloney-Refaie v Bridge at School, Inc*, 958 A 2d 871, 881 (Del Ch 2008).
[110] Ibid.
[111] *Medi-Tec of Egypt Corp v Bausch & Lomb Surgical*, 2004 WL 415251, at *7 (Del Ch 4 March 2004).

insufficient to satisfy the requisite fraud or injustice. Consequently, it is unlikely that Y will be found personally liable, unless X can demonstrate some fraud or injustice beyond not getting paid on the contract. Based on the facts provided, Y 'expects the transaction [with Company X] to deliver great benefits to Company A', and the fact that Y miscalculated would not appear to create the ground for a piercing claim.

Any attempt to hold Shareholders B and C personally liable also would be likely to fail. Despite the fact that it could be argued they failed to oversee Y's actions, as shareholders, US law imposes no duty on B and C qua shareholders to actively monitor the actions of the other shareholders or the board of directors. Limited liability is purposefully designed to encourage investors to purchase shares in the company, without requiring the shareholder to then actively manage or oversee the company.

Successful causes of action brought by creditors directly against directors are rare within the US.[112] Generally speaking, 'directors do not owe creditors duties beyond the relevant contractual terms'.[113] The typical justification for this rule is that

> [w]hile shareholders rely on directors acting as fiduciaries to protect their interests, creditors are afforded protections through contractual agreements, fraud and fraudulent conveyance law, implied covenants of good faith and fair dealing, bankruptcy law, general commercial law, and other sources of creditor rights.[114]

L. South Africa

i. The Position of Y: Personal Liability based on Section 424 of the 1973 Companies Act

It is a basic premise of South African corporate law that the majority shareholder has no duties, fiduciary or otherwise, towards the minority shareholder.[115] Shareholders also do not owe fiduciary duties to the company.[116]

---

[112] A 'de facto directors and officers' doctrine is generally recognised by courts in the US. See, eg, *In re Walt Disney Co. Derivative Litigation*, 906 A.2d 27, 48–49 (Del 2006) (finding that there is no basis for qualifying the defendant as a de facto officer); *SEC v Solucorp Indus.*, Ltd., 274 F Supp 2d 379 (SD NY 2003) (discussing de facto officer for purposes of s 16 of the Securities Exchange Act); *Prickett v American Steel & Pump Corp.*, 253 A.2d 86, 88 (Del Ch 1969) (defining the term 'de facto director' as 'one who is in possession of and exercising the powers of that office under claim and color of an election, although he is not a director'). It appears that courts have not used the doctrine to establish liability toward creditors. C is also unlikely to qualify as a de facto director in the hypothetical case.

[113] *Simons v Cogan*, 549 A 2d 200, 304 (Del 1988).

[114] *North American Catholic Educational Programming Foundation, Inc, v Gheewalla*, 930 A 2d 92, 99 (2007).

[115] See *Pender v Lushington* [1877] 6 ChD 70, 75; *Sammel v President Brand Gold Mining Co Ltd* 1969 (3) SA 629 (A), 680 (on the rule that shareholders may vote as they please); *Amdocs SA Joint Enterprise (Pty) Ltd v Kwezi Technologies (Pty) Ltd* 2014 (5) SA 532 (GJ) and PA Delport (ed), *Henochsberg on the Companies Act 71 of 2008* (Durban, LexisNexis, South Africa, Service issue November 2016) 168.

[116] See *Brouze and others v Wenneni Investments (Pty) Ltd and another* 2015 (4) All SA 543 (SCA) where the Court referred to *Hulett and others v Hulett* 1992 (4) SA 291 (A), 307G–I where long friendships of mutual trust have been seen as quasi-partnerships, but it was not the case *in casu* (para 113). A shareholders' agreement can also expressly exclude the existence or establishment of such a relationship (eg a partnership) between shareholders (para 113). The Court confirmed that, as a general rule, directors have fiduciary duties to the company and not to the shareholders individually (para 114). This case is discussed in PA Delport and I Esser, 'Corporate Law' in *The Annual Survey of South African Law* (Cape Town, Juta, 2015) 279–81.

In this case Company A has entered bankruptcy, which means that section 424 of the Companies Act of 1973 is relevant.[117] X can hold Y liable on the basis of section 424. Section 424 provides that:

> When it appears, whether it be in a winding-up, judicial management or otherwise, that any business of the company was or is being carried on recklessly or with intent to defraud creditors of the company or creditors of any other person or for any fraudulent purpose, the Court may, on the application of the Master, the liquidator, the judicial manager, any creditor or creditor or contributory of the company, declare that any person who was knowingly a party to the carrying on of the business in the manner aforesaid, shall be personally responsible, without any limitation of liability, for all or any of the debts of other liabilities of the company as the Court may direct.

Section 424 is confined to the winding-up of an insolvent company[118] and applies to two types of wrongful trading, namely reckless trading and fraudulent trading. Section 424 provides a specific list of people with *locus standi* (ie the Master, the liquidator, *any creditor* or member or contributory of the company). Actual knowledge of the legal consequences is not necessary in terms of section 424; knowledge of the fact from which the conclusion may properly be drawn that the business was conducted recklessly or fraudulently is sufficient.[119] 'Recklessness' implies the existence of an objective standard of care that would be observed by the reasonable man in the conduct of the business of the company. A departure from that standard will constitute negligence. 'Recklessly' in the context of section 424 means 'gross negligence' (thus a serious departure from this standard).[120]

> The test for recklessness is objective insofar as the defendant's actions are measured against the standard of conduct of the notional reasonable person and it is subjective insofar as one has to postulate that notional being as belonging to the same group or class as the defendant, moving in the same spheres and having the same knowledge or means to knowledge.[121]

Actual dishonesty is not a requirement. In determining whether the business of the company has been carried on 'recklessly' the court will have regard to the scope of the operations, the role, functions and powers of the director, the amount of the debt involved, the extent of the company's financial difficulties and the prospects, if any, of recovery.[122] In *Fourie NO v Newton*,[123] the Court held that to act 'recklessly' consists of an entire failure to give consideration to the consequences of one's actions.

---

[117] Chapter 14 of the 1973 Act has survived the implementation of the 2008 Act. Item 9 of sch 5 to the 2008 Act provides that c 14 of that Act continues to apply with respect to the winding-up of insolvent companies, as if that Act had not been repealed.

[118] If the company is not in winding-up, s 22 of the Companies Act 2008 applies where the business of the company is carried on recklessly, with gross negligence, with intent to defraud any person or for any fraudulent purpose, see ch 2 at II K, above. An 'insolvent company' is a company that is commercially insolvent.

[119] *Howard v Herrigel NO* 1991 (2) SA 660 (A), 673–74. See also In *R v Thornton* 1960 (3) SA 600 (AD), 611.

[120] *Ex parte Lebowa Development Corporation Ltd* 1989 (3) SA 71 9T) 111C. See FHI Cassim (ed), *Contemporary Company Law* (Cape Town, Juta, 2012) 591.

[121] See *S v Van As* 1976 (2) SA 921 (SCA), 928C–E. See also *Philotex (Pty) Ltd and Others; Braitex (Pty) Ltd and Others v Snyman and Others* 1998 (2) SA 138 (SCA), 143G–J to 144A–B.

[122] *Fisheries Development Corporation of SA Ltd v Jorgensen; Fisheries Development Corporation of SA Ltd v AWJ Investments (Pty) Ltd* 1980 (4) SA 156 (W). See also *Philotex v Snyman* 1998 (2) SA 138 (SCA), 144B and *McLuckie v Sullivan* 2011 (1) SA 365 (GSJ).

[123] [2010] JOL 26517 (SCA); *Engelbrecht NO and Others v Zuma and Others* [2015] 3 All SA 590 (GP). See Cassim, *Contemporary Company Law* (n 120) 592.

Factors like the scope of the operations, the role, functions and powers of the director, the amount of the debt involved, the extent of the company's financial difficulties and the prospects, if any, of recovery will be taken into account. Details regarding this are not provided in the case study. It seems, however, that the conduct of Y has indeed been 'reckless'. He concluded a contract, on behalf of Company A, with X when Company A was already approaching insolvency. Y also had knowledge of this fact. X will thus be able to approach the court to hold Y personally liable, based on section 424.

ii. Piercing of the Corporate Veil

The Companies Act 2008 now has – for the first time in South African law – a provision that permits the courts to pierce or disregard the separate legal personality of a company. Section 20(9) provides that:

> If, on application by an interested person or in any proceedings in which a company is involved, a court finds that the incorporation of the company, any use of the company, or any act by or on behalf of the company, constitutes an unconscionable abuse of the juristic personality of the company as a separate entity, the court may—
>
> (a) declare that the company is to be deemed not to be a juristic person in respect of any right, obligation or liability of the company or of a shareholder of the company or, in the case of a non-profit company, a member of the company, or of another person specified in the declaration; and
>
> (b) make any further order the court considers appropriate to give effect to a declaration contemplated in paragraph (a).

Section 20(9) does not, however, override the common law principles.[124] Piercing of the veil, in terms of the common law, is rather problematic as there are no clear illustrations in the case law as to when the court will pierce the veil. In *Cape Pacific Ltd v Lubner Controlling Investments (Pty) Ltd*,[125] the Court held that the court can disregard the separate legal personality of a company but that it is not clear when this will be done.[126] In *Cape Pacific*, a number of general principles were laid down. The Appellate Division made it clear that the court has no general discretion to lift or pierce the corporate veil and made it clear that no general principles will be formulated for when the veil should be lifted. The Court stated that where there is fraud or dishonesty or improper conduct the 'need to preserve the separate corporate identity would in such circumstances have to be balanced against policy considerations which arise in favour of piercing the corporate veil'. The Appellate Division in *Cape Pacific*

---

[124] *Ex parte application of Gore NO* [2013] JOL 30155 (WCC), para 34: it (s 20(9)) is supplemental to, rather than substitutive of, the common law in respect of piercing (or lifting) the corporate veil. See Delport, *Henochsberg* (n 115) 100(4). There was some doubt whether piercing was allowed under the common law and part of the inherent jurisdiction of the courts, see eg *Botha v Van Niekerk* 1983 (3) SA 513 (W), 523; *Al-Kharafi & Sons v Pema and Others NNO* 2010 (2) SA 360 (W), para 36; *Ex parte application of Gore NO* case above, para 27. See also *Prest v Petrodel Resources Ltd and Others* [2013] UKSC 34 in respect of the position in the UK.

[125] 1995 (4) SA 790 (A).

[126] At 802. See also *Hülse-Reutter v Godde* 2001 (4) SA 1336 (SCA), para 20.

rejected the test laid down in *Botha v Van Niekerk*.[127] The *Botha v Van Niekerk* test was based on 'unconscionable injustice' suffered by the plaintiff as a result of improper conduct by the defendant.[128] In *Cape Pacific*, it was held that this test is too rigid and that a more flexible approach should be adopted. In *Hülse-Reutter*,[129] the Court took a strict approach saying that piercing the corporate veil should always be used as last resort.

South African courts clearly uphold the independence of the corporate entity. They will not easily or readily pierce or lift the corporate veil.[130] A close analysis of the specific facts and policy considerations and a measure of judicial judgement will determine whether the veil is lifted or not.[131]

Abuse of the juristic personality and actions which show scant regard for the separate entities of companies will also amount to recklessness and therefore possible liability in terms of s 22 of the Companies Act 2008 and/or s 424 of the 1973 Act.[132]

When considering section 20(9) it is important to note that reference is made to 'unconscionable abuse', similar to the test referred to in *Botha v Van Niekerk*, discussed above. This concept is, however, not defined. Section 20(9) is similar to section 65 of the Close Corporations Act 1984 and case law on section 65 can provide useful guidance on the interpretation of section 20(9).[133] However, in terms of section 65 a corporation will not be regarded as a separate legal entity in cases of 'gross abuse', which is thus different to 'unconscionable abuse'.[134]

Any interested person can bring an application in terms of this section, but 'interested person' is not defined.[135]

The piercing of the corporate veil on the set of facts is thus possible under section 20(9) or even under the common law. For the interested party to succeed with section 20(9) the court must find that the acts of Y constituted 'unconscionable abuse'. In *TJ Jonck BK h/a Bothaville Vleismark v Du Plessis NO*,[136] it was held that a member of a close corporation was personally liable for the debts of the corporation based on section 64 of the Close Corporations Act 1984 (this is similar to section 424). However, the Court went further stating that the plaintiff could also have succeeded on the basis

---

[127] 1983 (3) SA 513 (W), 805.

[128] At 525.

[129] 2001 (4) SA 1336 (SCA), para 23.

[130] Cassim (n 120) 50.

[131] In *Faiza Ben Hashem v Shayif and Another* [2008] EWHC 2380 (Fam), the Court set out the criteria for piercing the corporate veil in the UK, but see *Prest v Petrodel Resources Ltd and Others* [2013] UKSC 34. The criteria as in the *Faiza Ben Hashem* case above should also be applicable in the context of South African company law. See Delport, *Henochsberg* (n 115) 87.

[132] Delport (n115) 100(4): 'However, it is submitted that the circumstances to pierce the corporate veil are used as a ground to implement these sections is unnecessary as the sections are a statutory basis for piercing the veil under the circumstances as provided for in the particular sections'.

[133] See, eg, *Airport Cold Storage (Pty) Ltd v Ebrahim* 2008 (2) SA 303 (C); confirmed on appeal: 2008 (6) SA 585 (SCA). See Delport, *Henochsberg* (n 115) 100(4).

[134] 'Gross abuse' refers to the consequences of the act, while 'unconscionable abuse' refers to the conduct that gives rise to the remedy: *Ex parte application of Gore NO* (n 124) para 34.

[135] See *Ex parte application of Gore NO case*, ibid, para 35 where an 'interested person' was defined as any person with direct and sufficient interest in the relief sought.

[136] 1998 (1) SA 971 (O), 986. See also *Bellini v Paulsen and Another* [2013] 2 All SA 26 (WCC).

of section 65 (similar to section 20(9)) because the member's actions constituted a gross abuse of the juristic personality of the corporation.

To follow the common law route the plaintiff, X, will have to follow the *Cape Pacific* decision where it was held that when 'fraud, dishonesty or improper conduct are present the separate legal personality of the company [should] be balanced against policy considerations favouring the piercing of the corporate veil'.[137] In *Henochsberg* it is submitted that: 'The existence of a statutory remedy as in s 20(9) is supplemental rather than substitutive of the common law and the provision of the remedy also detracts from the notion that the remedy of piercing the corporate veil is drastic or exceptional (*Ex parte application of Gore NO* case para 34)'.[138] Thus, if the requirements of section 20(9) of the Companies Act 2008 are not satisfied, the corporate veil may nevertheless be pierced under the common law.[139] The position will be the same with regards to B, as duly appointed director.

iii. The Position of B

B, as a duly appointed director, can be held liable for a breach of her duty of care, skill and diligence. As discussed previously, the standard of care is measured with a dual test.[140] This test is both objective and subjective.[141] By not attending to any of the company's business and not monitoring the conduct of X, B did not act reasonably and therefore does not comply with the minimum standard expected. The business judgment rule, discussed before, will not provide any relief to B. Section 76(4) introduced a safe harbour provision into South African company law stating that a director is presumed or deemed to have acted in accordance with sections 76(3)(b) and (c) if the director has taken reasonably diligent steps to become informed about the matter and the director made a decision, or supported a decision of a committee or the board, with regard to that matter, and the director had a rational basis for believing, and did believe, that the decision was in the best interests of the company. There should have been no self-dealing or proper disclosure if necessary. On compliance with these requirements the courts will not review the decision that was taken by the director.[142] B clearly does not comply with these requirements.

A further question is whether X can also hold B liable based on section 424. Here the definition/meaning of 'knowledge' is relevant. As explained above 'knowledge', in terms of section 424, does not relate to actual knowledge of the legal consequences; knowledge of the fact from which the conclusion may properly be drawn that the business was conducted recklessly or fraudulently is sufficient.[143] However, the definition

---

[137] *Cape Pacific Ltd v Lubner Controlling Investments (Pty) Ltd* 1995 (4) SA 790 (A), 803.
[138] Delport, *Henochsberg* (n 115) 89.
[139] MK Havenga (ed), *Company Secretarial Practice* (Cape Town, Juta, 2016) paras 2.3, 2.3.2.
[140] See ch 2 at II K, above.
[141] See Companies Act 2008, s 76(3). See Cassim (n 120) 558–61.
[142] See Cassim (n 120) 563–64 on the business judgment rule.
[143] *Howard v Herrigel NO* 1991 (2) SA 660 (A), 673–74. See ch 2 at II K, above.

in s 1 of the Companies Act 2008 is much wider and includes 'imputed' knowledge.[144] Whether the extended meaning of 'knowledge' in terms of the Companies Act 2008 will apply to the provisions of section 424 (and other sections in Chapter XIV in respect of 'knowledge') is uncertain. 'It is, however, submitted that the incorporation of Chapter XIV into the 2008 Act by means of Schedule 5, will, by necessary implication, indicate that it was the intention of the legislature.'[145]

Imputed knowledge will be present where a person in a particular position or post should have the knowledge and cannot aver that he or she does not have the knowledge (eg, a financial director has knowledge about the financial affairs of the company). Secondly when a person is in a position, and as a result of that position reasonably ought to have investigated, which would then have provided the knowledge. This would apply in addition to a duty to act. Thirdly, if a person is in a position, and as a result of that position, reasonably ought to have taken other measures, which if taken would reasonably have expected to give her the actual information. The imputed knowledge 'duties' are, however, qualified by 'reasonably', which would indicate that the test for the required actions is the common law test of that of the reasonable person with the knowledge and experience of the particular person.[146]

Based on this set of facts it is submitted that B has 'imputed knowledge' and can, if this definition of 'knowledge' is followed, be liable under section 424.

iv. The Position of C

The first question to address is whether C will qualify as a 'de facto' or 'shadow' director and whether directors' duties apply to de facto and/or shadow directors. The partially codified duties in the Companies Act 2008 apply to directors and directors are defined as:

(1) 'director' includes an alternate director, and – (a) a prescribed officer; or (b) a person who is a member of a committee of a board of a company, or of the audit committee of a company, irrespective of whether or not the person is also a member of the company's board.[147]

The definition of a 'prescribed officer' is relevant in this regard. A 'prescribed officer' is defined in section 1 as 'a person who, within a company, performs any function

---

[144] Section 1 states that: '"knowing", "knowingly" or "knows", when used with respect to a person, and in relation to a particular matter, means that the person either—

  (a) had actual knowledge of the matter; or
  (b) was in a position in which the person reasonably ought to have—

    (i) had actual knowledge;
    (ii) investigated the matter to an extent that would have provided the person with actual knowledge; or
    (iii) taken other measures which, if taken, would reasonably be expected to have provided the person with actual knowledge of the matter'

[145] Delport, *Henochsberg* (n 115) 29.
[146] Ibid, 28.
[147] Companies Act 2008, s 75(1).

that has been designated by the Minister in terms of section 66(10)'. Regulation 38 describes a prescribed officer in the following terms:

> Despite not being a director of a particular company, a person is a "prescribed officer" of the company for all purposes of the Act if that person—
>
> exercises general executive control over and management of the whole, or a significant portion, of the business and activities of the company; or
>
> regularly participates to a material degree in the exercise of general executive control over and management of the whole, or a significant portion, of the business and activities of the company.

It has been submitted that a company secretary and shadow directors will qualify as 'prescribed officers'.[148] A 'shadow director' is someone in accordance with whose instructions or directions directors of a company are accustomed to act[149] and due to the influence they have on major decisions should be regarded as a 'prescribed officer'.[150] In the present case, C is not appointed as a director but his advice is afforded great weight by Y. It can be argued that C is thus a shadow director and therefore a 'prescribed officer'; however, he does not hold a position 'within' the company as required in section 66(1) and could therefore fall outside the definition. He could, however, in terms of the common law be liable as principal on whose instructions the directors act.[151]

The aforementioned section 424 of the Companies Act 1973 applies to 'any person who is knowingly a party to the carrying on of a company's business' either recklessly or fraudulently. This section has been interpreted widely by the courts and any natural or juristic person, even one who is not a member, director or officer of the company, can be subject to this section. It is submitted that section 424 is wide enough to include the activities of a shadow director.[152]

III. Conclusion

The solutions to this case show considerable diversity in outcomes and reasoning. Yet, there are also a number of common concepts discussed in most, if not all, of the legal systems.

---

[148] Delport, *Henochsberg* (n 115) 30(2).

[149] Havenga, *Company Secretarial Practice* (n 139) para 8.2.

[150] Delport, *Henochsberg* (n 115) 30(2) but see also K Idensohn, 'The Regulation of Shadow Directors' (2010) *South African Mercantile Law Journal* 326 where it is argued that a person must hold an office within the company.

[151] *S v Shaban* 1965 (4) SA 646 (W); *S v De Jager* 1965 (2) SA 616 (A).

[152] See Idensohn, 'The Regulation of Shadow Directors' (n 150) 340 and see *Philotex (Pty) Ltd & Others v Snyman & Others; Braitex (Pty) Ltd & Others v Snyman & Others* 1998 (2) SA 138 (SCA), 142; *Gordon NO and Rennie NO v Standard Merchant Bank Ltd & Others* 1984 (2) SA 519 (C), 527. See also FHI Cassim, 'Fraudulent or Reckless Trading and Section 424 of the Companies Act' (1981) 98 *South African Law Journal* 162, 168–69.

A. The Liability of Shareholders

i. Piercing the Corporate Veil

In all countries discussed in the hypothetical case, the starting point is that shareholders enjoy the benefits of limited liability. This is treated as a way of promoting the ability of companies to attract capital, and it is often also seen as a consequence of the concept of the company as a separate legal entity.[153] Exceptionally, 'piercing the corporate veil' is allowed in many legal systems.[154] In Japanese law, this requires 'abuse of juridical personality' or a 'straw man case'. German case law has developed the categories of undercapitalisation, 'intermingling' of private and company capital and destruction of the economic basis of the company. The Spanish solution also mentions undercapitalisation or abuse of law. It is worth mentioning that South Africa codified the 'piercing the corporate veil' doctrine in 2008.[155] Dutch case law also knows the concept of veil piercing, but direct veil piercing is rarely recognised. In the UK, veil piercing is only allowed if a company is a 'mere façade' etc, and in the US, it is equally rare that the corporation is regarded as the 'alter ego' of the dominant shareholder. Finnish and Italian law only seem to accept veil piercing in cases of groups of companies, while the Polish and Latvian solutions indicate that courts have not yet developed a veil-piercing doctrine.

   To some extent, these differences can be explained by the fact that in both civil and common law countries, veil piercing is a matter of case law. Thus, the different categories have evolved as a consequence of the circumstances that have arisen in the courts. In addition, the importance of veil piercing depends on other questions of company law, for instance, whether special provisions for groups of companies operate or whether the requirement for minimum capital makes undercapitalisation of new firms less likely.[156]

ii. 'Fictitious Company' Approach

As to the present case, the 11 legal solutions mentioned up to this point all agree that the circumstances of the case do not provide sufficient information to conclude that Y should be personally liable under the principles of 'veil piercing'. However, French law would probably adopt a different result. The French solution does not use the terminology of 'veil piercing', but states that in some cases the courts will regard companies as fictitious. In particular, this will be the position if the company is dominated by one person, as Y dominates Company A, and the other shareholders are simply nominal shareholders. To put the French approach into context, it is worth noting that, historically, the concept of the company meant that there had to be a group of shareholders. Only gradually have legal systems allowed one-person companies.[157]

---

[153] See, eg, M Siems, *Convergence in Shareholder Law* (Cambridge, Cambridge University Press, 2008) 69.
[154] For a comparative account, see K Vandekerckhove, *Piercing the Corporate Veil: A Transnational Approach* (The Hague, Kluwer, 2007).
[155] South African Companies Act 2008, s 20(9).
[156] See, eg, Siems, *Convergence in Shareholder Law* (n 153) 70.
[157] See Siems, ibid.

In France, however, vestiges remain of the previous law. The public company in a narrow sense (SA) requires at least seven shareholders, while there are special forms of one-person public companies.[158] Thus, the French case law may be a 'side effect' of this late development.

iii. 'De Facto' or 'Shadow' Director

Finally, with respect to C, the question arises as to whether he is not only a shareholder but also a 'de facto director'. Most legal systems discussed here have a concept of de facto directors. In particular, the Spanish Company Act defines a 'de facto director' and in South Africa, the definition of a 'prescribed director' (as a 'de facto' or 'shadow' director) was codified by the Companies Act 2008; on the other hand, in the case of Germany and Poland, the solutions refer to the legal certainty of appointments. In any case, C only holds a small amount of the shares in Company A and the present scenario does not offer enough evidence to suggest that C has acted as if he was a director.

B. Liability as Directors

i. Director's Liability to Creditors

When a company is approaching insolvency, the directors may be required to call a general meeting,[159] and when the company is insolvent, the directors have to file for bankruptcy, although the precise point in time differs between countries. In the present case, we cannot assume that Y (or B) have violated these duties, possibly leading to liability towards the creditors.[160]

Share capital rules can also play a role. In the Italian solution, it is said that insufficient assets may lead to the liability of directors who have to preserve the share capital's integrity. The Finnish solution distinguishes between different cases, with liability being possible if the contract between X and Company A was concluded when the company had lost half of its capital. Similar rules may exist in other countries; nevertheless, with respect to the scenario in the hypothetical case, it does not take us any further forward since we do not know the precise financial position of Company A. Irrespective of these uncertainties, some legal systems adopt the position that it is possible for Y to be personally liable since he contracted with X while Company

---

[158] For the 'entreprise unipersonelle à responsibilité limitée' and the 'SAS unipersonelle', see French Commercial Code, Arts L 223-4 and 227-1.

[159] For the EU, see Art 19 of Directive 2012/30/EU of the European Parliament and of the Council of 25 October 2012 on coordination of safeguards which, for the protection of the interests of members and others, are required by Member States of companies within the meaning of the second paragraph of Article 54 of the Treaty on the Functioning of the European Union, in respect of the formation of public limited liability companies and the maintenance and alteration of their capital, with a view to making such safeguards equivalent (OJ L315/74 14/11/2012) which now became Art 58 of Directive (EU) 2017/1132 of the European Parliament and of the Council of 14 June 2017 relating to certain aspects of company law ([2017] OJ L169/46). See also the Finnish solution at II G, above.

[160] See the Polish solution to this case at II H, above.

A was approaching insolvency. The basis of this may either be found in the general rules on directors' duties or there may be specific rules which apply. Furthermore, it is important to address whether or not creditors can personally sue directors for such a breach of law. For these purposes, a distinction can be made between the following three groups of countries.

First, some countries may treat Y's behaviour as a breach of duty but would not allow personal enforcement by X. In the UK, when a company approaches insolvency, the directors have to take creditors' interests into account or even cease trading. However, these duties are owed to the company, not to the creditors.[161] Thus, they can only be enforced by the liquidator acting on behalf of the company. French law is similar. A director can be personally liable for the debts of a company when managerial errors contributed to the existence of irretrievable debts. However, the law also states that the sums paid by the directors form part of the debtor's assets and must be distributed to all creditors on a pro rata basis.[162]

Second, the German, Spanish and Latvian solutions regard it is as unlikely that there is a breach of law. In the present scenario, these three legal systems apply the general rules of directors' duties, since the company was not yet insolvent at the moment the contract was formed.[163] It is regarded as doubtful that there is a breach of duty since Y cannot be blamed for committing Company A to a contract where he had the expectation that this would benefit Company A. In this respect, the Latvian solution explicitly refers to the business judgment rule.[164] However, if there were a breach of duty, in Germany and Spain it is possible that the creditor X can sue Y directly if recourse against Company A proves ineffective.

Third, in Japan it seems to be a fairly straightforward process to permit X to proceed with a claim against Y. Despite criticism from academics, the Japanese courts have held that entering into a contract where it could be anticipated that the company will not fulfil its obligations amounts to a breach of duties. In addition, presumably influenced by the German law on this issue, Japanese law allows enforcement of such a breach by creditors under certain conditions. Moreover, as the Japanese solution explains, the law-maker has further extended the list of duties enforceable by creditors since small companies, which in Japan are often incorporated as public companies, had tended to disregard them.

ii. Director B's Liability

In the present scenario, shareholder B was appointed as a director but she has not been involved in the running of the Company. Seven solutions (France, Finland, Germany, Spain, Japan, UK, Netherlands) suggest that a director may be liable for breaching

---

[161] The position is the same in the US: see, eg, J Armour, G Hertig and H Kanda, 'Creditor Protection' in R Kraakman et al (eds), *The Anatomy of Corporate Law* (3rd edn, Oxford, Oxford University Press 2017) 129.

[162] French Commercial Code, Art L 651-2(3).

[163] For the difference between the UK law on 'wrongful trading' and the counterpart in German law, see T Bachner, 'Wrongful Trading – A New European Model for Creditor Protection?' (2004) 5 *European Business Organization Law Review* 293.

[164] See also ch 2, above.

his or her director's duty to monitor the conduct of other directors (or the CEO). In France, B would certainly be held to have breached her duty to monitor Y and could be liable (but also note that in France the sums paid by the directors must form part of the debtor's assets and be distributed to all creditors on a pro rata basis, on which, see II B above); in Finland too, failing to fulfil such a duty may lead to liability in damages.

However, some solutions suggest that in the present scenario B may not actually be liable. In Germany, an informal understanding that she should not be involved in the running of the basis may constitute wilful ignorance that can lead to a breach of duty, but, in the present scenario, this omission is unlikely to lead to a gross violation of duty, which is necessary for a direct claim available to a creditor. Similarly, in Spain, B could be committing a breach of the duty of care to be diligently informed about the business of the company and also to monitor other directors, but there does not seem to be enough evidence for this. In Japan, a director, as a member of the board, is under a duty to monitor all the business conduct of the representative director of the company. But, for example, a nominal director who had never received any remuneration or compensation from the company may not be liable for a breach of such a duty.

In some other jurisdictions, a director's failure to monitor other directors' (or CEO) conduct is liable for breach of duty only in very limited situations. In the UK, such a claim can be enforced only by a liquidator of the company. In the Netherlands, B can be held liable if she was closely involved in the company entering into the agreement.

In addition, some solutions suggest that B may be liable for a breach of other duties. In Italy, B could be held liable either for a violation of the duty to act on an informed basis or, more generally, for having violated her duties as director. In Latvia, B's actions could give rise to a liability claim should a certain threshold be met following the assessment of relevant objective criteria (but also note that in Latvia Y as the CEO may not be liable due to the application of the business judgment rule). In South Africa, B could be liable based on 'imputed knowledge'. In Poland, the outcome would be different depending on whether it is a limited liability company or a public company. Concerning the first, B may be liable based on a breach of fiduciary duties. However, B may be relieved of liability by showing that a petition for a declaration of the bankruptcy of the company has been filed. Concerning the latter, B's liability will be hard to prove since it would have to be based on tort law.

C. Conclusion

Overall, French and Japanese law are most protective to the creditor in the current scenario. US law seems to be the least interested in creditor protection, with the US solution referring to contractual solutions for creditors. Yet, as a whole, it is difficult to make a general assessment on whether countries favour the interests of directors, shareholders or creditors.[165] The company laws of most countries provide various

---

[165] For this question, see also J Armour, S Deakin, V Mollica and M Siems, 'How Do Legal Rules Evolve? Evidence from a Cross-Country Comparison of Shareholder, Creditor and Worker Protection' (2009) 57 *American Journal of Comparative Law* 579, 614–15.

tools of creditor protection, with many of them not concerned with directors' duties but safeguarding the assets of the company (such as capital requirements).

In terms of sources of law and legal families, the solutions show a mix of case law and codified law in all countries. The principle of 'piercing the veil' is not codified in any of the relevant legal systems other than South Africa. As far as there is codified law, for example, on directors' duties, case law also matters. This can clearly be seen in the Japanese situation, where the courts have further strengthened the pro-creditor law.

The solutions have also shown that questions of creditor protection are more complex than, say, shareholder protection because they touch on many areas of law apart from company and insolvency law, including contract, property, tort, civil procedure, accounting and securities law. Additional complications arise as a result of the need for the law to provide a balance between different types of creditors, such as secured and unsecured creditors, and by virtue of the fact that some laws are applicable to creditors regardless of whether the debtors are legal or natural persons, whereas others are specific to the creditors of companies.[166] All these points cannot be discussed in this book in detail, but in the next chapter we will deal with another typical problem of creditor protection in company law.

---

[166] For an overview, see M Siems, L Herzog and E Rosenhäger, 'The Protection of Creditors of a European Private Company (SPE)' (2011) 12 *European Business Organization Law Review* 147. For a detailed analysis of UK law, see L Gulliver and J Payne, *Corporate Finance Law: Principles and Policy* (2nd edn, Oxford, Hart Publishing 2015) 146–359.

7

Capital Maintenance

MICHAŁ ŻUREK AND KAMIL SZMID (EDITORS)

Main topics: capital maintenance rules; challenge to a decision to pay dividends; and disguised distributions.

Related topics: piercing the corporate veil (see chapter 6, above); non-payment of dividends (see chapter 8, below); abuse of shareholders' rights (see chapter 9, below); enforcement of directors' duties (see chapter 10, below).

I. Scenario

Builpod (the Company) is a limited liability company which manufactures steel structures for the construction industry. The Company purchases steel from a local steel producer named Steel Factory, whereas other raw materials are delivered by Multi-Steel (its 90 per cent shareholder). Current commitments of the Company to Steel Factory for delivered steel to date amount to €150,000. The Company's assets consist of its premises, production line and leased vehicles. The Company has recently experienced a sudden decrease in demand for its products due to the collapse of the real estate market. It has failed to meet the financial commitments which it owes to Steel Factory.

The management board of the Company prepared its annual accounts as at 31 December 2016. These showed that the Company had incurred a loss of €100,000 in the previous financial year. This could be contrasted with the financial years ended 31 December 2014 and 31 December 2015, where the Company had made profits of €180,000 and €20,000, respectively, which had not been distributed to shareholders as dividends. The balance sheet of the Company as at 31 December 2016 was as follows.

Assets		Liabilities	
Fixed assets	800,000	Issued share capital	500,000
Current assets	200,000	Current liabilities	200,000
		Non-current liabilities	200,000
		Net profit (loss) for the period	(−100,000)
		Accumulated profits brought forward	200,000
Total	1,000,000	Total	1,000,000

The shareholders' meeting held on 30 June 2017 passed a resolution approving the distribution of a dividend in the amount of €50,000. The management paid out the dividend in early July 2017. In August, the Company ordered technical equipment worth €120,000 from MultiSteel and duly paid the purchase price. It turns out that the market value of these goods had been overestimated by €60,000.

Steel Factory sued the Company for payment of its outstanding invoices (€150,000). However, Steel Factory's proceedings against the Company were ineffective and its claim remained unsatisfied. Steel Factory seeks to challenge (i) the dividend distribution and (ii) the payment to MultiSteel. Advise Steel Factory on how to proceed and whether it has a reasonable prospect of success.

II. Case Studies

A. Poland

i. Assessment of the Dividend Distribution

The primary authority for deciding whether a dividend should be paid out of the annual distributable profits of a limited liability company rests with the shareholders of that company. A shareholder has the right to be paid a dividend if the payment of the dividend is approved by the shareholders in general meeting.[1] According to Article 191, section 1 of the Polish Commercial Companies Code 2001 (CCC), a shareholder is entitled to participate in the profits posted in the company's financial accounts where this is sanctioned in terms of a resolution of the shareholders in general meeting.

a. Conditions Imposed on the Making of a Distribution

The distribution process involves the management board preparing the Company's accounts within three months of the financial year end. The Company's accounts must be approved by an 'ordinary' meeting of the shareholders and such meeting must be

---

[1] A Szajkowski and M Tarska in S Sołtysiński, A Szumański, A Szajkowski and J Szwaja (eds), *Kodeks Spółek Handlowych. Komentarz* (Warsaw, CH Beck, 2014) 350; A Opalski, *Kapitał zakładowy, zysk, umorzenie* (Warsaw, LexisNexis, 2002) 114.

convened no later than six months after the financial year end. The shareholders are not bound to follow the management board's recommendations of the amount to be distributed as a dividend and they may pass a resolution which differs from that proposal. Nevertheless, the shareholders are unable to approve the distribution of an amount by way of dividend which exceeds that provided for by the CCC.

The facts of the hypothetical case do not suggest any apparent procedural transgressions, since the accounts were prepared, the ordinary shareholders' meeting was convened and the statutory deadline of six months was met.

b. Distributable Amounts

Article 192 of the CCC provides for an earned surplus test in terms of which the amount distributable amongst the shareholders of a company in each financial year cannot exceed the result of the following calculation: first, the profit for the financial year is increased by (i) undistributed profits from previous years and (ii) sums drawn from supplementary and reserve capital accounts which may be distributed (ie distributable reserves) and have been created out of profits from previous years. Second, this amount must be reduced by (i) uncovered losses,[2] (ii) own shares,[3] and (iii) any amounts generated from profits in past financial years which by virtue of the CCC or the company's articles of association must be allocated to the supplementary or reserve capital accounts.[4]

Consequently, a dividend can be declared if net profits, profits carried forward and funds created out of profits (+) are higher than the Company's losses, including losses carried forward and other accounting items which operate to decrease the distributable profit (−).[5]

---

[2] This is a reference to the losses carried forward from previous financial years, including losses incurred in the relevant financial year, since the most authoritative opinion directs that the incurring of losses in the relevant financial year does not preclude the making of a dividend payment.

[3] This is a reference to shares purchased by the company (similar to Art 21 of Directive 2012/30/EU of the European Parliament and of the Council of 25 October 2012 on coordination of safeguards which, for the protection of the interests of members and others, are required by Member States of companies within the meaning of the second paragraph of Article 54 of the Treaty on the Functioning of the European Union, in respect of the formation of public limited liability companies and the maintenance and alteration of their capital, with a view to making such safeguards equivalent (OJ L315/74 14/11/2012)). The reason why 'own shares' decrease the amount available for distribution is that they must be recorded in the company's balance sheet under a separate heading as part of the company's undistributable capital reserves and are represented as a negative value (CCC, Art 200, para 2). Until this undistributable capital redemption reserve is extinguished or redeemed, it is treated as a loss which limits the sums to be distributed.

[4] This is a reference to that part of the previous year's profits of the company which must be capitalised as an undistributable reserve by virtue of the CCC or the company's articles of association. The CCC provides that the following reserves cannot be distributed:

— sums standing in the asset revaluation reserve of the company (Accountancy Act, Art 31, s 5);
— sums standing in the share premium reserve; and
— sums standing in particular capital reserves under the articles of association of the company for purposes other than the payment of a dividend (eg expected losses in previous financial years).

There are also provisions which apply to public companies that require that at least 8% of its profits for a given financial year are transferred to supplementary capital accounts until such capital reaches at least one-third of the share capital so that losses can be financed.

[5] Similar is Art 17(1) of Directive 2012/30/EU (n 3).

When applied to the facts of the hypothetical case, the above test results in the following calculation: €200,000 (retained earnings) less €100,000 (loss in the previous financial year), which is equivalent to €100,000 in earned surplus which can be distributed. The loss incurred during the previous financial year does not preclude the feasibility of the distribution,[6] nor does the fact that the Company had outstanding invoices payable to Steel Factory immediately prior to the distribution. The balance sheet as at 31 December 2016 disclosed current assets of €200,000 against current liabilities of €200,000, resulting in a 1:1 ratio, which may indicate a somewhat inadequate level of cashflow on the part of the Company. The circumstances may imply that the Company is experiencing significant financial hardship; however, this does not preclude a lawful distribution of dividends so long as the requirements of the test in Article 192 of the CCC are met, ie the equation stipulated above is positive.

After the distribution of €50,000 as a dividend, the balance sheet of the Company would be as follows.

Assets		Liabilities	
Fixed assets	800,000	Issued share capital	500,000
Current assets	150,000	Current liabilities	200,000
		Non-current liabilities	200,000
		Earned surplus	50,000
Total	950,000	Total	950,000

The capital maintenance rules which dictate the maximum dividend payable entail consideration of the structure of the shareholders' equity only and overlook the structure of the Company's assets and liabilities. Thus, the financial liquidity and cashflow position of the Company are factors which are irrelevant for the purposes of dividend distribution. The only remedy available which is based on the argument that the dividend resulted in a reduction of the Company's cashflow position would be an action which sought to revoke the shareholders' resolution approving the distribution on the basis that it was invalid. It could be challenged under Article 249 of the CCC as being (i) contrary to best practice and (ii) prejudicial to the Company's interests.[7] However, the right to bring an action is vested only in the shareholders and the members of the Company's governing bodies (ie the members of the management board or supervisory board), which means that Steel Factory would be unable to challenge such a shareholders' resolution.

Therefore, up to a maximum of €100,000 could be lawfully distributed as a dividend by the Company in accordance with the provisions of the CCC. The conclusion

---

[6] See, eg, A Szumański in W Pyzioł, A Szumański and I Weiss (eds), *Prawo spółek* (Bydgoszcz, Branta, 2006) 642; I Komarnicki, *Prawo akcjonariusza do udziału w zysku* (Warsaw, CH Beck, 2007) 97–99; A Opalski, 'Dywidenda po nowelizacji kodeksu spółek handlowych' (2004) *Prawo Spółek* 2–7. This seems to confirm the permissibility of the dividend distribution. For a different view, see S Sołtysiński in S Sołtysiński, A Szumański, A Szajkowski and J Szwaja (eds), *Kodeks Spółek Handlowych. Komentarz* (Warsaw, CH Beck, 2014) 353.

[7] Komarnicki, *Prawo akcjonariusza do udziału w zysku* (n 6) 167.

is that the dividend distribution will be legally effective and any challenge is unlikely to be successful.

It is noteworthy that this conclusion would differ under a previous draft bill aimed at reform of the capital structure of the limited liability company. The Polish government attempted to introduce a solvency test as a prerequisite of a legitimate distribution of a dividend as a part of company law reform.[8] The draft bill provided that the prerequisite for the distribution to shareholders would be the issuance of a solvency certificate under which it would be stated that the company is solvent and able to fulfil its due obligations within a year since the distribution date (in Article 192 draft CCC). Under this proposal, the board would have to pass the resolution and issue a certificate that the company will meet its due obligations within the next year. Thus, under those rules, the board of Builpod would be in breach of this obligation and be held liable for the distribution towards the Company if – as in this case – the Company failed to meet its due obligations within the subsequent year.

ii. Disguised Distribution

When the Company and MultiSteel concluded the contract to buy technical equipment at a price which was €60,000 higher than the market price, the Company was in fact using the contract as a means of diverting its profits to the parent company, ie it made a so-called disguised profit payment. In Polish law, the prohibition on making hidden distributions is set out *expressiv verbis* in Article 355, section 3 of CCC as follows:

> Any payment or remuneration for services or other activities undertaken for the benefit of the company by its founders or shareholders, or by companies or cooperatives affiliated therewith or in a relationship of subordination or dominance thereto, must not exceed the usual amount of payment or remuneration adopted in business dealings.

Thus, the law requires the market price to be adopted in any dealings between the shareholders and a public company. Although this provision has no counterpart in the provisions devoted to private limited liability companies, the disguised payment prohibition also applies to such companies by virtue of the *numerus clausus* principle of statutory payments which are made from company assets for the benefit of its shareholders.[9] According to this principle, no transfers of property between shareholders and the Company can be made in the absence of valid legal grounds.[10]

In addition, one must consider whether or not the payment amounts to a breach of the rules which prohibit the depletion of the Company's legal capital. In

---

[8] A first draft bill of the reform project was published by the Codification Commission of the Civil Law of the Ministry of Justice in December 2010 in the journal *Commercial Law Review*; another one was put forward in 2015. Although those proposals seem to have been removed from the governmental agenda, the initiative of making capital maintenance rules more flexible can be found in a study for Simplified Joint Stock Company (*Prosta Spółka Akcyjna*) which resembles the French *par actions simplifiée* and would have no par value shares, minimum capital in the amount of 1 PLN and an insolvency test as a prerequisite for distribution.

[9] Opalski, *Kapitał zakładowy, zysk, umorzenie* (n 1) 71; K Oplustil, 'Gloss to the Supreme Court Judgment', 16 April 2004, I CK 537/03.

[10] *Cf* the judgment of the Appeals Court in Białystok, 21 February 2006, I Aca 629/05.

accordance with that prohibition, shareholders are not entitled to draw profits from the Company if that leads to its net assets being reduced below the value of its share capital (Article 189, section 2 of the CCC).[11] This provision is designed to protect the creditors of a limited liability company by ensuring that the company is unable to dispose of assets equivalent to the amount of its share capital for the benefit of its shareholders. Therefore, any payment to the shareholders is possible only if the share capital is covered, ie that there are sufficient assets unconnected to company commitments which are at the very least equivalent to the value of the share capital. Some legal commentators argue that the prohibition does not apply to claims arising from civil law contracts concluded between shareholders and the company, since it refers only to payments associated with the *corporate* relationship,[12] but *de lege lata* it seems that there is no adequate normative basis for making such a distinction.

In the instant case, as a result of the transaction which involved MultiSteel ordering technical equipment, the Company reduced the value of its current assets by €60,000 (the difference between the purchase price and the actual value of the goods) to €890,000 (950,000 – 60,000 = 890,000). Since the liabilities of the Company equated to €400,000, the coverage of the share capital was reduced to €490,000 (890,000 – 400,000). The result is that the payment breaches the coverage of share capital (€500,000) and, thereby, the principle which requires share capital to be preserved (Article 189, section 2 of the CCC). This can be illustrated by making the necessary modifications to the balance sheet of the Company as follows.

Assets		Liabilities	
Fixed assets	800,000	Issued share capital	500,000
Current assets	30,000	Current liabilities	200,000
Goods	60,000	Non-current liabilities	200,000
		Earned surplus	50,000
		Loss on the goods	–60,000
Total	890,000	Total	890,000

A legal transaction which constitutes a disguised payment to shareholders or which breaches the prohibition against the depletion of the coverage of the share capital is void on the basis that it circumvents the civil law (Civil Code, Article 58, section 1, in conjunction with Article 191 of the CCC) or as being contrary to company law (CCC, Article 189, section 2). A payment made in breach of the law also renders the beneficiaries of the disguised payment (the shareholders) and members of the Company's governing bodies (on the basis that they negligently permitted the payment to be made) duly liable to reimburse the benefits they have received in contravention of the law (CCC, Article 198). Under the proposed draft bill of the CCC,[13] Article 189

---

[11] Art 189, s 2 of the CCC states that the shareholders may not receive, under any title, any payments from the company assets needed to fully finance the share capital.

[12] W Jurcewicz, 'W sprawie interpretacji art. 14 § 3 i art. 189 § 2 k.s.h.' (2003) 7 *Przegląd Prawa Handlowego* 24.

[13] See the final paragraph of (i), above.

would be superseded by a very clear rule to the effect that the value of any consideration paid by the company in a transaction could not exceed the market value ('arm's
length principle' of private dealings between shareholder and the company), whereby
the management board should check the effect of the transaction on the company's
solvency (ie perform a solvency test before the transaction is made) and should the
management board anticipate the insolvency within one year of the distribution, it
would be obligated to refrain from proceeding with the transaction. This would have
improved the position of creditors; however, it would not have solved the problem of
the lack of the standing of creditors against board members in a lawsuit (ie the non-
enforceability of the claim by creditors).

The claim for reimbursement against the shareholders and management members
vests in the Company. However, this claim does not vest in the creditors. Consequently,
in light of the above regulations, the creditors of the Company have no right to claim
directly from the shareholders.

Nevertheless, there is potentially some scope for the creditors to exercise certain
rights in this case based on the civil law. On the basis of the Civil Code, Article 527, any
creditor who is wronged by a debtor is afforded the right to seek a declaration rendering the debtor's conduct ineffective in certain circumstances:

> If a third party has gained a material benefit to the detriment of a creditor as a result of the
> conduct of a debtor, such creditor may demand that the said conduct be declared ineffective
> in law if the debtor acted deliberately to the detriment of the creditor and the third party
> knew, or ought to have been aware of, the same, if he had exercised due diligence.

Moreover, under Article 532 of the Civil Code the creditor may in such a case, in
priority to the creditors of the third party, vindicate his/her rights in the property of
the third party where such property was removed from the debtor's estate or did not
enter it. This so-called *actio pauliana* (which governs fraudulent transfers claims, claw-
back rules, transactions defrauding creditors, or transactions at undervalue) makes
it possible for a creditor – without formally applying for the opening of insolvency
proceedings – to claim directly from the third party who obtained the benefit and
enforce execution directly against that person in respect of any assets which were transferred out of the debtor's estate. However, it is uncertain whether the *actio pauliana*
would be applicable in the present case, since it requires the creditor (Steel Factory)
to prove, amongst other things, that Builpod acted with the intention to harm the
creditors. Another weakness of the *actio pauliana* is that the debtor is generally free to
choose which creditor to pay (ie at least on the ground of civil law, there is no statutory
order to satisfy the claims).[14] Therefore some of the creditors may be satisfied to the
detriment of others which contradicts the principle of the equal treatment of creditors
at the vicinity of insolvency.[15]

---

[14] *Cf* the judgment of the Appeals Court in Krakow 28 January 2004 I Aca 1213/03, the judgment of the
Supreme Court, 23 July 2003, II CKN 299/01 Lex 1217/02.

[15] The rule also known as 'evenhandedness' or '*par conditio creditorum*' or '*pari passu*'. See, eg, RC Clark,
'Duties of the Corporate Debtor to Its Creditors' (1977) 90 *Harvard Law Review* 505; T Bachner, *Creditor
Protection in Private Companies, Anglo-American Perspectives for a European Legal Discourse* (Cambridge,
Cambridge University Press, 2009) 47. See also G Wagner, 'Distributions to Shareholders and Fraudulent
Transfer Law' (2006) 6 *European Business Organization Law Review* 217.

258   MICHAŁ ŻUREK AND KAMIL SZMID (EDITORS)

iii. Liability of the Parent Company for the Liabilities of the Subsidiary Company

In the instant case, it is necessary to examine whether the disguised distribution of the assets of the Company (which impeded the Company's ability to meet its financial commitments) to the parent company justifies the creditor in seeking financial recourse against the assets of the parent company under laws which regulate corporate groups. The Polish rules which regulate corporate groups, which are set out in Article 7 of the CCC, require certain agreements concluded between the parent company and the subsidiary company to be registered with the Companies Register, namely those agreements providing for (i) the management of the subsidiary company by the parent company and (ii) the transfer of profits from the subsidiary company to the parent company.[16]

The facts of the case are devoid of any factors that would enable the one-off sale agreement to be classified as what is known as a 'holding agreement'. The aforementioned Article 7 of the CCC does not provide sufficient grounds for the courts to pierce the veil of incorporation to render MultiSteel liable for the debts and/or liabilities of the Company.[17] In the case at hand, whilst no holding agreement has been entered into, MultiSteel as the majority shareholder of the Company controls 90 per cent of the votes at the Company's shareholders' general meeting. Thus, we are dealing with a de facto holding situation. The question is whether MultiSteel as the majority shareholder of the Company may be held to account for the Company's liabilities in these circumstances in the absence of a formally concluded holding agreement. The academic legal literature is dominated by the traditional concepts of autonomy and the separate legal personality of a limited company, which is treated as negating the potential for any liability on the part of the parent company for the obligations or liabilities of the subsidiary company, whether it be a contractual or de facto holding relationship.[18] However, recent court decisions have endorsed the concept of shareholder liability vis-a-vis the creditor of the company, with this liability being based on the acts of the

[16] CCC, Art 7, para 1, 2 and 3: 'Where a parent company and a subsidiary company conclude a contract which controls the management of the subsidiary company or the transfer of such subsidiary company's profit, an extract from such contract, containing the provisions which determine the scope of liability of the parent company for (i) any losses sustained by the subsidiary company as a result of the parent company's failure to properly perform any of its obligations under the contract and (ii) the obligations and liabilities of the subsidiary company towards its creditors, shall be registered in the public company file of the subsidiary company held by the Polish Companies Register. If the contract does not regulate or exclude the liabilities of the parent company referred to in paragraph 1, such agreement shall nonetheless also be subject to registration. The management board of the parent company or the subsidiary company, or the member of the management board managing the affairs of the parent company or the subsidiary company shall notify the registration court of the circumstances subject to disclosure under paragraphs 1 and 2. If such notification is not made within three weeks from the date when the contract was concluded, it shall result in the nullity of the provisions which limit or exclude the liability of the parent company for the debts or obligations of the subsidiary company or its creditors'.
[17] T Targosz, 'Art. 7 k.s.h.—czy rzeczywiście zalążek regulacji prawa holdingowego?' (2003) 1 *Rejent* 130; A Karolak, 'Prawne mechanizmy ochrony spółki córki oraz jej wirzycieli w strukturze holdingowej' (2001) 5 *Prawo Spółek* 2–12; see also T Sójka, 'Umowa przewidująca odprowadzanie zysku przez spółkę akcyjną a zasada utrzymania kapitału zakładowego' in M Cejmer, J Napierała and T Sójka (eds), *Europejskie Prawo Spółek* (Krakow, Zakamycze, 2005) 247.
[18] M Romanowski, 'W sprawie potrzeby nowej regulacji prawa grup kapitałowych w Polsce' (2008) 7 *Przegląd Prawa Handlowego* 4–12.

creditor (eg misrepresentation regarding the assets owned by the company).[19] Creditors can also be protected under traditional rules of civil law (outside of company law) such as the *actio pauliana* or a claim for an annulment of the transfer made in the vicinity of insolvency (the latter being available however only after the insolvency proceedings are instituted).[20]

iv. The Potential for the Creditors of the Company to Successfully Recover Payments from the Members of the Management Board

Article 299 of CCC directs that the members of the management board will be jointly and severally liable for the obligations of the company if recourse against that company has proved ineffective. The board members may extricate themselves from such liability by demonstrating that: (1) a petition for declaration of bankruptcy of the company was filed or composition proceedings with the creditors were instituted in time; (2) that the failure to file a petition for declaration of bankruptcy or institute composition proceedings with the creditors was not attributable to their own fault; or (3) the creditors suffered no loss notwithstanding the fact that (i) no petition for declaration of bankruptcy was filed or (ii) no composition proceedings were instituted. Therefore, an effective method of Steel Factory pursuing its claim for payment of €150,000 may be grounded in the personal and joint and several liability of the members of the management board of the Company for the Company's liabilities.

The existence of personal liability on the part of the members of the management board of the Company does not stem from the illegality of the non-payment of Steel Factory's outstanding invoices of €150,000. Instead, it stems from the ineffectiveness of enforcement against the Company.[21] In terms of the facts of the case, Steel Factory's lawsuit of against Company board members would prove the most effective way to recover creditor's claims.

v. Conclusions

The Company could distribute a dividend in the amount of €50,000. However, the payment for the technical equipment which leads to the depletion of the share capital is prohibited by Article 189 of the CCC, which results in the transaction being treated as null and void. Nevertheless, the creditor (Steel Factory) has no legal right in company law to claim the payment of outstanding invoices directly from MultiSteel. Claw-back rules (such as the *actio pauliana*) may prove more useful but there are prerequisites

---

[19] Supreme Court Judgment dated 24 listopada 2009 r. V CSK 169/09. Emerging concept of treating the company and its subsidiary company as a single economic unit (resembling French Rozenblum doctrine) can be traced also in the jurisdiction; see A Opalski, *Prawo zgrupowań spółek* (Warsaw, CH Beck 2012) 610–20.

[20] M Romanowski, 'Wnioski dla prawa polskiego wynikające z uregulowań prawa grup kapitałowych w wybranych systemach prawnych państw UE, Japonii i USA' (2008) 2 *Studia Prawa Prywatnego* 23. The Codification Commission of the Civil Law of the Ministry of Justice presented a draft Bill regulating the group of companies. It provides that the parent company can pursue the interest of the dominant company unless it infringes the justified right of the creditors and minority shareholders (influenced by the French Rosenblum doctrine) However, the Bill has not been adopted by Parliament.

[21] M Litwińska-Werner, 'Nadużycie formy spółki' (2007) 3(4) *Studia Prawa Prywatnego* 81–102.

which are difficult to satisfy in court proceedings. Polish company law has also started to develop rules imposing liability on parent companies for the commission of torts vis-a-vis creditors (eg acting directly to the detriment of creditors by, for example, giving orders to the board member, rather than to the detriment of the company itself). Steel Factory has the right to sue the members of the management board of the Company for payment of the outstanding invoices of €150,000, if the enforcement proceedings against the Company are unsuccessful. Claims against board members of the company which failed to satisfy its creditors are exceptional, aiming to protect creditor interests in the case of breach of directors' duty to apply for insolvency, as well as for the acts made in the vicinity of insolvency.

B. France

i. Introduction

In France, a large company such as Builpod would probably be structured as a simplified public limited company (*Société par actions simplifiée* (SAS)) or a public limited company (*Société anonyme* (SA)) rather than as a limited liability company (*Société à responsabilité limitée* (SARL)). However, the applicable rules are similar. In the case of an SARL, the authority to decide whether a dividend should be paid out of the annual distributable profits belongs to the shareholders' general meeting.[22] The situation is identical in the case of an SA.[23] The board of directors proposes an amount and the decision is made by the shareholders. In an SAS, the situation is also identical, since Article L 227-9 al. 2 of the Commercial Code provides that decisions on the annual accounts have to be taken by a collective decision of the shareholders. In addition, the provisions of the Commercial Code on the ability of a company to pay a dividend and the limits on the amount that can be paid are included in the same provisions of the Commercial Code, particularly Article L 232-12, which applies to the SARL, the SA and the SAS.

ii. Assessment of the Dividend Distribution

French law applies the principle of intangibility of capital (*principe de fixité ou d'intangibilité du capital social*). Therefore, no dividends can be distributed from the issued capital. The financial liquidity and cashflow position of the company are irrelevant to determining whether a distribution of a dividend is lawful or not. Article L 232-11 of the Commercial Code indicates what can be used to pay the dividends:

> The distributable profit consists of the profit for the period, less the losses brought forward, plus the sums carried forward pursuant to the law or the memorandum and articles of association, plus the profit brought forward. The general meeting may, moreover, decide to distribute sums taken from the reserves available to it. In which case, the shareholders'

---

[22] Commercial Code, Art L 232-11.
[23] Commercial Code, Art L 232-11.

decision must expressly indicate the reserve from which such sums are to be taken. The dividends are nevertheless taken primarily from the distributable profit for the period. Unless there has been a share capital reduction, no distribution can be made to the shareholders when the share capital is, or would thereby become, lower than the amount of the capital plus the reserves which the law (*statutory reserves*) or the memorandum and articles of association require in order for a distribution to take place. Any revaluation reverse is not distributable. It may be wholly or partly incorporated into the capital.

In substance, this article provides that the amounts which can be distributed under French company law are as follows:

1. the profit from the company's financial year; and
2. the company's accumulated profits shown in a distributable reserve (*réserves*).

According to Article L 232-11 al. 3 of the Commercial Code, the statutory reserve (*réserve légale*) cannot be distributed. A company must set aside at least 5 per cent of its income from its profits as statutory reserve each year as long as the statutory reserve does not represent 10 per cent of its issued capital.[24] The statutory reserve is not distributable. In the Company's case, there does not seem to be any statutory reserve. However, it is assumed that the amount of €500,000 of issued share capital also includes the statutory reserve since, like the issued capital, it cannot be distributed.

One final issue is not dealt with by Article L 232-11, namely whether additional paid-in capital (*prime d'émission*) can be distributed or not as the case may be. There were conflicting views amongst authors as to whether the additional paid-in capital is profit or a form of capital. The French Cour de cassation took the latter view in a decision reached in 1952.[25] Since additional paid-in capital is not treated as issued capital, the French courts adopt the position that it is not subject to the principle of intangibility of capital. Therefore, it can also be distributed. In the Company's case, there is no indication that there is any additional paid-in capital.

The distribution of a dividend in violation of these rules may be punished criminally as a fictitious dividend.[26] The managers of an SARL may be held criminally liable in such a case.[27] The same applies to the CEO, the directors[28] and senior executive officers (*Directeurs généraux délégués*)[29] of an SA, as well as to their equivalents in an SAS.[30] Turning to the potential civil liability, the distribution of an illegal dividend may be treated as a nullity. The French Commercial Code provides that, in the case of a decision by the ordinary shareholders' meeting (SA) or an ordinary decision of the shareholders (SAS and SARL), 'The nullity of acts or deliberations ... may result only from the breach of a mandatory provision of this Title [*Title on Common provisions applying to commercial companies*] or of the acts governing contracts'.[31]

---

[24] Commercial Code, Art L 232-10.
[25] Cass Com (Cour de cassation, Commercial Chamber), 9 July 1952, *JCP* G 1953, II, 7742 with a note by Bastian.
[26] Commercial Code, Art L 232-11 al 3.
[27] Commercial Code, Art L 241-3 2°.
[28] Commercial Code, Art L 242-6 1°.
[29] Commercial Code, Art L 248-1.
[30] Commercial Code, Art L 244-1.
[31] Commercial Code, Art L 235-1.

Article L 232-11 of the Commercial Code is a mandatory provision. Therefore, when it is breached, the sanction is the nullification of the dividend payment. The legal action seeking a declaration that the dividend is a nullity may be brought by any interested person, including a creditor.

The shareholders must also reimburse the fictitious dividend to the company if they were aware that the dividend was fictitious or they ought to have been aware of this.[32] This disgorgement action can be raised by the company or a creditor.[33]

Turning to the Company's situation, during the 2017 shareholders' general meeting, which approved the 2016 accounts, the Company voted in favour of the distribution of a dividend of €50,000 which was paid in early July 2017. Since the 2017 shareholders' meeting deals with the 2016 fiscal year, no loss was incurred and the payment of the dividend (€50,000) is valid since it is less than the accumulated profits (€200,000). Under French company law, the fact that the shareholders decided to distribute a dividend during a calendar year in which they incurred losses is irrelevant, since the possibility of distributing a dividend depends on whether the financial statements regarding the previous financial year allowed for such a distribution. The Company made profits in 2014 and 2015 well in excess (€200,000) and a loss of €100,000 in 2016, which means that there was a remaining €100,000 distributable for the 2016 financial year. This is more than the amount of the dividend (€50,000) distributed for the 2016 financial year. Therefore, the payment of the €50,000 dividend in 2016 or in 2017 is valid and Steel Factory cannot challenge the decision.

iii. Disguised Distribution

In August 2017, the Company ordered technical equipment worth €120,000 from MultiSteel, its 90 per cent shareholder, and duly paid the purchase price. It turns out that the market value of these goods had been overestimated by €60,000. The fact that the Company overpaid by €60,000 for the technical equipment could be considered to be a disguised distribution. However, under French company law, there is no specific rule or case law on disguised distributions such as imbalanced transactions. Only tax law deals with a disguised distribution (*distribution camouflée de dividendes*). Therefore, the fact that the issued capital would be impaired by the loss due to the overpayment will not jeopardise the payment of the €50,000 dividend.

The situation would be dealt with in France through the application of the rules on conflicted/related transactions (*conventions réglementées*). Under French company law, in the case of an SARL, contracts such as the purchase of equipment entered into between a company and a manager or any shareholder (regardless of the amount held) are not subject to any requirement for prior authorisation but only to *ex post* approval by the shareholders.[34] The situation is the same in the case of the simplified public company (SAS).[35]

---

[32] Commercial Code, Art L 232-17.
[33] J Hémard, F Terré and P Mabilat, *Sociétés commerciales*, vol 3 (Paris, Dalloz, 1978) n° 532.
[34] Commercial Code, Art L 223-19.
[35] Commercial Code, Art L 227-10.

In both cases, there is an exemption from approval for contracts which are common and entered into under normal terms and conditions. It is likely that the purchase was a current operation of the Company since it is common for a company manufacturing steel structures to acquire technical equipment. However, the contract was not entered into under normal terms and conditions since the price paid to the majority shareholder was inflated. Therefore, the procedure on related parties transactions ought to have been applied.

However, the fact that the procedure has not been followed cannot be sanctioned by the nullity of the act. An action for damages could be initiated by the minority shareholders against the directors.

In the case of a public company (SA), contracts such as the purchase of equipment entered into between the company and a director or a shareholder holding more than 10 per cent of the voting rights are subject to the prior authorisation of the board.[36] Agreements are then subject to the *ex post* approval of the general meeting of the shareholders[37] and any interested directors are prohibited from voting.[38] These provisions do not also apply to agreements relating to current operations entered into under normal terms and conditions.[39]

With regard to the purchase of the equipment at an inflated price by the subsidiary, there was an obligation to have a board resolution since the contract is concluded both with a shareholder holding more than 10 per cent of the voting rights who is also probably a director of the Company. Therefore, the procedure relating to conflicted transactions ought to have been applied. If MultiSteel participated in the vote or the authorisation was not given by the board of directors, the transaction can be treated as void if it has a detrimental effect upon the Company. Indeed, this appears to have been the case. However, disinterested shareholders can avoid the nullity by ratifying through a vote.[40] In the Company's case, it is doubtful whether the disinterested shareholders would approve such a transaction.

However, even if there was a defect in the procedure, a creditor such as Steel Factory cannot raise a legal action to invalidate the purchase contract since the procedure on related parties transactions of the Commercial Code, and especially the requirement to have an *ex ante* authorisation by the board of directors, was established in order to protect the shareholders rather than the creditors.[41] Therefore, as in the case of an SA and an SARL, the only remedy is an action for damages, which could only be initiated by the minority shareholders against the directors.

Although not a shareholder, Steel Factory could consider suing the directors for damages on the grounds that they did not follow the procedure on related parties transactions of the Commercial Code or that the overpayment for the assets was detrimental to the interests of the Company's creditors. However, with regard to the former legal ground, it is very unlikely that a creditor would be recognised as having

[36] Commercial Code, Art L 225-38.
[37] Commercial Code, Art L 225-41.
[38] Commercial Code, Art L 225-40.
[39] Commercial Code, Art L 225-39.
[40] CA Paris (Court of Appeal of Paris), 18 December 1990, *Bull Joly*, 604.
[41] Cass Com (Cour de cassation, Commercial Chamber), 15 March 1994, *RJDA* 5/94 n° 541.

the requisite standing in a French court to sue the directors for damages in respect of a breach of the rules on conflicted transactions, since a creditor is barred from raising legal proceedings to invalidate the purchase contract. On the second legal ground, Steel Factory would also be unable to secure damages from the directors. The rationale for this is that French company law dictates that only the company itself can be sued and not the individual managers (SARL) or directors (SA and SAS). When the managers or the directors act in their official capacity as directors, they are shielded from liability towards third parties as long as they acted within the scope of their functions. The French Cour de cassation is very reluctant to find directors personally liable towards third parties for acting outside the scope of their responsibilities (*faute séparable des fonctions*). There must be intentional fault of a specific gravity which cannot be linked to the individual's functions or responsibilities as a director. Taking into account that it is a very rare case where such fault has been found by the Cour de cassation,[42] it is highly probable that MultiSteel, as a manager or director, would be shielded from personal liability.

iv. Liability of the Parent Company for the Financial Obligations of the Subsidiary Company

The French courts recognise the possibility of piercing the corporate veil. However, the conditions attached are very restrictive. There are two possible grounds for piercing the corporate veil. None of them would apply to the Company's situation. The first is the concept of the fictitious company (*société fictive*).[43] If a company is fictitious, its debts can be attributed to the parent company. This concept implies that the fictitious company does not exist because there is no real activity, there are no regular operations of the company or there was no real willingness on the part of the shareholders to create a company. The courts tend to apply different criteria in order to declare a company fictitious, with no one factor being essential. In the Company's case, the Company is clearly a real company with operations, a majority shareholder and minority shareholders. Therefore, the scope for Steel Factory to successfully pierce the corporate veil on this basis is non-existent.

The second ground for the corporate veil to be pierced is the commingling of assets (*confusion de patrimoine*).[44] If there is a commingling of assets, the debts of the subsidiary can be attributed to the parent company. This concept applies in the case of bankruptcy proceedings. The French courts are generally unenthusiastic when it comes to acceptance of the commingling of assets ground. Here again, the existence of an imbalanced transaction is not enough for a French court to pierce the corporate veil.

---

[42] See, eg, Cass Com (Cour de cassation, Commercial Chamber), 20 May 2003 (Madame SEUSSE c/ Société Sati), *Revue des sociétés* 2003, 479 with a note by JF Barbiéri, D 2003, Jur 2623, with a note by B Dondero and AJ 1502, with an observation by A Lienhard, *RTD com* 2003, 523, with an observation by J-P Chazal and Y Reinhard and 741, with an observation by C Champaud and D Danet, *RTD civ* 2003, 509, with an observation by P Jourdain.

[43] eg Cass Com (Cour de cassation, Commercial Chamber), 18 November 1986, D 1987, som 73 and 9 June 2009, *Revue des sociétés* 2009, 781.

[44] B Grelon and C Dessus-Larrivé, 'La confusion de patrimoine au sein d'un groupe' (2006) *Revue des sociétés* 281.

v. Summary and Conclusions

The French Commercial Code and the French courts are relatively liberal when it comes to the payment of dividends. In addition, there is no such concept as a disguised distribution. Therefore, in the hypothetical case, the creditor would enjoy little protection in France.

C. Germany[45]

i. Main Principles

The annual accounts of a German limited company (GmbH) are to be drafted according to the relevant rules of the German Commercial Code (see GmbHG, § 42). Thereafter, the accounts and, if required, the auditor's report have to be sent to the shareholders for approval, who also decide on the distribution of profits (GmbHG, §§ 42a, 46(1)). The amount of profits which may be distributed is specified in § 29 of the GmbHG: the shareholders are entitled to the annual net profit (plus the undistributed profits less the uncovered losses from the previous years), insofar as this amount has not been transferred to the supplementary or reserve capital accounts. Profits can also be distributed from the supplementary or reserve capital accounts. These rules are very similar to those in Polish law. Thus, the distribution of profits in the hypothetical case complied with § 29 of the GmbHG.

A further limitation is that the assets of the company which are required for the maintenance of the share capital may not be distributed to the shareholders (GmbHG, § 30). It is therefore necessary to calculate whether the value of the Company's assets less its liabilities and distributed profits is not less than the issued share capital. In this case, €1,000,000 less €400,000 and €100,000 is €500,000, which is equivalent to the Company's issued share capital.

If the resolution of the general meeting to distribute profits had been unlawful, this could not have been challenged by a creditor. Conversely, any shareholder could raise an action for the avoidance of a resolution of the general meeting.[46] Since the relevant criteria for a challenge are not specified in the GmbHG, the courts use the relevant rules of the law on public companies (AktG, §§ 241–49) by analogy. However, the strict time limit of one month (AktG, § 246(1)) is only regarded as a guide in order to determine whether an action has been filed within a reasonable period.[47]

ii. Disguised Distributions

Like Polish law, German law has a concept of 'disguised distributions'. German public companies are strictly prohibited from making such distributions (AktG, §§ 57 and 58(5)).

---

[45] Abbreviated statutes: AktG = Law on Public Companies; GmbHG = Law on Private Limited Companies; InsO = Insolvency Code.

[46] It will only be in extreme cases that a decision of the general meeting will be regarded as void.

[47] BGH (German Federal Supreme Court), BGHZ 101, 113, 117; 111, 224, 226; W Zöllner in *Baumbach & Hueck's GmbHG* (21st edn, Munich, Beck, 2017) Anh nach § 47, para 145.

The German law on private companies on this issue is not codified. However, here too, disguised distributions are unlawful under certain requirements. First, one is required to establish whether there is a 'disguised distribution'. This is a reference to any payment made to a shareholder (not being a formal distribution of profits) without adequate consideration. A typical example is the sale of goods to a shareholder below the market price.[48]

There are four reasons why such distributions may be unlawful.[49] First, assets required for the maintenance of share capital may not be distributed to the shareholders (GmbH, § 30). This is calculated in the same way as under Polish law. Second, in the absence of shareholder agreement, disguised distributions violate the principle of equal treatment of the shareholders. Third, such distributions may involve a breach of fiduciary duties. There may be cases where undervalue transactions can be justified by the business judgment rule.[50] However, if the beneficiary is a related party, there is little doubt that the directors are in breach of their duty of loyalty to the company.[51] Fourth, if the other shareholders do not approve of the distribution, this also entails the infringement of the powers of the general meeting, since the general meeting is usually entitled to decide about the distribution of profits (see above). Thus, in the present case, the disguised distribution is unlawful for a variety of reasons.

In the case of public companies, a special provision (AktG, § 62) sets out the remedies for a violation of capital maintenance laws.[52] Creditors can enforce such a violation if recourse against the company proved ineffective and insolvency proceedings have not yet been initiated (AktG, § 62(2)). In some cases, they can also enforce general breaches of directors' duties.[53] Similar provisions do not exist for private companies, and the predominant view rejects the drawing of any analogy.[54] Thus, the enforcement of disguised distributions also lies with the company itself.[55] Since creditor protection is most relevant in the insolvency of a company, it is also worth mentioning that in this case the insolvency administrator (InsO, § 148(1)) represents the company on behalf of the interests of the creditors.

The Polish solution indicates that the law on groups of companies may be relevant in the present case. In the German law on public companies, the law on groups of companies is codified in detail (AktG, §§ 291–338). However, no such rules exist for private companies and the predominant view also rejects drawing any analogy. Instead, one must consider whether there has been a violation of fiduciary duties among the shareholders.[56] This can be enforced by the shareholders themselves,[57] but not the creditors of the company.

---

[48] BGH, NJW 1987, 1194; L Fastrich in *Baumbach & Hueck's GmbHG* (21st edn, Munich, Beck, 2017) § 29, paras 68–69.

[49] Fastrich, ibid, paras 71–76.

[50] See ch 2 at II C, above.

[51] For this duty, see ch 3 at II E, above.

[52] Due to this special remedy, the BGH, NZG 2013, 496 held that a violation of AktG, § 57 does not affect the validity of the transaction.

[53] See ch 6 at II C, above.

[54] See, eg, Fastrich (n 48) § 31, paras 6, 31 and 43.

[55] For the possibilities of shareholder actions, see eg ch 10 at II E, below.

[56] See, eg, W Beurskens, *Baumbach & Hueck's GmbHG* (21st edn, Munich, Beck, 2017), Schlussanhang paras 15–16.

[57] See, eg, ch 10 at II E, below.

D. Italy[58]

According to Article 2478-*bis* of the CC, an Srl's financial statements must be prepared in accordance with the rules applicable to Spas and must be presented to the shareholders for their approval within 120 days (or 180 days in particular situations) of the financial year end. As part of this process, the shareholders must also decide on the distribution of profits. In addition, Article 2478-*bis*, paragraph 4 of the CC stipulates that only profits that have been 'really attained' and that are indicated in the financial statements can be distributed amongst the shareholders. Finally, Article 2478-*bis*, paragraph 6 of the CC provides that any dividends distributed in violation of the rules provided by the Civil Code do not need to be repaid if the shareholders received these profits in good faith and on the basis of financial statements that mentioned these profits and were approved by the shareholders.

In terms of the Italian rules on the preparation of a company's financial statements, the Company would be allowed to distribute €50,000, as indicated in the hypothetical case. In fact, the balance sheet of the Company indicates that the value of the Company's assets less its liabilities – and less its share capital – generated an 'accumulated profits brought forward' of €200,000, which was eroded only in part by the loss of €100,000 incurred during the previous financial year. In brief, in Italy the Company would be entitled to distribute a maximum of €100,000.

However, it should be stressed that Italian law would require a part of the accumulated profits to be allocated to a capital account called the 'legal reserve'. According to Article 2430 of the CC, the legal reserve is created by setting aside at least 5 per cent of the Company's annual net profits until this reserve has reached 20 per cent of the issued share capital.[59] This reserve cannot be distributed amongst the shareholders. Considering that the Company's balance sheet indicates that it has €200,000 of 'accumulated profits brought forward', a minimum of €10,000 of these profits would have been attributed to the 'legal reserve', meaning that only a distribution of €90,000 would have been permitted.

Another important issue is the date on which it was decided to distribute the dividend. If the resolution approving the financial statements and the distribution of the profits is taken as 30 June 2017, it would have been decided 182 days after the Company's financial year end. Thus, the resolution would have been taken in violation of Article 2478-*bis* of the CC. However, for several reasons, Steel Factory would not be allowed to challenge the validity of the profit distribution: first, it is unclear whether the approval of the financial statements after 120–180 days would put at risk the validity of a late resolution;[60] second, Article 2478-*bis*, paragraph 6 of the CC would protect the shareholders that received payments in good faith; and, third, even

---

[58] Abbreviations: CC = Italian Civil Code (codice civile); Spa = public company (*Società per azioni*); Srl = private limited company (*Società a responsibilità limitata*).

[59] Generally, on the legal reserve in Italian law, see P Balzarini, 'Commento *sub* art. 2430' in P Marchetti, LA Bianchi, F Ghezzi and M Notari (eds), *Commentario alla Riforma delle società. Obbligazioni. Bilancio* (Milan, Giuffrè-Egea, 2006) 617 ff.

[60] D Corrado, 'Commento *sub* art. 2434-*bis*' in Marchetti et al, *Commentario alla Riforma delle società. Obbligazioni. Bilancio* (eds) (n 59) 659 ff, 662 ff.

if the resolution were invalid, it is unlikely that a third party, particularly in the hypothetical case, would have standing to challenge the resolution.[61]

With regard to the transaction between the Company and MultiSteel in respect of the transfer of the technical equipment, Steel Factory may have several remedies. However, none are based on the rules on capital maintenance or directly relate to the problem of disguised distributions.

Article 2475-*ter*, paragraph 1 of the CC on the conflict of interest of directors may form the basis of an action for damages pursuant to Article 2476 of the CC. However, it is unclear whether creditors may file a direct action against directors of an Srl.[62] In addition, even if in some cases the conflict of interest may make the transaction voidable, the plain wording of Article 2475-*ter* of the CC grants only the company the right to challenge the validity of the agreement.

Since the Company is arguably subject to the 'direction and coordination' of MultiSteel, a second remedy available to Steel Factory would be an action pursuant to Article 2497 of the CC.[63] According to this provision, any companies and entities entrusted to carry out the direction and coordination of another company who act in their own interests or in the interests of other parties are directly liable for losses suffered by the shareholders of the companies subject to such direction and coordination, or by the creditors of those companies for the losses caused to the integrity of the corporate assets. It is important to highlight, however, that such liability is excluded if, among other things and in light of the impact and effect of the direction and coordination, no loss is suffered by the company. Thus, it would be necessary to know if, in general, the activity of direction and coordination carried out by MultiSteel was detrimental to the Company.

In conclusion, the distribution of dividends may not be challenged by Steel Factory. On the other hand, the transaction between the Company and MultiSteel may result in an award of damages for Steel Factory, both directly for a violation of the rules on the direction and coordination of companies or indirectly for a violation of the rules on the conflict of interests of the directors.

E. Spain

i. Introduction

In Spain, the annual accounts of the *Sociedad de Responsabilidad Limitada* (SL) have to be prepared in accordance with the rules set out in Articles 253–84 of the Ley de Sociedades de Capital (LSC) – Corporate Enterprises Act.[64] Directors are required to formulate the annual accounts within three months after the end of the financial year (LSC, Article 253.1) and the general shareholders' meeting must meet within the first

---

[61] *Cf* Corrado ibid, 681 ff.
[62] *Cf* ch 6 at II D, above.
[63] *Cf* ch 10 at II F, below.
[64] Real Decreto Legislativo 1/2010, de 2 de julio, por el que se aprueba el texto refundido de la Ley de Sociedades de Capital (LSC).

six months of the company's financial year in order to approve the annual accounts of the previous financial year (LSC, Article 164.1).[65] After the general shareholders' meeting is called, any shareholder must be afforded the opportunity to obtain the annual accounts and the auditor's report from the company (LSC, Article 272.2). The general meeting decides on the approval of the annual accounts (LSC, Article 272.1), as well as the dividends to be distributed to shareholders (LSC, Article 273).

In accordance with the LSC, once the formalities required by the law or the company's by-laws (for example, the constitution of capital reserves) have been attended to, dividends may be distributed, either from the company's profits or distributable capital reserves, but not from statutory capital reserves (LSC, Article 273.2). An additional requirement is that the distribution of dividends must not result in the company's net asset value being lower than its issued share capital (LSC, Article 273.2).[66] Indeed, if there are losses from previous financial years that result in the net asset value being lower than the issued share capital, then profits must be applied to cover such losses (LSC, Article 273.2). If the Company's general shareholders' meeting approves the annual accounts corresponding to the year 2016 in June 2017 and decides to distribute a dividend of €50,000, then the Company's net asset value would be €650,000 (ie €500,000 plus €200,000 minus €50,000); €650,000 is higher than the Company's issued share capital (€500,000). Therefore, the distribution of the dividends would be in accordance with Spanish company law. It is important to note that there is a legal requirement that 10 per cent of a company's annual profits in each financial year must be allocated to the statutory capital reserve until this reaches at least 20 per cent of the issued share capital of the company (LSC, Article 274.1); it is assumed that such an undistributable reserve was already in place in the hypothetical case.

ii. Disguised Distributions

Spanish law does not directly address the concept of disguised distributions by specific legal provisions. Nevertheless, scholars have recognised the existence of the phenomenon, which may have different purposes, ranging from the generation of tax savings for the company to the attribution of advantages to certain shareholders.[67]

The payment made by the Company to MultiSteel, its 90 per cent shareholder, concerning a purchase above market value can be considered a disloyal and discriminatory disguised distribution since a majority shareholder has benefited and the other shareholders have been excluded. Such types of disguised dividends, which are explained in the case of chapter 10, below, may involve the breach of certain duties by the directors of the Company and by MultiSteel towards the Company.

---

[65] Unless otherwise specified in the by-laws, the end of the financial year of a company is the 31 December in each calendar year (LSC, Art 26).

[66] See JL Iglesias Prada and J García de Enterría, 'Las Cuentas Anuales de las Sociedades de Capital' in A Menéndez and Á Rojo (eds) *Lecciones de Derecho Mercantil*, vol II (12th edn, Cizur Menor (Navarra), Civitas-Thomson Reuters, 2014) 540–44.

[67] A comprehensive study on disguised distributions and, notably, on disguised dividends in Spain is offered by B Bago Oria, *Dividendos encubiertos. El reparto oculto del beneficio en sociedades anónimas y limitadas* (Cizur Menor (Navarra), Civitas, 2010). An analysis of the different reasons behind disguised dividends is set out at 87–93.

Moreover, disguised dividends that bring the net asset value of the company below the share capital are considered to be a fraud on creditors.[68] The purchase of assets by the Company from MultiSteel at a price above the market value decreases the Company's net asset value by €60,000, thus reducing it to €590,000 (€500,000 plus €200,000 less €50,000 and €60,000). Since €590,000 is above the Company's issued share capital valued at €500,000, the capital maintenance rules are not breached. However, it is interesting to note the consequences of a distribution which defrauds a company's creditors. Whilst some scholars take the view that such transactions are null and void, imposing an obligation on the benefited shareholders in restitution, most jurisprudential and doctrinal analyses do not advocate the nullity of the transaction as a mechanism for the protection of creditors.[69] It is also worth stressing the point that creditors will tend to seek amounts owed to them rather than the nullity of the transactions giving effect to the distribution of disguised dividends.[70] This can be attributed to the fact that the latter remedy would simply repatriate the assets back to the company, whereas the main purpose of the creditors is to ensure that the amounts owed to them are paid.[71] There are circumstances where there may be compliance with capital maintenance rules, but where nonetheless there has been a fraud on the creditors, for example, where disguised dividends are aimed at committing fraud on creditors and executed prior to an insolvency situation – these dividends may indeed be challenged and judicially revoked afterwards.[72] Another possibility for creditors affected by fraud is to file a revocatory action (Código Civil (CC) – Civil Code,[73] Article 1111), which is however limited to those circumstances where the creditor cannot retrieve amounts in any other way (CC, Article 1291) and when the debtor does not have any other goods for the payment of the debt.[74]

F. The Netherlands[75]

i. Dividend Payments

Under Dutch law, the board of directors is responsible for the preparation of the annual accounts and for providing these draft annual accounts to the shareholders of the company.[76] The annual accounts are then adopted by the general meeting.[77] Resolutions regarding the adoption of the annual accounts cannot be made subject to the approval of a statutory body of the corporation and/or a third person.[78]

---

[68] See, eg, ibid, 96–102, 109, 112–13 and 121.
[69] See, eg, ibid, 150.
[70] See, eg, ibid, 150.
[71] See, eg, ibid, 150–51.
[72] See, eg, ibid, 118–20.
[73] Real Decreto de 24 de julio de 1889 por el que se publica el Código Civil.
[74] See, eg, Bago Oria, *Dividendos encubiertos. El reparto oculto del beneficio en sociedades anónimas y limitadas* (n 67) 120.
[75] Abbreviations: DCC = Dutch Civil Code; HR = Hoge Raad = Dutch Supreme Court; OK = Ondernemingskamer = Enterprise Chamber; Rb. = Rechtbank = District Court. An unofficial translation of Dutch company law as incorporated in bk 2 of the Dutch Civil Code can be found on www.dutchcivillaw.com/civilcodebook022.htm.
[76] DCC, Art 2:110/210-1.
[77] DCC, Art 2:101/210-3.
[78] DCC, Art 2:101/210-4.

Dutch law uses different regimes for dividend payments by private companies (BV) and public companies (NV). For public companies, the relevant legislation states that the company profits should be for the benefit of the shareholders. The profits are distributed after the annual accounts have been adopted by the general meeting, in terms of which it is shown that such a distribution is permitted.[79] The distribution can only take place to the extent that the distributable profits exceed the sum of the paid and called up capital and the statutory reserves.[80]

Even if the allocation of profits by the shareholders is acceptable based on the minimum requirements with regard to the reserves, as mentioned above, a dividend payment can under extraordinary circumstances still lead to shareholder and director liability. The Supreme Court ruled in the Nimox case that where a shareholder uses his voting rights in order to allocate profits, he or she can be held liable towards creditors if the shareholder should have seriously considered that the company would not be able to meet its obligations towards its creditors after the allocation of the profits.[81] However, it should be noted that this concerned a case in which the company had only one shareholder. It is unlikely that a minority shareholder would be held liable under the same circumstances. In a subsequent case, the Supreme Court ruled that the members of the board of directors can also be held liable to creditors if they prepare and approve the resolution regarding the allocation of the profits, if – from the position of the board of directors – it was to be reasonably expected that the company could not pay its creditors as a result of the allocation of the profits.[82] Alongside this liability of directors and shareholders, the shareholder that knew or ought to have known that the dividend distribution was not permitted is under an obligation to repay the received dividend to the company.[83]

For private companies, the relevant legislation states that the general meeting is empowered to allocate (in an appropriate way) the profits that have been determined on the basis of the adopted annual accounts, to the extent that the equity of the private company exceeds the reserves which have to be maintained on the basis of the articles of incorporation and/or the law.[84] The articles of incorporation and/or the law do not always prescribe that reserves should be maintained. It is therefore even possible to allocate profits to the extent that this creates a negative equity capital position for the company.[85]

The rules of private companies with regard to the liability of shareholders and directors for the allocation of profits were amended in 2012. This legislation dictates that a distribution by the shareholders shall have no effect where the board of directors has not approved it.[86] The board of directors can only withhold its approval if it

---

[79] DCC, Art 2:105-1 and 3.
[80] DCC, Art 2:105-2.
[81] HR 8 November 1991, *NJ* 1992/174, with a note by Maeijer (*Nimox*).
[82] HR 6 February 2004, *JOR* 2004/67, with a note by Van den Ingh.
[83] DCC, Art 2:105-8.
[84] DCC, Art 2:216-1.
[85] G van Solinge and MP Nieuwe Weme, *Mr. C. Assers Handleiding tot de beoefening van het Nederlands Burgerlijk Recht. 2. Rechtspersonenrecht.Deel IIa. NV en BV. Oprichting, vermogen en aandelen* (Deventer, Kluwer, 2013) 204.
[86] DCC, Art 2:216-2.

knew or reasonably ought to have foreseen that the private company would no longer be able to continue its payments towards creditors after the distribution. If the private company is not able to meet its obligations after the distribution, then the members of the board of directors who knew that this would be the position as a result of the distribution, or who could have reasonably foreseen this, will be jointly and severally liable towards the private company for compensation in respect of the deficit which has arisen on account of the distribution.[87] Moreover, the shareholder who has acquired the distribution while he or she knew or reasonably ought to have foreseen that the private company would no longer be able to continue its payment obligations towards creditors is also liable towards the private company for compensation in respect of the deficit which has arisen as a result of the dividend payment. This mechanism shows that for private companies the legislator has provided for the specific internal liability of directors and shareholders towards the company, which can only be invoked by the company or bankruptcy trustee but not by the creditors. In addition to this specific internal liability, it is possible for directors and shareholders of a private limited liability company to be held liable to – among others – creditors based on general tort law and the law of directors' liability.[88] On those grounds their liability could be higher than the deficit that was generated by the dividend distribution.

The question whether the dividend distribution that was made by Builpod is invalid should be assessed on the basis of the aforementioned rules. The relevant question is whether (i) Builpod was *unable* (not 'unwilling') to meet its obligations towards Steel Factory and (ii) the members of the board of directors or shareholders knew or could have reasonably foreseen that as a result of the distribution the obligations could not be met. This seems unlikely in light of the financial position of the Company based on the information provided in the case.

ii. Payment to MultiSteel

Whether it is allowed to only pay certain creditors is the question that under Dutch law will normally be discussed within the scope of the liability of the members of the board of directors towards a particular creditor.[89] In that case, the question is whether a member of the board of directors creates a de facto inability to pay, with the foreseeable disadvantaging of certain creditors because of a selective payment. The relevant criterion is whether the acts or omissions of the member of the board of directors towards the creditor is in the given circumstances so careless that it is possible to treat this as an illustration of personal serious blame (*persoonlijk ernstig verwijt*) of the director.[90]

The starting point is that members of the board of directors are allowed to only pay certain creditors, as long as this is for the benefit of the company as a whole, even

---

[87] DCC, Art 2:216-3.

[88] van Solinge and Nieuwe Weme, *Mr. C. Assers Handleiding tot de beoefening van het Nederlands Burgerlijk Recht. 2. Rechtspersonenrecht. Deel IIa. NV en BV. Oprichting, vermogen en aandelen* (n 85) 212.

[89] J Barneveld, *Financiering en vermogensonttrekking door aandeelhouders* (Deventer, Kluwer, 2013) 495.

[90] HR 8 December 2006, *NJ* 2006/659, with a note by Maeijer (*Ontvanger/Roelofsen*); HR 23 May 2014, *NJ* 2014/325, with a note by Schilfgaarde.

if there is a risk that the other creditors will not be paid.[91] The principle of *paritas creditorum* only applies if the company is declared bankrupt or if the company is de facto insolvent and there is no reasonable justification to assume that the company will be able to avert insolvency. In the Coral/Stalt case the Supreme Court stated that a company that has decided to cease its activities and foresees that it cannot pay all of its creditors cannot give the creditors that are part of the company group any preferential treatment over other creditors, unless there is some justification for doing so.[92]

A different question is whether paying a shareholder too much for the goods can be viewed as a material dividend payment under Dutch law. The Supreme Court has ruled that the rules regarding dividend payments – as described above – do not apply to such *material* dividend payments.[93] Although this judgment was originally challenged in the literature,[94] the view of the Supreme Court now finds more support, in part because of the changes to the regulation regarding dividend payments in private companies.[95] The interests of creditors and fellow shareholders will therefore be protected in the case of a material dividend payment under more general legal norms such as the liability of directors, the *actio pauliana* and the standards of reasonableness and fairness. Moreover, the shareholder that is involved in the related party transaction resulting in a material dividend payment could be held liable on the basis of general tort law if the transaction turns out to be unlawful.

The excessive purchase price paid for the technical equipment cannot be viewed as a (material) dividend distribution, which means that the rules for dividend payments do not apply. Owing to the fact that the financial position of the Company and timetable in the case are unclear, it is difficult to assess whether the directors and/or shareholder could be held liable. This will depend on the timing of the transactions with Steel Factory and Multisteel and the financial position of the Company at that time.

G. Finland

i. Distribution of Assets

Assets of a Finnish limited liability company may be distributed to the shareholders only as provided in the Companies Act (CA). The methods for distribution of the assets relevant to this case[96] are the distribution of profits (dividend) and the distribution of the assets from the reserves of unrestricted equity (CA, chapter 13, section 1(1)). Other transactions that reduce the assets of the company or increase its liabilities without a sound business reason constitute an unlawful distribution of assets.[97]

---

[91] This was already confirmed by the Supreme Court in: HR 22 mei 1931, *NJ* 1931, p 1429.

[92] HR 12 June 1998, *NJ* 1998/727, with a note by Van Schilfgaarde (*Coral Stalt*).

[93] HR 1 October 1997, *BNB* 1997/401.

[94] For an overview of the literature, see van Solinge and Nieuwe Weme (n 85) 180.

[95] Barneveld, *Financiering en vermogensonttrekking door aandeelhouders* (n 89) 431; ML Lennarts, 'De voorgestelde regeling van uitkeringen aan aandeelhouders van een bv nader beschouwd', WPNR 2007/6731.

[96] Pursuant to the CA, the assets may also be distributed by way of a reduction in the share capital, the acquisition and a redemption of shares and the dissolution and deregistration of the company (CA, c 13, s 1 (1)).

[97] CA, c 13, s 1 (3).

The distribution of assets shall be based on the financial statements most recently adopted (and audited).[98] The CA further requires that a solvency test is undertaken prior to any distribution of assets. Pursuant to the solvency test, assets are not to be distributed if it is known or should be known at the time of the resolution on the distribution that the company is insolvent or that the distribution will cause the insolvency of the company.[99] The general meeting resolves on the distribution of assets and is generally bound by the board's proposal for the distribution amount.[100] An unlawful distribution of assets constitutes a criminal offence and may lead to personal liability of the directors or shareholders of the company.[101] The recipient of unlawfully distributed assets also has an obligation to refund the company if the recipient knows or should have known that the distribution was in violation of the CA or the articles of association.[102]

In the present case, the distributable reserves (ie reserves of unrestricted equity) are comprised of the Company's profits from current and previous financial years from which losses are deducted. This amount may be distributed unless the articles of association provide otherwise. At first glance, therefore, it seems that €100,000 (the accumulated profits (€200,000) less the loss (€100,000)) would be distributable. However, a solvency test must be undertaken prior to any distribution of assets.

Furthermore, in the present case, the Company has failed to meet its financial commitments to Steel Factory (€150,000) on more than a temporary basis. The case does not reveal when the market collapsed or when the Company's severe difficulties in meeting its financial obligations began. For the purposes of the case, we assume that the Company's difficulties began before the general meeting in June 2017, and this led to the Company's insolvency. Therefore, it seems that the general meeting's resolution to distribute €50,000 as dividends from (to simplify) €100,000 of distributable reserves was made when it was known or ought to have been known that the distribution might lead to insolvency and consequently that the resolution may fall foul of the requirements of the CA. If the distribution of the dividends is deemed unlawful, the dividends must be refunded to the company if the shareholder in question knew or should have known that the distribution of assets was unlawful. Actions against a resolution by the general meeting can only be brought by a shareholder of the company; consequently, Steel Factory, as a creditor, would not be in a position to challenge the dividend distribution and demand a refund based on the CA. Furthermore, whether or not a distribution of assets is unlawful is often difficult to resolve in practice.

ii. Steel Factory's Options

Should the distribution of assets be deemed unlawful, Steel Factory has two options: (i) to sue the Company based on breach of contract and demand a court order for

---

[98] CA, c 13, s 3.

[99] CA, c 13, s 2.

[100] The general meeting may only resolve to distribute larger amounts if the articles of association requires so (CA, c 13, s 6(1)) or if the shareholders, with a minimum of 10% of all shares before a resolution on the use of the profits, demand that the so-called minority dividend is distributed (CA, c 13, s 7).

[101] CA, c 22 and CA, c 25, s 1(1).

[102] CA, c 13, s 4.

precautionary measures (injunction), although Steel Factory would likely not be successful in enforcing its claim, presumably owing to the Company's insolvency; or (ii) to hold the directors and/or the shareholders personally liable for damages based on chapter 22 of the CA. Shareholders who deliberately or negligently contribute to the unlawful distribution are liable for damages to a creditor.[103] The board of directors are obliged not to enforce unlawful resolutions made by the general meeting,[104] and having done so they are liable for damages to creditors,[105] with a reversed burden of proof. Naturally, the directors should not have proposed an unlawful distribution in the first place and may be liable to the creditors for damages if they indeed put such a proposition forward to the general meeting. Furthermore, Steel Factory can also bring a claim for damages in conjunction with possible criminal proceedings. The damages may in that case also be based on the Tort Liability Act,[106] under which damages can be granted for economic loss arising from punishable acts if the directors' conduct is considered particularly reprehensible.

iii. Disguised Distributions

Like, for example, Polish and German law, Finnish law has a concept of 'disguised distributions'. The transaction whereby the Company purchased equipment from the majority shareholder MultiSteel was seemingly overpriced and caused a loss for the Company. No sound business reasons for this transaction have been presented. As described above, such transactions are unlawful by virtue of the CA irrespective of whether the recipient is a shareholder.[107] Therefore, the (overpriced) assets must be refunded.[108] The recipient, MultiSteel, having a 90 per cent share of the Company, probably cannot argue that it was not aware of the unlawfulness.[109] Therefore the transaction will likely constitute a disguised distribution of assets. It is also worth noting that the transaction may also be a breach of the principle of equal treatment of shareholders enshrined in the CA.

Steel Factory's options are the same as described above in section (ii). As the Company is apparently insolvent, Steel Factory's best option would be to initiate proceedings against the directors for damages. Here, the shareholders were not formally involved in the decision-making. However, MultiSteel, to whom the disguised dividends were paid, may be held liable for damages if MultiSteel has contributed to the unlawful resolution in its capacity as majority shareholder.

---

[103] CA, c 22, s 2.
[104] CA, c 6, s 2.
[105] CA, c 22, s 1(2).
[106] Vahingonkorvauslaki (412/1974), s 5(1).
[107] Undervalue sales, overpriced purchases and loans taken with interest rates higher than average are all examples of transactions that prima facie lack sound business reason and therefore violate the fiduciary duties of the directors.
[108] CA, c 13, s 4.
[109] Only a party who knew or should have known about the unlawfulness is under an obligation to indemnify.

H. Latvia

i. Dividend Payments

By virtue of sections 174, 179 and 180 of the Commercial Code, the annual accounts of a Latvian limited liability company (*sabiedrība ar ierobežotu atbildību* (SIA)) must be prepared at the end of each business year and submitted to the general meeting of shareholders and the supervisory board, if the latter has been formed, together with a proposal by the board of directors on the application of the profits, if any.[110]

The distribution of profits to the shareholders is done in accordance with section 161 of the Commercial Code by way of the payment of dividends. In terms of section 161(4) of the Commercial Code, dividends may not be determined, calculated and paid out if the annual accounts reveal that the own funds of the company are less than the total amount of the company's issued share capital. There is nothing to suggest that this requirement has not been complied with.

ii. Payment to MultiSteel

However, the purchase from and payment to MultiSteel may have contravened the rule on the equal treatment of shareholders in section 161(2) of the Commercial Code, whereby dividends must be paid to shareholders in proportion to the total of the par value of the shares owned by them. If the payment to the shareholder MultiSteel is viewed as a disguised payment of dividends, the result would be that such payment to MultiSteel would have been to the exclusion of the other shareholders. Furthermore, section 161(5) of the Commercial Code may have been violated, which provides that dividends are to be determined and calculated only once a year: if the payment to MultiSteel is seen as a disguised payment to a shareholder, this payout and the normal payout by way of the statutory procedure would have occurred twice during 2017. In addition, the payment has not complied with the requirement that payments must be based on a resolution passed by the meeting of shareholders in terms of sections 161(2) and (5), 180(4) and 210(5) of the Commercial Code: the decision to order and pay for goods from MultiSteel was taken by the management and not by the meeting of shareholders.

Whilst it may be debated whether the above rules on the procedure for the payment of dividends have been complied with, the payment by the Company to MultiSteel has clearly violated the statutory prohibition on unjustified dividend payments to shareholders: section 182(1) of the Commercial Code prohibits any payments to shareholders, other than by way of dividend payments or in the event of a reduction of share capital. The law expressly prescribes a presumption that a purchase by a company from a shareholder at a price higher than usual is unjustified and therefore prohibited in terms of section 182(2) of the Commercial Code.[111] Whether prices for goods are 'higher than usual' depends on the respective current market prices of goods

---

[110] Likums 'Komerclikums', Latvijas Vēstnesis 158/160 (2069/2071), 13 April 2000.
[111] Judgment of the Latvian Supreme Court in case No C30821212 of 16 December 2016.

of equal quality, but also requires an overall assessment of the consequences of the transaction for the purchasing company. In the absence of any evidence of benefits accruing to the Company, the purchase of goods from MultiSteel at a price 50 per cent above the current market price would be viewed as being within the scope of conduct prohibited by the law and would therefore constitute an unjustified payment.

Unjustified payments to shareholders, as well as dividends paid out in contravention of the rules on the payment of dividends, result in an obligation to return payments to the Company by virtue of section 162(1) and (2) of the Commercial Code. The Company's claim for reimbursement here is not available to third parties: the wording of the Commercial Code and the location of the provision within the section of the Commercial Code which deals exclusively with relations between the shareholders and the company leaves no room for its application to non-shareholders by way of an extrapolative interpretation. The payment must be returned, but in order for Steel Factory to force the Company to make such a claim against MultiSteel, a separate statutory entitlement would be required, which is not available. Therefore, Steel Factory has no legal grounds to challenge the payment to MultiSteel.

I. The UK[112]

i. Introduction

The provisions of company law which regulate the payment of dividends[113] of a private limited company are found in the common law capital maintenance principle,[114] Part 23 of the CA 2006 (CA 2006, sections 829–53)[115] and regulations 30 to 35 of the Model Articles.[116] Like Polish law, the primary authority for deciding whether a dividend should be paid out of the annual distributable profits of a limited liability company rests with the shareholders of that company. Model Article 30(1) and (2) directs that a company may by ordinary resolution of its shareholders declare dividends, but a dividend must not be declared unless the directors have made a recommendation as to its amount and a dividend must not exceed the amount recommended by the directors. The directors have the power to recommend to shareholders what part of the profits available for distribution shall be carried to reserve or otherwise be set aside or be carried forward, and what part shall be made available for dividend. There is no requirement for a private limited company to hold a general meeting of

---

[112] Abbreviations: CA 2006 (the Companies Act 2006); Model Articles (Model articles of association of private companies limited by shares (in reg 2 of and sch 1 to the Companies (Model Articles) Regulations 2008, SI 2008/3229), private companies limited by guarantee (in reg 3 of and sch 2 to the Companies (Model Articles) Regulations 2008, SI 2008/3229) and public limited companies (in reg 4 of and sch 3 to the Companies (Model Articles) Regulations 2008, SI 2008/3229).

[113] Also referred to as 'distributions'.

[114] This is the rule in *Trevor v Whitworth* (1887) 12 App Cas 409 (HL) 423 (Lord Watson) that a company's share capital should not be returned to shareholders, except in the limited circumstances sanctioned by the CA 2006.

[115] CA 2006, s 851(1) clarifies that pt 23 of the CA 2006 operates in parallel with, and does not supersede, the common law rules which regulate the payment of dividends.

[116] See eg Model Articles, regs 30–35 of sch 1.

its shareholders to approve the company's annual accounts. Regulation 30(4) of the Model Articles directs that dividends of a private limited company are paid by reference to each shareholder's holding of shares on the date of the resolution or decision to declare or pay it.[117] However, this is subject to anything to the contrary stipulated in the articles, for example, where the articles direct that account will be taken of the shares of members which are not fully paid up.[118]

ii. Payment of €50,000 as a Dividend

Section 829 of the CA 2006 defines a 'distribution' as every description of distribution of a company's assets to its members, whether in cash or otherwise, subject to certain exceptions. Most importantly, section 830 of the CA 2006 stipulates that a company may only make a distribution out of profits available for the purpose. A company's profits available for distribution are its accumulated, realised profits, so far as they are not previously utilised by distribution or capitalisation, less its accumulated, realised losses, so far as they are not previously written off in a reduction or reorganisation of capital duly made. Section 853(4) of the CA 2006 directs that references to 'realised profits' and 'realised losses' are to such profits or losses of the company as fall to be treated as realised in accordance with principles generally accepted at the time when the accounts are prepared, with respect to the determination for accounting purposes of realised profits or losses. Thus, whether a realised profit or loss exists is ascertained mainly in accordance with generally accepted accounting principles (GAAP),[119] which are referred to as Financial Reporting Standards (FRS) and Statements of Standard Accounting Practice (SSAP) duly promulgated by the UK Financial Reporting Council.[120]

The relevant FRS is FRS 102. This stipulates that profits are to be treated as realised only in accordance with the relevant technical guidance of the Institute of Chartered Accountants in England and Wales (ICAEW) and the Institute of Chartered Accountants in Scotland (ICAS).[121] ICAEW and ICAS are the professional accountancy bodies in the UK and have issued detailed technical guidance on realised profits and losses in terms of section 830 of the CA 2006.[122] Sections 836 and 837 of the CA 2006 stipulate that whether a distribution may be made is determined by reference to the company's profits, losses, assets, liabilities, provisions, share capital and reserves (including undistributable reserves), duly based on the company's last annual accounts, ie the company's individual accounts that were last circulated to members of the company in accordance with section 423 of the CA 2006.[123] Since the Company

---

[117] See also *Birch v Cropper* (1889) LR 14 App Cas 525 (HL).
[118] *Hoggan v Tharsis Sulphur and Copper Co* (1882) 9 R 1191.
[119] *Gallagher v Jones* [1994] Ch 107 (CA).
[120] See https://frc.org.uk/Our-Work/Corporate-Governance-Reporting/Accounting-and-Reporting-Policy.aspx.
[121] See FRS 102, at paras [A4.25–A4.29] (https://frc.org.uk/Our-Work/Publications/Accounting-and-Reporting-Policy/FRS-102-The-Financial-Reporting-Standard-applicab.pdf).
[122] See paras 3.1–3.75 at 27–41 of TECH 02/17 at www.icaew.com/-/media/corporate/files/technical/legal-and-regulatory/company-law/tech-02-17bl-guidance-on-distributable-profits.ashx?la=en ('TECH 02/17').
[123] Accounts are drawn up in accordance with GAAP. See CA 2006, ss 395 and 396.

is not a plc, the financial liquidity, cashflow and net asset position[124] of the Company are factors which are irrelevant for the purposes of dividend distribution in the case of private limited companies.[125] This is in stark contrast to the Polish solution.

For the purposes of this UK solution, it is assumed that: (i) the retained earnings of €100,000 qualify as realised profits (rather than unrealised profits) in terms of ICAEW/ICAS TECH 02/17; (ii) the loss of €100,000 is a realised loss (rather than an unrealised loss); (iii) there has been no significant deterioration in the financial position of the Company since the annual accounts date of 31 December 2016;[126] (iv) the directors of the Company have recommended the payment of €50,000 as a dividend; and (v) the dividend has been approved by the shareholders by ordinary resolution[127] in accordance with Regulation 30 of the Model Articles. When applied to the facts of the case, like the Polish solution, the UK test results in the equivalent of €100,000 in earned surplus which can be distributed by the Company. Neither the loss of €100,000 incurred during the previous financial year nor the fact that the Company had outstanding invoices payable to Steel Factory immediately prior to the distribution functions to impair the lawfulness of the distribution. Therefore, up to a maximum of €100,000 could be lawfully distributed as a dividend by the Company, the dividend distribution of €50,000 will be legally effective and any challenge by Steel Factory would be unsuccessful. Indeed, once the dividend has been paid, the remaining €50,000 may be distributed in the same financial year.

iii. Disguised Distributions

Like Polish law and German law, UK law has a concept of 'disguised distributions', ie that where distributions/dividends are paid otherwise than out of profits available for distribution, this will represent a breach of the statutory rules in section 830 of the CA 2006.[128] Moreover, if a distribution is made by the Company to a shareholder such as MultiSteel otherwise than out of distributable profits or outside the course of a winding-up or a formal reduction of capital, that payment will be unlawful and will breach the common law capital maintenance principle enunciated in *Trevor v Whitworth*.[129] These statutory and common law rules are designed to protect creditors from being leap-frogged in the queue for receiving value.

It is submitted that the conclusion of the contract between the Company and MultiSteel amounted to a diversion of profits to the parent company and could be potentially described as a disguised distribution, since more than adequate

---

[124] In other words, the aggregate of the Company's assets less the aggregate of its liabilities.

[125] In terms of s 831(1) and (2) of the CA 2006, it is impermissible for a plc to pay a dividend (a) if the aggregate of its assets less the aggregate of its liabilities (referred to as its 'net assets') is less than the aggregate of its called up share capital and undistributable reserves and (b) if, and to the extent that the distribution does not reduce the amount of those assets to less than that aggregate.

[126] *Cf* the Finnish solution to this case at G, above. If this assumption were incorrect, the payment of the dividend might breach the common law capital maintenance principle.

[127] The hypothetical case specifically confirms this.

[128] See E Ferran and L C Ho, *Principles of Corporate Finance Law* (2nd edn, Oxford, Oxford University Press, 2014) 212–15 and 227–29; and E Micheler, 'Disguised Returns of Capital—An Arm's Length Approach' (2010) 69 *Cambridge Law Journal* 151.

[129] *Trevor v Whitworth* (n 114) (Lord Watson).

consideration was given in exchange. Whether a transaction amounts to a disguised distribution to shareholders is a question of substance rather than form.[130] Where an arm's length and good faith transaction between a company and a shareholder has proved with hindsight to have been detrimental to the company, the court must inquire into the true purpose and substance of the impugned transaction by investigating all the relevant facts, which might include the states of mind of those orchestrating the corporate activity. However, sometimes the states of mind of the directors will be irrelevant, and what they did was enough by itself to establish the unlawful character of the transaction, however well-meaning the directors who negotiated the transaction were. If the court concludes that there was a genuine arm's length transaction, then it would stand even if it might appear with hindsight to have been a bad bargain for the company; however, if it was an improper attempt to extract value by the pretence of an arm's length sale, it would be held to be unlawful.[131] Here, the state of knowledge or intention on the part of the Company or its directors is unclear from the facts of the hypothetical case. However, if one assumes that there was subjective knowledge or intention on the part of the directors of the Company that the assets were acquired by the Company from MultiSteel at overvalue, then there is a strong argument that the distribution was (i) a disguised return of capital to the extent that the overpayment was not covered by distributable profits and (ii) an unlawful distribution in breach of the rules in section 830 of the CA 2006 and the common law capital maintenance principle. As noted above, only €50,000[132] remained distributable as a dividend subsequent to the payment of the dividend of €50,000 in June 2017. Since the acquisition of the technical equipment from MultiSteel was overvalued by €60,000, this leaves a deficit of €10,000. The €10,000 shortfall would be treated as an unlawful distribution which depletes the capital base of the Company in contravention of Part 23 of the CA 2006 and the common law rules.[133]

Where there has been a distribution in contravention of section 830 of the CA 2006 and there is sufficient evidence to demonstrate that MultiSteel knew or had reasonable grounds for believing that it was made in contravention of section 830 of the CA 2006, section 847 of the CA 2006 directs that shareholders such as MultiSteel will be liable to repay it (or that part of it, as the case may be) to the Company.[134]

---

[130] *Aveling Barford v Perion* (1989) 5 BCC 677; *MacPherson v European Strategic Bureau Ltd* [2002] 2 BCC 39; *Progress Property Co Ltd v Moorgarth Group Ltd* [2010] UKSC 55, [2011] 1 WLR 1. Interestingly, most of the cases where it has been argued that there has been a disguised distribution have involved the sale of assets by a company at undervalue, rather than the situation in the hypothetical case which concerns the acquisition of assets by the Company from a shareholder at overvalue. However, it is submitted that the principles are the same, ie whether the Company has sufficient distributable profits to cover the extent of the underpayment or overpayment, as the case may be.

[131] *Progress Property Co Ltd v Moorgarth Group Ltd* [2011] 1 WLR 1, 10–11 (Lord Walker).

[132] In other words, realised profits, less realised losses, less any dividend paid in the same financial accounting year (€200,000 – €100,000 – €50,000 = €50,000).

[133] As noted above, since the Company is not a plc, its net asset position is irrelevant for the purposes of calculating the lawful dividend distribution and s 831 of the CA 2006 does not apply, on which, see the example provided in Ferran and Ho, *Principles of Corporate Finance Law* (n 128) 215–16.

[134] In the case of *It's A Wrap (UK) Ltd (In Liquidation) v Gula* [2006] EWCA Civ 544, [2006] BCC 626 (CA), the Court of Appeal ruled that a shareholder such as MultiSteel would be disentitled from claiming that it was not liable to return a distribution to the Company on the grounds that it did not know of the restrictions on the making of distributions in the CA 2006 and the consequences of those rules when properly applied to the facts.

However, the difficulty for Steel Factory is that section 847 of the CA 2006 only gives the Company the right to seek recovery, which is also the case under the common law rules. As such, neither section 849 of the CA 206 nor the common law gives a creditor such as Steel Factory the right to raise legal proceedings to compel MultiSteel to repay the Company in respect of the disguised distribution of €10,000. For that reason, Steel Factory will have no right to sue MultiSteel in terms of section 847 of the CA 2006.

Furthermore, in light of the cases of *Flitcroft's Case*,[135] *Bairstow v Queens Moat Houses plc*[136] and *Re Marini Ltd*,[137] a director who knowingly and deliberately authorises the payment of an unlawful dividend will be liable to account for the unlawful dividend to the extent that it is not covered by undistributable reserves, since this will be treated as a breach of section 171 or 174 of the CA 2006. However, once again, since Steel Factory is a creditor of the Company, the duties of the directors in sections 171 and 174 of the CA 2006 are owed to the Company only.[138] As the Company is not insolvent or on the verge of insolvency, it is submitted that it is unlikely that Steel Factory would be successful in any action it raised against the directors of the Company, since no duty is owed directly by the directors to the Company's creditors.[139]

Finally, it should be noted that the Polish solution indicates that the law on groups of companies may be relevant in the present case. However, no equivalent exists in UK company law and the law on piercing the corporate veil would be of no assistance to Steel Factory for the same reasons identified in the UK solution in chapter 6, above.

iv. Summary and Conclusion

The dividend of €50,000 paid by the Company is lawful and Steel Factory would be unsuccessful if it attempted to challenge it. Furthermore, although the value of €10,000 of the overpayment of €60,000 to MultiSteel amounts to an unlawful and disguised distribution by the Company in contravention of Part 23 of the CA 2006 and the common law capital maintenance principle, if Steel Factory was minded to sue MultiSteel or the directors of the Company, it is submitted that both claims would have no reasonable prospect of success.

J. The US

i. Appropriateness of the Dividend

In the US, corporate dividends are determined by the board of directors of a corporation, not by the shareholders.[140] The board of directors of a corporation may declare

---

[135] *Re Exchange Banking Co, Flitcroft's Case* (1882) LR 21 Ch D 519 (CA).

[136] *Bairstow v Queens Moat Houses plc* [2000] BCC 1025 (QB) 1033–34 (Nelson J). Nelson J's judgment was appealed to the Court of Appeal, but it was dismissed; see *Bairstow v Queens Moat Houses plc* [2001] EWCA Civ 712, [2002] BCC 91 (CA). See also *Re Paycheck Services 3 Ltd.* [2010] UKSC 51, [2011] BCLC 141.

[137] *Re Marini Ltd* [2003] EWHC 334 (Ch), [2004] BCC 172 (Ch).

[138] See CA 2006, s 170(1).

[139] See eg the UK solution in ch 6 at II J, above.

[140] See eg Delaware General Corporation Law (DGCL), § 173.

a dividend on shares of capital stock out of the corporation's 'surplus'.[141] Surplus is defined as 'the net assets of the corporation over the amount so determined to be capital'. A company's net assets are the 'amount by which total assets exceed total liabilities'.[142] The capital mentioned in the definition of surplus, often called 'legal capital', refers to the amount by which the stock value exceeds the aggregate par values of capital stock. In cases such as the hypothetical problem where no par value is assigned to the stock, the board of directors must state the amount of legal capital (called 'stated capital') or all the money in the no-par issuance will be deemed legal capital.

Assuming that the Company never provided a stated capital for the no-par issuance, the dividend paid still passes Delaware's 'impairment of capital' test. The Company's net assets in 2016 were €600,000. If the entire value of the issuance (€500,000) were considered legal capital, this still leaves a residue of €100,000 which the Company may employ to pay dividends.

Even if the Company's financial statements showed negative 'net assets', the board of directors of the Company would be given some latitude in the calculation of the 'surplus' available for distribution to shareholders. In the US, directors are given:

> Reasonable latitude to depart from the balance sheet to calculate surplus, so long as they evaluate assets and liabilities in good faith, on the basis of acceptable data, by methods that they reasonably believe reflect present values, and arrive at a determination of the surplus that is not so far off the mark as to constitute actual or constructive fraud.[143]

Consequently, even if the Company's distribution was slightly in excess of €100,000, the court would be likely to find that the directors had reasonable latitude to distribute the dividend. Moreover, even if there is no surplus, Delaware law permits the payment of a dividend out of the company's net profits for the fiscal year and/or the preceding fiscal year ('nimble dividends').[144] This option would seem to be typically useful in situations where a corporation has accumulated losses in the past, but has returned to making profits in more recent years.

Despite the wide latitude granted to the board of directors with regard to dividends, the board of directors does not have unlimited discretion in this area. If the board of directors commits any 'wilful or negligent violation' in the declaration or payment of dividends, the directors individually are jointly and severally liable to the corporation and 'to the creditors in the event of dissolution or insolvency'.[145]

If the Company were a limited liability company (LLC) rather than a closely held corporation, it would not be possible to make 'distributions' of the sort described in the hypothetical case if 'at the time of the distribution, after giving effect to the distribution, all liabilities of the limited liability company ... exceed the fair value of the assets of the limited liability company'.[146] Even if this occurred in the hypothetical

---

[141] DGCL, § 170(a)(1).
[142] DGCL, § 154.
[143] *Klang v Smith's Food & Drug Centers, Inc*, 702 A 2d 150 (Del 1997).
[144] DGCL, § 170(a)(2).
[145] DGCL, § 174.
[146] Delaware Limited Liability Company Act (DLLCA), § 18-607(a).

case, however, this statute 'creates a *corporate* cause of action against LLC members who improperly receive a distribution of those assets'. However, it does not create a cause of action for a third party like Steel Factory.[147]

ii. Payment to MultiSteel

In Delaware, there is no company law that directly addresses 'disguised distributions'. Further, there is no company law requiring all transactions between shareholders and the corporation or members and the LLC to be at market price. Notwithstanding this statutory silence, the Delaware courts would be reluctant to uphold a conflict-of-interest transaction that is 'unfair'. Generally speaking, shareholders have standing to challenge such transactions via fiduciary duty litigation, but the creditors of the Company would not have any standing to bring such a lawsuit.

iii. Fraudulent Transfer Law

Another avenue – independent of company law – that Steel Factory could pursue against the Company is to try to recover the payment to MultiSteel through Delaware's fraudulent transfer statute.[148] Under this statute, a transfer of assets by an insolvent corporation to a third party with actual intent to delay the creditor's ability to collect or without receiving reasonably equivalent value for the exchange may be voidable at the instance of one of the corporation's creditors.[149] If Steel Factory could demonstrate that the Company was insolvent at the time of the transfer and that the Company did not receive reasonably equivalent value for its consideration, Steel Factory may be able to nullify the transaction entirely.

Creditors might even succeed in attacking the dividend payment as a fraudulent transfer. The (federal) bankruptcy courts have applied an equivalent provision in the Bankruptcy Code[150] in a number of cases to dividend payments that were made shortly before a company's bankruptcy filing.[151]

K. South Africa

In 1999 the capital maintenance principle was in effect abolished by the Companies Amendment Act.[152] The new regime was based on the liquidity and solvency principles. The Companies Act 2008 followed a similar approach. Distributions are now dealt with

---

[147] *Pepsi-Cola Bot Co of Salisbury, Md v Handy*, 2000 WL 364199 (Del Ch 15 March 2000).
[148] See, eg, 6 Del Code §§ 1301–12.
[149] 6 Del Code § 1304.
[150] 11 U.S. Code § 548.
[151] *Global Crossing Estate Representative v Alta Partners Holdings LDC (In re Global Crossing, Ltd.)*, 385 B.R. 52 (Bankr. S.D.N.Y. 2008); *Adelphia Communs. Corp. v Rigas (In re Adelphia Communs. Corp.)*, 323 B.R. 345, 376 FN 104 (Bankr. S.D.N.Y. 2005); *Pereira v Equitable Life Ins. Soc'y of the United States (In re Trace Int'l Holdings, Inc.)*, 289 B.R. 548, 561 (Bankr. S.D.N.Y. 2003); *In re Dondi Financial Corp.*, 119 B.R. 106 (Bankr. N.D. Tex. 1990).
[152] Act 37 of 1999.

in section 46. Distributions are essentially broken down into three types of distributions, namely: a transfer of money or other property to a shareholder in that capacity; the assumption of an obligation; or the forgiveness or waiver of an obligation of a shareholder.[153] Dividends fall under the first type of distribution. There is, however, no definition of 'dividends' in the Act. Ordinarily a 'dividend' refers to the distribution by a company of profits of the company. A distribution must be authorised by the board of directors.[154] No shareholder approval is required for a distribution.[155] The board must not make any proposed distribution unless it has applied the solvency and liquidity test and it has acknowledged, by resolution, that it has reasonably concluded that the company will satisfy the test immediately after completion of the proposed distribution.[156] When 120 business days have passed since the board's acknowledgement and the company has not yet made the distribution then the board is required to reconsider the solvency and liquidity test.[157] Once an acknowledgement has been made the company has to proceed with the distribution. This is also the case if, within the 120 days, the company no longer satisfies the liquidity and solvency test.

Thus, in the case of the distribution in hand, the board, and not the shareholders, will have to approve it for it to be lawful.[158] No shareholder approval is required. The board will only approve the distribution if the solvency and liquidity test is satisfied. The solvency aspect of the test is satisfied if the assets would exceed or equal the liabilities following a distribution. The liquidity aspect means that the company should be able to pay its debts as they become due and payable in the ordinary course of business for a period of 12 months after the date on which the test is considered or, in the case of the transfer of money or other property (like a dividend), 12 months following the distribution. The solvency and liquidity test is a purely objective test. The hypothetical reasonable bystander must be satisfied with the solvency and liquidity of the company.[159] The board should make a proper enquiry to determine if the solvency and liquidity test is satisfied. The test must be satisfied 'immediately after completing the proposed distribution'.[160] Based on the information provided, it is submitted that the liquidity test has not been satisfied. The solvency test will be complied with as there will be €50,000 of accumulated profits left after the payment of the dividend. The liquidity element is problematic as the company will not be able to pay its debts as they become due and payable: the current liabilities exceed the current assets.

The payment that was made to MultiSteel for technical equipment ordered worth €120,000 is also problematic. Section 22(1) determines that the company must not carry on its business recklessly, with gross negligence, with intent to defraud any person or for any fraudulent purpose.

---

[153] Definition of 'distribution' in s 1 of the Companies Act 2008.

[154] FHI Cassim (ed), *Contemporary Company Law* (Cape Town, Juta, 2012) 267 ff.

[155] The MoI can also impose any prohibitions, conditions or requirements relating to distributions.

[156] Companies Act 2008, s 46(1)(b) and (c). The solvency and liquidity test is set out in s 4.

[157] Companies Act 2008, s 46(3)(a).

[158] Unless the distribution is pursuant to an existing obligation or a court order (s 46(1)(a)(ii)). This is not the case *in casu*.

[159] K van der Linde, 'The Solvency and Liquidity Approach in the Companies Act 2008' (2009) *Tydskrif vir die Suid-Afrikaanse Reg* 224, 235.

[160] Companies Act 2008, s 46(1)(b).

Based on the facts and the interpretation of 'recklessness' under section 22(1)[161] it seems as if the management did conduct the affairs of the Company in a reckless manner by ordering technical equipment at a price double its market value at a time when it experienced a sudden decrease in demand for its products due to the collapse of the real estate market.

L. Japan

i. Assessment of the Dividend Distribution

Under the Companies Act 2005 (CA) in Japan, a company may distribute dividends of any surplus to its shareholders.[162] Whenever a company intends to distribute dividends of surplus, it must decide to do so by resolution of a shareholders' general meeting. At the shareholders' general meeting, the type and total book value of the dividend, the arrangements for the payment of the dividend to the shareholders and the date on which the distribution of the dividend of the surplus takes effect should all be decided.[163] The amount of the surplus is basically calculated by subtracting the aggregate of the company's liabilities, stated capital and reserves from the amount of assets and the book value of treasury shares.[164]

The Company may distribute dividends up to the amount of the surplus calculated under Article 446(1) of the CA. The total book value of the sums to be delivered to shareholders may not exceed 'the distributable amount'.[165] If the Company pays dividends in excess of the distributable amount, the payment is illegal and is in breach of Article 461 of the CA.

ii. Disguised Distribution and Liability Related to Dividend Distribution

When the Company (Builpod) and MultiSteel concluded the contract to buy technical equipment at a price which was €60,000 higher than the market price, the Company was in fact using the contract as a means of diverting its profits to the parent company; thus, it can be regarded a so-called disguised profit payment.[166]

If the dividend paid is illegal on the basis that it exceeds the distributable amount, a shareholder in receipt of such dividends is obliged to pay to the Company the equivalent of the book value of the dividend.[167] A creditor of the Company is also entitled to require a shareholder who received the dividend to pay the Company the money equivalent to the book value of the dividend.[168]

---

[161] For a detailed discussion of s 22, see ch 2 at II K (ii), above.
[162] CA, Art 453.
[163] CA, Art 454(1).
[164] CA, Art 446.
[165] CA, Art 461(2).
[166] See Polish Solution at A, above.
[167] CA, Art 462(1).
[168] CA, Art 463(2).

If the payment of the dividend is made in violation of the law, shareholders who received the dividend, and directors and officers who were involved in the illegal payment of the dividend are jointly and severally liable to reimburse to the Company an amount equivalent to the book value of the dividend.[169]

If the director made the payment to the Company under Article 462(1) of the CA, he or she may claim against any shareholder who received the dividend. However, if the shareholder did not recognise the fact that the dividend payment exceeded the distributable amount, the director or officer who made the payment to the Company may not claim against such shareholder.[170] Some commentators argue that in such a case, the payment of the dividend is not invalid because Article 463(1) of the CA refers to the payment of 'the amount deliverable on the date on which the said act took effect'. However, such a view would lead to uncertainty since the validity of the payment would depend on the knowledge of the shareholder. Thus, the prevailing theory stresses that all transactions relating to the payment of the dividend become invalid if the payment made was in excess of the distributable amount.

In conclusion, in the hypothetical case, Steel Factory may take an action to pursue the liability of the directors of the Company and MultiSteel and to require them to repay the relevant sums to the Company.

III. Conclusion

A. Introduction

The case solutions illustrate how the jurisdictions examined address the issue of creditor protection of a company in financial difficulties where distributions are made to shareholders and assets are transferred at undervalue.

B. Distributions

Each of the jurisdictions imposes restrictions on distributions, ie each of them provides for the maximum permissible amount of a company's equity which can be paid to shareholders as a dividend. The restrictions vary from the traditional concept of nominal capital maintenance 'via accounting-based profit distribution restrictions',[171] which are typical for continental Europe, to the solvency-based mode.

In the first model, distributions must not be made which are in breach of legal capital requirements, ie the nominal value of the issued share capital and amounts treated

---

[169] Ibid.

[170] CA, Art 463(1).

[171] C Kuhner, 'The Future of Creditor Protection through Capital Maintenance Rules in European Company Law' in M Lutter (ed), *Legal Capital in Europe* (Berlin, Walter de Gruyter, 2006) 341–64.

as capital either by statute, case law or the company's charter.[172] The most common method of restricting distributions under this model stems from the application of the so-called 'balance sheet surplus test'. According to this test, the distribution is made out of the surplus of the company's net assets (aggregate assets less aggregate liabilities) over the legal capital. Interestingly, the balance sheet surplus test seems to be followed both by common law countries (as inferred from the US and South African solutions) and civil law jurisdictions (as in Germany, Italy or Latvia). The two most significant weaknesses of this test which the hypothetical case amply demonstrates are that (i) it is based only upon the historical financial situation of the company, since the limits on distributions are derived from the company's balance sheet in the previous set of financial statements, and (ii) it fails to take into account the nature and structure of the company's equity capital and consequently its liquidity and cashflow position. For example, in the present case, although the Company may have a large portfolio of fixed assets but no cash to discharge its due contractual obligations, it would nevertheless have the ability to make a dividend distribution. Moreover, the distributions regime based on the 'balance sheet surplus test' requires reliable regulations to determine the calculation of the balance sheet and for the purposes of simplicity we have assumed that the conventions on the calculation of the balance sheet would show the same values in each jurisdiction. Nevertheless, the same regulations would be much less protective in jurisdictions which apply more liberal accounting principles. The advantage of this system is that it is clear and it is a relatively straightforward way of controlling distributable amounts *ex ante*.

In some jurisdictions, the 'earned surplus test' is applied, according to which a distribution may be made only out of the company's profits available for that purpose, which is further defined either by law or soft law (as in the UK). The application of the earned surplus test leads to similar results to the 'balance sheet surplus test'.

Meanwhile, a solvency-based model assumes that a distribution cannot be made if payment would lead to the company's insolvency. The main example is Finnish, Dutch and South African law, which requires a solvency test to be exercised prior to the distribution. In terms of Finnish law, assets cannot be distributed if this would render the company insolvent according to the information available (and information that ought to be available) at the time of the decision. In the UK, soft law precludes the company's assets from being distributed to shareholders where there has been 'significant deterioration in the financial position of the Company since the annual accounts date'. The shift from traditional capital maintenance rules to a more modern test based on company liquidity has increasingly become popular as evidenced by the company law reforms that have taken place in Finland, the Netherlands and South Africa. In consequence, in those jurisdictions, financial liquidity appears to be a relevant factor in the case of dividend distributions. US law relies more on the concept of fraudulent transfers than liquidity which makes a dividend distribution made on the verge of insolvency vulnerable to action by the creditor against the recipient.

---

[172] For example, the threshold for statutory reserves in French and Italian law is 5% of the company's annual profit which is accumulated until the statutory reserves reach 10% or 20% of the share capital and in Finland restricted capital includes revaluation reserves.

Capital maintenance rules seem not to play an important role in curbing shareholders' opportunism that is aimed at making a transfer from a company's funds to a (related) individual's personal estate. The modernisation of the capital structure of limited liability companies in many jurisdictions, which includes decreasing the level of minimum share capital required for incorporation, has contributed to a decline in importance of the capital maintenance rules. This stems from the fact that capital maintenance rules without minimum legal capital are practically redundant as an instrument of creditor protection. The erosion of capital maintenance rules caused by reducing the amount of share capital needs to be viewed in the light of several circumstances:

Firstly, the trend away from the traditional European model of creditor protection based on capital maintenance to a more flexible solvency model may incidentally cause a regulatory gap. The reason for this is that in countries where legal capital rules traditionally do not play an important role for creditor protection, regulatory instruments are allocated either to insolvency law or are placed on the verge of corporate and insolvency laws like fraudulent transfers in US law and liability of the management board members for wrongful trading in UK law. Therefore, relaxing rules on capital maintenance must be combined with giving consideration to the strengthening of alternative protection mechanisms which would fill the gap, such as directors' duties to consider creditors in the vicinity of insolvency,[173] shadow directors' liability, piercing of the corporate veil or avoidance provisions in case of insolvency.[174]

Secondly, legal capital can play an important role for new companies. Reduction of the statutory minimum capital required at an entry level boosted the number of limited liability companies being set up; however, some studies show that the quality of those 'light' capital companies and their added value for the economy are doubtful.[175] In the American model of creditor protection, the obligation to maintain some capital after the distribution may be derived from fraudulent-transfers law rather than corporate law.[176] Therefore, minimum share capital is still significant at preventing the entrance of ill-judged and economically unjustified entries to the market, while it loses its relevance as companies grow.[177] Some studies also show that the lack of a minimum legal capital requirement may lead to competition between extremely different forms of conducting business activity such as business as a company or as an individual trader.[178]

---

[173] *West Mercia Safetywear Ltd v Dodd* (1988) 4 BCC 30 (CA). See also A Keay, *Company Directors' Responsibilities to Creditors* (Abingdon, Routledge-Cavendish, 2007).

[174] Bachner, *Creditor Protection in Private Companies, Anglo-American Perspectives for a European Legal Discourse* (n 15) 47.

[175] W Niemeier, 'What Kind of Companies will a "One-Euro-EPC" Generate?' in H Hirte and C Teichmann, *The European Private Company – Societas Privata Europea* (SPE) (Berlin, Waler de Gruyter, 2012) 33.

[176] The insufficiency of capital to meet obligations after making distribution is regarded as a 'badge of fraud'; see, eg, DG Baird, 'Legal Approaches to Restricting Distributions to Shareholders: The Role of Fraudulent Transfer Law' (2009) *European Business Organization Law Review* 7, 199; Wagner, 'Distributions to Shareholders and Fraudulent Transfer Law' (n 15).

[177] M Żurek 'W poszukiwaniu optymalnego modelu regulacji struktury majątkowej spółki z o.o. – ujęcie prawno-ekonomiczne' (2016) *Przegląd Prawa Handlowego* 5–29.

[178] See Żurek, ibid, 38. See also K Kułak, 'Francuskie „bezkapitałowe" spółki kapitałowe – uwagi na tle projektu reformy struktury majątkowej spółki z o.o.' (2011) *Przegląd Prawa Handlowego* 10–48.

Thirdly, the flexibility of capital maintenance rules rises with the availability of credit risk information and the development of public electronic registers to inspect the financial results of the company.[179]

The Polish attempt to modernise capital maintenance rules of the limited liability company reveals – what can be traced also in the country reports – that adequate level of creditor protection does not stem solely from capital maintenance rules but is an effect of combination of different considerations such as: (i) minimum legal capital should be reasonably low as not to hinder access to the legal form of limited liability companies; (ii) in the case of possible board liability for the distribution of dividends, the board should be able to defend itself with the business judgment rule, explaining that it observed due care and diligence in performing the solvency test and making the distribution, (iii) the board's duty to periodically monitor the solvency of the company should be combined with a duty to convene the shareholders' meeting when the forecast of the financial liquidity indicates a risk for the company as a going concern; (iv) the obligation of the company to recapitalise profits by setting-off some percentage of the profits is an often utilised instrument of capital maintenance rules and can protect the company's assets.[180] At the point when the company is nearing insolvency, capital maintenance rules can only support the assessment whether the distribution was made legally. But the major role seems to be played by crisis governance rules such as board liability for breach of its duties, in particular the duty to consider creditors' interests when the company is facing the risk of insolvency underpinned by the liability of so called shadow directors.[181]

[179] W Schön, 'Creditor Protection in the Closed Corporation' in G Bachmann, H Eidenmüller, A Engert, H Fleischer, and W Schön *Regulating the Closed Corporation* (Berlin, Walter de Gruyter, 2013) 167; H Merkt, 'Creditor Protection Through Mandatory Disclosure' (2006) 7 *European Business Organisation Law Review* 95. On the margin of the reform of the company law in Poland there are laws enacted to strengthen credit information agency and establish registry of tax debts: see Act of 7 April 2017 on amendment to some acts in order to facilitate debt recover, see also the improvement of the mandatory disclosure of electronic access to documents (including financial statements) filed with court register in Directive (EU) 2017/1132 of the European Parliament and of the Council of 14 June 2017 relating to certain aspects of company law.

[180] In many jurisdictions (expressly mentioned in solutions under French, German, Italian and Spanish law), it is required that some portion of the profit is allocated to the statutory reserve until this reaches some portion of the share capital (usually 10–20 % of share capital). This concept is designed to build capital buffers during company lifetime ('going concern'), especially when minimum share capital is eliminated; however, it is argued that the correct level should rather be marked by level of company actual debts than the level of own funds. Such a model would be based on financial indicator known as D/E ratio (debt/equity ratio) and was presented during the discussions on the modernisation of Polish limted liability; see A Nowacki, 'Uwagi o projektowanych zmianach struktury majątkowej spółki z o.o.' (2011) *Przegląd Prawa Handlowego* 9–40 and Żurek 'W poszukiwaniu optymalnego modelu regulacji struktury majątkowej spółki z o.o. – ujęcie prawno-ekonomiczne' (n 177).

[181] Usually decisions that allow for the continuation of profitable activity would add value to creditors in accordance with the entity value maximisation rule (to be contrasted with the decision of managers to make transaction at undervalue with the shareholder in the analysed case). On fiduciary duties of the directors towards creditors when the company is on the verge of insolvency, see Keay, *Company Directors' Responsibilities to Creditors* (n 173); A Chaver and J Fried, 'Managers' Fiduciary Duty Upon the Firm's Insolvency: Accounting for Performance Creditors' (2002) 55 *Vanderbilt Law Review* 1815. For the American literature, see also RS Silberglied 'Litigating Fiduciary Duty Claims in Bankruptcy Court and Beyond: Theory and Practical Considerations in an Evolving Environment' (2015) 10 *Journal of Business and Technology Law* 181 and famous case *Credit Lyonnais Bank Nederland, N.V. v Pahe Communications Corp.*, 17 Del J Corp L 1099, 1155 (Del Ch 1991).

Another discernible pattern in the majority of case solutions is that board liability for illegal distributions can be enforced by the company itself as opposed to the creditor itself. As long as the management that is liable for the unlawful distribution controls the company, it is unlikely that the board will file an action on behalf of the company.[182] Therefore, some solutions suggest that institutions outside of company law such as avoidance rules might prove helpful to creditors who would like to recover the distribution from the shareholders (see in particular, the Dutch, US, Finish and Polish solutions).[183]

C. Disguised Distributions

The jurisdictions examined employ a variety of strategies to address related party transactions and the transfer of assets at undervalue (tunnelling of profits) to the detriment of creditors.[184] Nevertheless, certain patterns can be traced in the solutions to the hypothetical case: (i) those which prohibit directly or indirectly disguised distributions, for example, Germany, the UK, Finland, Poland and Latvia; (ii) those which do not specifically regulate disguised distributions but provide other remedies for imbalanced transactions, for example, Italy and France or US.

German law defines a disguised distribution as a payment to a shareholder (not being a formal distribution of profits) without adequate consideration. The definition in the UK is more lenient insofar as it allows a distribution to be made so long as it is paid out of distributable profits, to the extent that any overpayment which falls outside distributable profits would be treated as unlawful. Rules on disguised distributions are either specifically addressed by statute or case law (for example, Latvian law, which prescribes that an acquisition by a company from a shareholder at a price higher than usual is presumed to be unjustified and therefore prohibited, or Finnish law, which provides that any transaction designed to make a loss for the company is unlawful), or derived from the rules on capital maintenance or the principle of equal treatment of shareholders of a private company (as in Germany and Poland) in the jurisprudence or academic literature. French and Italian law lack any rules on undervalue transactions with shareholders, but they employ rules on disclosure and authorisation in terms of which transactions with shareholders (above certain thresholds) need to be authorised

---

[182] This problem may be solved when the control over the company's assets is transferred to the court-appointed administrator (official receiver) in insolvency proceedings. The lack of sufficient funds is, however, a major obstacle for instituting insolvency proceedings in many jurisdictions; see B Hannigan, *Company Law* (Oxford, Oxford University Press, 2009) 217; eg this concerns the question whether the assets of the company in insolvency comprise claims brought against directors (eg in case of wrongful trading).

[183] Avoidance rules in order to substitute for the diminishing importance of capital maintenance rules are in need of review in many jurisdictions: see, eg, A Engert, 'Life without Legal Capital: Lessons from American Law' in M Lutter, *Legal Capital in Europe* (Berlin, Walter de Gruyter, 2006) 646; Bachner (n 15) 39. However, as stated in the Polish solution to this case, partly due to ill-designed prerequisites, these rules are hardly suitable for challenging claims aimed at recovery of illegal distributions.

[184] Transparency and approval of related party transactions is now also addressed in Article 9c Directive (EU) 2017/828 of 17 May 2017 amending Directive 2007/36/EC as regards the encouragement of long-term shareholder engagement ([2017] OJ L132/1), which has to be transposed by the Member States by 10 June 2019.

by the corporate bodies. At the other extreme, we have the US solution, where there is no requirement for the transaction between the shareholders and the company to be struck at the market price. However, there is the possibility that the transaction may be challenged via fiduciary duty litigation.

When it comes to an assessment of the practical effectiveness of all the above rules, it is of the utmost importance that the creditor (Steel Factory) can bring an action in order to challenge the illegal transfer of assets (dividend payment or undervalue transaction) and retrieve those assets for the company. Interestingly, we find that in none of the company laws of the jurisdictions examined, except for Japan, would the creditors enjoy standing to raise a direct action in court designed to repay illegally transferred assets to the company. Instead, we find that the company rules are aimed at protecting either the company or minority shareholders, as opposed to the creditors.

The hypothetical case involved a limited liability company. Therefore, the first important issue was the distinction between full publicly held corporations and privately held ones.[185] Limited liability companies and public companies whose shares are not listed on a stock exchange (ie a closed public company) are examples of such privately held corporations. Here, a functional argument can be made that the legislature should distinguish between companies with a dispersed shareholding structure where the management board (or the board of directors in a one-tier model system) exerts more control over the company's affairs than that undertaken in the case of privately held companies and companies with a concentrated shareholding structure when it comes to drawing up the rules on the liability of directors towards creditors.

As mentioned above, certain patterns can be traced in the solutions to the hypothetical case. These patterns of legal thought underlie the different legal rules. We have identified five groups of provisions relating to undervalue transactions, which basically lead to functionally similar results. For example, the first pattern of legal thought is that if the company's assets are illegally pumped out of the company (either by the directors or shareholders), they continue to be treated as a part of the company's property. Thus, the creditors of the company have the right to satisfy their claims thereon and reach these assets, despite the fact that title to the assets vests in a third party. However, the protection afforded to the creditors is different from that available in the case of a security *in rem*, since the creditor may not only satisfy its claims by calling on the former assets of the company but may also reach the personal assets of the 'wrongdoer' (as in the case of the application of the piercing the corporate veil doctrine or the damages-based liability of the directors towards creditors for a breach of fiduciary duties). The question of whether the protection of the creditors is stronger than that which could be obtained under contract (for example, under a security *in rem* contract) remains open since a company's creditors are not entitled to any priority of claims over the assets of the wrongdoer. Therefore, these strategies for retrieving the company's debts may be used only as supplementary to capital maintenance rules.

The rules regarding the payment of dividends, including the concept of disguised dividends in Poland, France, Germany, Finland, Latvia and the US, are often designed

---

[185] This issue was considered by many of the authors of the solutions in the context of the discussion on the liability of directors towards creditors.

to ensure the equal treatment of shareholders (see the Polish, German and Spanish solutions). As a result, these strategies are typically treated as constituting rights in favour of the company and its shareholders and are of little assistance to the creditors. The remaining legal patterns are: duties of directors (Germany, the UK and, possibly, the US); the liability of a parent company under the piercing the corporate veil doctrine or the law on group company holding relationships (Poland, Italy, Germany, the UK and the US); and fraudulent conveyance laws (the US, Spain and Poland).

One of the important questions addressed by the hypothetical case was whether creditors can invoke the rules on the duties of directors (management board members) and sue the directors in respect of a breach of these rules. In France, although damages are theoretically available because the directors failed to follow the proper procedure, it is very doubtful that a creditor would be recognised as having standing to sue the directors (of both public and closed companies) for damages in a French court in respect of losses suffered as a result of a breach of the rules on conflicted transactions. Moreover, the creditor would not be entitled to nullify the contract and the directors acting in their official capacity would be shielded from liability towards third parties as long as they acted within the scope of their functions. This can be contrasted with German law. Whilst directors' duties are not owed to creditors in the case of private companies, in the case of public companies, creditors are entitled to enforce a breach of capital maintenance rules if recourse against the company proved to be ineffective and insolvency proceedings have not yet been opened (AktG, paragraph 62(2)).[186] Furthermore, in certain circumstances, the creditors may also enforce general breaches of directors' duties.[187] Thus, it could be inferred that the mandatory law on public companies in Germany provides for greater responsibilities of directors towards creditors on the ground that the creditors are the 'real' owners of the company and the agency costs associated with separation of ownership and control are greater. This suggests that there is no need for special directors' duties towards creditors in the case of privately held companies, since the controlling shareholder may often also be the chairman of the board and chief executive of the company. Thus, imposing a stringent fiduciary duty on directors would be fruitless if they commonly act as both shareholders and directors simultaneously and are able to manipulate matters acting in the capacity of a director in order to advance their own interests as a shareholder. On the other hand, the German example is striking because it enables creditors to have recourse directly against the director of the stock corporation, even though insolvency proceedings have

---

[186] AktG, § 62(1): 'Shareholders shall repay the stock corporation for any benefits they have received from the stock corporation contrary to the provisions of this Act. If such amounts were received in the form of dividends, the obligation to repay such amounts to the stock corporation shall arise only if the shareholders knew, or due to negligence did not know, that they were not entitled to receipt thereof. (2) Claims of the stock corporation may also be asserted by the stock corporation's creditors if they are unable to obtain satisfaction from the stock corporation. If insolvency proceedings have been instituted over the stock corporation's assets, the receiver or the trustee shall exercise the rights of the stock corporation's creditors against the shareholders during the course of the insolvency proceedings'.

This provision could constitute the basis for an action against a director if he or she has obtained an unlawful benefit as a shareholder of the stock corporation.

[187] Other breaches of directors' duties of care may only be enforced by the creditors if recourse against the company proved ineffective and there was a gross violation of directors' duties (AktG, § 93(5)). This enables direct recourse against the director irrespective of whether he or she is a shareholder of the company or not.

not been initiated and irrespective of whether the company is on the verge of insol-vency or not. Spanish law also permits creditors recourse against a shareholder where a transaction entered into by the company and a shareholder amounts to a disguised dividend. In such a case, the creditor will be entitled to sue the shareholder directly on the basis that the disguised dividend is a fraud on the creditors. If established, the doctrine of fraud on the creditors imposes an obligation of restitution on the share-holder who has benefited from the transaction.

The remaining jurisdictions base a creditor's rights of recourse upon the solvency test in the context of a claim for a breach of a director's fiduciary duties. For exam-ple, under Finnish law, the creditors can demand damages from the directors if the company is insolvent. The transfer of assets at undervalue is unlawful by virtue of law.[188] Latvia and Italy do not recognise fiduciary duties owed by directors towards creditors. In the UK, the common law courts have adopted the position that the duty to take account of creditors' interests is owed by directors to the company – rather than directly to the creditors[189] – when a company is insolvent or nearing insolvency.[190] The end result is that a creditor is denied standing to sue in respect of a breach of directors' duties and only a future liquidator of a company would have title to sue the director. Under US law, although the conflict transaction will be treated as unfair, creditors will not have standing to bring a lawsuit.[191]

We have also grouped liability on the basis of the piercing the corporate veil doctrine and the techniques imposing liability on the parent company for the subsidiary in the same category, which can be referred to as the 'guarantee strategy'. This category is different because the creditor's right of recourse against the third party does not depend on whether the company is successful or effective in seeking recourse against the third party, akin to liability under the fiduciary duties (the German solution is an example). In turn, German law differentiates between the limited liability company

---

[188] The transaction was seemingly designed to make a loss and no sound business reasons have been advanced in favour of the decision.

[189] *Yukong Line Ltd of Korea v Rendsburg Investments Corp of Liberia* [1998] 1 WLR 294 (QB); *West Mercia Safetywear Ltd v Dodd* (1988) 4 BCC 30 (CA); *Re Halt Garage (1964) Ltd* [1982] 3 All ER 1016 (Ch); *Kuwait Asia Bank EC v National Mutual Life Nominees Ltd* [1991] 1 AC 187 (PC).

[190] Whether a company is on the verge of insolvency is an issue for objective assessment and directors must take independent financial and legal advice to confirm the position. In such circumstances, the duty to have regard to the interests of the company's creditors arises because it is the creditor's position in the company's liquidation that will be affected by the director's actions. Since the director's duty to take into account the interests of creditors when the company is insolvent or nearing insolvency is owed to the company rather than directly to the creditors, it is only indirectly through a liquidator acting on behalf of the company that the creditors' interests are represented.

[191] The question continues to be debatable in the US. eg, in *Credit Lyonnais Bank Nederland v Pathe Communications Corp* (1991) 17 Delaware Journal of Corporate Law 1099 (not reported in A 2d), the Court of Chancery opined that when a corporation is 'in the vicinity of insolvency', its directors should not consider the shareholders' welfare alone, but should consider the welfare of the community of interests that constitute the corporation. In another case (*Geyer v Ingersoll Publications Co*, No 12, 406 1992 Del Ch Lewis 132 (Del Ch 18 June 1992)), the Court of Chancery ruled that directors owe a direct duty to manage the corporation on behalf of creditors when the corporation is insolvent but not yet in bankruptcy. However, how far fiduciary duties should protect creditors in circumstances of near-insolvency remains a hot topic. See, eg, HTC Hu, 'Risk, Time, and Fiduciary Principles in Corporate Investment' (1990) 38 *UCLA Law Review* 277; L Lin, 'Shift of Fiduciary Duty upon Corporate Insolvency: Proper Scope of Directors' Duty to Creditors' (1993) 46 *Vanderbilt Law Review* 1485.

and the stock corporation. Although the mechanism and legal provisions appear to be completely different, the pattern is similar. Therefore, the strategy is to govern the situation where a dominant shareholder administers the company through either a formal transfer of profits agreement or in disregard of corporate governance principles (the piercing the corporate veil doctrine). For example, under UK law, if the company is a mere façade concealing the true facts or has been formed to evade existing legal obligations, the court will pierce the corporate veil. However, it seems that the application of the piercing the corporate veil doctrine possesses certain defects when compared to liability under group company holding law. Besides the fact that in the case of the application of the piercing the corporate veil doctrine (as in other 'guarantee strategy' examples) no priority will be given over assets of the company where they have been commingled with the personal assets of shareholders, creditors will also be confronted by obstacles by virtue of the burden of proof. Therefore, it would appear that capital maintenance rules and directors' fiduciary duties towards creditors (Germany) better serve the purposes of creditor protection in comparison to the piercing the corporate veil doctrine.

On the other hand, some jurisdictions (such as the Poland, US and Spain) provide for the so-called claw-back rules or the *Actio Pauliana*, which afford creditors a remedy where debtors transfer their assets to third parties or prefer certain creditors over others in the period leading up to the company's insolvency. These doctrines allow creditors to rescind transactions at undervalue if corporate assets are diverted near insolvency. This doctrine is particularly important in the US, where there are no capital maintenance rules.

Part 3

Shareholder Protection

8

Shareholders and Shareholder Law

PIERRE-HENRI CONAC (EDITOR)

Main topics: legal consequences of a failure to pay dividends; legal challenges to a merger; exclusion of shareholders as a result of a merger.

Related topics: payment of dividends in breach of capital maintenance rules (see chapter 7, above); abuse of shareholders' rights (see chapter 9, below); enforcement of directors' duties (see chapter 10, below).

I. Scenario

A non-listed public company (Family Company A) has a controlling shareholding in another non-listed public company (Family Company B), holding 70 per cent of the shares. The shares of Family Company A are held (90 per cent) by another non-listed public holding company (Family Holding Company C). The position may be illustrated as follows:

Family Company C

↓ 90 per cent

Family Company A

↓ 70 per cent

Family Company B

For a period of 10 years, and despite the steady build-up of profits over that time which have led to an increase in the fair value of the shares of Family Company B, the controlling shareholder Family Company A has refused to vote in favour of any dividend in the hope of buying back the 30 per cent of the shares of Family Company B held by the five minority shareholders A, B, C, D and E. Each time the matter has come before the ordinary general meeting of the shareholders (which has the competence to decide on this issue), the board of directors has recommended that the shareholders do not vote in favour of any dividend but instead retain the profits in Family Company B. Some family members hold senior positions in Family Company A and Family Company B and so receive a satisfactory level of remuneration. Therefore, they do not feel they have any need to receive dividends. A minority shareholder of Family Company B, namely shareholder A, has decided to sue the majority shareholder Family Company A for damages in respect of the failure to vote in favour of the payment of a dividend for such a long period.

Meanwhile, for valid business reasons, the management of Family Company B decides to merge Family Company B with Family Company A by having Family Company A absorb Family Company B. Family Company A has other assets as well as its investment and participation in Family Company B. The share exchange ratio, as approved by the auditors, is for 20 shares of Family Company B to be exchanged for one share of Family Company A. The minority shareholders of Family Company B have several complaints.

First, minority shareholder A of Family Company B has decided to sue to obtain a court order annulling the merger on the ground that Family Company A, although authorised by law to vote on the merger, had a conflict of interest and should have refrained from voting. Second, minority shareholder B of Family Company B has a complaint that he did not receive the formal notice of the extraordinary shareholders' meeting to consider the approval of the merger, although he was able to participate since he heard about the meeting from another shareholder. Indeed, all of the shareholders were actually present at the extraordinary shareholders' meeting. Finally, in the course of the merger, several minority shareholders, namely shareholders C, D and E of Family Company B, who held only 18 shares each, were unable to become shareholders of Family Company A, receiving cash instead. They sue and seek the annulment of the merger on the ground that they were unjustifiably deprived of their status as shareholders. How would the rules of company law resolve each of these issues in your own country?

II. Case Studies

A. France

i. Action by a Minority Shareholder for Not Having Received a Dividend for 10 Years

A minority shareholder of Family Company B has decided to sue the majority shareholder for damages on the basis of the latter's failure to vote in favour of a dividend for a long period of time. This is a classic situation which has frequently given rise to court decisions in France. However, there is no specific legal provision addressing this issue in French law. Indeed, according to case law dating back to 1961,[1] in such a

---

[1] Cass Com (Cour de cassation, Commercial Chamber), 18 April 1961, *JCP* 1961, p 12164, with a note by DB.

situation, a minority shareholder may sue the company in order to seek the annulment of the decision of the general meeting of the shareholders not to distribute a dividend on the ground of 'abuse by the majority'. Alternatively, the minority shareholder may sue the majority shareholders for damages.

a. Action for Annulment or for Damages

The action for annulment rests upon Article 1844-10 of the Civil Code, which governs the annulment of juridical acts of companies (except those of the extraordinary share-holders' meeting). In the case of such an action, the statutory limitation period is three years.[2] However, this is not the preferred method for shareholders to protect themselves, since it does not result in the immediate payment of a dividend.

The action for damages rests upon general tort law (Civil Code, Article 1382) and requires a plaintiff to demonstrate fault, loss and a causal link between the two. The action for damages is directed at the majority shareholders (ie Family Company A). The statutory limitation period is five years (Civil Code, Article 2224).

b. Legal Elements Required to Demonstrate 'Abuse by the Majority'

The 'abuse by the majority' is defined by case law as a resolution taken by the majority shareholders which is contrary to the social interest of the company and which has the sole objective of favouring the majority shareholders to the prejudice of the minority shareholders.[3] Several factors must be taken into account in the determination of an 'abuse by the majority' claim. However, the French courts are reluctant to nullify the resolution or to hold majority shareholders liable for deciding to retain profits in the company. First, the French courts will consider whether there is a commercial ration-ale for retaining the profits within the company, such as for the purposes of financing investments. However, this does not seem to be the situation in the instant case. A second factor is the length of the period of non-payment of a dividend. Here, the period is 10 years. This is particularly long and the courts have ruled in a previous case that such a period may constitute an abuse by the majority[4] and, indeed, have done so in the case of shorter periods of time.[5] The fact that the majority shareholders have entered into a contract of employment with, and hold positions in, Family Company A and Family Company B are also matters which would be taken into account by French courts. This is exactly the situation in the instant case and therefore it is further suggestive of an abuse by the majority.

---

[2] Commercial Code, Art L 235-9.

[3] Cass Com (Cour de cassation, Commercial Chamber), 30 November 2004, *Bull Joly*, 2005, p 241, with a note by P Le Cannu.

[4] Cass Com (Cour de cassation, Commercial Chamber), 6 June 1990, *Bull Civ IV*, n° 171, *Revue des sociétés*, 1990, p 606, with a note by Y Chartier.

[5] CA Rouen (Court of Appeal of Rouen), 4 April 2001, *RJDA*, January 2002, n° 111. In this case, the period was 4 years. See also Cass Com (Cour de cassation, Commercial Chamber), 1 July 2003, 99-19328 (*SARL Mécano soudure et autres c/ Balice*), *Bull Joly*, 2003, p 1137, with a note by A Constantin. In this case, the period was 8 years.

Another important issue is that Family Company B is not listed. Therefore, unlike a listed company, the minority shareholders are unable to sell their shares on the market.[6] In the circumstances, it is more than reasonably likely that the French courts would rule that there has been an abuse by the majority.

ii. Action by Minority Shareholders against the Merger

We now consider the complaints of the minority shareholders of Family Company B against the merger of Family Company A and Family Company B.

a. Action for Annulment of the Merger

First, shareholder A of Family Company B has decided to sue to obtain a court order annulling the merger on the ground that Family Company A, although authorised by law to vote on the merger, had a conflict of interest and should have refrained from voting. Any shareholder can file an action seeking the annulment of an extraordinary general shareholders' meeting which approved a merger.[7] The merger is subject to a vote of the extraordinary shareholders' meeting of Family Company B, which requires a majority of two-thirds of the shares cast.[8] The action to annul a merger is subject to a shorter statutory limitation period of six months instead of three years, which runs from the date of the final registration of the merger in the Commercial Register.[9]

It can be argued that Family Company A has a conflict of interest and should be prohibited from voting on the merger since it is the majority shareholder of Family Company B and also the beneficiary of the transfer of the assets of Family Company B. The conflict of interest arises from the fact that Family Company A has an interest in undervaluing the shares of Family Company B in order to (i) reduce the amount to be paid to the minority shareholders of Family Company B and (ii) minimise the extent of the dilution of Family Company C's stake in Family Company A. However, there is no provision in the French Commercial Code which prevents Family Company A from voting on the merger on the basis of the existence of a conflict of interest. In addition, in the absence of a legal provision, the French courts have refused to invalidate the exercise of a shareholder's voting rights on the basis of a conflict of interest.

A case from 2006 provides an illustration of the reluctance of the French courts to deprive a shareholder of his or her voting rights in such circumstances.[10] In this case, a minority shareholder claimed that the majority shareholder should have been deprived of the right to vote on a decision to convert all of the founder's shares into ordinary shares. The majority shareholder was the main holder of the founder's shares and stood to benefit from an overvaluation of the founder's shares. The minority

---

[6] If the company was listed, they could sell the shares in a liquid open market. However, this would not exclude the possibility of an action for abuse by the majority since the shares would trade at a discount compared to shares which would be yielding a dividend.

[7] Commercial Code, Arts L 235-8 al 1 and L 235-1.

[8] Commercial Code, Art L 232-6 al 2.

[9] Commercial Code, Art L 235-9 al 2.

[10] Cass Com (Cour de cassation, Commercial Chamber), 19 September 2006 (*Société groupe Partouche*), *Revue des sociétés*, 2007, p 540, with a note by D Schmidt.

shareholder considered that the share exchange ratio was not favourable to the shareholders. He argued that the majority shareholder should have been prohibited from voting, since it was the main beneficiary of the share conversion. In the absence of any legal or regulatory provision, the Court refused to prohibit the majority shareholder from casting his vote. The decision also referred to the possibility of the majority shareholder being prohibited from voting because of a provision in the company's articles of association. However, in this particular case, there was no such provision in the articles of the company. The reasoning of that case also applies to a merger situation since the majority shareholder can benefit from an overvaluation of the shares of the absorbing company (ie Family Company A) and so has a conflict of interest.

In another case decided by the French courts, a minority shareholder tried to prevent the majority shareholder from voting on the ground that the majority shareholder received the assets of the absorbed company, whereas the minority shareholder received shares of the absorbing company. The minority shareholder alleged that this conferred a special benefit (*avantage particulier*) upon the majority shareholder and therefore it ought to have been prohibited from voting.[11] However, the Court held that this was not a special benefit and therefore the majority shareholder could vote.[12]

As such, the first possible course of action available to a minority shareholder who complains about the share exchange ratio and who is seeking to declare the shareholders' meeting void is to sue on the basis of an 'abuse by the majority'. He or she can also seek damages from the majority shareholder or can sue the auditors of the merger (*commissaire à la fusion*), who are appointed by the court, for having declared that the relative values assigned to the shares of the companies participating in the operation are sound and that the exchange ratio is fair.[13] The minority shareholders can also sue them for having made a mistake when assessing the value of the contributions in kind.[14] However, all of these actions have a low probability of success, especially because, despite the existence of judicial guidelines, there is still an admitted level of subjectivity in assessing the respective value of the merging companies.

b. Failure to Receive Notice

Second, another minority shareholder of Family Company B (Shareholder B) has a complaint that he did not receive a formal notice of the extraordinary shareholders' meeting to consider the approval of the merger, although he was able to participate since he heard about the meeting from another shareholder. Indeed, all of the shareholders were actually present at the extraordinary shareholders' meeting.

In the case of public companies, a specific provision of the French Commercial Code provides that 'any meeting may be cancelled if incorrectly convened'.[15] Since shareholder B did not receive notice of the extraordinary shareholders' meeting, this

---

[11] Commercial Code, Arts L 225-10 and L 225-147.
[12] CA Douai (Court of Appeal of Douai), 7 July 1994 (*Adam et autres c/ SA La Redoute*), *Bull Joly*, 1994, n° 9, p 994, with a note by P Le Cannu.
[13] Commercial Code, Art L 236-10.
[14] Commercial Code, Arts L 225-147 and L 236-10.
[15] Commercial Code, Art L 225-104.

provision applies. However, the same article adds that 'an application for cancellation shall not, however, be admissible where all the shareholders were present or represented'. This is also the situation in the instant case. Therefore, despite the procedural irregularity, B would be unsuccessful in an action seeking the annulment of the shareholders' meeting. A similar solution is provided by law in the case of limited liability companies (*Société à responsabilité limitée* (SARL))[16] and has been extended by the courts to apply to civil companies (*Sociétés civiles*).[17]

c. Exclusion as a Shareholder from the Company as a Result of the Merger

Finally, in the course of the merger, several minority shareholders (C, D and E) of Family Company B, who held only 18 shares each, were unable to become shareholders of Family Company A, receiving cash instead. They sue and seek the annulment of the merger on the ground that they were unjustifiably deprived of their status as shareholders.

By applying a share exchange ratio which implies that some minority shareholders will not be able to become shareholders of the absorbing company unless they succeed in buying other subscription rights, these minority shareholders are effectively excluded from Family Company A since they are only allowed to receive cash in exchange for their shares. The adoption of the share exchange ratio can lead to the expropriation of some or all of the shares of the minority shareholders.

An action has been raised several times before the French courts on this basis but without success. In one particular case which came before a French court of appeal, it was held that the minority shareholder should have received at least one share of the absorbing company.[18] However, the court held that this was not a sufficient reason to justify the annulment of the merger since it is not one of the reasons for an annulment which are allowed by the law. The action for annulment raised on the ground of an 'abuse by the majority' was also rejected by the court because the minority shareholder was unable to establish that the merger was contrary to the interests of the absorbed company and that the true motive for the merger was to oust him as a shareholder from the company.

Another more recent decision of the French Supreme Court (*Cour de cassation*) is even less encouraging for the minority shareholder.[19] In this case, a company reduced its share capital to zero, and subsequently issued new shares which could be subscribed, through the issuance of subscription rights, by the previous shareholders. The ratio was calculated in such a way that a shareholder was required to hold at least two shares in order to receive one from the company and there was a majority shareholder who held 3,997 shares of the 4,000 shares in issue. Therefore, only three shares were held by minority shareholders. One of the minority shareholders held only one share and

---

[16] Commercial Code, Art L 223-27.

[17] Cass Com, 8 February 2005 (Locatelli), *Revue des sociétés*, 2006, p 94, with a note by M Menjucq and A Taste.

[18] CA Rouen (Court of Appeal of Rouen), 6 July 2004 (*Pingault v Axe conseils expertise*).

[19] Cass Com (Cour de cassation, Commercial Chamber), 1 July 2008 (*Société ITM Entreprises contre Société Kerris*), pourvoi numéro 07-20.643, Juris-Data numéro 2008-044663.

could not acquire another subscription right in order to buy one new share and remain a shareholder of the company. The minority shareholder complained that the true purpose of the operation was to exclude him from the company. The Court held that the ratio applied was not fraudulent and that it did not amount to an indirect suppression of the minority shareholder's subscription rights. The reasoning of this case also applies to a merger situation where the share exchange ratio does not enable all of the shareholders to become shareholders of the absorbing company. Therefore, unless the minority shareholder is able to prove that the true objective of the process was to oust him from the company (*fraus omnia corrumpit*) or that there was an 'abuse by the majority', he will be unable to prevent the majority shareholder from proceeding with the merger and excluding him as a shareholder.

iii. Conclusion and Summary

Under French company law, it is possible for minority shareholders to succeed in an 'abuse by the majority' claim against a majority shareholder, but such proceedings tend to be fraught with difficulty. This is particularly the case in the context of a merger: minority shareholders benefit little in terms of judicial protection where the group is controlled. There is no prospect of legislative change either, since Parliament has been keen to facilitate mergers rather than hamper them. In addition, French judges tend to have a formalistic approach and to apply the law (both statutory and case-based) cautiously in this area. However, there are specific rules for listed companies. In such cases, the securities regulator can force the majority shareholder to make a tender offer for the shares of the company.[20]

B. Germany[21]

i. Action by Minority Shareholder A for Not Having Received a Dividend for 10 Years

There is no mandatory right to dividends for shareholders of public companies in Germany. Although the provisions for the payment of a dividend have a statutory basis (AktG, §§ 58(4), 60, 174(1)), this is merely an entitlement to bring about a decision on profit utilisation. Only after this decision is made is there a claim to the distribution of a dividend. The resolution for the annual dividend presupposes the adoption of the annual accounts. The general meeting is usually only responsible for the decision on use of the operating results (AktG, §§ 119(1) (no 2), 174(1)). Adoption of the annual accounts must as a rule be made by the supervisory board (AktG, § 172), unless it does not approve them or the executive and supervisory boards resolve to leave the adoption to the general meeting (AktG, § 173).

The provisions regulating the amount payable by way of dividend follow a compromise solution. In order to meet both the shareholders' pecuniary interest and the

---

[20] General Regulation of the French *Autorité des marchés financiers* (AMF), Art 236-6.
[21] Abbreviated statutes: AktG = Law on Public Companies; BGB = Civil Code; GmbHG = Law on Private Limited Companies; UmwG = Transformation Act.

company's self-financing interest, the management and the supervisory board can place half of the company's annual surplus into reserves as a maximum (AktG, § 58(2) (s 1)). However, the articles of association can deviate from this 'halving rule' (AktG, § 58(2)(s 2)). Moreover, the management has considerable room for manoeuvre through the accounting provisions on the ascertainment of profits. For example, it can often control the amount of the dividend in accordance with its interests by valuing certain items of income and expenditure and its reserves and liabilities.[22] It is also debated whether the improper exercise of management discretion is able to justify liability for damages.[23]

In the present case, the main complaint of the minority shareholders relates to the conduct of the majority shareholder. In general, German law requires a resolution of a shareholders' general meeting to be justified to the shareholders by some objective reason[24] and the shareholders' duty of loyalty to the company must not be infringed by the resolution.[25] However, these general principles are restricted by a special provision for the avoidance of shareholder resolutions on the distribution of profits (AktG, § 254): these resolutions can be challenged if the general meeting allocates profits to its reserve account even though this is unnecessary from a reasonable business perspective, and by doing so the shareholders do not receive at least a profit of 4 per cent of the issued share capital.[26] This action can only be filed by a shareholder who holds at least a 5 per cent share of the registered capital or a stock exchange value of €500,000. It has to be made no later than one month after the general meeting. In addition, any shareholders can challenge a resolution of the general meeting if it confers special benefits upon a third person or another shareholder (AktG, § 243(2)).[27]

Since § 254 of the AktG is intended to apply to extreme cases only[28] and since the words 'reasonable business perspective' leave considerable discretion to the management, it is often not clear whether such a claim would be successful. Yet, a typical example of a special benefit under § 243(2) of the AktG is where the majority fails to distribute profits in order to put pressure on the minority to sell its shares to the majority for a low price.[29] Thus, in the present case, it is not unlikely that the non-distribution of profits will be held to be unlawful.

ii. Action by Minority Shareholders against the Merger

As in France, the general meetings of the merging companies have to approve a merger. There is an exception for the acquiring company's general meeting if this company already owns 90 per cent of the shares of the acquired company (UmwG, § 62). This is

[22] See M Siems, *Convergence in Shareholder Law* (Cambridge, Cambridge University Press, 2008) 73–74.
[23] *Cf* H Henze in *Großkommentar zum AktG* (Berlin, de Gruyter, 2000) § 58, para 45.
[24] See BGH (German Federal Supreme Court), BGHZ 71, 40; BGHZ 83, 319.
[25] See BGH, BGHZ 103, 184, 194–95 (Linotype); BGHZ 129, 136, 148 (Girmes); NJW 1999, 3197.
[26] Although this is not expressly stated in this provision, this excludes the general principles mentioned above. See, eg, J Koch, *Münchener Kommentar zum Aktiengesetz, Band 4* (4th edn, Munich, Beck, 2016) § 254, para 8.
[27] This is not excluded by AktG, § 254. See, eg, Koch, ibid, § 254, paras 4 and 9.
[28] Koch, ibid, § 254, para 3.
[29] Koch, ibid, § 254, para 9.

not the case here since Family Company A only held 70 per cent of the shares of Family Company B.

A violation of the law usually leads to the voidability of the decision of the general meeting (AktG, § 243(1)). In the present case, the first reason could be that Family Company A's vote should not count, owing to the presence of a conflict of interest. However, with the exception of individual provisions which are not applicable here,[30] it is a matter of debate whether in such a situation the right to vote is excluded in the case of public companies by analogy with the laws on associations and private companies (BGB, § 34; GmbHG, § 47(4)(s 2)). Even if this question is answered in the affirmative, however, the exclusion of voting rights does not cover topics which concern the corporate structure of a company, such as a merger. Thus, Family Company A could vote in the general meeting.[31]

Second, there was the failure to notify all shareholders. Under German law, a failure to give notice is irrelevant if all the shareholders attend the meeting and no shareholder objects to this failure at the general meeting (AktG, § 121(6)). It is unclear whether the second requirement is fulfilled in the present case. If there was an objection, this would lead to the nullity (and not only voidability) of the resolution (AktG, (§ 241 (no 1)). Shareholders can, however, file an action for nullity with effect *inter omnes* (AktG, §§ 249(1)(s 1), 248(1)). If no legal action seeking a declaration of nullity is lodged within three years of the entry of the resolution(s) made at the general meeting in the commercial register (AktG, § 242(2)), then the resolutions and the meeting are unimpeachable.

Third, minority shareholders C, D and E complain that the share exchange ratio deprived them of their right to become shareholders of the surviving company. In Germany, this cannot lead to the avoidance of the merger. The remedy for any complaint about the share exchange ratio is limited to compensation only (UmwG, §§ 14(2), 15).[32] Therefore, if this complaint is successful, there can only be an increase in monetary compensation. In the interests of legal certainty, the share exchange ratio cannot be changed.

C. Italy

i. Action by Minority Shareholder A for Not Having Received a Dividend for 10 Years

The question of whether shareholders of a *Società per azioni* (Spa) have an enforceable right to the distribution of profits generated by the company is a classic – and somewhat unresolved – problem of Italian law. The approach to this issue, which is currently accepted by legal scholars and the courts generally, is that shareholders do

---

[30] AktG, §§ 136, 142(1), (2), 243(2)(s 1).

[31] See H Diekmann, in J Semler and A Stengel (eds), *UmwG* (3rd edn, Munich, Beck, 2012) § 65, para 21. According to some scholars, the position differs in the case of the GmbH, on which, see, eg, W Zöllner and U Noack in *Baumbach & Hueck's GmbHG* (21st edn, Munich, Beck, 2017) § 47, para 90.

[32] For the procedure itself, see the special law: *Spruchverfahrensgesetz* (SpruchG) of 17 July 2003, BGBl. I 838.

not have such a right and thus the majority may decide to carry forward the annual profits even if minority shareholders are against this decision.[33]

The freedom afforded to majority shareholders, however, is not without its limits. In fact, in approving the financial statements and in deciding to carry forward profits, shareholders must respect the general principles governing company law. Among these principles, an important role is played by Article 1375 of the Civil Code (CC), which requires the parties to a contract to perform it in good faith. This is a principle which applies to shareholders in the general meeting when they are considering a resolution to approve a company's financial statements.[34]

In practice, a shareholder may challenge a resolution of the general meeting based on a purported violation of Article 1375 of the CC. However, it will be difficult to succeed in such an action. In fact, majority shareholders have no duty to put forward any imperative reasons in favour of the resolution against the distribution of profits. Indeed, on the contrary, a minority shareholder that challenges the resolution must prove that the company has no interest in carrying the profits forward and, in conclusion, only actions taken against blatant abuses of the majority will have any chance of success.

ii. Action by Minority Shareholder A against the Merger

a. Action for Annulment of the Merger

With regard to the issues raised by the merger, a principle of Italian company law which may be relevant for the solution to this case is set out in Article 2504-*quater* of the CC. According to this provision, once the authentic instrument of merger has been entered in the Company Registers of the companies involved in the transaction, the validity of the merger cannot be challenged, and shareholders and third parties are only allowed to file an action for damages. Thus, in Italian company law, the validity of a resolution of the general meeting that approves a merger can be challenged only before the conclusion of the merger has been published, and in such a case the suspension of the execution of the resolution is not an automatic consequence of the action.[35]

Turning to the problem of conflict of interest, Article 2373 of the CC stipulates · that the resolutions of the general meeting may be challenged if a shareholder has a direct or indirect conflict of interest, insofar as (a) his or her vote was necessary for the approval of the resolution and (b) the resolution may cause loss to the company. However, whether this provision is of any application to a resolution which approves a merger has been questioned.[36] Indeed, since the rules currently in force provide some guarantee to the shareholders by allowing them to receive opinions from external experts on the fairness and reasonableness of the exchange ratio, the potential for the application of the rules on a conflict of interest of the shareholders is reduced.[37]

---

[33] See, eg, G Campobasso, *Diritto commerciale: Diritto delle società* (9th edn, Turin, Utet, 2015) 484.

[34] P Balzarini, 'Commento *sub* art. 2433' in P Marchetti, LA Bianchi, F Ghezzi and M Notari (eds), *Commentario alla Riforma delle società. Obbligazioni. Bilancio* (Milan, Giuffrè-Egea, 2006) 633 ff, 635 ff.

[35] The suspension is decided by a court in light of the different interests involved.

[36] See, eg, P Menti, 'Commento *sub* art. 2502' in G Cian and A Trabucchi (eds), *Commentario breve al Codice Civile* (12th edn, Padua, CEDAM, 2016) 3131 ff, 3134.

[37] Ibid.

b. Failure to Receive Notice

Where a general meeting has not been properly convened owing to a failure to notify all shareholders in advance, the relevant resolution may be challenged by any interested party within a period of three years in accordance with Article 2379, paragraph 1 of the CC. However, Article 2379-*bis*, paragraph 1 of the CC adds that a resolution, which is void for lack of notice, cannot be challenged by those persons who authorised the continuation of the meeting. This principle must also be read in conjunction with Article 2366, paragraph 4 of the CC, which stipulates that the general meeting is deemed to be correctly convened when the entire body of shareholders participates in the meeting and the majority of the members of the corporate bodies are present. In this situation, however, any participant in the meeting may refuse to discuss any topic on which he or she considers himself or herself not adequately informed. In light of this regulatory framework, in Italian company law, any action undertaken by shareholder B for lack of notice of the general meeting would be unsuccessful.

c. Exclusion as a Shareholder from the Company as a Result of the Merger

Finally, with regard to the exclusion of shareholders C, D and E from Family Company A as a consequence of the exchange ratio of the merger, at least one precedent[38] excludes the validity of pure cash-out mergers where a shareholder owns only a minimal number of shares.[39] Legal scholarship, on the other hand, supports a more permissive approach and has considered the possibility of the exclusion of small shareholders in the absence of an abuse by the majority shareholders.[40]

D. Spain

i. Introduction

The first element required for the distribution of dividends[41] is that a balance sheet must be approved by the general shareholders' meeting (Ley de Sociedades de Capital

---

[38] Trib Benevento 3/11/1992.

[39] Another limitation to the possible abuses created by the determination of a specific share exchange ratio is set out in art 2501-*ter*, para 2 of the CC, which excludes any cash consideration from exceeding 10% of the par value of the shares assigned to the shareholders in the context of a merger.

[40] C Santagata, 'Le Fusioni' in GE Colombo and GB Portale (eds), *Trattato delle società per azioni*, vol 7** 1 (Turin, Utet, 2004) 211 ff.

[41] Dividends are those profits distributed amongst the shareholders of the company. However, dividends constitute one amongst a diverse set of possibilities for the allocation of the company's profit. Profits may be used to create different capital reserves in the balance sheet of the company, either in terms of statute or determined in accordance with the company's by-laws. The distribution of dividends can only take place once those capital reserves have been covered. The by-laws may establish that part of the profits are distributed to the founders of the company or the directors. Preferential shares may also entitle preferential shareholders to preferential dividends or, in the case of non-voting shares, to the right to receive an annual dividend of a minimum amount. It is worth mentioning that dividends can also be distributed on the basis not of profits, but by releasing sums held in distributable capital reserves that the company may have created over a period of time. On these issues, see F Sánchez Calero, *Principios de Derecho Mercantil*

(LSC) – Corporate Enterprises Act, Article 273.1)[42] and, second, that the net asset value of the company (ie its current assets less its current liabilities) is equal to or higher than the share capital of the company (LSC, Article 273.2). It seems that both these criteria are satisfied in the case of Family Company B. The general shareholders' meeting decides on the allocation of the company's profits and thus also on the potential distribution of dividends. However, the distribution of dividends is not compulsory and the general meeting may agree, even if profits have been generated, that none of them will be distributed as dividends and instead may decide that the profits are retained as part of the company's capital reserves in its balance sheet.[43]

The fact that the general shareholders' meeting may decide not to distribute dividends does not mean that, in adopting such a decision, it can act in a biased manner.[44] Indeed, those decisions could be challenged, particularly in instances of biased deprivation of dividends, adopted in the interest of certain groups of shareholders, to the extent that the purpose of distributing dividends is not to further the interest of some shareholders but the general company's interest, common to all shareholders.[45] Moreover, such behaviour could constitute an abuse of law (Código Civil (CC) – Civil Code,[46] Article 7.2), which would result in the decision being treated as challengeable (LSC, Article 204.1).[47] Therefore, in the case of Family Company B, the decision adopted with the support of Family Company A could in principle be challenged by shareholder A on the basis of Article 206.1 of the LSC. However, in order for A to be entitled to do so he or she would have to represent at least 1 per cent of the share capital of Family Company B, unless the by-laws of the latter set a lower percentage (LSC, Article 206.1). The claim should be brought against the company itself, not against the majority shareholders (LSC, Article 206.3). It could also be argued that the behaviour of Family Company A is in breach of the duty of loyalty owed by shareholders towards Family Company B, which requires them to abstain from interested conduct that may produce loss or harm to the company. Such a breach may lead to the obligation to compensate in damages.[48]

ii. The Merger

The merger between Family Company A and Family Company B must be approved by the general shareholders' meeting of both companies, according to Article 40.1 of the

---

(15th edn, Navarra, Thomson-Aranzadi, 2010) 305–08; and JL Iglesias Prada and J García de Enterría, 'Las Cuentas Anuales de las Sociedades de Capital' in A Menéndez and Á Rojo (eds) *Lecciones de Derecho Mercantil*, Vol II (12th edn, Cizur Menor (Navarra), Civitas-Thomson Reuters, 2014) 540–44.

[42] Real Decreto Legislativo 1/2010, de 2 de julio, por el que se aprueba el texto refundido de la Ley de Sociedades de Capital (LSC).

[43] Subject to the satisfaction of certain requirements, where the general shareholders' meeting decides not to declare a minimum dividend, the law provides for the appraisal rights of shareholders of non-listed companies who voted in favour of the distribution of dividends (LSC, Art 348 *bis*).

[44] In this sense, see STS (Sentencia Tribunal Supremo) of 26 May 2005, in which the Spanish Supreme Court recognised the abusive character of an SL failing to distribute dividends.

[45] Sánchez Calero, *Principios de Derecho Mercantil* (n 41) 309.

[46] Real Decreto de 24 de julio de 1889 por el que se publica el Código Civil.

[47] See Á Rojo, 'Artículo 204. Acuerdos impugnables' in Á Rojo and E Beltrán (eds), *Comentario de la Ley de Sociedades de Capital* (Cizur Menor (Navarra), Civitas-Thomson Reuters, 2011) 1040–41.

[48] See V Ribas Ferrer, *El deber de lealtad del administrador de sociedades* (Madrid, La Ley, 2010) 325–28.

Ley sobre Modificaciones Estructurales de las Sociedades Mercantiles (LMESM) – Act on Structural Changes in Corporations.[49] A violation of this provision, for example, where invalid but decisive votes are cast in favour of the merger, may result in the decision being treated as challengeable (LSC, Article 204).[50] The controlling shareholder – Family Company A – may be in a situation of conflict of interest when voting on the merger. There has been a debate in the legal literature whether shareholders of SAs affected by conflict-of-interest situations are subject to a general duty to abstain from voting.[51] Article 190.1 of the LSC restricts the voting rights of shareholders when it comes to certain specific conflict-of-interest situations; yet, the decision concerning the merger between Family Company A and Family Company B would not fall under the scope of this provision. Otherwise, in instances of conflict of interest not listed in Article 190.1 of the LSC, shareholders – such as Family Company A – are not deprived of their voting rights but, if and when the vote of a shareholder affected by the conflict of interest is decisive for the adoption of a decision and the latter is challenged – as shareholder A plans to do – then the company and the shareholder(s) who was/were affected by the conflict of interest must prove that the challenged decision was in the company's interest (LSC, Article 190.3). It is also possible that the by-laws of a company prescribe provisions which set abstention duties applicable to shareholders in a conflict-of-interest situation.[52]

When it comes to the issue of the failure to give notice of the shareholders' meeting to all shareholders, Article 40.2 of the LMESM provides that any notice concerning the convening of a shareholders' meeting to decide on a merger must be given at least one month prior to the date of the meeting. If these formalities are violated, the agreements adopted by the shareholders' meeting would contravene the law and might be considered challengeable.[53] According to the LSC, it is possible to challenge decisions of the shareholders' meeting on the grounds that there was a breach of the rules concerning the manner in which the notice of the meeting must be provided (LSC, Article 204.3(a)). In the instant case, it is unclear whether Family Company B failed to give notice to shareholder B or whether the latter did not receive notice of the meeting despite Family Company B complying with the notice rules. However, the general shareholders' meeting of Family Company B could be treated as a universal general meeting, which is regulated by Article 178 of the LSC. This provision stipulates that general shareholders' meetings at which all the share capital of the company is present/represented and in which those present accept by unanimity the business of the meeting, are validly constituted, without the need of any prior notice. The use of universal shareholders' meetings by SAs for the adoption of agreements concerning mergers is also accepted (LMESM, Article 42; LSC, Article 178.1).[54] Thus, if these elements were

---

[49] Ley 3/2009, de 3 de abril, sobre Modificaciones Estructurales de las Sociedades Mercantiles.

[50] See MA Martí, *La Nulidad de la Fusión de Sociedades* (Cizur Menor (Navarra), Aranzadi, 2002) 90.

[51] See eg Ribas Ferrer, *El deber de lealtad del administrador de sociedades* (n 48) 328–43; and J Costas Comesaña, *El deber de abstención del socio en las votaciones* (Valencia, Tirant lo Blanch, 1999) 48–53.

[52] See Costas Comesaña, *El deber de abstención del socio en las votaciones* (n 51) 53.

[53] On challengeable agreements, see A Briganty Arencibia, 'Notas sobre la impugnación de acuerdos sociales: su problemática' in *Abogados del Estado, Elementos Esenciales del Derecho Societario* (11–13 May 2004), Centro de Estudios Jurídicos, Madrid.

[54] In this regard, see also J Soria Sorjús, 'Consideraciones sobre el procedimiento de fusión de sociedades anónimas acordadas en junta universal', *Diario La Ley*, 2011, N° 7680.

present in this case, shareholder B would have no legal grounds to challenge the agreement regarding the merger.

Turning to shareholders C, D and E, we are told that they were unable to become shareholders of Family Company A under the approved share exchange ratio. Spanish law does not explicitly regulate such a situation and therefore there is some debate on this issue. Some scholars in the field are of the view that in such cases there are specific conditions that have to be respected by majority shareholders, directors and the company.[55] The first prerequisite is that the majority must be able to provide justification for the merger being in the interests of the company and that the issue to be resolved is of a technical nature – so as to avoid the use of the exchange ratio as an instrument designed to exclude some shareholders from the absorbing company. This has to be explained and justified by the directors of the companies that participate in the merger in their report concerning the merger programme (LMESM, Article 33).[56] The second condition is that the company must offer the affected shareholders all possible alternatives in order to avoid their exclusion – these solutions also have to be included by the directors in their report on the merger programme.[57] Commentators are also of the view that additional conditions are applicable when it is clear that the only possible option is the exclusion of the concerned shareholders. In particular, justification would need to be given for the proposition that the viability of the company would be threatened if the merger did not proceed. If that were to be the case and some shareholders were finally to be excluded, they would have the right to receive compensation.[58] Therefore, the possibilities of shareholders C, D, and E being able to challenge the merger on the ground of the unfairness of the share exchange ratio would very much depend on whether the aforementioned criteria were satisfied or not as the case may be. In any event, arbitrary or abusive decisions by majority shareholders concerning the exchange ratio would result in the decision on the merger being found to be challengeable.[59]

E. The Netherlands[60]

i. Action by Minority Shareholder for Not Having Received a Reasonable Dividend

For public limited liability companies (NV) it is stated that the company's profits are for the benefit of the shareholders, unless otherwise provided for in the articles

---

[55] See A Pérez Troya, *La tutela del accionista en la fusión de sociedades* (Madrid, Civitas, 1998) 225–28. The same author has developed a very comprehensive study about the determination of the share exchange ratio in merger processes in A Perez Troya, *La determinación del tipo de canje en la fusión de sociedades* (Madrid, Marcial Pons, 1998).

[56] A Pérez Troya, *La determinación del tipo de canje en la fusión de sociedades* (Madrid, Marcial Pons, 1998) 227.

[57] Ibid, 227–28.

[58] Ibid, 228.

[59] Whether such an agreement would be void or voidable is debated among scholars; in this regard, see Martí, *La Nulidad de la Fusión de Sociedades* (n 50) 95–96.

[60] Abbreviations: DCC = Dutch Civil Code; HR = Hoge Raad = Dutch Supreme Court; OK = Ondernemingskamer = Enterprise Chamber; Rb. = Rechtbank = District Court. An unofficial translation of Dutch company law as incorporated in bk 2 of the Dutch Civil Code can be found at www.dutchcivillaw.com/civilcodebook022.htm.

of association.[61] In most cases the articles of association include a clause that it is the general meeting that decides on the allocation of profits. For private limited liability companies (BV) the relevant legislation states that the general meeting decides on the allocation of the profits, unless the articles of association shift this power to another corporate body.[62] Therefore, in practice, generally in both private and public companies the general meeting will decide on the allocation of the profits, unless a more elaborate system for the allocation of profits between shareholders is included in the articles of association or a shareholders' agreement.

As a general rule, the shareholders are allowed to vote in their own interests[63] and the minority shareholders should accept the consequences of resolutions that are the result of the voting of the majority shareholders.[64] However, majority shareholders need to act reasonably and fairly towards the minority shareholders[65] and are not allowed to abuse their power as a majority shareholder.[66] The court will need to take a reserved approach when assessing the dividend policy of a company as de facto set out by the majority shareholder and should judge whether the interests of the involved stakeholders have been properly taken into account when formulating the dividend policy.[67] There is also specific case law governing the situation in which the majority shareholder stipulates the dividend policies and this is to the detriment of the minority shareholder. The Supreme Court has ruled that if a majority shareholder de facto withholds a reasonable dividend from minority shareholders over a number of years without there being a justification for this policy in the interests of the company itself, this can be unlawful because the minority shareholders should receive a reasonable dividend if possible.[68] Additionally, such a resolution of the shareholders can also be in violation of the reasonableness and fairness test and therefore be voidable. In one case, the Court of Appeal of Arnhem even decided on behalf of the general meeting/company what dividend payments the minority shareholders should receive instead.[69]

Minority shareholder A of Family Company B therefore has a right to a reasonable dividend, if Family Company B is financially strong enough to distribute dividends and there is no important reason preventing the company from distributing a reasonable dividend in the company's interests. This is possible but not certain since the case does not mention these facts and any assessment will also depend on considerations of reasonableness and fairness. The fact that the other shareholders do not need dividends since they receive money from the company by means of management fees is not a valid reason to preclude minority shareholder A from receiving dividend payments.

---

[61] DCC, Art 2:105-1.

[62] DCC, Art 2:216-1.

[63] HR 30 June 1944, *NJ* 1944/465 (*Wennex*); HR 13 November 1959, *NJ* 1960/472 (*Melchers*); HR 19 February 1960, *NJ* 1960/472 (*Aurora*).

[64] HR 17 May 1991, *NJ* 1991/645, with a note by Maeijer (*Lampe/Tonnema*).

[65] DCC, Art 2:8.

[66] DCC, Art 3:13.

[67] HR 12 July 2013, ECLI:HR:2013:BZ9145.

[68] HR 9 July 1990, *NJ* 1991/51, with a note by Maeijer (*Sluis*).

[69] Hof Arnhem 26 May 1992, *NJ* 1993/182, with a note by Maeijer (*Uniwest*).

ii. Conflict-of-Interest Shareholder

As stated above, the general rule is that shareholders are allowed to vote in their own interests. Moreover, Dutch law has no mandatory rules with regard to shareholders that have a conflict of interest. These shareholders are allowed to vote just as other shareholders and can even vote in accordance with their conflicting interest. However, the acts of the shareholder with a conflicting interest will still have to be reasonable and fair and should not constitute an abuse of power. Therefore, in practice, shareholders could be limited in their freedom if this would lead to an unreasonable result for other stakeholders.

iii. Convening a General Meeting and Taking Binding Resolutions

Public and private companies have different rules with regard to the way in which a general meeting is convened. There are also differences in legislation with regard to the minimum period for the issuance of a notice convening a general meeting. For public companies, it is stated that if no notice has been sent to the shareholders (in time), no legally valid resolutions can be passed by the general meeting unless the resolution is passed with a unanimous vote at the general meeting where the entire issued share capital is present.[70] For private companies a different rule applies. If no notice has been sent to the shareholders (in time), no legally valid resolutions can be passed by the general meeting unless two conditions are satisfied. First, that all persons entitled to attend the general meeting have approved decisions to be taken; and secondly, that the directors and supervisory directors have been provided with the opportunity to give their advice and views on the resolutions to be passed before the actual decision is taken.[71] If a resolution is passed without correctly applying these rules, the resolution is voidable on the basis of Article 2:15, paragraph 1, sub a DCC.

iv. Opposing a Merger

The general meetings of the merging companies need to approve a merger by means of a shareholder resolution.[72] If no lawful resolution is passed, any party with a legitimate interest can request the courts to nullify the merger.[73] As discussed above, in the case of the resolutions passed by the general meetings of these companies, these resolutions might very well be voidable, because the general meetings were not convened correctly (although it will ultimately depend on what happens during the general meeting). Moreover, if the court decides not to nullify the merger notwithstanding that there are grounds to nullify it, the court has the power to make an order that the claimant should be adequately compensated for any damages.[74]

The shareholders in the merging companies will become shareholders in the acquiring company in accordance with their former share interest and the share

---

[70] DCC, Art 2:115.
[71] DCC, Art 2:225.
[72] DCC, Art 2:317-1.
[73] DCC, Art 2:323-1.
[74] DCC, Art 2:323-5.

exchange ratio.[75] The starting point is therefore that the shareholders in the merging companies will become shareholders in the merged company.[76] In the case of a national merger (between two companies incorporated in the Netherlands), it is not possible to prevent a shareholder from receiving shares in the merged company and to provide the exiting shareholder with cash instead, unless there are very specific circumstances.[77] One of these circumstances arises when certain shareholders are unable to receive shares, as a result of the share exchange ratio of the merger.[78] This seems to be the case for this merger, since shareholders C, D and E only hold 18 shares each. These shareholders will therefore in principle only have a right to cash instead of shares. However, if the merger is solely focused on ousting the minority shareholders, such a merger could be in violation of the requirements of the reasonableness and fairness test.[79] In that case the minority shareholders could try to annul the shareholder resolution approving the merger on the ground that it is contrary to the reasonableness and fairness test.[80] This in turn could give the minority shareholders grounds to request the court to annul the entire merger.[81] The case scenario states that there are valid business reasons for the merger, but it gives no information as to whether a different share exchange ratio could have been used. If this share exchange ratio was used for the sole purpose of ousting the minority shareholders, it could lead to the shareholder resolution approving the merger being treated as voidable. In such a case, the merger would therefore be voidable.

F. Finland

i. Claim by a Minority Shareholder for Not Having Received a Dividend in 10 Years

Minority shareholder rights with regard to the payment of dividends are protected by virtue of chapter 13, section 7(1) of the Companies Act 2006 (CA) (the so-called minority dividend). Shareholders with at least 10 per cent of all shares can make a demand at the ordinary general meeting that at least half of the profits earned in the financial period, less the amount not to be distributed under the articles of association, are distributed as dividends. Minority dividends in excess of 8 per cent of the equity of the company are not allowed. Moreover, the distribution of profits is not possible without creditors' consent if it would put the company's solvency at risk.[82]

---

[75] DCC, Art 2:331-2.

[76] G van Solinge and MP Nieuwe Weme, *Mr. C. Assers Handleiding tot de beoefening van het Nederlands Burgerlijk Recht. 2. Rechtspersonenrecht.Deel IIa. NV en BV. Oprichting, vermogen en aandelen* (Deventer, Kluwer, 2013) 445.

[77] See DCC, Arts 2:311-2; 2:325-4; 2:333-1; 2:310-4. Art 2:333-3; 2:333-2; 2:333a; 2:330a; 2:333h-3 for the exceptions.

[78] DCC, Art 2:311-2.

[79] HR 14 September 2007, *NJ* 2007/610, with a note by Maeijer (*Versatel I*); Hof Amsterdam (OK) 20 December 2007, *JOR* 2008/36, with a note by Van der Korst (*Shell*).

[80] DCC, Art 2:15-1 under b.

[81] DCC, Art 2:323.

[82] See the Finnish solution in ch 7, above, for the general conditions for the distribution of assets, including the solvency test.

In the present case, the minority shareholders have failed to demand the distribution of the minority dividend for each fiscal year. A claim for damages for a failure to distribute during the last ten years is therefore unlikely to succeed.

ii. Minority Shareholders' Action against the Merger

a. Claim for Annulment of the Merger

The resolution to merge is taken by the general meeting and requires a majority of two-thirds of the votes cast and shares represented at the meeting.[83] The resolution may be rejected or deemed void on the same grounds as other resolutions of the general meeting. The time limit for rejection is three months from the date of the general meeting. A void resolution is not subject to said time limit. However, an action relating to a merger resolution may not be brought once six months have passed from registration of the merger.[84]

A resolution of the general meeting may be challenged where: (i) the procedural provisions in the CA or the articles of association have been breached and the breach may have had an impact on the contents of the resolution or on a shareholder's rights; or (ii) the resolutions violate substantive provisions of the CA or the articles of association. A resolution is deemed void, for example, where no notice of the general meeting has been delivered or the resolution is clearly contrary to the principle of equal treatment.[85]

It is very rare that a conflict of interest between a shareholder and other shareholders (or the company) would render a resolution of the general meeting voidable. A shareholder may vote for resolutions in line with their own financial interests, such as in the present case, without an obligation to be loyal to other shareholders. A shareholder may also vote in matters concerning agreements between the shareholder and the company.[86] Restrictions on a shareholder's right to vote due to a conflict of interest concern only the instances provided in chapter 5, section 14 of the CA, namely civil actions that the company brings against the shareholder, the discharge of the shareholder from liability in damages and from other liability towards the company. Therefore, shareholder A's claim in this case would not succeed.

It should be noted that a shareholder of the merging company opposing the merger may, at the general meeting resolving on the merger, demand that his or her shares are redeemed. An opportunity to make this demand before the resolution on the merger should be reserved for the shareholders.

---

[83] CA, c 16, s 9 and c 5, s 27.
[84] CA, c 21, ss 1 and 2.
[85] CA, c 21, ss 1 and 2 see the Finnish solution in ch 10 at II I, below.
[86] J Mähönen and S Villa, *Osakeyhtiö I – Yleiset opit* (Helsinki, Talentum, 2015) 413–14 find that while shareholders generally are not bound by a duty of loyalty to other shareholders, a majority shareholder might owe obligations to other shareholders that are similar to those of the directors. They base their view on the wording of the principle of equal treatment of shareholders in c 1, s 7. However, this view has not been affirmed by case law and the current position is that shareholders are free to act as they wish.

b. Failure to Receive Notice

In the context of a merger, the provisions governing the notices of meetings are stricter than usual. In addition to the provisions of the articles of association governing the notice, every shareholder should receive notice of the general meeting by a letter sent to the shareholder's known address.[87] If the addresses of all the shareholders are unknown, the notice must also be published in the Official Gazette. The notice may not be sent before the merger plan has been registered. In the present case, shareholder B has not received any notice, neither by letter nor, it seems, via the Official Gazette.[88]

As stated above, if the notice is not delivered, the resolution passed by the general meeting might be treated as void.[89] Even if the resolution is void, a claim against a merger resolution must be brought within six months of the registration of the merger, otherwise the resolution will stand.

However, a matter that has not been dealt with in accordance with the procedural provisions of the CA or the articles of association may only be resolved if the shareholders, who are affected by the omission, consent to the resolution being made.[90] In the present case, the general meeting has taken place, all shareholders have participated and none of the shareholders have pled during the general meeting that the general meeting was summoned in an unlawful manner. Thus, the shareholders may not challenge the merger resolutions afterwards and plead that the general meeting was not summoned in accordance with the CA.[91]

c. Exclusion as a Shareholder from the Company as a Result of the Merger

The minority shareholders C, D and E complain that the share exchange ratio deprived them of their right to become shareholders of the surviving company. It is unlikely that this would lead to the annulment of the merger. In some situations, the minority shareholders receiving only cash as a result of the merger may constitute a breach of the duty of equal treatment of shareholders. This duty stipulates that all shares carry the same rights in the company unless the articles of association provide otherwise. The general meeting or the board may not pass resolutions or other measures that are conducive to conferring, for example, an undue benefit to a shareholder at the expense of another.[92] The equal treatment of the shareholders in a merger is protected by the requirements to draw up a detailed merger plan. Amongst other requirements, the share exchange ratio and the nature of the consideration for the merger must be provided in detail in the merger plan.[93] It is generally accepted that some shareholders may receive cash only given that their shareholdings are small enough to receive only

---

[87] CA, c 16, s 10.

[88] The case scenario does not reveal whether the shareholder has informed the company of a possible change of address or whether the merger plan was published in the Official Gazette, but it is assumed that neither of these has taken place.

[89] CA, c 21, s 2.

[90] CA, c 5, s 15.

[91] J Kyläkallio, O Iirola and K Kyläkallio, *Osakeyhtiö I* (Helsinki, Edita, 2015) 454.

[92] CA, c 1, s 7.

[93] Explanatory notes of the CA, Hallituksen esitys 109/2005, 149.

a fraction of a share in the surviving company as in this case. As stated above, in mergers the main remedy for the minority shareholders is the right to initiate the redemption procedure and have their shares redeemed at a fair price.

G. Poland

i. Action by a Minority Shareholder for Not Having Received a Dividend for 10 Years

Like other EU Member States, Polish law (Commercial Companies Code (CCC)) provides for the protection of minority shareholders against abuses perpetrated by the majority shareholders. However, the case law which has considered this issue has not been particularly illuminating to date.

A minority shareholder may, depending on the cause of the suit, bring an action to revoke a resolution where it is contrary to the company's articles or good practice and prejudicial to the interests of the company or intended to wrong a shareholder (CCC, Article 422). Furthermore, a minority shareholder may bring an action to have an unlawful resolution of the shareholders' meeting pronounced invalid (CCC, Article 425). In light of the facts of the hypothetical case, the first possibility – namely the action to revoke the merger resolution – would appear to be the most suitable.

The phrase 'prejudicial to the interest of the company' is very broad. Generally, it encompasses everything that may cause damage to the company's assets, including the draining of financial resources from a subsidiary by a dominant company or majority shareholder. Another phrase, 'intended to wrong a shareholder', is also very broad. For example, the failure to pay dividends where the company has ample liquidity may be regarded as intended to wrong a shareholder. However, it must be stressed that there is no need to prove that a particular shareholder suffered damage; rather, it is enough to demonstrate that this was the objective behind the resolution.

Generally, the success of this action depends on whether sufficient proof is presented by the shareholder as the *onus probandi* is on the shareholder in any challenge to revoke such a resolution. On the basis of facts given, the challenge may turn out to be successful.

ii. Action by Minority Shareholders against the Merger

a. Action for Annulment of the Merger

Shareholder A of Family Company B has decided to sue to obtain a court order annulling the merger on the ground that Family Company A, although authorised by law to vote on the merger, had a conflict of interest and should have refrained from voting. According to Article 509 of the CCC, subsequent to the date of the merger, any action to set aside or secure a declaration of invalidity of a resolution of a shareholder's meeting or general meeting of each of the merging companies that has been adopted by a three-quarters majority of votes representing at least half of the initial capital of the company may be only brought against the absorbing/bidder company or any newly formed company, unless more stringent terms are provided by the company's articles. An action to revoke or declare a merger invalid is subject to a shorter statutory limitation period of one month, which runs from the date of adoption of the resolution (CCC, Article 509, item 2).

Like the position in French law, there is no provision in the CCC which prohibits the company from voting on the merger on the basis of a possible conflict of interest. A court reviewing such a case would probably refuse to declare such a resolution invalid as long as it is not detrimental to the minority shareholders. There is not a great deal of case law on this subject. This may be attributable to the detailed procedure for mergers set forth in the CCC. According to Article 498 of the CCC, a plan for the merger of companies requires an agreement between the merging companies. Furthermore, such a plan should contain inter alia the ratio of exchange of shares of the target company for shares of the bidding company. The merger plan must be submitted to the registration court, which appoints an expert to examine the merger plan with regard to its viability and procedural regularity. The expert draws up a detailed opinion and submits it to the registration court. The opinion contains a statement as to whether the share exchange ratio has been determined appropriately. Furthermore, the merger resolution must contain agreement to the merger plan. Thus, the share exchange ratio is subject to an examination by an independent court.

Finally, minority shareholders can raise an action against the absorbing/bidder company on the basis of Article 509 in order to set aside or to seek a declaration that a resolution approving the merger is invalid where they claim that the adoption of the merger resolution amounted to an abuse of their rights. An action to revoke the merger resolution may be brought by a shareholder who voted against the resolution and demanded that his or her objection be put on record when the resolution was adopted. In addition, a shareholder who was unduly prevented from participating in the general meeting is also entitled to raise an action to revoke the merger resolution.

b. Failure to Receive Notice

Shareholder B of Family Company B complains that he did not receive notice of the extraordinary shareholders' meeting to consider the approval of the merger, although he was able to participate since he heard about the meeting from another shareholder.

In the case of public companies, Article 422 of the CCC provides that in the event of a general meeting being improperly summoned, a shareholder has a right to bring an action to revoke the resolutions passed at that general meeting. Therefore, since shareholder B has not received notice of the extraordinary shareholders' meeting, this provision would be applicable. However, there is an exception: the same article adds that a shareholder may not bring an action to revoke the resolution of a general meeting where he or she was absent from the general meeting. Therefore, despite the procedural irregularity, B would be unsuccessful in any action he might bring that seeks the revocation of the shareholders' meeting.

c. Exclusion as a Shareholder from the Company as a Result of the Merger

It should be mentioned that Polish law requires a higher majority than 70 per cent in order to approve a merger. According to Article 506, section 1 of the CCC, a merger of companies requires a resolution of a shareholders' meeting or general meeting of each of the merging companies, adopted by a three-quarters majority of votes representing at least half of the initial capital of the company, unless more stringent terms are provided by the company's articles. Family Company A has a controlling shareholding in Family Company B, but only to the extent of 70 per cent of the latter's share capital. Therefore, in order to finalise the merger with Family Company B, Family Company A would need to secure the votes of at least another 5 per cent of Family Company B's shareholders. Shareholders C, D and E held 18 shares each. However, there is no further information in the hypothetical case as to how much those shares are when expressed as a percentage of the company's overall share capital.

If Family Company A had 75 per cent of the votes in Family Company B, the solution to the case would be as follows: in terms of Article 498 of the CCC, a merger plan must be prepared consisting, inter alia, of the share exchange ratio of the absorbed company for shares of the absorbing company and, if applicable, the amount of any additional payments. According to Article 500, section 1 of the CCC, a merger plan must be submitted to the registration court of the merging companies together with the merger application. As noted above, Article 502, section 2 of the CCC directs that the merger plan must then be examined by an expert as to its viability and procedural regularity. The registration court with jurisdiction in the seat of the absorbing company must appoint the expert upon a joint request of the companies subject to the merger. The expert, within the period specified by the court, which must be no longer than two months from the date of his or her appointment, is bound to draw up a detailed written opinion and submit it together with the merger plan to the registration court and the management boards of the merging companies. The opinion must contain at least: (i) a statement whether the share exchange ratio, referred to in Article 499, section 1, sub-section 2, was determined appropriately; (ii) an indication of the method or methods used for determining the share exchange ratio proposed in the plan together with an evaluation of the grounds for their application; and (iii) an indication of particular difficulties connected with the valuation of the shares of the merging companies. In the hypothetical case, we are told that the share exchange ratio was approved by the auditors. However, there is no further information as to whether the auditors were appointed by the registered court or merely chosen by the management boards. Polish law would find that the merger would be dismissed by the registered court if the expert's opinion on the share exchange ratio was negative. It must be stressed that according to Article 493, section 2 of the CCC, the merger will be completed on the day it is entered into the register with jurisdiction in the seat of the absorbing/bidding company (day of merger). Such entry shall result in the removal of the absorbed/target company.

Assuming, however, that the merger was approved by the court, there will be no possibility for the minority shareholders to annul the merger resolution on the basis of a challenge to the share exchange ratio. According to Article 509, section 1 of the CCC, subsequent to the date of completion of the merger, any legal action to set aside the merger resolution or seeking a declaration of its invalidity may be brought only against the absorbing company. However, Article 509, section 2 supplements this provision by adding that the merger resolution may not be challenged if the only objection to it concerns the appropriateness of the share exchange ratio referred to in Article 499, section 1, sub-section 2. However, this does not limit the right of a minority shareholder to seek redress in accordance with the general rules of company law.

H. Latvia

i. Action by a Minority Shareholder for Not Having Received a Dividend for 10 Years

The Latvian law dealing with public companies set out in the Commercial Code[94] does not prescribe a general prohibition on the sustained failure to pay dividends out of profits, as found in § 254 of the German AktG.[95] The only provision we find is one which stipulates that 'a decision of the shareholders that the dividends ... are left at the disposal of the company is void' (Commercial Code, section 161(7)). This is not the position in the hypothetical case, however, since no dividends were to be paid out at all and the complaint of the minority shareholder is directed against that failure.

The conduct of the majority shareholders could enable the minority shareholders to sue pursuant to section 286(1)(no 1) of the Commercial Code. This directs that a court may declare a decision taken by a meeting of the shareholders as void if it contradicts commercial morality: the conduct of the majority shareholders constitutes a form of coercion designed to force the sale of the shareholdings of the minority shareholders and this clearly contravenes acceptable moral standards of commercial practice and tradition in Latvian law.

The right to bring a legal action in court on such a basis may be exercised by any shareholder if he or she voted against the disputed decision and requested that this be recorded in the minutes or, if the voting was conducted by a secret ballot, if he or she has objected to the disputed decision and requested that this be recorded in the minutes (Commercial Code, section 287(1)(no 2)). In the hypothetical case, the consequences of a minority shareholder's failure to request that his or her vote against the disputed decision be recorded in the minutes must be determined. In principle, the record in the minutes is purely for evidential purposes in the sense that it enables a shareholder to prove how he or she voted. However, any difficulty in providing evidence of his or her objection in the minutes does not affect the minority shareholder's substantive right to bring an action to challenge the failure to pay dividends, since it is acceptable for other forms of evidence to be provided. However, there is an exception where the recording of any objection is a statutory requirement, in which case a minority shareholder would have to show that both conditions are fulfilled. If the shareholder fails to fulfil only one of the conditions, an action may not be raised. Although it can be debated whether such an interpretation is in line with the aims of the relevant provision, the wording of the law clearly requires both the vote and its recording. Therefore, legal proceedings may not be brought.

[94] Likums 'Komerclikums', Latvijas Vēstnesis 158/160 (2069/2071), 13 April 2000.
[95] See also the German solution at B, above.

ii. Action by Minority Shareholders against the Merger

a. Action for Annulment of the Merger

Family Company A may not be prohibited from taking part in the vote concerning the mergers of the two companies. The statutorily prescribed cases for the restriction of voting rights in public companies are laid down in section 280 of the Commercial Code. This stipulates that a shareholder has no voting rights if he or she is a member of the council or of the board of directors, a liquidator, an auditor or a company controller and the subject of the resolution is that he or she should be removed, that the shareholders have no confidence in him or her, that an action ought to be raised against him or her, that the company be entitled to exercise certain rights against him or her, or that he or she be released from his or her obligations or liability towards the company. However, none of these circumstances are relevant in the context of the hypothetical case and the end result is that Family Company A was entitled to participate in the vote.

b. Failure to Receive Notice

There was a failure to comply with the rules on providing advance notice of a meeting of the shareholders of a public company in section 273(1) of the Commercial Code, whereby such a meeting must be intimated not later than 30 days prior to the planned meeting of shareholders. The impact of this failure is that a court may declare any resolutions of the general meeting of shareholders as void in terms of section 286(1)(no 4) of the Commercial Code. However, a shareholder who was present at the general meeting of shareholders is not entitled to bring a legal challenge in court – only those shareholders who were not present may do so (Commercial Code, section 287(3)). Hence, shareholder B of Family Company B would not be entitled to challenge the merger vote.[96]

c. Exclusion as a Shareholder from the Company as a Result of the Merger

Latvian law neither prohibits nor authorises the exclusion of unwanted shareholders from a newly merged public company. Since the principle of autonomy of the parties to enter into contracts is recognised in Latvia, such conduct is permitted. A public company may not be forced to accept a shareholder against its interests and wishes. Furthermore, conduct of this nature on the part of the majority shareholder does not contravene the rules on the reorganisation of companies in terms of sections 334, 343, 346 and 284 of the Commercial Code. The issue of whether shareholders C, D, and E may sue for damages requires additional information and evidence: according to the general principles for raising legal proceedings for compensation for damages,[97] there must be evidence of negligence on the part of the parties it is alleged have breached a legal requirement, resulting in losses.

---

[96] However, the entitlement to bring an action is permitted in the case of the supervisory board and the board of directors by virtue of s 287(1) of the Commercial Code.
[97] See also ch 2, above.

I. The UK[98]

i. Action by a Minority Shareholder for Not Having Received a Dividend for 10 Years

In terms of UK company law, shareholders have no automatic right to be paid a dividend. A company can choose whether to make a payment and it may set the amount of that payment.[99] When voting on the ordinary resolution to declare a dividend, the majority shareholders owe no duty or obligation to the minority shareholders and may vote in accordance with their own self-interest.[100] The payment of a satisfactory level of remuneration in lieu of dividends to those shareholders who hold senior positions in Family Company B is prima facie lawful since Family Company A owns 70 per cent of the share capital of Family Company B and therefore has sufficient power to defeat any ordinary resolution.

However, it is possible that the persistent non-payment of dividends may constitute 'unfair prejudice'[101] against the minority shareholder. The legal concept of 'unfair prejudice' is set out in section 994 of the CA 2006, which provides that a member of a company may petition the court on the basis that its 'affairs are being or have been conducted in a manner that is unfairly prejudicial to the interests of members generally or of some part of its members (including at least himself)'.[102] What is 'fair' or 'unfair' will depend on the context in which the term is being applied. However, it will generally entail some breach of the terms on which the shareholders had agreed in advance in writing, verbally or tacitly that the affairs of the company should be conducted and there will be cases in which equitable considerations make it unfair for those conducting the affairs of the company to rely upon their strict legal powers or rights.[103] Thus, 'unfair prejudice' may arise where powers and rights adumbrated in the company's articles of association or company law rules are applied in a manner which equity would regard as contrary to good faith.

In the present case, the minority shareholder A of Family Company B alleges that the directors' recommendation not to vote in favour of a dividend payment and Family Company A's failure to vote in favour of the ordinary resolution approving the payment of dividends amount to unfair prejudice.[104] In the absence of a satisfactory level of remuneration, minority shareholder A's only entitlement is to a payment of

---

[98] Abbreviations: CA 2006 (the Companies Act 2006); Model Articles (Model articles of association of private companies limited by shares (in reg 2 of and sch 1 to the Companies (Model Articles) Regulations 2008, SI 2008/3229), private companies limited by guarantee (in reg 3 of and sch 2 to the Companies (Model Articles) Regulations 2008, SI 2008/3229) and public limited companies (in reg 4 of and sch 3 to the Companies (Model Articles) Regulations 2008, SI 2008/3229).

[99] The internal procedures which a company has to follow if it decides to pay a dividend are set out in its articles of association, which are based on the Model Articles. See the analysis in the UK solution in ch 7 at II I, above.

[100] *Pender v Lushington* (1877) 6 Ch D 70 (Ch) 75–76 (Sir George Jessel MR); *NW Transportation Co. v Beatty* (1887) 12 App Cas 589 (PC) 593 (Sir Richard Baggallay); *Re Ringtower Holdings plc* (1989) 5 BCC 82 (Ch) 101 (Peter Gibson J); and *Re Astec (BSR) plc* [1999] BLC 59 (Ch) 83–85 (Parker J).

[101] *Re Sam Weller & Sons Ltd* [1990] Ch 682 (Ch) 693 (Peter Gibson J).

[102] CA 2006, s 994(1)(a).

[103] *O'Neill v Philips* [1999] 1 WLR 1092 (HL) 1098–99 (Lord Hoffmann).

[104] This is despite the fact that Family Company B has experienced a steady build-up in its profits and in the fair value of its shares during the 10-year period in which dividends have not been paid.

dividends which he is being denied by the majority. Thus, based on the authority of *Re Sam Weller & Sons Ltd*,[105] the activities of the directors and Family Company A clearly constitute 'unfair prejudice' as they 'unfairly' affect the interests of the minority shareholder to his financial prejudice.

Section 996 of the CA 2006 stipulates the remedies which are available to the successful minority shareholder A. The court 'may make such order as it thinks fit for giving relief in respect of the matters complained of'.[106] Furthermore, section 996(2)(b)(ii) of the CA 2006 sets out a non-exhaustive list of possible orders which can be made, including an order which requires the company 'to do an act that the petitioner has complained it has omitted to do', such as pay out a dividend to the successful minority shareholder, or an order for the buyout of the minority shareholder's shares.

ii. Action by Minority Shareholders against the Merger

In terms of UK law, if Family Company A wishes to merge with Family Company B, it will be required to acquire the shares of the 30 per cent minority shareholders of Family Company B. In order to achieve this, Family Company A will require the consent of the 30 per cent minority shareholders of Family Company B. If those minority shareholders refuse to consent to the merger, the majority cannot, under UK law, force the minority to sell their shares in order for the merger to proceed. However, all is not lost for Family Company A. Part 26 of the CA 2006 prescribes a procedure referred to as a 'compromise or scheme of arrangement' which can be used to achieve a merger.[107] Part 26 applies 'where a compromise or arrangement is proposed between a company and its creditors or any class of them or its members or any class of them'.[108] A compromise is only applicable where there is a dispute about the rights of members or creditors or a difficulty in enforcing those rights.[109] Meanwhile, a 'scheme of arrangement' (hereinafter 'scheme') is much wider than a 'compromise' and is not dependent on the existence of a dispute about members' or creditors' rights. Section 900 of the CA 2006 clarifies that a scheme can be used 'for the purpose of or in connection with a scheme for the amalgamation of two or more companies'.

There are three principal steps in a scheme. First, the scheme must be proposed between the company and its members and an application must be made to the court to summon meetings of all, or of classes, of the members or creditors to approve it.

---

[105] *Re Sam Weller & Sons Ltd* (n 101) at 693 (Peter Gibson J).
[106] CA 2006, s 996(1).
[107] For the differences between UK and US law on this topic, see M Ventoruzzo, 'Freeze-Outs: Transcontinental Analysis and Reform Proposals' (2010) 50 *Virginia Journal of International Law* 841, 900–02. In the case of a private limited company, there is also the option of using a so-called 'drag along' provision where this is provided for in the company's articles of association. This provision enables the majority of the shareholders (usually in excess of 75%) to accept an offer to buy their shares from the merging company and to force the remaining minority shareholders to also accept such an offer. As there is nothing to suggest that such a provision is contained in Family Company B's articles of association, this is not examined in more detail here. For an example of a 'drag-along' provision, see *Arbuthnott v Honeyman* [2015] EWCA Civ 536, [2015] 2 BCLC 627.
[108] CA 2006, s 895.
[109] *Sneath v Vallley Gold Ltd* [1893] 1 Ch 477 (Ch) 492 (Lindley LJ).

Second, meetings of the members and separate classes of shareholders must be held to seek approval of the scheme. A 75 per cent majority of the members of each class of members (as the case may be) must be obtained. Finally, the scheme is sanctioned by the court.[110] The court will only sanction a scheme if certain requirements are fulfilled. As Maugham J pointed out in *Re Dorman Long & Co*,[111] the courts have two duties when approving schemes:

> The first is to see that the resolutions are passed by the statutory majority in value and number ... at a meeting or meetings duly convened and held. The other duty is in the nature of a discretionary power ... What [the court has] to see is whether the proposal is such that an intelligent and honest man, a member of the class concerned and acting in respect of his interest, might reasonably approve.[112]

Moreover, in the case of *Re Equitable Life Assurance Society (No 2)*,[113] it was ruled that the court could withhold its sanction if there were 'some blot on the scheme' in the form of some material oversight or miscarriage.

Assuming that the above three matters are satisfied and the court is of the opinion that an adequate and effective explanatory statement accompanying the notice of the scheme meeting was sent to each member or creditor in compliance with section 897(1) and (2) of the CA 2006, the court will approve the scheme. For the purposes of this hypothetical case, it is assumed that (i) Family Company A has been able to persuade at least 5 per cent of the remaining shareholders of Family Company B to vote in favour of the scheme and (ii) that the court has sanctioned the scheme on the basis that there is nothing in the facts of the case to suggest that each of the above factors will not be satisfied. If the court approves the scheme, it becomes binding on the company and all members, and so any dissentients become bound by the scheme.[114] However, the merger in this case raises several difficult questions, as illustrated by the complaints brought by the minority shareholders, each of which will now be dealt with in turn.

a. Action for Annulment of the Merger

A shareholder owes no fiduciary duties to the company or other shareholders of the company.[115] As a result, a shareholder's vote on the scheme may be exercised in whatever way he or she sees fit.[116] The courts will only order that a member must vote in a particular way if they are seeking to restrain him or her from acting perversely.[117] This does not seem to be the case here. Thus, shareholder A will not be successful in obtaining a court order annulling the scheme merger on the ground that Family Company A had a conflict of interest and should have refrained from voting. However,

---

[110] See CA 2006, ss 896–99.

[111] *Re Dorman Long & Co* [1934] Ch 635.

[112] Ibid at 655–57. Author's annotations in square brackets.

[113] *Re Equitable Life Assurance Society (No 2)* [2002] EWHC 140 (Ch), [2002] BCC 319.

[114] CA 2006, s 899(3).

[115] See the UK solution in ch 6 at II J, above.

[116] In this respect, a shareholder differs from a director of a company: see *Northern Counties Securities Ltd v Jackson & Steeple Ltd* [1974] 1 WLR 1133 (Ch) 1144 (Walton LJ).

[117] See *Standard Chartered Bank Ltd v Walker* [1992] 1 WLR 561 (Ch) 566 (Vinelott J).

like the UK solution to the case in chapter 3, above, there is the possibility that Family Company A will be treated as a person connected to a director of Family Company B and so the directors' duties to avoid a conflict of interest in terms of section 175 of the CA 2006 may be engaged.

b. Failure to Receive Notice

Section 307(2) of the CA 2006 prescribes that the members of a public limited company such as Family Company B must be given at least 14 days' notice in the case of a general meeting which is not an annual general meeting. Every member of the company (whether entitled to vote or not) and every director is entitled to receive notice of the meeting.[118] Failure to give notice results in the outcome of the meeting being declared invalid. However, an accidental failure to give notice to one or more members does not affect the validity of the meeting or resolution.[119] In the context of a meeting to vote on a scheme, in the case of *Re Equitable Life Assurance Society (No 2)*,[120] it was held that the failure to send out a notice to the members could be categorised as a minor oversight and accidental and could be condoned by the court. In the present case, this means that shareholder B cannot object to the outcome of the general meeting of shareholders on the basis that he was not given notice of the meeting. In particular, his participation in the meeting indicates his acceptance of the decision.

c. Exclusion as a Shareholder from the Company as a Result of the Merger

If the merger proceeds on the basis of a court-approved scheme, the effect is that shareholders C, D and E will be unable to annul the merger on the ground that they were unjustifiably deprived of their status as shareholders. Any argument that the court-approved scheme sanctioning the forced sale of the shares of C, D and E in Family Company B to Family Company A amounts to a violation of Article 1 of the First Protocol of the Human Rights Act 1998 is unlikely to be successful. Article 1 of the First Protocol entitles C, D and E to the peaceful enjoyment of their possessions and prohibits the unlawful deprivation of their property. However, as noted in the case of *Re Equitable Life Assurance Society (No 2)*,[121] for Article 1 of the First Protocol to be engaged in the context of a court-approved scheme, it is necessary to demonstrate an arbitrary and unjust deprivation of property or some form of confiscation of property. Since the three shareholders have been given some consideration for their shares in good faith, it is unlikely that their objections will succeed. Overall, therefore, C, D and E

---

[118] CA 2006, s 310.

[119] CA 2006, s 313. The 'accidental omission' provision does not cover the deliberate omission to give notice to a troublesome member, nor does it cover a deliberate omission based on a mistaken belief that a member is not entitled to attend the meeting: *Musselwhite v Musselwhite & Son Ltd* [1962] Ch 964. However, if the omission is 'accidental', it applies even if the meeting is called to pass a special resolution: *Re West Canadian Collieries Ltd* [1962] Ch 370.

[120] *Re Equitable Life Assurance Society (No 2)* (n 113).

[121] Ibid.

are unlikely to succeed in having the merger annulled on the ground that they were unjustifiably deprived of their status as shareholders.

iii. Conclusion and Summary

Whilst the minority shareholder A is likely to be successful in persuading a court that the persistent failure of Family Company B to pay a dividend amounts to unfair prejudice in terms of section 994 of the CA 2006, it is extremely unlikely that shareholders A, B, C, D and E will be successful in challenging (i) the proceedings of the general meeting of the shareholders of Family Company B which approved the merger and/or (ii) the court-approved scheme of arrangement.

J. The US

i. Action by a Minority Shareholder for Not Having Received a Dividend for 10 Years

Traditional corporate law in the US envisages centralised management by the board of directors and majority rule by the shareholders when their vote is required.[122] Contrary to the assumptions of the hypothetical case, the decision whether to declare a dividend normally lies with the board of directors in the US. In a situation such as this one, the majority shareholder will have a very strong influence on any decision. The traditional assumption of majority rule, however, places a minority shareholder in a vulnerable position, especially in closely held corporations. This hypothetical case illustrates the plight of the minority shareholder. The majority shareholders, who also participate in the management of the corporation, have refused to declare dividends for a substantial amount of time, thereby eliminating one of the primary means by which the minority shareholders can capitalise on their financial investment in Family Company B. Furthermore, as the company's stock is non-listed, there is no readily available market for the minority shareholders to sell their shares, leaving them with very few options to exit.

In the US, a substantial divergence of approach exists amongst the states on how to respond to instances of alleged oppression by the majority shareholders against those in minority positions. Delaware has generally been unsympathetic to any claims of minority oppression. In the well-known case of *Nixon v Blackwell*, the Delaware Court refused to fashion a new judicial remedy for minority shareholders, instead relying on the minority shareholder's ability to bargain for protections in the shareholder agreement prior to buying into a minority position.[123] The Court felt that 'it would do violence to normal corporate practice and our corporation law to fashion an *ad hoc* ruling which would result in a court-imposed stockholder buyout for which the parties had not contracted'.[124] Consequently, such a claim would in all likelihood fail in Delaware.

[122] See, eg, Delaware General Corporation Law (DGCL), §§ 141 and 216.
[123] *Nixon v Blackwell*, 626 A 2d 1366 (Del 1993). For a more recent discussion, see *Blaustein v Lord Balt. Capital Corp.*, WL 1810956 (Del Ch 30 April 2013).
[124] Ibid.

Other states have been more hospitable to claims of minority oppression. In *Dodge v Ford Motor Co*,[125] an iconic American case, the Michigan Supreme Court ordered Ford Motor Company to pay dividends, stating that 'a refusal to declare and pay further dividends appears to be not an exercise of discretion on the part of the directors, but an arbitrary refusal to do what the circumstances required to be done'.[126] While *Dodge* is often read by legal academics as the source of the doctrine of shareholder primacy, recent commentary has started to coalesce around the idea that '*Dodge v. Ford Motor Co.* is best viewed as a minority oppression case'.[127] The implication of this reading is that judges will not routinely order the distribution of dividends, but will do so only when the withholding of dividends is part of a plan to oppress minority shareholders.

The Massachusetts courts have been at the forefront of minority oppression law for decades, holding that shareholders in close corporations owe each other a heightened fiduciary duty.[128] When a minority shareholder brings a claim of minority oppression in Massachusetts, the majority shareholders are given an opportunity to 'demonstrate a legitimate business purpose for this action'.[129] In evaluating the majority shareholders' actions, the majority 'must have a large measure of discretion, for example, in declaring or withholding dividends, deciding whether to merge or consolidate, establishing the salaries of corporate officers, dismissing directors with or without cause, and hiring and firing corporate employees'.[130] Once the majority has asserted its business purpose:

> It is open to the minority stockholders to demonstrate that the legitimate objective could have been achieved through an alternative course of action less harmful to the minority's interest. If called upon to settle the dispute, our courts must weigh the legitimate business purpose, if any, against the practicability of a less harmful alternative.[131]

Under the Massachusetts approach to minority oppression, the members of the board would have to demonstrate that their decision to withhold dividends had a legitimate business purpose. The burden would then pass to the minority shareholder to show that the business purpose could have been accomplished without withholding the dividend.

ii. Action by Minority Shareholders against the Merger

a. Action for Annulment of the Merger

Shareholder A argues that the merger should be annulled because Family Company A should have been precluded from voting owing to its conflicting interests in the transaction. However, the merger can be approved by a simple majority of the shareholders and there is no requirement that the shareholders be disinterested.[132] Nevertheless,

---

[125] *Dodge v Ford Motor Co*, 170 NW 668 (Mich 1919).
[126] Ibid, 683.
[127] DG Smith, 'The Shareholder Primacy Norm' (1998) 23 *Journal of Corporation Law* 277, 320.
[128] See, eg, *Donahue v Rodd Electotype Company of New England*, 328 NE 2d 505 (Mass 1975).
[129] *Wilkes v Springside Nursing Home, Inc*, 370 Mass 842 (Mass 1976).
[130] Ibid.
[131] Ibid.
[132] See, eg, DGCL, §§ 216 and 251(c).

minority shareholder A has two potential remedies. First, a minority shareholder who is dissatisfied with the merger consideration may pursue an appraisal of his or her shares from the Delaware Court of Chancery.[133] Second, a minority shareholder may sue a controlling shareholder for breach of fiduciary duty.

Most board actions (including a merger with a third party) are evaluated under the business judgment rule. Under this standard of review, challenges to a merger are usually dismissed unless the plaintiff can prove that the terms of the transaction are so egregious that no rational person in good faith could assert that such corporate action was fair and not as a result of the violation of the board's fiduciary duties.[134] However, when a controlling shareholder initiates a going-private transaction or acquires its subsidiary corporation, as contemplated in the hypothetical case, the controlling shareholder is subject to an 'uncompromising duty of loyalty'.[135] In evaluating this duty, the Delaware courts apply the 'entire fairness' standard, which:

> [H]as two basic aspects: fair dealing and fair price. The former embraces questions of when the transaction was timed, how it was initiated, structured, negotiated, disclosed to the directors, and how the approvals of the directors and the stockholders were obtained. The latter aspect of fairness relates to the economic and financial considerations of the proposed merger, including all relevant factors: assets, market value, earnings, future prospects, and any other elements that affect the intrinsic or inherent value of a company's stock.[136]

Controlling shareholders often use a special committee of independent directors and condition the transaction on a non-waivable majority-of-the-minority vote as a means of ensuring procedural fairness. These devices have the effect of shifting the burden of proof under the entire fairness standard to the plaintiffs,[137] but they do not change the standard of review from entire fairness to the business judgment rule.[138] The usual remedy in such cases is an award of damages rather than the annulment of the merger.

With the *MFW* decision of 2013, the Delaware courts finally created an avenue for controlling shareholders to structure a merger transaction with a subsidiary in a way that would give it the protection of the business judgment rule. The transaction must be subject to (i) negotiation and approval by a special committee of independent directors fully empowered to say no; and (ii) approval by an uncoerced, fully informed vote of a majority of the minority investors.[139] The rationale is that, in this situation, the process replicates the scheme of a non-conflicted merger under the DGCL, namely negotiation by a disinterested group of directors and approval by disinterested shareholders. The case thus incentivises controlling shareholders to structure bids with maximum protection for the minority, but also allows them to avoid the cost and uncertainty of litigation involving the entire fairness review.

---

[133] DGCL, § 262.

[134] For a discussion on the business judgment rule, see *Sinclair Oil Corp. v Levien*, 280 A. 2d. 717 (Del 1971); *Cede & Co. v Technicolor*, Inc. 634 A. 2d. 345 (Del 1993).

[135] *Weinberger v UOP, Inc*, 457 A 2d 701, 710 (Del 1983). For a discussion on the standard of review, see *Glassman v Unocal Exploration Corp.*, 777 A.2d 242 (Del 2001).

[136] Ibid, 711.

[137] *Kahn v Lynch Communications Systems, Inc*, 638 A 2d 1110 (Del 1994).

[138] *In re PNB Holding Co Shareholders Litig*, 2006 WL 2403999 (Del Ch 18 August 2006).

[139] See *In re MFW Shareholders Litigation*, 67 A.3d. 496 (Del Ch 2013); *Kahn v. M & F Worldwide Corp.*, 88 A.3d 635 (Del 2014) (affirming).

The end result of shareholder A challenging the merger will largely depend on the structure chosen for the merger by Family Company A and Family Company B's board. If the terms of the merger have the aforementioned structural protections built in, the merger will be subject to a more deferential business judgment standard review (in which case, shareholder A's challenge will most likely be dismissed). Otherwise, if the entire fairness review applies and a breach of fiduciary duty is found, damages will most likely be awarded. If shareholder A sued prior to the consummation of the merger, the court might issue an injunction against the transaction.

b. Failure to Receive Notice

All meetings which require the shareholders to vote on a matter or matters enjoin the company to give all shareholders written notice stating the place, date and hour of the meeting, the means of remote communication that can substitute for physical presence and 'in the case of a special meeting, the purpose or purposes for which the meeting is called'.[140] However, it is provided that the 'attendance of a person at a meeting shall constitute a waiver of notice of such meeting'.[141] Consequently, because all shareholders were in attendance, their presence at the meeting constitutes a waiver and defeats any claim by shareholder B that the shareholder meeting ought to be annulled owing to lack of notice.

c. Exclusion as a Shareholder from the Company as a Result of the Merger

The hypothetical case states that several minority shareholders of Family Company B were unable to participate in Family Company A because their shareholdings were below the share exchange rate of 20:1. Instead of shares in Family Company A, the shareholders have received cash. In the US, this transaction is called a 'cash-out merger' and is a legal transaction.

A typical cash-out merger involves a controlling shareholder, such as Family Company A, who announces a tender offer to acquire the shares of the minority shareholders at a premium. If the controlling shareholder can then acquire 90 per cent or more of the company's shares, the company can engage in a short-form merger and cash out the remaining minority shareholders at the tender offer price.[142] For a corporation listed on a national stock exchange, if the controlling shareholder is unable to acquire at least 90 per cent of the outstanding shares, the controlling shareholder must then persuade the board to adopt a resolution to approve the merger and then submit it for approval by a majority of the minority stockholders.[143] If the merger is so approved, the transaction will proceed.

However, section 203 of the DGCL's majority of the minority provisions do not apply to corporations such as Family Company B that are not listed on a national

---

[140] DGCL, § 222.
[141] DGCL, § 229.
[142] See, eg, DGCL, § 253.
[143] See DGCL, § 203(a).

exchange. Consequently, the only limitation on the controlling shareholder's actions is that the board of Family Company B's approval of the merger must comply with the board's 'uncompromising duty of loyalty' to the shareholders, as measured by the entire fairness standard.[144] When a merger involves two interested companies such as those presented in the hypothetical case, the corporations will often establish procedures to ensure that the transaction is nonetheless structured on an 'arm's length' basis.[145]

Resolution of this issue in the present case would require a detailed analysis of the dealings of the two corporations and the price offered for the minority shares. Based on the facts presented in the case, there is no reason to call into question the fairness of the merger unless any of the minority shareholders C, D or E could come forward with evidence of unfair dealings or an inadequate price for their shares.

K. South Africa

i. Action by a Minority Shareholder Challenging the Failure to Receive a Dividend for 10 Years

There is no definition of the term 'dividend' in the Companies Act 2008 but it will ordinarily refer to a distribution by a company of its profits. The Act draws no distinction between the distribution of profits and any other distributions. Distributions have to comply with the requirements set out in the Companies Act. The payment of a dividend qualifies as a distribution and must be in line with section 46.[146] It is important to note that no shareholder approval is required for a distribution.

Unless the Memorandum of Incorporation (MoI) provides otherwise, a company is not obliged to distribute its profits by way of dividends. When voting on the ordinary resolution to declare a dividend, the majority shareholders owe no duty or obligation to the minority shareholders and may vote in accordance with their own self-interest.[147] In this case, it is not stated whether the MoI makes provision for this. The process to distribute the dividend is thus a matter for internal management. However, when exercising the discretion to distribute a dividend, the directors have a fiduciary duty 'to consider the interests and legitimate expectations of the shareholders when deciding on how much must be distributed to them, and must bear in mind that one of the major benefits to members is the payment of dividends'.[148] The directors may be acting for an 'improper purpose' if they do not distribute a dividend which could, with entire propriety and commercial ease, be paid out to members.

---

[144] *Weinberger v UOP, Inc* (n 135).
[145] Ibid.
[146] See Case Study 7 above on 'distributions'.
[147] *Pender v Lushington* [1877] 6 Ch D 70 (Ch) 75–76 (Sir George Jessel MR) and *Re Astec (BSR) plc* [1999] BLC 59 (Ch) 83–85 (Parker J).
[148] *Ex Parte Glossop* [1988] 1 WLR 1068 (Ch).

However, it is possible that the persistent non-payment of dividends may constitute 'unfair prejudice'[149] against the minority shareholder. Section 163 is relevant in this regard, which determines that:

(1)   A shareholder or a director of a company may apply to a court for relief if—

(a)   any act or omission of the company, or a related person, has had a result that is oppressive or unfairly prejudicial to, or that unfairly disregards the interests of, the applicant;

(b)   the business of the company, or a related person, is being or has been carried on or conducted in a manner that is oppressive or unfairly prejudicial to, or that unfairly disregards the interests of, the applicant; or

(c)   the powers of a director or prescribed officer of the company, or a person related to the company, are being or have been exercised in a manner that is oppressive or unfairly prejudicial to, or that unfairly disregards the interests of, the applicant.

In order to succeed, the applicant will have to show that the conduct (in this case not declaring a dividend) was 'oppressive' or 'unfairly prejudicial' and thus unfairly disregarding the interests of the applicant.[150] The scope of section 163 is thus wide as 'interests' are also included, which has a much wider scope than the term 'rights'.[151] It is worth noting that 'the word "unfairly" qualifies the word "prejudicial"'.[152] 'Moreover, the word "unfairly", in this context, is used in the sense of "unreasonably".[153]

> The section thus contemplates that although an act or omission of a company, or the conduct of its affairs, may be prejudicial to a shareholder or shareholders, it may nevertheless not be unreasonable that this should be the case. Mere prejudice is therefore not sufficient, since the prejudice must be 'unfair'.[154]

Mere dissatisfaction with or disapproval of the conduct of a majority shareholder does not render the acts unfairly prejudicial. Instead, the conduct must be unreasonable or unethical and interests unfairly prejudiced must result in commercial unfairness affecting the applicant in his or her capacity as a dissenting minority.[155] The courts are, apparently, more inclined to intervene in cases between shareholders, especially in

---

[149] *Re Sam Weller & Sons Ltd* [1990] Ch 682 (Ch) 693 (Peter Gibson J).

[150] See PA Delport (ed), *Henochsberg on the Companies Act 71 of 2008* (Durban, LexisNexis, South Africa, Service issue November 2016) 572(2). 'Shareholder interests would appear to be intertwined with shareholder expectations. It does not appear that the shareholder expectations which are to be considered are those that a shareholder has as his own individual "wish list". It must be expectations which could be said to have been (or ought to have been considered as) part of the compact of the shareholders'. The basis of the 'legitimate expectations' can be an understanding based on an informal arrangement or understanding between shareholders and will be relevant if this can be proved as a fact (see *O'Neill and Another v Phillips and Others* [1999] 2 All ER 961 (HL); *McMillan NO v Pott* 2011 (1) SA 511 (WCC); *Peel v Hamon J&C Engineering (Pty) Ltd* [2013] 1 All SA 603 (GSJ), para 61; *Visser Sitrus (Pty) Ltd v Goede Hoop Sitrus (Pty) Ltd and Others* 2014 (5) SA 179 (WCC), para 61).

[151] *Utopia Vakansie-Oord Bpk v Du Plessis* 1974 (3) SA 148 A.

[152] Delport, *Henochsberg* (n 150) 573. According to case law on s 252, the predecessor of s 163.

[153] Ibid, 573. *Garden Province Investment v Aleph (Pty) Ltd* 1979 (2) SA 525 (D), 531.

[154] Delport, *Henochsberg* (n 150) 572. 'Oppression' as a separate ground, connotes an element at least of unfairness, if not something worse: *Visser Sitrus (Pty) Ltd v Goede Hoop Sitrus (Pty) Ltd and Others* 2014 (5) SA 179 (WCC), para 55.

[155] *Count Gotthard SA Pilati v Witfontein Game Farm (Pty) Ltd and Others* [2013] 2 All SA 190 (GNP), paras 19.5 and 17.12. See Delport, *Henochsberg* (n 150) 572(2).

the case of 'quasi-partnership' companies and also because the (majority) shareholders are not restricted by, for instance, fiduciary duties.

It might be easier to rely on a breach of duty in this case. The fact that no dividends were paid as satisfactory remuneration payments are made is relevant here. The Australian case of *Sanford v Sanford Courier Service Pty Ltd*[156] is relevant in this regard and will also be applicable in South African law. Here, it was held that the restriction of dividends was unfair. In this case, the minority was excluded from management and excessive remuneration paid to directors out of profits.

ii. Action by Minority Shareholders against the Merger

a. Action for Annulment of the Merger

Mergers, other than a consensual share swap between all the relevant shareholders, can only be implemented in terms of the procedures prescribed in sections 114 or 113 and 116 of the Companies Act 2008. These procedures must, however, be implemented in terms of section 115.

Section 114 regulates schemes of arrangement. This is an arrangement that is proposed between the company and shareholders, ie Family Company B and its shareholders. The shareholders in Family Company B (excluding Family Company A) will receive shares in Family Company A. The scheme of arrangement has two elements in that it must be an arrangement, as defined in the common law and in section 114(1), and it must be between the company and its shareholders. A third party, such as Company A can be part of the arrangement, but not to the exclusion of the 'primary' parties, being the company and its shareholders.[157] The scheme must be implemented in terms of section 115.

Section 115(2) requires a special resolution (75 per cent majority) from the company implementing the scheme and the quorum must equate to at least 25 per cent of the voting rights entitled to vote on that matter. However, votes of an acquiring party, a person related to an acquiring party or a person acting in concert with them must be excluded from calculating the quorum requirements and in determining the 75 per cent majority.[158] A related party is defined in section 2 and includes a holding company. Family Company A will therefore not be able to vote at the section 115 meeting and there will not be an actionable conflict of interest as in the facts above.

If the proposed resolution were approved by at least 85 per cent of the votes exercised on the proposal, any shareholder falling within the 15 per cent who voted against the resolution could, within five business days of the resolution, require the company to seek court approval. The company must then seek court approval within 10 business days after the vote, or treat the resolution as a 'nullity'.[159] Any person who voted against the resolution, which in effect would mean that if the dissenting vote was less than 15 per cent, can apply to the court for the resolution to be reviewed, if the court

---

[156] (1987) 5 ACLC 394.
[157] See Delport, *Henochsberg* (n 150) 410 and the authorities there cited.
[158] Companies Act 2008, s 115(4).
[159] Companies Act 2008, s 115(5).

grants that person leave in terms of section 115(6). The court would take into account the setting aside of the resolution in terms of section 115(7) if the resolution was manifestly unfair to any class of the holders of the company's securities, or the vote is materially tainted by a conflict of interest, inadequate disclosure, failure to comply with the Act, the MoI or rules of the company, or any other significant or material procedural irregularity.

The notice of the section 115 meeting must set out the requirements of section 115 as well as the rights of a shareholder in terms of section 164. Upon such notice, the shareholder can request the company to desist from putting the arrangement to the vote.[160] If the company proceeds nonetheless and the arrangement is approved in terms of section 115, the dissenting shareholder can require the company to acquire her shares in terms of section 164. The value will be the fair value as determined by the directors as at the date immediately preceding the resolution,[161] or the shareholder may approach the court to determine a fair value.[162]

The boards of directors of Company A and Company B can also propose a merger between the two companies in terms of sections 113 and 116, if the companies are solvent and liquid. However, the proposal must be approved by a special resolution of the shareholders of the companies. This process must also be implemented in terms of section 115. This would, however, not be possible as Company A would not be able to have a quorate meeting as 90 per cent of the shares are held by its holding company, which would make the 25 per cent quorum of 'non-related' parties impossible.[163]

b. Failure to Receive Notice

Every shareholder of a company is entitled to receive notice of a shareholders' meeting.[164] If there was a material defect in the giving of the notice of a sharehold- ers' meeting, the meeting may proceed, only if every person who is entitled to exercise voting rights in respect of any item on the meeting agenda is present at the meeting and votes to approve the ratification of the defective notice or the material defect relates to a matter on the agenda that can be separated.[165] *In casu*, there is thus a material defect and the notice was not valid unless all the shareholders at the meeting ratified it, which they did not do.

c. Exclusion as a Shareholder from the Company as a Result of the Merger

As stated above, there must be an arrangement that is between the company and its shareholders. In *Ex parte NBSA Centre* Ltd[166] a full bench of the High Court expressed

---

[160] Companies Act 2008, s 164(3).
[161] Companies Act 2008, s 164(11) and (16).
[162] Companies Act 2008, s 164(14).
[163] Companies Act 2008, s 115(2).
[164] Companies Act 2008, s 62. Section 1 defines a shareholders' meeting as a meeting of those holders of that company's issued securities who are entitled to exercise voting rights in relation to that matter at any meeting with respect to any particular matter concerning a company.
[165] Companies Act 2008, s 62(4) and (5).
[166] 1987 (2) SA 783 (T).

doubt, in effect, whether an expropriation for cash, other than an acquisition of shares by the company itself, can be an 'arrangement'. If these shareholders followed the requirements of section 164, ie by giving a written notice of objection to the resolution any time before the resolution is voted on, then any one of them can apply to court for review and the court can determine if the arrangement was manifestly unfair to any class of the holders of the company's securities, or the vote is materially tainted by a conflict of interest, inadequate disclosure, failure to comply with the Act, the MoI or rules of the company, or any other significant or material procedural irregularity. If the merger was implemented in terms of sections 113 and 116, then the shareholders will only have rights as minority shareholders in terms of the common law and/or section 163.[167]

L. Japan

i. The Right to Receive Dividends of a Surplus

A shareholder has the right to receive dividends of surplus profits[168] with respect to the shares he or she holds (CA, Article 105(1)(i)). However, this merely confers an entitlement to bring about a decision on how the profits of the company are applied.[169] Whenever a stock company intends to distribute a dividend of a surplus, it must take a decision on that matter by resolution at a shareholders' meeting (CA, Article 454(1)).

ii. The Majority Shareholders' Duties and Liability

The notion of majority shareholders owing duties and being potentially liable on such a ground to minority shareholders has not been accepted by the courts in Japan: such theories are considered too vague to be effective or are treated as involving the application of other principles of law.[170] Therefore, in the present case, it would be difficult for a minority shareholder of Family Company B to obtain redress from the majority shareholder in damages on the basis that the latter had failed to vote in favour of the payment of any dividend for a sustained period of time.

However, if a director entered into an irregular transaction which was detrimental to the company under pressure from a controlling shareholder which also harmed the company's interests, the director will be liable to the company for damages arising as a result thereof in terms of the CA, 423(1).[171]

iii. Approval of the Merger Agreement

Turning to the merger of the companies, both the absorbed company and the absorbing company must obtain the approval of the merger agreement by a resolution at

[167] See (i) above in respect of s 163.
[168] The notion of 'surplus' was introduced into the Companies Act 2006 (CA) as a starting point for the calculation of the distributable amount (CA, Art 461(2)(i)).
[169] Supreme Court, 24 January 1919, in *Minroku* 25, 30.
[170] K Egashira, *Kabushikigaisha-hô* [*Laws of Stock Corporations*] (7th edn, Tokyo, Yuhikaku, 2017) 449.
[171] Ibid.

a shareholders' meeting before the day immediately preceding the effective date of completion of the merger (CA, Articles 783(1) and 795(1)). An exception applies where the absorbing company's general meeting already owns 90 per cent or more of the shares of the absorbed company (CA, Article 796(3); Ordinance of the Ministry of Justice, Article 196). However, this is not the case here since Family Company A only held 70 per cent of the shares of Family Company B.

iv. Voting by a Person Having a Special Interest at the Shareholders' Meeting

A shareholder may raise a claim to revoke the resolution by filing an action within three months of the date of the resolution of the shareholders' meeting on the ground that the resolution was grossly improper. A resolution will be grossly improper if a shareholder having a special interest in that resolution exercises his or her voting right (CA, Article 831(1)(iii)). Therefore, in the present hypothetical case, minority shareholders of Family Company B will be entitled to sue to obtain a court order annulling the merger on the ground that Family Company A had a conflict of interest and should have refrained from voting at the shareholders' meeting.

v. Failure to Give Notice about the Extraordinary Shareholders' Meeting

In the present hypothetical case, there was a failure to notify all of the shareholders of Family Company B about the extraordinary shareholders' meeting. However, such a failure to give notice is irrelevant if all shareholders (including proxies) attend the shareholders' meeting and understand that the purpose of the meeting and the resolution of the meeting is within the scope or range of that purpose.[172]

vi. Appraisal Rights by Dissenting Shareholders

In the context of the implementation of an absorption-type merger, dissenting shareholders are entitled to demand that the absorbed stock company purchase, at a fair price, the shares held by such shareholders (CA, Articles 785–88). With regard to the rights of minority shareholders C, D and E to challenge the share exchange ratio, we turn to that issue at (viii), below.

vii. Proceedings to Invalidate Acts Concerning the Organisation of a Company

Proceedings which seek to invalidate an absorption-type merger of a company can only be raised by filing an action within six months of the completion date on which the merger became effective (CA, Article 828(1)). Such proceedings may be filed by a person who was a shareholder of the absorbed company at the completion date on which the merger became effective or by a shareholder of the absorbing company who did not give approval to the merger (CA, Article 828(2)).

---

[172] Supreme Court, 20 December 1985, in *Minshû* 39(8), 1869.

viii. Invalidity of the Merger and the Inequality of the Share Exchange Ratio

There is currently some debate as to whether a complaint about the share exchange ratio can be a cause of action justifying the invalidation of a merger. Some academic commentators have insisted that the inequality of the exchange ratio can supply a cause of action to invalidate the merger.[173] However, the courts have not followed this line on the ground that dissenting shareholders are entitled to demand that their shares be purchased.[174] Hence, in the present hypothetical case, it is unlikely that minority shareholders C, D and E of Family Company B will be able to successfully annul the merger on the ground that they were unjustifiably deprived of their status as shareholders. However, these dissenting minority shareholders can demand that their shares be purchased at a fair price.

ix. Demanding Cessation of Restructuring

In addition, under the 2014 Amendments of Companies Act, shareholders may demand a cessation of the restructuring,[175] unless it is a 'simple form restructuring'. This includes the rules that, if shareholders of a disappearing stock company are likely to suffer disadvantages, the shareholders may demand that the disappearing stock company cease an absorption-type merger in cases where (i) the absorption-type merger violates the applicable laws and regulations or the articles of incorporation; or (ii) the absorption-type merger is grossly improper in light of the financial status of the disappearing stock company or the surviving company.

In the present case, the minority shareholders of Family Company B will be entitled to demand that Company B cease the merger on the ground that the resolution governing the merger was grossly improper because Family Company A had a material conflict of interest.[176]

III. Conclusion

A. Introduction

The main conclusion to be drawn from this case relating to minority shareholders' protection regarding ordinary (lack of distribution of dividends) and extraordinary (merger) decisions of the general meeting is that there is a general convergence as to the solutions which would have been reached in the different jurisdictions. However, in certain areas, such as the failure to distribute a dividend, some jurisdictions are less protective (Delaware and Japan) than the average, while others seem more protective

---

[173] See, eg, H Kanda, *Kaisha-hô [Corporations Law]* (20th edn, Tokyo, Koubundou, 2018) 375.
[174] Tokyo High Court, 31 January 1990, in *Shiryôban Shôji Hômu* 77, 193.
[175] CA, Art 784-2, 796-2, 805-2.
[176] Egashira, *Kabushikigaisha-hô* (n 170) 892–93.

(Finland). In addition, a distinction does not appear to exist as to the level of protection between common law and civil law jurisdictions.

B. Action by a Minority Shareholder in Respect of the Failure to Receive a Dividend for 10 Years

Regarding the failure to distribute a dividend, which constitutes a typical form of abuse by controlling shareholders, most legal systems examined would allow an action to be filed with a reasonable prospect of success. The minority shareholders would probably prevail in nine jurisdictions either because of the application of a standard (France, Spain, Netherlands, Poland, Latvia, the UK, Massachusetts and South Africa) or a specific rule (Germany and Finland).[177] In two other jurisdictions, it is unlikely that the application of the standard would lead the minority shareholders to prevail, although the possibility is not ruled out in the case of Italian law. Only in two jurisdictions (Delaware and Japan) does it seem that the minority shareholders would probably not prevail.

Therefore, there do not appear to be any major differences arising between common law and civil law countries. The courts in the UK and in some US states (Massachusetts and Michigan) for the common law jurisdictions, and in France, Spain and Germany for the civil law jurisdictions would probably grant relief to the minority shareholders. However, there are three principal differences which can be identified.

First, all jurisdictions rely on a standard for the judge to apply, which varies according to each jurisdiction. However, whatever name the relevant standard might take, ultimately it is a form of duty of loyalty. It is called an abuse by the majority in France and Italy, an abuse of law or biased non-payment of dividends in Spain, unfair prejudice against minority shareholders in the UK and South Africa, a contradiction to morality in Latvia, a breach of the principle of equal treatment in Finland, an intention to wrong a shareholder in Poland, a duty of loyalty in Germany and a breach of fiduciary duties in the US and Japan. Two countries (Germany and Finland) have an additional specific provision regarding the refusal to vote in favour of a dividend, regardless of the duration of the situation, which would be applicable in the hypothetical case. However, the right to invoke such rules in both jurisdictions is limited to large minority shareholders. It could be argued that the existence of such provisions significantly reinforces the protections afforded to minority shareholders because the courts would otherwise, by the application of the standard, require that the lack of dividend be repeated over a long period of time. In addition, the courts might be reluctant to apply the standard which makes the rule useful.

Second, the decision on whether or not minority shareholders are entitled to some form of relief ultimately rests with the courts. The difference here seems to lie more

---

[177] For a discussion of the distinction between legal commands which are crafted as standards and those which are drawn as rules in the field of company law, see MA Eisenberg, 'The Divergence of Standards of Conduct and Standards of Review in Corporate Law' (1993) 62 *Fordham Law Review* 437; CS Diver, 'The Optimal Precision of Administrative Rules' (1983) 93 *Yale Law Journal* 65; L Kaplow, 'Rules versus Standards: An Economic Analysis' (1992–93) 42 *Duke Law Journal* 557.

with the fact that the courts in some countries (Spain, Italy, Delaware and Japan) are apparently more reluctant to intervene in corporate affairs than in other jurisdictions. Here again, the more restrictive approach adopted by the courts does not seem to be correlated to whether they are located in common law or civil law jurisdictions.

Third, jurisdictions have different views as to the appropriate remedy available. This could also be reflective of different jurisdictional approaches to judicial intervention and remedies. In addition to the nullification of the decision not to distribute a dividend, the other remedies available include damages paid by the majority shareholder (France and Spain, on the basis of a breach of the majority shareholder's duty of loyalty towards the company), a court order requiring the dividend to be paid out to the successful minority shareholder (the UK and in one case in the Netherlands) or to all shareholders (Finland, in the event of the minority dividend rule), or even the redemption of the shares (Finland, in the event of an abuse).

C. Action by Minority Shareholders against the Merger

i. Action for Annulment of the Merger

We now turn to the possibility of the controlling shareholder being prohibited from voting on the merger resolution. It is alleged that such a prohibition arises owing to the existence of a conflict of interest on the part of Family Company A as the controlling shareholder. All jurisdictions, whether grounded in the common law or the civil law, would not prevent the controlling shareholder from voting. Italy has a general rule which allows resolutions of the general meeting to be challenged if a shareholder has a direct or indirect conflict of interest (CC, Article 2373). However, it would probably not apply in this case as it is debatable whether it applies to mergers. Therefore, it appears that barring a statutory provision to the contrary, the courts in common law and civil law jurisdictions alike are very reluctant to deprive a controlling shareholder, in a conflicted transaction, of his or her right to vote in the shareholders' general meeting.

Although it does not prohibit the controlling shareholder from exercising its vote, Delaware confers increased protection for minority shareholders by applying an uncompromising duty of loyalty (entire fairness standard) in such a case.

ii. Failure to Receive Notice

With regard to the failure to provide notice of an extraordinary shareholders' meeting, all jurisdictions adopt a very pragmatic approach and would bar the shareholder from suing for nullification. Therefore, there is also a large degree of convergence in this area of the law. However, jurisdictions adopt two different approaches. Most countries provide that if a shareholder did not receive notice of a general shareholders' meeting but nevertheless took part in the meeting, he or she is barred from suing for nullification of the meeting (the UK, Delaware, Italy, Finland, Latvia and Poland). Other countries provide for a different rule according to which no action for nullification can be filed where all of the shareholders were present at the meeting (Italy, France, Spain,

Germany and Japan). Some of these countries (Germany, South Africa and Japan) require in addition that no shareholder has objected to the failure to provide notice. This second approach is similar to the first one in the sense that if all shareholders are present, none of them can request the nullification of the meeting. However, the second approach does not exclude the possibility, like for instance in France,[178] that a shareholder who would have been present at the meeting may sue for nullification as long as other shareholders were not invited and present at the meeting.

iii. Exclusion as a Shareholder from the Company as a Result of the Merger

Finally, as to the share exchange ratio which leads to the exclusion of some minority shareholders of the absorbed company since they do not hold enough shares to receive at least one share of the absorbing companies, all jurisdictions would refuse to consider that the minority shareholders were entitled to receive at least one share of the absorbing company. Therefore, all jurisdictions take the view that there is no right to stay in the company which is subject to a merger. However, at least in some countries (France, Italy and Netherlands), the merger could be declared void if it could be proved that the share exchange ratio was designed – for instance, through a reduction of the number of shares of the absorbing company in order to increase the individual price of each share – to prevent the minority shareholders from being entitled to receive at least one share of the absorbing company. Likewise, in Spain, if the share exchange ratio could be considered to be an arbitrary or abusive decision of the majority shareholders, the merger would be treated as void or voidable.[179] Furthermore, the excluded minority shareholders would be entitled to receive compensation in respect of their exclusion under Spanish law.

---

[178] Cass Civ 3rd (French Court of Appeal, Third Civil Chamber), 21 October 1998, n° 1257, *RJDA*, 12/98, n° 1371.

[179] Whether such an agreement would be void or voidable is debated among scholars; in this regard, see Martí (n 50) 95–96.

9

Abuse of Shareholder Rights

MATHIAS SIEMS (EDITOR)

Main topics: shareholders' right to ask questions and demand answers at shareholders' meeting and legal challenges to a merger.

Related topics: shareholders and shareholder law (see chapter 8, above); requirements of general meeting (see chapter 10, below).

I. Scenario

AB Public Company (AB), listed on the main domestic stock exchange, plans to merge with another public company. In the general meeting – which has been called in order to decide about this plan – Prof X, who holds one AB share, opposes this plan. In particular, he intends to ask 100 questions concerning various technical details of the merger. The chairman of the general meeting – who is also the chairman of AB's board – informs Prof X that he is only allowed to ask up to 40 questions. After Prof X has asked 40 questions, the chairman and his fellow board members respond to 30 of them but declare that, unfortunately, they are unable to provide answers to the remaining 10 questions because these questions are concerned with very specific details of the merger to which they are not able to respond on the spot.

Prof X's opposition is unsuccessful and the general meeting approves the merger with an overwhelming majority. Four weeks later, Prof X files a claim for the annulment of this decision. He also applies to the competent register in order to block the registration of the merger until the court has resolved his annulment claim. AB's board is concerned by this, since any delay may jeopardise the merger. Prof X is aware of these circumstances and therefore he offers to drop his claim if the company pays him a settlement fee of €50,000. AB's board rejects this proposal.

The lawyer representing AB argues that Prof X's claim can under no circumstances be successful because: (i) shareholders have no statutory right to ask questions at the general meeting; (ii) it was impossible for the board to respond to all 100 questions;

(iii) any violation of the procedure at the general meeting would not be material since the clear majority of shareholders would have nevertheless approved the merger; (4) the claim for annulment was filed too late; and (5) Prof X abused his right to challenge the decision of the general meeting because (a) a single shareholder cannot be allowed to prevent the registration of a multi-million euro merger by the competent register and (b) the settlement offer showed that Prof X had no legitimate motive but simply an intention of having the 'nuisance value' of his claim bought off.

How will the court decide?

II. Case Studies

A. Germany[1]

i. Introduction

Under German law, a resolution is void in law only in particularly extreme circumstances (AktG, § 241). In all other cases, the unlawfulness of a resolution of a general meeting leads to its voidability (AktG, § 243). Therefore, in the usual case, an annulment claim is necessary and it must comply with a number of formal and substantive requirements.

ii. Standing to Sue and Time Limit

A shareholder who takes part in the general meeting has standing to sue in respect of a decision of the general meeting if he or she acquired the shares before the date of service of the notice of the general meeting and his or her objection against the decision is recorded in the minutes (AktG, § 245(1)(a)). This can be assumed in the present case because Prof X openly opposed the merger at the general meeting. It is immaterial for his standing to sue that he holds one share only, and it is also unnecessary to examine whether he is personally affected by the decision in question.

An annulment action has to be filed within one month (AktG, § 246(1)) of the date of the passing of the resolution. In the interests of legal certainty and for the purposes of respecting the decision of the shareholder majority, the resolution is treated as unchallengeable after this time limit. Prof X has also complied with this requirement.

iii. Cause of Action

An annulment action can be based on any violation of the law[2] or the articles of association (AktG, § 243(1)). In the present case, there may be a breach of § 131(1)

---

[1] Abbreviated statutes: AktG = Law on Public Companies; BGB = Civil Code; StGB = Criminal Code; UmwG = Transformation Act.

[2] This is not limited to company law; see U Hüffer and J Koch, *Aktiengesetz* (12th edn, Munich, Beck, 2016) § 243, para 5.

of the AktG. According to this provision, a shareholder has the right to demand that the management board responds to his questions at the general meeting.

The questions have to be asked by a shareholder taking part in the meeting and they have to be answered by the management board. However, this does not mean that the board members are necessarily excused from compliance with this obligation if they have no personal knowledge about a particular fact (as may be the case here); rather, they are deemed to have knowledge of all circumstances of which, in principle, they ought to know.[3]

The shareholder has to demand the information at the general meeting. It is neither necessary nor sufficient that he or she has notified the board in advance of the meeting of the impending demand. The question can concern any business of the company (which the courts interpret widely).[4] However, there has to be some connection to the agenda of the general meeting (AktG, § 131(1))(s 1)).[5] This can be difficult to determine,[6] but in the present case, this requirement is very likely to be fulfilled because Prof X's questions relate to the merger which was to be decided by the meeting. In particular, according to the orthodox view, it is irrelevant that details of the proposed merger have already been circulated before the general meeting because the individual right to demand information is treated as being independent of general forms of disclosure.[7]

The board has the right to refuse to answer the question in some specific instances, enumerated in § 131(2) AktG, for instance, if disclosure of the requested information can seriously damage the interests of the company. In addition, there are a number of general reasons which constrain the right to demand information: first, the ability of the general meeting to function properly;[8] second, the fiduciary duty of shareholders towards other shareholders;[9] third, the general principle of abuse of law, which is based on the principle of good faith (BGB, § 242);[10] and, fourth, the general bar of impossibility (BGB, § 275).[11]

In the present case, it is unlikely that answering all questions would be regarded as seriously damaging to AB or the functioning of the general meeting. However, it is possible that asking 'too many questions' would be treated as either a breach of fiduciary duty towards the other shareholders (because one shareholder should not monopolise the general meeting) or as an abuse of law based on the sub-category

---

[3] See M Siems in G Spindler and E Stilz (eds), *Kommentar zum Aktiengesetz* (3rd edn, Munich, Beck, 2015) § 131, para 17.

[4] Ibid, § 131, para 23.

[5] BGH (German Federal Supreme Court), BGHZ 198, 354 confirmed that this requirement complies with Art 9(2) of the Directive 2007/36/EC of 11 July 2007 on the exercise of certain rights of shareholders in listed companies ([2007] OJ L184/17).

[6] Ibid, § 131, paras 28–33.

[7] Ibid, § 131, para 5.

[8] Ibid, § 131, para 59; C Decher, *Großkommentar zum Aktiengesetz* (4th edn, Berlin, de Gruyter, 2001) § 131, para 276.

[9] Ibid, § 131, para 59. For the fiduciary duty among shareholders, see generally BGH, BGHZ 103, 184, 194 ('Linotype').

[10] Ibid, § 131, para 60; Hüffer and Koch, *Aktiengesetz* (n 2) § 131, para 33.

[11] Ibid § 131, para 61; Hüffer and Koch (n 2) § 131, para 10.

of excessive behaviour. For instance, it is clear that a shareholder cannot demand 25,000 pieces of information.[12] However, whether asking 100 questions is excessive has not yet been decided. Since the onus is on AB to prove that one of the exceptions has been fulfilled,[13] it is not unlikely that Prof X would be held to have the right to ask all of his questions.

The failure to respond to the 10 questions could be justified because no-one is obliged to perform an impossible obligation (BGB, § 275). However, the courts have held that the management board has the duty to prepare for questions which are likely to be asked at the general meeting.[14] Large public companies therefore often install 'back offices' that can quickly provide the management board with information while the general meeting is under way.[15] Since the extent of this duty can be a matter of debate, more information would be needed about the 10 questions which were not answered by the management board. Overall, it is therefore possible that the court would hold that there is a breach of § 131(1) of the AktG.

iv. Violation of Law Not Immaterial

According to the first sentence of § 243(4) of the AktG, a violation of § 131(1) of the AktG only leads to an annulment of the resolution if a hypothetical shareholder would regard this information as material to his or her voting decision. Moreover, according to its second sentence, an inaccurate response to a question about the amount of a shareholder's cash compensation does not invalidate the decision of the general meeting if the amount of compensation can be reassessed in a special compensation procedure ('*Spruchverfahren*').[16]

The first sentence does not require a causal link between the breach of the law and the outcome of the general meeting. The courts have used a causality requirement in the past;[17] however, an amendment in 2005[18] made it clear that only 'relevance' is necessary and not 'causality'. Moreover, § 243(4)(s 1) of the AktG has to be proven by the company.[19] Thus, according to the first sentence of this section, AB would have to show that the possibility can be excluded that the answers to Prof X's questions would have influenced the other shareholders. It may be difficult for the company to provide such evidence.

The second sentence relates to the problem that allowing any action against decisions of the general meeting may block the entry of the resolution in the commercial

---

[12] OLG Frankfurt (Higher Regional Court Frankfurt), AG 1984, 25.

[13] BayObLG (Bavarian Supreme Court), AG 2000, 131; OLG Koblenz (Higher Regional Court Koblenz), ZIP 2001, 1093, 1095.

[14] KG (Berlin Court of Appeal), AG 1996, 131, 134; OLG Düsseldorf (Higher Regional Court Düsseldorf), AG 1992, 34, 35.

[15] Siems in Spindler and Stilz, *Kommentar zum Aktiengesetz* (n 3) § 131, para 17.

[16] Spruchverfahrensgesetz (SpruchG) of 17 July 2003, BGBl I 838. Similar the prior case law of the German Federal Supreme Court in BGHZ 146, 179 (MEZ); BGH, NJW 2001, 1428 (Aqua-Butzke).

[17] BGH, BGHZ 14, 264, 267; BGHZ 36, 121.

[18] Gesetz zur Unternehmensintegrität and Modernisierung des Anfechtungsrechts (UMAG) of 22 September 2005, BGBl I 2802.

[19] Hüffer and Koch (n 2) § 243, para 61.

register, resulting in the danger of an abuse of law.[20] It is therefore provided that any objection against the cash compensation that shareholders may receive in the case of mergers (UmwG, § 29) is only examined in a special compensation procedure (UmwG, §§ 32, 34). However, Prof X has challenged the entire merger and not just the compensation. Thus, the possibility of succeeding in an annulment action cannot be excluded in the present scenario.

v. No Abuse of the Right to Sue

AB advances two reasons why it should be held that there has been an abuse of Prof X's' rights as a shareholder. The first reason relates to the fact that Prof X attempted to block the entry of the merger in the commercial register until the final outcome of the avoidance proceedings. Usually, this is done by filing an application to the registry court, which can then postpone the entry in the register. However, in the present case, this application is not actually necessary. A claim made against a resolution of the general meeting to merge with another company leads to the automatic blocking of the register (UmwG, § 16(2)). In this respect, it is held that the mere fact that a shareholder filed a claim against a decision of the general meeting is perfectly legitimate and cannot be seen as putting undue pressure on the company.[21] In addition, since a 2009 reform, it has become easier for companies to make the case that an exception is applied so that the decision of the resolution can be entered in the commercial register (UmwG, § 16(3));[22] notably, they can do so where a shareholder does not hold shares representing an amount of at least €1,000, which may be possible in the present case.

Second, the settlement offer of Prof X could be regarded as a form of extortion. The German courts have indeed considered whether such behaviour can be treated as extortion under criminal law (StGB, § 249).[23] With respect to company law, it has been discussed whether directors who give in to this pressure violate the principle of capital maintenance (AktG, § 57(1)).[24] In the present case, it matters whether the general principle of abuse of law[25] has the capacity to bar the annulment claim. The courts have considered a number of criteria in order to determine whether this is the case: for instance, it has been held to be irrelevant that the shareholder owned only one share,[26] that he or she decided to extort the company before or after he or she filed the claim,[27] or that the claim would actually be successful.[28] Instead, what is decisive is whether the plaintiff would have had a legitimate reason for the 'settlement fee' or whether he

---

[20] For more detail on this, see (v), below.

[21] BGH, NJW 1992, 2821, 2822.

[22] Gesetz zur Umsetzung der Aktionärsrechterichtlinie (ARUG) of 30 July 2009, BGBl I 2479. A corresponding release procedure (*Freigabeverfahren*) has also been provided for other cases (AktG, § 246a), initially with the UMAG reform of 2005 (see n 18 above).

[23] Ibid, 2823.

[24] Ibid, 2821.

[25] See (iii), above.

[26] OLG Köln (Higher Regional Court Cologne), BB 2003, 2307, 2308; OLG Stuttgart (Higher Regional Court Stuttgart), AG 2003, 456, 457.

[27] BGH, NJW 1992, 569.

[28] BGH, NJW 1989, 2689, 2692; NJW-RR 1990, 350, 353.

or she only wanted to receive an unsubstantiated monetary benefit.[29] For instance, it therefore matters whether the 'settlement fee' could have been seen as compensating the shareholder for his or her efforts or for the diminution of the value of his or her shares.

Here, there is no indication why Prof X should have received €50,000 in compensation. However, it can be argued that when one engages in settlement negotiations, one usually begins with a demand for a sum which is higher than the sum which one eventually expects to receive. Moreover, an abuse of rights is a rare exception which has to be proven by the company. Thus, it would be for AB to provide more evidence in order to show that Prof X had the sole aim of blackmailing it.

vi. Conclusion

Disruptive shareholders have played an influential role in the practice of German corporate governance and company law, in particular as far as general meetings are concerned. Thus, the complaint has been made that general meetings of public companies often take an entire day because the management board is keen to answer every question in order to reduce the risk of shareholder claims.[30] The literature has also identified around 40 'professional plaintiffs' who often hold only one share of each listed company and challenge many of their resolutions in order to have the 'nuisance value' of their claim bought off.[31]

The German law-maker has reacted to this problem with the 2005 and 2009 company law reforms, which have led to a halving of claims filed against resolutions of the general meeting.[32] However, the debate is still ongoing, and in November 2015 the German government indicated plans to initiate a major review of the law challenging resolutions of the general meeting.[33] Indeed, it may be said that the present case study shows that the legislature and the courts have not yet found a way to prevent this kind of disruptive behaviour.

B. France

i. Introduction

Under French company law, the solution would be the same irrespective of whether AB was incorporated as a public limited company (*Société anonyme* (SA)) or a

---

[29] BGH, BGHZ 107, 296 (DM 1.5 million); NJW 1992, 569 (DM 10 million); NJW 1992, 2821 (DM 1.5 million).

[30] S Rößler-Tolger, *Der räuberische Aktionär – eine schwindende Bedrohung?* (Karlsruhe, Verlag Versicherungswirtschaft, 2007) 132 (between 7 and 13 hours).

[31] T Baums, A Keinath and D Gajek, 'Fortschritte bei Klagen gegen Hauptversammlungsbeschlüsse – Eine empirische Studie' (2007) *Zeitschrift für Witschaftsrecht und Insolvenzpraxis (ZIP)* 1629.

[32] See W Bayer, T Hoffmann und T Sawada, 'Beschlussmängelklagen, Freigabeverfahren und Berufskläger – Ergebnisse einer im Auftrag des BMJ erstellten empirischen Studie und Überlegungen de lege ferenda' (2012) *Zeitschrift für Wirtschaftsrecht (ZIP)* 897.

[33] Beschlussempfehlung des Rechtsausschusses des Bundestags, BT-Drs. 18/6681 of 11 November 2015 at p 12. The 2018 coalition agreement repeats this ambition: Koalitionsvertrag zwischen CDU, CSU und SPD, 7 February 2018, p 131.

simplified public limited company (*Société par actions simplifiée* (SAS)). An SAS cannot offer shares to the public (except in the case of crowdfunding) although its shares can be listed on a non-regulated market. Provisions of the Commercial Code on the general shareholders' meeting in an SA do not apply to an SAS because the SAS is free not to have a shareholders' meeting. However, with regard to the treatment of written and oral questions at a shareholders' meeting, the approach of the courts is based on general principles included in the Civil Code or provisions of the Commercial Code that are applicable to both the SA and the SAS. Under French company, law, the arguments raised by the lawyer representing AB would be dealt with in the following way.

ii. The Statutory Right of Shareholders to Ask Written and Oral Questions at the General Shareholders' Meeting

In the case of an SA, the general shareholders' meeting is chaired by the chairman of the board of directors (or the chairman of the supervisory board), unless the articles of association provide otherwise.[34] If the chairman of the board of directors does not chair the meeting, the chairman is elected by the shareholders. For an SAS, there is no equivalent provision, but the articles of association will usually provide for a similar arrangement.

The shareholders of an SA have the right to ask written questions in advance of the general shareholders' meeting.[35] These questions have to be answered by the board of directors or by the management board, depending on the structure of the company. The chairman of the board, as the chairman of the meeting, is usually the person who will answer the questions during the meeting. Alternatively, he or she may appoint another person to fulfil that role, for example, the chief financial officer or the general counsel. There is no specific provision that regulates written questions for an SAS, although the articles of association can cater for such a right. However, in the case of AB, the issue concerns oral questions rather than written questions.

The chairman of the meeting has the duty to organise and direct the discussion during the shareholders' meeting. He or she is in charge of organising the question-and-answer session. Usually, the session will consist of answering the written questions and then taking oral questions from the shareholders attending the meeting. The Commercial Code does not include any rule or limitation on the number of written questions that a shareholder may send in advance of the meeting or that he or she may express orally.

There is no provision in the Commercial Code on oral questions. However, the right of shareholders to participate in a general shareholders' meeting includes the right to ask oral questions during the meeting and is guaranteed by the Civil Code.[36] Therefore, it applies to all types of companies. The violation of this right is punished by criminal sanctions in the case of commercial companies.[37]

---

[34] Commercial Code, Art L 225-100.
[35] Commercial Code, Art L 225-108 al 3.
[36] Civil Code, Art 1844.
[37] Commercial Code, Art L 242-9°1.

Therefore, under French company law, shareholders have a statutory right to ask written and oral questions at the general meeting. Since the right of shareholders to ask questions is considered to be a fundamental right, the chairman of the meeting will usually be cautious not to be too authoritative and certainly not to end the question-and-answer session if the shareholders wish to continue.

iii. The Inability of the Board to Answer Oral Questions on Specific Details

The right of shareholders to ask questions is not absolute. It is subject to certain general limitations. First, certain commentators take the view that written questions (their position is the same in the case of oral questions) which relate to the same subject can be answered as one.[38] In this way, it is possible to reduce the number of questions to a more limited number. Second, the power of the chairman of the meeting includes, preferably after a discussion with the secretarial board of the meeting (*bureau*), the right to end a long list of questions by one single shareholder in order to give the other shareholders the opportunity to ask questions. Finally, some questions can be left unanswered for valid reasons, for example, questions whose answers would involve the communication of trade secrets.

Although there are few cases on this issue, the French courts tend to adopt a reasonable approach to written and oral questions. For instance, a decision of the Paris Court of Appeals held that a company could not be held liable for not answering a written question on a complex matter which was received on the eve of the general shareholders' meeting.[39] The case concerned a written question, but the reasoning applies all the more to a technical oral question asked during the course of the shareholders' meeting itself.

Therefore, under French case law, the chairman of AB would probably have the legal right not to answer the final 10 questions of Prof X provided they concerned very specific details of the merger to which he could not respond on the spot. In such a case, the practice in France is to ask the shareholder to contact the relevant department of the company in order to receive an answer after the meeting.

iv. Abuse of the Right to Ask Questions in Order to Have a Claim Bought Off

Under French law, any right can give rise to liability in the case of an abuse, including the right to participate in the general shareholders' meeting and to ask questions. French courts tend to protect companies from the abusive behaviour of shareholders.

In a case decided in 2004 by the Paris First Degree Commercial Court, the Court held that a shareholder could not use his or her right to ask questions where the shareholder's motive for doing so was something other than being informed.[40]

---

[38] *Code des sociétés et des marchés financiers* (Paris, Dalloz, 2010), Commentary under Commercial Code, Art L 225-108.

[39] CA Paris (Court of Appeal of Paris), 23 April 1985: *RJ Com* 1986 143, with a note by P Le Cannu.

[40] T com Paris 2e ch (Second Chamber of the Tribunal of Commerce of Paris), 11 May 2004, n° 2003078521 (*SA Suez cl D*), *Bull Joly Sociétés*, 1 October 2004 n° 10, p 1238.

In this case, the shareholder had admitted in writing that he would remove his questions if he secured a better deal on a transaction to which the company was a party. It was held that the company was entitled to receive one symbolic euro in non-monetary damages. The case was very close to the situation in the hypothetical case. Therefore, Prof X could face civil liability for abusing his right to ask questions since he has clearly stated that his aim in asking the questions was not to be informed about AB's affairs, but to find a legal argument which would enable him to try to annul the merger and blackmail AB.

v. Annulment of the Meeting for the Failure to Allow Oral Questions

Under French company law, it is provided that:

> The nullity of ... an act amending the articles of association may result only from the breach of a provision of this Title [referring to the title on common provisions applying to commercial companies] expressly providing for such nullity or of the acts governing contracts.[41]

A merger implies amending the articles of association. Therefore, the nullification of the meeting approving a merger, such as that of AB, can only be achieved if a provision in the relevant Book of the Commercial Code (Articles L 210-1–L 249-1) expressly provides so or if the provisions governing the nullity of contracts are satisfied. The situation is very different from an ordinary shareholders' meeting where many more causes for nullification are prescribed since: 'The nullity of acts or deliberations ... may result only from the breach of a mandatory provision of this Title [*title on Common provisions applying to commercial companies*] or of the acts governing contracts'.[42]

Written questions are regulated by Article L 225-108 of the Commercial Code, which does not include the annulment of the shareholders' meeting as a sanction. Oral questions are not regulated by the Commercial Code and the shareholders' meeting cannot be declared void on the basis of a violation of the right to ask oral questions.

Therefore, there is little risk that the extraordinary shareholders' meeting of AB which approved the merger will be nullified on the ground that the chairman and his fellow board members did not answer the final 10 questions of Prof X.

vi. Summary and Conclusion

French law is very restrictive when it comes to the possibility of nullification of acts, deliberations and decisions of companies. This situation dates back to the 24 July 1966 Commercial Companies Act,[43] which reduced the causes of nullification and replaced them with criminal sanctions in order to, among other things, prevent companies from being blackmailed. Therefore, in France, behaviour such as that of Prof X would be very uncommon and would not trigger severe consequences for a company such as AB.

---

[41] Commercial Code, Art L 235-1.
[42] Commercial Code, Art L 235-1.
[43] Loi n°66-537 du 24 juillet 1966 sur les sociétés commerciales.

C. Italy

Italian company law distinguishes between resolutions that are void and resolutions that are voidable. A resolution is void in three specific situations only: (a) when the general meeting has not been convened; (b) when there are no minutes of the meeting; and (c) when the content of the resolution is impossible or unlawful (Italian Civil Code (CC), Article 2379). Meanwhile, a resolution is treated as voidable not in specific cases, but, generally, if it has not been adopted in conformity with the law or with the by-laws of the company (CC, Article 2377).

Any interested party may challenge a void resolution. By contrast, only the share-holders who did not take part in the decision, the directors and the members of the board of auditors may challenge a voidable resolution. As a general rule, a challenge to a void resolution must be filed within three years of the date of the resolution's entry in, or filing with, the Company Register or of the date of the transcription of the deci-sion in the register of the general meeting if the resolution should not be entered in, or filed with, the Company Register. On the other hand, according to Article 2377 of the CC, a challenge to a voidable resolution must be filed within 90 days of the date of the resolution or, if the resolution has to be entered in the Company Register, within 90 days from the entry date or, if the resolution has only to be filed in the Company Register, within 90 days of the date of the filing of the resolution.[44]

The facts presented in the hypothetical case do not fall within one of the three cases indicated in Article 2379 of the CC. Therefore, the validity of the resolution may be challenged only by filing an action under Article 2377 of the CC. However, it is uncer-tain whether a failure to inform the shareholders may be treated as a legitimate cause of action under Article 2377 of the CC. Indeed, Italian scholars[45] and courts[46] have recognised that the shareholders have a right to be informed.[47] However, this right has traditionally found its most typical expression in Article 2374 of the CC. This provi-sion stipulates that, during the general meeting, the shareholders who represent at least one-third of the share capital of the company may request a brief postponement[48] of any discussion of the topics on which they declare themselves insufficiently informed. On the other hand, notwithstanding that Italian law gives the shareholders of a company the general right to be informed, the scope of this right is limited, and direc-tors have been considered not to be obliged to answer the questions presented by the shareholders.[49]

However, more recently, Legislative Decree no 27 of 2010, which transposed Directive 2007/36/EC into Italian law, introduced a new provision that applies to listed companies – Article 127-*ter* of the Consolidated Law on Finance (CLF).

---

[44] Italian law recognises a distinction between 'entering' a resolution in the Company Register and 'filing' a resolution in the Company Register.

[45] See, eg, A Serra, 'Il procedimento assembleare' in P Abbadessa and GB Portale (eds), *Il nuovo diritto delle società, Liber amicorum Gian Franco Campobasso*, vol 2 (Turin, Utet, 2006) 37 ff and 68 ff.

[46] Cass Sez Un (Corte di Cassazione, Joint Chambers) 27/2000.

[47] C Montagnani, 'Commento *sub* art. 2374' in G Niccolini and A Stagno D'Alcontres (eds), *Società di capitali. Commertario*, vol 1 (Naples, Jovene, 2004) 517 ff, 520 ff.

[48] No longer than 5 days.

[49] Corte di Cassazione (n 46). *Cf* also Montagnani, 'Commento *sub* art. 2374' (n 47).

This also expressly allows the shareholders of listed companies to submit questions prior to the general meeting. Afterwards, this provision was amended by Article 3 of Legislative Decree no 91 of 18 June 2012, as rectified by the notice published in the Official Gazette no 155 of July 5, 2012. This provision, which is applicable only to listed companies, empowers '[a]ll those with voting rights' to 'submit questions on the items on the agenda even prior to the shareholders' meeting'. According to this provision, the questions received before the meeting must be answered at the latest during the said meeting. The notice calling the meeting must specify the term within which questions raised prior to the shareholders' meeting must reach the company, which may not be less than three days prior to the date of the shareholders' meeting, or five days if the notice calling the meeting establishes that the company should provide a reply to the questions received before the meeting. Certainly, this provision now grants shareholders of listed companies the right to ask questions and to receive an answer; however, it is still not completely settled if the lack of any reply may be treated as a legitimate cause of action under Article 2377 of the CC.[50] Thus, in light of the foregoing, on the merits of the hypothetical case, there is probably a positive chance of successfully challenging the validity of the resolution passed at the general meeting.

Finally, even if Prof X were allowed to challenge the validity of the resolution by filing an action under Article 2477 of the CC, there are at least two different reasons why he would not be permitted to unilaterally block the entry of the resolution approving the merger in the Company Register: (i) under Article 2378 of the CC, Prof X may request a suspension of the execution of the resolution taken by the general meeting. In this situation, however, the decision is taken by a court by taking into account a comparison of the harm which the plaintiff and the company may incur, and the plaintiff may be required to offer an adequate guarantee for any possible damage that may be suffered by the company; and (ii) only shareholders that own at least one-one thousandth (in closely held companies the threshold is 5 per cent) of the share capital of the company may file an action to avoid the resolutions of the general meeting. Meanwhile, shareholders who do not meet this threshold are only allowed to file an action for damages and may not challenge the resolution.

In conclusion, the action filed by Prof X based on a purported violation of the shareholders' right to information could succeed on its merits. However, even if he has a legitimate cause of action, he could not secure the suspension of the execution of the resolution that approved the merger, since he would only be allowed to file an action for damages and not to challenge the validity of the decision.

D. Spain

Under Spanish company law, shareholders are allowed to ask the directors of a *Sociedad Anónima* (SA) various questions about the items included in the agenda of

---

[50] F Pasquariello, 'Commento *sub* art. 2366' in A Maffei Alberti (ed), *Commentario breve al diritto delle società* (3rd edn, Padua, CEDAM, 2015) 512 ff, 525; *cf* R Guidotti and F Pasquariello, 'Commento *sub* art. 127-*ter*' in F Vella (ed), *Commentario T.U.F.*, t 2 (Turin, Giappichelli, 2012) 1396 ff and 1398, commenting on the original wording of this provision.

the general meeting (Ley de Sociedades de Capital (LSC) – Corporate Enterprises Act, Article 197).[51] Moreover, in the case of listed companies, shareholders may request clarification about the auditor's report and the publicly accessible information provided by the company to the Comisión Nacional del Mercado de Valores (CNMV) – the Spanish Securities Markets Commission – after the last general shareholders' meeting (LSC, Article 520.1). This right can be exercised in two ways. First, up to the fifth day – seventh day for non-listed companies (LSC, Article 197.1) – prior to the date of the general meeting, shareholders may make a written request for information to the directors of the company (LSC, Article 520.1). In such a case, the directors are required to provide the information, in writing, before the date of the general meeting (LSC, Article 197.1). Second, during the course of the general meeting, shareholders may verbally request information or clarifications about items included in the agenda of the general meeting (LSC, Article 197.2). Hence, under Spanish company law, shareholders such as Prof X have a statutory right to ask questions. Nevertheless, it is necessary to point out that the by-laws of an SA may establish that, in order to attend the general meeting, shareholders must be in possession of a minimum number of shares; however, the minimum required cannot exceed 0.1 per cent of the share capital of the company (LSC, Article 179.2). If the by-laws of AB impose such limitations, this would impede the right of Prof X to attend the meeting and, assuming that he was unable to overcome this requirement for a minimum 0.1 per cent shareholding through other means, he could only exercise his right to information in the form of questions to the directors by written means before the deliberations of the general meeting.[52]

The directors of a Spanish SA may give an answer to shareholders' questions during the course of the general meeting. However, in the hypothetical case, providing an answer to the 100 questions asked by Prof X may pose certain difficulties for the directors of AB, who may not be able to answer all of them. In such cases, Spanish company law provides an alternative solution consisting of the imposition of an obligation on the directors of an SA to give a written answer to the questions within seven days after the date of the general meeting (LSC, Article 197.2). Thus, the directors of AB would be required to provide an answer within such period to the remaining 70 questions which Prof X posed.

The directors have, however, an element of discretion in deciding whether to supply the requested information and may decide not to do so when: (a) such information is not necessary to safeguard the rights of shareholders; (b) there are objective grounds to consider that the information may be used to advance interests different from the interests of the company; or (c) the publication of such information may harm the company or related group companies (LSC, Article 197.3). Some scholars indeed take the view that when minority shareholders abuse information rights in order to benefit or advance interests different from those of the company – such as appears to be the situation in Prof X's case – then directors have the right to decide not to answer the

---

[51] Real Decreto Legislativo 1/2010, de 2 de julio, por el que se aprueba el texto refundido de la Ley de Sociedades de Capital (LSC).

[52] See JA García-Cruces, 'Artículo 197. Derecho de información en la sociedad anónima' in Á Rojo and E Beltrán (eds), *Comentario de la Ley de Sociedades de Capital* (Cizur Menor (Navarra), Civitas-Thomson Reuters, 2011) 1388–89.

questions.[53] It is also worth pointing out that in the case of listed companies, when shareholders ask a specific question and the relevant information was already available to all shareholders on the website of the company in a clear, express and direct manner and in a question-and-answer format, then directors may simply refer shareholders to the website of the company (LSC, Article 520.3).

However, when the request for information is supported by shareholders who represent at least 25 per cent of the share capital of the company – or a lower percentage if prescribed in the by-laws of the company, provided that it is higher than 5 per cent of the share capital – then the directors of the company are not entitled to refuse to supply it (LSC, Article 197.4). However, this does not seem to apply in Prof X's case.

Some scholars have proposed that the failure of the directors of a company such as AB to comply with the obligation to answer the questions within the seven days following the general shareholders' meeting would not automatically result in the agreements adopted by the shareholders being treated as void. This is on the ground that the shareholders' right to information is considered to be instrumental to the right to vote. Therefore, if it was not possible to give an answer to all the questions during the general meeting, then the information would lose its instrumental character.[54] It could also be argued that a shareholder such as Prof X exhibited a lack of diligence in the exercise of his rights. In this regard, if Prof X considered that the answers to the questions which he asked during the general shareholders' meeting were essential to enable him to decide how to vote, then he ought to have made use of the right to request the information prior to the meeting (LSC, Article 197.1), which would have avoided the risk that his questions could not be adequately answered during the course of the meeting. This could even affect the right of Prof X to challenge the merger. However, directors would still be bound to provide the requested information and the failure to do so might lead to consequences in terms of liability.[55] This interpretation of the legal literature seems to have been adopted by a reform of Spanish company law of the year 2014,[56] which introduced a new paragraph in Article 197 of the LSC whereby the failure of directors to answer questions during or after the meeting entitles shareholders to request compliance with such obligation as well as compensation for damages, but not to challenge the decisions adopted by the shareholders' general meeting (LSC, Article 197.5).

Assuming that Prof X nonetheless wished to proceed to challenge the merger – and that there were other valid reasons for it to be challenged – he would most likely not be entitled to do so because only shareholders who represent at least 0.1 per cent of the share capital of a listed company can challenge decisions of the shareholders' general

[53] In this regard, see F Vicent Chuliá, *Compendio Crítico de Derecho Mercantil* (Barcelona, Bosch, 1991) 530–31, who makes reference to the STS (Sentencia Tribunal Supremo) of 26 December 1969 in support of this view.

[54] This argument is developed by M García-Villarrubia, 'Ejercitado por un accionista el derecho de información durante la celebración de la junta general sin que sea posible satisfacerlo en dicho momento y adoptado el correspondiente acuerdo ¿qué consecuencias tiene el incumplimiento por parte de los administradores de la obligación de facilitar por escrito la información dentro de los siete días siguientes al de la terminación de la junta?' *El Derecho* (1 February 2011).

[55] Ibid.

[56] Ley 31/2014, de 3 de diciembre, por la que se modifica la Ley de Sociedades de Capital para la mejora del gobierno corporativo.

352   MATHIAS SIEMS (EDITOR)

meeting, unless the by-laws set a lower percentage (LSC, Articles 206.1 and 495.2(b)). Decisions of the shareholders' general meeting that are against the public order can be challenged by any shareholder, but this does not appear to be relevant or applicable in the case of the decision approving the merger. Subject to the satisfaction of certain conditions, the merger could be challenged even after it had been registered at the Companies Register. The deadline is three months from the date of the merger (Ley sobre Modificaciones Estructurales de las Sociedades Mercantiles (LMESM) – Act on Structural Changes in Corporations,[57] Article 47; Código de Comercio – Code of Commerce,[58] Article 21; and Reglamento del Registro Mercantil (RRM) – Regulations of the Companies Register,[59] Article 9). Therefore, in the instant case, Prof X would have proceeded within the deadline. Shareholders representing at least 1 per cent or 5 per cent of the share capital of a company – depending on whether its shares are admitted to trading or not in secondary markets (Ley de Enjuiciamiento Civil (LEC) – Civil Procedure Act,[60] Article 727.10) – can also request the suspension of the validity of agreements during the course of court proceedings. Hence, Prof X could ask for the suspension of the agreement concerning the merger if he owned a percentage of the shares that is equal to or higher than 1 per cent of AB's share capital. However, it should be noted that the suspension of the agreement regarding the merger could only be requested before it had been registered at the Companies Register.[61]

The motivations and behaviour of Prof X suggest that he engaged in conduct amounting to an abuse of law (Código Civil (CC) – Civil Code,[62] Article 7.2) when he proceeded to challenge the merger. The behaviour of Prof X would have to be considered by the court when it decided on his claim in relation to the validity of the agreement.[63]

E. The Netherlands[64]

i. Challenging Resolutions by a Corporate Body of the Company

Under Dutch law there is the possibility to challenge resolutions that are passed by a corporate body of the company. Since the provisions regarding the challenging of resolutions are provided in the general provisions of Book 2 of the Dutch Civil Code,[65]

---

[57] Ley 3/2009, de 3 de abril, sobre Modificaciones Estructurales de las Sociedades Mercantiles.
[58] Real Decreto de 22 de agosto de 1885 por el que se publica el Código de Comercio.
[59] Real Decreto 1784/1996, de 19 de julio, por el que se aprueba el Reglamento del Registro Mercantil.
[60] Ley 1/2000, de 7 de enero, de Enjuiciamiento Civil.
[61] See, eg, MA Martí, *La Nulidad de la Fusión de Sociedades* (Cizur Menor (Navarra), Aranzadi, 2002) 53–54.
[62] Real Decreto de 24 de julio de 1889 por el que se publica el Código Civil.
[63] Proposals for reform aimed at avoiding the abusive use of the right to challenge agreements are analysed by J Sánchez-Calero, 'Propuestas de revisión de la impugnación de acuerdos (Especial referencia a las sociedades cotizadas)' *Comunicación presentada a la Jornada Internacional 'Reflexiones sobre la Junta General de las sociedades de capital'* (Ilustre Colegio Notarial de Madrid, 20 April 2009).
[64] Abbreviations: DCC = Dutch Civil Code; HR = Hoge Raad = Dutch Supreme Court; OK = Ondernemingskamer = Enterprise Chamber; Rb. = Rechtbank = District Court. An unofficial translation of Dutch company law as incorporated in bk 2 of the Dutch Civil Code can be found on www.dutchcivillaw.com/civilcodebook022.htm.
[65] Title 1 of bk 2 of the Dutch Civil Code.

these rules apply to all Dutch private legal persons, including private limited liability companies (BV) and public limited liability companies (NV).

On the basis of Article 2:14 DCC, unless the law suggests otherwise, a resolution of a corporate body of the legal entity is null and void (nietig) if the resolution is in violation of the law or the articles of association. On the basis of Article 2:15 DCC, a resolution of a corporate body of the legal entity is voidable (vernietigbaar) if the resolution (a) has been passed in conflict with the provisions of the law or articles of association that regulate the way in which resolutions are made, (b) is in conflict with the standards of reasonableness and fairness that are imposed by Article 2:8 DCC, or (c) is in conflict with the (internal) by-laws of the legal person.

If a resolution is null and void, every party that has a legitimate interest can request the court to order that the resolution is null and void.[66] In case of a resolution that is voidable, Article 2:15, paragraph 3 DCC states that a claim can only be filed against the legal entity by someone who has a legitimate interest in compliance with the requirements which have not been observed or upon request of the legal entity itself. The right to claim that the resolution is voidable lapses after one year from the date on which (i) either sufficient publicity has been given to the resolution or (ii) the interested party has become aware of the resolution and/or has been given sufficient notice thereof.[67]

ii. Information Rights of Shareholders

Under Dutch law, the board of directors and supervisory board have the obligation to provide the general meeting with all requested information, unless a substantial interest of the company opposes the provision of this information to the general meeting.[68] A question has been raised in the literature as to whether this means that individual shareholders have the right to request information from the board of directors and supervisory board during the general meeting or whether only the general meeting itself as a corporate body is allowed to request information. The Supreme Court ruled that shareholders individually have the right to ask for information during the general meeting.[69] In principle, shareholders have no right to information outside the general meeting, although there is no rule prohibiting shareholders from requesting information. The board of directors and supervisory board should, however, be cautious of providing information to individual shareholders outside the general meeting, because this could violate the principle of equality of shareholders.[70]

Although in principle the individual shareholders do not have any rights to information outside of the general meeting, there are exceptions under extraordinary circumstances. One of those circumstances is when all other shareholders are members of the board of directors and have additional information in that capacity.[71]

---

[66] DCC, Art 3:303.
[67] DCC, Art 2:15-5.
[68] DCC, Art 2:107/217-2.
[69] HR 9 July 2010, *NJ* 2010/544, with a note by Van Schilfgaarde (*ASMI*).
[70] DCC, Art 2:92/201-2.
[71] Hof Amsterdam (OK) 6 June 2011, *JOR* 2011/282, with a note by Blanco Fernandez.

Under those circumstances the only shareholder that is not a member of the board of directors should also be provided with more information outside of the general meeting if the circumstances require it. Another example is the case of a liquidation of an estate where the holder of the depositary receipt for shares requires information about the company in order to determine the value of the depositary receipts of shares. Under those circumstances the Enterprise Chamber of the Court of Appeal of Amsterdam has ruled that information has to be provided by the board of directors outside of the general meeting.[72]

In principle, a shareholder can use the rights that are attached to his position as a shareholder, including the right to ask for information during the general meeting, in his own interest.[73] However, a shareholder will have to act reasonably and fairly towards the other shareholders and the company itself[74] and is not allowed to abuse the rights that he or she has as a shareholder.[75] A right can be abused, amongst others, when it (i) is exercised for no other purpose than to damage another person; (ii) it is exercised for a purpose other than that for which it was granted or (iii) should, given the disparity between the interests which are served by its implementation and the interests which are damaged as a result thereof, reasonably be stopped or postponed.[76] In particular, the third criterion requires a balancing of the interests of the different parties that are involved in using the power to ask for information.

iii. Prevention of the Merger

Under Dutch law, it is not possible for an individual shareholder to prevent the registration of a (national) merger. The merger takes effect as soon as the civil notary passes the deed of the merger.[77] However, afterwards the merger can be declared void by the court under certain circumstances[78] at the request of a member of the board of directors, shareholder or other interested party. The only ground for annulment that this specific shareholder, Prof X, could potentially invoke is that the resolution of the general meeting is null and void or voidable. If that was indeed the case, the court can nullify the merger on that ground.[79] Such an action needs to be claimed within six months of the deed of merger being filed with the Chamber of Commerce.[80] However, considering what was mentioned under (i) and (ii) above, there seems to be little reason to assume that the resolution regarding the merger would indeed be treated as null and void or voidable.

---

[72] Hof Amsterdam (OK) 17 February 2009, *ARO* 2004/45.

[73] B Kemp, *Aandeelhoudersverantwoordelijkheid, De positie en de rol van de aandeelhouder en aandeelhoudersvergadering* (Deventer, Kluwer, 2015) ch 5.

[74] DCC, Art 2:8.

[75] DCC, Art 3:13.

[76] DCC, Art 3:13-2.

[77] MJ Kroeze, *Mr. C. Assers Handleiding tot de beoefening van het Nederlands Burgerlijk Recht. 2. Rechtspersonenrecht. Deel I*. De rechtspersoon* (Deventer, Kluwer, 2015) 438.

[78] As mentioned in DCC, Art 2:323.

[79] DCC, Art 2:323-1.

[80] DCC, Art 2:323-3.

iv. Conclusion

Prof X has an individual right to ask for information during the general meeting and he can, in principle, put forward as many questions as he wants. The board of directors should answer these questions unless a substantial interest of the company points against the provision of this information. Given the fact that in the hypothetical case it seems that Prof X is abusing his rights as a shareholder and, although it is dependent on the relevance of the questions that he puts forward, it seems likely that the court will decide in favour of the lawyer representing AB. Moreover, the request to nullify the merger was filed in time (within six months), but the grounds for a voidable merger are probably not present since it was not reasonable and fair to assume that the board would allow 100 questions to be put forward by a single shareholder. As such, the board could not be expected to be able to provide an answer to all of the questions.

F. Finland

i. Introduction

Like German law, a resolution of a general meeting will only be void in particularly extreme situations. Pursuant to chapter 21, section 2 of the Companies Act 2006 (CA), a resolution of the general meeting will be void where:

1. no notice has been delivered of the general meeting or the provisions on the notice have been materially breached;
2. the resolution requires the consent of a shareholder and such consent has not been obtained;
3. the resolution is clearly contrary to the principle of equal treatment of the shareholders and the consent of the shareholder has not been obtained; or
4. according to the law, the resolution could not have been passed even with the consent of all shareholders.

In other cases, the unlawfulness of a resolution of a general meeting may lead to its voidability. Voidable resolutions may be challenged pursuant to the CA.

ii. Standing to Sue and Time Limit

Any shareholder can bring a claim against a company on the grounds that a resolution is unlawful. There is no requirement that the shareholder holds a minimum number of shares or that he or she be present at the meeting or that he or she has voted against the resolution. The resolution can be challenged regardless of whether the plaintiff-shareholder has suffered any loss or been otherwise affected by the resolution.[81]

A claim to challenge an unlawful resolution must be filed within three months of the date of the resolution being passed. Consequently, Prof X has complied with this requirement.

---

[81] J Mähönen and S Villa, *Osakeyhtiö III – Corporate Governance* (Helsinki, Talentum, 2012) 298–99.

iii. Cause of Action

A resolution by the general meeting may be challenged pursuant to chapter 21, section 1 of the CA where: (i) the procedural provisions of the CA or the articles of association have been breached and the breach may have had an impact on the content of the resolution or otherwise on the rights of a shareholder; or (ii) the resolution is otherwise contrary to the CA or the articles of association. This case concerns shareholders' rights to request information, which is safeguarded by chapter 5, section 25 of the CA, and a violation would consequently fall within the ambit of (ii) above.

If requested by a shareholder, the board of directors and the CEO are obliged to provide more detailed information on the circumstances that may affect the evaluation of a matter dealt with by the general meeting. The board of directors and the CEO, as well as the supervisory board (if relevant), are under an obligation to ensure that this right is realised before the meeting is convened.[82] Thus, the directors are presumed to be reasonably prepared to answer questions and give information. As under German law, this right of the shareholders must be exercised at the general meeting.

The request must be directly connected to the matter at hand, except in cases concerning financial statements where the obligation applies to more general information on the financial position of the company.[83] A merger includes financial and other important considerations and therefore a more extensive right to information would be justifiable.

Consequently, Prof X has a right to information, unless the information requested clearly is irrelevant to the evaluation of the proposed merger. The board is excused from and must refuse to answer questions that would cause significant harm to the company.[84]

The right to request information has generally not been abused in Finland, in part perhaps, because of the following provision in chapter 5, section 25(2) of the CA: if the question cannot be answered on the basis of information available at the meeting, the board is obliged to provide an answer in writing within two weeks.

Unlike German law, there are no general reasons that would restrict the right to demand information such as fiduciary duties owed by shareholders to other shareholders.

iv. Consequences of a Breach

The general meeting must pass resolutions on the basis of sufficient and correct information. If not, the resolution might be void or voidable. The resolution to restrict the number of questions to 40 of the 100 initially asked and then to answer only 30 may be a breach of the right to information if the chairman of the general meeting has not reached the conclusion that the information requested is irrelevant for the purposes of evaluating the proposed merger. However, the annulment of the resolution would require a breach of the provisions of the CA and the breach may have had an effect

---

[82] CA, c 5, s 10.
[83] CA, c 5, s 25(1).
[84] CA, c 5, s 25(1).

on the contents of the resolution or otherwise on the rights of a shareholder or the resolution is otherwise contrary to the CA or the articles of association.[85] Taking into account the nature of Prof X's questions and the fact that he owns only one share, it is likely that the breach of the right to information would have had no effect on the outcome of the merger resolution. Therefore, it is unlikely that Prof X's claim would succeed.

The registration of the merger following the approval of the merger resolution at the general meeting can only be successfully opposed by a creditor.[86] Therefore, as a shareholder, Prof X cannot hinder the registration. As in German law, compensation issues are dealt with in separate proceedings.[87]

v. 'Abuse of Right to Sue'

As pointed out in the Finnish law solution to chapter 8 above, the minority protection mechanism in a merger is the right to have shares redeemed. Therefore, a shareholder of the merging company who opposes the merger may, at the general meeting that is to decide on the merger, demand that his or her shares be redeemed. As pointed out above, any shareholder owning even one share can bring a claim against a company on the grounds that a resolution of the general meeting is unlawful. Therefore, Prof X may take legal action against the company and challenge the resolution of the general meeting even if Prof X's claim is unlikely to succeed. Negotiations of a settlement would be viewed as in the ordinary course of matters. However, in some situations, the invocation of one's legal rights may fall under the general legal principle of chicanery. The said principle stipulates that a person's principal objective in using his or her legal rights must not be to maliciously harm another party.[88]

G. Poland

i. The Shareholder's Right to Information

The shareholder's right to information in a public company includes the possibility of shareholders asking questions of the members of the management board at the general meeting, outside the general meeting and in a manner combining both. The management board is entitled to refuse to answer a question posed at the general meeting if: (i) the question does not relate to any matter tabled on the agenda of the meeting; (ii) answering the question could expose a particular member of the management board to legal liability, for example, by disclosing a business secret (Commercial Companies Code (CCC), Article 428 or in the case of a publicly listed company,

---

[85] CA, c 21, s 1.
[86] CA, c 16, s 15.
[87] Redemption proceeding as per CA, c16, s 13(3) and (4).
[88] On the principle of the chicanery, see M Hemmo, 'Irtisanomisvapaus ja pitkäkestoiset liikesopimukset' (1996) *Defensor Legis* 328, 334–35 and S Villa, *Välipääomarahoitusinstrumentit* (Lakimiesliiton kustannus, Helsinki, 2001) ch 3.7.8.5.

revealing inside information held by a board member before it is publicly disclosed to participants in the regulated market); and (iii) the question relates to data already published on the company's website, for example, the question is deemed to have been answered if the company has presented relevant information in the Frequently Asked Questions section of its website (CCC, Article 428, section 4). The management board is required to refuse to give any answer which could damage the company or subsidiary or related entity, for example, by revealing trade secrets or confidential information protected by law (CCC, Article 428 section 2).

In contrast, if a shareholder abuses his or her right to information, for example, by heckling, this does not in itself justify the management board refusing to provide answers. An abuse by the shareholder of his or her right to information may be deemed at most an expression of bad corporate practice.[89]

The management board of AB could – in respect of the 10 detailed questions (provided that they are not covered by information published on its website) – take advantage of the possibility of providing written information outside the general meeting. This method, which constitutes a combined way of fulfilling the information duty, can be invoked for 'important reasons' (CCC, Article 428, section 5). It is arguable that the need to verify and investigate a few of the issues queried would constitute such an important reason. The deadline for providing answers to such questions is two weeks from the date of making such a request to that effect at the general meeting. A breach of that deadline may render the company liable to the shareholder in damages (Civil Code, Article 471) and also make the management board liable to the company in damages (CCC, Article 483).

ii. Challenging the Resolution of the General Meeting

A shareholder may challenge a resolution passed at the general meeting by suing the company. A breach of the shareholder's right to information (CCC, Article 428) may constitute grounds for treating the resolution as invalid (CCC, Article 425). It ought to be emphasised that shareholders have a right to information irrespective of the amount of share capital of the company that they hold.

It should be stressed that registration proceedings will not be suspended by a challenge to a resolution of the general meeting. However, owing to the fact that a challenge has been made, the registration court may suspend registration proceedings after conducting a hearing (CCC, Article 423, section 2). The objective of this provision is to place the adverse consequences of registration or refusal thereof on the entity which is least likely to be successful in winning the case if it came before a commercial court. Moreover, if a shareholder raises a baseless legal action seeking the invalidity of a resolution purely for vexatious or nuisance purposes, that party will be penalised by being held liable for 10 times the cost of proceedings and the fees of one professional attorney (CCC, Article 423, section 2).

---

[89] A Szumański in S Sołtysiński, A Szumański, A Szajkowski and J Szwaja, *Kodeks Spółek Handlowych. Komentarz* (Warsaw, CH Beck, 2013) 543.

Any shareholder who voted against a resolution passed at a general meeting and requested that his or her protest be recorded in the minutes of the meeting is entitled to raise a legal action seeking the invalidity of the resolution. The deadline for challenging a resolution that specifically concerns a merger between companies has been shortened by Article 509, section 2, sentence 1 of the CCC and amounts to one month only, whereas under general provisions it may amount to six months or two or even three years.[90]

In a number of cases, the Supreme Court has considered the approach that ought to be applied where the validity of a resolution passed by the general meeting is challenged for having formal (procedural) irregularities. As far as an action for annulment of the resolution is concerned, the violation of procedural regulations only matters if it has an impact on the merits of those resolutions.[91] In the hypothetical case, the shareholder's right to information has indeed been violated but the plaintiff will have to demonstrate that this has impacted on the merits of the resolution. It is unlikely that the court would issue a judgment confirming such impact of Prof X on the majority shareholders and consequently the result of the voting.[92] Even if such proof is demonstrated, Article 509, section 3 of the CCC provides that procedural irregularities which only concern the share exchange ratio in the merger process (eg failure to inform shareholders on the method of calculation of the assets of the company being acquired or of companies merging) cannot be invoked as a legitimate reason for challenging the merger resolution.[93] Although the case does not specify what Prof X is mostly concerned about, the exchange ratio of shares is a central issue for the minority shareholders' rights in the merger process which cannot be questioned by Prof X in an action for annulment of the resolution (although it is possible in an action to redress damage).

In a recent judgment, the District Court seems to have curbed the excessive use of the right to information, holding that the shareholder's right to information concerns the company itself rather than information concerning other entities (or the merger).[94] Providing that the 'technical details of the merger' pertain only to the AB company and the requested information does not breach the duty to protect inside information of the public company, management will be precluded from avoiding the duty to answer the questions. This does not mean, however, that his claim for annulment will

---

[90] See A Szumański in S Sołtysiński, A Szumański, A Szajkowski and J Szwaja, *Kodeks Spółek Handlowych. Komentarz* (Warsaw, CH Beck, 2008) 1374.

[91] See the judgment of the Supreme Court, 8 December 1998, I CKN 243/98, *OSN* 1999, issue 6/116.

[92] See the judgment of the Supreme Court dated 21.02.2012 VCSK 9/12) in which the Court stated that the resolution to merge is under the strong protection of Art 509 of CCC, which limits both the grounds of the action for an annulment or for a declaration of the invalidity of the resolution (procedural irregularities connected with establishing exchange ratio are excluded) and the time within which a resolution can be challenged to 1 month from its adoption.

[93] Ibid.

[94] Decision of the District Court in Krakow, dated 26.01.2016, XII Ga 437/15. In the judgment the Court seemed to be reluctant to hold that the procedural infringements (as opposed to the merits of the resolution itself) will give rise to an action for declaration of invalidity of a resolution. The Court drew a line between the right to be informed, which is protected by a separate action seeking an injunction (resolution that the management board is obligated to provide the information according to Art 429 of CCC), and the right to file an action for the annulment of the resolution.

be successful. It will be difficult for Prof X to demonstrate that failure to answer his questions is a legitimate reason to challenge the resolution: firstly, owing to the limitations of the grounds on which such a claim will be based (exclusion of information regarding exchange ratio and other entities than AB company itself), and, secondly, due to the very low probability that Prof X will demonstrate that procedural irregularities have influenced the merits of the resolution (the result of the voting). In our opinion, therefore, the court will decide in favour of AB Company.

H. Latvia

i. The Shareholder's Right to Ask Questions

The question of whether individual shareholders of a Latvian public company have a statutory right to ask questions at the general meeting of shareholders must be decided on the basis of the Commercial Code and the Financial Instrument Market Law. In general, individual shareholders have no statutory right to ask questions at the general meeting of shareholders in a Latvian public company (*akciju sabiedrība* (AS)). According to sections 274 and 276 of the Commercial Code,[95] a meeting of the shareholders may take decisions only regarding those issues on the agenda which are indicated in the publication or notice regarding the convening of the meeting. Although it is not prohibited for a shareholder to pose additional, spontaneous questions during the meeting of the shareholders, there is no statutory right on which a shareholder can rely in order to do so.

In principle, additional issues may be included in the notice regarding the meeting. However, only shareholders or groups of shareholders who hold no less than 5 per cent of the share capital of a company are entitled to do so in terms of section 274(2) of the Commercial Code. If Prof X was able to meet this threshold requirement, section 274(2) of the Commercial Code stipulates that he would still be required to request the general meeting of shareholders to include additional issues in the agenda of the meeting within seven days of the date of the publication of the advertisement of the general meeting or within five days of the day when he received the notice.

With regard to public companies, the Financial Instrument Market Law contains additional regulations. According to section 54.2 of the Financial Instrument Market Law, individual shareholders have the right to submit additional questions to be included in the agenda which are indicated in the publication or notice regarding the convening of the meeting within seven days after the publication or notice regarding the convening of the meeting. Together with these questions, shareholders are obliged to submit a draft of suggested decisions on those questions, if necessary, or explanations. The board of directors examines the questions and other documents and decides if they should be included in the agenda. Where the board of directors declines all questions and suggestions, individual shareholders have the right to submit them during the shareholders' general meeting.

---

[95] Likums 'Komerclikums', Latvijas Vēstnesis 158/160 (2069/2071), 13 April 2000.

ii. The Right to Have Questions Answered

Unless the general meeting decides to include some of the questions on the agenda, there was no obligation imposed on AB to answer the 100 questions posed, since they were not initially included on the agenda of the general meeting

iii. Challenging Resolutions of the Shareholders' General Meeting

The shareholders' general meeting takes decisions by a majority of votes of the shareholders with voting rights present at the meeting, unless the law or the articles of association of the public company prescribe a higher threshold in terms of section 284(1) of the Commercial Code. However, a decision taken by the majority does not operate to cure any procedural violation. In principle, therefore, decisions passed by a majority of the shareholders may be challenged and declared invalid.[96] As such, it is of some importance to identify the nature of the possible violation and whether it falls within the scope of section 286 of the Commercial Code.[97] In the hypothetical case, assuming that Prof X holds 5 per cent of the share capital of AB, it is submitted that no statutorily recognised breach can be established on the basis of section 286 of the Commercial Code.

iv. The Period for the Commencement of Action

In the hypothetical case, any legal action will not be precluded based on a statute of limitation. According to section 288(2) of the Commercial Code, the period for the commencement of an action to declare a decision of a meeting of shareholders as void is three months from the date of the meeting.

---

[96] Judgment of the Latvian Supreme Court in case No. SKC-37 of 10 February 2010.
[97] 'Section 286. Declaration of a Decision Taken by a Meeting of Stockholders as Void

(1) A court may declare a decision taken by a meeting of shareholders as void if:

1) it contradicts the purposes of the company, the public interest or morality;
2) it infringes the rights of third persons;
3) it contradicts the law or the articles of association;
4) the provisions of the law or of the articles of association regarding the convening of the meeting or the announcement of information associated with it have been violated;
5) shareholders were unlawfully not allowed to participate in the meeting;
6) shareholders were unlawfully not allowed to become acquainted with draft decisions, the list of shareholders participating at the meeting or the minutes of the meeting of shareholders;
7) shareholders were unjustifiably refused information requested and this has significantly affected their approach to voting on the relevant issue;
8) the voting provisions were not observed at the meeting and thereby the results of the voting were significantly affected, or the provisions of law for the number of votes given were not observed; or
9) the requirements referred to in section 284, paragraph three were not observed.

(2) The declaration of a decision taken by a meeting of shareholders as void shall not affect the rights of third persons obtained in good faith.'

v. The Rights of Shareholders

If it is presumed that the right of Prof X to have his questions heard has been violated, even though it may delay or even render a multi-million euro merger impossible, his conduct is not invalid or illegal. If an entitlement to ask questions exists, its exercise may not be treated as illegal, for example, on the ground that the importance of the right to ask questions is disproportionately small in comparison to the success of the merger for the future of AB. A shareholder is free to exercise his or her rights without limitation.

vi. The Conduct of Prof X in Raising Action

In the event that a single shareholder brings an action in order to reach a settlement with the company and therefore for personal financial gain, such conduct would not render the action itself invalid. According to the principles of Latvian law, an action in court may only be declared invalid if the statutorily defined conditions for the claim are not met or cannot be established. In the event that Prof X has fulfilled all procedural as well as material requirements, he may bring the action before the court. The intention to bring the action for financial gain alone is not sufficient to declare the claim invalid, even if his intention clearly deviates from the arguments laid down in the action. Such conduct may however result in an obligation of Prof X towards AB to compensate any losses sustained by AB if an action for damages is brought against him.

I. The UK[98]

i. Introduction to Shareholder Rights

In terms of section 319A of the CA 2006, a statutory obligation is imposed on a traded company such as AB.[99] It directs that at 'a general meeting of a traded company, the company must cause to be answered any question relating to the business being dealt with at the meeting put by a member attending the meeting'. However, there are four statutory exceptions to this rule, whereby a chairman may refuse to answer questions if:

1. answering the question would interfere unduly with the preparation for the meeting;[100]
2. answering the question would involve the disclosure of confidential information;[101]
3. the answer has already been given on a website in the form of an answer to a question;[102] or
4. it is undesirable in the interests of the company or the good order of the meeting that the question be answered.[103]

---

[98] Abbreviations: CA 2006 (the Companies Act 2006).
[99] In terms of CA 2006, s 360C, a 'traded company' is a company with shares which (a) carry rights to vote at general meetings and (b) are admitted to trading on a regulated market (such as the London Stock Exchange) by or with the consent of the company.
[100] CA 2006, s 319A(2)(a)(i).
[101] CA 2006, s 319A(2)(a)(ii).
[102] CA 2006, s 319A(2)(b).
[103] CA 2006, s 319A(2)(c).

The chairman of the meeting should attempt to answer all questions which are posed at the meeting. However, in circumstances where the answer is not available for the chairman to provide, he or she can either nominate a representative to answer the question or a full answer could be deferred and provided after the meeting. In its guidance on section 319A of the CA 2006, the Institute of Chartered Secretaries and Administrators (ICSA)[104] notes that the chairman must be sure that one of the exceptions above applies when refusing to answer a question. Moreover, the chairman should be able to refer to the relevant provisions of section 319A of the CA 2006 when deciding how to answer a particular question at a meeting. Finally, it is directed that the chairman should use his or her discretion in good faith.

Therefore, it is perfectly lawful for the chairman of AB to (i) defer the provision of answers to Prof X's 100 questions if he is unable to provide a full answer at the general meeting or (ii) refuse to provide an answer to each of Prof X's questions if (a) the question would involve the disclosure of confidential information or (b) it is undesirable in the interests of the company or the good order of the meeting that the question be answered at the general meeting. If (ii)(b) is invoked in support of a decision not to answer Prof X's questions, the chairman should explain why a response to the question would be undesirable on an objective basis (rather than on the basis of his subjective opinion). In the context of the hypothetical case, it would appear to be valid on an objective basis for the chairman to refuse to answer more than 30 questions if this would result in the disclosure of confidential information about the merger or if it would disrupt the good order of the general meeting. On the facts of the case, it is unclear whether confidentiality would be compromised, but there is sufficient basis to hold that the good order of the general meeting would be impaired.

ii. Consequences of a Violation of Procedure

It is possible for shareholders to challenge the conduct of the chairman at the meeting. If it can be established that the chairman violated or deprived the member of a right, such as the right to ask questions, then the validity of the resolution passed at the meeting to approve the merger may be called into question.[105] Any challenge must be progressed without undue delay. However, as Kosmin and Roberts point out:

> A minority shareholder who has an insufficient number of shares to prevent the passing of a particular resolution may find it very difficult to obtain any effective relief unless he can show serious prejudice to his rights as a member and the possibility that the outcome of the meeting might have been different had his rights been recognized.[106]

Therefore, the courts are generally reluctant to scrutinise the conduct of general meetings and, in particular, to challenge the chairman's exercise of discretion unless there is evidence of bad faith. In Re Piccadilly Radio plc,[107] Millet J made it clear that

---

[104] ICSA, 'Guidance on the Implementation of the Shareholders' Rights Directive', 8: see www.icsa.org.uk/knowledge/resources/shareholder-rights-directive.
[105] Henderson v Bank of Australasia (1890) LR 45 Ch D 330 (CA).
[106] L Kosmin and C Roberts, Company Meetings: Law, Practice and Procedure (Oxford, Oxford University Press, 2008) 139.
[107] Re Piccadilly Radio plc (1989) BCC 692 (Ch).

364 MATHIAS SIEMS (EDITOR)

applicants must have clear and compelling grounds before making any court application to challenge a general meeting of a company or any resolution passed at that
meeting. This is particularly the case when the company is involved in, for example, a
contested takeover or merger bid, or in a similar struggle for control of the company,
as such applications may unnecessarily hold up vital company business which could
lead to considerable losses.

As such, in the hypothetical case, it is extremely unlikely that Prof X would have
valid grounds to challenge the merger resolution. First, even though Prof X and other
shareholders of AB have a statutory right to ask questions, it was impossible for the
board to respond to all 100 questions and the decision of the chairman to refuse to
answer more than 30 questions is likely to be justified within his discretion on the basis
of the exceptions considered above. As a consequence, there has been no breach of
procedure at the general meeting of AB. However, even if there had been a violation
of procedure, Prof X has an insufficient number of shares to prevent the passage of the
resolution which was adopted by an overwhelming majority. Therefore, he cannot rely
on the case law mentioned above which allows shareholders to challenge the conduct
of the chairman at the meeting unless he can demonstrate bad faith on the part of the
chairman. Otherwise, it is unlikely that the courts will investigate the conduct of the
meeting. Since there is no evidence of bad faith on the part of the chairman of AB,
Prof X's legal challenge is destined to be unsuccessful.

iii. Summary and Conclusion

There would appear to be an absence of bad faith on the part of the chairman of
AB in refusing to answer more than 30 of the questions posed by Prof X. Moreover,
the chairman has valid grounds for a refusal to answer more than 30 questions under
section 319A(2)(b) and (c) of the CA 2006 on the basis that this may result in the
disclosure of confidential information about the merger or that it would disrupt the
good order of the general meeting. The end result is that there has been no breach of
procedure at the general meeting of AB and so Prof X would be unable to persuade a
court to invalidate the meeting and/or the resolution passed at the meeting to approve
the merger.

J. The US

Delaware corporations must hold an annual meeting of stockholders to elect directors,
unless directors are elected by written consent in lieu of an annual general meeting.[108] While matters such as the merger described in the hypothetical case may be
decided at an annual general meeting, Delaware law also provides for the calling of
special meetings to vote on particular issues that may arise in between annual general
meetings.[109]

---

[108] See, eg, the Delaware General Corporation Law (DGCL), § 211(b).
[109] DGCL, § 211(d).

Stockholders in a Delaware corporation have equitable standing to sue on behalf of the corporation in a so-called 'derivative' action.[110] The DGCL specifies the following requirements:

> In any derivative suit instituted by a stockholder of a corporation, it shall be averred in the complaint that the plaintiff was a stockholder of the corporation at the time of the transaction of which such stockholder complains or that such stockholder's stock thereafter devolved upon such stockholder by operation of law.[111]

Even though he is a holder of only one share, Prof X is entitled to bring a derivative claim under this provision.

In addition to these standing requirements, a derivative plaintiff must meet the requirements of Court of Chancery Rule 23.1, which include a requirement that the complaint 'allege with particularity the efforts, if any, made by the plaintiff to obtain the action the plaintiff desires from the directors or comparable authority and the reasons for the plaintiff's failure to obtain the action or for not making the effort'. This is referred to as the 'demand requirement'. In addition, derivative litigation cannot be dismissed or compromised without the approval of the Court of Chancery, and the recovery, if any, flows only to the corporation, not directly to the shareholders.

In some instances, a shareholder is injured directly, not derivatively through injury to the corporation. In these cases, holding one share of stock is sufficient to provide standing, and the additional procedural requirements associated with derivative litigation are inapplicable. Whether Prof X's claim is a derivative claim or a direct claim depends on the nature of the alleged harm. The Delaware Supreme Court articulated the standard for distinguishing derivative and direct claims in *Tooley v Donaldson, Lufkin & Jenrette, Inc*: 'The analysis must be based solely on the following questions: Who suffered the alleged harm—the corporation or the suing stockholder individually—and who would receive the benefit of the recovery or other remedy?'[112]

Delaware law does not provide for the 'annulment' of a merger, but plaintiffs often challenge mergers by asking a court for an injunction. An injunction is appropriate only if the shareholder challenges the transaction prior to its implementation/consummation.[113] In Delaware, the statute of limitations for such claims is three years.[114] Consequently, even though Prof X waited four weeks before filing his claim, he is still well within the period prescribed in the statute of limitations.

As for the cause of action, Prof X has no obvious claim. Delaware statutes regulate quorum and voting requirements, notice requirements and certain voting procedures in connection with annual and special meetings,[115] but the statutes do not regulate the conduct of the meetings, as argued by Prof X. Under the DGCL, therefore, AB would

---

[110] See, eg, *Schoon v Smith*, 953 A 2d 196 (Del 2008).

[111] DGCL, § 327.

[112] *Tooley v Donaldson, Lufkin & Jenrette, Inc*, 845 A 2d 1031 (Del 2004).

[113] See, eg, DGCL, § 251(d) (outlining the process by which a merger becomes effective following shareholder approval). If the merger was already deemed to be effective, the cause of action would be for rescission of the merger: see, eg, *Crescent/Mach I Partners, LP v Turner*, 846 A 2d 963 (Del Ch 2000).

[114] See, eg, Del Code Ann 10, § 8106; see also *Baron v Allied Artists Picture Corp*, 717 F 2d 105 (3d Cir 1983) applying a 3-year statute of limitations found in Del Code Ann 10, § 8106 to a cause of action seeking to enjoin a merger.

[115] DGCL, §§ 212–32.

be correct in arguing that a shareholder has no statutory right to ask questions from the floor at shareholder meetings and a corporation is under no obligation to answer those questions.

Unless the company's by-laws provide otherwise, AB's board of directors manages the meeting. The board of directors must perform this obligation in accordance with its fiduciary duties,[116] but the case offers no facts to suggest self-dealing or other inappropriate behaviour by the board.

However, the board may otherwise be subject to an affirmative duty to disclose certain information to shareholders. In submitting the merger to a shareholder vote, the board would solicit for shareholders' proxies and would thus be required to disclose certain information to shareholders under the securities laws.[117] Moreover, the Delaware courts have held that directors and controlling shareholders owe shareholders a fiduciary duty to disclose all facts that are material to the transaction when seeking their approval of a transaction.[118] Prof X might be able to seek an injunction on these grounds. Finally, independent from the shareholder meeting, Prof X might submit a request to inspect AB's books and records, in respect of which he must establish a 'proper purpose'.[119]

Consequently, unless Prof X produces evidence of fraud or other information demonstrating that the results of the meeting were somehow tainted, the fact that he was unable to fully participate at the shareholder meeting will not be sufficient to enable him to successfully challenge the merger. However, he might be able to argue that the disclosure made by directors about the merger was materially deficient. It is possible that the Delaware courts would accept AB's defence that the merger would have been nevertheless approved, at least if there was a controlling shareholder in favour of the transaction.[120]

---

[116] eg, the courts may hold directors to a reasonableness standard for actions affecting votes on mergers. See, eg, *Mercier v Inter-Tel, Inc*, 929 A.2.d 786 (Del Ch 2007) (upholding a board's decision to delay the meeting to avoid the rejection of a merger); *Portney v Cryo-Cell Int'l, Inc*, 940 A.2d 43 (Del Ch 2008) (finding that CEO's filibustering conduct constituted a breach of his fiduciary duty and ordering a new meeting).

[117] See Sch 14A, 17 CFR 240.14a-101.

[118] *Lynch v Vickers Energy Corp.*, 383 A.2d 278 (Del 1977) (the fiduciary duty of candour requires disclosure of all 'germane facts' to communications requiring shareholder action); *Bershad v Curtiss- Wright Corp.*, 535 A.2d 840 (Del 1987) (assessing director liability for a failure to disclose to shareholders turns on issues of materiality and drawing on federal case law definition of material); *Rosenblatt v Getty Oil Co*, 493 A.2d 929 (Del 1985). The Delaware courts have further clarified that directors do not owe shareholders an underlying duty of disclosure absent mandatory or voluntary communications to shareholders. The rationale is not to overload shareholders with information. See *Malone v Brincat*, 722 A.2d. 5 (Del 1998); *Brody v Zhauca*, 697 A.2d. 749 (Del 1997); *Stroud v Grace*, 606 A.2d 75 (Del 1992) (Delaware corporations are under a fiduciary duty to disclose fully and fairly all material information within the board's control when it seeks shareholder action); *In re J.P. Morgan Chase & Co. Shareholder Litigation*, 906 A.2d 766 (Del 2006); *In re Wayport, Inc Litigation*, 76 A.3d 296 (Del Ch 2013). See also L Hamermesh, 'Calling Off the Lynch Mob: The Corporate Director's Fiduciary Disclosure Duty' (1996) 49 *Vanderbilt Law Review* 1087; Z Barclift, 'Senior Corporate Officers and the Duty of Candor: Do The CEO And CFO Have A Duty To Inform?' (2006) 41 *Valparaiso University Law Review* 269, 283–86; S German, 'What They Don't Know Can Hurt Them: Corporate Officers' Duty of Candor to Directors' (2009) 34 *Delaware Journal of Corporate Law* 221, 226–33.

[119] DGCL, § 220(b). For a discussion of possible purposes, see, eg, *Thomas & Betts Corp v Leviton Mfg Co, Inc*, 685 A.2d 702 (Del Ch 1995).

[120] *Glinert v Wickes Companies, Inc*, 1992 WL 165153 (finding that in spite of a violation of the duty of candour, defendants held voting control over the company); see also *Virginia Bankshares, Inc v Sandberg,*

K. South Africa

Shareholders have wide powers at a general meeting. Even a single shareholder can raise matters at general meetings and question directors.[121] The question, *in casu*, however, concerns the rights of shareholders, especially minority shareholders, in the context of a merger. For the approval of a merger, a special resolution is necessary and this must happen at a meeting called for that purpose with a quorum of 25 per cent of the voting rights present.[122] This shareholder approval requirement provides protection for minority shareholders, but it also provides flexibility to prevent a troublesome minority from frustrating a merger.[123]

Once the merger has been approved by the requisite majority, ie by way of a special resolution passed at a meeting for that purpose with a quorum of at least 25 per cent of people entitled to exercise their voting rights on the matter, the dissenters are not generally able to frustrate the merger. There are only two grounds on which a company cannot proceed to implement the merger, despite the adoption of the requisite special resolution. For instance, if a shareholder who voted against the merger makes a successful application for leave to apply to the court for a review of the transaction. This must, however, happen within ten business days after the vote.[124] *In casu*, this did not happen as Prof X did not file a claim until four weeks after the decision was taken. The only possibility available for Prof X is to rely on section 164 of the Companies Act 2008. Section 164 makes provision for a new remedy, the appraisal remedy.

The appraisal remedy is only applicable in certain circumstances.[125] In broad terms this remedy is triggered when a company passes a special resolution to amend the rights of a class of shares in terms of the Memorandum of Incorporation that materially or adversely affects the rights of that shareholder or undertakes a fundamental transaction (like a merger).[126] In these circumstances, dissatisfied or minority shareholders do not have to go along with the decision made by the company as they have the right to opt out of the company by withdrawing the fair value of the shares by exercising their appraisal rights. This remedy is only available to those shareholders who are entitled to vote on the resolution. Moreover, he or she must have voted against the resolution and mere abstention will not suffice. To make use of this remedy a shareholder

---

501 U.S. 1083 (1990) (securities law case denying the materiality of disclosure violation because minority shareholders' approval was not needed). The presence of a controlling shareholder raises the question of that individual's conflict of interest, which would likely require the latter to show the entire fairness of the transaction.

[121] *Byng v London Life Association Ltd* [1990] Ch 170, 188.

[122] Companies Act 2008, s 115(2)(a). See the discussion in ch 8 at II K, above.

[123] FHI Cassim (ed), *Contemporary Company Law* (Cape Town, Juta, 2012) 661.

[124] Companies Act 2008, s 115(3)(b) read with 115(6).

[125] See s 164 of the Companies Act 2008. See also HGJ Beukes, 'An Introduction to the Appraisal Remedy as proposed in the Companies Bill: Triggering Actions and the Differences between the Appraisal Remedy and Existing Shareholder Remedies' (2008) *South African Mercantile Law Journal* 479 (but see A Pike, 'An Alternative view of the Appraisal Remedy' (2015) *South African Mercantile Law Journal* 678); HGJ Beukes, 'An Introduction to the Appraisal Remedy in the Companies Act 2008: Standing and the Appraisal Procedure' (2010) *South African Mercantile Law Journal* 176 and J Yeats, 'Putting Appraisal Rights into Perspective' (2014) *Stellenbosch Law Review* 328.

[126] As regulated in Companies Act 2008, ch 5.

should have sent a notice of objection to the company before the relevant resolution was voted on.[127] Such a shareholder will then be able to make a demand for payment of the fair value of his or her shares by delivering a written notice to the company. This demand must be made within 20 business days after receiving the adoption of the resolution. The shareholder will then have no further rights other than to get paid the fair value for the shares.

In casu, this would have been an option available to Prof X but he did not comply with the prerequisite requirements,[128] discussed above, in order to make such a demand.

L. Japan

i. The Accountability of Directors

A duty of accountability applies to directors at the shareholders' meeting in terms of the Companies Act (CA). When requested by the shareholders to provide explanations on such matters, a director, an accounting adviser, a company auditor or an executive officer is obliged to provide all necessary explanations with respect to certain matters at the shareholders' meeting (CA, Article 314).

However, this duty does not apply where the explanations sought are not relevant to the matters which are the purpose of the shareholders' meeting, or in cases where such explanations are to the serious detriment of the common interest of the share-holders, or in other cases prescribed as justifiable grounds by the applicable Ordinance of the Ministry of Justice (CA, Article 314, proviso). Moreover, Article 71(1) of the Ordinance of the Ministry of Justice stipulates that a director can refuse to answer any question which requires a degree of research in order to be answered properly. However, on the other hand, it also provides that a director cannot refuse to answer a question when the shareholder provides advance notice of the question he or she intends to ask before the date of the shareholders' meeting.

In the hypothetical case, there would be justification for Prof X to be restricted to 40 questions as it would be very difficult for the board to respond to all 100 questions. Moreover, there would also be justification for the chairman and his fellow board members to respond to only 30 questions, since the remaining 10 questions concerned very specific details of the merger to which they could not respond on the spot.

ii. Legal Proceedings Seeking the Annulment of a Resolution Passed at a Shareholders' Meeting

A shareholder is entitled to challenge a resolution passed at a shareholders' meeting by raising a legal action within three months of the date of the resolution being passed: (i) when the procedures adopted to call the shareholders' meeting violated the laws and regulations or the articles of incorporation of the company or are grossly improper; (ii) when the contents of the resolution of the shareholders' meeting violate the articles

---

[127] Companies Act 2008, s 164(3).
[128] Companies Act 2008, s 164(5).

of incorporation of the company; or (iii) when a grossly improper resolution is passed as a result of a person exercising a voting right who has a special interest in the resolution of the shareholders' meeting (CA, Article 831(1)).[129] However, in cases where an action is raised, even if the procedures for calling the shareholders' meeting are in violation of laws and regulations or the company's articles of incorporation, the court may dismiss the claim if it finds that the violation is not sufficiently serious and will not affect the resolution (CA, Article 831(2)).

In the hypothetical case, Prof X complies with the time limit requirements in respect of the legal action seeking to challenge a resolution of the shareholders' meeting. However, there may be no cause of action as it is justifiable that Prof X was restricted to 40 questions and that the chairman and his fellow board members responded to only 30. Furthermore, if there is any violation of the procedure at the general meeting, it would not be material, since the clear majority of shareholders would nonetheless have approved the merger.

iii. Legal Action Against a Director Pursuant to a Derivative Suit

A shareholder owning the shares of a company for a consecutive period of six months or more[130] may demand that a public company raise a legal action against a director (CA, Article 847(1)). If the company fails to initiate such proceedings within 60 days of the date of the demand, the shareholder who has made such a demand may bring such action himself or herself on behalf of the company (CA, Article 847(3)). Moreover, the shareholder may immediately file an action pursuing the director on behalf of the company if the company is likely to suffer irreparable harm if the shareholder is required to wait for the aforementioned 60 days before commencing such proceedings himself or herself (CA, Article 847(5)). Turning to the hypothetical case, it is submitted that Prof X can raise an action to pursue the director since Prof X has complied with the requirements for commencing such action.

However, when a shareholder raises such an action, the court may, in response to a petition by the director, order such a shareholder to provide reasonable security for the action (CA, Article 847(7)). If the director intends to file such a petition, the onus lies on him or her to establish a prima facie case that the shareholder's action has been raised in bad faith (CA, Article 847(8)).

iv. Blocking the Entry of the Merger in the Competent Register and Abuse of this Right

The aforementioned rules governing legal actions against directors do not apply where the purpose of the shareholder in initiating such action is to make unlawful gains[131] or to enable a third party to inflict damage or loss on the company

---

[129] Furthermore, with regard to a resolution of a shareholders' meeting, a declaration of invalidity of that resolution may be sought by raising an action which seeks to establish that the contents of the resolution violate laws and regulations (CA, Art 830(2)).
[130] In cases where a shorter period is prescribed in the articles of incorporation, compliance is required in order to demand that the company file an action to pursue the liability of a director (CA, Art 847(1)).
[131] Nagasaki District Court, 19 February 1991 in *Hanrei Jihô* 1393, 138.

(CA, Article 847(1), proviso). In the present hypothetical case, Prof X attempted to block the entry of the merger in the commercial register until the final resolution of the legal claim he raised. However, as in German law, this application is not actually necessary.[132] A registrar is bound to dismiss an application for registration where any ground exists for the invalidation, revocation or rescission of any matter to be registered (Commercial Registration Act, Article 24, no 11).

v. The Provision of Benefits in Response to the Shareholder's Actions: Civil Consequences

Prof X's settlement offer might be treated as a form of extortion. The law provides that a public company must not give property or benefits to any person in respect of, or in response to, the exercise by a shareholder of his or her rights (CA, Article 120(1)). If the company gives such benefits to a specific shareholder without rendering a charge, it is presumed that this has been done in respect of, or in response to, the exercise by a shareholder of his or her rights. The same presumption applies where the company gives property or benefits to a specific shareholder for value where the benefit received by the company or its subsidiary is insignificant in comparison to the value of the benefits received (CA, Article 120(2)). In addition, if the company provides a benefit in violation of these provisions, the recipient of such a benefit is obliged to return the same to the company or its subsidiary and if the recipient has tendered anything to the company or its subsidiary in exchange for such benefit, he or she is entitled to have that benefit returned (CA, Article 120(3)). Finally, if the company gives property or benefits in violation of the provisions, any person involved in the provision of such benefits is jointly and severally liable to the company for payment of an amount equivalent to the value of the benefit so given (CA, Article 120(4)).[133]

vi. The Provision of Benefits in Response to the Shareholder's Actions: Criminal Consequences

When any one of the persons listed in Article 960(1)(iii)–(vi) of the CA or any other employee of a public company provides property or benefits on the account of such company or its subsidiary in respect of, or in response to, the exercise by a shareholder of his or her rights, such person will be punished by imprisonment for a period not exceeding three years or a fine of not more than three million yen (CA, Article 970(1)). These provisions also apply to any person (hereinafter 'Person') who has, knowingly, received the benefits or caused such benefits to be given to a third party (CA, Article 970(2)) and any person who has requested the Person to provide him or her or a third party with the benefits on the account of the company or its subsidiary in respect of, or in response to, the exercise by a shareholder of his or her rights (CA, Article 970(3)).

---

[132] See the German solution at A, above.

[133] However, this does not apply if such persons (excluding the directors who gave such benefit) have proven that they did not fail to exercise due care in discharging their duties (CA, Art 120(4), proviso). Exemptions from the obligations may not be given without the consent of all shareholders (CA, Art 120(5)).

When a person who has committed any of the said crimes intimidates the Person with regard to the commission of such crime, the former person will be punished by imprisonment for a period not exceeding five years or a fine of not more than five million yen (CA, Article 970(4)). It is also possible that a person who has committed any one of the said crimes will be punished by the imposition of both imprisonment and a fine in light of all the circumstances (CA, Article 970(5)).

In the hypothetical case, there is no indication why Prof X should have received €50,000 in compensation. Thus, it would be for the defendant to provide more evidence in order to show that Prof X had the sole aim of blackmailing the company.[134]

vii. 'Sôkaiya' and 'Lump-Sum Answer' at the Shareholders' Meeting

In Japan, the revision of the Commercial Code in 1981 introduced the director's duty of accountability at the shareholders' general meeting.[135] This resulted in a large list of questions being submitted to the company by professional special shareholders known as 'sôkaiya'[136] prior to the date of the shareholders' meeting. Many companies who were concerned about the potential confusion which might be engendered at shareholders' meetings and the amount of time which might be taken up with researching and answering questions adopted a strategy whereby they would lump all questions relating to similar matters together and answer them in bulk. As a result, there have been many lawsuits seeking to challenge resolutions passed at a shareholders' meeting on the basis of a breach of the accountability duty. However, the courts have accepted the legitimacy of such a 'lump-sum question and answer' technique.[137]

III. Conclusion

A. Introduction

In terms of German law, it is possible that Prof X's claim would thwart the merger. In Germany, however, many also call for a change of law: it is considered unacceptable that a single shareholder can disrupt a general meeting by asking an excessive number of questions and then block a multi-million Euro project, decided by the meeting, on the basis that not all of his or her questions were answered. Similarly, the Japanese solution indicates that in Japan some shareholders have attempted to abuse the duty of accountability of directors. In contrast to German law, however, most of the other countries examined here would not allow such a claim for a variety of different reasons.

---

[134] See the German solution at A, above.

[135] Art 237, no 3 of the former Commercial Code (Art 314 of the CA is the successor to this provision).

[136] For more details on the 'sôkaiya', see eg MD West, 'Information, Institutions, and Extortion in Japan and the United States: Making Sense of the Sokaiya Racketeers' (1999) 93 *Northwestern University Law Review* 767, 771–78.

[137] Tokyo High Court, 19 February 1986, in *Hanrei Jihô* 1207, 120.

B. Standing to Sue and Time Limits

The formal requirements for a claim are likely to be fulfilled in most of the juris-dictions under consideration inasmuch as every single shareholder has the requisite standing to sue. In contrast to the law of derivative actions, the legal systems do not usually impose significant hurdles, since a claim against a decision of the general meet-ing is based on the shareholders' own rights of participation. The exceptions are Italy and Spain where law reforms have imposed minimum thresholds for actions that chal-lenge a resolution passed at a general meeting (though shareholders could still sue for damages): in Italy shareholders have to hold at least 0.1 per cent of the share capital of the company or 5 per cent of the share capital in the case of a closely held company, and in Spain it is 0.1 per cent for listed companies or 1 per cent for other companies.[138]

Most civil law jurisdictions impose time limits for legal actions to be raised which seek to challenge resolutions and decisions reached at shareholders' meetings in some circumstances. This is attributable to the distinction between void and voidable reso-lutions, with the latter requiring shareholders to challenge the resolution within, say, one month (Germany), 90 days (Italy), three months (Finland, Latvia and Japan), six months (Poland), or one year (the Netherlands). The UK, the US and South Africa do not have provisions governing the challenge of resolutions passed at the share-holders' meeting, while case law accepts that shareholders can, generally speaking, do so without strict time limits. For the present scenario, it also needs to be consid-ered that some countries provide special time limits for merger decisions, for example, 10 days (South Africa), one month (Poland), three months (Spain), and six months (the Netherlands). In the hypothetical case, Prof X has met all of these deadlines with the exception of the ten-day deadline of South African law.

C. Cause of Action

The crucial substantive question is whether shareholders have a right to ask ques-tions in the general meeting. Shareholders of all but one of the legal systems under investigation have such a right. This is no surprise, since in the EU, Article 9 of the Shareholder Rights Directive of 2007 provides:

1. Every shareholder shall have the right to ask questions related to items on the agenda of the general meeting. The company shall answer the questions put to it by shareholders.

2. The right to ask questions and the obligation to answer are subject to the measures which Member States may take, or allow companies to take, to ensure the identification of share-holders, the good order of general meetings and their preparation and the protection of confidentiality and business interests of companies. Member States may allow companies to provide one overall answer to questions having the same content.

---

[138] Codice Civile, Art 2377 as amended and introduced by Decreto legislativo 17 gennaio 2003, n 6. Riforma organica della disciplina delle società di capitali e società cooperative, in attuazione della legge 3 ottobre 2001, n 366; LSC, articles 260, 495 as amended by Ley 31/2014, de 3 de diciembre, para la mejora del gobierno corporativo de las empresas.

Member States may provide that an answer shall be deemed to be given if the relevant information is available on the company's Internet site in a question and answer format.[139]

For some Member States, such as Latvia, Italy and the UK, this was a new right. Thus, here, we have some convergence of the law, with this Directive's provision being based on the German model.[140] Nevertheless, a degree of variation between the Member States remains. In German law, the right to ask questions is clearly focused on the general meeting, whereas in some of the other legal systems, individual questions can also be asked before or responded to after the meeting. For instance, French and Italian law allow for questions to be asked in advance and then answered during the meeting. Spanish, Finnish and Polish law provide that the directors can also answer in writing seven days (Spain) or two weeks (Finland and Poland) after the meeting. Thus, in the present case, the directors of AB could have rectified their failure to answer all of the questions on the spot.

Naturally, there are situations where the directors do not have to answer all questions posed, such as for reasons of confidentiality (see also the aforementioned provision). The current situation is more difficult to judge since none of the legal systems have fixed rules on the extent to which directors have to prepare for questions at the meeting and what maximum number of questions per shareholder may be acceptable. Only in Germany and France is there some case law on this issue; in Japan and the Netherlands there are some legislative provisions which specify (in Japan) or imply (in the Netherlands) that directors are not expected to answer all details, with the likely result being that the claim would not have been successful.

In Spain, the company by-laws may provide that shareholders must hold a minimum number of shares (which cannot exceed 1 per cent of the share capital of the company) in order to attend a general meeting. Thus, a single shareholder, such as Prof X, may be excluded from the right to ask questions in large public corporations. Other countries no longer allow such a restriction – for instance, in 2001, France repealed a similar provision, which allowed a minimum threshold.[141]

No right to ask questions exists under US law. In some cases, fiduciary duties may be significant if the directors do not disclose relevant facts in respect of a transaction they propose ('duty of candour' in the US) – a form of reasoning that could possibly also be applied in other countries in relevant circumstances. For the remaining difference, two possible explanations can be offered. On the one hand, US law is often said to give directors and managers more flexibility than their counterparts in other parts of the world. Thus, individual rights of shareholders can be regarded as the exception.[142] On the other hand, in the US model of corporate governance, proxy

---

[139] Directive 2007/36/EC of 11 July 2007 on the exercise of certain rights of shareholders in listed companies ([2007] OJ L184/17). This Directive was modified by Directive (EU) 2017/828 of 17 May 2017 amending Directive 2007/36/EC as regards the encouragement of long-term shareholder engagement ([2017] OJ L132/1); yet, Art 9 has remained unchanged.

[140] See M Siems, 'The Case Against Harmonisation of Shareholder Rights' (2005) 6 *European Business Organization Law Review* 539.

[141] See M Siems, *Convergence in Shareholder Law* (Cambridge, Cambridge University Press, 2008) 109.

[142] For suggestions as to how this ought to be changed, see LA Bebchuk, 'The Case for Increasing Shareholder Power' (2005) 118 *Harvard Law Review* 833; LA Bebchuk, 'Letting Shareholders Set the Rules'

voting plays a greater role than elsewhere.[143] Thus, the general meeting itself is less important, making discussions and debates obsolete.

D. Consequences of a Breach of the Law

If we assume that there has been a breach of company law, the question remains whether the merger itself can be challenged, in particular whether it will be automatically blocked as a result of a claim against the resolution. Countries use different tools to address this issue, some general, but some also specifically related to mergers and other special resolutions.

At a general level, Spanish law seems to have the clearest answer as a failure to answer questions at the general meeting can lead to a claim for damages but not the annulment of the subsequent resolution. In the UK, resolutions of the general meeting may only be challenged if there are 'clear and compelling grounds' for a 'serious violation of rights'. One of the factors to be considered is whether an overwhelming majority has approved the resolution. Thus, it is unlikely that Prof X's challenge would be successful. Similarly, in some of the other countries (Finland, Japan, Poland and the US), it is seen as relevant that a clear majority of shareholders would nonetheless have approved the merger. By contrast, the German solution indicates that it would have been for the company to prove that the answers to the questions would not have been material (ie, that it can be excluded that it would have influenced the other shareholders).

Specifically on mergers, French law provides that, in contrast to other resolutions, mergers can only be challenged in a restricted number of circumstances – and a violation of the right to ask questions in the general meeting is not one of them. In some of the other country reports (eg, Finland, South Africa), it is also mentioned that for mergers, and some other topics decided by special resolution, the main legal remedy is not to challenge the resolution but instead, to seek an appraisal remedy, ie to leave the company and receive fair compensation.[144]

Insofar as it is possible to file a claim against the merger, Italy, Spain, Finland, the Netherlands, Poland and the US would not take the view that a claim would automatically block the effect of a resolution. Instead, the shareholders would be required to apply for an injunction. In addition, Polish law provides for an interesting rule, whereby shareholders can face a penal sanction of 10 times the cost of proceedings if they raise a baseless or vexatious set of legal proceedings.

(2006) 119 *Harvard Law Review* 1784; LA Bebchuk, 'The Myth of the Shareholder Franchise' (2007) 93 *Virginia Law Review* 675. For the opposite view, see, eg, WW Bratton and ML Wachter, 'The Case Against Shareholder Empowerment' (2010) 158 *University of Pennsylvania Law Review* 653 and S Bainbridge, 'Director Primacy and Shareholder Disempowerment' (2006) 119 *Harvard Law Review* 1735.

[143] See *Stoud v Grace*, 606 A 2d 75, 86 (Del Supr 1992) ('Realities in modern corporate life have all but gutted the myth that shareholders in large publicly held companies personally attend their annual meetings').

[144] Such appraisal rights are also prevalent in the US and Japan, see comparison in Siems, *Convergence in Shareholder Law* (n 141) 206–07.

A final issue to consider is whether it is lawful for Prof X to offer to drop his claim if the company pays him a settlement fee. German, French and Japanese law may treat this behaviour as a form of extortion. Conversely, the Finnish and Latvian solutions are less critical of this behaviour since they may regard it as an acceptable form of bargaining.

E. Conclusion

Overall, most of the legal systems would not allow Prof X's claim: Italian law would not grant such a claim to an individual shareholder; in South Africa the claim would have been filed too late, US law does not have such a thing as a right to ask questions at the general meeting; Spanish, Finnish and Polish law would enable AB to answer these questions after the general meeting; Japanese and Dutch law would presumably accept the refusal to answer questions that are too detailed; French law protects the validity of mergers except in exceptional cases; UK law requires a severe violation of the law in order to challenge a resolution of the general meeting; and in Germany, his action would be treated as an abuse of law.

Is one of these solutions preferable? It is submitted that the desirability of affording a shareholder a right to ask questions in the general meeting is open to debate.[145] Naturally, shareholders should have sufficient information to enable them to decide on the issues put before the general meeting. However, public companies – and in particular those which are listed on a stock exchange – are, in any case, already obliged to disclose information to the general public as well as specifically to shareholders. Thus, an individual right conferred in favour of shareholders to ask questions seems to be an anomaly. Of course, there may be situations where the general forms of disclosure produce gaps. Yet, it would not be realistic to assume that the directors can answer all such questions in the general meeting on the spot. Instead, the law should ask shareholders to submit such questions in advance of the meeting.

From a comparative perspective, the case offers the following insights: at a general level, legal systems do not appear to be fundamentally different; all legal systems enable shareholders to challenge decisions of the general meeting while also accepting the interests of legal certainty and reliability. The common law jurisdictions seem to rely more on case law than the civil law jurisdictions. However, UK law has deviated from its common law origin by virtue of the introduction of a statutory right to ask questions. Within the civil law world, there is also some diversity: for example, only Italy fails to allow a single shareholder the right to challenge decisions of the general meeting and only France provides for the special protection of resolutions approving a merger.

---

[145] See also Siems (n 3) § 131, para 10; Siems (n 141) 125–26 and 350–51.

10

Shareholders' Rights and Litigation

DAVID CABRELLI (EDITOR)

Main topics: ability of a shareholder to raise a derivative action against a director or third parties; validity of decisions taken by the board of directors in breach of procedures.

Related topics: undervalue transactions (see chapter 7, above); shareholders and shareholder law (see chapter 8, above); abuse of shareholders' rights (see chapter 9, above).

I. Scenario

Venture Capitalist (VC) invested substantial funds in exchange for a 76 per cent share of Portfolio Company (PC), a large private company specialising in nanotechnology and created by Founder one (8 per cent shareholder), Founder two (8 per cent shareholder) and Founder three (8 per cent shareholder). In connection with this investment, VC was entitled to nominate two of PC's four directors. The remaining two directors are Founder one and Founder two.

After two years, Founder two resigns from his directorship on the board of PC, sells his 8 per cent shareholding to VC and is appointed as a consultant to PC pursuant to a consultancy contract which pays him an annual fee of £100,000. The articles of association of PC provide that the termination of any contract in excess of £75,000 must be approved by no less than a 75 per cent majority of the shareholders of PC.

Nonetheless, VC's two nominee directors and Founder one subsequently adopt a board resolution terminating Founder two's consultancy contract with PC. Founder two seeks to challenge this board resolution on the basis that it is a matter for the shareholders and not the board, and as a result the board's decision is invalid. Would Founder two be successful in your country (i) if Founder three was in favour of the termination of his contract and (ii) if Founder three was not in favour of the termination of Founder two's contract, for example, by his expressing dissent at a shareholders' meeting, in writing or by his conduct?

Founder two's litigation leads to tensions in relations between VC, Founder one and Founder three. After a great deal of pressure, Founder three agrees to sell his shares to VC. Thereafter, VC's two nominee directors pass a majority board resolution which resolves for PC to transfer valuable intellectual property (IP) at less than market value to a company ABC, which is wholly owned by VC. The transfer is ratified by shareholder resolution since VC now owns 92 per cent of the shares of PC and voted in favour of it. Founder one sues (i) VC's two nominee directors for breach of their duties as directors and (ii) VC itself. Founder one is seeking to recover the property from ABC on behalf of and for the benefit of PC. Would Founder one be successful in your country?

II. Case Studies

A. The UK[1]

i. Validity of the Decision to Terminate Founder Two's Consultancy Contract

a. Introduction

The directors and PC appear to be in breach of the articles of association when the board of directors decides to terminate Founder two's consultancy contract. However, the difficulty lies in enforcing the breach of the articles.

b. Where Founder Three is in Favour of Termination

If Founder three was in favour of the termination of Founder two's consultancy contract, there are two reasons why Founder two would be unable to challenge the validity of the board decision. Both of these reasons are based on rules contained in the common law and the CA 2006.[2] First, since Founder two was no longer a shareholder of PC when the board of directors made the decision to terminate the consultancy contract, he is precluded from enforcing the provision that no less than a 75 per cent majority of the shareholders of PC must approve the termination. Founder two is unable to enforce a breach of the articles of association since he is an 'outsider'.[3]

The second obstacle to Founder two challenging the validity of the board decision is the common law 'unanimous assent' rule. In the case of *Re Duomatic Ltd*, the rule was articulated in the following terms:

> [W]here it can be shown that the shareholders who have a right to attend and vote at a general meeting of the company assent to some matter which a general meeting of the

---

[1] Abbreviations: CA 2006 (the Companies Act 2006).
[2] CA 2006, s 281(4).
[3] *Eley v Positive Government Security Life Assurance Co* (1876) 1 Ex D 88 (CA) and *Hickman v Kent or Romney Marsh Sheep-Breeder's Association* [1915] 1 Ch 881 (Ch) 896–97 (Astbury J).

company could carry into effect, that assent is as binding as a resolution in general meeting would be.[4]

Thus, if a decision is taken by the directors or shareholders of the company without passing the requisite resolution in terms of any of the conditions set out in the company's articles of association or the CA 2006, provided that there is clear evidence to the effect that all[5] of the shareholders assented to that course of action, the failure to pass that resolution cannot be challenged. However, the common law has developed limitations upon the unanimous consent rule. First, if the directors merely inform the shareholders of the decision, that is not enough. Nor is it sufficient for the directors to demonstrate to the court that the shareholders would have consented if their consent had been actively sought.[6] Hence, the unanimous assent rule requires some positive act by, or some conduct consistent with, assent from[7] all of the shareholders. Since the hypothetical case specifically states that the nominee directors of VC and Founder one voted in favour of the resolution, in terms of the case law, it is clear that assent may be communicated through shareholder representatives.[8] Moreover, since Founder three was in favour of the decision to terminate Founder two's consultancy contract, it is clear that there has been universal assent.

At a more fundamental level, the unanimous assent rule will be inapplicable where the provision in the articles of association or the CA 2006 was intended to protect either creditors or future members.[9] Thus, it must be ascertained whether the purpose of the provision of the articles of association which stipulates that the termination of any contract in excess of £75,000 must be approved by no less than a 75 per cent majority of the shareholders of PC is for the benefit of the shareholders, creditors or future shareholders of PC. On balance, it is submitted that the objective of this provision is to protect existing shareholders, rather than future shareholders or creditors. First, the inclusion of such a provision in the articles of association is unusual. Second, there is no suggestion that the creditors of PC had any role in negotiating the inclusion of such a provision for their own benefit. In summary, since the provision is designed for the benefit of the existing shareholders and there is evidence that all of the shareholders agreed to the decision adopted by the board either expressly or by their conduct, the unanimous assent rule applies and thus precludes Founder two from challenging the board resolution to terminate his consultancy contract.

c. Where Founder Three is Not in Favour of Termination

If Founder three was not in favour of the termination of Founder two's contract, the unanimous assent rule cannot apply to 'cure' the absence of the shareholder resolution

---

[4] *Re Duomatic Ltd* [1969] 2 Ch 365 (Ch) 373 (Buckley J).
[5] A majority of the shareholders is insufficient: *Extrasure Travel Insurances Services Ltd v Scattergood* [2002] EWHC 3093 (Ch), [2003] 1 BCLC 598 (Ch) [153]–[154] (Mr Jonathan Crow).
[6] *EIC Services Ltd v Phipps* [2004] EWCA Civ 1069, [2004] 2 BCLC 589 (CA) [133]–[137] (Neuberger J).
[7] *Re Bailey, Hay & Co Ltd* [1971] 1 WLR 1357 (Ch).
[8] *Euro Brokers Holdings Ltd v Monecor (London) Ltd* [2003] EWCA Civ 105, [2003] BCC 573 (CA).
[9] *Re Torvale Group Ltd* [2000] 2 BCC 626 (Ch) 632–37 (Neuberger J) and *Kinlan v Crimmin* [2006] EWHC 779 (Ch), [2007] 2 BCLC 67 (Ch) [42]–[45] (Phillip Sales).

passed by no less than a 75 per cent majority of the shareholders of PC. This is so, since all of the shareholders must assent and the approval of a majority of the shareholders is not enough.[10] In such circumstances, prima facie, it would appear to be the case that Founder two could raise legal proceedings to challenge the failure to pass a shareholder resolution. Nevertheless, Founder two would still be precluded from enforcing the articles of association since he would remain an 'outsider'. Whilst outsiders such as Founder two would have standing to raise proceedings for a declaration that the unanimous assent rule cannot be applied to cure the failure to pass a resolution of not less than 75 per cent of the shareholders duly approving the termination of the consultancy contract, this is not the same as enforcing the articles of association. Cases such as *Wright v Atlas Wright (Europe) Ltd*[11] and *Re RW Peak (Kings Lynn) Ltd*,[12] where outsiders have been successful in invoking the inapplicability of the unanimous assent rule as a means of challenging a failure to pass a requisite resolution, concerned breaches of the Companies Acts, which stipulate a requirement to pass a resolution – not the articles of association. For that reason, the outcomes of these cases do not affect the rule that outsiders cannot enforce the articles and so here, Founder two's action would be unsuccessful.

ii. Action by Founder One against VC's Two Nominee Directors and VC

a. Introduction

By virtue of section 260(1) and (3) of the CA 2006, Founder one may seek to recover PC's property from ABC pursuant to a statutory action known as a 'derivative claim'. The derivative claim[13] must be raised in the name of Founder one on behalf of and for the benefit of PC against VC's two nominee directors in order to recover the property from ABC. The proceedings must allege negligence, breach of fiduciary or other duty or breach of trust on the part of the two nominee directors. Prior to any consideration of the merits of the derivative claim, Founder one must first obtain permission/leave of the court to continue with the claim. It is worth emphasising at this point that section 260(3) of the CA 2006 enables both VC and/or ABC to be sued.[14] If successful,

---

[10] *Extrasure Travel Insurances Services Ltd v Scattergood* (n 5) [153]–[154].

[11] *Wright v Atlas Wright (Europe) Ltd* [1999] BCC 163 (CA). Here, the resolution ought to have been passed in terms of the Companies Act 1985 to sanction the approval of a director's service contract which endured for more than 5 years.

[12] *Re RW Peak (Kings Lynn) Ltd* [1998] BCC 596 (Ch). Here, the resolution ought to have been passed in terms of the Companies Act 1985 to sanction an own share buyback.

[13] Sections 260–64 of the CA 2006 apply to England, Wales and Northern Ireland, and ss 265–69 apply to Scotland only. In Scotland, a derivative action is known as 'derivative proceedings' rather than a 'derivative claim'. Sections 260–64 and 265–69 are not identical, but are in more or less the same terms. However, for the purposes of simplicity, this solution will use the provisions of ss 260–64 which apply to England, Wales and Northern Ireland only as a proxy for the whole of the UK.

[14] A derivative claim can be taken against VC or ABC in terms of s 260(3) of the CA 2006, where it is alleged that they were involved in a breach of duty by a director. eg, in proceedings concerning the transfer of funds or property of PC by a director to ABC in breach of duty, the proceedings may also be brought against ABC where it is alleged that they had knowledge of their source or nature.

Founder one would be able to recover the property from ABC and any gain or profit enjoyed by VC as a result of the breach. These remedies would be based on the equitable principles of knowing receipt and/or knowing assistance in the case of ABC and VC.

b. The Basis of a Derivative Claim

Founder one would allege a breach of duty on the part of VC's two nominee directors, ie that by transferring valuable IP belonging to PC at less than market value to ABC, which is wholly owned by VC, the directors have clearly breached their statutory duties as follows:

- in section 172 of the CA 2006, whereby the director must act in a way he or she considers is likely to promote the success of the company;
- in section 175 of the CA 2006 to avoid conflicts of interest without first having the arrangement with ABC authorised by the directors of PC in advance; and
- in section 177 of the CA 2006 to declare to the other directors any direct or indirect interest they may have in the proposed transaction or arrangement between PC and ABC.

Furthermore, in terms of section 182 of the CA 2006, directors of a company owe a duty to declare to the other directors any direct or indirect interest they may have in the existing transaction or arrangement between PC and ABC. A failure to comply with this duty is a criminal offence in terms of section 183(1) of the CA 2006.

The sale of property of PC at undervalue to ABC amounts to a breach of sections 172, 175, 177 and 182 of the CA 2006, whether the directors acted fraudulently or negligently in sanctioning such sale.[15] It represents: (i) a decision which VC's two nominee directors would not have genuinely considered to be likely to promote the success of the company (in breach of section 172 of the CA 2006); (ii) a conflict of interest without director authorisation (in breach of section 175 of the CA 2006); and (iii) a breach of the duty to declare to the other directors any direct or indirect interest that the two nominee directors may have had in the proposed and/or the existing transaction or arrangement between PC and ABC (in breach of sections 177 and 182 of the CA 2006).

c. Permission to Continue the Derivative Claim

Whilst there has been a breach of duty by the directors, this does not mean that Founder one's derivative claim will be automatically successful. He must first obtain permission from the court to continue his derivative claim to a full hearing, where the

---

[15] See *Alexander v Automatic Telephone Co* [1900] 2 Ch 56 (CA) (directors benefiting themselves), *Cook v Deeks* [1916] 1 AC 554 (PC) (directors diverting contract/business away from the company in their own favour) and *Daniels v Daniels* [1978] Ch 406 (Ch) (directors negligently selling assets of company to themselves at undervalue).

merits of the claim are fully considered before the court. The criteria to be applied by the court at this preliminary stage are contained in section 263(2) and (3) of the CA 2006. In terms of section 263(2) of the CA 2006, the court must refuse permission to continue the derivative claim if it is satisfied that:

1. a person acting in accordance with section 172 of the CA 2006 (the duty of a director to promote the success of the company) would not seek to continue the claim;[16] or
2. the alleged negligence, default, breach of duty or breach of trust on the part of the director had been ratified by the company after it occurred.[17]

Founder one satisfies the test in point (1), above, since it is submitted that there is insufficient material for a court to be satisfied that no hypothetical director acting in accordance with section 172 of the CA 2006 would continue the derivative claim.[18] However, point (2) is a more formidable hurdle, since each of the purported breaches of duty on the part of VC's two nominee directors appear to have been ratified by a clear majority of the shareholders. Without more, the terms of section 263(2)(c)(ii) of the CA 2006 suggest that Founder one's application for permission to continue his derivative claim would be unsuccessful. However, there are two issues which may preclude the court from applying point (2), above, as a reason to refuse such permission:

a. First, section 239 of the CA 2006 governs ratification by ordinary resolution[19] of the conduct of a director amounting to negligence, default, breach of duty or breach of trust. Any votes by the directors or persons connected with them must be disregarded. Thus, the votes of VC must be ignored for the purposes of the vote on ratification if it can be taken to be connected with its two nominee directors on the board of PC. Sections 252(2)(b) and 254(2) of the CA 2006 dictate whether VC is connected to the directors and the general rule is that the directors must each (i) own shares in VC representing at least 20 per cent of the nominal value of its equity share capital or (ii) be entitled to exercise or control the exercise of more than 20 per cent of the voting power of VC at any general meeting of VC. From the hypothetical case, it is unclear whether each of the two nominee directors will satisfy either of the tests in section 254(2) of the CA 2006. If they do not, then, prima facie, it would appear that the court must refuse Founder one permission to continue his derivative claim in terms of section 263(2)(c)(ii) of the CA 2006. However, this is subject to what is said in the point immediately below.
b. Second, section 239(7) of the CA 2006 preserves the common law of ratification. Crucially, the common law recognises a class of non-ratifiable wrongs. However, it has never been particularly clear as to where the line between ratifiable and non-ratifiable

---

[16] CA 2006, s 263(2)(a).
[17] CA 2006, s 263(2)(c)(ii).
[18] In *Franbar Holdings Ltd v Patel* [2008] EWHC 1534 (Ch), [2008] BCC 885 (Ch) [30], William Trower QC suggests that this is the appropriate approach to apply. See also *Airey v Cordell* [2006] EWHC 2728 (Ch), [2007] BCC 785 (Ch), 800–01 (Warren J), *Iesini v Westrip Holdings Ltd* [2009] EWHC 2526 (Ch), [2010] BCC 420 (Ch) [86] (Lewison J) and *Re Seven Holdings Ltd* [2011] EWHC 1893 (Ch) [9] (David Donaldson QC).
[19] In terms of s 282(1) of the CA 2006, an ordinary resolution is a resolution passed by a simple majority of the shareholders.

wrongs is to be drawn.[20] In the case of *Daniels v Daniels*,[21] it was held that the negligent transfer of property of the company at undervalue to a third party which confers some benefit on the directors and the majority shareholders could not be ratified by the shareholders of the company, ie such action by the directors was a non-ratifiable wrong. That being the case, the effect of the combination of section 239(7) of the CA 2006 and the common law is that ratification is impossible in the case of VC's two nominee directors transferring PC's IP at undervalue to ABC. This is the case notwithstanding the position regarding the application of section 254(2) of the CA 2006. As a result, the court is disentitled from applying section 263(2)(c)(ii) of the CA 2006 to refuse Founder one permission to continue his derivative claim.

In ascertaining whether the derivative claim should be continued, the court must have regard to a variety of factors listed in section 263(3) of the CA 2006. Section 263(4) of the CA 2006 also stipulates that the court must consider the views of independent shareholders. With regard to section 263(3)(a) of the CA 2006, whether Founder one is acting in good faith in seeking to continue the claim is relevant. Here, the test is subjective,[22] ie one must assess the state of mind and motivations of Founder one in seeking to claim. It is submitted that there is nothing to suggest that Founder one is not acting in good faith, for example, that he has some ulterior motive or is seeking to pursue some agenda in attempting to continue the claim. On the contrary, his sole desire appears to be to make sure that the value he would extract from his shareholding in PC would be full and fair if he were to sell his shares at some point in the future. As for section 263(3)(d) of the CA 2006, the ratifiability of the breach must be considered. As explained above, the alleged breach of directors' duty is one which cannot be ratified under the common law. In terms of section 263(3)(e) of the CA 2006, whether PC has decided not to pursue the claim against the directors is a factor which must be considered. Here, it is evident that PC has not chosen to raise a claim. For the purposes of section 263(3)(f) of the CA 2006, the court must consider whether the breach of duty by VC's two nominee directors could be pursued personally by Founder one. Notwithstanding the provisions of sections 994(1) and 996(2)(c) of the CA 2006,[23] it is very difficult for Founder one to pursue the recovery of the property of PC in terms of his own personal right to present an unfair prejudice petition under section 994 of

---

[20] Davies and Worthington have suggested that the common law confines non-ratifiable wrongs to the decisions of directors which involve the misappropriation of the company's property: PL Davies and S Worthington, *Gower's Principles of Modern Company Law* (10th edn, London, Sweet & Maxwell, 2016) para 16–124 at 574–76, contrasting *Cook v Deeks* [1916] 1 AC 554 (PC) and *Menier v Hooper's Telegraph Works* (1874) LR 9 Ch App 350 (CA) with *Regal (Hastings) Ltd v Gulliver* [1967] 2 AC 134 (HL), *NW Transportation Co v Beatty* (1887) 12 App Cas 589 (PC) and *Burland v Earle* [1902] AC 83 (PC). See also C Riley, 'Derivative Claims and Ratification: Time to Ditch Some Baggage' (2014) 34 *Legal Studies* 582. This approach was endorsed in *Franbar Holdings Ltd v Patel* (n 18) [47] (William Trower QC). In *Franbar Holdings* [44]–[45], William Trower QC held that the effect of s 239(7) of the CA 2006 is that any acts which, pursuant to any common law rule of law, are incapable of being ratified will continue to apply to invalidate the purported ratification.

[21] *Daniels v Daniels* (n 15).

[22] *Wishart v Castlecroft Securities Ltd* [2010] CSIH 2, 2010 SC 16 [36] (Lord Reed).

[23] This section gives the court the power to authorise a shareholder to raise proceedings in the name and on behalf of the company where PC's affairs have been conducted in an unfairly prejudicial manner to Founder one's interests as a shareholder.

the CA 2006. The restoration of property to the company from a third party pursuant to section 996(2)(c) of the CA 2006 is not a common remedy which is granted by the court, since it is not a personal remedy and remedies granted in terms of a success-ful section 994 unfair prejudice petition are usually confined to relief in respect of harms which are personal to the shareholder.[24] Whilst the factual allegations made by Founder one in the derivative claim give rise to causes of action that he could pursue in his own right under section 994 of the CA 2006, the remedy being pursued in terms of this derivative claim is not personal to Founder one and is one which belongs to the company. Nor is there any suggestion that Founder one has presented a section 994 unfair prejudice petition. For these reasons, like the decision of the Inner House of the Court of Session in the Scottish case of *Wishart v Castlecroft Securities Ltd*,[25] the application of 263(3)(f) of the CA 2006 does not weigh in favour of the refusal of permission to continue the derivative claim. With regard to section 263(4) of the CA 2006, there are no independent shareholders to consider; all are interested in this case. Meanwhile, section 263(3)(b) of the CA 2006, which enjoins a court to determine the importance a person acting in accordance with section 172 of the CA 2006 would attach to continuing the claim, is the most problematic of the five relevant criteria. In *Franbar Holdings Ltd v Patel*,[26] William Trower QC stipulated that the court must have regard to a wide range of factors which a hypothetical director would be expected to take into account, namely:

- the size of the claim;
- the company's ability to fund the proceedings;
- the prospects of success of the claim;
- the ability of the company to make a recovery on any award of damages;
- the disruption which would be caused to the development of the company's business by having to concentrate on the proceedings; and
- the costs of the proceedings and any damage to the company's reputation and business if the proceedings were to fail.[27]

In Founder one's case, it is submitted that consideration of each of these factors would result in a balance in favour of Founder one being given permission to continue the claim. There is no suggestion that Founder one has the option of enforcing a personal right against VC's two nominee directors or VC itself in a shareholders' agreement. Nor, for the reasons given above, is it reasonable to suggest that Founder one's claim would be best pursued as a personal unfair prejudice petition under section 994 of the CA 2006. Moreover, VC has not made an offer to buy out Founder one's shares. For these reasons, in terms of section 263(3)(b) of the CA 2006 above, the hypothetical

---

[24] See *Kung v Kou* (2004) HKCFAR 579 and the discussion in Davies and Worthington, *Gower's Principles of Modern Company Law* (n 20) para 20-16 to 20-17 at 677–78. Contrast this with *Franbar Holdings Ltd v Patel* (n 18) [50]–[52].

[25] *Wishart v Castlecroft Securities Ltd* [2010] CSIH 2, 2010 SC 16.

[26] *Franbar Holdings Ltd v Patel* (n 18) [44]–[45].

[27] *Franbar Holdings Ltd v Patel* (n 18) [36]; *Iesini v Westrip Holdings Ltd* (n 18) [85] (Lewison J) and *Re Seven Holdings Ltd* (n 18) [12].

director would be likely to attribute importance to the continuation of the derivative claim.

iii. Conclusion

Thus, since the purported ratification is ineffective for the reasons advanced above, the effect of the application of the criteria in section 263 of the CA 2006 is such that the court would be compelled to rule that Founder one should be given permission to continue his derivative claim; the nature of the alleged breach of duty on the part of VC's two nominee directors is such that it is reasonably clear that their actions in selling the property of PC at undervalue to ABC clearly amounted to a breach of sections 172, 175, 177 and 182 of the CA 2006. In the subsequent consideration of the claim on its merits, it is probable that the court will hold that Founder one ought to be successful in his derivative claim. The outcome would be that Founder one would be entitled to recover the property from ABC on behalf of and for the benefit of PC, since ABC was in knowing receipt of the property from PC. Moreover, if VC enjoyed a gain or generated a profit as a result of the breach of duty on the part of VC's two nominee directors, this gain could be disgorged. However, there is no suggestion of VC having made such a profit in the hypothetical case and so litigation on the part of Founder one against VC pursuant to the statutory derivative action would serve no purpose.

B. The US

i. Introduction

Two distinct forms can be used to create a privately held limited liability entity in the US.[28] One form, the limited liability company (LLC), is the preferred entity for many companies with a small number of owners. The other form, the traditional corporation, still dominates among venture capital portfolio companies.

ii. Founder Two

Founder two seeks to challenge the board resolution to cancel his consultancy contract because such matters are explicitly reserved for the shareholders in the articles of association. Under the Delaware General Corporation Law (DGCL), the 'business and affairs of every corporation … shall be managed by or under the direction of the board of directors'.[29] The decision to terminate a contract of the sort described in the hypothetical case would generally fall within this large grant of authority. The only basis for doubt regarding the board's authority in this case is the fact that the certificate of incorporation provides that the termination of any contract in excess of £75,000 must be approved by no less than a 75 per cent majority of the shareholders of PC.

---

[28] See ch 2 at II J, above.
[29] DGCL, § 141(a).

The rights of creditors of a corporation, such as Founder two, may be affected by provisions in the certificate of incorporation, and in some instances, the courts allow creditors to stand in for stockholders, bringing derivative claims against the board of directors.[30] Generally speaking, however, creditors have no standing to sue the corporation or the directors for violations of the governance provisions in the certificate of incorporation. The rights of creditors are defined by their contracts with the corporation, unless the termination process contemplated by the certificate of incorporation became a term of that contract. Therefore, Founder two would lack standing to sue because he had sold his shares prior to accepting the consultancy contract.

Delaware law has a doctrine comparable to the 'unanimous assent' rule in the UK, though it is even more lenient. Under the DGCL, it is provided that:

> [A]ny action which may be taken at any annual or special meeting of … stockholders, may be taken without a meeting, without prior notice, and without a vote, if a consent or consents in writing, setting forth the action so taken, shall be signed by the holders of outstanding stock having not less than the minimum number of votes that would be necessary to authorize or take such action at a meeting at which all shares entitled to vote thereon were present and voted.[31]

The various written documents required by this provision must be delivered to the corporation and must fulfil various formal requirements (eg the writing must bear the date of the signature of each signing stockholder), but in this case, these matters seem quite straightforward since VC owns a sufficient number of shares to give unilateral consent. As a result of the fact that Delaware allows less than unanimous consent, whether Founder three favours the termination of the consultancy contract and expresses his dissent is irrelevant.

iii. Founder One

Delaware law recognises two forms of shareholder litigation: direct and derivative. In a direct lawsuit, a shareholder brings claims for injuries that are separate from any injuries to the corporation. In a derivative lawsuit, a shareholder brings a claim on behalf of the corporation against the directors. In deciding whether a claim is direct or derivative, the Delaware courts ask: 'Who suffered the alleged harm – the corporation or the suing stockholder individually – and who would receive the benefit of the recovery or other remedy?'[32] With respect to Founder one's claim, the alleged harm was inflicted on the corporation, suggesting the existence of a derivative claim.

To bring a derivative action, a shareholder must satisfy certain procedural requirements. To understand these procedural obstacles, it must first be understood that the Delaware courts generally presume that directors faithfully fulfil their duties to the corporation.[33] Consequently, before a derivative claim by a shareholder can even

---

[30] See, eg, *North American Catholic Educational Programming Foundation, Inc v Gheewalla*, 930 A 2d 92 (Del 2007) (conferring standing on creditors to bring a derivative action where the corporation is insolvent).
[31] DGCL, § 228(a).
[32] *Tooley v Donaldson, Lufkin, & Jenrette, Inc*, 845 A 2d 1031 (Del 2004).
[33] *Beam Ex Rel Martha Stewart Living Omnimedia, Inc v Stewart*, 845 A 2d 1040, 1049 (Del 2004).

be brought against a director, the shareholder must overcome this presumption in favour of the directors.

Prior to filing a derivative claim, a shareholder must first demand that the board of directors take action to remedy the problem (commonly referred to as the 'demand requirement').[34] If the board refuses, the shareholder can challenge the board's refusal to act upon the shareholder's demands in court. It should be stressed that this is only a challenge of the board's decision to act upon demand, not a challenge to the board's alleged misconduct. In these proceedings, the courts are generally deferential to the board's judgement and will evaluate the decision in light of the deferential business judgment rule.[35]

The demand requirement, however, is not mandatory. In situations where the board would be unwilling to act upon demand because of some conflict of interest, the Delaware courts have been willing to excuse demand because such actions would be futile. When evaluating whether the shareholder appropriately determined that demand would be futile, the court will look to see whether 'the pleaded facts create a reasonable doubt that a majority of the board could have acted independently in responding to the demand'.[36] A director's independence is questioned once a shareholder can demonstrate that the director is so '"beholden" to an interested [party] that his or her "discretion would be sterilized"'.[37] Under the facts of the case, the directors of VC do not appear to be independent; therefore, demand would be futile.

Assuming that Founder one can navigate these procedural hurdles, he can challenge the fairness of the IP transaction. At the time of the IP transaction, VC held 92 per cent of PC's stock. As a controlling shareholder, VC retains fiduciary duties to the minority shareholders to continue to advance the interests of PC, not VC's interests.[38] Furthermore, the directors of VC owe fiduciary duties to PC and the minority shareholders. Thus, both VC and its directors would be defendants in the derivative litigation, and their actions must be able to pass the exacting 'entire fairness' analysis described earlier in this book.[39]

The shareholder vote purporting to ratify the transfer of IP would not extinguish or otherwise affect the duty of loyalty claim in this case. In cases involving transactions between a corporation and its controlling shareholder, a fully informed ratifying vote of a majority of the disinterested shareholders has the limited effect of shifting the burden of proof under the entire fairness standard from the defendants to the plaintiffs.[40] In this case, Founder one is the only disinterested shareholder, and he did not vote to ratify the transaction. Thus, the vote by VC would have no effect on the litigation.

Under an entire fairness standard, the courts will look at both the details of the corporation's dealings and the price paid in the contract. In this hypothetical problem,

---

[34] See eg Chancery Rule 23.1.
[35] Ibid and accompanying text.
[36] *Beam Ex Rel Martha Stewart Living Omnimedia, Inc v Stewart* (n 33) at 1049.
[37] Ibid at 1050 (citing *Grimes v Donald*, 673 A 2d 1207, 1217 (Del 1996)).
[38] See *In re Loral Space and Communications Inc*, 2008 WL 4293781 *21 (Del Ch 19 September 2008).
[39] See ch 8 at II J, above.
[40] *In re Wheelabrator Technologies Inc Shareholders Litigation*, 663 A 2d 1194, 1203 (Del Ch 1995).

the IP was transferred by PC at less than the market rate, even though the IP was apparently valuable. Further, the transfer was to ABC, a corporation wholly owned by VC. These facts strongly suggest self-dealing and call into question the fairness of the transaction.

Remedies in derivative litigation may be recovered from any of the defendants. Although PC probably has insurance in place for the VC directors, insurance companies do not write policies to insure against directors' breaches of loyalty. As a result, most cases involving meritorious claims relating to the duty of loyalty are settled by the parties to the litigation without any admission of wrongdoing by the defendants. Settlements of derivative lawsuits in Delaware must be approved by the Court of Chancery, and compensation awarded in the settlements typically flows to the corporation. In addition, successful plaintiffs may receive attorneys' fees in recognition of their efforts on behalf of the corporation. In this case, it is also possible that PC would be able to recover the IP from ABC, assuming that ABC knew that VC or its directors had acted in violation of their fiduciary duties in transferring the IP.[41]

C. South Africa

i. Challenging the Board Resolution by Founder Two

In casu, the board of directors did not act in line with the provisions of the Memorandum of Incorporation (MoI), requiring a special resolution of the shareholders of PC to terminate a contract in excess of £75,000. The relevant issue is thus whether Founder two can enforce the MoI in these circumstances. The MoI is the founding document of the company. It sets out the rights, duties and responsibilities of the shareholders, directors and others within the company. It is the sole governing document of the company. The MoI is binding between the company and each shareholder (in their capacity as shareholders only),[42] between the shareholders *inter se*, between the company and each director or prescribed officer and between the company and any other person serving the company as a member of a board committee.[43] The binding nature of the MoI is probably contractual owing to the terms of the legislation.[44] The usual remedies, for a breach of the constitution, will thus apply namely an interdict or a declaratory order.

As a shareholder and director Founder two would have these remedies available to him (in his capacity as shareholder or based on the fact that he is a director exercising the functions of a director), but having sold his shares and resigned as a director,

---

[41] See *Paramount Communications Inc v QVC Network Inc*, 637 A 2d 34, 50–51 (Del 1994).
[42] See *Rosslare (Pty) Ltd v Registrar of Companies* 1972 (2) SA 524 (D), 528.
[43] Companies Act 2008, s 15(6).
[44] FHI Cassim (ed), *Contemporary Company Law* (Cape Town, Juta, 2012) 142. It can, however, be amended by way of a special resolution. See also *Pender v Lushington* [1877] 6 ChD 70, 80. When a shareholder enforces his or her rights, qua shareholder, directly against the company, it is not clear which range of provisions of the MoI may be directly enforced by a shareholder against a company. Here the distinction between personal and corporate rights is important.

this is no longer the case. As the MoI is generally unenforceable by outsiders or third parties there are few remedies available to Founder two.[45] However, one possible way to enforce a provision of the MoI, as an outsider, is to rely on the provisions of the MoI being applicable by implication, ie as implied terms.[46]

Whether Founder three was in favour of the termination or not does not make a difference as Founder two will still not be able to enforce the MoI because he was an outsider. The only possibility is for Founder two to rely on the application of the provisions of the MoI and that it is an implied term of the contract not to act in contravention of the MoI.

ii. Litigation against VC's Two Nominee Directors for Breach of their Duties as Directors and against VC itself

Founder one can institute a derivative action (as shareholder) on behalf of PC as the two directors of PC (VC's nominees) breached their duties to PC. The nominee directors breached their fiduciary duty to the company to act in its best interests. They sold valuable IP rights of PC to ABC at far less than its market value. As stated before, in the context of the duty to act in the best interests of the company, the issue is whether or not the director, subjectively, based on objective facts, believed that he or she acted in the best interests of the company. It is about the state of mind of the relevant director. Directors must thus exercise their powers in what they consider, and not what the courts consider, is in the best interests of the company.[47] But this subjective test is not without its limits.[48] The absence of a reasonable ground may be the basis for finding that a director did not act in the best interests of the company.[49] It has been held that the test is to determine whether the reasonable person would regard the actions of the director in question as reasonable.[50] There must be reasonable grounds for the belief of the directors that they were acting in the best interests of the company. This is clearly not the case *in casu*.

---

[45] Cassim, *Contemporary Company Law* (n 44) 143. See *Melhado v The Porto Alegre New Hamburgh & Brazilian Railway Co* (1874) LR 9 CP 503; *In re Tavarone Mining Co* (1873) LR 8 Ch App 956, 960. See PA Delport (ed), *Henochsberg on the Companies Act 71 of 2008* (Durban, LexisNexis, South Africa, Service issue November 2016) 77:

> It may be noted, however, that the correctness of the proposition that the articles can never as such constitute a contract between the company and a person otherwise than in his capacity as a member has been questioned (see Davies and Worthington 64–66). And in our law it may be possible for such a contract to arise on the basis of a *stipulatio alteri* (cf *Isaacs Geshen & Co (Pty) Ltd v Ellis* 1964 (2) PH A59 (N) (at 298); *Corporate Law* 80 and SJ Naudé *Die Regsposisie van die Maatskappydirekteur* (Durban, Butterworths 1970) 60–68 also in respect of rights by third parties based on the Memorandum of Incorporation.

[46] Delport, *Henochsberg* (n 45) 75; HS Cilliers et al, *Cilliers and Benade Corporate Law* (Durban, Butterworths, 2000) 81. And see *De Villiers v Jacobsdal Saltworks (Michaelis & De Villiers) (Pty) Ltd* 1959 (3) SA 873 (O), *De Freitas v Chamdor Meat Packers (Pty) Ltd* 2015 JDR 1934 (GJ) and *Trinity Asset Management (Pty) Ltd v Investec Bank Ltd* 2009 (4) SA 89 (SCA) para 22.

[47] Re *Smith & Fawcett Ltd* [1942] Ch 304, 306. See also *Hogg v Cramphorn Ltd* [1967] Ch 254, 268.

[48] See Cassim, *Contemporary Company Law* (n 44) 524.

[49] *Gethning v Kilner* [1972] 1 WLR 337, 342. This is discussed in Cassim (n 44) 524.

[50] See *Shuttleworth v Cox Brothers & Co (Maidenhead) Ltd* [1927] 2 KB 9, *Teck Corp Ltd v Millar* (1972) 33 DLR (3d) 288 (BCSC); *Charterbridge Corporation Ltd v Loyds Bank Ltd* [1970] Ch 62.

Once Founder one has established this breach he can rely on section 165 of the Companies Act 2008. Section 165 provides for a statutory derivative action and expressly abolishes any right at common law of a person other than a company to bring or prosecute any legal proceedings on behalf of the company. A derivative action is thus brought by a person to protect the interests of the company. A shareholder or shareholders will typically institute a derivative action.[51] Provision is made for judicial discretion to grant leave to an applicant for derivative proceedings. A person has to apply to the court for leave to bring the proceedings in the name or on behalf of the company.[52] The governing criterion is provided in section 165 on whether or not the court should grant leave to bring the application or not. The court may only grant leave to the applicant to bring the proceedings if the applicant is acting in good faith, the proceedings involve the trial of a serious question of material consequence to the company and it is in the best interests of the company that the applicant be granted relief.[53] Based on the facts provided, it would appear that Founder one should be able to succeed with an application for leave to institute proceedings. The fact that VC, as majority shareholder, ratified the sale of the IP rights will not make a difference. It is specifically stated that a shareholder is not barred from invoking section 165 if a shareholder or shareholders ratified the wrong.[54] The court may, however, take the ratification into account when making any judgment or order.[55]

VC itself is not a director and Founder one will thus not be able to hold VC to account for a breach of duties. The only possible basis to hold VC accountable is based on the common law principles of agency: VC appointed the nominee directors. The sale of the IP rights to ABC is to the advantage of VC as ABC is wholly owned by VC.

A final aspect to consider relates to the disposal of all or a greater part of the assets of a company. If the sale of the IP rights concerns a greater part of the assets of PC, then section 112 of the Companies Act 2008 is applicable.[56] In order to comply with section 112, the disposal has to be approved by a special resolution of the shareholders, in accordance with section 115. If the transaction did not receive the requisite shareholder approval then the company cannot dispose of the assets.[57] The procedure for this is similar to the procedure for a merger, discussed in previous cases. A special resolution must be adopted at a meeting called for that purpose and the quorum for

---

[51] See s 165(2) for the categories of applicants to whom s 165 can apply.

[52] This person must have served a demand on the company to commence or continue legal proceedings, or take related steps to protect the legal interests of the company. See s 165(2). The company may apply within 15 business days to a court to set aside the demand on the ground that it is vexatious or without merit. Within 60 business days after receiving the demand the company must either initiate or continue legal proceedings or take related steps to protect its legal interests or serve a notice on the person who made the demand refusing to comply with it.

[53] On the good faith requirement, see *Dowling v Colonial Mutual Life Assurance Society* [1915] HCA 56, (1915) 20 CLR 509, 521–22, 21 ALR 425, 433; *IOC Australia Pty Ltd v Mobil Oil Australia Ltd* [1905] HCA 28, (1975) 11 ALR 417, 426–27. See Delport, *Henochsberg* (n 45) 585 for a detailed discussion of s 165.

[54] Companies Act 2008, s 165(14).

[55] Cassim, *Contemporary Company Law* (n 44) 794.

[56] See s 1 definition of 'all or greater part of the assets or undertaking'.

[57] S 112(2), read with s 115(1) of the Companies Act 2008.

the meeting is constituted by the presence of sufficient persons to exercise, in aggregate, at least 25 per cent of all the voting rights that are entitled to be exercised on that matter.[58] It is, however, important to note, for the purposes of the special resolution, that any voting rights controlled by an 'acquiring party, or a person related to an acquiring party' are disqualified from voting. *In casu* VC will thus be disqualified from voting as VC is a related party. The disposal in terms of section 112 will thus not be possible.

D. France

The solution to this problem will differ depending on whether PC is a public limited liability company (*Société anonyme* (SA)), a simplified public limited company (*Société par actions simplifiée* (SAS)) or a limited company (*Société à responsabilité limitée* (SARL)). However, in France, PC would probably not be a limited company since this would offer less flexibility, especially as to financing. The SAS would be the most likely company form used in this case. However, for the sake of completeness, the case is considered below from the perspective of the SA, the SAS and the SARL.

i. Solution under French Law in the Case of a Public Company (SA)

a. Introduction

The first issue to consider is whether a provision in the articles of association of a public company (SA) which gave a 75 per cent majority of the shareholders (under French company law, it would be in the general shareholders' meeting) the power to terminate any contract in excess of £75,000 would be valid under French company law. According to the French Commercial Code and case law, each corporate organ (the board of directors and the shareholders' meeting) has a specific role and one organ cannot supersede the other organ's legal functions.

The powers of the chief executive officer (*Directeur général*) are not specified. The Commercial Code only provides that 'the general management of the company is assumed, under the responsibility of either the chairman of the board, or by another individual person appointed by the chairman of the board and who receives the title of chief executive officer'.[59] The chief executive officer (CEO) and the board of directors have competing powers.

In principle, the decision to terminate a contract belongs to the CEO or, when the importance of the contract justifies it, to the board of directors as opposed to the general shareholders' meeting. However, the French courts cater for some flexibility in the separation of powers between the different organs of the company. Therefore, it is possible for the articles of association of the company to shift some of the decision-making powers from one organ to another, as long as no organ is overly deprived of

---

[58] Companies Act 2008, s 115(2)(a).
[59] Commercial Code, Art L 225-51-1 al 1.

its legal responsibilities.[60] Therefore, the provision in the articles of association granting the shareholders the power to decide on the termination of contracts in excess of £75,000 is valid.

Regarding the 75 per cent majority, under French company law, the majority is set by the Commercial Code at 50 per cent for ordinary business matters.[61] It is not considered possible for the majority level indicated by the Commercial Code to be raised.[62] Therefore, the provision regarding the 75 per cent special majority would be void. However, a similar result could be achieved through a shareholders' agreement.

The fact that this reinforced majority would be void under French company law does not affect the solution of the case.

b. Validity of the Decision to Terminate Founder Two's Consultancy Contract

On the face of it, it would appear that the directors and the company are in breach of PC's articles of association when the board of directors decides to terminate Founder two's consultancy contract. However, the difficulty lies in enforcing the breach of the articles.

Breach of the Articles of Association
Under French company law, the decision by the board of directors to terminate Founder two's consultancy contract is a breach of PC's articles of incorporation. Therefore, the decision is invalid.

However, a second issue is whether the invalidity of the decision can be cured either because the majority shareholder and Founder one (representing together 92 per cent of the shares and 75 per cent of the votes at the level of the board of directors) were in favour of the termination or because Founder three would have also voted in favour of terminating the contract, which would have meant that there would have been unanimity in voting. The French courts take a very restrictive view where precise requirements have not been followed, even though the decision would have been the same if the appropriate organ would have been called to decide it. The courts are very deferential to the allocation of powers decided by the legislature and by the articles of association. Therefore, in the first situation, the fact that there would have been a majority in favour of terminating the contract at the level of the board of directors and at the shareholders' level would not cure the invalidity of the decision.

In the second case, where Founder three would have voted in favour of the termination and there would therefore have been unanimity of the shareholders, the French courts would also treat the decision as invalid. Because of the respect for formalism

---

[60] Cass Civ (Cour de cassation, Civil Chamber), 4 June 1946, Motte, with a note by J Noirel, in *Les grands arrêts de la jurisprudence commerciale*, T 1,2e éd, 1976, n° 69, 297; and also CA Aix-en-Provence (Court of Appeal of Aix-en-Provence), 28 September 1982, *Rev sociétés* 1983, 773, with a note by J Mestre.
[61] Commercial Code, Art L 225-37.
[62] Y Guyon, *Traité des contrats, Les sociétés* (Paris, LGDJ, 1999) n° 165.

above substance, there is no equivalent in French law of the 'unanimous consent' doctrine in UK law.

A similar situation as that experienced by PC has been considered by the courts. In one case decided in 2000, the issue was whether shareholders, through unanimous consent, could implicitly modify the articles of association. The French Cour de cassation held that implicit modifications of the articles of association, even with the unanimous consent of the shareholders, were not valid.[63] Therefore, the decision by the board of directors of PC, whether unanimous or not, would not be valid under French law.

Enforcement of the Breach of the Articles of Association

Another issue to be decided concerns the applicable sanction. Two types of sanctions are possible under French company law: nullification (*nullité*) and damages.

Nullification   The French Commercial Code provides that: 'The nullity of acts or deliberations ... may result only from the breach of a mandatory provision of this Title (*Title on Common provisions applying to commercial companies*) or of the acts governing contracts'.[64] The violation of the articles of association is not a mandatory provision of the 'Title on Common provisions applying to commercial companies'. Nor is it a violation of the acts governing contracts, be it general contract law or the provisions on corporate contracts included in the French Civil Code.[65]

In an early case, the French Cour de cassation held that a violation of the by-laws was equivalent to a violation of the laws which governed contracts, since the articles of association are themselves a contract.[66] However, the Cour de cassation has since changed its approach on this issue.[67] For instance, in two recent cases (in 2000 and 2005), the Cour de cassation decided that the appropriate sanction for a violation of the by-laws was not nullification. The first case concerned a non-commercial company (*société civile*),[68] and the second case an Economic Interest Grouping (*groupement d'intérêt économique* (GIE)),[69] which is a business vehicle close to the general partnership (*société en nom collectif*). This approach also applies to the public company since the text relating to the GIE[70] on this point is drafted in an identical way to the text applicable to public companies.

Therefore, under French law, the decision to terminate the contract is not void.

---

[63] Cass Civ 1re (Cour de cassation, First Civil Chamber), 21 March 2000 (*F Le Garrec c/G. Vincent*), *Rev sociétés* 2000, with a note by Y Guyon, 509.

[64] Commercial Code, Art L 235-1.

[65] Civil Code, Art 1832 ff.

[66] Cass Com (Cour de cassation, Commercial Chamber), 1974, D 1974 1975 102, with a note by Y Guyon, *RTD com* 1975. 107 with a note by Chartier.

[67] J-P Legros, 'La violation des statuts est-elle une cause de nullité?' (1991) *Droit des sociétés chron* 1.

[68] Cass Civ 3e (Cour de cassation, Third Civil Chamber) 19 July 2000, n° 98-17.258, *RJDA* 12/00 n° 1122, *Bull Joly* 2001 70 with a note by L Grosclaude, *Dr sociétés* 2000 comm n° 170 with a note by T Bonneau.

[69] Cass Com (Cour de cassation, Commercial Chamber) 14 June 2005, n° 02-18.864, *RJDA* 10/05 n° 1123, *Bull Joly* 2005 1412 with a note by P Le Cannu, D 2005 AJ 1777 with a note by A Lienhard.

[70] Commercial Code, Art L 251-5.

Damages   The only action that can be used by Founder two is an action for damages. Under French law, Founder two can sue PC, but not the directors, for breach of contract and claim damages. In order to attain damages, Founder two must prove fault, loss and a causal link. The requisite fault is that the termination took place without a decision by the competent organ of PC. The termination should have been decided by the general shareholders' meeting. The loss is the termination of the contract and the loss of payments deriving from the execution of the contract. There is a causal link between the fault and the loss, since the invalid decision of the board led to the termination of the contract.

However, there are two additional issues to discuss under French company law. The first is whether a person who is no longer a shareholder, such as Founder two, can invoke the violation of the articles of incorporation since he or she is not a party to that contract. Since 2006, the French Cour de cassation has adopted the approach that the violation of a contract, such as the articles of incorporation of a company, is always a fault which can be invoked by a third party.[71] Therefore, Founder two, although no longer a shareholder and not a party to the articles of incorporation, can invoke the violation of the articles of association since they are a contract.

A second issue concerns who could be sued by Founder two. Under French company law, only the company itself can be sued and not the individual directors. The reason is that the directors acted in their official capacity as directors and are shielded from liability towards third parties, such as Founder two, as long as they acted within the scope of their responsibilities. The Cour de cassation is very reluctant to hold directors personally liable towards third parties for acting outside the scope of their functions (*faute séparable des fonctions*). There has to be intentional fault of a specific gravity which cannot be linked to the individual director's responsibilities as a director. Given the rare cases where such fault has been admitted by the Cour de cassation,[72] it is highly probable that VC, Founder one and Founder three – if he had voted in favour of the termination – would be considered to be shielded from individual liability. Therefore, the action for damages can only be directed at PC itself.

PC can easily call a shareholders' meeting to vote on the termination of the contract. Therefore, the damage would probably be limited to the amount of money that Founder two should have received between the invalid decision of the board and the subsequent decision at the general shareholders' meeting.

---

[71] Cass Ass Plé (Cour de cassation, Plenary Assembly), 6 October 2006, n° 05-13255: *Bull Civ*, ass Plén, n°9; D 2006, 2825, with a note by G Viney; *RTD Civ* 2007, 115 with an observation by J Mestre and B Fages, and with an observation by P Jourdain, 123.

[72] eg Cass Com (Cour de cassation, Commercial Chamber), 20 May 2003 (*Madame Seusse c/ Société Sati*), *Rev sociétés* 2003, 479, with a note by JF Barbiéri, D 2003, Jur 2623, with a note by B Dondero and AJ, 1502, with an observation by A Lienhard, *RTD com* 2003, 523, with an observation by JP Chazal and Y Reinhard and 741, with an observation by C Champaud and D Danet, *RTD civ* 2003, 509, with an observation by P Jourdain.

c. Action by Founder One against VC's Two Nominee Directors and VC

Founder one can sue VC's nominee directors and VC itself on civil grounds and also on criminal grounds.

Action on Civil Grounds: Nullification

Under French company law, a contract, such as a contract for the sale of assets, entered into between a company and a director or a shareholder holding more than 10 per cent of the voting rights of a public company is subject to the prior authorisation of the board.[73] Contracts where one of the persons mentioned above is 'indirectly interested' are also covered. Agreements authorised by the board of directors are then subject to *ex post* approval by the shareholders' general meeting[74] where the interested director and the interested shareholder cannot vote.[75] These provisions do not apply to agreements relating to current operations entered into under normal terms and conditions.[76]

In the case of the transfer of valuable assets from PC to ABC, there was an obligation to obtain board authorisation since VC is indirectly interested in the contract both as a director, given that VC has two nominee directors on the board of PC, and as a shareholder holding more than 10 per cent of the voting rights. The exemption for current operations entered into under normal terms and conditions is not applicable since the transfer of valuable IP is not a current operation of the company. In addition, the price was less than market value, which means that the terms and conditions were not normal.

The interested director cannot vote on the prior approval by the board of directors.[77] In the case of PC, VC's two nominee directors participated in the vote. The sanction under French case law is that contracts entered into with the prior authorisation of the board of directors, but including the vote of the interested directors – whether or not the vote was essential to approve the contract or not – may be cancelled if they have prejudicial consequences for the company.[78] Furthermore, the solution is the same when a contract is entered into without the prior authorisation of the board of directors, ie it may be cancelled if it has prejudicial consequences for the company.[79]

The Commercial Code holds that the shareholders can ratify the decision which was not approved by the board of directors, with a special vote after a report is produced by the statutory auditors.[80] It is probable that the courts would adopt the

---

[73] Commercial Code, Art L 225-38.
[74] Commercial Code, Art L 225-41.
[75] Commercial Code, Art L 225-40.
[76] Commercial Code, Art L 225-39.
[77] Commercial Code, Art L 225-40.
[78] CA Aix-en-Provence (Court of Appeal of Aix-en-Provence) 15 May 1990, *Dr sociétés* 1991, n° 379; Cass Com 18 October 1994, *RJDA* 12/94 n° 1307.
[79] Commercial Code, Art L 225-42.
[80] Commercial Code, Art L 225-42 al 3.

same solution if the contract was approved irregularly. However, in the case of PC, VC voted at the general shareholders' meeting and there was no special report of the shareholders explaining why VC participated in the vote. As an interested shareholder, VC was prohibited from voting.[81] Therefore, no valid shareholder ratification has been effected and the decision would continue to be treated as a nullity.

Since the sale has been entered into below market value, the contract is detrimental to the interests of PC. Therefore, a court – despite the fact that it has discretion to decide whether or not the annulment of the contract would be detrimental[82] – would probably declare the contract to be void. Therefore, Founder one, as a shareholder, can seek the nullification of the contract.[83]

Action on Civil Grounds: Damages
Since the authorisation by the board of directors of PC was not valid, Founder one can also sue against VC's nominee directors and VC itself for damages.[84] According to the Commercial Code, the failure by the board of directors to authorise the contract makes an 'interested person' liable.[85] The 'interested person' is VC, together with the other directors who authorised the contract. Founder one is protected against liability since he voted against the sale of the assets. An invalid authorisation, such as that of PC in the hypothetical case, is treated by the French courts as a failure to authorise. Therefore, an action can be raised against VC for damages. In addition, the Commercial Code provides that nominee directors incur the same liability as if they were directors in their own name.[86] Therefore, VC's nominee directors can also be sued for damages.

However, Founder one is unable to sue VC and the nominee directors *directly* for damages. The reason for this is that he only suffered derivative losses, namely the loss of value of his shares in PC. The damaged party is PC itself and PC is the only party who can sue. The French courts refuse to allow actions by shareholders for damage inflicted on a company, except if the shareholder can prove a specific and different damage from that of the company. Here, if Founder one sues for monetary damages, he would be unable to establish the existence of some specific monetary damage.

As a matter of principle, the action has to be raised by PC, which means by the CEO, the chairman of the management board or by the board of directors. However, the Commercial Code permits one or several shareholders (*action sociale ut singuli*) to raise a derivative action. The plaintiff only needs to be a shareholder when he or she initiates the suit and will be entitled to do so even if he or she holds only one share. There is no judicial scrutiny of this derivative action, but akin to the position in the US, the shareholder must first request the company to act. The legal costs of the action must be borne by the shareholder, although the benefit of the suit is for the company.

---

[81] Commercial Code, Art L 225-40 al 4.
[82] Cass Com. (Cour de cassation, Commercial Chamber), 22 November 1977, *Bull civ IV*, n° 276.
[83] See, eg, CA Amiens (Court of Appeal of Amiens), 1 December 1966, D 1967, 244 with a note by Dalsace.
[84] Commercial Code, Art L 225-42.
[85] Commercial Code, Art L 225-42 al 1.
[86] Commercial Code, Art L 225-20 al 1.

Therefore, Founder one is entitled to seek damages against VC and the two nominee directors in the name of PC.

Action on Criminal Grounds

A breach of the director's duty of loyalty can result in a criminal offence on the basis of an 'abuse of corporate assets'.[87] This provision punishes, among others, directors of a public limited company who:

> [U]se the company's property or credit, in bad faith, in a manner which they are aware is contrary to the interests of the company, for personal purposes or to favour another company or undertaking in which they have a direct or indirect interest.

The penalty is imprisonment for a term of up to five years (with no minimum). The transfer of assets below market value to a majority shareholder (VC), even indirectly through a wholly-owned subsidiary (ABC), would most probably be considered by a court to be an abuse of corporate assets.

In French law, a minority shareholder such as Founder one, acting derivatively in the name of the company (*action sociale ut singuli*), has the power to initiate a criminal prosecution and request civil damages by filing a criminal complaint (*plainte avec constitution de partie civile*) with the Dean of the Examining Magistrates (Doyen des Juges d'Instruction) of the Civil First Degree Court (Tribunal correctionnel). A 2007 Act[88] imposed a requirement whereby the shareholder must first raise his or her suit with the local Attorney-General and must then wait for a period of three months before filing his or her suit with the Dean of the Examining Magistrates.[89] In order for the complaint to be admissible by an examining magistrate, it is sufficient that the circumstances which gave rise to the complaint allow the examining magistrate to consider it 'possible' that there is a link between the losses suffered by the company and the alleged abuse of corporate assets. Case law has long made it clear that the examining magistrate has a duty to investigate, so long as he or she has deemed it to be the case that this undemanding standard has been met.

Therefore, Founder one can also cause VC and VC's nominee directors to be sued criminally for an abuse of corporate assets.

ii. Solution under French Law in the Case of a Simplified Public Company (SAS)

a. Introduction

The first issue to consider is whether the provision in the articles of association of an SAS giving the power to terminate any contract in excess of £75,000 to the shareholders rather than the CEO or the board of directors would be valid. The SAS is a more flexible corporate vehicle than a public company and such a provision in the articles is treated as valid.

---

[87] Commercial Code, Art L 242-6 al 3.
[88] Loi n°2007-291 du 5 mars 2007 tendant renforcer l'équilibre de la procédure pénale, JO 6 mars 2007, 4206.
[89] Criminal Procedure Code, Art 85.

Regarding the 75 per cent majority, in the case of an SAS, the Commercial Code leaves it to the articles of association to decide the majority.[90] Therefore, contrary to the case of an SA, this provision is valid in an SAS.

b. Validity of the Decision to Terminate Founder Two's Consultancy Contract

Breach of the Articles of Association
In French company law, the decision by the board of directors of an SAS to terminate Founder two's consultancy contract is a breach of the articles of incorporation. Therefore, the decision is also invalid. As in the case of an SA, a second issue is whether the invalidity of the decision can be cured either because the majority shareholder and Founder one (representing together 92 per cent of the share capital and 75 per cent of the votes at the level of the board of directors) were in favour of the termination or because Founder three would have also voted in favour of terminating the contract, which would have meant that there would have been unanimity in voting. Although there is no case law on this issue, there is no reason to think that the restrictive principles applied in the case of a public company would be applied differently in the case of an SAS. Therefore, the decision by the board of directors of PC, if it was incorporated as an SAS, whether unanimous or not, would not be valid under French law.

Enforcement of the Breach of the Articles of Association
Nullification   The same article of the Commercial Code on nullification of acts of a company applies to the SA and the SAS. Therefore, as in the case of the SA, the decision of the board of directors of SA to terminate the contract is not void.

Damages   The solution here would be the same as in the case of an SA.

c. Action by Founder One against VC's Two Nominee Directors and VC

Action on Civil Grounds: Nullification
In the case of an SAS, contracts entered into between the company and a director or a shareholder holding more than 10 per cent of the voting rights of a public company are not subject to the prior authorisation of the board of directors, since this organ is not compulsory in the SAS. Instead, they are subject to the *ex post* approval of the shareholders.[91] The transaction will be subject to the related parties transactions regime if it is concluded with a 10 per cent (or more) shareholder. However, that is not the situation in the hypothetical case, since the deal was done with a subsidiary (ABC) of PC's majority shareholder (VC). However, the related parties transactions regime will nonetheless apply where there has been the interpositioning of a person,[92] ie ABC for VC. Therefore, it is assumed that the regime would apply here. This provision does

---

[90] Commercial Code, Art L 227-9.
[91] Commercial Code, Art L 227-10.
[92] *Mémento Francis Lefebvre Sociétés commerciales*, 2015, n° 60431.

not apply to agreements relating to current operations entered into under normal terms and conditions.[93] However, as stated above, this exemption would not be applicable here.

Commentators adopt the view that the interested shareholders in a related parties transaction in an SAS cannot be excluded from the vote, unless the articles of association provide so.[94] Therefore, the approval of the general shareholders' meeting would probably be considered valid by the courts, although there is no case law on this issue. The solution can also be applied to the vote of VC authorising the sale at the level of the board of directors. This decision would probably also be considered valid by the courts.

Action on Civil Grounds: Damages

Despite the fact that the authorisation by the board of directors of PC and VC at the general shareholders' meeting of PC is probably valid in the case of an SAS, Founder two could probably sue for damages. Article L 227-10 of the Commercial Code states that contracts which have not been approved can give rise to an action for damages. However, as in the case of an SA, where a similar provision exists, this article cannot be construed as barring an action for damages in the case of approval of the contract by the shareholders. The reason is that, according to Article L 225-253 of the Commercial Code, no decision of the general shareholders' meeting can have the effect of extinguishing or preventing the raising of a suit. This article also applies to an SAS because it is not listed among the articles of the Commercial Code which is expressly stipulated as not applying to the SAS.[95] Therefore, an action for damages may be raised against VC. In addition, as in the case of a public company, the Commercial Code provides that nominee directors in an SAS incur the same liability as if they were directors in their own name.[96] Therefore, VC's nominee directors can also be sued for damages.

Action on Criminal Grounds

The solution here would be the same as in the case of an SA.

iii. Solution under French Law in the Case of a Limited Company (SARL)

a. Introduction

The first issue to consider is whether the provision in the articles of association of an SARL giving the shareholders (rather than the managers) the power to terminate any contract in excess of £75,000 would be valid. Like the SAS, the SARL is a more flexible corporate vehicle than a public company and such a provision in the articles is treated as valid.

---

[93] Commercial Code, Art L 227-11.
[94] *Mémento Francis Lefebvre Sociétés commerciales*, 2015, n° 60432; PL Périn, *SAS – La société par actions simplifiée* (Paris, Joly éditions, 2005) n° 640.
[95] Commercial Code, Art L 227-1 al 3.
[96] Commercial Code, Art L 227-7.

Regarding the 75 per cent majority, in the case of an SARL, the Commercial Code allows the articles of association to increase the majority.[97] Therefore, akin to the SAS, this provision is valid in the case of an SARL.

b. Validity of the Decision to Terminate Founder Two's Consultancy Contract

Breach of the Articles of Association

In an SARL, there is no board of managers (*Conseil de gérance*). If it is provided for by the articles of association, each individual manager alone can represent the company vis-a-vis third parties. Assuming that there is a board of managers, a decision by the board of PC to terminate Founder two's consultancy contract is a breach of the articles of incorporation. The solution here is the same as in the case of the SA and the SAS.

Enforcement of the Breach of the Articles of Association

Nullification   The same article of the Commercial Code on the nullification of acts of a company, which applies to the SA and the SAS, also applies to the SARL. Therefore, once again, in the case of the SARL, the decision to terminate the contract is not void.

Damages   The solution here would be the same as in the case of an SA and an SAS.

c. Action by Founder One against VC's Two Nominee Directors and VC

Action on Civil Grounds: Nullification

In the case of an SARL, contracts entered into between the company and a manager or a shareholder are subject only to the *ex post* approval of the shareholders.[98] The Commercial Code also covers contracts where a manager or a shareholder of the SARL is also manager or director or general partner of the other company.[99] In the case of ABC, it is very likely that VC is also a director of ABC, since ABC is wholly owned by VC. Therefore, the requirement to obtain an approval should apply.

This transaction is not an operation entered into under normal terms and conditions and this exemption, which also exists for SARL, is not applicable here.[100]

As an interested shareholder, VC was prohibited by the Commercial Code from voting.[101] However, the Commercial Code does not provide for the nullification of the transaction in this case.

Action on Civil Grounds: Damages

Article L 223-19 of the Commercial Code stipulates that related parties transactions which have not been approved, or which have been irregularly approved as in the case

---

[97] Commercial Code, Art L 223-30; CA Douai (Court of Appeal of Douai), 9 February 1973: *Journ Sociétés* 1973, 318 with a note by Bosvieux.

[98] Commercial Code, Art L 223-19 al 1.

[99] Commercial Code, Art L 223-19 al 5.

[100] Commercial Code, Art L 223-20.

[101] Commercial Code, Art L 223-19 al 1.

of VC's participation in the vote, can give rise to an action for damages.[102] Therefore, an action for damages may be raised against VC. Nominee managers are not allowed in an SARL since managers must be individual persons.[103] Therefore, VC's nominee managers can be sued for damages.

Action on Criminal Grounds

The solution would be the same as in the case of an SA or an SAS since the abuse of corporate assets also applies to an SARL.[104]

iv. Summary and Conclusion

With regard to PC and the abuses by VC, Founder two would probably be successful in obtaining damages for the termination of his consultancy contract regardless of whether PC is incorporated as an SA, an SAS or an SARL. However, in all cases, he would not be able to obtain the nullification of the decision. On the second issue, Founder one would probably be successful in obtaining the nullification of the transfer of assets and damages if PC is incorporated as an SA. However, this would be restricted to damages if PC is incorporated as an SAS or an SARL. Nevertheless, irrespective of the form of the corporate vehicle, Founder one could trigger criminal proceedings on the basis of an 'abuse of corporate assets'.

E. Germany[105]

i. Validity of the Decision to Terminate Founder Two's Consultancy Contract

The powers of the general meeting can be found in the codified company law (listed in GmbHG, § 46). However, restrictions and extensions are also possible.[106] In particular, 'the directors are bound to observe the restrictions on the scope of their authority to represent the company which are imposed by the articles or, unless the articles otherwise provide, by resolution of the members' (GmbHG, § 37(1)).

The main difficulty in relation to the first part of the case is whether the implicit decision of the directors and Founder three can be regarded as a decision of the general meeting. A rule of German law provides that 'where a meeting is not duly called, resolutions can be passed thereat only if all the members are present' (GmbHG, § 51(3)). In addition, it is necessary that the shareholders do not object to the failure to follow a proper procedure.[107] Another provision stipulates that 'a meeting is not necessary,

---

[102] Commercial Code, Art L 223-19 al 4; Cass Com (Cour de cassation, Commercial Chamber), 13 February 1996: *RJDA* 5/96, n° 566.

[103] Commercial Code, Art L 223-18.

[104] Commercial Code, Art L 241-3 4°.

[105] Abbreviated statutes: AktG = Law on Public Companies; GmbHG = Law on Private Limited Companies.

[106] See, eg, W Zöllner and U Noack in *Baumbach & Hueck's GmbHG* (21st edn, Munich, Beck, 2017) § 46, para 92.

[107] Ibid, § 51, para 31.

if all shareholders agree in writing on a particular resolution or if all shareholders agree to conduct a written procedure' (GmbHG, § 48(2)).

In the present case, it is not clear whether Founder three objected to the procedural faults rather than only the subject matter itself. Furthermore, for a valid decision, it depends on the way Founder three has expressed his opinion: if it was in voiced at the general meeting or in writing, this would be accepted by the German courts. However, if he expressed his consent in a different form (for example, if one of the directors asked him for his opinion in advance of, or after, the board meeting), the mainstream opinion is that this type of 'staggered resolution' is not accepted as valid, even if all shareholders agree.[108]

In the latter case, the decision of the directors on the termination of the contract is void by analogy with § 241(no 1) of the AktG.[109] However, this does not mean that the termination itself would be void. It is explicitly stated that 'a restriction on the power of directors to represent has no legal effect against third parties' (GmbHG, § 37(2)). An exception is made if the other person is a director or shareholder of the company.[110] Since this exception does not extend to former shareholders, Founder two's consultancy contract has been validly terminated.

ii. Action by Founder One against VC's Two Nominee Directors and VC

As explained in the German solution in chapter seven, an undervalue transaction with a shareholder or (as here) a related party of a shareholder[111] violates a number of provisions of German company law. In particular, the transaction constitutes a breach of capital maintenance rules (GmbHG, § 30) and of the directors' duty of loyalty (GmbHG, § 43(1)). As a result of both of these legal infringements, it follows that the directors are liable to compensate the company (AktG, § 43(2), (3)). In addition, the related party ABC is obliged to return the received benefits (AktG, § 31(1)).[112]

The claims under capital maintenance law, both against the directors and the related party, cannot be waived (AktG, §§ 43(3)(s3), 31(4)). In principle, it would be possible for the general meeting to ratify a breach of the directors' duty of loyalty (GmbHG, § 46(no 8)). However, since VC was in a conflict of interest situation, its vote was invalid (AktG, § 47(3)).[113] Nevertheless, in a normal case, a minority shareholder would have to raise an action challenging the resolution of the general meeting which ratified the directors' breach.[114] In the present scenario, however, this has not been necessary owing to the fact that it is not possible to waive any infringement of capital maintenance laws.

---

[108] BGH (German Federal Supreme Court) NZG 2006, 428; Zöllner and Noack, ibid, § 48, para 41.

[109] BGH, ibid; Zöllner and Noack, ibid, § 48, para 42 (others, however, regard the decision as only voidable).

[110] See Zöllner and Noack, ibid, § 37, para 41.

[111] L Fastrich in *Baumbach & Hueck's GmbHG* (21st edn, Munich, Beck, 2017) § 30, para 26a.

[112] Ibid, § 31, para 13 (a direct claim against a related party is possible in exceptional circumstances).

[113] This could either be based on the first or the second sentence of this paragraph, on which, see, eg, Zöllner and Noack, *Baumbach & Hueck's GmbHG* (n 106) § 47, paras 77–78.

[114] See, eg, Zöllner and Noack (n 106) § 47, para 104. On this action, see ch 7, above.

The aforementioned provisions cannot be directly enforced by a minority share-holder (such as Founder one). The mainstream position is that shareholders are not permitted to sue the directors of a private company since they have no direct contrac-tual relationship with them;[115] an analogy with the derivative suit in the law of public companies (AktG, § 147a)[116] is also rejected.[117] However, the minority shareholders may call a general meeting (GmbHG, § 50(1)) and propose that the shareholders vote in favour of a resolution to sue the directors for a breach of the duty of loyalty, a violation of the rules on capital maintenance and the failure to enforce the compensa-tion claim against ABC (GmbHG, § 46(no 8)). If the majority of shareholders reject this proposal, Founder one could then raise an action seeking a declaratory judgment, which will state that the majority has to approve his proposal. However, in the present case, this course of action is not feasible since the minority right to call a meeting requires a 10 per cent stake in ABC and Founder one only holds 8 per cent of ABC's shares.

A better way for Founder one to proceed would be to sue the majority share-holder VC. In general, this is possible. Insofar as private companies are concerned, the courts have held that, by analogy with the situation in partnerships, shareholders owe fiduciary duties to one another.[118] The position depends on the extent to which the shareholders of a particular company are not only investors but also 'economic owners' of the company. In the hypothetical case, VC has clearly violated its fiduciary duties since the undervalue transaction between PC and VC's subsidiary only had the objective of 'tunnelling' profits at the expense of the minority shareholder.

In procedural terms, the courts have allowed minority shareholders to sue the majority in their own name with the aim of compensating the company.[119] Such an *actio pro socio* usually requires the minority shareholder to pursue any internal reme-dies available. If it is obvious that these means would not be feasible (for example, as in the hypothetical case, because the majority completely dominates the company), an immediate claim against the majority shareholder is admissible. Unlike Polish law (see J., below), there is no time limit before which a shareholder can raise the *actio pro socio*. Thus, Founder one can successfully sue VC for the benefit of PC.

F. Italy[120]

In the case of the Srl in Italian law, the balance of power between the directors and the shareholders is governed by the interaction between Articles 2475 and 2479 of the CC. According to Article 2475 of the CC, unless otherwise provided in the articles of association of the company, the direction of the company is entrusted to

---

[115] BGH, WM 1982, 928; Fastrich in *Baumbach & Hueck's GmbHG* (n 111) § 13, para 39.
[116] See also ch 4 at II C, above.
[117] See, eg, Zöllner and Noack (n 106) § 43, para 32.
[118] Fastrich (n 111) § 13, para 24.
[119] Fastrich (n 111) § 13, paras 36–39 and BGH (German Federal Supreme Court), BGHZ 65, 15.
[120] Abbreviations: CC = Italian Civil Code (*codice civile*); Spa = public company (*Società per azioni*); Srl = private limited company (*Società a responsabilità limitata*).

one or more directors. Article 2479 of the CC, on the other hand, says that the share-holders must decide on the matters reserved within their competence by the articles of association, as well as on the decisions that one or more directors or shareholders that represent at least one-third of the share capital of the company submit to them for their approval. An analysis of the hypothetical case in light of this legal framework reveals that the provision requiring the approval of the shareholders to terminate any contract in excess of £75,000 falls within the scope of Article 2479 of the CC.

Even if the decision on the termination of the contract is reserved to the share-holders, the legal action raised by Founder two will be unsuccessful under Italian law, and the opinion of Founder three will have no effect on the outcome of the litigation. In fact, Italian company law makes a clear distinction between the power to manage the company and the power to represent the company vis-a-vis third parties. While the first power is given to the board acting as a corporate body (CC, Article 2475), the power to represent the company and thus also to terminate the contract is given indi-vidually to one or more members of the board. The relationship between the powers to manage the company and to represent the company is governed by Article 2475-*bis*, paragraph 2 of the CC. This provision is interpreted so that limitations on the power to manage the company imposed on directors may never be relied on as against third parties in the absence of evidence that such third parties deliberately acted to damage the company.[121]

In addition, given that the possibility of challenging the resolutions of the board of an Srl is not specifically addressed in Italian law, with the exception of resolutions passed in a conflict-of-interest situation, many scholars exclude this possibility.[122] Moreover, even if we accept that – as in the case of the Spa – a resolution of the board could be challenged, a third party would not have the requisite standing to sue. Furthermore, a breach of the articles of association is the basis for an action against the directors, which cannot be directly presented by third parties. In conclusion, the termination of the contract is valid and the resolution cannot be challenged. Thus, the only remedy available would be an action for damages against the directors. However, Founder two is probably not allowed to raise such an action.[123]

Turning to the transfer of the IP to ABC at a discounted price, three issues should be kept separate: (i) the power to represent PC vis-a-vis third parties; (ii) the resolution taken in conflict of interest by the board of directors; and (iii) the conflict-of-interest situation inherent in the resolution adopted by the shareholders.

Starting with the first issue, according to Article 2475-*ter*, paragraph 1 of the CC, any agreements concluded in conflict of interest, entered into by the directors with the power to represent the company, are voidable upon PC's request if the conflict was known or could have been known by the third party, ie ABC.

---

[121] *Cf* P Morandi, 'Commento *sub* art. 2475-*bis*' in A Maffei Alberti (ed), *Commentario breve al diritto delle società* (3rd edn, Padua, CEDAM, 2007) 1370 ff, 1373 ff.

[122] See, eg, M Ventoruzzo, 'Commento *sub* art. 2475-*ter*' in P Marchetti, LA Bianchi, F Ghezzi and M Notari (eds), *Commentario alla Riforma delle società. Società a responsabilità limitata* (Milan, Giuffrè-Egea, 2008) 599 ff, 653 ff.

[123] *Cf* M Ventoruzzo, 'Commento *sub* art. 2388' in P Marchetti, LA Bianchi, F Ghezzi and M Notari (eds), *Commentario alla Riforma delle società. Amministratori* (Milan, Giuffrè-Egea, 2005) 299 ff, 327 ff.

With regard to the second issue, Article 2475-*ter*, paragraph 2 of the CC stipulates that the resolutions of the board of directors adopted with the decisive vote of a director in a conflict-of-interest situation may be challenged by the other directors (in this case by the director appointed by Founder one). This provision also stipulates that any rights acquired in good faith by third parties pursuant to any action performed in order to put into effect the decision are not prejudiced.

Turning to the third issue, unless the articles of association of a company provide specific powers to the shareholders on the matter, in terms of Article 2475 of the CC, there is a presumption that the power to manage the company is vested in the board of directors. It is also important to highlight that, according to Article 2479-*ter*, paragraph 2 of the CC, the resolutions of the shareholders may be challenged if it is proved that they may cause loss to the company and, as in the instant case, if they have been adopted with the decisive votes of interested shareholders.

In brief, after the successful challenge of the resolution of the board of directors of PC, the transfer of IP to ABC may also be challenged, and the action will succeed as it will probably not be difficult to prove that ABC was acting in bad faith and was aware of the conflict of interest. In addition to this remedy, directors are also liable for a violation of the duty of loyalty and any shareholder may raise such a legal action (CC, Article 2476, paragraph 3).

Finally, it is important to stress that in the hypothetical case, the rules on the direction and coordination of companies may also have a role to play. According to Article 2497 of the CC, any company or entity carrying out the direction and coordination of companies that acts in its own interests or in the interests of other parties is directly liable for any losses suffered by the shareholders of such company or entity subject to such direction and coordination. However, this type of liability does not arise if, among other things, no loss is caused as a result of the direction and coordination. This liability also extends to any party who participated in the conduct that caused the loss, including any party (like ABC) that in bad faith took advantage of the conduct. It must also be underlined that this type of liability supplements and does not replace the rules on the conflict of interest of the directors illustrated above.[124]

G. Spain

i. Founder Two's Challenge to the Termination of the Consultancy Contract

Spanish company law sets out certain specific issues which have to be debated and agreed by the shareholders in general meeting (Ley de Sociedades de Capital (LSC) – Corporate Enterprises Act,[125] Article 160), such as the appointment of directors, mergers or increases in share capital among others. The law also provides that the general meeting must decide on any matter specified in the by-laws

---

[124] M Ventoruzzo, 'Commento *sub* art. 2391' in Marchetti et al, *Commentario alla Riforma delle società. Società a responsabilità limitata* (n 122) 468 ff.
[125] Real Decreto Legislativo 1/2010, de 2 de julio, por el que se aprueba el texto refundido de la Ley de Sociedades de Capital (LSC).

(LSC, Article 160(j)). The LSC also permits the by-laws of a *Sociedad de Responsabilidad Limitada* (SL) to set majority requirements which, without requiring unanimity, are higher than those established by law (LSC, Article 200). Therefore, PC is entitled to include a clause in its by-laws requiring qualified shareholder approval as regards the termination of contracts.

As explained in chapter 8, above, according to the law, a general shareholders' meeting will be treated as validly constituted without the need for any prior notice when all the share capital is present or represented at the meeting and those present accept, by unanimity, the deliberations of the meeting (LSC, Article 178.1). If the decision by VC's two nominee directors and Founder one is adopted under such circumstances and with the presence/representation and agreement of Founder three, then it would be theoretically possible to treat the agreement as indeed having been validly adopted by the general shareholders' meeting. If Founder three was present at the meeting and accepted its deliberations, then whether he agreed with the decision or not would have no effect on the validity of the agreement, to the extent that even if he disagrees with the termination of the contract, the decision of the general meeting would be valid.

However, if we assume that the court rejects the idea that the decision to terminate the consultancy agreement was taken at a valid general shareholders' meeting and that it is instead treated as a resolution of the board of directors, then such a decision would be in clear violation of PC's by-laws and would thus be challengeable (LSC, Articles 251.2 and 204.1). However, Founder two would face important limitations upon his ability to raise legal proceedings, since the law only allows directors, and shareholders representing at least 1 per cent of the share capital of a company, to challenge the resolutions of the board of directors (LSC, Article 251.1). Founder two is neither a director nor a shareholder, and thus he would not be entitled to raise such an action. With regard to the termination of the contract itself, the law states that any restrictions[126] on the power of the directors to represent the company will have no effect vis-a-vis third parties (LSC, Article 234.1) and therefore the contract would have been validly terminated.

ii. Action by Founder One

The decision to sell the assets of PC to ABC at less than market value, which was adopted with the votes of VC's two nominee directors and ratified by the general shareholders' meeting of PC, would be treated as a disguised distribution aimed at tunnelling profits at the expense of PC's minority shareholders. By voting in a conflict-of-interest situation in relation to which they ought to have abstained, VC's two nominee directors are liable for a breach of their duty of loyalty towards PC (LSC, Article 229.1). As explained in chapter 3, above, the votes of VC's two nominee directors would be invalid and if they were decisive for the purposes of the adoption of the decision to

---

[126] This is a reference to voluntary restrictions such as those set out in the by-laws of the company. In this regard, see G Esteban Velasco, 'Artículo 234. Ámbito del poder de representación' in Á Rojo and E Beltrán (eds), *Comentario de la Ley de Sociedades de Capital* (Cizur Menor (Navarra), Civitas-Thomson Reuters, 2011) 1683–84.

transfer the IP – as would seem to be the case here – then the decision would have been adopted without compliance with the majority requirements and could thus be challenged by directors and by shareholders who represent at least 1 per cent of the share capital of the company (LSC, Article 251.1). Therefore, Founder one, who is a director and owns 8 per cent of the shares of PC, would be entitled to take action. The decision of the general shareholders' meeting of PC to ratify the resolution of the board of directors to transfer PC's IP harms the interests of PC to the benefit of one of its shareholders, namely VC, and thus that decision is challengeable (LSC, Article 204.1)[127] by those shareholders who represent, at least, 1 per cent of the share capital of PC (LSC, Article 206.1). Moreover, directors are also entitled to challenge such decisions (LSC, Article 206.1).[128] Therefore Founder one could also proceed to challenge the decision by the general shareholders' meeting of PC to ratify.

Founder one would also be entitled to raise a claim for damages against VC's two nominee directors on the board of PC for a breach of their duties of loyalty (LSC, Article 227) which are owed towards PC[129] and more particularly for a breach of their duty to abstain from voting in respect of a decision where they had a conflict of interest (LSC, Articles 228 and 229.1) which amounts to behaviour that may render them liable to PC (LSC, Article 236). Claims against directors for damages to the company are normally brought by the company with the agreement of the general shareholders' meeting (LSC, Article 238.1). However, shareholders representing a percentage equal to or higher than 5 per cent of the share capital of the company can directly bring a suit for damages against the company themselves when such suit is grounded on an alleged breach of the duty of loyalty by the directors (LSC, Article 239.1), as is the case with VC's two nominee directors. To the extent that Founder one owns 8 per cent of the share capital of PC, he would be entitled to bring the suit against VC's two nominee directors in defence of PC's interests – for example, if PC failed to do so, which, in the instant case, would be highly likely owing to VC's majority shareholding.

VC was in a clear conflict-of-interest situation in relation to the sale transaction and, notwithstanding this, exercised its vote in favour of the transfer of the IP to ABC. Spanish company law establishes certain restrictions on the voting rights of shareholders affected by conflicts of interest (LSC, Article 190). However, such limitations concern very particular circumstances[130] and it is unlikely that VC's situation would fall within any of them.[131] Nevertheless, the behaviour of VC does constitute a breach of the 'corporate contract' and its duty of loyalty which is owed

---

[127] See B Bago Oria, *Dividendos encubiertos. El reparto oculto del beneficio en sociedades anónimas y limitadas* (Cizur Menor (Navarra), Civitas, 2010) 335.

[128] On the parties entitled to challenge shareholders' agreements, see especially Á Rojo, 'Artículo 206. Legitimación para impugnar' in Á Rojo and E Beltrán (eds), *Comentario de la Ley de Sociedades de Capital* (Cizur Menor (Navarra), Civitas-Thomson Reuters, 2011) 1458–61.

[129] See, eg, Bago Oria, *Dividendos encubiertos* (n 127) 397–98.

[130] See MM Curto, 'Artículo 190. Conflicto de intereses en la sociedad de responsabilidad limitada' in Á Rojo and E Beltrán (eds), *Comentario de la Ley de Sociedades de Capital* (Cizur Menor (Navarra), Civitas-Thomson Reuters, 2011) 190.

[131] Some scholars take the view that a general prohibition applies precluding controlling shareholders from acting or taking decisions in situations of conflict of interest. See, eg, V Ribas Ferrer, *El deber de lealtad del administrador de sociedades* (Madrid, La Ley, 2010) 337–43.

towards PC.[132] Notwithstanding this, commentators take the view that the scope for an individual shareholder, such as Founder one, to be successful in an *actio pro socio* is very limited.[133] This does not exclude the potential for VC to be liable for the losses sustained by PC; the fact that the sale transaction was entered into with ABC does not alter the scope for such liability to arise because ABC is wholly owned by VC, who is the party that receives the benefit from the transaction.[134] The normal consequence of a disguised distribution in contravention of the duty of loyalty is that the concerned shareholder must restore its value.[135] However, in the case of a synallagmatic contract – such as the sale of assets to ABC – the party harmed by the implementation of the contract – in the instant case PC – could choose between compensation for damages or restitution of the assets (Código Civil (CC) – Civil Code,[136] Article 1124).[137]

H. The Netherlands[138]

i. The Validity of the Decision to Terminate Founder Two's Consultancy Contract

The general meeting has the powers that have been granted to it on the basis of codified company law and the articles of association of the company.[139] Moreover, the general meeting has any power not assigned to the board of directors or another corporate body.[140] The board has the broad power to manage and represent the company vis-a-vis third parties as well as to determine its strategy.[141] This strongly limits the residual power of the shareholders, because many acts will constitute managing and representing the company or will be related to the determination of the strategy of the company. The power of the board generally includes the power to terminate contracts on behalf of the company, unless the articles of association contain a specific clause stating that shareholder approval is required.

Dutch law does not include any specific procedural rules regarding the manner in which the board of directors should pass resolutions. Legislation prescribing that resolutions should be passed by a corporate body only apply to shareholders passing resolutions in the general meeting. Therefore, it will normally be assumed that, unless

[132] See, eg, Bago Oria (n 127) 381–82.
[133] See FJ Alonso Espinosa, 'Introducción a la Teoría General del Derecho Español de Sociedades' (Universidad de Murcia, 2010) 37–39.
[134] See, eg, Bago Oria (n 127) 329–31 and 400–01.
[135] See, eg, Bago Oria (n 127) 387–90.
[136] Real Decreto de 24 de julio de 1889 por el que se publica el Código Civil.
[137] See, eg, Bago Oria (n 127) 390–93.
[138] Abbreviations: DCC = Dutch Civil Code; HR = Hoge Raad = Dutch Supreme Court; OK = Ondernemingskamer = Enterprise Chamber; Rb. = Rechtbank = District Court. An unofficial translation of Dutch company law as incorporated in bk 2 of the Dutch Civil Code can be found on www.dutchcivillaw.com/civilcodebook022.htm.
[139] HR 13 Juli 2007, *JOR* 2007/178, with a note by Nieuwe Weme (*ABN AMRO*); HR 9 Juli 2010, *JOR* 2010/228, with a note by Van Ginneken (*ASMI*).
[140] DCC, Art 2:107217-1.
[141] DCC, Art 2:129/239-1 and 2:130/240-1.

stated otherwise in the articles of association or by-laws, the board will pass resolutions by means of a majority vote.[142] Although not explicitly mentioned in the law itself, it is also generally assumed that the board of directors can only act based on a resolution of the board of directors.[143] This is, however, an internal rule only, which in principle does not have any external affect towards third parties. The starting point is that both the board jointly and all directors individually can legally represent the company.[144] It is only possible to limit this power *externally* if the law provides for such a limitation. It is, for instance, possible to stipulate that the company can only be represented by two directors together, which is a common clause in the case of joint ventures.

Although normally the board of directors would have the power to terminate a contract on behalf of the company, it is possible to include a provision in the articles of association that prescribes that certain resolutions of the board of directors require the approval of another corporate body within the company. Frequently this corporate body is the shareholders' general meeting or the supervisory board. Even if such a clause is included in the articles of association, this mandatory approval clause only has effect internally within the company.[145] Therefore, in principle, the contract is legally terminated, even if the approval of the shareholders was not provided. In theory, it is possible that in cases of extreme misuse of these powers a third party can nevertheless state that the contract was not validly terminated by the board of directors.[146] This could for instance be the case when the director has a clear conflict of interest when acting on behalf of the company in order to profit from it personally.

Even though in principle the contract is validly terminated notwithstanding that the mandatory shareholder approval as mentioned in the hypothetical case under discussion was not provided, the act of the board of directors could have internal consequences for the individual directors that terminated the contract on behalf of the company, because they could be held liable. Under Dutch law, generally the directors that acted in breach of the provisions that are included in the articles of association in order to protect the legal entity will be liable on the basis of serious fault.[147] Moreover, acting in violation of the articles of association could lead to an inquiry procedure before the Enterprise Chamber of the Court of Appeal of Amsterdam, which court could conclude that the directors have mismanaged (*wanbeleid*) the company because they acted contrary to the terms of the articles of association.

Whether Founder three was or was not in favour of termination of the consultancy contract with Founder two will in principle not be a major point, given the fact that (i) Founder three is only a shareholder, (ii) the company was still legally represented by the board of directors and (iii) a violation of the mandatory approval in the articles

---

[142] BF Assink and WJ Slagter, *Compendium Ondernemingsrecht, Deel 1* (Deventer, Kluwer, 2013) § 51.

[143] MJ Kroeze, *Mr. C. Assers Handleiding tot de beoefening van het Nederlands Burgerlijk Recht. 2. Rechtspersonenrecht. Deel I*. De rechtspersoon* (Deventer, Kluwer, 2015) 67.

[144] DCC, Art 2:130/240-2.

[145] This can also be derived from DCC, Art 2:107a-2. This article, which is only applicable for public companies, states that certain resolutions are subject to approval of the general meeting but that the absence of such approval does not affect the power of representation of the board of directors.

[146] HR 17 December 1982, *NJ* 1983/480, with a note by JMM Maeijer (*Bibolini*).

[147] HR 29 November 2002, *NJ* 2003/455 (*Berghuizer Papierfabriek*).

of association does not have external effect. However, whether or not Founder three was (also) in favour of the termination of the consultancy contract could influence the way in which the broader legal norms of reasonableness and fairness and abuse of power are perceived by the court. If all parties involved except for Founder two were in favour of terminating the consultancy contract, it might be defendable to state that no interests were affected as a result of the failure to attain shareholder approval, because all other shareholders were in favour anyway. It has to be noted however, that such a form of practical reasoning has been rejected by the Supreme Court in a case in which the mandatory advisory vote of the directors was not included when one of the members of the board of directors was dismissed by the general meeting. In that case the defendant stated that casting the advisory vote would not have made a difference, because the defendant as a shareholder would still have voted in favour of the dismissal of the director. The Supreme Court took a more formal approach stating that even though this might have been the case, this still meant that the resolution to dismiss the director was voidable on the basis of Article 2:15, paragraph 1, sub 1 DCC.[148]

ii.   Action by Founder One against VC's Two Nominee directors and VC

Under Dutch law, the members of the board of directors of a public and a private company are not allowed to vote on resolutions if the directors have a conflict of interest.[149] Whether there is a conflict of interest depends on all circumstances of the case. A potential conflict of interest is in itself not enough, since there have to be actual circumstances that can affect the way the interested members of the board are influenced in their behaviour, as a result of which they would not be able to act objectively and with integrity.[150] The mere fact that the director acts in various capacities is not sufficient for a conflict-of-interest situation to arise.[151] If one or more directors have a conflict of interest, the other directors will have to vote on the resolutions and the conflicted directors are not allowed to be present during the relevant deliberation.[152] Conflicted directors are however still allowed to represent the companies towards third parties. If all directors have a conflict of interest, the resolution is voted on by the supervisory board, if one is present. If there is no supervisory board or all members of the supervisory board also have a conflict of interest, the general meeting votes on the resolution unless the articles of association provide otherwise. It is possible to include a provision in the articles of association that under such circumstances the conflicted directors can vote on the resolution.[153]

Dutch law has no mandatory legislation regarding the regulation of conflicts of interest in the case of shareholders, unless the articles of association provide or

---

[148] HR 10 March 1995, *NJ* 1995/595, with a note by Maeijer (*Janssen Pers*).
[149] DCC, Art 2:129/239-6.
[150] HR 29 June 2007, *NJ* 2007/420, with a note by Maeijer (*Bruil/Kombex*).
[151] PJ Dortmond, *Mr E.J.J. van der Heijden Mr W.C.L van der Grinten Handboek voor de naamloze en de besloten vennootschap* (Deventer, WEJ Tjeenk Willink, 2013) nr 233.1.
[152] DCC, Art 2:129/239-6.
[153] Dortmond, *Mr E.J.J. van der Heijden Mr W.C.L van der Grinten Handboek voor de naamloze en de besloten vennootschap* (n 151) nr 233.1.

incorporate such rules.[154] Shareholders are therefore in principle allowed to vote in accordance with their own interests, even if these interests are not directly related to their position as a shareholder of the company. However, when a shareholder acts in such a way it is possible that the shareholder might abuse his powers and/or act in violation of standards of reasonableness and fairness.[155]

First of all, the question is whether the two directors have a conflict of interest. Since they voted in favour of a resolution as a result of which intellectual property rights were transferred for less than market value, this would indeed suggest that the directors have a conflicting interest. However, it will depend on all circumstances of the case whether there is indeed such a conflict. The fact that a director is a nominee of VC is not of itself sufficient. Assuming for the sake of argument that the two VC nominee directors do indeed have a conflict of interest, they would not be permitted to participate in voting on the board resolution regarding the transfer of the intellectual property to ABC. In this case, Founder one was the only member of the board of directors without a conflict of interest and therefore he would have to decide on the proposed board resolution. The fact that a general meeting ratified the board resolution does not affect matters, since the general meeting does not have any (direct) powers in this regard.

Moreover, the resolution also seems to be voidable on the basis of the standards of reasonableness and fairness.[156] Although two of the directors are nominated by VC and therefore practically represent VC in the board of directors, the individual board members still have to focus on the interests of the company as such.[157] If an enterprise is connected with the company, the interests of the company are generally formed by promoting the lasting success of that enterprise.[158] The transfer of valuable intellectual property under market value would be in violation of the interest of PC as a company and therefore could be deemed voidable based on the reasonableness and fairness criteria.

Alongside the voidability of the board resolution, the directors that voted on the resolution whilst having a conflict of interest could potentially be held liable by the company or, in case of insolvency, the creditors and bankruptcy trustee. It should also be mentioned that since the sale of assets was below market value it could be argued that the directors acted contrary to the interests of the company which can increase their risk of liability. If the shareholder's sole loss is a loss in the value of their shares, the minority shareholder will generally not be able to raise a direct suit against the directors.[159] The lawsuit would primarily have to be initiated by the company itself as the directors owe their duty to the company and Dutch law does not allow a derivative action. Shareholders can, however, initiate direct action on the basis of a tort claim against the directors if it can be established that those directors have directly violated

---

[154] This can, eg, be done on the basis of DCC, Art 2.12.
[155] This was, eg, the case in: HR 29 September 2006, *NJ* 2006/639, with a note by Maeijer (*The Mill Resort*).
[156] DCC, Art 2:15-1 sub 1.
[157] HR 4 April 2014, *NJ* 2014/286, with a note by Van Schilfgaarde (*Cancun*).
[158] Ibid.
[159] HR 2 December 1994, *NJ* 1995/288, with a note by Maeijer (*Poot/ABP*); Assink and Slagter, *Compendium Ondernemingsrecht, Deel 1* (n 142) § 14.

a specific duty of care (*specifieke zorgvuldigheidsnorm*) against those shareholders. A mere loss in share value is however insufficient.

The action to hold the directors liable could be combined with an action to nullify the resolution, but this is not mandatory. Even when the resolution is not legally affected the directors who voted with a conflict of interest can potentially be held liable.[160]

I. Finland

i. *Validity of the Resolution to Terminate Founder Two's Consultancy Contract*

The powers of the general meeting can be found in Chapter 5 of the Companies Act 2006 (CA) and as a rule, the general meeting passes resolutions on matters that fall within its competence by virtue of the CA. However, it may be provided in the articles of association that the general meeting may pass a resolution on matters that would otherwise fall within the general competence of the board or the managing director. Further, by unanimity, shareholders may also in individual cases otherwise make resolutions on matters falling within the general competence of the board or the managing director.[161] The main question in relation to the first part of the case is whether the implicit resolution of the directors and Founder three can be regarded as a resolution of the general meeting. Shareholders may pass a resolution on a matter within the competence of the general meeting also by a dated written resolution of the shareholders without holding a meeting. However, such a written resolution must be unanimous.[162]

Therefore, on the one hand, it seems that the board has exceeded its powers (pursuant to the articles of association) and, on the other hand, that the resolution does not meet the procedural requirements of a written unanimous resolution of the shareholders. Pursuant to chapter 5, section 15 of the CA, a matter that has not been dealt with in accordance with the procedural provisions of the CA or the articles of association may only be resolved if the shareholders, who are affected by the omission, consent to the resolution being passed. Where Founder three is in favour of termination and the resolution of the shareholders is in writing, dated, numbered and signed, the resolution is valid. In addition, Founder three's consent would validate the breach of the procedural requirements.

Where Founder three is opposed to the termination and Founder two is no longer a shareholder of the company, Founder two does not have the right to challenge a resolution of the company. However, Founder two has an option to seek damages for the loss. Pursuant to the CA, the directors are liable for damages for any loss that they, in violation of the CA or the articles of association, have caused deliberately or negligently to a third party, such as Founder two.[163]

---

[160] Dortmond (n 151) nr 233.1.
[161] CA, c 5, s 2.
[162] CA, c 5, s 1.
[163] CA, c 22, s 1(2).

ii. Action by Founder One against VC's Two Nominee Directors and VC

Under Finnish law, derivative claims are based on chapter 22, section 7 of the CA. A shareholder may bring a claim in his or her own name on behalf of the company against the directors, a shareholder or the chairman of a general meeting, but only for damages. In order to recover the assets of the company, the basis for the action must be found in other provisions.

The basis for a derivative claim in this case is that VC's two nominee directors negligently or deliberately breached their fiduciary duties and violated the provisions of the CA. The transfer of IP at undervalue to VC's subsidiary ABC may constitute a disguised distribution of the assets and thus an unlawful distribution of assets.[164] VC's two nominee directors were in breach of their duty of care and duty of loyalty.[165] Furthermore, the transaction may have been contrary to the objectives of the company.[166] Furthermore, a disguised distribution violates the principle of equal treatment.[167] The provisions in chapter 1, sections 5, 7 and 8 of the CA are treated as the source of the authority of the board of directors. If the directors violate these provisions, they are deemed to have acted without authority and the resolution is treated as void.[168] In that case, the transfer of IP to ABC does not bind PC and must be returned to PC. However, a shareholder cannot raise a derivative claim to recover assets.

Shareholders are entitled to bring a claim in their own name on behalf of the company when: (1) it is likely that the company will not take action; and (2a) the shareholders represent at least 10 per cent of the shares in the company; or (2b) if it would violate the principle of equal treatment if the claim for damages was not enforced.[169] Founder one, as a shareholder, would indirectly suffer loss as a result of the damage PC suffers because of the unlawful distribution of the IP. The value of Founder one's investment would decrease because of the transfer of PC's assets to ABC. At the same time, VC's assets would increase, since ABC is VC's subsidiary. Thus, even if Founder one owns only 8 per cent of the shares of PC, he can raise an action against VC's nominee directors and VC as a shareholder for damages and such damages would be awarded to PC.[170]

Founder one is also a director of the board. The two other directors are VC's nominee directors who may have been conflicted to participate in this matter because of the existence of a possible conflict of interest.[171] If the VC's nominee directors were

[164] As discussed in the Finnish solution in ch 7 at II G, above.
[165] CA, c 1, s 8.
[166] CA, c 1, s 5, assuming the purpose is to generate profits for the shareholders.
[167] CA, c 1, s 7.
[168] CA, c 6, s 28(1).
[169] CA, c 22, s 7.
[170] In exceptional circumstances, damages are paid to a shareholder directly. The Supreme Court held in KKO 2000:89 that a shareholder was entitled to damages directly from the directors as the shareholder otherwise would not have had sufficient legal protection. In practice, the shareholder would not have been able to reverse the effect of the board's unlawful resolution, which significantly reduced the value of the shareholder's shares.
[171] CA, c 6, s 4. Conflicts of interests are discussed in the Finnish solution in ch 3 at II I, above.

conflicted, the resolution to transfer the IP is invalid and must not be enforced.[172] If enforced, the directors are liable in damages for any losses sustained by PC, a shareholder or a third party.[173] However, the CA does not regulate how resolutions of the board may be invalidated and this matter is yet to be clarified by case law. In this case, the only disinterested person who could act on behalf of PC (according to the case scenario) would be Founder one – as director[174] – and in practice Founder one would also presumably be obliged to do so in order to avoid liability in damages. Therefore, Founder one as a director is likely to have authority to act on behalf of PC in order to recover the assets. However, in contrast, in his capacity as a shareholder, Founder one does not have this option.

Consequently, Founder one presumably is able to bring an action to have the board resolution declared void and the assets recovered. To the extent that the IP cannot be recovered and for additional loss the company has suffered, Founder one, as a shareholder, is entitled to bring an action on behalf of PC against VC's nominee directors and VC as shareholder.[175]

VC as shareholder is liable in damages for loss that it negligently or deliberately caused to PC by contributing to the violation of the CA. When the loss has been caused in order to benefit a related party (such as ABC), negligence is presumed.[176]

It is worth noting that, since VC owns more than 90 per cent of the shares of the company, the redemption procedure under chapter 18 of the CA is applicable. The threshold for the redemption right and obligation has been set to nine-tenths of the shares and votes in a company. When crossing the threshold, the majority shareholder is entitled and obliged to redeem the remaining shares at a fair price. Therefore, both Founder one or VC may initiate the redemption process.

J. Poland

i. Validity of the Decision to Terminate Founder Two's Consultancy Contract

The breach of the provision of PC's articles of association, which provides that the termination of any contract in excess of £75,000 must be approved by no less than 75 per cent of the shareholders of PC, will invoke Article 17, section 3 of the Commercial Companies Code (CCC). According to this provision, where the articles of association require that a decision must be approved by a particular body of the company, the validity of such a decision is not affected by the absence of such approval. However, the liability of the directors for a breach of the articles of association in such circumstances is not precluded. The duty of board members to obey the

---

[172] CA, c 6, s 2(2).

[173] CA, c 22, s 1.

[174] When the majority of the board is disqualified, the matter can be referred to the general meeting. In this case, VC holds 92 per cent of the shares of PC.

[175] CA, c 22, ss 1 and 2.

[176] A company and another person are related parties if one controls the other or otherwise has significant influence over the financial and business resolutions of the other (CA, c 8, s 6(2)).

articles of association and resolutions of shareholders is stipulated in Article 207 of the CCC:

> [I]n relation to the company, the members of the management board are subject to the limitations stipulated in this section (of the CCC), in the articles of association and, unless the articles of association provide otherwise, in the resolutions of the shareholders.

Whether informal decisions of the directors and Founder three can be regarded as demonstrating the approval of the general meeting depends on the form in which this decision was taken. The resolutions of shareholders are adopted either at the shareholders' general meeting or in the absence of such a meeting. Where a resolution is passed by a group of shareholders outside the shareholders' general meeting, it is valid in terms of Article 227, section 2 of the CCC provided that:

- the shareholders give their unanimous assent in writing for the decision which is to be taken; or
- all shareholders agree for their votes to be cast in writing (which otherwise would not modify the threshold required to pass a resolution).[177]

The prevailing view amongst leading commentators is that passing a resolution in accordance with the above informal procedure does not affect the validity of the decision.[178] Assuming that the consent of Founder three was given in writing or voting in writing was held, the decision to terminate the consultancy contract would be validly approved.

On the other hand, where Founder three is not in favour of termination of the consultancy contract (dissenting resolution), the decision of directors to terminate would have legal effect as far as the internal decision-making process is concerned but towards Founder two it would be legally binding – the consultancy contract would be terminated. There is a rule of Polish law that the powers of directors to represent the company cannot be restricted vis-a-vis third parties (CCC, Article 204, section 2)[179] and accordingly the termination of the contract would be fully legally binding with respect to third parties such as Founder one (*pro foro externo*). With regard to the internal effect (in the sphere of corporate governance) of the breach of the articles of association of PC, the directors would be held liable to PC (on the basis of Article 293 of the CCC, as commented upon below). Therefore, as an outsider, Founder two would be unable to enforce a breach of the articles and Founder two's consultancy contract is validly terminated irrespective of the legal defects in the shareholders' resolution.

ii. Action of Founder One against VC's Nominee Directors and VC

By approving an undervalue transaction with a related party, VC's nominee directors acted to the detriment of PC. Management board members are liable for losses

---

[177] M Litwińska-Werner, *Kodeks Spółek Handlowych. Komentarz* (2nd edn, Warsaw, LexisNexis, 2005) 606.
[178] S Szumański in A Szajkowski in S Sołtysiński, A Szumański, A Szajkowski and J Szwaja, *Kodeks Spółek Handlowych. Komentarz* (2nd edn, Warsaw, CH Beck, 2005) 283.
[179] Ibid, 277.

sustained by the company which are attributable to their acts or omissions in breach of the law or the provisions of the articles of association unless they were not at fault (CCC, Article 293). The necessary prerequisite for liability under Article 293 of the CCC is that the company demonstrates a breach of specific legal provisions or the articles of association, so it is insufficient to allege unprofessional conduct, or conduct taken without the observance of due care.

It could be argued that the directors of PC breached the following provisions:

- Article 189 of the CCC, which prohibits the depletion of the company's share capital;[180]

- Article 209 of the CCC, which prohibits a director from voting on any matter which gives rise to a conflict of interest between himself or herself and the company; or

- prohibition of the 'tunnelling of profits' in terms of Article 189 § 1 of CCC in connection with Article 58 of the Civil Code.

The shareholders can also ratify the wrong and waive the liability of the directors by holding an annual general meeting and granting approval of the directors' performance of their duties.[181] However, the facts of the hypothetical case suggest that the ratification was granted by the shareholders in extraordinary general meeting. Therefore, the conduct of the directors does not seem to have been ratified in accordance with the requirements of Polish law.

Under Article 293 of the CCC, the directors are liable towards the company for any breach of duty which causes loss to the company. Only the directors have the power to commit PC to a legal action to recover any losses incurred by PC. Therefore, as long as the directors represent PC vis-a-vis third parties, one cannot reasonably expect them to raise a legal action on behalf of PC against themselves.

The most workable option for Founder one would be to sue the majority shareholder VC in his own name but on behalf of PC. According to Article 295 of the CCC, when a company fails to raise an action seeking redress for losses it has sustained within one year of the date of the occurrence of the conduct giving rise to that loss, the entitlement to raise an action is transferred to the shareholders (the so-called *actio pro socio*). Therefore, that right is only vested in the shareholder after the expiry of the aforementioned one-year period. Beyond that, the *actio pro socio* can be raised irrespective of the wrong ratified by the shareholders' general meeting (CCC, Article 296). In such proceedings, Founder one would raise an action in his own name but on behalf of PC and he would have to demonstrate that PC had suffered loss. Thus, Founder one can successfully sue VC for the benefit of PC in accordance with the

---

[180] In the case of a Polish limited liability company (Sp z o.o.), the prohibition of disguised distributions is interpreted on the basis of Art 189 § 1 of the CCC which states that the shareholders may not receive, under any title, any payments from the company's assets that are needed to fully finance the share capital. The majority view is that transactions falling under this prohibition are those arising between shareholders and the company which are not provided for consideration at the fair market value in exchange for the company contribution: see A Opalski, *Prawo zgrupowań spółek* (Warsaw, CH Beck, 2012) 431.

[181] Judgment of the Supreme Court-Civil Chamber, 25 November 2004, III CK 592/2002.

provisions regulating the *actio pro socio* if PC did suffer a loss as a consequence of the transfer.

Turning now to the possibility of Founder one raising a legal action against shareholder VC or ABC for his own direct benefit, there is no straightforward legal basis which provides for the liability of a shareholder towards another shareholder for a breach of the duty of loyalty. In legal doctrine, it is provided that the 'economic owners of the company are obliged to honestly cooperate with each other which means that they owe each other duties of loyalty'.[182] According to the rule that damages can be sought only by the directly injured party (PC), it would not be possible to seek damages resulting from the depreciation of the value of assets of the company.[183]

The claim of Founder one that is aimed at the recovery of property directly against ABC will not be successful. The end result is that Founder one should be successful in any proceedings raised on behalf of PC in terms of the *actio pro socio*, but any direct action against VC would prove fruitless.

K. Latvia

i. Validity of the Decision to Terminate Founder Two's Consultancy Contract

The powers of the general meeting in Latvian limited liability companies (*sabiedrība ar ierobežotu atbildību* (SIA)) are laid down in section 210 of the Commercial Code.[184] The meeting of the shareholders must be convened in accordance with the formal notification requirements in sections 213 and 214 of the Commercial Code. It is possible for the shareholders to make decisions by written procedure without convening a meeting in terms of section 215 of the Commercial Code. However, in the present case, it is doubtful whether a valid decision of the shareholders has been taken to terminate the contract in satisfaction of the requirements in section 215 of the Commercial Code. If the decision is void, this does not result in the contract itself being void, since it is not possible to restrict the rights of the board of directors to represent and bind the company in dealings with third parties by virtue of section 223(3) of the Commercial Code. Since Founder two is no longer a shareholder of PC, he is treated as a third party for the purposes of this provision. Therefore, the decision to terminate the contract with Founder two is valid, irrespective of whether Founder three was in favour of the termination of his contract or not.

---

[182] On the duty of loyalty of shareholders, see D Wajda, *Obowiązek lojalności w spółkach handlowych* (Warsaw, CH Beck, 2009) 361 and Judgment of the Supreme Court, 16 October 2008, III CSK 100/08, OSNC 2009 no 1, issue 30. A Opalski, 'Obowiązek lojalności w spółkach kapitałowych' (2008) 2 *Kwartalnik Prawa Prywatnego* 469.

[183] A Opalski in *System Prawa Prywatnego. Prawo spółek kapitałowych Vol 17B* (Warsaw, CH Beck, 2016) 449; K Oplustil, *Instrumenty nadzoru korporacyjnego (corporate governance) w spółce akcyjnej* (Warsaw, CH Beck, 2010) 796; M Olechowski, 'O relacji między szkodą poniesioną przez spółkę akcyjną a szkodą poniesioną przez akcjonariusza – polemika' (2007) 9 *Przegląd Prawa Handlowego* 19; M Kaliński, 'Szkoda poniesiona przez spółkę akcyjną a szkoda poniesiona przez akcjonariusza w świetle przepisów kodeksu spółek handlowych i kodeksu cywilnego – polemika' (2009) 9 *Przegląd Prawa Handlowego* 52.

[184] Likums 'Komerclikums', Latvijas Vēstnesis 158/160 (2069/2071) 13 April 2000.

ii. Action by Founder One against VC's Nominee Directors and VC

Any action by Founder one against the board members first requires a breach of duty.[185] The Supreme Court of Latvia has confirmed on several occasions that if the particulars of a claim (the loss, whether it has already arisen or is merely anticipated, the performance or non-performance of the member of a board and the causal link between the loss and performance or non-performance of the member of the board) are established, the member of such board would have few valid excuses. In particular, the director would be obliged to prove that he or she had acted as an honest and careful manager in the particular circumstances without any hint of negligence. Furthermore, the member of a board cannot be held liable if he or she acted in good faith to implement a legitimate decision of the shareholders.

Assuming that the two directors were in breach of duty, Founder one would be entitled to raise a claim against the directors on the basis of a breach of the prohibition on competition in relation to members of the board of directors of a company (Commercial Code, section 171). If the directors have contravened the aforementioned prohibition, PC may bring an action against the members of the board of directors on the basis of a decision taken by a meeting of the shareholders. The company has the duty to bring an action against the members of the board in the case mentioned above and also if that is requested by a minority of shareholders who jointly represent not less than 20 per cent of the equity capital or whose participation in the equity capital of the company is not less than €71,100 (Commercial Code, sections 171, 172).

The claim against VC can be based on section 168(1) of the Commercial Code, which states that a person who in bad faith persuades a member of the board of directors to act against the interests of the company or its shareholders will be liable to the company for any losses incurred as a result of such activities. Section 168(1) of the Commercial Code is not applicable if the influence was exerted by using one's voting rights at a meeting of shareholders or by lawfully using one's decisive influence in accordance with the Groups of Companies Law (Commercial Code, section 168(4)). In this case the transfer is ratified by shareholder resolution since VC now owns 92 per cent of the shares of PC and voted in favour of it.

According to the Groups of Companies Law, a group of companies is an aggregate of a dominant undertaking and one or several dependent companies. A dominant undertaking is defined as an undertaking that has a decisive influence over one or more companies and that is located in Latvia or in another state. Meanwhile, a dependent company is a company that is under the decisive influence of a dominant undertaking and is located in Latvia (Groups of Companies Law, section 2(2), (3)). A decisive influence will arise on the basis of a 'group of companies' contract, as well as on the basis of participation (Groups of Companies Law, section 3(1)) and may be direct or indirect (Groups of Companies Law, section 4(1)). It is provided that if a dominant undertaking exercises a decisive influence upon a dependent company without the mediation of another dependent company, it has a direct decisive influence upon such company. Meanwhile, if a dominant undertaking exercises a decisive influence upon a dependent

---

[185] See, eg, the Latvian solution in ch 2 at II A, above.

company via its influence over another dependent company or such persons as act in their own name but for the benefit of the dominant undertaking or the company dependent upon it, it will be treated as having an indirect decisive influence upon such company (Groups of Companies Law, section 4(2) and (3)). In the current case PC is a dependent company, but ABC has an indirect decisive influence through VC.

According to section 29(1) of the Groups of Companies Law, a dominant under-taking may not use its influence in order to induce a dependent company to conclude a transaction disadvantageous to it or carry out another measure disadvantageous to it unless compensation is paid for losses incurred as a result of such transaction or measure. If a dominant undertaking induces a dependent company to conclude a transaction disadvantageous to it or to carry out another measure disadvantageous to it and by the end of the accounting year does not in fact compensate the losses caused as a result of such transaction or measure or, further, does not grant the rele-vant right to claim compensation for such losses, the dominant undertaking has the duty to compensate the losses incurred by the dependent company as a result of such action. The dominant undertaking has the obligation to compensate losses suffered by shareholders of the dependent company as a result of such action, irrespective of the losses incurred by them that are indirectly attributable to the losses caused to the dependent company.

However, ABC will not be obliged to compensate the losses suffered by PC or Founder one if it proves that an honest and conscientious manager of an independent undertaking also would have concluded the transaction transferring the valuable IP to ABC.

The representatives of a dominant undertaking, who have induced a dependent company to conclude a transaction disadvantageous to it or to carry out another measure disadvantageous to it are liable as joint debtors together with the dominant undertaking (Groups of Companies Law, sections 33, 34). It follows that ABC and VC are jointly liable in respect of the transfer of IP. The preconditions to the claim are similar to the preconditions imposed in respect of proceedings raised against the members of the board: loss must have already arisen or be anticipated; there must have been performance or non-performance by VC or ABC; and a causal link must be established between the loss and performance or non-performance of VC or ABC.

If a dispute arises with respect to whether VC has acted with the care of an honest and able manager, the burden of proof lies with VC or the executive body of the dependent company (Groups of Companies Law, sections 33 and 34).

According to section 29(4) of the Groups of Companies Law, Founder one is enti-tled to bring an action for compensation for losses in its own name but for the benefit of PC.

L. Japan

i. Authority of the Shareholders' Meeting and Delegation

Shareholders' meetings may resolve the matters provided for in the Companies Act, the organisation, operations and administration of the company, and any and all other matters regarding the company (Companies Act (CA), Article 295(1)). However, in the case of a company with a board of directors, a shareholders' meeting may resolve only the matters provided for in the CA and the matters provided for in the articles of incorporation (CA, Article 295(2)). Moreover, a provision of the company's articles of incorporation will not be effective if it provides that the directors, executive officers and board of directors may determine a particular matter which, pursuant to the provisions of the CA, requires a resolution of the shareholders' meeting (CA, Article 295(3)).

ii. Termination of Founder Two's Consultancy Contract

In the present case, the directors and the company appear to be in breach of the articles of incorporation when the board of directors decides to terminate Founder two's consultancy contract.[186] However, Founder two was no longer a shareholder of PC when the board of directors made the decision to terminate the consultancy contract. Therefore, if Founder three was in favour of the termination of Founder two's consultancy contract, Founder two would lack any standing to sue to challenge this board resolution. Likewise, if Founder three was not in favour of the termination of the contract, on the same basis, Founder two would be unable to challenge the board resolution. However, if the directors of PC deliberately or negligently cause loss to a third party in performing their duties, such directors will be held liable for damages arising as a result thereof (CA, Article 429(1)). As such, it is possible for Founder two to obtain compensation from the directors of PC who were in breach of the articles of incorporation.

iii. Undervalue Transactions and the Liability of the Directors

In the hypothetical case, VC's two nominee directors pass a majority board resolution which resolves for PC to transfer valuable IP at less than market value to a company ABC which is wholly owned by VC. A director owes a duty of loyalty to the company (CA, Article 355), so when the board of directors enters into an undervalue transaction with a shareholder or a related party under pressure from a major shareholder, it is liable for the losses sustained by the company (CA, Article 423(1)). It follows that VC's two nominee directors are liable to compensate PC (CA, Article 423(1)). If PC fails to take legal proceedings against the directors, Founder one would be entitled to take a shareholder derivative action on behalf of PC against VC's two nominee directors. A shareholder owning the shares consecutively for the preceding six months or more may demand that PC file an action to pursue the liability of a director. If PC does not file an action to pursue such liability within 60 days from the date of the demand, the shareholder who has made such a demand may file an action to pursue such liability on behalf of PC.[187]

---

[186] See, eg, the solution under UK law at II A, above.
[187] CA, Art 847(1)–(3).

iv. Duties and Liability of Majority Shareholders

If fiduciary duties exist amongst shareholders, one would assume that VC would have violated such duties since the only objective of the undervalue transaction entered into between PC and its subsidiary ABC was to tunnel profits at the expense of the minority shareholder. On that basis, it would be possible for Founder one to be successful if he sued the majority shareholder VC for the losses sustained by PC as a result of the undervalue transaction struck with VC's subsidiary. However, the notion that majority shareholders owe fiduciary duties to minority shareholders has not been accepted by the Japanese courts on the basis that it is too vague a proposition or that it is simply an instantiation of other principles of company law.[188] Therefore, in Japanese law, it would not be possible for Founder one as a minority shareholder to successfully sue the majority shareholder VC or its subsidiary ABC for the benefit of the company.

However, if a director made an irregular transaction which was detrimental to the company under pressure from a controlling shareholder and harmed the company's interests, the director would be liable to the company for damages arising as a result thereof in terms of the CA, 423(1).[189]

III. Conclusion

A. Introduction

The legal systems examined would all reach the conclusion that Founder two would not be able to challenge the termination of his consultancy contract where Founder three was in favour of termination. However, the grounds for this outcome vary according to whether the jurisdiction is grounded in the common law or civil law traditions. Only in France, Japan and Finland would Founder two have a right to attain damages, namely against PC in France in the case of an SA, an SAS or an SARL,[190] and against the directors of PC in Finland and Japan. As for South Africa, Founder two may have a right of action in damages against PC based on the doctrine of implied terms in contract law. Where Founder three is not in favour of termination, there is no change in the legal position in any of the jurisdictions under scrutiny which denied Founder two a right to damages and so Founder two would have no right of relief.

In all of the countries under review, Founder one would be successful in his claim, but the party from whom a remedy would be obtained would differ, as would the party entitled to a remedy (ie Founder one or PC). Only in a limited number of jurisdictions

---

[188] K Egashira, *Kabushikigaisha-hô* [*Laws of Stock Corporations*] (7th edn, Tokyo, Yuhikaku, 2017) 449.
[189] Ibid.
[190] Cass Ass Plé (Cour de cassation, Plenary Assembly), 6 October 2006, n° 05-13255: *Bull Civ*, ass Plén, n° 9; D 2006, 2825, with a note by G Viney; *RTD civ* 2007, 115 with an observation by J Mestre and B Fages, and with an observation by P Jourdain, 123.

would recovery of the property from ABC be possible, for example, Spain and Latvia. Generally, Founder one would have no right of relief directly against VC, but rather, if successful in any claim against VC, Founder one would have to watch as PC enjoyed the remedy. Spain is one jurisdiction which is an exception to this trend.

B. Termination of Founder Two's Consultancy Contract: Where Founder Three is in Favour of Termination

There are two issues here: first, whether third parties such as Founder two can challenge a board resolution or a breach of PC's internal governance provisions; and, second, if so, whether the unanimous assent of all of the shareholders of PC[191] precludes Founder two from (i) challenging the board decision to terminate his consultancy contract or (ii) enforcing the breach of PC's internal governance code.

i. Challenging a Board Resolution or a Breach of PC's Internal Governance Provisions

The common law in the UK would preclude Founder two from enforcing any purported breach of PC's internal governance provisions as he is a third party and has no legal standing to sue. In the UK, there is no procedure whereby the validity of a board resolution could be contested. The position in US law and South African law is identical. The outcome in most of the civil law countries would be identical, for example, in Spain, Italy, Germany, Poland, the Netherlands, Latvia and Japan, but the reasoning would differ. Unlike the UK, South Africa and the US, the legal proceedings would focus on whether Founder two had the ability to challenge the board resolution rather than his right to enforce the breach of the articles of the company. This is an approach which is not encountered in the common law countries and the 'mixed' jurisdiction of South Africa. In all of the civil law countries bar France, Founder two would lack standing to sue and so have no right to challenge the board resolution as a procedural violation of the articles on the ground that he is a creditor and not a shareholder[192] or a director. Although the board resolution might be void or voidable, this will not disturb the fact that the consultancy contract has been terminated. In Italy, Germany, Poland, the Netherlands, and Latvia, this is grounded in the rule that the rights of the board of directors to represent the company in relation to third parties may not be restricted. Subject to what is said below about French and Finnish law, the end result is that Founder two could not challenge the termination of his consultancy contract where Founder three is in favour of that decision.

---

[191] Howsoever manifested and in the absence of a written shareholder resolution.

[192] Some civilian jurisdictions such as Spain (LSC, Art 251.1) impose a minimum threshold requirement on shareholders to sue to challenge a board resolution, namely 1 per cent of the issued share capital of the company. Meanwhile, other civilian jurisdictions permit any shareholder to sue regardless of the value of their shareholding.

ii. The Effect of the Unanimous Assent Rule

In the UK, a procedural violation (such as a board decision adopted in breach of a provision of the articles which directs that it is a decision for the shareholders) of the articles of association of a company will nevertheless be valid and not void if there is evidence (written or otherwise) that the decision taken commanded the unanimous assent of the shareholders of the company. This is known as the informal 'unanimous assent' rule and since that is the case here, this is another reason why Founder two would be unable to challenge the failure to pass a shareholder resolution. US law recognises a similar doctrine, but it is more liberal than the UK position, since the consent of only 75 per cent of the shareholders would be needed to cure the procedural violation, provided it is given in writing.[193] Whilst it is not a shareholder resolution, the board resolution signed by VC would be sufficient to satisfy the latter requirement in the US. Turning to the civil law countries, French law has specifically rejected the existence of a 'unanimous assent' rule[194] and Italian law does not recognise such a concept. Although Germany, Finland and Poland have a rule which is similar to the UK's unanimous consent doctrine, this only applies if all shareholders give written approval of the board decision, which cannot be assumed in the present case.[195] For example, in German law, dissent expressed orally or manifested through conduct, is insufficient. Likewise, although Spain does recognise a rule akin to the UK's 'unanimous assent' principle, it only applies where all of the shareholders of the company are present at a meeting and signify their agreement to a decision. Thus, the outcome described in the paragraph immediately above would not change, since the hypothetical case does not inform us that Founder two was present at a shareholders' general meeting.

It is French, Japanese and Finnish law which would both diverge from the other civil law jurisdictions in the outcome. French law would provide Founder two with a right to damages against PC (irrespective of whether it was an SA, an SAS or an SARL) for a breach of the articles notwithstanding that he is a third party.[196] South African law may also recognise that Founder two has a right to attain damages from PC on a contractual basis, namely the doctrine of implied terms in contract. Meanwhile, in Finnish law, Founder two would have a right to damages directly from the directors of PC where they have deliberately or negligently caused loss to Founder two in breach of the articles.[197] Likewise, Japanese law would allow Founder two to sue the directors of PC directly to obtain damages.

---

[193] It can perhaps be referred to as the 'supermajority assent' rule.

[194] The Cour de cassation in Cass Civ 1, 21 March 2000 (*F Le Garrec c/G. Vincent*), *Revue des sociétés* 2000, with a note by Y Guyon at 509.

[195] Nevertheless, in German, Finnish and Polish law, even if the requirements of the unanimous consent rule were satisfied, although the decision of the board would be void (this can be contrasted with French law, where the board resolution would not be valid, but not void (ie a nullity) and so the termination of the consultancy contract would be valid), this would not cure the invalidity of the termination of Founder two's consultancy contract which could not be challenged by Founder two anyway, since he is a third party (see above). Likewise, in Italy and Spain, the invalidity of the board resolution on the basis that it is null and void would not permit Founder two to challenge, since he is not a shareholder or a director.

[196] See references in n 190, above.

[197] Limited Liability Companies Act 2006, c 22, s 1(2) (Osakeyhtiölaki 624/2006).

C. Termination of Founder Two's Consultancy Contract: Where Founder Three is Not in Favour of Termination

Where Founder three is not in favour of termination, there is no change in the legal position in the majority of the jurisdictions under scrutiny, ie Founder two would have no right of relief. However, it is only in UK law that one of the grounds for such an outcome would be removed, ie the unanimous consent rule would no longer be applicable, which can be contrasted with US law, where the functional equivalent of that rule (the 'supermajority assent' rule) will remain satisfied. It should also be recalled that in certain jurisdictions, such as Germany, it is a legal requirement that Founder three's dissent is expressed in writing and conduct on his part which suggests disapprobation will not be sufficient.

D. Shareholder Derivative Action by Founder One against VC's Two Nominee Directors and VC

i. General Introduction

In each jurisdiction, VC's two nominee directors would be in breach of their duty to avoid a conflict of interest and duty, or to act in the best interests of PC. The main focus here was on how Founder one as a shareholder and/or director might seek to challenge that breach of duty. Each jurisdiction would indeed offer Founder one a remedy, but the party or parties against whom litigation ought to, or could be, raised, the nature of those legal proceedings, the nature of the remedy and the grounds for receiving such a remedy vary quite markedly across the countries.

ii. Action against VC's Two Nominee Directors

Turning first to the potential liability of VC's two nominee directors and the nature of the proceedings which would be taken against them, in the UK, the US, Spain, South Africa, France, Japan and Finland, Founder one's action would be derivative in nature and PC would be entitled to any remedy.[198] This can be contrasted with Italy, where Founder one would have a direct personal action against VC's two nominee directors,[199] and Germany and the Netherlands, where the law does not permit a derivative action in the case of the GmbH. In Dutch law, any direct action against VC's two nominee directors would lie in tort law – assuming a duty of care owed by such directors to Founder one could be established – to enable Founder one to recover personal losses sustained (rather than reflective losses, such as diminutions in PC's share price/value, which are irrecoverable) and could be accompanied by a challenge to the resolution passed by the directors transferring PC's IP to ABC. The legal bases

---

[198] However, in Finnish law, it would also be possible for Founder one as shareholder to receive damages.
[199] In Spain, it would be theoretically possible for Founder one to raise a direct personal action against VC's 2 nominee directors, but the opportunity for success would be very limited: Alonso Espinosa, 'Introducción a la Teoría General del Derecho Español de Sociedades' (n 133) 37–39.

on which such derivative actions would be raised against VC's two nominee directors differ. For example, under French and Finnish law, the derivative action would focus on challenging the board resolution which transferred the IP to ABC. This can be contrasted with the UK, South Africa, the US and Spain, where the derivative action would be used to enforce a breach of duty by VC's two nominee directors. In Spain, the derivative action could also be deployed in order to challenge the resolution of the shareholders ratifying the conduct of VC's two nominee directors which, if successful, would entitle PC to recover damages.

There are certain initial conditions or requirements which must be fulfilled in order to raise a derivative action, presumably to enable the court to weed out vexatious claims, and in the UK and South Africa, this involves an application to the court for leave to continue a derivative claim. However, the requirements are not uniform. In the UK, those criteria generally centre around whether the shareholders of PC had validly ratified the directors' breaches of duty and whether the motivations of Founder one in seeking a remedy on behalf of PC were honest and bona fides. The legal position in South Africa is similar to that of the UK to the extent that the court will evaluate the good faith of the shareholder, and whether the proposed proceedings are in the best interests of the company or involve a serious question of material consequence to the company. However, in South Africa, the ratification of the director's breach will carry less significance than is the case in the UK. The UK can be contrasted with the US, France, Japan and Spain, which impose a form of 'demand requirement', ie Founder one would be required to show that he had demanded that the PC's directors (i) commit PC to litigation against VC's two nominee directors or (ii) hold a general meeting to enable the shareholders to vote on such litigation, and that PC's directors had failed to do so. US law would also require Founder one to dislodge the business judgment rule, ie the presumption that the majority of PC's board acted independently in responding to the demand.[200] Spanish and Finnish law impose a minimum shareholding requirement (5 per cent in Spain and 10 per cent in Finland) and the latter also imposes a five-year time limit within which the derivative suit must be commenced. French law is particularly unusual in that it would be possible for Founder one to take separate derivative proceedings in the name of PC under the criminal law.[201]

iii. Personal Action by Founder One against VC

Civilian jurisdictions such as Germany and Italy would enable minority shareholders such as Founder one to recover damages from VC pursuant to a personal action. The action would be grounded in VC's breach of fiduciary duty which it owes personally to Founder one as a minority shareholder. However, in Germany, Founder one's *actio pro socio* would only give PC a right to recover from VC as a result of Founder one's action against VC.[202] Similarly, in Poland, Founder one could raise an *actio pro socio* in order to recover damages from VC in respect of the breach of duty by VC's

---

[200] On the facts of the hypothetical case, Founder one should have no difficulty in rebutting this presumption.

[201] This is known as the *plainte avec constitution de partie civile*.

[202] In Germany, although the action is personal, it very much resembles the derivative claim.

two nominee directors owed to PC or for a breach of the capital maintenance rules. However, Founder one could only commence the *actio pro socio* if PC had not initiated legal action within one year of the date of occurrence of the wrong committed by VC's two nominee directors and, if successful, PC would be entitled to a remedy, not Founder one. Interestingly, Founder one would also be entitled to sue VC in Finland and France, but this would not be a personal action. Instead, the action would be derivative in nature and any legal redress would flow to PC rather than Founder one. In France, the derivative action would be grounded in a challenge to the effectiveness of the board and/or shareholder resolutions rather than any concept of shareholder fiduciary duties, whereas in Finland, the derivative action against VC would be based on the breach of duty by VC's two nominee directors. The US also recognises the existence of such controlling shareholder obligations and would permit Founder one to raise a derivative action against VC to enforce those obligations.[203] Meanwhile, although UK law is crafted in a way that enables a shareholder such as Founder one to raise derivative proceedings against VC, this is not based on any notion of shareholder fiduciary duties. Instead, like Finnish law, Founder one would pursue VC for a remedy which would flow to PC in respect of losses sustained by PC as a result of the breaches of duty by VC's two nominee directors. In South African law, since VC itself is not a director, Founder one will be unable to hold VC to account for a breach of duties and the only potential way that VC may be held accountable is based on the common law principles of agency.

iv. Recovery of the IP from ABC

With regard to the recovery of the IP from ABC, this would indeed be possible in Italy, Germany, Latvia, the UK, South Africa, Spain and the US, but the nature of the proceedings would differ. In Italy, the legal action would be personal and the legal ground for recovery would be that ABC was acting in bad faith in receiving the IP. In the UK, Spain and the US, the action would be derivative and deployed to enable Founder one to sue ABC to effect the recovery of the IP for PC. In the UK, the legal ground for recovering from ABC would be that it was in 'knowing receipt' of the IP, ie that it had knowledge that VC's two nominee directors caused PC to transfer the IP to it in breach of duty. Finally, in Latvia, recovery of the IP from ABC would be grounded in the specialist 'groups of companies' law which would enable Founder one to recover from VC and ABC for the benefit of PC.

v. Status and Relevance of Shareholder Ratification Resolution

As for the status and relevance of the shareholder ratification resolution of PC, Poland would treat it as a nullity on the basis that it was tainted by the votes of VC. UK law

---

[203] However, in the UK, there is a functional equivalent to the controlling shareholders' fiduciary duties in s 994 of the Companies Act 2006, whereby Founder one would have a right to petition the court to have his shares bought out by the majority shareholders at a fair price without a discount if he could show that the affairs of the company had been conducted in a manner unfairly prejudicial to his interests.

would likely follow suit, but would treat the ratification as ineffective rather than void; likewise, in Italy, the resolution would be challengeable but not void. In French and German law, the ratification resolution would be effective but insufficient to carry the vote, since VC would be prohibited from voting and procedural requirements had been breached. Finally, in Spain, the shareholder ratification resolution would be voidable.[204]

E. Conclusion

Overall, most of the legal systems would not allow Founder two's claim, irrespective of Founder three's views, but Founder one would be entitled to recover from someone. With regard to Founder two's options, the solutions reveal that the unanimous assent rule is by no means a phenomenon unique to the common law and is recognised by some civilian systems, whereas there is a clear divide between the common law and civil law when it comes to challenging the validity of board resolutions. Moreover, we learn that company law will not permit outside third parties such as Founder two to challenge board resolutions of a company (in the civilian jurisdictions) or enforce a breach of a company's internal governance provisions (in the common law jurisdictions). To that extent, there is functional convergence in the result, but formal divergence in the company law rules. The only oddities are French, Japanese and Finnish law, which provide Founder two with a right to claim damages from PC or the directors of PC, notwithstanding that he is a third party.[205]

As for Founder one's potential claim, we learn that derivative actions are common to both common law, 'mixed' and civil law jurisdictions, as is the concept of controlling shareholders' fiduciary duties. Personal actions are also possible in some jurisdictions, as is the *actio pro socio* which is a form of hybrid between a personal and derivative action. Most jurisdictions allow the derivative action to be deployed to sue both VC's two nominee directors and VC itself, but a shareholder will not be able to raise it as of right and instead conditions and requirements are imposed which must be satisfied. Moreover, the legal grounds on which the derivative or personal actions were based would vary. The shareholder ratification resolution in most jurisdictions would be tainted by VC voting in its own self-interest, and although it would be irrelevant, its status would differ depending on the country concerned.

From a comparative perspective, this case offers the following insights. On a general level, legal systems do not appear to be fundamentally different: all legal systems enable shareholders to challenge decisions of the board which are tainted by the self-interest of the directors or the majority shareholders in one shape or form. There is no evidence that the differing shareholding structures in common law and civil law countries has influenced the content of the company law, particularly since one would not expect to find controlling shareholders' fiduciary duties in common law jurisdictions,

---

[204] See, eg, Bago Oria (n 127) 335.
[205] See references in n 190, above.

and in light of the fact that they do indeed exist in US law.[206] As one would expect, common law jurisdictions rely more on case law than the civil law jurisdictions. As for discrepancies in the level of shareholder protection in common law and civil law jurisdictions, there does not appear to be any evidence for the legal origins theorem. Having said that, the requirement in Polish law that a shareholder must wait for one year before initiating the *actio pro socio* and the 5 per cent and 10 per cent minimum shareholding thresholds under the derivative action in Spain and Finland do appear to curtail the shareholder's access to justice. With regard to legal transplant theories, it is too early to tell whether the reception of the *actio pro socio* into Polish law from German law has been successful.

Is one of these solutions preferable? It is suggested that the most preferable solution would deny Founder two any relief on the basis that he is a creditor and has the means to protect himself in contract, whilst enabling Founder one to challenge the greatest number of parties (ie VC's two nominee directors, VC and ABC) on the ground that the decision of PC to transfer the IP has clearly entailed the misappropriation of PC's assets for the (indirect) benefit of VC, the controlling shareholder. With that in mind, the juxtaposition of the unanimous assent rule alongside the inability of Founder two as an outsider to challenge in the UK and the US result in their solutions being the most preferable with regard to Founder two. Meanwhile, with regard to Founder one's position, it is likely that most routes for relief would be available in Italy, the UK, South Africa and the US, and for that reason, it is suggested that the solutions in these jurisdictions are the most desirable.

---

[206] In asking country experts to elaborate upon whether Founder one would be entitled to relief from VC, the intention was to draw out whether the company law systems of civilian jurisdictions had developed principles or rules whose aim was specifically to minimise majority/minority shareholder horizontal agency costs, eg by imposing legal obligations on the majority not to act against the interests of the minority and providing the latter with a right of legal action against the former in order to enforce the same. There was ample evidence of this in the country solutions. Many commentators (E Berglöf, 'A Note on the Typology of Financial Systems' in K Hopt and E Wymeersch (eds), *Comparative Corporate Governance: Essays and Materials* (Berlin, De Gruyter, 1997) 151–64; J Armour, S Deakin and S Konzelmann, 'Shareholder Primacy and the Trajectory of UK Corporate Governance' (2003) 41 *British Journal of Industrial Relations* 531, 533; B Cheffins, 'Putting Britain on the Roe Map: The Emergence of the Berle-Means Corporation in the United Kingdom' in JA McCahery, P Moerland, T Raaijmakers and L Renneboog (eds), *Corporate Governance Regimes: Convergence and Diversity* (Oxford, Oxford University Press, 2002) 147–70) argue that the agency costs which arise in civilian jurisdictions are attributable to a misalignment of the interests of majority shareholders and minority shareholders, rather than a misalignment between the interests of directors and shareholders, the latter being the case in common law jurisdictions. The majority/minority agency cost is attributable to the presence of 'blockholder' shareholders and the absence of a diffuse shareholder owner-ship base in corporations registered in Civil law countries. See, eg, the discussion in J Armour et al, 'What is Corporate Law' in R Kraakman et al, *The Anatomy of Corporate Law: A Comparative and Functional Approach* (3rd edn, Oxford, Oxford University Press, 2017) 25–28 and the review of the literature in B Cheffins, *Corporate Ownership and Control: British Business Transformed* (Oxford, Oxford University Press, 2008) 4–7.

11

Limitations on the Shareholder's Right to Transfer Shares

CORRADO MALBERTI AND MARCO VENTORUZZO (EDITORS)

Main topics: validity of restrictions on a shareholder's right to transfer his or her shares; possibility of inheriting shares.

Related topics: shareholders and shareholder law (see chapter 8, above); abuse of shareholders' rights (see chapter 9, above); enforcement of shareholders' rights, breach of directors' duties and shareholder litigation (see chapter 10, above).

I. Scenario

Mr Rossi, Mr Verdi and Mr Bianchi are three engineers who, after 20 years of service in a famous Italian motorcycle company based in Milan, decide to leave their job and establish an innovative firm that manufactures custom-made motorcycles. They plan to found a (non-listed) public company with limited liability (called 'Rovebi'), in which each of them holds the same number of shares.

Since their organisational and managerial skills complement each other well, the three engineers think that their business plan will succeed only if the shareholding structure of the company remains stable. In particular, they would like both to prohibit transfers of shares in the case of the death of a shareholder and to give the shareholders a right of pre-emption in the case of any transfers *inter vivos*. Therefore, they instruct a lawyer to prepare draft by-laws which, among other things, will address these issues. Draft Article 11 of Rovebi's by-laws is worded as follows:

Article 11 Transfer of shares

11.1 Transfers of shares shall be made only in accordance with the rules set forth in this article. Transfers of shares not made in accordance with the rules set forth in this article shall have no effect as against the company, and shall not be entered in the company's register of members or register of transfers.

11.2 In the event of the death of a shareholder his or her shares shall be transferred to the surviving shareholders in proportion to their respective shareholdings in the company as calculated on the date of the death of the shareholder.

11.3 If during his or her lifetime a shareholder wishes to dispose of his or her shares (the 'Offering Shareholder'), he or she is first obliged to follow the pre-emptive rights procedure in favour of the remaining shareholders. The Offering Shareholder shall offer the first right of purchase/refusal to the other shareholders of the company. The Offering Shareholder's notification shall include the number of the shares to be transferred, the proposed price, a note of the identity of the third party that wishes to acquire the shares and the other terms of the proposed agreement to purchase to be entered into between the Offering Shareholder and the said third party. If any of the other shareholders agree to acquire such shares in full or part thereof, such shares shall be transferred to the shareholders thereof. In a case of acceptance by more than one shareholder, the shares shall be transferred to each of such shareholders in proportion to their respective shareholding in the company on the date of the offer in accordance with the terms of the said proposed agreement. If none of the shareholders accept the offer within 20 (twenty) days of receipt of the notice, the Offering Shareholder may transfer the offered shares to a third party or parties who is or are identified in the notice, provided that under no circumstances shall the number and the price of the shares and the terms and conditions upon which the shares are proposed to be transferred to such third party or parties be more favourable for the buyer than those terms on which they were offered to the other shareholders who had refused.

11.4 Any dispute arising among or between the shareholders pertaining to the price and the other terms of the proposed agreement shall be settled by an arbitrator appointed by the board of directors.

How would this clause be evaluated in your legal system? Would the effect of this clause be different if it had been included in a shareholders' agreement rather than the by-laws of the company? Insofar as a provision is not lawful in your jurisdiction, would it have made a difference if the company were established as a private company?

II. Case Studies

A. Italy[1]

i. Introduction

The draft Article 11 of Rovebi's by-laws raises at least four issues under Italian law: (i) the enforceability of the pre-emption clause, depending upon whether it is contained in the company's by-laws or in a shareholders' agreement; (ii) the validity and enforceability of the part of the pre-emption clause which gives a third party the power to

---

[1] Abbreviations: 2003 Corporate Law Reform = Legislative Decree no 6 of 2003 (d lgs n 6/2003); App = Court of Appeals (Corte d'appello); Cass = Italian Supreme Court (Cassazione); CC = Italian Civil Code (codice civile); Spa = public company (*Società per azioni*); Trib = tribunal (Tribunale).

decide the purchase price; (iii) the kinds of alienation which fall within the scope of the pre-emption clause; and (iv) the validity and enforceability of a pre-emption clause which limits the transfer of shares in the case of the death of a shareholder.

ii. The Enforceability of the Pre-emption Clause, Depending Upon Whether it is Contained in the Company's By-laws or in a Shareholders' Agreement

Article 2355-*bis* of the CC, which is a provision introduced by the 2003 Corporate Law Reform, addresses the extent to which it is valid for a company or its shareholders to place limitations or qualifications on a shareholder's right to transfer the shares of an Spa. According to the first paragraph of this article, the by-laws of an Spa may limit or remove a shareholder's right to transfer shares. However, while qualified limitations are not subject to time limits, any complete prohibition on a shareholder's right to transfer shares must not exceed a period of five years. With the exception of Article 11.2,[2] the limitations on the free disposal of a shareholder's shares contained in Article 11 of Rovebi's by-laws are restricted to a right of pre-emption in favour of the other shareholders, ie there is no outright prohibition on a shareholder's right to transfer shares.

It is settled law that pre-emption clauses may be included in the by-laws of an Spa.[3] However, the legal effect of these clauses remains unclear. According to one theory, where these provisions are included in the by-laws of an Spa, they have the same effect as if they were contained in a shareholders' agreement.[4] In terms of this approach, any breach of a pre-emption clause ought to be treated as a contractual breach, which will normally result in an award of damages. However, this view is not endorsed by the majority of the Italian courts and legal commentators, who argue that a breach of a pre-emption clause should not simply result in an award of contractual damages. Instead, the proponents of this approach suggest that third parties who have acquired the shares in breach of the pre-emption clause should not be allowed to take the place and 'step into the shoes' of the selling shareholder in the Spa. There are several grounds for reaching this particular conclusion. First, there are some older decisions where it was held that the contract between the shareholder and the third party should be considered void.[5] On the other hand, more recent decisions have not treated the transfer as void, but have simply concluded that the agreement would be denuded of legal effect.[6] However, those who advocate this theory debate whether the transfer is deprived of legal effect vis-a-vis the company[7] or whether the transfer is also of no effect between the parties to the agreement.[8] Finally, other scholars suggest that any breach of a pre-emption clause also confers upon the shareholders an implied

---

[2] The issues which are raised by Art 11.2 of the by-laws are analysed in detail below.

[3] See, eg, Cass 3702/1957; Cass 2763/1973.

[4] See, eg, S Gatti, *L'iscrizione nel libro dei soci* (Milan, Giuffrè, 1962) 112; Trib Bassano del Grappa 15/9/1993.

[5] See, eg, Cass 3702/1957; Cass 2763/1973.

[6] See, eg, Trib Milano 23/9/1991; Trib Napoli 4/6/1993; Trib Roma 18/3/1998.

[7] In particular, the transfer of the shares should not be entered into the company's registers or records.

[8] L Stanghellini, 'Commento *sub* art. 2355-*bis*' in P Marchetti, LA Bianchi, F Ghezzi and M Notari (eds), *Commentario alla Riforma delle società. Azioni* (Milan, Giuffrè-Egea, 2008) 559 ff, 562 ff.

right to repurchase the shares from the third party who had acquired them in breach of that provision.[9]

Having examined the wording of Article 11.3 of Rovebi's by-laws, it is submitted that the pre-emption clause is valid and enforceable in terms of Italian law. This can be contrasted with the legal position if the same pre-emption clause had been contained in a shareholders' agreement. Whilst a breach of such a pre-emption clause in Rovebi's by-laws would neither result in any alteration of the shareholding structure as against the company nor possibly any modification in the legal ownership of the shares (ie the transfer would be of no legal effect, with title remaining with the vendor shareholder), in circumstances where the pre-emption clause was included in a shareholders' agreement, any transfer of shares in breach of that clause would nevertheless be lawful and title would be conveyed to the third party who had acquired those shares.

iii. The Validity and Enforceability of a Pre-emption Clause which Gives a Third Party the Power to Decide the Purchase Price

Pre-emption clauses which confer upon third parties the power to decide the price payable are traditionally treated with suspicion by Italian scholars and the Italian courts. These provisions may play an important role where the vendor shareholder and the proposed third party acquirer seek to circumvent the pre-emption clause by setting a high – and perhaps artificial – price for the transfer. These provisions, however, are also problematic on other grounds, since they may permit shareholders to exercise the rights expressed in the pre-emption clause at a price which is particularly low. Indeed, in these circumstances, pre-emption clauses are similar to share transfer clauses which require the approval of the board or the shareholders to the transfer, since if the price decided by the third party is rather low, the vendor shareholder may not consider the exercise of the other shareholders' rights as a viable option: effectively, the vendor would then become 'locked into' the company. Thus, the vendor shareholder's decision not to exercise the right in such circumstances may become functionally similar to a clause which requires the vendor to secure the prior approval of the board or the shareholders to the transfer. For this reason, Article 11.4 of Rovebi's by-laws should also be examined in light of the way the law treats clauses which limit or qualify the right of a shareholder to transfer shares, which are known in Italian company law as *clausole di gradimento*.

Prior to the enactment of the 2003 Corporate Law Reform, the Italian courts generally recognised the validity of pre-emption clauses which gave a third party the power to decide the price payable for the shares.[10] However, before 2003, in Italian law, any *clausola di gradimento* which made transfers of shares conditional upon a completely discretionary approval of the board or of the shareholders was simply not allowed. This approach was endorsed in 1978 by the Corte di Cassazione,[11] which declared that

---

[9] G Campobasso, *Diritto commerciale. Diritto delle società* (9th edn, Turin, Utet, 2015) 237; contra Trib Napoli 4/6/1993; Trib Roma 18/3/1998.
[10] Cass 91/1970; Trib Roma 9/12/1987; Trib Napoli 29/6/1990; Trib Alba 14/1/1998; contra Trib Trieste 19/12/1993, which treated this clause as void.
[11] Cass 2365/1978.

these clauses were void, and in 1985 by the legislature,[12] which, taking a slightly different approach, stated that these clauses were simply 'without legal effect'.

Since the introduction of the 2003 Corporate Law Reform, the legal approach
adopted towards completely discretionary *clausole di gradimento* has changed. The
current wording of Article 2355-*bis*, paragraph 2 of the CC directs that these *clausole
di gradimento* will continue to have no legal effect where the by-laws do not confer
(i) a right to withdraw in favour of the shareholders who intend to transfer their shares
or (ii) a right to sell out in favour of the shareholders who intend to transfer their
shares at a price equal to that provided for in the case of withdrawal.[13] This change of
approach towards *clausole di gradimento* has also resulted in the application of a new
reading of pre-emption clauses contained in the by-laws of an Spa which permit the
exercise of a right to purchase at a price decided by a third party. The predominant
view is that the law stipulates that these clauses are subject to challenge[14] where they
involve the determination of the purchase price at a level which is different from that of
the proposed offer and significantly lower than that fixed in the case of withdrawal.[15]

In brief, in order to determine the validity of pre-emption clauses that confer upon
a third party the power to set the price, it is necessary to ascertain the risk of potential
breaches of Article 2355-*bis*, paragraph 2 of the CC. Having examined the specific
provisions of Article 11.3 of Rovebi's by-laws in more detail, it would appear that it is
probably not per se invalid or unenforceable. Nevertheless, in order to avoid any risk of
invalidity and unenforceability, it would be advisable if the wording of the clause had
made reference to a price floor equal to that provided for in the case of withdrawal.

iv. The Types of Alienation which Fall within the Scope of the Pre-emption Clause

Another traditional problem raised by pre-emption clauses concerns the categories of
alienation which may trigger its application. Pre-emption clauses are generally structured around a sale of shares and, arguably, they may be applied to all transfers made
in consideration of fungible goods offered by the third party seeking to acquire the
shares. Things become more complicated, however, when the transfer is gratuitous or
when it is made in consideration of goods transferred which are not fungible. In these
circumstances, two different issues need to be examined.

First, it is necessary to consider whether pre-emption clauses which explicitly
include acts of alienation other than a conventional sale fall within the ambit of
the rules which may regulate the by-laws of a company. Generally, this question is

---

[12] Art 22 of Law no 281 of 1985.

[13] Stanghellini, 'Commento *sub* art. 2355-*bis*' (n 8) 575 ff.

[14] Ibid, 584 ff; Consiglio Notarile di Milano – Commissione per i principi uniformi in tema di società,
'Massima n 85 – Limiti di efficacia della clausola di prelazione c.d. "impropria" negli statuti di s.p.a.
(art. 2355-*bis* c.c.)' in *Massime notarili in materia societaria* (Milan, Ipsoa, 2007) 250. Interestingly, the
Consiglio Notarile di Milano suggests that this clause should have no effect if (i) it exceeds the 5-year period
indicated in Art 2355-*bis*, para 1 of the CC on the complete prohibition of the transfer of shares and (ii) the
price decided by the third party is significantly lower than that calculated according to the rules provided in
the case of a withdrawal.

[15] Moreover, a right of withdrawal or sell-out at a price equal to that provided for in the case of withdrawal
is not granted.

answered in the affirmative.[16] In these cases, the only difficulty which may arise from an explicit extension of the scope of the rights in the pre-emption clause derives from the interpretation of the terms of the relevant agreement of sale and purchase entered into between the shareholder and the purchaser, and, in particular, from the determination of the consideration paid by the shareholder exercising those rights under the pre-emption clause. It is common for pre-emption clauses which do not replicate the terms of the proposed agreement of sale and purchase between the shareholder and the purchaser to be treated in a similar fashion to those pre-emption clauses which involve the price being decided by a third party. Thus, in these situations, the consideration paid to exercise the right of pre-emption should probably be equal to or higher than the value calculated following the criteria set forth in the case of withdrawal.[17]

The second and closely related issue which is raised by such clauses concerns the extent of their scope, in circumstances where the wording is ambiguous and does not directly refer to gratuitous alienations or to transfers made in consideration of goods which are not fungible – which, of course, is the case in Article 11.3 of Rovebi's by-laws. The Italian courts which have had the opportunity to examine this issue have strictly interpreted any provisions which grant rights of purchase to shareholders in terms of a pre-emption clause and, generally, they have rejected any extension of the scope of these clauses.[18] Thus, we can conclude that, in its current wording, Article 11.3 of Rovebi's by-laws probably does not engage the pre-emption clause in circumstances where a shareholder proposes to enter into a gratuitous transfer of his or her shares or in the case of a transfer of shares which is made in consideration of goods which are not fungible.

v. The Validity and Enforceability of a Clause which Limits the Transfer of Shares on the Death of a Shareholder

According to Article 458 of the CC, which is the cornerstone of the Italian law of succession, persons may not conclude contracts with third parties which (i) appoint their heirs or successors or (ii) stipulate irrevocable directions with regard to the distribution of their estate or legacies after their death. Hence, according to this provision, individuals cannot covenant with third parties in a contract *inter vivos* as to who will become the beneficiary of their estates after their death. Before the enactment of the 2003 Corporate Law Reform, the scope of this provision was debated and it was unclear whether any limitations on share transfers applicable in the case of the death of a shareholder were valid[19] or void.[20]

---

[16] Stanghellini (n 8) 593.

[17] Ibid, 593 f.

[18] See Cass 93/1989, which excluded the possibility that a gift of shares may trigger the pre-emption procedure; Trib Venezia 7/11/2003, dealing with a subscription of shares by means of a contribution in kind of shares of another company. *Cf* CA Busi, 'Le clausole di prelazione statutaria nella s.p.a.' (2005) *Rivista del notariato* 453 ff, 497 ff, who argues that this restrictive interpretation should probably be reconsidered after the 2003 Corporate Law Reform.

[19] See, eg, Cass 3609/1994, which reversed the decision of the Court of Appeal of Rome mentioned in n 20, below, but see also Cass 1434/1975.

[20] See, eg, App Roma 28/4/1992.

The 2003 Corporate Law Reform resolved this issue by introducing Article 2355-*bis*, paragraph 3 of the CC, which applies principles to such clauses that are similar to those provided for in the context of share transfer clauses which require the approval of the board or the shareholders to the transfer (ie *clausole di gradimento*). Hence, any limitation on the right to transfer shares in the case of the death of a shareholder may have effect and be enforced, but only insofar as a right of withdrawal or a right of sell-out at a price which is at least equal to that provided for in a case of withdrawal is conferred in favour of the successors of the deceased shareholder.[21] Thus, in light of the wording of this paragraph, the doubts expressed before the 2003 Corporate Law Reform concerning the ability to limit the transfer of shares in the case of death have lost most of their significance.

It is also important to emphasise that, traditionally, the courts treated clauses such as Article 11.2 of Rovebi's by-laws as void on the basis that they fell within the compass of Article 458 of the CC.[22] A similar conclusion may be reached under the provisions introduced pursuant to the 2003 Corporate Law Reform. The reason for this conclusion is that a provision such as Article 11.2 does not confer upon the successors of the deceased shareholder an equitable sum duly calculated according to the criteria used in the case of withdrawal, and so it does not satisfy the requirements stipulated in Article 2355-*bis* paragraph 3, of the CC. It follows that this provision is undoubtedly of no legal effect. In addition, taking into account the wording of Article 458 of the CC and the approach followed in the court decisions indicated above, the validity of this clause is probably also doubtful.

vi. Summary and Conclusion

Pre-emption clauses play a fundamental role in Italian company law, since they facilitate the maintenance of a stable shareholding structure in a company. For this reason, the consequences of a violation of these clauses are different from those resulting from the violation of a shareholders' agreement. However, since these clauses achieve this goal by limiting the freedom of the shareholders to choose the party to whom they may transfer their shares, they also create important limitations on the right of shareholders to exit a company. Obviously, these limitations are not burdensome when a shareholder wishes to conclude a simple sale and when the pre-emption clauses are structured so as to substitute the purchasing third party with the other shareholders, and the other terms of the proposed agreement remain unchanged. Things, however, become more complicated when the pre-emption clause grants to a third party the power to decide the purchase price or when the actual identity of the counterparty plays a role in determining the means by which the alienation is to be structured. Similarly, although the limitations on the transfer of shares on the death of a shareholder

---

[21] *Cf* Stanghellini (n 8) 606 ff.
[22] Cass 1434/1975; Trib Vercelli 19/11/1992, which, examining the case of 2 unincorporated business entities, declared this clause void since, in the first case, the value of the shares of the deceased shareholder which were transferred to the other shareholders was not given to his successors, and since in the second case, only the par value of the shares that were transferred to the other shareholders was given to the successors of the deceased shareholder.

arguably clash with well-established principles of Italian succession law, they may also play an important organisational role.

The Italian legislature addressed these issues in the 2003 Corporate Law Reform. Article 2355-*bis* of the CC states that the constraints imposed on the right of share-holders to exit do not put at risk the legal validity of share transfer clauses (i) which require the approval of the board or the shareholders to the transfer (a *clausola di gradimento*) and (ii) which limit the transfer of shares on the death of a shareholder. However, in order not to be denuded of their legal effect, these clauses must grant a sum at least equal to that provided for in the case of withdrawal, in the first case, to the exiting shareholder and, in the second case, to the successors of the deceased shareholder. This principle arguably operates as a general rule which is also applicable to other limitations of the right to transfer shares such as pre-emption clauses which (i) grant to a third party the power to decide the purchase price and (ii) include (a) gratuitous transfers or (b) transfers made in consideration of goods which are not fungible.

B. France

The solution here will differ depending on whether the company is a public limited company (*Société anonyme* (SA)) or a simplified public limited company (*Société par actions simplifiée* (SAS)), since there are some specific provisions applicable to an SAS.

i. Solution under French Law in the Case of a Public Company (SA)

a. Introduction

Pre-emption clauses are valid under French law. They can be found in a compa-ny's by-laws or in a shareholders' agreement. Unlike a share transfer clause (*clause d'agrément*), a pre-emption clause in the case of an SA is not regulated by the Commer-cial Code but by general contract law and by case law. The validity of pre-emption clauses included in the by-laws has been confirmed by the Paris Court of Appeals[23] and later by the Cour de cassation.[24] Therefore, Article 11.1 of Rovebi's by-laws would be valid under French law. The validity of a pre-emption clause included in a sharehold-ers' agreement has also been confirmed by the courts.[25] The legal position in respect of pre-emption clauses is the same regardless of whether the clause is included in the by-laws or in a shareholders' agreement.

Practitioners distinguish between pre-emption clauses, in terms of which the share-holders decide whether to purchase the shares after an offer has been made by the vendor shareholder to a third party acquirer, and preference clauses (*clause de préfé-rence*), whereby the vendor shareholder must provide the other shareholders with a

---

[23] CA Paris, 14 March 1990, *Bull Joly* 1990, p 353, *Rev jurisp Com* 1990, 256 with a note by Goyet; *Rev soc Somm* 643; *RTD Com* 1990, 413 with a note by Y Reinhard.
[24] Cass Com (Cour de cassation, Commercial Chamber), 15 February 1994 n° 460: *RJDA* 6/94 n° 671.
[25] CA Angers (Court of Appeal of Angers), 20 September 1988, *Rev soc* 1989 somm 288; Cass Com (Cour de cassation, Commercial Chamber), 15 October 1996, *Bull Joly* 1997, 126 with a note by Th Massart.

right to purchase the shares regardless of whether there is a potential purchaser. In the case of Article 11.3 of Rovebi's by-laws, the clause is clearly a pre-emption clause of the first type since it requires the offering shareholder to indicate 'the identity of the third party that wishes to acquire the shares and the other terms of the proposed agreement to purchase'.

Case law provides shareholders with a significant amount of freedom when it comes to the drafting of pre-emption clauses. Moreover, there is no requirement to indicate a time limit or long-stop date before which a shareholder must decide to exercise the right of pre-emption (or not as the case may be).

There is some debate amongst academic commentators as to whether the right to purchase shares pursuant to a pre-emption clause can be split unevenly among the shareholders. Some commentators are of the view that the distribution of shares amongst the shareholders must be proportional to their rights in the share capital.[26] According to these commentators, any clause failing to abide by this rule would violate the principle which provides that the company is formed for the 'common interest of the shareholders'.[27] This analysis is not shared by other commentators on the basis that shareholders can adopt, to a certain extent, provisions that provide for unequal rights and it is opined that this is the preferable view.[28] In addition, the wording of Article 1833 of the Civil Code is too general to be able to prohibit the uneven split of rights amongst the shareholders. In the case of Rovebi, there would be no difficulty since the beneficiaries are the two other shareholders.

The issues raised under Italian law now will be presented under French company law in the same order and with the same headings.

b. The Enforceability of the Pre-emption Clause, Depending Upon Whether it is Contained in the Company's By-laws or in a Shareholders' Agreement

If a pre-emption clause included in the by-laws is violated, the transfer is valid between the parties but has no effect vis-a-vis the company. The company is not obliged to consider the buyer as the new shareholder, but the transfer is not void. This is well settled in the case law.[29] According to the case law, if the purchaser acted fraudulently, the sale is void.[30] The Cour de cassation recently allowed the beneficiary of a pre-emption right to substitute himself or herself for the purchaser in the case of fraud.[31] However, for a sale in violation of the pre-emption clause to be considered fraudulent, it must be proven that the purchaser knew of the existence of the pre-emption right and that he or she also knew that the beneficiary would have purchased the shares. These conditions are very strict and make the substitution or nullification of a sale in violation of a pre-emption clause very difficult. However, in 2016, French contract law

---

[26] P Le Cannu, *Bull Joly* 1990, p 325 n° 22.

[27] Civil Code, Art 1833.

[28] *Mémento Francis Lefebvre Sociétés commerciales* 2015 n° 68612.

[29] *Mémento Francis Lefebvre Sociétés commerciales* 2015 n° 68630.

[30] Cass Civ 3ème (Cour de cassation, Third Civil Chamber), 26 October 1982, *Bull Civ. III* n° 165, p 129.

[31] Cour de cassation, ch mixte (Cour de cassation, Mixed Chamber) 26 May 2006 (*Daurice Pater, épouse Père c/ M. Jean Solari*), Revue des sociétés 2006, 808 with a note by JF Barbieri.

was reformed: preference clauses are now officially recognised[32] and specific performance in the case of the violation of contracts is favoured.[33] Therefore, it is possible
that case law may evolve making it easier to hold a sale void and allow substitution to
take place.

If a pre-emption clause is included in a shareholders' agreement and is violated,
the situation is identical as when the pre-emption clause is included in the by-laws.
According to case law, the transfer is valid between the parties but has no effect vis-a-vis
the company.

c. The Validity and Enforceability of a Pre-emption Clause which Gives a Third Party the Power to Decide the Purchase Price

As a first point, under French case law, a pre-emption clause is not considered a share
transfer clause in disguise for two reasons. First, they only give a preferential right to
the other shareholders to acquire shares rather than deciding whether or not to admit
a new shareholder. Second, they do not impose an obligation on the shareholder to
purchase the shares in the case of a refusal, which is the case for a share transfer clause
included in the by-laws.[34] Therefore, the issue of whether a pre-emption clause can be
considered a functional equivalent to a share transfer clause, which could give rise to
the issue of validity, has not been relevant under French law.

A pre-emption clause which gives a third party the power to decide the purchase
price is considered valid by French courts. The French courts have dealt with the issue
of the risks associated with a situation where a third party decides on the price, for
example, if the parties agree on an inflated price in order to circumvent the pre-emption
right, through the concept of fraud. An attempt to circumvent the pre-emption right
through the mechanism of an inflated price can be dealt with by the other shareholders
by raising the argument of fraud.[35] However, this is usually not a very efficient legal
tool in the French courts.

A more efficient protection consists of drafting the pre-emption clause in a particular manner, whereby the vendor shareholder is not entitled to sell his or her shares to
the indicated third party acquirer for a price less than the one stated to the company
where a shareholder beneficiary refuses to take up the pre-emption right. In addition,
the French courts have accepted[36] that a provision can be included in a pre-emption
clause whereby in a case where the other shareholders wish to use their pre-emption
rights, the price will not be the one indicated by the offering shareholder but will be
determined by an expert.[37]

---

[32] Civil Code, new art 1123.

[33] Civil Code, new art 1221 and 1222.

[34] CA Paris (Court of Appeal of Paris), 14 March 1990, *Bull Joly* 1990, 353, *Rev jurisp Com* 1990, 256 with
a note by Goyet; *Rev soc Somm* 643; *RTD Com* 1990, 413 with a note by Y Reinhard.

[35] CA Paris (Court of Appeal of Paris), 6 May 1994, *Dr sociétés* 1994, n° 140, with a note by H Le
Nabasque.

[36] Cass Com (Cour de cassation, Commercial Chamber), 15 October 1996, *Bull Joly* 1997, 126 with a note
by Th Massart.

[37] Civil Code, Art 1843-44.

d. The Types of Alienation which Fall within the Scope of the Pre-emption Clause

French courts take a very restrictive view of the scope of application of pre-emption clauses since these clauses are an exception to (i) the principle that shares can be freely transferred and (ii) the general principle that a shareholder has a free right to dispose of his or her property. In two recent cases, the Cour de cassation once again confirmed its very restrictive view on the scope of pre-emption clauses. In the first case, the provision applied to the transfer of the shares of the company. However, the shares had been sold indirectly through the sale of the shares of the holding company. The Court considered that the clause did not apply to an indirect sale such as the sale of the company owning the shares.[38] In another very recent case, the Cour de cassation held that the term 'disposal' (*cession*) did not cover the situation where the shares were transferred to a third company through a contribution in kind (*apport*).[39] Similarly, the Cour de cassation has also taken a restrictive view on whether a 'transfer' included a transfer through a merger.[40] To be included, it has to be stated explicitly. Taking into account French case law, the wording of Article 11.3 of Rovebi's by-laws would only cover the direct sale of shares and not indirect sales or gratuitous transfers of shares.

e. The Validity and Enforceability of a Clause which Limits the Transfer of Shares on the Death of a Shareholder

A clause included in the by-laws of a limited liability company (*Société à responsabilité limitée*) which seeks to transfer the shares of a deceased shareholder to his or her heirs potentially engages the law of succession. Indeed, in 1986, the Cour de cassation held[41] that the clause was a valid '*post mortem*' promise and not a prohibited pact on future succession (*pacte sur succession future*).[42] Although the decided case concerned a limited liability company, the decision was based on the Civil Code and applies to all types of companies. However, a note of caution should be struck, since the latter position does not seem to be endorsed by all commentators and therefore is subject to a particular degree of uncertainty.[43]

However, in the case of an SA, the Commercial Code provides that a share transfer clause (*clause d'agrément*) cannot be used to block the transfer of shares on the death of a shareholder to his or her heirs.[44] A clause which limits the transfer of shares on the death of a shareholder is similar to a share transfer clause in its effect. As a consequence, a clause which would bar the heirs from receiving the shares of the defunct shareholder in a public company, such as Article 11.2 of Rovebi's by-laws, is not valid under French law.

---

[38] Cass Com (Cour de cassation, Commercial Chamber), 15 September 2009, n° 08-11.627.
[39] Cass Com (Cour de cassation, Commercial Chamber), 15 September 2009, n° 08-21.037.
[40] Cass Com (Cour de cassation, Commercial Chamber), 3 June 1986, D 1987 Jur 95, with a note by JJ Daigre; *Rev sociétés* 1987, 52, with a note by Y Reinhard.
[41] Cass Civ 1 (Cour de cassation, First Civil Chamber), 8 July 1986: *Bull Civ* I, n° 202, p 195.
[42] Civil Code, Art 1130.
[43] ANSA CJ, 7 April 1993, n° 237.
[44] Commercial Code, Art L 228-23.

ii. Solution under French Law in the Case of a Simplified Public Company (SAS)

Since the SAS is open to any person without restriction, it is highly probable that Rovebi would be incorporated in France as an SAS rather than as an SA. On certain points, the solution is different for an SAS than for an SA. In the same vein as an SA, pre-emption clauses are not included in the Commercial Code. However, they are valid even when they are included in the company by-laws.[45]

a. The Enforceability of the Pre-emption Clause, Depending Upon Whether it is Contained in the Company's By-laws or in a Shareholders' Agreement

If a pre-emption clause concerning an SAS is included in the by-laws and is violated, unlike the situation in the SA, the transfer is void.[46] The same solution applies to all sales of shares in violation of provisions included in the by-laws of an SAS. Therefore, the other shareholders are more protected than they would be in the case of an SA.

If a pre-emption clause concerning an SAS is included in a shareholders' agreement and is violated, the situation is identical as in the case of an SA. According to case law, the transfer is valid between the parties but has no effect vis-a-vis the company.

b. The Validity and Enforceability of a Pre-emption Clause which Gives a Third Party the Power to Decide the Purchase Price

The solution here would be the same as in the SA.

c. The Acts of Alienation which Fall within the Scope of the Pre-emption Clause

The restrictive interpretation of the French courts regarding limitations to the right to sell shares are applicable in the same manner to an SAS since they are based on general company law principles and not provisions which are specific to a particular type of company.

d. The Validity and Enforceability of a Clause which Limits the Transfer of Shares on the Death of a Shareholder

The issue of whether the articles of association or a shareholders' agreement could limit the transfer of shares in the event of the death of a shareholder in a SAS is the subject of debate. Article L 227-14 of the French Commercial Code states that 'the articles of association can subject any transfer (*cession*) of shares to the prior approval of the company'. The issue is whether the term transfer (*cession*) can also cover a transfer triggered by the death of a shareholder. This is a matter of interpretation. If it does include transfer by death, then the clause is invalid because Article L 228-23 of the Commercial Code, which prohibits such a clause in an SA, will apply since it has

---

[45] CA Versailles (Court of Appeal of Versailles), 24 February 2005 (*Cts Cassado c. SAS Cofradim Résidences*) *JCP* E, 10 mars 2005, n° 385, p 406.
[46] Commercial Code, Art L 227-15.

not been set aside by the special provision of Article L 227-14. Most commentators are of the opinion that the term 'transfer' in Article L 227-14 also covers transfers for the reason of death.[47] Other authors are not so sure since they argue that this interpretation relies on giving a wide construction to the term 'transfer' in Article L 227-14 of the Commercial Code, whereas the courts have given a narrow reading of the same term in Article L 223-23 of the Commercial Code.[48] The *Cour* de cassation has still to decide on this issue. Therefore, the validity of Article 11.2 of Rovebi's by-laws, if it were an SAS, is open to doubt.

iii. Summary and Conclusion

Share transfer and pre-emption clauses are very common in France and the courts take a liberal approach to them because they reflect contractual freedom. Case law on the issue is well settled and, apart from the creation of the SAS in 1994, which reinforced significantly the efficiency of such clauses where they are included in the by-laws of an SAS (compared to an SA), there have not been many legislative developments since.

C. Germany[49]

In principle, the shares of German public companies (AGs) can be freely sold.[50] In the case of bearer shares (AktG, § 10(1)),[51] the articles of association cannot change this. It would not make sense to immediately reverse the greater fungibility of bearer shares by making provision in the articles of association. Legal certainty is also served, since a restriction on the sale of bearer shares would be hard to enforce. For registered shares (AktG, §§ 10(1), 67), by contrast, some restrictions in the articles of association are feasible for non-listed public companies. In the hypothetical case, it is assumed that the shareholders of Rovebi only hold registered shares.

According to § 68(2) of the AktG, the articles of association may provide that the transfer of registered shares is subject to the approval of the management board, the supervisory board or the shareholders' general meeting. The articles can also specify the reasons when a transfer can be refused. The decision to allow or reject the transfer is, generally speaking, at the discretion of the management. While there is no requirement for a substantive justification to refuse the transfer, it is held that management must take appropriate account of the interests of the company and the shareholders.[52]

---

[47] M Germain and PL Perrin, *Juris-Classeur Sociétés Traité*, fasc 155-30, n° 9; *Mémento Francis Lefebvre Sociétés commerciales*, 2012, n° 60700; J Mestre and D Velardochio, *Lamy Sociétés commerciales*, 2010, n° 4045.

[48] See especially B Saintourens, *L'héritier de l'associé* (Mélanges Bernard Bouloc, Dalloz, 2006) 1025 and 1035.

[49] Abbreviated statutes: AktG = Law on Public Companies; BGB = Civil Code; GmbHG = Law on Private Limited Companies.

[50] BGH (German Federal Supreme Court), WM 1987, 174 and 175.

[51] Note that a recent reform restricted the possibility of public companies to issue bearer shares, Gesetz zur Änderung des Aktiengesetzes (Aktienrechtsnovelle 2016) of 30 December 2015, BGBl I 2565.

[52] BGH, NJW 1987, 1019, 1020; U Hüffer and J Koch, *Aktiengesetz* (12th edn, Munich, Beck, 2016) § 68, para 15.

If the transfer of shares is rejected, it would be invalid (BGB, § 182). As in Italian law, this would be different if the restriction was instead contained in a shareholders' agreement.

The law on German public companies is mandatory unless stated otherwise to the contrary (AktG, § 23(5)): this is referred to as the principle of rigidity of the articles (*Prinzip der Satzungsstrenge*) whereby the articles of association can only deviate from company law if expressly permitted by law and thus other restrictions are not allowed. § 68(2) of the AktG does not apply to a transfer in the case of succession.[53] Moreover, it is not possible to restrict the class of purchasers to particular specified persons only or to give the other shareholders a right of first refusal. Since the duties of shareholders are explicitly mentioned in the Act (AktG §§ 54, 55), the articles of association cannot impose additional obligations.[54] A shareholders' agreement, however, would be accepted in Germany. This is based on the position whereby private agreements are strictly separated from positive company law.[55]

Overall, a provision like the draft Article 11 would be void under the German law of public companies. In the present case, one would therefore recommend the use of a private company (GmbH). Here, rights of first refusal in favour of existing shareholders can be provided in the articles (GmbHG, § 15(5)). Furthermore, although it is not possible to preclude shares from being inherited, the articles may impose a duty on the heir to transfer the shares to the other shareholders.[56]

D. Spain

In principle, the shares of the *Sociedad Anónima* (SA) in Spain are freely transferable.[57] However, the by-laws of the company may impose limitations on the freedom to transfer shares (Ley de Sociedades de Capital (LSC) – Corporate Enterprises Act,[58] Article 123.1). Any transfer of shares made in breach of the by-laws is of no effect vis-a-vis the company and, in such cases, directors must not register the purchaser in the register of members.[59] Therefore, Article 11.1 of Rovebi's by-laws, which requires transfers of shares to be made in accordance with certain criteria set out in the by-laws, is, as such, valid under Spanish law. In the case of registered shares,

---

[53] Ibid, § 68, para 11.

[54] BayObLG (Bavarian Supreme Court), AG 1989 173; T Baums and M Möller, 'Venture Capital: U.S.-amerikanisches Modell und deutsches Aktienrecht' in T Baums, K Hopt, and N Horn (eds), *Corporations, Capital Markets and Business in the Law (Liber Amicorum Buxbaum)* (The Hague, Kluwer, 2000) 33, 75.

[55] However, this has also been criticised in the literature. See U Noack, *Gesellschaftervereinbarungen bei Kapitalgesellschaften* (Tübingen, Mohr, 1994).

[56] L Fastrich in *Baumbach & Hueck's GmbHG* (21st edn, Munich, Beck, 2017) § 15, para 13.

[57] See JL Iglesias Prada and J García de Enterría, 'Las Sociedades de Capital. Las Acciones y las Participaciones Sociales. Las Obligaciones (I)' in A Menéndez and Á Rojo (eds) *Lecciones de Derecho Mercantil*, vol I (12th edn, (Cizur Menor (Navarra), Civitas-Thomson Reuters, 2014) 469.

[58] Real Decreto Legislativo 1/2010, de 2 de julio, por el que se aprueba el texto refundido de la Ley de Sociedades de Capital (LSC).

[59] See F Sánchez Calero, *Principios de Derecho Mercantil* (15th edn, Navarra, Thomson-Aranzadi, 2010) 227–28.

the main general conditions for those restrictions to be valid are that they must be expressly set out in the by-laws of the SA and indicate the specific content and scope of the restriction (LSC, Article 123.1; and Reglamento del Registro Mercantil (RRM) – Regulations of the Companies Register,[60] Article 123.1). Those provisions of the by-laws that make shares practically non-transferable are void (LSC, Article 123.2).[61]

The main types of restrictions on the transfer of shares that may be set out in the by-laws of the company are: first, those making the validity of a transfer dependent on authorisation by the company; second, those establishing a pre-emption right in favour of shareholders, the company or third parties; and, third, those setting out the rights of the shareholders, the company, or third parties to purchase the shares of a shareholder affected by certain events (eg a shareholder who is held criminally liable).[62] Article 11.3 of Rovebi's by-laws establishes a transfer restriction in the form of a right of pre-emption. In such cases, the law requires that the by-laws precisely delimit the transfers to which the rights of pre-emption apply (RRM, Article 123.3). This condition is fulfilled in the hypothetical case. Moreover, the specifications contained in Article 11.3 of Rovebi's by-laws regarding notification by the offering shareholder and those concerning the way in which shareholders exercise their rights of pre-emption are in accordance with Spanish law.[63]

Any restrictions pertaining to *mortis causa* transfers must be expressly indicated in the by-laws (LSC, Article 124.1). In those cases, the company may refuse to register the transfer of the shares to the heir in the register of members. However, if it decides to do so, it must either suggest a purchaser to acquire the shares from the heir or the company itself may acquire the shares for their reasonable value (LSC, Article 124.2).[64] These situations concern instances in which the shares have already been transferred to the heir where he or she is afterwards required to re-transfer them to other persons.[65] However, as an alternative, another variant of such a clause may provide that in the case of the death of a shareholder, that shareholder's shares must be

---

[60] Real Decreto 1784/1996, de 19 de julio, por el que se aprueba el Reglamento del Registro Mercantil.

[61] See Iglesias Prada and García de Enterría, 'Las Sociedades de Capital. Las Acciones y las Participaciones Sociales. Las Obligaciones (I)' (n 57) 472; and A Perdices, 'Artículo 123. Restricciones a la libre transmisibilidad' in Á Rojo and E Beltrán (eds), *Comentario de la Ley de Sociedades de Capital* (Cizur Menor (Navarra), Civitas-Thomson Reuters, 2011) 991–92.

[62] See Iglesias Prada and García de Enterría (n 57) 473–74.

[63] The regulation of rights of pre-emption is analysed in depth by Perdices, 'Artículo 123' (n 61) 993–94. These types of clauses have been used by major Spanish SAs, eg Bolsas y Mercados Españoles (BME), the holding group which owns the main Spanish stock exchanges. During the process of demutualisation of BME, a provision in BME's by-laws, corresponding to the year 2004 version, read as follows:

> Until the Company's shares are subject to an organised trading regime their transfer shall be governed by the rules set forth below: Any shareholder seeking to transfer all or some of his shares for valuable consideration or at no cost to any person, including another shareholder, must notify the Board of Directors in writing, specifying the number of shares that he wishes to transfer, the name, address and nationality of the person to whom he wishes to transfer them, the price or valuable consideration of each share and the conditions of the transaction. This notification of the proposed transfer shall have the effect of an irrevocable contract offer. Within fifteen calendar days of receiving the notification, the Board of Directors shall notify the rest of the shareholders in case they wish to make use of their right of pre-emption to acquire the shares.

[64] See Iglesias Prada and García de Enterría (n 57) 474–75.

[65] See A Perdices, 'Artículo 124. Transmisiones *mortis causa*' in Á Rojo and E Beltrán (eds), *Comentario de la Ley de Sociedades de Capital* (Cizur Menor (Navarra), Civitas-Thomson Reuters, 2011) 1002.

directly transferred to the remaining shareholders.[66] Article 11.2 of Rovebi's by-laws is an example of this second option.

Article 11.4 of Rovebi's by-laws submits any disputes between shareholders to arbitration where the dispute concerns the price and the other terms and conditions governing the transfer of shares. The determination of the price by a third party is accepted by Spanish law (for example, Código Civil (CC) – Civil Code,[67] Articles 1447 and 1690,[68] and RRM, Article 123.7). Moreover, the settlement of corporate disputes by an arbitrator is explicitly accepted by Article 11 (*bis*) of the Ley Arbitral (LA) – Arbitration Act –,[69] which permits the incorporation of clauses in a company's by-laws which provide for the submission of disputes to arbitration (LA, Article 11 (*bis*) 2-3).

Finally, it should be stressed that there would be important differences in the legal position depending on whether the clauses under consideration in the hypothetical case were included in the by-laws or in a shareholders' agreement. In this context, any clauses establishing restrictions on the transfer of registered shares will only have effect vis-a-vis the company if they are included in the by-laws registered in the Companies Register (LSC, Article 123.1). This means that if the restrictions of the type considered in this hypothetical case were contained in a shareholders' agreement rather than the company's by-laws, they would only have legal effect amongst the shareholders who were party to such agreement.[70]

When it comes to the *Sociedades de Responsabilidad Limitada* (SLs), the approach of Spanish company law is that their shares should be subject to transfer restrictions;[71] indeed, clauses in the by-laws of SLs that result in the almost free transferability of their shares would be void (LSC, Article 108.1). If Rovebi was a private limited company, the clauses discussed above would also be valid according to Spanish company law.[72]

E. The Netherlands[73]

Shares in a Dutch public limited liability company (NV) can be transferred freely from a shareholder to a third party, unless the articles of association impose restrictions on the transfer of shares.[74] These restrictions may not be such that a transfer is impossible or extremely difficult. In practice, the articles of association frequently include such a restriction if the company is not listed. For a private limited liability company (BV)

---

[66] Ibid, 998 and 1002–03.

[67] Real Decreto de 24 de julio de 1889 por el que se publica el Código Civil.

[68] In this regard, see STS (Sentencia Tribunal Supremo) of 22 March 2010.

[69] Ley 60/2003, de 23 de diciembre, de Arbitraje.

[70] See Sánchez Calero, *Principios de Derecho Mercantil* (n 59) 227.

[71] Iglesias Prada and García de Enterría (n 57) 472.

[72] For a detailed discussion about restrictions on the transfer of shares in both SAs and SLs, see Iglesias Prada and García de Enterría (n 57) 471-7.

[73] Abbreviations: DCC = Dutch Civil Code; HR = Hoge Raad = Dutch Supreme Court; OK = Ondernemingskamer = Enterprise Chamber; Rb. = Rechtbank = District Court. An unofficial translation of Dutch company law as incorporated in bk 2 of the Dutch Civil Code can be found on www.dutchcivillaw.com/civilcodebook022.htm.

[74] DCC, Art 2:87.

the rules follow a different logic. Unless the articles of association state otherwise, a valid transfer of shares requires that the shareholder who wants to dispose of one or more of his or her shares first has to offer those shares to the other shareholders in proportion to the number of shares that are held by each of them at the moment that such an offer is made.[75] This means that for a private company it is possible to ensure that the shares can be freely transferred, but this has to be stated explicitly in the articles of association. Moreover, the transfer of shares can be excluded in the articles of association for a fixed period of time.[76] A transfer in violation of such an exclusion in the articles of association is invalid. An arrangement to exclude transferability in the articles of association requires the consent of all the holders of shares to which the exclusion of transferability relates.[77]

It is generally assumed that, under Dutch law, it is possible in both public and private limited liability companies to put additional obligations on the shareholders with regard to the transferability of shares.[78] For the private limited liability company this is certainly possible as a result of the changes to the law governing private companies in 2012.[79] In the case of the public limited liability company, a minority view in the literature takes the position that these restrictions are only possible if all shareholders consent to these restrictions beforehand.[80] Thus, assuming the position of the majority view, the agreements made by the engineers are valid. However, the shareholders/contracting parties will always have to act reasonably and fairly towards each other.[81] Therefore, if the agreement leads to a situation in which this standard of reasonableness and fairness is violated, this could affect the validity of the agreement under those specific circumstances.

Whether the suggested clause would have the same effect if it was not included in the articles of association but in the shareholders' agreement is still debated and therefore unclear under Dutch law. Although the Supreme Court has never clearly ruled on this matter and legislation does not include any reference to shareholders' agreements in this regard, there is a strong tendency in the Netherlands to suggest that clauses in shareholders' agreements also have a 'corporate effect' in the sense that they are not just contractual obligations but also affect the company law obligations of the company.[82] This position is defended even more strongly if the company is

---

[75] DCC, Art 2:195-1.
[76] DCC, Art 2:195-3.
[77] DCC, Art 2:195-3.
[78] G van Solinge and MP Nieuwe Weme, *Mr. C. Assers Handleiding tot de beoefening van het Nederlands Burgerlijk Recht. 2. Rechtspersonenrecht.Deel IIa. NV en BV. Oprichting, vermogen en aandelen* (Deventer, Kluwer, 2013) 295–96.
[79] DCC, Art 2:192.
[80] See JMM Maeijer, *Mr. C. Assers, Handleiding tot de beoefening van het Nederlands Burgerlijk Recht. 2. Vertegenwoordiging en rechtspersoon. Deel III. De naamloze en de besloten vennootschap* (Zwolle, WEJ Tjeenk Willink, 2000) 98; WCL van der Grinten, *Van der Heijden Handboek voor de naamloze en de besloten vennootschap* (Deventer, WEJ Tjeenk Willink, 1992) nr 172.
[81] DCC, Art 2:8, 6:2 and 6:248.
[82] RGJ Nowak, 'Rechtsgeldigheid en doorwerking van buitenstatutaire governance-afspraken' WPNR 2014/7014; WJM van Veen, 'Opnieuw: contractuele ontslagreglingen, doorwerking en het belang van de vennootschap' WPNR 2016/7089. See also District Court The Hague 1 August 2012, *JOR* 2012/286; Rb. (pres.) 16 January 2014, *JOR* 2014/157.

also a party to the shareholders' agreement.[83] However, there is also a minority view suggesting that shareholders' agreements only create contractual obligations between the parties to the contract and do not have any effects from a company law perspective, especially if the company is not a party to the shareholders' agreement. If this latter view were adopted, a violation of the shareholders' agreement would only result in a breach of contract. This is not viewed differently for the public and private limited liability company.

F. Finland

i. Limitations on Transferability in the Articles of Association

Under Finnish company law, it is presumed that shares are freely transferable.[84] Nevertheless, share transferability may be limited by including restrictions thereon in the articles of association, however, only as far as permitted by the Companies Act 2006 (CA). Two types of restrictions are permitted:[85] redemption articles and consent articles.[86] Such articles are common in private companies and are also allowed in public companies, except for listed companies.

In relation to redemption articles, it is stipulated in section 7, chapter 3 of the CA that it may be provided in the articles of association that a shareholder, the company or another person has the right to redeem shares due to be transferred to a third party by a shareholder other than the company. The redemption clause must indicate who is entitled to the right of redemption and, where there are several persons who have that right, how their order of precedence is to be determined.

Consent articles are regulated by section 8, chapter 3 of the CA. Pursuant to the said provision, it may be provided in the articles of association that the acquisition of shares by way of a transfer requires the consent of the company. Before the consent is given, the acquirer of the shares must have no shareholder rights in the company except the right to payment in the event that assets are distributed and the pre-emptive right in a share issue.

Therefore, pursuant to the CA redemption articles confer on a shareholder, the company or another person the right to redeem shares that an existing shareholder[87] transfers to a third party. Unlike Articles 11.2 and 11.3 in the present case, redemption and consent articles are applicable only once the shares have been transferred.[88] Unless

---

[83] See for an overview of the different views on this aspect: Nowak, 'Rechtsgeldigheid en doorwerking van buitenstatutaire governance-afspraken' (n 82); R de Leeuw, 'Rechtsgeldigheid en doorwerking van een aandeelhoudersovereenkomst in de persoonsgebonden BV: een stappenplan voor de praktijk', *Maandblad voor Ondernemingsrecht* 2016/10.

[84] CA, c 1, s 4.

[85] CA, c 3, s 6.

[86] The articles of association may also include provisions stipulating that a shareholder who owns a certain percentage of all shares is obliged to redeem the shares of other shareholders. The Supreme Court treated this as the Finnish incarnation of a poison pill in KKO 2005:122 and found it valid on the grounds that it did not restrict the transferability of the shares.

[87] Excluding the company.

[88] J Mähönen and S Villa, *Osakeyhtiö II – Pääomarakenne ja rahoitus* (Helsinki, Talentum, 2014) 202.

the contrary is stipulated in the articles of association, the board of directors must notify the persons who have the right to redemption within one month of the date of notification of the transfer. A possible demand for redemption must then be presented to the company.[89]

Redemption articles are applicable to all acquisitions, including inheritance and transfers based on estate division.[90] Meanwhile, consent articles prescribe that an acquisition by way of transfer, excluding inheritance and transfers based on estate division (but including gifts), requires the consent of the company.[91] Without consent, the transfer will not be entered into the shareholder register.

Unless the contrary is provided for in the articles, the redemption price is equal to the fair price of the shares, which is usually the agreed price in the transfer.[92] However, there are no obstacles to the insertion of an article such as Article 11.4 in the articles of association of a Finnish company. Thus, a third party can resolve the price if the parties are unable to agree.

To summarise, Article 11 in the present case would not be a valid article in Finland, with the exception of Article 11.4. However, under the CA, a similar outcome would be achievable by a different formulation of the redemption and consent clauses. The main observation is that instead of the pre-emptive redemption and consent proce-dures, the articles should have been triggered by an actual transfer of the shares.

ii. Limitations on Transferability in a Shareholders' Agreements

Article 11 would be valid in a shareholders' agreement. However, a shareholders' agreement binds only the parties to it, and only constitutes a contractual obligation, which means that generally Article 11.1 would not be enforceable against third parties.

iii. Limitations on Freedom of Contract

In extreme cases, clauses in contracts and articles in the articles of association can be adjusted by the courts by the virtue of section 36 of the Contracts Act. In KKO 1999:42, the Supreme Court considered the validity of a redemption article, which at the time of drafting represented fair value, but at the time of interpretation represented approximately one-tenth of the fair value (as a result of inflation). As a result, the redemption price had become so low that the owners of the shares were discouraged from selling them. Therefore, the Supreme Court found that the redemption article blocked the free transferability of shares. The Supreme Court adjusted the clause, pegging the redemption price in the article to the agreed transfer price or, if not agreed, to a fair price to be resolved at the time of transfer.

---

[89] CA, c 3, s 7(2).

[90] A redemption clause must at the very least contain a specification of what kind of clause it is (ie that it is a redemption clause), indicate who has the right to redemption and how their precedence is to be determined (CA, c 3, s 7(1)).

[91] Provisions about the clause and the procedure are found in c 3, s 8 of the CA.

[92] CA, c 3, s 7(2), para 3.

G. Poland

i. Introduction

The hypothetical case concerns a company with limited liability, which is not listed on a stock exchange. In Poland there are two types of companies with limited liability: (i) *Spółka akcyjna* (a public company); and (ii) *Spółka z ograniczoną odpowiedzialnością* (a limited liability company). Both types of companies may function and be structured as 'private in fact' by shareholders, but the public company (*Spółka akcyjna*) is usually treated as more open, whose shares should be freely sold. It is clear that the public company (*Spółka akcyjna*) appeals to a wider public and anonymous shareholders, whereas limited liability companies are usually more closed.[93] The legal definition of a public company is linked to the fact that its shares are dematerialised within the meaning of the Act on trading in financial instruments. Thus, Polish legal doctrine differentiates between public and non-public companies for the purpose of the above Act and less frequently uses such expressions as a 'private' company as the opposite of a 'public' company.

ii. Inclusion of the Pre-emption Clause in the Company's By-laws

Turning first to the public company in Poland (*Spółka akcyjna*), pursuant to Article 337, section 1 of the Commercial Companies Code (CCC), the shares of a company are freely transferable. In the case of bearer shares of a public company, the articles of association cannot provide otherwise. Such a provision would be null and void in accordance with Article 303, section 3 of the CCC, which stipulates as follows: 'where permitted by this Act, the company's articles may contain provisions different from those provided in the Act'. Some commentators also invoke the principle of rigidity of the articles as in the German law doctrine (*Prinzip der Satzungsstrenge*).[94] In general, this principle means that the articles of association can only deviate from company law if 'expressly' permitted by law, which does not permit the purpose and function of a given rule of law to be taken into account as part of the process of interpretation.[95] Furthermore, the presumption of mandatory rules must be applied.[96] Since Article 333, section 2 of the CCC only allows restrictions of registered shares (the articles of association may provide that the transfer of registered shares is subject to the approval of the company or otherwise restrict the freedom of disposal of registered shares), it is

---

[93] See, eg, A Chmurski, 'Spółki z ograniczoną odpowiedzialnością według dekretu z d. 8 lutego 1919 r.' (Warsaw, Instytut Wydawniczy, 'Biblioteka Polska', 1920) 8–9.

[94] See S Sołtysiński in S Sołtysiński (ed), *System prawa prywatnego*, t 17b. *Prawo spółek kapitałowych* (Warsaw, CH Beck, 2010) s 7.

[95] Ibid.

[96] A Szumański, 'Nowe polskie prawo spółek handlowych' (2001) 1 *Prawo Spółek* 3 and S Sołtysiński in S Sołtysiński, A Szajkowski, A Szumański and J Szwaja, *Kodeks spółek handlowych. Komentarz, t. III* (Warsaw, CH Beck, 2008) 92. The presumption in favour of mandatory rules is also accepted by the supporters of deregulation of company law. See, eg, K Oplustil and J Bą k, 'Ius Cogens w prawie spółki akcyjnej – analiza prawno-ekonomiczna' (2007) 2 *HUK* 182. However, the rule is questionable in its application to the regulation of the internal affairs of a corporation, which do not affect third parties, on an economic analysis of law perspective.

not possible to include a transfer restriction in the articles of association which applies in the case of bearer shares. Moreover, the articles of association may only limit the disposal of registered shares, but it is not possible to exempt the disposal completely or temporarily (for example, a provision in the by-laws that shares may not be sold during the first five years of the company's life). In accordance with Article 338 of the CCC, it is only possible to conclude a special agreement restricting the disposal of a share or a fraction thereof for a period of no longer than five years from the date of the contract.

Moreover, the doctrine also dictates that the articles of association may not limit a transfer of shares so that it is subjected to the consent of the board, the supervisory board or the shareholders' general meeting. The articles of association must specify a time limit for the identification of the buyer, the price or the manner of determining the same, including the manner of payment. Otherwise, registered shares may be sold without any restrictions (CCC, Article 337 section 4, sentences 2–3). Furthermore, it is not possible to bypass the above limitations of law by granting the beneficiary an irrevocable power of attorney to vote the shares or to transfer the dividend receivables to the beneficiary on the ground that this would distort the nature of the company.[97] It should be stressed that the free transferability of shares is strongly rooted in the nature of the corporation and has its functional and economic justifications. Nevertheless, there are many other means by which the transfer of registered shares may be limited. Typical controls and restrictions on the transfer of shares include: (i) the right of pre-emption (*prawo pierwokupu*); (ii) the right of first refusal (*prawo pierwszeństwa*); (iii) the right of first offer; and (iv) the requirement to obtain the consent of the company, the other shareholders or the supervisory board.[98]

There is a difference under Polish law between a right of pre-emption and a right of first refusal. A right of pre-emption is governed by the provisions of the Civil Code (it has a narrower scope and mandatory provisions which cannot be altered), whereas the right of first refusal is purely contractual. Despite the similarity, it is possible to distinguish contractually between a right of first refusal and a right of first offer. A right of first refusal involves the vendor shareholder being under an obligation to offer its shares to the other shareholders before it can transfer its shares to a third party. The offer must be on the same terms and conditions as those offered by the third party. The other shareholder with the right of first refusal then has a fixed period of time in which to accept. If that shareholder does not acquire the shares of the vendor shareholder, it will obviously find itself in a company with a new co-shareholder. The right of first offer is different from the right of first refusal. In the case of the former, the vendor shareholder first offers its shares to the other shareholders before approaching a third party. There would be a period of time for acceptance after which, if the other shareholders do not buy, the vendor shareholder is free to sell to a third party.[99]

---

[97] A Szumański, 'Ograniczona wolność umów w prawie spółek handlowych' (1999) 5 *Gdańskie Studia Prawnicze* 418.

[98] M Davies and A Siemiątkowski, *Joint Ventures in Poland – A Legal Guide* (Warsaw, Wydawnictwo, CH Beck, 2009) 61; S Sołtysiński in S Sołtysiński, A Szajkowski, A Szumański and J Szwaja (eds), *Kodeks handlowy. Komentrz, t. II* (Warsaw, CH Beck, 1998) 333; J Frą ckowiak in W Popiołek, W Pyzioł, J Frąckowiak, A Witosz and A Kidyba (eds), *Kodeks spółek handlowych. Komentarz* (Warsaw, LexisNexis, 2008), note 6 to Art 337 of the CCC.

[99] Davies and Siemią tkowski, *Joint Ventures in Poland* (n 98) 61.

In light of the aforementioned explanation, the right prescribed in the hypothetical case would be categorised as a right of first refusal.

If Rovebi was a limited liability company (*Spółka z ograniczoną odpowiedzialnością*), the conclusions would be almost the same. Pursuant to Article 182, section 1 of the CCC, a company's by-laws may make the transfer of a share or a fraction thereof, or the pledging of a share, contingent upon the consent of the company or otherwise restricted. The main difference is that the limited liability company may not issue any documents evidencing freely transferable registered or bearer shares, so solving the hypothetical case in the context of the limited liability company is easier. Restrictions on the transfer of shares are common in limited liability companies and the principle of free transferability of shares does not apply here. Generally, the idea is that a limited liability company is a commercial arrangement between certain parties and if those parties were to be changed, this might alter the whole balance of the constitution of the limited liability company. However, on the other hand, commercial entities are reluctant to be bound for an indefinite period of time in a commercial venture with no possibility of exit and therefore no possibility of profit-taking, minimising their losses or changing their business focus. A common compromise is to allow the transfer of shares but with certain restrictions. Often the transfer provisions are subject to intensive negotiations and are quite lengthy. There is no standard way of dealing with this matter in Poland.[100]

With regard to the wording of Article 11.2 of Rovebi's by-laws, it must be stated that the CCC does not regulate this issue explicitly in the case of the public company. One might attempt to apply the above-mentioned Article 337 of the CCC and argue that clause 11.2 is an example of 'other restrictions on the disposal of registered shares'.[101] However, it must be stressed that there is a dispute amongst commentators as to whether Article 337 of the CCC applies to disposals *mortis causa*.[102] Some commentators claim that any disposal *mortis cause* must be consistent with Article 941 of the Civil Code, which provides that disposals *mortis causa* are only allowed if prescribed in the form of a testamentary document (will).[103] Undoubtedly, the wording of Article 11.2 is inconsistent with Article 941 of the Civil Code. As a result, such a provision would be null and void. These commentators further assert that the by-laws may provide for the automatic (compulsory) redemption of shares in the case of a shareholder's death (according to Article 359, section 1 of the CCC, a company's articles may provide for the redemption of shares on the occurrence of certain identified events without any requirement for the prior approval of the shareholders in general meeting by resolution).[104] Redemption is possible since it does not entail a transfer or an obligation to transfer shares, and thus is in accordance with Article 941 of the Civil Code. In this case, Article 359, section 2 of the CCC applies, whereby compulsory redemption is subject to the payment of compensation which must be no lower than the value of the company's net assets attributable to a share,

---

[100] Ibid.
[101] See A Nowacki, *Umorzenie akcji* (Warsaw, CH Beck, 2007) 106–07.
[102] See S Sołtysiński in Sołtysiński et al, *Kodeks handlowych. Komentrz, t. II* (n 98) 508.
[103] Ibid.
[104] Ibid.

as shown in the financial statements of the company in the previous financial year, duly reduced by any amounts distributed amongst the shareholders (CCC, Article 359, section 2, sentence 3). This begs the question as to whom compensation should be paid in respect of redeemed shares where the shareholder has already died. The only possible answer is that payment must be made to the heirs of the deceased shareholder. It may be argued that any other solution would deprive the heirs of their legal rights and would be contrary to the rules on social harmony (CCC, Article 304, section 4). As mentioned before, there is, however, another possible interpretation of Article 337 of the CCC in conjunction with Article 941 of the Civil Code. It could be argued that Article 337 of the CCC is *legi speciali* to Article 941 of the Civil Code.

The issue is explicitly regulated in case of the limited liability company (*Spółka z ograniczoną odpowiedzialnością*). According to Article 183, section 1 of the CCC, the company's articles of association may limit or exclude the right of heirs of a deceased shareholder to join the company in the place of a deceased shareholder. In such a case, the company's articles must determine the terms of paying off such heirs, on pain of invalidity of the limitation or exclusion. According to the majority of legal opinion, the exclusion of the right of heirs may entail an obligation to transfer the shares to the other shareholders.[105] It is said that Article 183, section 1 of the CCC precludes the application of the law of succession.[106] However, there is also a minority view which is to the contrary, ie that the exclusion of heirs to join the company should always lead to the automatic redemption of their shares.[107] Turning to Article 11 of Rovebi's by-laws, this clearly provides for the possibility of limitation or even the exclusion of an heir's right to join Rovebi as a shareholder.

However, notwithstanding the fact that the terms of clause 11.2 of Rovebi's by-laws appear to comply with Article 183, section 1 of the CCC in the case of the limited liability company and Article 337, section 2 of the CCC with respect to the public company, it must be stressed that Article 11.2 is likely to be unenforceable and invalid since there is no mechanism to compensate and pay off the heirs of the deceased shareholder. It would be advisable to supplement the wording of the clause with such a provision.

iii. Inclusion of the Clause in the Shareholders' Agreement

The conclusion of a shareholders' agreement is allowed on the basis of the principle of freedom of contract which is provided for in Article 353(1) of the Polish Civil Code.[108]

---

[105] See M Rodzynkiewcz, *Kodeks spółek handlowych. Komentarz* (Warsaw, LexisNexis, 2009) 314–15; E Marszałkowska-Krześ in J Jacyszyn and E Marszałkowska-Krześ, *Kodeks spółek handlowych. Komentarz. Orzecznictwo* (Warsaw, Libarta, 2001) 296; R Pabis, *Spółka z ograniczonąodpowiedzialnością. Komentarz* (Warsaw, CH Beck, 2003) 137; JA Strzępka and E Zielińska in JA Strzępka, E Zielińska, W Popiołek, P Pinior and H Urbańczyk (eds), *Kodeks spółek handlowych. Komentarz. Orzecznictwo* (Warsaw, CH Beck, 2003) 514; A Szajkowski in S Sołtysiński, A Szajkowski, A Szumański and J Szwaja, *Kodeks spółek handlowych. Komentarz, t. II* (Warsaw, CH Beck, 2002) 273–74.

[106] See A Kidyba, *Kodeks spółek handlowych. Komentarz, t. I* (Krakow, Zakamycze, 2005) 794.

[107] See R Potrzeszcz and T Siemiątkowski in R Potrzeszcz, T Siemiątkowski, JP Naworski and K Strzelczyk, *Komentarz do kodeksu spółek handlowych, t. II* (Warsaw, LexisNexis, 2011), note 2 to Art 183 of the CCC.

[108] See, eg, A Rataj, 'Umowy wspólników (akcjonariuszy) spółek kapitałowych' (2006) 1 *Monitor Prawniczy* 48; J Okolski and A Opalski, 'Porozumienia akcjonariuszy' (1999) 2 *Przeglą d Prawa Handlowego* 6;

Some commentators are also of the opinion that restrictions on the transfer of bearer shares is permitted in a shareholders' agreement.[109] If Article 11.3 of Rovebi's by-laws was included in a shareholders' agreement rather than the by-laws of the company, it would certainly be binding between the parties to such an agreement. However, such provisions in a shareholders' agreement would not be binding vis-a-vis the company. Furthermore, any shareholder in breach of such provisions of the shareholders' agreement would be liable on the basis of Article 471 of the Civil Code (contractual liability or organisational liability). However, these provisions would not be binding upon a new shareholder, since he or she would not be a party to the agreement. Turning to Article 11.2 of Rovebi's by-laws, if inserted into a shareholders' agreement, it might be considered null and void as inconsistent with Article 941 of the Civil Code on the same basis as the articles of association.

In the case of a shareholders' agreement applicable in the context of a public company, the law provides for a maximum 10-year period for a right of first refusal (CCC, Article 338, section 2). However, it is possible to conclude another agreement after the lapse of this period. The CCC does not stipulate any time limits for validity of the agreement in the case of a limited liability company.

iv. Conclusion

According to Polish law, the right prescribed in Article 11.3 of Rovebi's by-laws would be effective in both the case of the public company (*Spółka akcyjna*) and the limited liability company (*Spółka z ograniczoną odpowiedzialnością*). It would also be possible to conclude provisions in a shareholders' agreement to the same effect. However, such provisions in a shareholders' agreement would not bind the company and new shareholders who were not a party to the agreement. Furthermore, Article 11.2 of Rovebi's by-laws would be invalid under Polish law. Nevertheless, it would be possible to achieve the same result by adopting different wording or by including provisions for the redemption of shares.

H. Latvia

Latvian public limited companies (*akciju sabiedrība* (AS)) must keep a register of shareholders by virtue of section 234 of the Commercial Code.[110] Under statute, shareholders may alienate any shares they own by independent valuation. The general principle is that shareholders may freely alienate their shares (Commercial Code, section 238(1)). However, the articles of association may provide specific procedures for

---

M Spyra, 'Zobowiązanie prawa do głosu w spółce akcyjnej, dopuszczalność, konstrukcja, skuteczność' (2000) 3 *Transformacje Prawa Prywatnego* 85; Ł Gasiński, 'Dopuszczalność zawierania umów (porozumień) akcjonariuszy co do sposobu wykonywania prawa głosu' (2000) 10 *Przeglą d Prawa Handlowego* 46; Ł Gasiński, *Umowy akcjonariuszy co do sposobu wykonywania prawa głosu w prawie polskim i amerykańskim* (Warsaw, CH Beck, 2006).

[109] See J Okolski and A Opalski, 'Porozumienia akcjonariuszy' (1999) 2 *Przeglą d Prawa Handlowego* 9; A Wiśniewski, *Prawo o spółkach – podręcznik praktyczny. Spółka akcyjna, t. III* (Warsaw, Twigger, 1993) 140.

[110] Likums 'Komerclikums', Latvijas Vēstnesis 158/160 (2069/2071), 13 April 2000.

the sale of registered shares. The exact same approach is taken when addressing private limited liability companies (*sabiedrība ar ierobežotu atbildību* (SIA)) as prescribed by section 188 of the Commercial Code.

Latvian law distinguishes between registered shares and bearer shares. The rights arising from registered shares belong to the person who, as a shareholder, is recorded in the register of shareholders. Section 238(2) of the Commercial Code directs that the articles of association may: (a) provide that the sale of registered shares requires the consent of the board of directors or the general meeting of shareholders; (b) include the grounds on which such consent may be refused; and (c) specify the right of first refusal of other shareholders to the shares to be sold. If such right of first refusal has been provided for in the articles of association, the time period for the utilisation thereof must not exceed one month from the date when the notice regarding the sale of the shares was submitted to the board of directors. The board of directors must, after receipt of such notice, without delay publish it in accordance with the procedures of the Commercial Code. The shareholder may waive the right of first refusal prior to the end of the specified time period. Bearer shares are financial instruments according to the provisions of the Financial Instrument Market Law, and for this reason cannot be subject to restrictions on their transfer (Commercial Code, sections 228, 238(2)). In private companies, shareholders maintain the right to freely alienate their shares unless statutory or by-law prohibitions exist (Commercial Code, section 188(1)). Nonetheless, the making of a gift of shares, exchanging shares, or any other type of share alienation besides a sale has to be approved in a shareholders' meeting (Commercial Code, section 188(3)).

Article 11.2 of Rovebi's by-laws is not in conformity with Latvian law, although it is generally possible to bequeath registered shares to other shareholders as natural persons or even to Rovebi itself as a legal person.

It is commonly agreed that the provisions of section 238(2) of the Commercial Code are to be interpreted restrictively and apply only to the sale of registered shares. If we assume that Rovebi is a company with registered shares that are not publicly tradable, only their sale (as one of the various potential means of transferring registered shares) may be restricted. For example, the ability of an individual shareholder to make a gift of, exchange or otherwise alienate registered shares (except a sale) may not be limited by the articles. Therefore, since the transfer of registered shares in the event of the death of a shareholder does not constitute a sale, a provision such as Article 11.2 of Rovebi's by-laws restricting such a transfer would be treated as null and void. Similarly, the transfer of shares to shareholders would be contrary to the legislative framework of private companies, which prescribes that shares, in the event of a shareholder's death, are to be transferred to the respective heirs, unless by-laws prescribe their transfer to the company itself (Commercial Code, section 191(1)).

Turning now to the possibility of the other shareholders or the company inheriting a deceased shareholder's registered shares, the relevant provisions of the Civil Code must be taken into account. The inheritance of shares may take place on the basis of a testamentary document (will) or an inheritance contract. It is impossible under Latvian law to regulate issues of inheritance in the by-laws of a company.

Article 11.3 of Rovebi's by-laws is in principle in conformity with Latvian law. According to sections 189(1) and 238(2) of the Commercial Code, in the event that a shareholder sells his or her registered shares, the other shareholders of the company have the right of pre-emption/first refusal, as stipulated in Rovebi's by-laws. As stated before, the right of pre-emption concerns only a straight sale and does not apply to other forms of transfer, for example, by way of gift or barter. If two or more shareholders wish to invoke their rights of first refusal, but the number of the shares to be sold is not sufficient to divide them proportionately, the board of directors must organise a restricted auction amongst those shareholders in respect of the remaining shares that cannot be proportionately divided. The time period for the utilisation of the rights of first refusal may not exceed one month from the date when the notification regarding the sale was submitted to the board of directors. The shareholder may refuse the right of first refusal in writing before the end of the specified time period. The time period in Article 11.3 of Rovebi's by-laws may therefore remain 20 days.

With regard to the provision in Article 11.3 whereby a transfer to the shareholders takes place if any of the other shareholders agree to acquire such shares in full or part thereof, this complies only partly with Latvian law. The Civil Code states that if a shareholder with the right of pre-emption/first refusal wishes to invoke this right, then he or she must, unless otherwise agreed, fulfil the same conditions stipulated by the new third party purchaser. Usually a person with the right of pre-emption/first refusal enters into the sale contract on the same conditions which would apply to the third party purchaser. It is possible to agree other conditions on the right of pre-emption, but those conditions must be specified (Civil Code, section 1417). In the case of Article 11.3, it is not possible to consider those conditions as having been sufficiently specified and therefore a shareholder (or shareholders) who wishes to apply his or her pre-emption right must enter into the sale and purchase contract on the same conditions as a respective third party purchaser (with regard to the number of shares, the price payable and the terms of the transaction).

The effect of clause 11 would not be different if it had been included in a shareholders' agreement rather than the by-laws of the company, since sections 189(1) and 238(2) of the Commercial Code and the relevant provisions of the Civil Code are mandatory provisions. Therefore, they apply with equal effect to a company's by-laws and a shareholders' agreement.

I. The UK[111]

i. Introduction to Shares

UK company law recognises two types of shares: first, registered shares; and, second, bearer shares, which are known as 'share warrants'.[112] The former are much more common than the latter. In the current case, it is assumed that the shareholders of

---

[111] Abbreviations: CA 2006 (the Companies Act 2006); Model Articles (Model articles of association of private companies limited by shares (in reg 2 of and sch 1 to the Companies (Model Articles) Regulations 2008, SI 2008/3229), private companies limited by guarantee (in reg 3 of and sch 2 to the Companies (Model Articles) Regulations 2008, SI 2008/3229) and public limited companies (in reg 4 of and sch 3 to the Companies (Model Articles) Regulations 2008, SI 2008/3229)).
[112] CA 2006, ss 122 and 779.

Rovebi only hold registered shares. In UK company law, the shares of any member in a private company or plc are transferable in accordance with the company's articles.[113] In terms of section 771(1) of the CA 2006 and *Gilbert's Case*,[114] it is not necessary for the articles of a private company or plc to specifically confer a right to transfer on the members for such a right to exist in law. Instead, it is presumed that shares are freely transferable and if this is not what is intended, the articles must set out the extent to which the right to transfer is restricted. Thus, the articles of association of a private company or plc govern the transfer of shares and may specify that the power to transfer is restricted. However, by contrast, the Listing Rules[115] require the shares of a listed plc to be freely transferable at all times.[116]

Shares may be transferred by means of an instrument of transfer (known as a 'stock transfer form'), which is executed by or on behalf of the transferor.[117] In terms of the Model Articles, the directors of a private company have an unfettered and unqualified discretion to refuse to register the transfer of a share.[118] Meanwhile, for plcs, the Model Articles stipulate that the power of the directors to refuse to register the transfer of a share is fettered and limited to particular identified circumstances.[119] It must be stressed that such provisions in the Model Articles may be displaced by a plc whereby the director's power of refusal to register a transfer of shares is removed or further restrictions are placed on share transfers (such as those contained in Articles 11.1–11.4 of Rovebi's by-laws). If the directors elect to refuse to register the transfer, section 771(1) and (2) of the CA 2006 directs that the directors must give the purported transferee notice of such refusal and the reasons for such refusal as soon as practicable, and in any event within two months after the date on which the transfer is lodged with them.[120] However, it is unclear whether the share transfer remains valid.[121]

ii. Pre-emption Rights on Transfer

Prior to 1980, it was mandatory for private companies to include provisions in their articles of association conferring in favour of existing shareholders a right of first refusal in respect of shares which a shareholder had indicated he or she wished to sell

---

[113] CA 2006, s 544. See also *Re Bahia and San Francisco Railway Co Ltd* (1868) LR 3 QB 584, 595 (Lord Blackburn).

[114] *Gilbert's Case* (1869–70) LR 5 Ch App 559, 565 (Sir GM Giffard LJ).

[115] For full details of the legal status of the Listing Rules, see the UK solution in ch 4 at II I, above.

[116] Listing Rules, r 2.2.4(1).

[117] In the case of a private company, see the Model Articles, reg 26(1) of sch 1, and for a plc, see Model Articles, reg 63(1) of sch 3.

[118] Model Articles, reg 26(5) of sch 1.

[119] See Model Articles, reg 63(5) of sch 3, namely where: (i) the share is not fully paid up; (ii) the stock transfer form is not deposited at the company's registered office; (iii) the transfer is not accompanied by the share certificate to which it relates or such other evidence as the directors may reasonably require to show the transferor's right to make the transfer; (iv) the transfer covers more than one class of share; or (v) the transfer is in favour of more than five transferees.

[120] Any failure to do so can lead to fines on the part of the company and any officer of the company in default.

[121] See, eg, G Morse and R Smeardon (eds), *Palmer's Company Law* (London, Sweet & Maxwell, 2017) paras 6.445 and 6.461–6.464.

to a third party. In 1980, the law was changed so that it was no longer compulsory for such provisions to be inserted into the articles of association of a company. Notwithstanding the change in the law, it remains common for private companies and some non-listed plcs to continue to include such provisions in their articles. These provisions are known as 'pre-emption clauses on transfer'[122] and their purpose is to enable the company to restrict who can become a member and to ensure that an existing shareholder's share is not diluted outside his or her control.[123] The common law is clear to the effect that there is no limit on the nature of the restrictions on share transfers which can be contained in a non-listed company's articles of association, so long as the existence and extent of any restrictions are clearly stated in the articles.[124] Thus, there is no impediment to Rovebi including provisions such as Articles 11.1–11.4 in its articles of association.

Since the pre-emption clause on transfer is contained in Rovebi's by-laws, it amounts to a contract which binds each of the members and the company and the members *inter se* in terms of section 33 of the CA 2006. The effect is that these provisions are contractual in nature and the procedures contained therein, including any time limits, must be complied with fully. Otherwise, they will be deemed to have been breached[125] and a member will be entitled to take enforcement action, for example, by obtaining an injunction restraining the company from contravening the articles of association.[126]

Article 11.3 directs that the price to be paid by the existing shareholders for the shares will be no greater or lower than the price which the third party purchaser proposed to pay the vendor shareholder for them. Such a procedure in the pre-emption clause which seeks to ascertain the price to be paid for the shares will be held to be valid, since the methodology to be applied in fixing the price for the shares is a matter of construction of the clause[127] and it is submitted that the terms of Article 11.3 are unambiguous and clear.

iii. The Validity of Article 11.2

In terms of section 773 of the CA 2006, shares may be 'transmitted' from a deceased shareholder to a personal representative (for example, an executor or trustee) by operation of law, and the company may only recognise the transmittee as having any title

---

[122] The right of the existing shareholders under the pre-emption clause on transfer is referred to as their 'right of pre-emption'.

[123] *Lyle & Scott v Scott's Trustees* [1959] AC 763 (HL) 777 (Lord Reid).

[124] *Re Crawley & Co* (1889) 42 Ch D 209, 231; *Re Stockton, Malleable Iron Co* (1875) LR 2 Ch D 101 (Ch); *Re Smith and Fawcett Ltd* [1942] 1 Ch 304 (CA) 306 (Lord Greene MR).

[125] *Macro v Thompson (No 3)* [1997] 2 BCLC 36 (Ch) 67 (Walker J). See also Morse and Smeardon, *Palmer's Company Law* (n 121) para 6.460.

[126] *Johnson v Lyttle's Iron Agency* (1877) 5 Ch D 687 (CA) and *Wood v Odessa Waterworks Co* (1889) 42 Ch D 636 (Ch). However, the third party purchaser who had intended to acquire the shares will have no right of enforcement: *Williams v MacPherson* 1990 SLT 279.

[127] *Dashfield v Davidson (No 2)* [2008] EWHC 486 (Ch), [2008] BCC 662 (Ch). See also *McKillen v Misland Cyprus (Investments) Ltd* [2012] EWCA Civ 179, where it was held that the ascertainment of the meaning of pre-emption provisions in the articles of association is a matter of applying the law of interpretation of contracts.

to that share.[128] As regards the death of the shareholder, section 773 of the CA 2006 further provides that a transfer by the deceased's personal representative, even if he or she is not a member of the company, is as valid as if he or she had been. However, pre-emption clauses such as Article 11.2 of Rovebi's by-laws will be treated as lawful and valid. For example, in the case of *Cottrell v King*,[129] where a deceased's shares had transmitted to his personal representatives, been transferred by the personal representatives to the deceased's wife in terms of the deceased's will and the wife's name entered into the company's register of members, an existing shareholder was held to be entitled to an order rectifying the company's register of members to remove the wife's name. This was on the basis that the effect of the personal representative and the wife giving notice to the company (that the wife wished to take the deceased's shares by transfer) was to convert the existing shareholders' rights of pre-emption into an option to purchase the shares.[130] In that sense, the terms of the pre-emption clause must be followed. Otherwise, where a putative transferee takes the shares of a deceased shareholder without the prior exhaustion of the pre-emption provisions in Article 11.2, this will amount to a clear breach of the articles of association by the aforementioned putative transferee.[131]

iv. Pre-emption Rights in Shareholders' Agreements

There is no impediment to pre-emption rights being contained in a shareholders' agreement and such provisions will be held to be legally binding.[132] If the shareholders' agreement is breached, this is a breach of contract and enables an innocent party to raise an action for damages or some other remedy. However, one of the principal differences between a shareholders' agreement and the articles of association is that the former does not automatically bind new members of the company, whereas the articles do.[133] In addition, the company will not be bound by a provision of the shareholders' agreement where it purports to restrict or remove its ability to exercise a power which it possesses in terms of company law.[134]

v. Summary and Conclusion

The existence of Articles 11.1–11.4 in the articles of association of a non-listed plc such as Rovebi would be lawful in terms of UK company law. This would also be the case if these provisions were contained in a shareholders' agreement.

---

[128] In the case of a private company, see also the Model Articles, reg 27 of sch 1, and for a plc, see Model Articles, reg 65 of sch 3. In such circumstances, the prohibition on registering unless a proper instrument of transfer has been delivered does not apply.

[129] *Cottrell v King* [2004] EWHC 397 (Ch), [2004] BCC 307 (Ch).

[130] See also *Tett v Phoenix Property and Investments Co Ltd* (1986) 2 BCC 99, 140 (CA).

[131] Ibid.

[132] *Holt v Faulks* [2001] BCC 50 (Ch).

[133] CA 2006, s 33(1) states that the articles bind the company and the members, meaning those who at any one time are the members of the company.

[134] *Russell v Northern Bank Development Corp Ltd* [1992] 3 All ER 161.

J. The US

Restrictions on the transfer of shares are widely used in the US in the context of close corporations. They are designed to limit who is allowed to participate in the business. Transfer restrictions can appear in a separate shareholders' agreement or be included in the corporation's charter or by-laws.[135] To be valid, transfer restrictions must first comply with the formal statutory requirements, namely: (i) that the terms are written in a separate shareholders' agreement or are included in the corporation's charter or by-laws; and (ii) are noted conspicuously on the share certificates.[136] In addition to these formal requirements, all transfer restrictions must be for a proper, or 'reasonable', purpose.[137]

Here, the three engineers drafted an article to be included in either the shareholders' agreement or Rovebi's by-laws. So long as this restriction is conspicuously noted on the share certificates, the formal requirements will be satisfied, regardless of whether it is in the by-laws or in a separate agreement. The only remaining question is whether the restrictions are reasonable.

Their desire is to provide a right of first refusal to the other shareholders for any transfer made during the life of the shareholder and also to restrict transfers upon the death of the shareholders to the remaining shareholders. The first type of restriction, the right of first refusal, is expressly provided for in the DGCL.[138] Although no type of restriction is deemed valid *per se*,[139] the courts have been 'broadly deferential to the decisions of market participants when they decide to place restrictions on stocks',[140] especially the type of restrictions that are expressly provided for in the DGCL.[141] The reasonableness of a restriction on the transfer of shares upon the death of a shareholder has already been specifically addressed by the Delaware courts. It was found that the company's purpose, which sought to 'maintain some measure of choice in taking in new shareholders', was a reasonable one.[142] In light of the deferential approach taken by the Delaware courts, coupled with the fact that both types of restrictions have already been upheld as reasonable, the transfer restrictions in the hypothetical would likely be upheld.

If the engineers decided to form a limited liability company (LLC) rather than a corporation, they would be required to adjust their articles to take account of the unique nature of the interests in an LLC. Whereas shares in a corporation are freely transferable, LLC interests are restricted as a matter of default rule. Under the Delaware Limited Liability Company Act (DLLCA), '[a] limited liability company

[135] Delaware General Corporation Law (DGCL), § 202(a)–(b).
[136] Ibid.
[137] See, eg, *Capital Group Companies, Inc v Armour*, 2005 WL 678564 *5 (Del Ch 15 March 2005).
[138] See, eg, DGCL, § 202(c)(1).
[139] See, eg, *Capital Group Companies, Inc v Armour* (n 137) at *6.
[140] Ibid at *8.
[141] Ibid.
[142] *Mitchell Associates, Inc v Mitchell*, 1980 WL 268106 (Del Ch 5 December 1980).

interest is assignable in whole or in part except as provided in a limited liability company agreement',[143] but the assignee of such an interest:

> [S]hall have no right to participate in the management of the business and affairs of a limited liability company except as provided in a limited liability company agreement or, unless otherwise provided in the limited liability company agreement, upon the affirmative vote or written consent of all of the members of the limited liability company.

Of course, the members of an LLC could construct other transfer restrictions in their LLC agreement, and the Delaware LLC Act provides that: 'It is the policy of this chapter to give the maximum effect to the principle of freedom of contract and to the enforceability of limited liability company agreements'.[144]

K. South Africa

Securities[145] in a company can be acquired directly from the company through an issue and allotment of shares or can be acquired by transfer from the holder itself. *In casu*, the focus is on the transfer of shares (and not the issue or allotment). Section 51 of the Companies Act 2008 is relevant in this regard and provides that a company must enter in its securities register every transfer of any certificated securities. The transfer has to be evidenced by a proper instrument of transfer that has been delivered to the company or was effected by operation of law. Section 51(1)(a)(iv) states that restrictions can be placed on the transfer of securities.

The position with regard to the transfer of securities is different for a private and public company. The Memorandum of Incorporation (MoI) of a private company must restrict the free transferability of its securities. The Act does not, however, prescribe the manner or form of restriction.[146] This restriction on the transferability of its securities relates to the situation where one acquires shares in a company from an existing shareholder who wishes to dispose of the shares.[147] The company *in casu* is, however, a public company. Unlike a private company the securities of a public company may be freely offered to the public and there is no requirement that the securities (of a non-listed company) must be freely transferable. A company is, however, able to restrict the transferability of its securities by imposing restrictions by way of the MoI. This can be done by way of a pre-emptive clause, which will be part of the company's MoI. This usually involves a provision that a shareholder who wishes to dispose of its shares

---

[143] DLLCA, § 18-702.

[144] DLLCA, § 18-1101.

[145] Securities are defined as 'any shares, debentures or other instruments, irrespective of their form or title, issued or authorised to be issued by a profit company'.

[146] Companies Act 2008, s 8(2)(b)(ii)(bb). See also *Smuts v Booyens; Markplaas (Edms) Bpk v Booyens* 2001 (4) SA 15 (SCA) (decided under the previous, 1973, Companies Act). If any restriction on transferability in terms of the company's constitution is not complied with, then the shares are not transferable at all. It is not clear whether this strict application will be followed under the Companies Act 2008.

[147] Section 39 deals with the pre-emptive rights of existing shareholders in private companies to acquire new shares, which can be excluded in the MoI.

must first offer them to the other shareholders pro rata to their existing shareholdings under the terms and conditions and the price as provided for in the particular provision.[148]

The 'by-laws' referred to in the present case study are probably similar to the 'Rules of the Company'. This is a new concept introduced by the Companies Act 2008. The 'Rules of the Company' are binding rules, made by the board, that govern the internal affairs of the company. The Rules are subject to the MoI and the Act and will be void if they are inconsistent.[149] No model or prescribed set of rules are provided by the Companies Act. The Rules can be more easily amended than the MoI. A special resolution[150] is necessary to amend the MoI whereas the Rules can be amended by the board, subject to confirmation by the shareholders by way of an ordinary resolution.

The Rules will generally deal with internal matters that are not addressed in the Act. Pre-emptive rights can therefore be part of the MoI or the Rules, and can also be incorporated in a shareholders' agreement.[151]

It would be possible to have an article similar to article 11, referred to in the case study, under South African law, and it could be included in the MoI or in the by-laws (or Rules in the case of South African companies). This restriction can also be made applicable, in this manner, in respect of a public company because although a private company must restrict the transfer of its securities in its MoI as one of the requirements to be a private company, a public company can, by whatever means such as the MoI or Rules, restrict the transfer of its securities. If a public company is not listed, there is no requirement that the shares be freely transferable.

As stated above, the position on the transfer of shares is different in the case of private companies, compared to public companies. If it was a private company, section 8(2)(b) requires that the transferability of securities must be restricted and if these pre-emptive rights are contained in the Rules and not in the MoI, the company will not comply with one of the requirements of a private company. It is important to note that this restriction applies not only to shares, but to all securities, which is a much wider term.

L. Japan

i. The Special Treatment of Closely Held Corporations

Unlike a public corporation, any change in the shareholding proportion of shareholders is likely to cause serious friction in a closely held corporation, particularly

---

[148] The courts are generally reluctant to restrict the transferability of shares: *Greenhalgh v Mallard* [1943] 2 All ER 234, 237 (CA); *Bellairs v Hodnett* 1978 (1) SA 1109 (A), 1139. See FHI Cassim (ed), *Contemporary Company Law* (Cape Town, Juta, 2012) 243. The pre-emptive provisions are usually elaborate and complicated. See *Harilal v Rajman and Others* (1633/2016) [2017] ZAKZDHC 3 (11 January 2017).

[149] Companies Act 2008, s 15(4)(a).

[150] Companies Act 2008, s 16.

[151] Section 15(7) of the Companies Act 2008 regulates shareholders' agreements. See also *De Freitas v Chamdor Meat Packers (Pty) Ltd* 2015 JDR 1934 (GJ).

in connection with its organisation and management. Therefore, modern companies often include special provisions in their constitutions to regulate any changes in the proportions of their share capital.

The Companies Act 2005 (CA) in Japan sets out many provisions to protect the close nature of the company, in particular, by providing a comprehensive series of procedures for the transfer of shares. For example, the articles of incorporation of a company may determine that the company's approval is required for any purported acquisition by assignment of any of the shares it issues.[152] Any such shares requiring the company's approval are called 'Shares with Restrictions on Transfer'.[153]

Rather confusingly, the CA employs the word 'acquisition' to include both the transfer of shares by assignment and by general succession such as inheritance, merger and corporate divestiture. The CA in Japan regulates comprehensively changes in shareholdings both by assignment and general succession.

ii. Sale/Transfer of Shares

If a company decides to restrict the free transferability of its issued shares, it is required to amend the articles of incorporation by special majority voting in a general meeting.[154] The company is required to publish the amended articles of incorporations in the register book.[155] If a shareholder owning shares with restricted transferabil-ity intends to sell its shares to another shareholder or a third party, the transferor/shareholder may request that the company approve the proposed transfer. To enable the company to make such a decision, the transferor/shareholder must disclose mate-rial information such as the name of transferee, the class and number of shares to be transferred, and that the designation of a purchaser if the company determines not to give approval to the proposed transfer.[156] If the company fails to give notice to the transferor/shareholder within two weeks from when the company received the request, the company is deemed to have given its approval to the proposed transfer.[157] If the company decides not to give its approval to the transferor/shareholder, the company is required to purchase the proposed shares itself or to designate a person who can purchase the proposed shares (designated purchaser).[158]

If a transferor/shareholder has already sold its shares to another person without the approval of the company, the acquirer may request that the company give its approval to the transfer and that the company purchase the shares or designate a person who can purchase the shares.[159] The sale of the shares without the company's approval is effective between the parties to the sale because it does not deprive the shareholder of

---

[152] CA, Art 107(1).
[153] CA, Art 2(17).
[154] CA, Art 309(3)(i). The required supermajority is two-thirds unless a higher proportion is provided for in the articles.
[155] CA, Art 911(3)(vii).
[156] CA, Art 138.
[157] CA, Art 145.
[158] CA, Art 140.
[159] CA, Art 137.

an opportunity to participate in his or her investment.[160] Meanwhile, if the transferor/shareholder or transferee asked the company to approve a sale and the company takes the decision to purchase the shares itself, the company is required to obtain a special majority resolution at a shareholders' meeting.[161] The company or the designated purchaser is required to give notice to the transferor/shareholder or the transferee/acquirer by depositing the consideration for the proposed purchase of the shares based upon calculating the price of the net asset value per share.[162] When the company or the designated purchaser serves notice to the company or the transferee/acquirer, the law deems the contract for the sale of the proposed shares to have been effective at the time of notice. After having received the notice, both parties enter into an agreement for the sale of the shares, including the price. If the price offered does not satisfy the transferor/shareholder or the transferee/acquirer, either party may raise an action with the court to determine the sales price.[163] When an action for the determination of the price is raised, the court is required to take into consideration the company's financial situation.[164]

iii. 'Pre-emption' and 'Call Option' Clauses in Shareholders' Agreement

In practice, a company may enter into a shareholders' agreement to protect the close nature of the corporation. For example, if a shareholder seeks to sell or transfer shares which have a restriction on their transferability, he or she is required to give a notice to the other shareholders before the sale is concluded and such other shareholders have pre-emption rights to purchase the shares. This arrangement is legally effective; however, it is important to set out a method for the determination of the sale price on the exercise of the pre-emption right.[165]

A shareholders' agreement may also include a 'call option' clause therein. For example, if a shareholder owning shares with restricted transferability dies and his or her son succeeds him or her as a shareholder, the successor is required to sell those shares to the other shareholders of the company. Alternatively, if an employee/shareholder resigned from the company, the employee/shareholder is required to sell his or her shares to other shareholders, typically at the book value of the shares.[166] Such a shareholders' agreement is legally valid as a contract in general.

---

[160] Supreme Court, 15 June 1973, *Minshu*, vol 27 no 6 at 700.
[161] CA, Arts 140(2) and 309(2)(i). The required supermajority is two-thirds unless a higher proportion is provided for in the articles.
[162] CA, Arts 141–42.
[163] CA, Art 144.
[164] CA, Arts 144 and 870.
[165] K Egashira, *Kabushikigaisha-hô [Laws of Stock Corporations]* (7th edn, Tokyo, Yuhikaku, 2017) 243–44.
[166] The courts have ruled a number of times that a shareholders' agreement is valid on the ground that all of the parties to the agreement have understood it before entering into it. See, eg, Supreme Court, 17 February 2009, *HanreiJiho*, no 2038 at 144; Tokyo High Court, 29 June 1993, *HanreiJiho*, no 1465 at 146.

III. Conclusion

A. The Different Categories of Clauses in Companies' By-laws which Place Limitations on the Right to Transfer Shares

The comparative analysis provides useful insights into the scope and mechanics of limitations on the right to transfer shares in the jurisdictions under investigation. Before examining the different problems addressed in the hypothetical case in more detail, a preliminary matter that deserves attention is that of the various categories of clauses in a company's by-laws that limit the ability of shareholders to transfer their shares. In the jurisdictions under scrutiny, it is common for the limitations to belong to two different families: on the one hand, we have provisions that have particular traits in common with Italian pre-emption clauses, while on the other hand, we have clauses that make the transfer of shares conditional upon the approval of an organ of the company such as the shareholders' general meeting or, alternatively, that require the transferee to fulfil certain requirements to acquire ownership of the shares.

B. The Permissibility of Pre-emption Clauses in By-laws and Other Limitations on the Right to Transfer Shares

France, Spain and the Netherlands are the countries that are most similar to the Italian approach in dealing with the validity of limitations on the right to transfer shares. These three countries commonly accept pre-emption clauses in by-laws, although, as will be shown below, the legal consequences attached to these clauses may differ.

Common law jurisdictions, like the UK and Delaware, recognise the validity of pre-emption clauses. However, these two jurisdictions differ in that, while in the UK it appears that no general limitations are imposed on the inclusion of restrictions on the shareholder's right to transfer shares in non-listed companies,[167] in Delaware any limitation on the right to transfer shares must be made for a proper or reasonable purpose and is subject to *ex post* judicial review. South Africa, which in matters of company law has strong ties with common law countries,[168] also provides for the possibility to restrict the transferability of shares using pre-emption clauses.[169]

Polish and Latvian law recognise the validity of pre-emption clauses in the case of public companies. However, for these two countries, it is worth pointing out that in the relevant rules on the limitations of the shareholder's right to transfer shares,

---

[167] It is also worth noting that in the UK, before 1980, it was mandatory for private companies to include provisions in their by-laws that gave a right of first refusal to the existing shareholders. Thus, we may see here a decrease in the importance of clauses functionally similar to Italian pre-emption clauses.

[168] See also ch 12 and ch 13, below.

[169] Despite the fact that the South-African courts are generally reluctant to restrict the transferability of shares.

a greater degree of emphasis is apparently given to clauses that require the prior approval of the transfer.

On the opposite side of the spectrum, some legal systems do not allow shareholders to include pre-emption clauses in the by-laws of their companies: this is the case in Germany, Finland and, apparently, Japan. These three countries, however, permit provisions that make the transfer of the shares dependent upon approval. In particular, the Finnish approach deserves attention: if examined in light of a functional approach to company law, it can be seen that here redemption clauses may play a role that is similar to that of pre-emption clauses.[170]

C. The Consequences of an Alienation of Shares Made in Violation of a Limitation on the Right to Transfer Shares in a Company's By-laws

Turning to the legal effect of a share transfer made in breach of limitations included in a company's by-laws – and in particular pre-emption clauses – the solutions adopted by the examined jurisdictions commonly seek to strike a balance between, on the one hand, the interests of the parties and certainty in upholding the validity of the transfer, and, on the other hand, the interests of the company and of the other shareholders in ensuring that the shares are not freely circulated. Some jurisdictions treat share transfers that are made in breach of a pre-emption clause as invalid, like, apparently, the Netherlands, or void – for example, this is the solution adopted in France for the SAS. This approach is also followed in Germany for share transfers made in breach of a clause that imposes an obligation to attain prior approval of the transfer, which are considered invalid.[171]

However, unlike the position in German law, in other jurisdictions, a share transfer made in violation of a pre-emption clause is treated as valid and has legally binding effect between the parties to the share transfer contract. Nevertheless, these jurisdictions take the view that these share transfers are of no legal effect vis-a-vis the company itself.[172]

D. The Differing Consequences of Limitations on the Right to Transfer Shares Being Contained in a Company's By-laws or a Shareholders' Agreement

Another issue raised by the hypothetical case is whether different legal effects and consequences attach to pre-emption clauses depending upon whether they are included

---

[170] In fact, redemption clauses are accepted in Finland but operate in a different way from pre-emption clauses. Another example of the strict relationship between pre-emption clauses and the right of redemption may be found in France, where redemption of shares transferred in breach of a pre-emption clause is permitted in certain instances (cf the Italian approach to this problem).

[171] Interestingly, although Japanese law apparently does not recognise the validity of pre-emption clauses included in by-laws, it does recognise the validity of a transfer between parties made in violation of a clause that requires prior approval of the transfer.

[172] This is the solution adopted in Spain and – even if with some qualifications – France for SAs. However, in the UK, it has not been settled whether the transfer between the parties remains valid.

in a company's by-laws or a shareholders' agreement. In fact, many countries adopt the position that the same pre-emption clause would have different effects in such cases.

The most common approach (see, eg, Finland, Poland and Spain) is to treat provisions of shareholders' agreements as having no legal effect vis-a-vis the company, whilst recognising that the provisions of a company's by-laws would have such an effect. In a similar vein, UK company law distinguishes between provisions contained in the by-laws of a company and those that are simply a part of a shareholders' agreement by making it clear that the latter are binding only on the shareholders who entered into it and may not bind the company, whilst the former are binding on the company and on the present and future shareholders. Furthermore, German law makes a distinction between two particular situations: whilst the violation of a provision of a company's by-laws which imposes a limitation on the right to transfer shares would render the transfer invalid, a limitation included in a shareholders' agreement would have no such legal effect on the transfer.

An interesting solution is adopted by French law in the case of the SA: French law would not distinguish between limitations on the right to transfer shares included in a shareholders' agreement and limitations included in a company's by-laws. In both cases, the transfer would be considered valid as regards the parties to the share transfer contract themselves, but it would not have legal effect vis-a-vis the company.[173] The Latvian law too would not distinguish between by-laws provisions and shareholders' agreements, since the relevant Latvian provisions are mandatory and they would apply with equal effect to companies' by-laws and shareholders' agreements.

A pragmatic approach is adopted by Delaware law, where, as happens in France in the case of SAs, there is no difference in the treatment of pre-emption clauses included in a company's by-laws or in a shareholders' agreement. Both limitations on the right to transfer shares would have the same legal effect as long as the limitations were clearly noted on the share certificate.

Finally, in the Netherlands it is still not settled whether a pre-emption clause in a shareholders' agreement would have the same effect as a clause included in the company's by-laws. However, here, the trend appears to be one that recognises not only a contractual effect but also a broader 'corporate effect' to shareholders' agreement.

E. The Validity and Enforceability of a Pre-emption Clause which Gives a Third Party the Power to Decide the Purchase Price

The pre-emption clause in Rovebi's by-laws provides that any dispute between the shareholders pertaining to the price of the proposed transfer would be settled by a third party. Clauses of this type may become useful when a shareholder and a third party seek to circumvent the pre-emption clause by setting an artificially high price. As explained above, in the Italian legal system, a provision of this type would be considered problematic because it would make the pre-emption clause similar to a transfer clause, which requires the approval of the board or the shareholders to the transfer.

---

[173] However, a limitation on the right to transfer the shares of an SAS would be treated differently depending on whether it was included in the by-laws or in a shareholders' agreement.

Interestingly, in the other jurisdictions examined, this problem does not appear to be considered as relevant as it is in Italy. In Spain, a provision which permits a third party to determine the price for the shares is treated as valid. Likewise, in the UK, a similarly liberal approach is adopted: in brief, so long as the clause agreed on is 'unambiguous and clear', the matter would be left to the determination of the parties. Furthermore, in France, a similarly liberal approach prevails and the French courts have accepted the enforceability of pre-emption clauses that allow an expert to determine the price of the transfer. However, for artificially inflated prices, it would still be possible to invoke fraud as a rationale for a challenge. Finally, under Finnish law there are no obstacles to the insertion of a clause in the articles of association which would give a third party the power to determine the price if the parties were unable to agree.

F. The Types of Alienation Falling within the Scope of the Pre-emption Clause

An issue examined in the Italian solution concerned the nature of the types of alienation that may be considered as falling within the scope of a pre-emption clause. It should be noted that the other jurisdictions analysed pursuant to this project do not appear to be particularly concerned about this issue. However, one exception is Latvian law, where a distinction is made between sales on the one hand and gifts, exchanges and transmissions of shares on death on the other hand: the former may be restricted in the articles, whereas the latter may not. Another exception is Finnish law, where redemption clauses in articles of association are applicable to all acquisitions, including inheritance and transfers based on estate division, while consent clauses are interpreted more narrowly.

Finally, the only other two national solutions that addressed this problem adopt divergent approaches. In France, the concept of sale is very limited and does not take into account other types of transfer. Meanwhile, Japanese law adopts a broad interpretation of the concept of transfer. However, it should also be noted that here the analysis of the limitations on the right to transfer shares is made with regard to clauses that require prior approval of a share transfer rather than pre-emption clauses *strictu sensu*.

G. The Validity and Enforceability of Clauses in By-laws Limiting the Transfer of Shares on the Death of a Shareholder

Before examining the issues arising in the context of the validity and enforceability of clauses limiting the transfer of shares on the death of a shareholder, some preliminary comments should be made. In the legal systems examined, the law of succession does not limit *per se* the possibility of including limitations on the right to transfer shares in a company's by-laws. Confirmation of this conclusion can be found in the French legal system, where limitations of this nature are not treated as promises *mortis causa* that are prohibited pacts on a future succession (*pacte sur succession future*), but simply as *post mortem* clauses.[174] Even if we exclude the central relevance of the law of succession in assessing the permissibility of these clauses, the solutions adopted in the legal systems examined are heterogeneous and can be divided into three groups.[175]

First, there is a group of countries that do not recognise the validity of limitations on share transfers on the death of a shareholder. This is the position adopted in Germany and it is based on a general principle that shares should be freely transferable unless otherwise provided by the law.[176] A similar approach is followed by the French legal system in the context of the SA.[177]

Meanwhile, a second group of legal systems allows limitations on the right to transfer shares on the death of a shareholder. However, they also provide some protections to the heirs of the deceased shareholder. In Spain, for example, where the shares are initially transferred to the heir, the heir is entitled to receive the 'reasonable' value of the shares from the acquiring shareholders or the company itself may acquire the shares.[178] In Poland, a limited liability company's articles may limit or exclude the heir's rights to become a shareholder.[179] However, the validity of these limitations is recognised so long as the criteria for determining the sum to be paid to the heirs of the deceased shareholder is set out in the company deed. In Latvian law, it would not be possible to arrange the transfer of a shareholder's shares to the other shareholders in the event of that shareholder's death. However, it would be possible to provide in the by-laws that those shares ought to be transferred to the company itself. Similarly, Finnish law accepts the possibility of introducing a redemption clause in the event of the death of a shareholder in the articles of association.

Finally, there is a third group, which encompasses common law jurisdictions. Here, an even more permissive approach is applied, whereby limitations on the right to transfer shares on the death of a shareholder are permitted, with few protections given to the heirs. In Delaware, for example, a limitation of this nature on the right to transfer shares will be examined in light of a reasonableness criterion. Thus, there are no particular differences in the treatment of a limitation on the right to transfer shares on the death of a shareholder in comparison with other types of limitations. Likewise, UK law also embraces a liberal approach.[180]

---

[174] This principle was recognised in a case, which considered a limitation on the right to transfer shares included in the by-laws of a *Société à responsabilité limitée*.

[175] For further comparative analysis, see also S Kalss (ed), *Company Law and the Law of Succession* (Springer, Berlin, 2015).

[176] German law, however, allows – at least for GmbHs – by-laws to impose on the heirs that succeed the shareholder an obligation to transfer the acquired shares to the other shareholders.

[177] However, the position in relation to SASs is debated amongst scholars and remains unsettled in the case law.

[178] LSC, Art 124.2.

[179] See, eg, CCC, Art 183, s 1. This can be contrasted with the public company in Poland (*Spółka akcyjna*), where it is unclear whether the heir's rights may be limited, since it has been argued that such a limitation would be void on the basis of Art 941 of the Civil Code and Art 337 of the CCC.

[180] More precisely, in UK law, the right of pre-emption is converted into an option to acquire the shares.

H. The Determination of the Value of Shares whose Transferability is Limited

In the context of a discussion about limitations on the right to transfer shares, another point deserves attention, namely the methods employed by the different jurisdictions in order to assess the value of, and price payable for, the shares. In fact, a country may allow limitations on share transfers, whilst recognising that shareholders may have alternative exit strategies or be entitled to other forms of monetary compensation. This issue is particularly relevant in the context of the determination of the price to be paid by a third party where a pre-emption clause is engaged. However, this problem becomes particularly acute where the terms of the pre-emption clause do not necessitate a previous offer to sell the shares at a given price to a third party. This situation may arise in the following circumstances, namely: (i) where the company's by-laws impose a limitation on the right to transfer shares on the death of the shareholder; (ii) in the case of the exercise of a right of redemption of the shares; or (iii) when the company's by-laws require a party to give approval to the transfer of the shares and such approval is refused.

In the UK, it seems that shareholders enjoy a great degree of freedom in drafting the relevant provisions of the company's by-laws that determine the criteria to be employed in assessing the value and price of the shares. In Finland, with regard to redeemable shares, where the price of the transfer has not been previously agreed, the standard criterion of the 'fair price' of the shares will be applied.[181] Similarly, in Spanish law, in the context of limitations on the right to transfer shares on the death of a shareholder, the value of the shares of the heir will be determined in accordance with their 'reasonable' value, which in the case of a dispute amongst the parties would be decided upon by an arbitrator appointed by the board of directors in terms of Article 11.4 of Rovebi's by-laws.

According to Japanese law, where a provision of the by-laws requires a party to give its prior approval to the transfer, when such authorisation is refused, a shareholder is entitled to a right of exit from the company. The value of the shares is calculated taking as a reference the net asset value per share; alternatively, if the valuation is considered to be unsatisfactory, the court has the power to decide the value of the shares by taking into consideration the company's financial situation. Polish law also makes reference to the value of the net assets for determining the value of the shares in the case of redemption.

I. Conclusion

The solutions of the different jurisdictions examined demonstrate the current level of uniformity of the national company laws in this field. As stated above, the jurisdictions attempt to strike a balance between, on the one hand, the personal interest of a shareholder in exiting the company based on the free transferability of his or her shares and,

---

[181] In addition, if the price had been previously decided by the shareholders, judicial adjustments would be considered admissible at least under particular circumstances.

on the other hand, the competing interest of the shareholders as a group in maintaining an equilibrium amongst themselves and the similar interest of the company in preserving a shareholder structure with certain characteristics.

In general, pre-emption clauses play an important role in legal systems that emphasise the interests of the shareholders in preserving an equilibrium, whilst clauses which require prior approval of share transfers are probably more common in countries that attach greater importance to the interests of the company in maintaining a specific shareholder structure. However, the vast majority of the legal systems grant a considerable degree of freedom to the shareholders, and limitations on the right to transfer shares of a different nature are commonly permitted and are not treated unfavourably.

Another trend found in many legal systems concerns the different legal effects and consequences attaching to a limitation on the right to transfer shares, depending upon whether it is included in the by-laws of the company or in a separate shareholders' agreement. In addition, according to the company laws of some countries, transfers made in violation of a limitation in the company's by-laws will have legal effect between the parties to the transfer, but not vis-a-vis the company. Furthermore, limitations on the right to transfer shares on the death of a shareholder are also frequently allowed in the jurisdictions analysed. Nevertheless, when the transferability of the shares is restricted in the case of the death of a shareholder or for other reasons, many of the jurisdictions confer alternative protections, such as exit rights, in favour of the shareholders. This approach, however, creates an additional problem, namely how the value and price of the shares ought to be calculated.

In conclusion, this comparative analysis reveals that countries with the same legal origin tend to approach the issues raised by limitations on the right to transfer shares in a similar way. These comparable approaches, however, do not always result in analogous practical consequences: all legal systems display specific characteristics and the common trends seem to have a more general foundation that transcends the usual categorisations based on legal traditions and origins.[182]

---

[182] On these, see further ch 12 and 13, below.

Part 4

Conclusion

12

A Rule-Based Comparison and Analysis of the Case Studies

DAVID CABRELLI AND IRENE-MARIÉ ESSER

I. Introduction

Drawing on the data derived from the preceding ten chapters, a comprehensive comparative analysis can now be undertaken of the slew of company law rules identified in the 12 jurisdictions under review. The purpose of this exercise is to elicit a set of insights that make a genuine contribution towards the evolutionary progress of the subject of comparative company law. While the subsequent chapter 13 adopts a quantitative methodology to yield a series of findings – insofar as it codes company law rules, sources of company law and the product of such rules – this chapter will instead apply a rule-based comparative approach to produce a set of observations. Adopting a variant of the approach propounded by LoPucki specifically for comparative company law,[1] we identify the particular socio-economic and commercial problems in each of the case studies in the preceding chapters as our starting point. We then extract the relevant legal rules or principles applicable in each of the 12 jurisdictions from each of the case studies, and examine their nature, form and function, and how they seek to address these practical issues. Once identified, the governing rules are juxtaposed and assessed in order to achieve some higher purpose,[2] which in this chapter concerns the making of a meaningful contribution to four central propositions in comparative company law scholarship. A broader array of conclusions can be drawn from this process including the scrutiny of each of these four claims.

---

[1] L LoPucki, 'A Rule-Based Method for Comparing Corporate Laws' (2018) 94 *Notre Dame Law Review* (forthcoming). At this stage of the process, we apply steps 4 to 6 of LoPucki's methodology: steps 1 to 3 were adopted in the preceding 10 case studies, ie the formulation of a case study with a socio-economic problem or problems, the selection of a company entity type, and the application of the relevant legal rule or rules to resolve the case and produce a legal outcome.

[2] See HE Chodosh, 'Comparing Comparisons: In Search of Methodology' (1999) 84 *Iowa Law Review* 1025, 1049–52 for the proposition that there ought to be some higher purpose to any rule-based comparison.

We can evoke two themes that have been raised in contemporary comparative company law debates to explain in greater depth the textual and qualitative approach that we adopt in this chapter:

- First, relying on the division of comparative company law methodologies into seven distinct categories, each bearing a degree of relevance to the comparative exercise adopted in this and the following chapter,[3] we apply a complex amalgam of two of those seven strands. This will entail an evaluation of the *formal* company law rules recognised by the national reporters as applicable in their jurisdiction in the case findings, as well as the *effects and consequences* of the application of those rules. In essence, these two approaches involve rule-based and functional comparisons. The former enquires whether a rule of company law exists in more than one of the jurisdictions under review and is expressed in the same particular incarnation or form, whereas the latter is less formalistic and asks in what way the specific problems set out in the cases are tackled in each of the 12 countries in the same or similar ways, irrespective of the form that the relevant legal rules might take. The differences and similarities are then charted and the implications evaluated. It should be emphasised that each of these two instruments is applied in a selective and context-dependent manner. In certain cases, the method of formal comparison will be more appropriate as a tool, whereas in others, it will be the functional methodology that fits best.

- Secondly, we adopt the distinction between two particular categories that feature in the literature addressing taxonomy in comparative company law.[4] The first concerns the techniques for the evaluation of the differences and similarities in the form and function of the relevant legal rules that focus principally on the consequences for corporate law itself. This can be set apart from the second which involves consideration of non-legal factors. As will become apparent, two of the comparative company law themes analysed in this chapter are primarily law-focused in their nature – namely (i) the legal origins and (ii) convergence claims. These can each be distinguished from the two claims concentrating on the relevance of (iii) patterns of share ownership and (iv) shareholder primacy, both of which operate 'beyond the law', as such.

The beginning of section III sets out the anatomical features and precise steps of the rule-based comparative method applied in this chapter. The claim is made that the originality and significance of this chapter lies not only in the *nature and content* of the comparative results produced from the analysis of the governing rules drawn from the case studies, but also in *the assessment of their implications*. The novelty of the terms and effects of those results becomes all the more stark and insightful when they are compared with the results derived from the alternative methodological approach adopted in the subsequent chapter. In other words, having applied

---

[3] M Siems, 'The Methods of Comparative Corporate Law' in R Tomasic (ed), *The Routledge Handbook of Corporate Law* (London, Routledge, 2017) 13.

[4] M Siems, 'Taxonomies and Leximetrics' in J Gordon and W-G Ringe (eds), *The Oxford Handbook of Corporate Law and Governance* (Oxford, Oxford University Press, 2018) 228.

two differing comparative methodological approaches to subject the results drawn from the ten case studies to a measure of scrutiny, this and the next chapter adopt a kind of check and balance exercise to test the purchase of the respective comparative findings: the methodological techniques adopted in this and the next chapter are so diverse, that they may give rise to differing conclusions regarding the persuasiveness of the aforementioned four comparative propositions. As for the analytical rigour of the methodological approach employed, this is fully explained and justified at the inception of section III, with a particular focus on the four 'claims' tested in the comparative evaluations, to which we now turn in section II.

II. Aims and Implications of the Project and the Four Claims

One of the principal objectives of this book is to identify and understand possible differences and similarities in approach between legal systems in company law. By identifying the affinities between company law regimes as well as the extent, nature and scope of the disparities, the project has the potential to offer significant insights into the validity of four of the most central propositions in the field of comparative company law. These concern the claims that:

1. the pressures exerted by the increased pace of globalisation, international competition, interest groups, and imitation will inevitably lead to the convergence of company law rules (in terms of form or function) across all jurisdictions in the world, and in particular, assimilation to the US model of corporate law and governance ('the convergence claim');
2. the patterns and structures of shareholder ownership (dispersed/outsider v concentrated/insider) of listed public companies in a country's main stock exchange will influence the nature, content and strength of the shareholder protection rules applicable in that country ('the patterns of shareholder ownership claim');
3. countries have, and ought to have, a preference for a shareholder primacy model of corporate governance over that of a stakeholder or director primacy framework ('shareholder primacy claim'); and
4. the civilian legal origin of a country will influence the content, nature and scope of its company law rules to such an extent that it will be inferior to a country that has its origins in the common law with regard to the level of its shareholder/investor protection ('the legal origins claim').

Each of these four claims are cross-cutting and overlap to some degree, which may be attributed to the fact that each of them at some level addresses the extent to which a single, carefully prescribed framework can ever function as the optimal 'default operating' system of company law within a decontextualised environment. For example, stripped to their core, the legal origins and convergence claims concern whether it is practically and normatively sustainable for the company law rules applied in the Anglo-American common law system to claim superiority in formal and functional terms. As for the link between the shareholder primacy proposition and the claims surrounding the centrality of patterns or structures of shareholder ownership, these can both be understood as concerned about one of the ultimate questions in company law: namely in whose interests the corporation ought to be run, for instance the directors, shareholders generally, minority shareholders, majority shareholders, or creditors, etc, as well as the climate within which such a prioritisation of interests ought to be made and observed. For example, it is claimed that company laws in dispersed shareholder ownership regimes – ie where the patterns of shareholder ownership of listed public companies in a country's main stock exchange are predominantly diffuse – ought to be designed to protect shareholders as a class from the potential misconduct of directors, such is the latter's power. Conversely, the same claim puts forward the proposition that the corporate laws of insider corporate governance systems – ie where the patterns of shareholder ownership of listed public companies in a country's main stock exchange are predominantly concentrated in a few key blockholders – should be oriented around protecting minority shareholders from the possibility of controlling shareholders using their majority stake to misbehave and extract private benefits of control.

Since the legitimacy of each of these four propositions has a direct bearing on economic policy at an international[5] and national level, the extraction and analyses of the comparative findings (drawn from the ten case studies) that are presented in this chapter has the capacity to influence the shape of future legal developments. It is also significant for the investment potential of legal systems, since it is said that countries with more robust and sophisticated shareholder protection regimes are more likely to attract higher levels of inward investment. Since company law is one of the determinants of such protective capacities,[6] these results and their consequences assume importance. In the next section we present a detailed explanation of these four claims.

A. Claim 1: Convergence and Divergence in Corporate Law and Governance Systems

This work intends to make a contribution towards the convergence claim.[7] In 2001, Hansmann and Kraakman wrote a very important article arguing that the US model

---

[5] See, in particular, the 'Protecting Minority Investors' index of the World Bank's Doing Business Reports, www.doingbusiness.org/data/exploretopics/protecting-minority-investors, and the G20/OECD Principles of Corporate Governance, www.oecd.org/corporate/principles-corporate-governance.htm.

[6] Albeit only one; eg, securities laws, commercial laws, labour laws and inward investment rules are also going to have a bearing on a country's ability to attract overseas capital.

[7] JC Coffee, 'The Future as History: The Prospects for Global Convergence in Corporate Governance and its Implications' (1999) 93 *Northwestern University Law Review* 641, 679–80; DM Branson, 'The Very Uncertain Prospect of "Global" Convergence in Corporate Governance' (2001) 34 *Cornell International Law Journal* 321; JN Gordon and MJ Roe (eds), *Convergence and Persistence in Corporate Governance* (Cambridge, Cambridge University Press, 2004); B Cheffins, 'Putting Britain on the Roe Map: The Emergence of the Berle–Means Corporation in the United Kingdom' in JA McCahery, P Moerland, T Raaijmakers and L Renneboog (eds), *Corporate Governance Regimes Convergence and Diversity* (Oxford, Oxford University Press, 2002) 147–70; M Siems, *Convergence in Shareholder Law* (Cambridge, Cambridge University Press, 2008); J Gordon, 'Convergence and Persistence in Corporate Law and Governance' in J Gordon and W-G Ringe (eds), *The Oxford Handbook of Corporate Law and Governance* (Oxford, Oxford University Press, 2018) 28.

of corporate law would ultimately 'win out' in a competition with the more traditional managerial model of US corporate law and the stakeholder and state-oriented models of civil law countries.[8] Indeed, certain studies have supplied evidence of such convergence, with a number of factors such as securities law and stock market requirements coalescing to dilute the differences between company law regimes across the world.[9] This phenomenon is partly attributable to the growth of globalisation and, in particular, the pressures exerted by competition, interest groups and imitation. Convergence is not limited to growing similarities between the form, source and style of company laws. Instead, the phenomenon may occur at a number of levels, eg convergence in terms of the form or function of company law rules (ie specific rules designed to directly secure the protection of minority shareholders or creditors, or rules whose effect is to ensure such protection albeit indirectly (function)). Therefore, the evolutionary dynamic predicted by Hansmann and Kraakman and others is more nuanced and complicated than simply asking whether the form and sources of company laws have converged or are converging.

It is no exaggeration to say that Hansmann and Kraakman's article generated a reaction amongst comparative company law scholars across the world.[10] Many contested their arguments. For example, some commentators were of the view that the effect of regulatory competition amongst jurisdictions runs counter to convergence, leading inexorably to greater divergence amongst legal systems as each jurisdiction competes and engages in a 'race to the bottom' to attract incorporations.[11] Furthermore, cultural

---

[8] H Hansmann and R Kraakman, 'The End of History for Corporate Law' (2001) 89 *Georgetown Law Journal* 439; L Cunningham, 'Commonalities and Prescriptions in the Vertical Dimension of Global Corporate Governance' (1999) 84 *Cornell Law Review* 1133; A Chandler, *Scale and Scope: The Dynamics of Industrial Capitalism* (Cambridge, MA, Belknap Press, 1990); B Cheffins, 'Law, Economics and the UK's System of Corporate Governance: Lessons from History' (2001) 90 *Journal of Corporate Law Studies* 71, 76–89; R Kraakman et al, *The Anatomy of Corporate Law* (3rd edn, Oxford, Oxford University Press, 2017) 4–6. For criticism and commentary on this thesis, see A Winkler, 'Corporate Law or the Law of Business?: Stakeholder and Corporate Governance at the End of History' (2004) 67 *Law and Contemporary Problems* 109; C Williams and J M Conley, 'An Emerging Third Way? The Erosion of the Anglo-American Shareholder Value Construct' (2005) 38 *Cornell International Law Journal* 493; FA Gevurtz, 'The Globalization of Corporate Law: The End of History or a Never-Ending Story?' (2011) 86 *Washington Law Review* 475; M Walsh, P Spender, IL Fannon and K Hall, 'The End of the "End of History for Corporate Law"?' (2014) 29 *Australian Journal of Corporate Law* 147; Gordon, 'Convergence and Persistence in Corporate Law and Governance' (n 7); M Pargendler, 'Corporate Governance in Emerging Markets' in J Gordon and W-G Ringe (eds), *The Oxford Handbook of Corporate Law and Governance* (Oxford, Oxford University Press, 2018) 735. Hansmann and Kraakman have since written a reflection on their original article: H Hansmann and R Kraakman, 'Reflections on the End of History for Corporate Law' in AA Rasheed and T Yoshikawa (eds), *The Convergence of Corporate Governance: Promise and Prospects* (Basingstoke, Palgrave MacMillan, 2012) 32.

[9] Siems, *Convergence in Shareholder Law* (n 7); M Siems, 'Legal Origins: Reconciling Law and Finance and Comparative Law' (2007) 52 *McGill Law Journal* 55; see also more generally on the debate about convergence, BS Markesinis (ed), *The Gradual Convergence: Foreign Ideas, Foreign Influences, and English law on the Eve of the 21st Century* (Oxford, Clarendon Press, 1994).

[10] For example, a search in Google Scholar at https://scholar.google.co.uk/scholar?hl=en&as_sdt=0%2C5&q=hansmann+kraakman+%22end+of+history+for+corporate+law%22&btnG= leads to 2,250 citations as at 3 March 2018.

[11] RJ Daniels, 'Should Provinces Compete? The Case for a Competitive Corporate Law Market' (1991) 36 *McGill Law Journal* 138; P Rose, 'EU Company Law Convergence Possibilities after Centros' (2001) 11 *Transnational Law and Contemporary Problems* 121.

constraints, political-economic barriers[12] and the variations one encounters across jurisdictions in the legal rules on the protection of shareholders are other reasons advanced to explain why one ought to be sceptical about the potential for such convergence. Proponents of 'path-dependence' theory argue that the structure of a jurisdiction's corporate governance system and the shape of its company laws are conditioned by its cultural, social, economic and political past.[13] Hence, 'history matters', since once a jurisdiction has embarked upon a particular path, legal systems become 'locked in' to follow that same track and are conditioned by institutions built up within the system over the years. As a result, strong complementarities between different institutions in the system are generated, rendering it difficult and inefficient for that jurisdiction to suddenly shift direction by introducing an altogether novel set of institutions. For this reason, it is argued that the uniqueness of corporate governance systems ought to be strengthened and permitted to evolve organically in accordance with the existing legal, political, social and economic infrastructure.[14]

In what way can it be claimed that an analysis of the ten case studies will make a contribution towards assessing this broader convergence claim? The stated contribution can be made by adopting the fourth, fifth and sixth stages of LoPucki's framework for conducting exercises in comparative company law,[15] namely by (4) extracting the controlling or governing rules applied by the 12 jurisdictions under review to address a particular corporate or commercial problem, (5) juxtaposing them at close quarters, and (6) subjecting them to a comparative evaluation that is designed to detect exact or approximate convergence in the rules in terms of their forms or functions. The greater the number of examples of identical, approximate or similar governing rules that we can extract from the case studies, the more persuasive the convergence proposition will become. Of course, one of the limitations of this study is that the terms 'convergence' and 'divergence' incorporate implicit references to time trends which the methodology applied will inevitably struggle to cover, for instance in terms of whether and how the governing rules are similar or vary longitudinally over time. Nevertheless, there is evident utility in pursuing this approach insofar as some useful insights can be gleaned about the current legal position, which will provide indications of the purchase of the convergence claim.

---

[12] Cheffins, 'Putting Britain on the Roe Map' (n 7); Gordon and Roe, Convergence and Persistence in Corporate Governance (n 7); MJ Roe and M Vatiero, 'Corporate Governance and Its Political Economy' in J Gordon and W-G Ringe (eds), *The Oxford Handbook, of Corporate Law and Governance* (Oxford, Oxford University Press, 2018) 56.

[13] See B Cheffins, *Corporate Ownership and Control: British Business Transformed* (Oxford, Oxford University Press, 2008) 55–56; MJ Roe, 'Chaos and Evolution in Law and Economics' (1996) 109 *Harvard Law Review* 641, 653–60; RJ Gilson, 'Corporate Governance and Economic Efficiency: When Do Institutions Matter?' (1996) 74 *Washington University Law Quarterly* 327, 329–34; JC Coffee, 'The Future as History: The Prospects for Global Convergence in Corporate Governance and its Implications' (1999) 93 *Northwestern University Law Review* 641, 646–47, 660–61.

[14] LA Bebchuk and MJ Roe, 'A Theory of Path Dependence in Corporate Ownership and Governance' (1999) 52 *Stanford Law Review* 127; UC Braendle and J Noll, 'On the Convergence of National Corporate Governance Systems' (2006) 17 *Journal of Interdisciplinary Economics* 57; MJ Roe, 'Some Differences in Corporate Structure in Germany, Japan and United States' (1993) 102 *Yale Law Journal* 1928; Gilson, 'Corporate Governance and Economic Efficiency' (n 13).

[15] LoPucki, 'A Rule-Based Method for Comparing Corporate Laws' (n 1).

B. Claim 2: Share Ownership Structures and Patterns

The above-mentioned phenomenon is closely connected to the divergence in the patterns and structure of share ownership of the largest listed companies one finds in common law and civil law countries. In the capitalist market economies of common law jurisdictions such as the UK and the US, which are categorised as 'liberal market economies' in the 'varieties of capitalism' literature in the field of comparative political economy,[16] the corporate governance system is referred to as an 'outsider/arm's length' system of ownership and control. Ownership of the stakes of large public corporations quoted on the capital markets in such systems is widely dispersed with a general absence of dominant controlling shareholders.[17] Where a majority shareholder does exist, its holding expressed as a percentage of the total number of shares in a listed company tends to be low. This can be contrasted with 'coordinated market economies', in the varieties of capitalism literature where the corporate governance system is 'insider/control-oriented' in nature. This taxonomy roughly maps onto the company law regimes of the civil law jurisdictions where the share ownership of public corporations is concentrated in a single or a few blockholder controlling shareholders.[18] The patterns of shareholder ownership claim maintains that such systems tend to be characterised by weak minority shareholder protection, a phenomenon which is largely attributable to the ability of controlling shareholders to extract private benefits by virtue of their dominance and control.

The evidence for this division between dispersed and concentrated patterns of share ownership in common law and civil law countries can be found in the work of Stulz[19] and Franks & Mayer.[20] An article by Stulz published in 2005 sets out the

---

[16] See AP Hall and D Soskice, *Varieties of Capitalism: The Institutional Foundations of Comparative Advantage* (Oxford, Oxford University Press, 2001); B Hancké, M Rhodes and M Thatcher, *Beyond Varieties of Capitalism: Conflict, Contradictions, and Complementarities in the European Economy* (Oxford, Oxford University Press, 2007); D Hope and D Soskice, 'Growth Models, Varieties of Capitalism and Macroeconomics' (2016) 44 *Politics and Society* 209.

[17] See J Franks and C Mayer, 'Evolution of Ownership and Control Around the World: The Changing Face of Capitalism' ECGI Finance Working Paper No 503/2017, at 32–33, figs 13 and 16; S Deakin, R Hobbs, S Konzelmann and F Wilkinson, 'Anglo-American Corporate Governance and the Employment Relationship: A Case to Answer?' (2006) 4 *Socio-Economic Review* 155, 159–60; K Hopt, 'Comparative Corporate Governance: The State of the Art and International Regulation' (2011) 59 *American Journal of Comparative Law* 1, 9.

[18] See, eg, Kraakman et al, *The Anatomy of Corporate Law* (n 8) 24–28; M Becht and C Mayer, 'Introduction' in F Barca and M Becht (eds), *The Control of Corporate Europe* (Oxford, Oxford University Press, 2001); M Faccio and LHP Lang, 'The Ultimate Ownership of Western European Corporations' (2002) 65 *Journal of Financial Economics* 365; S Claessens, S Djankov and LHP Lang, 'The Separation of Ownership and Control in East Asian Corporations' (2000) 58 *Journal of Financial Economics* 81; R La Porta, F Lopez-de-Silanes, A Shleifer and R Vishny, 'Corporate Ownership Around the World' (1999) 54 *Journal of Finance* 471; RJ Gilson, 'Controlling Shareholders and Corporate Governance: Complicating the Comparative Taxonomy' (2006) 119 *Harvard Law Review* 1641.

[19] RM Stulz, 'The Limits of Financial Globalisation' (2005) 60 *Journal of Finance* 1595. See also G Aminadav and E Papaioannou, 'Corporate Control Around the World', NBER WP 23101 (Dec 2016) (figs 4a, 4b: Type of Control in 2012, 2007).

[20] Franks and Mayer, 'Evolution of Ownership and Control Around the World' (n 17). See also B Cheffins, 'The Undermining of UK Corporate Governance(?)' (2013) 33 *Oxford Journal of Legal Studies* 503; B Cheffins, SA Bank and H Wells, 'Questioning "Law and Finance": US Stock Market Development, 1930–70' (2013) 55 *Business History* 601; W-G Ringe, 'Changing Law and Ownership Patterns in Germany:

equally weighted (EW) and value-weighted (VW) average percentages of shares held by corporate insiders across countries in 2002, where shares held by corporate insiders are proxied by the block holdings reported by Worldscope.[21] As one would expect, in jurisdictions such as the UK and the US, the average stakes of the largest shareholders are low expressed as a percentage of total share ownership, in comparison with the position in Germany, Italy, Spain and France, where the stakes are much higher. Likewise, data provided by Franks and Mayer brings the findings up to the year 2012 regarding the average shareholding of controlling shareholders.[22] Once again, the average stakes of controlling shareholders in civilian jurisdictions such as Germany, Poland, Italy, France and Latvia are much higher than those found in the UK, Ireland and US.

The reason that such evidence is important is that the patterns of share ownership claim argues that the main focus of company laws in dispersed/outsider jurisdictions such as the UK and US is, and ought to be, on protecting shareholders as a class from the conduct of managers and directors that are prejudicial to the former's interests, the latter being in a position to further their own positions at the expense of the former.[23] Furthermore, a large degree of emphasis is placed on corporate disclosure and market control by outsiders. However, since the governance of companies in 'insider/control-oriented' systems tends to be closely coordinated between management and the blockholding controlling shareholders, many commentators[24] adhering to the patterns of shareholder ownership claim contend that company law protections in civil law jurisdictions ought to be – and in actual fact are – designed to protect minority shareholders. The argument runs that the 'agency costs' which arise in civilian 'insider/control-oriented' jurisdictions are horizontal, ie attributable to a misalignment in the interests of majority shareholders and minority shareholders, rather than a vertical misalignment between the interests of directors and shareholders generally as a class, which is predominant in common law jurisdictions.

Corporate Governance and the Erosion of Deutschland AG' (2015) 63 *American Journal of Comparative Law* 493; J Franks, C Mayer and H Miyajima, 'The Ownership of Japanese Corporations in the 20th Century' ECGI Finance Working Paper No 410/2014; K Reddy, N Mirza and Y Yin, 'The Relationship Between Ownership Identity, Ownership Concentration and Firm Operating Efficiency: Evidence from China 2005–2012' available at https://ssrn.com/abstract=2479274: each of these papers and articles comment on the UK, German, Japanese and Chinese positions in much greater detail. For the contrary argument that the US is no longer a dispersed shareholder ownership system, see RJ Gilson and JN Gordon, 'The Agency Costs of Agency Capitalism: Activist Investors and the Revaluation of Governance Rights' (2013) 113 *Columbia Law Review* 863.

[21] Stulz, 'The Limits of Financial Globalisation' (n 19) 1604 at fig 4. Franks and Mayer (n 17) also document the evolution of ownership and control of firms around the world over a 100-year period from the beginning of the 20th century to the present day.

[22] Franks and Mayer, 'Evolution of Ownership and Control Around the World' (n 17) 32–33, figs 13 and 16.

[23] Kraakman et al, *The Anatomy of Corporate Law* (n 8) 2 and 29–32.

[24] See Kraakman et al, *The Anatomy of Corporate Law* (n 8) 29–32; Cheffins, *Corporate Ownership and Control* (n 13) 4–7; E Berglöf, 'A Note on the Typology of Financial Systems' in K Hopt and E Wymeersch (eds), *Comparative Corporate Governance: Essays and Materials* (Berlin, De Gruyter, 1997) 151–64; J Armour, S Deakin and S Konzelmann, 'Shareholder Primacy and the Trajectory of UK Corporate Governance' (2003) 41 *British Journal of Industrial Relations* 531, 533.

In order to understand the possible 'agency costs' at play in a listed public company, it is also useful to consider Kraakman et al,[25] who expound a tripartite division of 'agency costs', namely between:

1. directors/managers and shareholders – 'vertical agency costs', which are prevalent in common law 'liberal market economies' such as the UK and the US where shareholdings are widely dispersed;

2. majority shareholders and minority shareholders – 'horizontal agency costs', encountered principally in civil law 'coordinated market economies' such as France, Germany and Italy, where shares are concentrated in the hands of a 'blockholder' or a few blockholder shareholders; and

3. shareholders and non-shareholder constituencies such as creditors, employees, suppliers, etc.

The debate as to which of the 'outsider/arm's length' or 'insider/control-oriented' systems of ownership and control is superior or more efficient has not been resolved: the jury is still out. The same can be said about the purchase of the central claim advanced by the patterns of shareholder ownership proposition that 'insider/control-oriented' civilian jurisdictions prioritise the diminution of horizontal agency costs whereas 'outsider/arm's length' systems such as the US and UK place greater emphasis on tackling vertical agency costs.

With its emphasis on case-oriented factual problem-solving across common law and civil law jurisdictions, the approach pursued in this book has the potential to test the descriptive relevance of the dichotomy struck in the literature between 'outsider/arm's length' and 'insider/control-oriented' systems of corporate governance. This can be best achieved by adopting a two-pronged approach. Firstly, the evidence from both Stulz's and Franks & Meyer's research will assist us in reaching conclusions regarding the share ownership patterns, stakes and structure of the 12 specific jurisdictions examined in this study. For instance, we can identify whether the US (Delaware), UK, Germany, France, Netherlands, Italy, Spain, Poland, Finland, Latvia, South Africa and Japan are outsider/dispersed or insider/concentrated systems. Secondly, the data derived from the ten case studies can be analysed alongside Stulz's and Franks & Meyer's findings. If the results from the ten case studies point towards the existence of legal techniques in civilian jurisdictions that prioritise or suggest a preference for the constraint of horizontal agency costs over vertical agency costs, this will furnish some support for the patterns of shareholder ownership claim adopted in the literature. Likewise, if the case-based methodology reveals that common law jurisdictions pay less attention to legal mechanisms whose purpose it is to restrict horizontal agency costs. The case-based approach is particularly well-suited to such an endeavour, since the solutions to the cases across the selected common law and civil law jurisdictions can be compared and contrasted in close juxtaposition where the interests of (i) majority shareholders and minority shareholders or (ii) directors and shareholders generally conflict with each other. The constituency favoured by each of the solutions can then be duly identified and evaluated within the broader framework of the patterns of shareholder ownership claim.

---

[25] See Kraakman et al, *The Anatomy of Corporate Law* (n 8) 29–32.

C. Claim 3: Shareholder and Stakeholder Theories

The debate concerning the normative role of the company and in whose interests it should be run is one of the most venerable in company law.[26] The most versed frameworks are those prioritising the interests of shareholders, stakeholders or directors. In shorthand, these are referred to respectively as the 'shareholder primacy', 'stakeholder' and 'director primacy' models. The shareholder primacy model[27] holds that it is a director's duty to maximise the wealth of a company for the benefit of shareholder welfare: shareholder wealth maximisation is thus the *ends* and fundamental objective of company law.[28] It can be contrasted with the stakeholder theory,[29] which posits that directors should run the company in the interests of a wider variety of stakeholders.[30] Finally, the director primacy model demands that the shareholders surrender power in exchange for the achievement of the shareholder wealth maximisation goal[31] and

[26] AA Berle, 'For Whom Corporate Managers Are Trustees: A Note' (1932) 45 *Harvard Law Review* 1365–72, 1372; AA Berle, 'Corporate Powers as Powers in Trust' (1931) 44 *Harvard Law Review* 1049–74, 1049; EM Dodd, 'For Whom are Corporate Managers Trustees?' (1932) 45 *Harvard Law Review* 1145–63, 1148; M Friedman 'The Social Responsibility of Business is to Increase Its Profits' *New York Times Magazine* (13 September 1970). For discussion, See Kraakman et al (n 8) 24–28;
[27] On shareholder primacy, see generally B Sheehy, 'Scrooge – The Reluctant Stakeholder: Theoretical Problems in the Shareholder–Stakeholder Debate' (2005) 14 *University of Miami Business Law Review* 193–240, 208 indicating that this does not mean that other parties (or stakeholders) should be ignored, but that shareholders should receive primacy when directors manage a company.
[28] However, shareholder welfare is not necessarily the same thing as maximising share market value: O Hart and L Zingales, 'Companies Should Maximize Shareholder Welfare Not Market Value' (2017) 2 *Journal of Law, Finance and Accounting* 247.
[29] The term 'stakeholder theory' was first used in 1963 at the Stanford Research Institute, although it can be traced back to work done by Dodd in the 1930s. See T Clarke, 'The Stakeholder Corporation: A Business Philosophy for the Information Age' (1998) 31 *Long Range Planning* 182–94; Sheehy, 'Scrooge – The Reluctant Stakeholder' (n 27) 200. On the stakeholder theory, see generally M Friedman, *Capitalism and Freedom* (University of Chicago Press, 1962); RE Freeman and WM Evan, 'Corporate Governance: A Stakeholder Interpretation' (1990) 19 *Journal of Behavioural Economics* 337–59; VS Baumfield, 'Stakeholder Theory from a Management Perspective: Bridging the Shareholder/Stakeholder Divide' (2016) 31 *Australian Journal of Corporate Law* 187; I Chiu, 'Operationalising a Stakeholder Conception in Company Law' (2016) 10 *Law and Financial Markets Review* 173 and SF Mansell, 'An Introduction to Stakeholder Theory' and 'The Philosophy of Stakeholder Theory' in *Capitalism, Corporations and the Social Contract: A Critique of Stakeholder Theory* (Cambridge, Cambridge University Press, 2013) chs 2 and 3.
[30] ET Penrose, *Theory of the Growth of the Firm* (3rd edn, Oxford, Oxford University Press, 1995) laid the intellectual foundations for the stakeholder theory in her concept of 'the company as a bundle of human assets and relationships'. See also Clarke, 'The Stakeholder Corporation' (n 29) 182–94 and JE Fisch, 'Measuring Efficiency in Corporate Law: The Role of Shareholder Primacy' (2006) 31 *The Journal of Corporation Law* 637, 647; MM Blair, *Ownership and Control: Rethinking Corporate Governance for the Twenty-First Century* (Washington, DC, The Brookings Institute, 1995) in the foreword states that corporations may be conceived as institutional arrangements for governing the relationships between all the parties that contribute company-specific assets, including, eg, employees who contribute specific skills (see also Clarke, 'The Stakeholder Corporation' (n 29) 171). See also Sheehy, 'Scrooge – The Reluctant Stakeholder' (n 26) 201 where he discusses the stakeholder theory, stating that economics and efficiency are not ultimate values and that the distribution of costs and benefits for society's resources are also important.
[31] Some of the literature is as follows: S Bainbridge 'Director v. Shareholder Primacy in the Convergence Debate' (2002) 16 *The Transnational Lawyer* 45; S Bainbridge, 'Director Primacy: The Means and Ends of Corporate Governance' (2003) 97 *Northwestern University Law Review* 546, 549; S Bainbridge, 'Director Primacy and Shareholder Disempowerment' (2005) 119 *Harvard Law Review* 1735; S Bainbridge, '*Unocal* at 20: Director Primacy in Corporate Takeovers' (2006) 31 *Delaware Journal of Corporate Law* 769; S Bainbridge, 'The Case for Limited Shareholder Voting Rights' (2006) 53 *UCLA Law Review* 601; S Bainbridge, 'Director Primacy' in CA Hill and BH McDonnell (eds), *Research Handbook on the Economics*

that the most efficient way for the corporation to achieve these ends is to concentrate management in the hands of the board of directors as the primary decision-making body in the company.[32] Seen from this perspective, although shareholder wealth maximisation is the *ends* of company law, a director primacy framework is the best *means* of achieving this goal. The shareholder primacy, stakeholder and director primacy theories are closely associated with the contractual (or contractarian/agency/*nexus-of-contracts*) theory of the firm.[33] The contractual model is based on the contractarian or agency theory, whereby the company is seen as a *nexus* of contracts.[34]

Jurisdictions such as South Africa and the UK have both recently introduced a framework known as 'enlightened shareholder value' which sits somewhere at a midway point, counterpoised between the shareholder primary and pluralist approaches or theories. Although the enlightened shareholder value approach provides for the protection of shareholders, other stakeholders' interests are also considered. However, their interests are subordinate to those of the shareholders. Ultimately, profit maximisation is the main goal of the directors and as such, the model is not entirely pluralist in configuration, to the extent that the directors would owe fiduciary duties directly to different stakeholders under the latter approach. In this way, the enlightened shareholder value and pluralist approaches both operate at some distance from the traditional shareholder-oriented understanding where the shareholders and their interests are the exclusive beneficiaries of the attention of directors when the latter manage the company.

of Corporate Law (Cheltenham, Edward Elgar, 2010); LE Strine Jr, 'Can We Do Better by Ordinary Investors? A Pragmatic Reaction to the Duelling Ideological Mythologists of Corporate Law' (2014) 114 *Columbia Law Review* 449; S Bainbridge, 'Director versus Shareholder Primacy in New Zealand Company Law as Compared to USA Corporate Law' (2014) *UCLA School of Law, Law-Econ Research Paper* 14-05; S Bainbridge, 'Preserving Director Primacy by Managing Shareholder Interventions' in J Hill and R Thomas (eds), *Research Handbook on Shareholder Power* (Cheltenham, Edward Elgar, 2015) 231.

[32] In the UK, eg, the company must have a board of directors regardless of its size in terms of ss 154–155 Companies Act 2006. The board is given the general authority to exercise all powers of the company for the management of the company's business in terms of Art 3 of the Model Articles for both private and public companies: see Schs 1, 2 and 3 to the Companies (Model Articles) Regulations 2008 (SI 2008/3229). This, it is argued, represents the default rule that the board of directors are the primary decision-making body in the firm, and as such are intended to be the focus of this nexus of contracts.

[33] On these theories, see generally, MC Jensen and W Meckling, 'Managerial Behavior, Agency Costs and Ownership Structure' (1976) 3 *Journal of Financial Economics* 305; EF Fama, 'Agency Problems and the Theory of the Firm' (1980) 88 *Journal of Political Economy* 288; EF Fama and MC Jensen, 'Separation of Ownership and Control' (1983) 26 *Journal of Law and Economics* 301; CA Hill and BH McDonnell, 'The Agency Cost Paradigm: The Good, the Bad, and the Ugly' (2015) 38 *Seattle University Law Review* 561; S Bottomley, 'From Contractualism to Constitutionalism: A Framework for Corporate Governance' (1997) 19 *Sydney Law Review* 277; A Keay, 'Directors' Duties to Creditors: Contractarian Concerns Relating to Efficiency and Over-Protection of Creditors' (2003) 66 *Modern Law Review* 665, 672; J Velasco, 'The Fundamental Rights of the Shareholder' (2006) 40 *University of California Davis Law Review* 407–67; H Hansmann and M Pargendler, 'The Evolution of Shareholder Voting Rights: Separation of Ownership and Consumption' (2014) 123 *Yale Law Journal* 100; for the theory that corporate law is also concerned with the minimisation of 'principal costs' as well as 'agency costs', see Z Goshen and R Squire, 'Principal Costs: A New Theory for Corporate Law and Governance' (2017) 117 *Columbia Law Review* 767.

[34] K Greenfield, 'The End of Contractariansim: Behavioral Economics and the Law of Corporations' in E Zamir and D Teichman (eds), *The Oxford Handbook of Behavioral Economics and the Law* (Oxford, Oxford University Press, 2014) 518; M Klausner, 'The "Corporate Contract" Today' in J Gordon and W-G Ringe (eds), *The Oxford Handbook of Corporate Law and Governance* (Oxford, Oxford University Press, 2018) 84.

The ten case studies and the conclusions drawn in respect of each of the 12 countries under review will be used to determine whether a specific jurisdiction is more in line with the shareholder primacy model, director primacy model or a framework that prefers the interests of the company's stakeholders' interests. Seen from this perspective, it is necessary to have a sound theoretical foundation concerning shareholder primacy and the more recent developments adopted by some jurisdictions involving the recognition of the interests of different stakeholders, such as employees, creditors and consumers. In the evaluation of the case studies the discussion will thus address whether a specific jurisdiction is more in line with models reflecting shareholder primacy, stakeholder protection or director primacy. A caveat should be sounded, however, that some of the case studies considering small private companies may lack relevance to this enquiry, since it may be that the shareholders, directors and stakeholders involved are bound up in the same single individual.

D. Claim 4: The Legal Origins Claim and its Critics

The 'legal origins' proposition is connected to the wider notion or theories of 'legal families' and 'path dependency' in the general comparative law literature.[35] The principal contention advanced by La Porta, Lopez-de-Silanes, Shleifer and Vishny ('LLSV') in a series of articles[36] is that corporate law regimes grounded in the tradition of the common law are more protective of shareholders than civilian systems:

> Compared to French civil law, common law is associated with (a) better investor protection, which in turn is associated with improved financial development, better access to finance, and higher ownership dispersion, (b) lighter government ownership and regulation, which are in turn associated with less corruption, better functioning labor markets, and smaller unofficial economies, and (c) less formalized and more independent judicial systems, which are in turn associated with more secure property rights and better contract enforcement.[37]

The argument posits that the direct correlation between regimes which protect shareholders and the sophistication of the state of the capital markets and financial development of a jurisdiction means that civil law countries suffer from a weaker level of stock market development. This has developed into a highly influential body of

---

[35] See, eg, M Siems, *Comparative Law* (Cambridge, Cambridge University Press, 2014) 41–93; U Mattei, T Ruskola and A Gidi, *Schlesinger's Comparative Law, Cases—Texts—Materials* (7th edn, Eagen, Thomson West, 2009) 258–64; J Husa, 'Legal Families' in J Smits (ed), *Elgar Encyclopedia of Comparative Law* (Cheltenham, Edward Elgar Publishing Ltd, 2006) 389; K Zweigert and H Kötz, *Introduction to Comparative Law* (3rd edn, Oxford, Clarendon Press, 1998) 72–73.

[36] See, eg, R La Porta, F Lopez-de-Silanes, A Shleifer and R Vishny, 'Law and Finance' (1998) 106 *Journal of Political Economy* 1113; La Porta et al, 'Corporate Ownership Around the World' (n 18); E Glaeser and A Shleifer, 'Legal Origins' (2002) 117 *Quarterly Journal of Economics* 1193; R La Porta, F Lopez-de-Silanes, C Pop-Eleches and A Shleifer, 'Judicial Checks and Balances' (2004) 112 *Journal of Political Economy* 445; R La Porta, F Lopez-de-Silanes and A Shleifer, 'What Works in Securities Laws?' (2006) 61 *Journal of Finance* 1; R La Porta, F Lopez-de-Silanes and A Shleifer 'The Economic Consequences of Legal Origins' (2008) 46 *Journal of Economic Literature* 285; S Djankov, R La Porta, F Lopez-de-Silanes and A Shleifer, 'The Law and Economics of Self-dealing' (2008) 88 *Journal of Financial Economics* 430.

[37] La Porta et al, 'The Economic Consequences of Legal Origins' (n 36) 298.

academic literature,[38] particularly via the Doing Business reports of the World Bank.[39] The ascendancy of the common law position is said to be attributable to a low level of government ownership and regulation of corporations, fewer formalised judicial procedures and the emphasis it attaches to the reasoned and incremental development of company law through a highly independent judiciary.[40] To claim that this scholarship is influential is undoubtedly correct.[41]

However, for obvious reasons, the 'legal origins' theorem has generated a great deal of controversy. The critiques[42] vary from concerns about the failure of the theory to consider the political determinants of corporate law and corporate governance systems to its deterministic and reductionist core of reasoning[43] and the adequacy of the methodological approach adopted by LLSV and the assumptions that underpin the conclusions drawn from the empirical results. For example, Roe refers to the tendency of governments of a 'left-wing' social democratic hue to favour the interests of labour over capital. In such systems, company laws protecting shareholders as

---

[38] The 'law and finance' literature is extensive: S Deakin and K Pistor (eds), *Legal Origin Theory* (Cheltenham, Edward Elgar, 2012); K Pistor, 'Law *in* Finance' (2013) 4 *Journal of Comparative Economics* 311; K Pistor, 'A Legal Theory of Finance' (2013) 4 *Journal of Comparative Economics* 315; GM Hodgson, 'Observations on the Legal Theory of Finance' (2013) 4 *Journal of Comparative Economics* 331; S Deakin, 'The Legal Theory of Finance: Implications for Methodology and Empirical Research' (2013) 41 *Journal of Comparative Economics* 338; M Siems, 'The Leximetric Research on Shareholder Protection' in J Hill and R Thomas (eds), *Research Handbook on Shareholder Power* (Cheltenham, Edward Elgar, 2015) 168; Siems, 'Taxonomies and Leximetrics' (n 4); R McQueen, 'How Corporate Law Matters: The Debate as the Interrelationship Between Legal Origin and Economic Performance' in R Tomasic (ed), *The Routledge Handbook of Corporate Law* (London, Routledge, 2017) 64; D Katelouzou and M Siems, 'Disappearing Paradigms in Shareholder Protection: Leximetric Evidence for 30 Countries, 1990–2013' (2015) 15 *Journal of Corporate Law Studies* 127; C Bruner, *Corporate Governance in the Common-Law World* (Cambridge, Cambridge University Press, 2012); B Cheffins, S Bank and H Wells, 'Shareholder Protection Across Time' (2016) 68 *Florida Law Review* 691; B Cheffins, S Bank and H Wells, 'Questioning "Law and Finance": US Stock Market Development, 1930–70' (2013) 55 *Business History* 601; AM Pacces, 'How Does Corporate Law Matter? Law and Finance and Beyond' in M Faure and J Smits (eds), *Does Law Matter? On Law and Economic Growth* (Antwerp, Intersentia, 2011) 297; AM Pacces, *The Future in Law and Finance* (The Hague, Eleven International Publishing, 2013).

[39] See www.doingbusiness.org.

[40] La Porta et al, 'The Economic Consequences of Legal Origins' (n 36) 286.

[41] R Michaels, 'Comparative Law by Numbers? Legal Origins Thesis, Doing Business Reports, and the Silence of Traditional Comparative Law' (2009) 57 *American Journal of Comparative Law* 765, 766.

[42] Some of the critical literature is as follows: MJ Roe, 'Corporate Law's Limits' (2002) 31 *Journal of Legal Studies* 233; MJ Roe, 'Legal Origins, Politics and Modern Stock Markets' (2006) 120 *Harvard Law Review* 460; M Siems, 'Shareholder Protection around the World: "Leximetric II"' (2008) 33 *Delaware Journal of Corporate Law* 111; J Armour, S Deakin, P Sarkar, M Siems and A Singh, 'Shareholder Protection and Stock Market Development: An Empirical Test of the Legal Origins Hypothesis' (2009) 6 *Journal of Empirical Legal Studies* 343; J Armour, S Deakin, P Lele and M Siems, 'How Do Legal Rules Evolve?: Evidence from a Cross-country Comparison of Shareholder, Creditor and Worker Protection' (2009) 57 *American Journal of Comparative Law* 579; RV Aguilera and CA Williams, '"Law and Finance": Inaccurate, Incomplete, and Important' (2009) *Brigham Young University Law Review* 1413; J Armour, S Deakin, V Mollica and M Siems, 'Law and Financial Development: What We are Learning from Time-Series Evidence' (2009) *Brigham Young University Law Review* 1435; K Pistor, 'Re-thinking the "Law and Finance" Paradigm' (2009) *Brigham Young University Law Review* 1647; J Armour and P Lele, 'Law, Finance and Politics: The Case of India' (2009) 43 *Law & Society Review* 491; S Deakin, P Sarkar and M Siems 'Is there a Relationship Between Shareholder Protection and Stock Market Development?' (2017) ECGI Law Working Paper No 377/2017.

[43] See R Schmidbauer, 'On the Fallacy of LLSV Revisited – Further Evidence About Shareholder Protection in Austria and the United Kingdom', available at https://ssrn.com/abstract=913968, 10–14.

a class are eschewed owing to the governmental preference to prioritise the demands of labour, which leads to a greater intensity in conflicts between the interests of shareholders and directors/managers. Greater opportunities arise for vertical agency costs which are attributable to the policy preferences of those 'left-wing' governments with a socialist tradition.[44]

Turning to the methodological deficiencies, the finding that robust shareholder rights lead to more effective and efficient capital markets and financial development was reached by LLSV on the basis of a limited range of coded variables and 'cross-sectional data on the [company] laws of countries in the late 1990s, with no systematic coding of legal change over time'.[45] Studies conducted on the basis of longitudinal time-series coding systems have demonstrated that the evidence for a correlation between legal origins and stock market development is much more tenuous.[46] Moreover, these studies revealed that the level of shareholder protection in civil law regimes has been catching up with common law jurisdictions in recent years.[47] Subsequent research has also identified many coding errors,[48] and when the index is re-calibrated to remove them, the correlations found by La Porta et al simply disappear.[49]

Moving on to the criticism of the assumptions underpinning the findings reached by LLSV, Pistor propounds three fallacies which lie at the heart of the 'legal origins' theorem. First, there is the 'extrapolation fallacy' whereby an unsubstantiated assertion is made that common law systems with stronger legal protections for shareholders invariably incentivise smaller investors to save their money in shares, leading to a broader investor base and greater capital market development.[50] Second, Pistor advances the 'transmission problem', which criticises the supposed unidirectional impact of legal origin on specific legal provisions in regulations, statutes and case law and more efficient economic outcomes.[51] Here, LLSV fail to address the possible feedback between legal origins, specific legal provisions and stock market development, ie reverse causality and the danger of drawing causal inferences from the data.[52] Finally, there is the 'exogeneity paradox' whereby LLSV assume that a country's legal origin is exogenous and thus independent of the political, social, economic and cultural context. Instead, there is evidence which shows that the state of a jurisdiction's stock market and economic development is dependent on a number of factors, including political and economic events and shocks.[53]

The case-based and rule-based comparative approach adopted in this work has the ability to offer some input into the legal origins paradigm. In particular, once extracted

---

[44] MJ Roe, *Political Determinants of Corporate Governance* (Oxford, Oxford University Press, 2003).

[45] Armour, Deakin, Mollica and Siems, 'Law and Financial Development' (n 42) 1437–38.

[46] Armour, Deakin, Sarkar, Siems and Singh, 'Shareholder Protection and Stock Market Development' (n 42).

[47] Armour, Deakin, Lele and Siems, 'How Do Legal Rules Evolve?' (n 42).

[48] S Cools, 'The Real Difference in Corporate Law Between the United States and Continental Europe: Distribution of Powers' (2005) 30 *Delaware Journal of Corporate Law* 697; U Braendle, 'Shareholder Protection in the USA and Germany – "Law and Finance" Revisited' (2006) 7 *German Law Journal* 257.

[49] H Spamann, 'The "Antidirector Rights Index" Revisited' (2010) 23 *The Review of Financial Studies* 468.

[50] Pistor, 'Re-thinking the "Law and Finance" Paradigm' (n 42) 1648–56.

[51] Ibid, 1656–59.

[52] H Spamann, 'Empirical Comparative Law' (2015) 11 *Annual Review of Law and Social Science* 131.

[53] Pistor, 'Re-thinking the "Law and Finance" Paradigm' (n 42) 1659–62.

from the ten case studies, the governing rules in each of the 12 jurisdictions under review can be measured and compared in terms of the level of shareholder, director, majority shareholder, minority shareholder, or creditor protection which they provide. This can be achieved by positioning the relevant rules alongside each other and then asking whether weak levels of shareholder protection correspond to those jurisdictions which are civilian, and strong levels in the case of common law jurisdictions. If the legal origins claim is valid, we would expect to find some correlation between common law regimes and enhanced rights and protection for shareholders generally at the expense of the protection and/or insulation from liability of (i) directors in respect of their decision-making and conduct, and/or (ii) creditors and other stakeholders. Although one cannot go so far as to contend that the findings of such a case-based methodology will operate to reveal the rationales for divergences in shareholder protection across the selected jurisdictions, there is considerable force in the view that it will serve to capture nuances in the level of shareholder protection which the cruder 'binary type' methodological approach of LLSV is unable to achieve. Moreover, it has the added attraction of possessing the capacity to expose the differences in the form and style of the legal rules which function to confer protection on the various constituencies whose interests are affected in each of the case studies. There are also clear overlaps here with the issues to be addressed in connection with propositions 2 and 3 above, as regards the prevailing pattern of shareholder ownership in a jurisdiction, and the orientation and nature of that jurisdiction's preferred theoretical model of corporate law.

III. Applying the Four Claims to the Hypothetical Cases

A. Methodology

The starting point to the methodology is first to isolate the relevant governing rule or rules (and their functions) applicable in each of the 12 jurisdictions considered in the ten case studies. These governing rules can be identified as the ones that 'correctly predict ... or produce' the legal outcome.[54] The extraction of the controlling rules is done on a case study-by-case study basis, with particular emphasis on the key corporate legal issues in the cases. Once abstracted from each of the ten case studies, in a similar fashion to the traditional rule-based comparative approach taken by the Common Core of European Private Law,[55] the controlling or governing rules (and their functions) are examined in close proximity to each other. This enables the

---

[54] LoPucki (n 1) at para [29] and D Crump, 'The Twilight Zone of the Erie Doctrine: Is There Really A Different Choice of Equitable Remedies in the "Court A Block Away"?' (1991) *Wisconsin Law Review* 1233, 1244.

[55] See the Common Core website at http://www.common-core.org/ with details of the Common Core approach.

similarities and differences between them to be articulated and is also viewed in light of the case study conclusions in each of chapters 2 to 11. In the case of each of these rules, when viewed alongside each other, they ought to be broadly comparable insofar as they should be directed to resolve the same set of facts, perform the same function, and produce a legal result. The important point here is that in each of the jurisdictions, it is the governing rules – rather than the legal conclusions, results or outcomes reached or produced – that are the primary subject of the comparative evaluation.[56] The subsequent exercise in rule comparison is very specific, as it is channelled through the prism of certain evaluative criteria. The aim of the application of these criteria is to offer up useful insights, and in this chapter, these evaluative criteria correspond to the four claims versed above. That is to say, that the end products of that formal and functional comparison will be dissected and explored in order to feed into each of the four central propositions identified earlier in this chapter, ie whether the particular rules and their functions suggest convergence of company laws, and what they have to say about the relevance and relative impact of outsider versus insider patterns of share ownership on company law. Further, this process will shed light on the constituencies and groupings whose interests are prioritised by the company laws of the 12 jurisdictions, as well as the relevance of legal origins to shareholder protection, stock market efficiency and inward capital investment. It should be stressed that in some case studies, the function and rule-based findings may offer no helpful conclusions or insights as regards any of the four claims. However, that will not always be the case as much will depend on the context. The irrelevance of some case studies can be attributed to them failing to touch on any of the issues underpinning the four propositions in question. It is perhaps also a by-product of affording the authors a free hand or licence to draft the case studies on their own terms without external interference.[57]

B. Claim 1: The 'Convergence' Debate

In this section III B, we focus on what the case studies can reveal about the force and purchase of the convergence claim. At the outset, it should be stressed that the fact patterns and results of case studies 1 and 2 in chapters 2 and 3 offered little insights into the convergence claim. For that reason, they are excluded from consideration.

i. Case Study 3 (Obligations of Directors in Takeovers)

The facts of case study 3 arise in the context of a takeover and address whether directors have the power to take action to ward off a takeover bid without interference from the shareholders. When the governing rules of the 12 jurisdictions are juxtaposed and evaluated, it is clear that they each recognise that the directors of target companies will

---

[56] However, this is not to say that the outcome, conclusion or result in the 12 jurisdictions will be irrelevant. As such, it will be taken into account as part of the evaluation albeit that it will not be the principal focus of the evaluative stage.

[57] See ch 1, above.

owe duties to the company where they attempt to influence matters to such an extent that a takeover bid is thwarted. However, notwithstanding that the EU Takeover Directive looms large and we would expect to find that each of the jurisdictions that are members of the European Union would recognise the board neutrality rule, instead, what we encounter is considerable divergence. This lack of uniformity is attributable to the existence of the opt-in and opt-out options in the EU Takeover Directive. Finally, in those jurisdictions that have accepted the board neutrality rule, we also witness a variety of governing rules that regulate the consequences of its breach. If we consider each of these findings as a whole, the conclusion can be reached that case study 3 supplies no evidence for the convergence claim. Instead, the various controlling rules of the 12 jurisdictions are notable for their diversity.

ii. Case Study 4 (Cross-Border Takeovers and Takeover Defences)

Case study 4 also covers takeover bids. It examines the liabilities of directors in the takeover context and whether jurisdictions recognise laws that require (i) shareholders (rather than directors) to decide on the rights issue of fresh shares and (ii) compliance with shareholder pre-emption rights on a rights issue of fresh shares, in the case of a shareholders' rights plan that is designed to ward off a takeover bid. First, the governing rules of each of the European countries on the regulation of the allotment and issue of shares are characterised by a level of convergence inasmuch as this activity falls outside the power of the board of directors and is reserved to the shareholders for decision. Likewise, rules are also found in each of the European countries conferring pre-emption rights on the allotment and issue of shares in favour of the existing shareholders. This is in stark contrast to the position in the US and Japan, where the directors are entitled to initiate share rights issues and shareholder pre-emption rights do not exist. However, the European jurisdictions vary in their approach to the ability of shareholders to waive or exclude their pre-emption rights. For instance, in the UK, no specific reason for waiver or exclusion needs to be given, whereas in Germany, Italy and Spain, the law imposes limitations on the potential for shareholders to do so. This divergence between the European countries becomes all the more the stark when the lawfulness of accounting for the interests of the employees in deciding on the shareholders' rights plan is placed under the microscope. French and German law would permit the interests of labour to be considered, whereas the opposite conclusion would be reached in terms of UK law. Once viewed in their entirety, the findings seem to neither substantiate nor challenge the convergence claim.

iii. Case Study 5 (Piercing the Corporate Veil)

Chapter 6 which narrates case study 5 addresses whether the 12 jurisdictions under review recognise the doctrine on piercing the corporate veil, ie circumstances in which the courts will look behind the veil of incorporation to impose liability on the shareholders, directors or other groups. It also addresses whether the 12 jurisdictions have a rule that recognises an individual as a director notwithstanding that he/she has not been formally appointed. Turning first to the veil piercing doctrine, with the exceptions of Poland and Latvia, this is an undisputed part of the legal firmament of each of the 12 jurisdictions. However, in each of the jurisdictions where veil piercing holds sway, a claim is rarely successful, either because the doctrine is only applicable in a limited range of circumstances (Italy and Finland), the conditions or requirements for its invocation are difficult to satisfy (Japan, Germany, Spain, UK and the US), or because other areas of the law are more effective in offering creditors relief (eg tort law in the Netherlands). Once again, we encounter divergence in both the recognition of the doctrine, as well as the extent of, and the conditions for, its operation. As for the existence of governing rules that acknowledge individuals as directors in the absence of any formal appointment, the position is mixed. The concept of a de facto or prescribed director exists in the corporate laws of the UK, Spain and South Africa, but other jurisdictions such as Germany and Poland prioritise formality in appointments and reject the unofficial ascription of director status. Here again, the findings suggest the existence of palpable variances in the approaches adopted by each of the jurisdictions. However, the opposite point can be made regarding the recognition of duties imposed on directors to monitor the conduct of other directors appointed to the board. In the majority of the 12 jurisdictions under review, the content of a director's duty of care will encompass such an obligation to monitor.

iv. Case Study 6 (Capital Maintenance)

The topic of this case study centres around the recognition of capital maintenance laws, rules controlling the payment of disguised distributions, and the regulation of managerial decisions to pay dividends. The US, South Africa and Japan do not recognise a capital maintenance principle – in the sense that capital can indeed be returned to the shareholders in these countries, subject to particular restrictions. As such, they are outliers to the extent that a capital maintenance doctrine does exist in each of the nine EU jurisdictions. Meanwhile, although the governing rules applicable in each of the 12 jurisdictions highlight the ubiquity of restrictions on dividend payments, there are marked variations in the nature of those limitations. Some jurisdictions adopt a 'balance sheet surplus' approach which can be compared to the 'earned surplus' approach applied in others. Likewise, the approaches towards the control of disguised distributions are characterised by an abundance of diversity, from a hard-line to more accommodating set of rules. Each of these findings are suggestive of little evidence for the convergence claim.

v. Case Study 7 (Shareholders and Shareholder Law)

This case study focuses on the legal recourse available to shareholders to challenge the failure of the company to pay a dividend, as well as the ability of shareholders to dispute a merger where a company fails to provide sufficient notice of a general meeting. With regard to the possibility of challenging the non-payment of dividends, there is considerable convergence in the 12 jurisdictions to the extent that they each have enabling governing rules. A variation can be seen in the attitude of those jurisdictions to the prospects of a successful suit, with some countries more protective of shareholders (Finland) than others (Delaware and Japan), such is the liberal orientation and nature of the former's controlling rules. Turning to the scope for shareholders to take legal proceedings to annul a merger, there is considerable convergence in the governing rules applicable in the 12 jurisdictions under review. In each country, this would not be possible, although the exact grounds for such a rule differ. As such, this case study so far is the strongest to provide support for the convergence claim.

vi. Case Study 8 (Abuse of Shareholder Rights)

The issues probed by this case study include the rights of shareholders to pose questions and demand answers at the general meeting of the company. The power of a shareholder to issue legal proceedings to block a merger approved at such a meeting is also raised by this case study. An examination of the governing rules applicable to the right to ask questions reveals a large degree of alignment across the jurisdictions with 11 of the 12 under review expressly recognising such an entitlement: the US is the sole country where this right is absent. The majority of the jurisdictions also empower shareholders to challenge resolutions approving a merger. However, a variety of conditions are placed on the assertion or successful application of such a right, some of which are general whereas others are tailored more to merger resolutions in particular. This gives rise to the conclusion that a material degree of legal convergence can be seen to applicable.

vii. Case Study 9 (Shareholders' Rights and Litigation)

In this case study, one of the central issues is whether a technical breach of company law or a company's constitution can be cured by the unanimous assent of the shareholders. The second key matter is the extent to which resolutions passed by the board of directors are subject to challenge by third parties who are not shareholders or directors. Finally, the case study considers whether shareholders are afforded the right to enforce a breach of a director's duties, for instance by raising shareholders' derivative proceedings or some other mechanism. With regard to the scope for curing technical breaches, a close analysis of the governing rules in each of the 12 jurisdictions reveals that most recognise a form of the unanimous assent rule (France and Italy are the exceptions). However, the conditions imposed on the operation of that rule differ; for instance, in some jurisdictions written approval is demanded and mere conduct is insufficient. To that extent, convergence is clearly applicable here. Likewise, each of the 12 jurisdictions denies third parties the right to challenge board resolutions, although the machinery adopted and reasoning for this outcome differs along the common law/civil law divide. As noted in the conclusion to this case study, this gives rise to functional convergence in the result, but formal divergence in the company law rules applicable. Turning to the possibility of shareholders challenging violations of directors' duties, derivative actions and other direct or indirect enforcement mechanisms are common to both common law, 'mixed' and civil law jurisdictions, as is the concept of controlling shareholders' fiduciary duties. However, as highlighted in the conclusion to the case study, there is considerable divergence across national boundaries as regards the party or parties against whom litigation ought to, or could be, raised, the nature of those legal proceedings, the nature of the remedy and the grounds for receiving such a remedy. In conclusion, there is clear convergence in the outcomes reached, but diversity in the rules that pertain in each of the jurisdictions, as well as the enforcement machinery and remedies, which suggests a complex amalgam of convergence and divergence.

viii. Case Study 10 (Limitations on the Shareholder's Right to Transfer Shares)

There are two principal company law issues examined in this case study. The first question is whether the 12 jurisdictions entitle companies and their shareholders to include and enforce shareholders' pre-emption rights on the transfer of shares in the constitutions of non-listed public companies. The second matter is inter-related, and probes the extent to which non-listed public companies are precluded from including provisions in their constitutions which prohibit or restrict the automatic transmission of the shares of deceased shareholders to their heirs or legatees. The vast majority of the jurisdictions will permit companies to include share pre-emption rights on transfer, but many impose diverse forms of *ex ante* or *ex post* restrictions or review on their application. However, in three countries, namely Germany, Finland and Japan, such pre-emption clauses are unlawful. To that extent, there is a modest degree of evidence for convergence. Having said that, what is particularly striking about the common law jurisdictions that recognise constitutional pre-emption restrictions on the transferability of shares is the comparatively few controls on such restrictions vis-a-vis the civilian countries. As for the legal validity of restrictions on the transferability of shares on the death of a shareholder, there is clear divergence in the approaches adopted between the common law and civilian countries. In the UK, USA and South Africa, very few (if any) checks or limitations are imposed on clauses which confer pre-emption rights in favour of shareholders where a fellow shareholder is deceased. However, this is not the case in the civilian jurisdictions where we encounter two distinct approaches. First, the position in Germany and France is that any restrictions on the free transferability of shares are not allowed. This can be contrasted with Spain, Poland, Latvia and Finland where such provisions are lawful, but numerous conditions are imposed. On balance, the governing rules of the 12 countries by and large suggest a lower degree of convergence than divergence in the legal positions.

ix. Conclusions

The findings to be drawn from each of the above case studies can be charted in a table.

Table 12.1 Results from case studies regarding the convergence claim

Case Study	Convergence?	Divergence?	Observation
3	x	✓	Mainly divergent
4	✓	✓	Mixed evidence
5	x	✓	Mainly divergent
6	x	✓	Mainly divergent

(continued)

Table 12.1 *(Continued)*

Case Study	Convergence?	Divergence?	Observation
7	✓	x	Mainly convergent
8	✓	x	Mainly convergent
9	✓	✓	Mixed evidence
10	x	✓	Mainly divergent
Total	4	6	Mainly divergent

What Table 12.1 demonstrates is that by and large, the convergence claim lacks substance. Indeed, the range of areas in which convergence is evident may be partly or directly attributable to European successes in harmonising company law. The results of this rule-based and function-based methodology are consistent with those produced in chapter 13, which in light of other mounting evidence, gives rise to the conviction that the convergence claim may be overstated. Indeed, if the authors were to hazard a view, it may well be that the convergence claim is simply a relic that has survived the initial post-Cold War period from which it is an abstraction.

C. Claim 2: Shareholder Ownership Patterns and Structures

This section III C which probes the validity of the patterns of shareholder ownership claim, is one of the main illustrations of the proposition made in section III A that the purchase of a number of the four claims II A to II D will not be assisted or advanced in any way by some of the ten case studies. In fact, this is one of the variables where comparatively few of the ten case studies have any bearing or anything useful to contribute: only case studies 2 and 5 have anything to offer by way of insights. There is also an irony associated with the fact that these two case studies are analysed for the purposes of testing this claim, which translates into an additional potential limitation. Case studies 2 and 5 cover private companies and non-listed plcs, rather than listed plcs. Since the fundamental premise of the patterns of shareholder ownership claim is that the characteristics of the ownership of shareholdings of the largest listed plcs in a jurisdiction will dictate the orientation of the controlling company law rules, this arguably leaves the methodology adopted open to the charge that the data produced from these case studies can only be irrelevant. However, this argument can be countered by the point that the governing rules identified as applicable in each of the 12 jurisdictions for the purposes of case studies 2 and 5 will nonetheless retain their relevance on the basis that they are the same irrespective of whether the company concerned is private or a non-listed or listed plc. For example, in case study 2, if the company concerned had been a listed plc, there would be no variation in the applicable UK company laws: the same point can be made about case study 5. As such, the fact that the governing rules would not change enables this counterpoint to be dismissed as overblown.

i. Case Study 2 (Duties of Nominee Directors)

This case study sheds light on the question whether shareholders will owe a duty to the company or minority shareholders when they exercise their voting powers. As discussed in section II B above, in 'insider/block-holder' systems of corporate governance where horizontal agency problems outweigh other agency concerns, the claim is made that the configuration of the applicable company laws ought to restrain the power of the majority shareholders – and not the directors. If this analytical framework is accurate, then a jurisdiction where the share ownership of public listed companies tends to be held in blocks, and not dispersed, should recognise legal rules or principles that impose a fiduciary duty on controlling shareholders that is owed to the minority shareholders or company when the former exercise their voting rights. In the final analysis, the findings from case study two will enable us to ascertain whether there is indeed a link between the pattern of share ownership of companies in a jurisdiction and the legal imposition of duties on majority shareholders.

In his article 'The Limits of Financial Globalization',[58] Stulz distinguishes countries with blockholder share ownership structures from countries where the share ownership tends to be more dispersed. His results are shown in columns 2 and 3 and the fourth column sets out the results that can be derived from case study 2:

Table 12.2 Results from case study 2

Jurisdiction	Blockholding[59]	Dispersed[60]	Is a shareholder fiduciary duty owed to the company or minority shareholders? No or Yes.
Latvia	✓ (78%)		NO RESULTS IN THIS CASE STUDY.
France	✓ (40%)		YES
Germany	✓ (51%)		YES
Italy	✓ (43%)		NO
Spain	✓ (51%)		YES
The Netherlands		✓ 23%	YES
Finland	✓ 31%		NO RESULTS IN THIS CASE STUDY.
Poland	✓ (68%)		YES
UK		✓ 11%	NO
US		✓ 15%	YES
South Africa	✓ (46%)		NO
Japan	✓ (41%)		YES

---

[58] Stulz, 'The Limits of Financial Globalisation' (n 19) 1604. See also Franks and Mayer, 'Evolution of Ownership and Control Around the World' (n 17) 32–33, figs 13 and 16.

[59] The standard adopted is that where the value-weighted average percentage of a single shareholder is > 30 = a blockholding jurisdiction. The mandatory bid rule in the law regulating takeovers is taken as a proxy for the relevant level of share ownership that constitutes a blockholding: the mandatory bid threshold is 30% in most EU Member States.

[60] Conversely, the position adopted is that a value-weighted average percentage of that is < 30 = a dispersed jurisdiction.

The countries *in italics* in Table 12.2 fail to adhere to the suggested link between the imposition of fiduciary duties on majority shareholders and the share ownership structure of a jurisdiction. In particular, South Africa and Italy are two 'insider/blockholding' jurisdictions which produce results that are in non-conformance with the underlying theory. Both South Africa and Italy have value-weighted average percentages of blockholder shareholders that are quite high, but neither of these countries recognise legal rules to the effect that the majority shareholders owe a fiduciary duty to the minority shareholders or the company when they vote. The US and the Netherlands are also outliers, although for the opposite reason. Both have a dispersed shareholder ownership structure, but the majority shareholders do owe a fiduciary duty to the company when exercising their rights. This fails to align with the underlying claim that the principal focus of company laws in dispersed/outsider systems of corporate governance will not be to subject majority shareholders to legal obligations to the company or minority shareholders. Taken as a whole, this exercise in evaluating case study 2 in chapter 3 demonstrates that the findings in respect of six out of the 12 jurisdictions are consistent with the patterns of shareholder ownership claim, whereas four of the 12 conflict with that proposition, and two of the jurisdictions are inconclusive.

ii. Case Study 5 (Piercing the Corporate Veil)

For the purposes of the patterns of shareholder ownership claim, the relevant issue in this case study is whether or not a majority shareholder can ever be treated as a shadow director and as such, be subject to directors' duties. If the theoretical proposition suggesting a link between patterns of share ownership and the legal recognition of majority shareholder duties is valid, the answer to this question should be positive in a system that is characterised by an insider/blockholder shareholder ownership structure. This is attributable to the majority (blockholder) shareholder having the capacity to exercise majority rule and instruct the directors on what to do. In contrast, in an 'outsider/dispersed' shareholder ownership system, since the shareholders are more diffuse, they would have insufficient powers of coordination to influence the behaviour and decision-making of directors, leaving the latter to exercise rule. The italicised countries do not adhere to this presumption.

Table 12.3 Results from case study 5

Jurisdiction	Blockholding[61]	Dispersed[62]	Shareholders treated as shadow directors?
Latvia	✓ (78%)		UNCLEAR
France	✓ (40%)		YES
Germany	✓ (51%)		NO
Italy	✓ (43%)		YES

(continued)

---

[61] >30% = a blockholding jurisdiction.
[62] <30% = a dispersed jurisdiction.

Table 12.3 *(Continued)*

Jurisdiction	Blockholding[61]	Dispersed[62]	Shareholders treated as shadow directors?
Spain	✓ (51%)		YES
The Netherlands		✓ 23%	YES
Finland	✓ 31%		UNCLEAR
Poland	✓ (68%)		NO
UK		✓ 11%	YES
US		✓ 15%	NO
South Africa	✓ (46%)		YES
Japan	✓ (41%)		YES

The findings set out in Table 12.3 reveal that for the countries *in italics* (ie Germany, the Netherlands, Poland and the UK) the governing legal rules do not conform to the patterns of shareholder ownership claim. In Germany and Poland, if the proposition were correct, then one would expect to encounter a legal rule in these jurisdictions that recognises that shareholders can constitute shadow directors and as such, owe duties to the company and/or minority shareholders. However, that is not the case. In the case of the Netherlands and the UK, the results are also inconsistent with the patterns of shareholder ownership proposition. The value-weighted average percentage of block-holders in the Netherlands and the UK is low, but there are legal rules that make it possible for shareholders to be treated as directors, which can result in liability for a failure to consider the interests of the company and/or minority shareholders. Turning to the jurisdictions that are not italicised, each of them bar Latvia and Finland (where the results are unclear) do indeed track the patterns of shareholder ownership proposition. In this way, the majority of the 12 jurisdictions conform, but a substantial minority do not.

iii. Conclusions

Of course, the findings derived from case studies 2 and 5 in chapters 3 and 6 provide a limited sample and are unrepresentative when expressed as a percentage of the total number of case studies, ie only 20 per cent. There is the added dimension of the corporate form of the companies covered by the two case studies, although that point can be closed off by the realisation that the governing rules in the jurisdictions would not change if the companies were listed plcs. The results are also mixed, with six of the 12 countries in case study 2 and six of the 12 countries in case study 5 exhibiting consistency with the primary claim that structures of shareholder ownership will dictate the nature and strength of fiduciary duties imposed on controlling shareholders. This is in comparison with four of the 12 jurisdictions in case studies 2 and 5 where no consistency between the orientation of the legal rules and shareholder ownership patterns could be discerned. Subject to the limitations expressed above regarding the lack of representativeness of the findings, on balance, they do cast a degree of doubt on the purchase and plausibility of the patterns of shareholder ownership claim. The best that can be said is that in the majority of cases, the claim will hold true, but in a substantial minority, the opposite will be the case. Of course, this is hardly a ringing endorsement of the underlying premise, which means that we perhaps ought to reserve a degree of scepticism about its accuracy and for the bolder claims made about its consequences.

D. Claim 3: Shareholder- or Stakeholder-orientated Approach

We now evaluate each of the case studies to determine whether the specific country in question leans more towards the shareholder primacy, stakeholder protection or director primacy models of corporate governance. This objective can be achieved by examining the governing rules for each of the 12 countries that can be derived from the case studies and then applying two subordinate questions, namely:

1.   Do any of the jurisdictions stand out in this context?
2.   What conclusions can be drawn from these controlling rules?

The product of the application of these questions are presented in separate tables on a case study-by-case study basis in the Annex to this chapter. As such, the detailed results and findings are not presented in this section. Instead, a composite Table 12.4 is presented towards the end of section III D setting out the extent to which the corporate governance systems of the 12 jurisdictions can be claimed to be predicated on a shareholder, stakeholder or director primacy framework.

i. Case Study 1 (General Case on Directors' Duties)

This case study primarily addressed directors' duties. Here, there are three issues that can be highlighted. First, whether there was a breach of the director's duty of care and skill. Secondly, whether shareholder ratification or authorisation is valid in the context of a breach of directors' duties. Finally, this case study also covers the extent to which creditors are protected in the 12 legal systems. Depending on how each of the jurisdictions dealt with these issues, it is possible to draw certain conclusions on their positions relating to shareholder primacy, director primacy and stakeholder protection.[63] For instance, a jurisdiction that recognises company laws that shield directors from liability for breach of their duties is suggestive of a director primacy system of corporate governance. In contrast, countries that permit shareholders to authorise a breach of directors' duties in advance, or to ratify such a breach *ex post facto*, are consistent with a framework that embraces a shareholder primacy regime. Finally, if it is not possible for directors to be insulated from liability for a breach of duty and the content of those duties specifically enjoins directors to further the interests of the company's stakeholders such as its creditors, suppliers, clients, employees or communitarian or environmental concerns, this provides some evidence of a stakeholder-oriented corporate governance system.

---

[63] See the discussion in ch 1, section III A, above.

ii. Case Study 2 (Duties of Nominee Directors)

The issues addressed in this case study do not make any useful contribution towards testing the validity of the shareholder primacy claim. As such, it is yet another illustration of the point made at section III A above.

iii. Case Study 3 (Obligations of Directors in Takeovers)

The facts of case study 3 enable us to extract findings regarding the force of the shareholder primacy claim, specifically in the context of a takeover. In some jurisdictions, the takeover rules will be more shareholder friendly. For example, if a jurisdiction recognises the 'board neutrality' rule, the directors of the target company are prevented from frustrating a takeover offer without the approval of the shareholders. It thus follows that the main purpose of the 'board neutrality' or 'anti-frustration' rule is to protect the shareholders of the target company from defensive measures taken by its own directors, ie to prioritise shareholder primacy. In the EU, companies have the option to opt in or to opt out of this rule. However, if a country opts out of this rule then the company must nonetheless have the right to implement board neutrality provisions in the company's articles or by-laws. The end result is that many European countries recognise a strong or weak form of the board neutrality rule. However, other jurisdictions reject it. This means that their legal systems legitimise governing rules that confer power on the directors to entrench their positions by frustrating a takeover bid and/or depriving the shareholders of the choice whether to accept or reject a bid. Since the rules are much more oriented towards directors, such a jurisdiction would be suggestive of a director primacy regime of corporate governance: the more countries adopting such an approach, the less purchase associated with the shareholder primacy claim. The relative positions of each of the 12 jurisdictions are set out in Table 4.1 in chapter 4.

iv. Case Study 4 (Cross-Border Takeovers and Takeover Defences)

This case study focuses on the protection offered to the employees of a target company in the takeover context. As such, it is possible to test the validity of the shareholder primacy claim inasmuch as the greater the number of jurisdictions that prioritise the concerns of stakeholders over shareholders, the less persuasive the proposition becomes. In other words, this case study asks to what extent takeover/company law rules allow directors to take decisions purely in the interests of employees (as stakeholders).

v. Case Study 5 (Piercing the Corporate Veil)

This case study probes the extent to which the law prescribes that directors must directly safeguard or protect the interests of creditors when a company is in the vicinity of insolvency or ultimately enters into bankruptcy. Bankruptcy or its vicinity are both situations where shareholder interests are in opposition to those of creditors as stakeholders. As such, in this particular environment, the extent to which shareholder or stakeholder primacy is in fact a model adopted by the jurisdictions under review can be subjected to close scrutiny. A second relevant issue in the context of this case study relates to the monitoring of directors by directors. If it can be shown that the law imposes no liability on a director for a failure to monitor the board, this is indicative of an approach leaning towards director primacy insofar as directors are insulated from legal reproach. In such a case, this acts as a counterpoint to the shareholder primacy claim.

vi. Case Study 6 (Capital Maintenance)

In this case study, the relevant issue is whether the law offers protection to creditors and specifically whether or not a creditor can challenge the illegitimate transfer of value from the company to the shareholders where this is disguised as a dividend. If this is legally permissible, then this points in the direction of an approach favouring the interests of stakeholders and casts doubt on the cogency of the shareholder primacy claim. Thus, once again, the tension in this regard is between the shareholder primacy claim and stakeholder protection.

vii. Case Studies 7 and 8 (Shareholder and Shareholder Law)

Case studies 7 and 8 both address the rights of shareholders. Where a broad range of rights are conferred in favour of shareholders, this provides support for the shareholder primacy claim. However, if shareholders enjoy a limited variety of legal rights, it can be argued that the interests of directors are prioritised; the greater the number of shareholder rights, the more powerful the impact on the balance of constitutional power struck between the shareholders and directors, with more restrictions imposed on the director's scope for manoeuvre and decision-making.

In case study 7, four specific issues were identified which should provide some insights concerning the legal position of shareholders relative to directors in each of the jurisdictions under review. These matters are as follows:

- the shareholder's right to receive a dividend;
- the shareholder's right to annul a merger;
- the shareholder's right to challenge the confiscation of property in exchange for cash; and
- a breach of the shareholder's right to receive notice of a general meeting.

The subject matter of case study 7 is similar to the issues addressed in case study 8, where the following rights of shareholders were considered:

- the shareholder's right to ask questions at a general meeting;
- whether the board has a duty to respond to all questions asked by shareholders at a general meeting;
- whether a decision taken at the general meeting will still be valid where all the other shareholders agree to it;
- whether it is possible for a shareholder to raise a legal claim to annul a resolution passed at a meeting; and
- whether there is a doctrine of abuse of shareholder rights.

The responses to these questions are considered in their totality to determine the extent of the global protection offered to shareholders in each of the jurisdictions under review.

viii. Case Study 9 (Shareholder Rights and Litigation)

The relevant question in this case study concerns the rights of enforcement of shareholders where a director (or a third party) has committed a breach of duty, for instance whether a shareholder can raise a derivative action or a variant thereof and whether the directors are protected from such claims because the governing rules of the jurisdiction generally exclude them. The strength of the actual derivative action is also assessed in terms of how likely it is to be successful: the stronger the scope for the derivative action to succeed, the better the protection for the shareholders. In this way, the shareholder primacy claim can be tested, since the lower the prospects of success, the more compelling the claim that a jurisdiction adopts a director primacy framework to insulate the board from liability. The data derived from each of the 12 jurisdictions is also combed for evidence of stakeholders having the right or power to raise derivative enforcement action, including the likelihood of success of such a claim. In such a case, evidence is supplied of the recognition of stakeholder claims against directors.

ix. Case Study 10 (Limitations on the Shareholder's Right to Transfer Shares)

This case study dealt with restrictions on the transfer of shares in the articles or by-laws of a company, for instance shareholder pre-emption rights on the transfer of a shareholder's shares or the transmission of shares on the death of a shareholder. Accordingly, the extent to which the interests of existing shareholders are protected in the context of pre-emption rights is subjected to analysis in this case study: the more heightened the shareholder protection, the more convincing the shareholder primacy claim. In this regard the competing interests of the company's stakeholders or the directors were not addressed in this assessment, but rather a measurement was taken of the power or strength of the shareholder protection mechanisms.

x. Conclusions

Based on the findings derived from the case studies above, it has been possible to ingather evidence concerning whether shareholders, stakeholders or directors are the primary consideration and focus of the company laws in each of the 12 jurisdictions reviewed in this book. The following Table 12.4 illustrates the findings (the separate tables, one per case study, are in the Annex):

Table 12.4 Results from case studies 1, 3, 4, 5, 6, 7, 8, 9 and 10 relative to shareholder, stakeholder or director primacy

Jurisdiction	Evidence of shareholder primacy										Evidence of stakeholder protection										Evidence of director primacy									
Case Study	1	3	4	5	6	7	8	9	10	T	1	3	4	5	6	7	8	9	10	T	1	3	4	5	6	7	8	9	10	T
Latvia	✓	✓			✓				✓	4	✓	✓			✓				✓	4	✓	✓			✓				✓	4
France						✓	✓	✓	✓	4	✓		✓	✓	✓					4	✓	✓								2
Germany		✓				✓	✓	✓	✓	5			✓	✓	✓					3	✓									1
Italy		✓	✓		✓	✓	✓	✓	✓	7	✓			✓						2	✓									1
Spain		✓	✓			✓	✓	✓	✓	6	✓			✓	✓					3	✓						✓			2
The Netherlands						✓	✓	✓	✓	4	✓	✓	✓	✓	✓					5	✓	✓						✓		3
Finland		✓	✓			✓	✓	✓	✓	6	✓			✓	✓					3	✓									1
Poland	✓					✓	✓	✓	✓	5				✓	✓					2		✓								1
UK	✓	✓	✓			✓	✓	✓	✓	7				✓	✓					2										0
US	✓				✓			✓	✓	4				✓						1	✓	✓	✓			✓	✓			5
South Africa		✓	✓			✓	✓	✓	✓	6	✓			✓	✓					3	✓									1
Japan	✓					✓	✓	✓	✓	5				✓	✓					2	✓	✓	✓							3

On the basis of these results, it is possible to reach a number of conclusions about the validity of the shareholder primacy claim. The first point that can be made is that although the results are rather mixed – as one might expect – and to some extent rather surprising, a clear majority of the 12 jurisdictions conform to the shareholder primacy claim. Table 12.4 demonstrates that the legal positions in South Africa, the UK, Italy, Spain, Finland and Poland tend to favour the protective capacity for shareholders, which provides a signal that such jurisdictions correspond to the shareholder primacy claim. This can be contrasted with the governing rules applicable in France which underscore an equally weighted preference for the protection of the interests of stakeholders and shareholders. Germany adopts a similar approach to France, albeit more attenuated to the extent that the shareholder primacy claim enjoys fractionally more salience. Meanwhile, the Netherlands is a jurisdiction which is an outlier to the extent that a majority of its governing rules are characterised by a preference for the advancement of the rights of stakeholders. As for the US, the findings match its caricature as a jurisdiction that adopts a director primacy approach to the extent that its prevailing philosophy is that the most effective means of heightening the interests and wealth of shareholders is to enlarge the discretionary powers of the directors and suppress shareholder interference in corporate decision-making. Finally, the relevant controlling legal rules applicable in Latvia demonstrate no preference for the interests of either of the three constituencies, and Japan exhibits a marginal partiality towards the shareholders over the directors and stakeholders.

E. Claim 4: Legal Origins

Each of the case studies is scrutinised for evidence of the legal origins claim. If this proposition is valid, we would expect to find some correlation between common law regimes and enhanced rights and protection for shareholders generally at the expense of the protection (i) and/or insulation from liability of directors in respect of their decision-making and conduct, and/or (ii) of creditors and other stakeholders. It should be stressed that South Africa is treated for these purposes as belonging to the common law family. This is despite the fact that it is a mixed legal system, ie a regime with a deep Romano-Dutch foundation with a common law superstructure. The justifications for this decision are twofold. First, the company laws of South Africa are largely based on English law. Secondly, company law is an area of law whose formation post-dates the original Romano-Dutch base. On a related theme, Japan is treated as a civilian system in this study, notwithstanding that it is also a mixed common law and civilian jurisdiction, with a framework grounded in German and US law. Once again, certain case studies repay little attention inasmuch as they fail to touch on the legal origins proposition. It is for that reason that we begin the discussion with case study 3.

i. Case Study 3 (Obligations of Directors in Takeovers)

From an evaluation of the findings from case study 3, there would appear to be no evidence for the legal origins theorem. First, the UK follows the EU approach towards the obligations of directors in takeovers, namely that they are subject to the 'board neutrality' rule: if the legal origins proposition held true, one would expect to find some deviation between the position in the UK and EU jurisdictions. To that extent, the UK, which is a common law jurisdiction, is fully aligned with the legal position in the EU. Moreover, the US and Japan diverge from the UK and EU positions and according to the legal origins theory, the ability of directors in the US and Japan to engage in frustrating action would provide shareholders with fewer legal protections and as such generate greater barriers to their companies accessing finance than companies situated in the UK and EU. However, there is no evidence to suggest that access to finance in the US and Japan is subject to a greater array of frictions and rigidities as a result of the failure of their legal systems to tackle managerial defensive action in a takeover context. It follows that case study 3 suggests that the legal origins claim is overplayed.

ii. Case Study 4 (Cross-Border Takeovers and Takeover Defences)

Three propositions can be derived from the takeover context in case study 4. First, the legal position in Italy, Spain and Germany is noteworthy in that a reason is needed for the pre-emption rights of existing shareholders to be excluded. However, that is not the case in the UK, where there are no restrictions on the power of an individual shareholder to waive pre-emption rights on the allotment and issue of new shares. This seems to substantiate the legal origins claim, as it underscores the comparatively liberal position of the UK in empowering shareholders to exercise their freedom of choice. Secondly, the governing rules regulating the shareholders' rights plan in the US, Japan and South Africa differ radically from the European jurisdictions. In the European countries, rights of pre-emption on the issue of fresh shares are uniformly required, whereas there are no such restrictions in Japan, US and South Africa. As such, we can characterise South African, Japanese and US law as less protective of shareholders than is the case in the EU. Although this suggests an element of alignment amongst the EU jurisdictions, it does represent a challenge to the convergence and legal origins claims more generally, since the UK and US have divergent laws and levels of shareholder protection in this context, notwithstanding that they are both common law countries. The fact that there are disparities in South African law and UK law also casts some doubt on a related claim that legal transplants are easy,[64] to the extent that the host jurisdiction South Africa would appear to have rejected the rule from which its company law was originally derived. Finally, consideration of the interests of constituencies such as employees in the takeover bid context is firmly scotched in the case of UK and US company law (unless this also furthers shareholder protection), which can be contrasted with the position in other EU jurisdictions such as Germany and France. This points towards some, albeit restricted, support for the legal

---

[64] See A Watson, *Legal Transplants: An Approach to Comparative Law* (2nd edn, Athens, GA, University of Georgie Press, 1993) 95; A Watson, 'Society's Choice and Legal Change' (1980) 9 *Hofstra Law Review* 1473; R Cotterrell, 'Is there a Logic of Legal Transplants?' in D Nelken and J Feest (eds), *Adapting Legal Cultures* (Oxford, Hart Publishing, 2001) 71, 82; DA Skeel, Jr, 'Corporate Anatomy Lessons' (2004) 113 *Yale Law Journal* 1519, 1569.

origins proposition insofar as shareholder interests do appear to enjoy greater levels of prioritisation in common law regimes such as the UK and US than civilian ones.

iii. Case Study 5 (Piercing the Corporate Veil)

The country solutions to the case study provide little support for the legal origins claim, since there is no discernible pattern distinguishing civil law and common law countries from each other as regards the adoption of a piercing the corporate veil doctrine. In fact, countries in both these comparative law camps accept it. The only minor factor separating them is that in the US, the courts are least protective of creditors and by implication more preferential to shareholders, whereas the position is the exact opposite in France and Japan. However, this perhaps tells us nothing, since in the case of some civilian jurisdictions such as the Netherlands, it is equally challenging as it is in the US to persuade a court to lift the veil of incorporation. This suggests that shareholders are also afforded an enlarged degree of priority over other constituencies in certain civil law countries.

iv. Case Study 6 (Capital Maintenance)

Turning first to legal controls on distributions, the governing rules applicable in each of the 12 jurisdictions demonstrate that limitations on the payments of dividends are pervasive. What differs from one jurisdiction to the next is the form that those restrictions take. For example, the majority of jurisdictions adopt a 'balance sheet surplus' approach and this is encountered in both common law (US and South Africa) and civilian countries (Germany, Italy, Latvia, etc). Turning to the controlling rules that apply in the context of disguised distributions, the conclusion to the case study provides evidence for clear divergence in the approaches adopted. Some jurisdictions prohibit such practices directly or indirectly (Germany, the UK, Finland, Poland and Latvia), whereas others do not, whilst recognising functionally equivalent legal rules to control the situation (Italy, France and the US). However, the most significant point is that of those states that adopt a restrictive approach against those that apply one that is more liberal and flexible, no dividing line can be seen along legal origins as regards the level of shareholder protection. Evidence in favour of the legal origins claim is also absent when it comes to an evaluation of the jurisdictions that have substituted solvency-based tests for principles of capital maintenance, which assess the liquidity of a company as part of the enquiry surrounding whether to authorise a distribution (Finland, the Netherlands and South Africa).

v. Case Study 7 (Shareholders and Shareholder Law)

A number of issues are touched upon in this case study which enable us to chart the relevance of the common law/civil law divide. The principal matters addressed are whether aggrieved shareholders are likely to obtain relief where the company fails to declare a dividend for a period of ten years and their prospects of success in challenging a merger resolution. As regards these issues, the conclusion to the chapter makes the point that there is no particular distinction in the governing rules applied in the common law and civilian countries. However, this is not entirely accurate. For example, the governing rules also demonstrate that shareholders have no legal power or right to declare a resolution approving a merger as void in the UK or US, which can be distinguished from civilian jurisdictions such as France, Italy and the Netherlands where this is a distinct possibility. Seen from this perspective, to the extent that shareholders experience greater protection in civilian countries than they do in those governed by the common law, case study 7 reveals some compelling evidence for the exact opposite of the legal origins claim.

vi. Case Study 8 (Abuse of Shareholder Rights)

The evidence to be derived from case study 8 suggests some, albeit a large measure of mixed, evidence for the legal origins claim. Both the civilian jurisdictions and some common law countries such as the UK recognise the rights of shareholders to ask questions and demand answers at a company's general meeting. However, other common law jurisdictions such as the US reject such rights. This leads to a mixed assortment of results. It is when we turn to the entitlements of shareholders to attack merger resolutions that we encounter alignment in the governing legal rules in each of the 12 jurisdictions. In each country, such a challenge would be permissible, albeit that the prospects of success and limitations placed on the ability to challenge would differ.

vii. Case Study 9 (Shareholders' Rights and Litigation)

In this case study, an examination of the rules governing the availability and operation of the unanimous assent rule demonstrate that shareholders in common law and civilian countries enjoy broadly similar degrees of shareholder protection. Likewise, in both systemic camps, shareholders have various legal means of challenging resolutions passed by the board of directors of companies which are sullied by the self-interest of the directors involved in the decision-making process. The various procedures for such challenges vary greatly, as do the eligibility requirements and conditions for their operation and availability, for instance via shareholder derivative proceedings, individual shareholder actions, or hybrids between such derivative and personal claims, etc. However, whilst there are such variations, the underlying premise of the legal origins claim does seem overdone in this context insofar as most of the 12 jurisdictions will provide shareholders with an avenue to obtain relief where the directors have engaged in some form of self-interested dealings or activities.

viii. Case Study 10 (Limitations on the Shareholder's Right to Transfer Shares)

A demarcation line between civilian and common law countries can be detected in this case study when the 12 jurisdictions are scrutinised for the recognition, operation and enforceability of existing shareholders' pre-emption rights on the intended transfer of another shareholder's shares to a third party. For example, common law countries tend to impose few, if any, restrictions on the ability of shareholders to invoke and enforce such pre-emption rights as a means of preventing the sale of shares in a non-listed public company to a third party outsider. In this way, shareholders enjoy high levels of protection of their interests and rights. This can be contrasted with civilian jurisdictions where one finds *ex ante* and *ex post* legal controls on the pre-emption rights of shareholders, which in certain cases, will translate into the failure of such provisions to bite. The same division in the legal position along common law/civilian lines can be seen in the case of the operation of existing shareholders' pre-emption rights which are applicable on the death of a shareholder. In common law countries such as the UK, US and South Africa, such clauses are not subjected to regulatory or legal limitations on their operability, which can be contrasted with civilian systems where there is more scope for them to be challenged.

ix. Conclusions

Table 12.5 sets out the various findings.

Table 12.5 Results from case studies regarding the legal origins claim

Case Study	Legal Origins?	Observation
3	x	No evidence
4	✓	Some, but mixed, evidence
5	x	No evidence
6	x	No evidence
7	x	No evidence, and in fact, some evidence of the opposite
8	✓	Some, but mixed, evidence
9	x	No evidence
10	✓	Clear evidence
Total	3	

The findings illustrated in Table 12.5 give rise to the proposition that there is scant evidence for the legal origins claim. With this final conclusion drawn, at this juncture, we now move to a discussion which tries to make sense of the composite results.

IV. Conclusions

A. Introduction

In this final section, we first explore the limitations inherent in this study. With those caveats in place, the conclusions that can be drawn from the evaluation of each of the four claims are presented. In the final analysis, the discussion then turns to the scrutiny of these results, as well as their relationship to the arguments presented in the existing comparative corporate law scholarship.

B. Limitations

There are of course, various limitations to our approach. Some have been identified in sections II and III above. However, others are more systemic. First, we recognise that it is impossible to extract and process all pertinent information on a legal system's approach to a particular corporate problem from the ten case studies. By dint of the nature of the study, this chapter presents a limited sample, particularly in the case of the evaluation of the plausibility of the patterns of shareholder ownership claim, which only draws on two case studies. Having said that, even with the restricted numbers of case studies in the latter case, the results drawn represent a sizeable proportion of the overall number of permutations arising from ten case studies and 12 jurisdictions.

Secondly, only a selection of the legal rules that act directly to regulate a socio-economic issue may have been spelled out in the national reports to the case studies, or extracted from the case studies in this chapter for the purposes of the evaluative exercise adopted in section III. Furthermore, certain extra-legal means of resolving the relevant problems may have been omitted. Nevertheless, we would argue that great value remains in pursuing a rule-based comparative approach in this study, especially when taken together with the numerical study of the legal rules and outcomes in the subsequent chapter. There is the distinct prospect that the application of differing comparative methodological approaches – in this and the following chapter – towards the evaluation of the governing legal rules adopted by the various jurisdictions in response to the corporate or socio-economic problem may generate diverse findings. Of itself, therefore, the application of diverse methodological techniques is extremely valuable in throwing structural variations of approach into sharp relief.

Thirdly, an inherent weakness of this study lies in the tendency to categorise legal rules in a binary manner, for instance that either a rule in country X says A, or it says B, or that it functions in manner C, and if not, then in manner D. However, by their very nature, legal rules are subject to a 'penumbra of uncertainty', particularly so at the borders.[65] Since they are mutable, they are not always capable of a single or fixed interpretation according to an 'either/or' or algorithmic approach.

Fourthly, we should stress that we have tended to focus on the controlling rule or rules that govern a particular corporate issue, rather than the conditions to the applicability of such rules, or the exceptions where they do not apply. The fifth point to make is that this exercise entails an assessment of the 'law in the books' rather than the 'law in action'. One of the oft-versed criticisms of comparative evaluations of the laws and rules of legal systems is that they only assess the actual hard law. If we factor in the point that laws do not enforce themselves but rely on extra-legal factors for their vitality and efficacy – such as the economic resources allocated towards enforcement, the configuration and force of procedural laws and safeguards, the position of legal institutions and fields that lay adjacent to corporate law (such as general commercial laws, private laws, etc), as well as the general population's respect for the law and properly functioning systems for civil dispute resolution (such as courts, arbitration systems, etc) – it soon becomes apparent that a simple analysis of the rules 'in the books' may be missing a fundamental trick.

---

[65] HLA Hart, *The Concept of Law* (2nd edn, Oxford, Oxford University Press, 1994) 125–27.

Finally, the methodology in this study is less mathematical, scientific and precise than the leximetric approach adopted in the subsequent chapter inasmuch as the comparative assessment of the relevant legal rules and their functions is much more impressionistic and qualitative in nature. Nevertheless, the technique pursued in this chapter follows faithfully the traditional rule-based method of comparative law, as adapted and particularised to comparative company law by LoPucki,[66] which has the capacity to pick up shades of difference which may be overlooked in more numerical evaluations of legal rules and their functions insofar as these adopt a cruder binary form of assessment of compared rules.

C. Results

The findings derived from the rule-based evaluation of the case studies can be illustrated in a table, as follows:

Table 12.6 Results from evaluation of case studies for evidence of four claims

Claim	Evidence	No Evidence
Convergence	x	✓
Patterns of Shareholder Ownership	x	✓
Shareholder Primacy	✓	x
Legal Origins	x	✓

Overall, the results of this chapter suggest that three out of the four primary claims are unsubstantiated, which does appear to support the positions of the various sceptical commentators discussed in section II. On their face, some of the findings appear to be coherent and in harmony with each other. For example, the separate findings that there is little evidence for both the patterns of shareholder ownership and legal origins claims are both consistent to the extent that the structure of shareholder ownership of corporations in common law jurisdictions tends to be dispersed (eg the UK and the US), unlike the position in civilian legal systems.

But if the results are indeed correct, then how can we explain their inherent inconsistencies? For instance, the proposition that there is substance to the shareholder primacy claim would appear to conflict with the simultaneous rejection of the convergence claim: one of the original arguments advanced by Hansmann and Kraakman for the convergence claim was that the superiority of the shareholder-oriented model would be the principal factor that would push forward the alignment of the formal corporate laws of legal systems.[67] The same inconsistency objection can be aimed at the conclusions validating the shareholder primacy claim whilst rejecting the legal origins proposition: if the results demonstrate that the nature and orientation of the legal rules in both common law and civilian countries prioritise the protection of

---

[66] LoPucki, 'A Rule-Based Method for Comparing Corporate Laws' (n 1).
[67] Hansmann and Kraakman, 'The End of History for Corporate Law' (n 8) 440–41.

shareholders, then how can it be argued with any confidence that civilian and common law legal systems exhibit a range of diversity? Likewise, as regards the doubt they cast on both the convergence and patterns of shareholder ownerships propositions, since the rejection of the argument that the governing company law rules vary according to the structure of shareholder ownership in a jurisdiction provides some indirect support for the convergence claim. These questions take us to a more in-depth discussion of the implications of the findings.

D. Analysis and Implications

The findings produced from case studies 3 to 10 doubt the descriptive accuracy, predictive power and normative bite of the convergence claim. This is perhaps ironic: it is unsurprising to the extent that it stretches credulity to assert that global divergences in the form or function of corporate laws will be crowded out overnight or even gradually as a result of the irresistible forces of globalisation and imitation; whilst at once surprising inasmuch as it fails to cohere with the additional finding that the shareholder primacy claim appears to be sound. Perhaps the answer to this conundrum lies in Jeff Gordon's notion of 'divergence-within-convergence'.[68] This notion can encompass three separate strands. The first is the idea that whilst convergence in corporate law is indeed taking place, it is masked by the fact that it is proceeding at such a glacial pace that the capacity to detect a measure of alignment is strained: however, subject to the caveat struck at section III A above, our findings do not substantiate this interpretation. Secondly, there is the argument that diversity in legal rules often occurs within the rubric of a convergent legal framework: the results do support this approach and the classic example is the convergence we can see across EU Member States in the field of corporate law.[69] This EU convergence may not translate into global convergence, which is exactly what the findings from this study bear out. Thirdly, there is the concept of convergence in principle, but divergence in practice. The results drawn from case studies 7 and 8 are an excellent illustration of the point as they establish the existence of a particular general legal principle that is expressed as a governing legal rule or rules, for instance the ability to challenge the non-payment of dividends or to challenge merger resolutions, but then go on to articulate considerable degrees of variation in the nature in form or function of the rules, as well as the machinery for their operation, or the conditions for, or exceptions to, their exercise.

The failure of the findings to cohere with the patterns of shareholder ownership proposition is an interesting outcome. This claim essentially hinges on the contention that the law is a passive recipient of reforms that stem from the economic infrastructure of a jurisdiction. In terms of this world view, it is the economic, commercial and social context that determines the shape that the law takes. Perhaps this claim fails to appreciate the salience of the converse proposition that the 'law matters'. In other words, that it is the law that influences the patterns of shareholder ownership rather than the opposite way round. Indeed, Cheffins's research furnishes some support for

---

[68] Gordon, 'Convergence and Persistence in Corporate Law and Governance' (n 7) 41–45.
[69] Case study 4 covering takeover rules is a good example of the point.

this proposition. He makes the argument that the dispersed system of shareholder ownership in the UK is partly attributable to legal reforms in stock exchange listing rules, and tax, takeover and pensions law.[70]

The success of the shareholder primacy claim aligns with the various claims made in the academic literature about the descriptive position in the corporate laws in many jurisdictions. However, it should not cloud the fact that the results suggest that the US is an outlier insofar as it eschews the standard shareholder-oriented model and clings to the vestiges of a managerialist approach to corporate governance in the guise of the director primacy model. A similar point can be made about the position in France, Germany and the Netherlands which exhibit affinities with a stakeholder-oriented model.

Turning to the persuasiveness of the legal origins claim, our results clearly provide little support for this proposition. This is reflective of recent mounting economic evidence derived from research conducted by economists and empirical legal researchers. For example, empirical research suggests that corporations operating in legal and corporate governance systems adopting the shareholder primacy norm with higher levels of shareholder protection will tend to (i) have lower firm-level profits[71] and (ii) invest fewer resources in product innovation, research and development than in stakeholder regimes.[72] These findings have an impact on the purchase of the legal origins claim, since in the case of companies trading in civilian jurisdictions conforming to the shareholder primacy claim with high levels of shareholder protection, the evidence indicates a reversal of the finding that firm-level profits will be suppressed.[73]

As for the apparent inconsistencies in the results mentioned in section III C above, on closer inspection, it can be argued that the rejection of the convergence claim alongside the substantiation of the shareholder primacy norm is not as puzzling as it might first seem. Table 12.4 demonstrates that many jurisdictions prioritise the interests of a complex mixture of parties' interests. As such, shareholder primacy provides the main, but not exclusive, explanation of what is going on. To overlook these 'side stories' would be to illegitimately discount the possibility that there is indeed some divergence in the legal positions of countries, which is hidden immediately beneath the headline narrative. In the case of the perceived mismatch in the findings that dismiss

---

[70] Cheffins, *Corporate Ownership and Control* (n 13) ch 9; B Cheffins, 'Does Law Matter? The Separation of Ownership and Control in the United Kingdom' (2001) 30 *Journal of Legal Studies* 459.

[71] Z Adams and S Deakin, 'Corporate Governance and Employment Relations' in J Gordon and W-G Ringe (eds), *The Oxford Handbook of Corporate Law and Governance* (Oxford, Oxford University Press, 2018) 1037; D Chai, S Deakin, P Sarkar and A Singh, *Corporate Governance, Legal Origin and the Persistence of Profits*, CBR WP Series No 465, December 2014.

[72] Adams and Deakin, ibid; J Graham, C Harvey and S Rajgopal, *The Economic Implications of Corporate Financial Reporting*, NBER Working Paper No 10050 (2005) 15–19; J Asker, J Farre-Mensa and A Ljungqvist, *Comparing the Investment Behavior of Public and Private Firms*, ECGI Finance Working Paper 282/10 (2012) 6; F Belloc, 'Law, Finance and Innovation: The Dark Side of Shareholder Protection' (2013) 37 *Cambridge Journal of Economics* 863, 885.

[73] Adams and Deakin, ibid; Chai et al, *Corporate Governance, Legal Origin and the Persistence of Profits* (n 71).

the legal origins claim but substantiate the shareholder primacy proposition, it may be that this can be explained by the close alignment of the controlling legal rules in the UK and EU. In addition, the results for another common law jurisdiction, namely the US, are positively ambivalent regarding the level of shareholder protection, as many of the entries in Table 12.4 show that the governing legal rules are just as, if not more, likely to prefer the interests of directors as they are of shareholders. Finally, the contention that the dual rejection of the patterns of shareholder ownership and convergence claims is incompatible, stretches matters too far. While the dismissal of the former is consistent with the convergence proposition, it does not necessarily provide *positive* support for it. It is equally plausible that there is no evidence of any convergence.

Annex: Supporting Tables and Evidence

Claim 3: Case Study 1 (General Case on Directors' Duties)

This annex provides a brief explanation of our findings as set out in Table 12.4. However, we will not provide a detailed elaboration for each case study, and the findings for each case study (bar case study 1) are illustrated only in a table. Instead, it is only for case study 1 that a detailed account is provided, which ought to be sufficient to furnish an indication of our thinking and how we reached our results.

Latvia

Here, there is some evidence of a system that does not favour the shareholder primacy claim, especially if one considers that shareholders do not have the authority to ratify the actions of the directors or to authorise them in advance. It is specifically stated that the ultimate authority does not reside with the shareholders and that they thus do not have the power to waive the breach in question. Mr B, in question, can still be liable even if the shareholders do approve his conduct.

By considering the law on directors' duties and possible breaches, in this case study, there is no evidence supporting either a shareholder-orientated or a stakeholder dominant system.

France

A rule, similar to the business judgment rule, is applicable in France. The courts in France generally do not second-guess the decisions of the board, as long as the company remains solvent. This shows some evidence of director primacy. There is also some evidence of stakeholder protection based on the protection offered to creditors (see para iii of case study 1, France). Shareholder approval or ratification is not possible which is in line with the director primacy norm.

Germany

The business judgment rule, developed through case law, is applicable in Germany. This is in line with the director primacy claim insofar as a presumption operates to insulate directors from liability. Shareholder approval is also not absolute, which is in line with the director primacy proposition, as *ex ante* authorisation is possible but not *ex post* ratification.

Italy

Legal principles similar to the business judgment rule are applied in Italy (see case study 1 on Italy). These principles protect directors when they perform their duties. It is stated that the position with regard to shareholder authorisation or ratification, in the case of a breach of duty by a director, is not clear. We therefore cannot draw any conclusions from this. There is some evidence of a stakeholder approach in the context of the position of creditors when a company is in financial trouble. It states that the directors must call a general meeting (see Article 2482-*bis* of the Civil Code), otherwise they will be held personally and jointly liable to the creditors and third parties for any loss suffered. This provides a high level of protection for stakeholders.

Spain

The business judgment rule has been recognised through case law for a long time and is now incorporated into legislation (since 2014, see Ley 31/2014). Creditors also receive a lot of protection as directors will be held liable, jointly, to the company, shareholders and the creditors in the case of a breach (see LSC, Articles 236.1 and 237). Directors also have additional duties in cases of corporate insolvency (this is regulated in Ley Concursal 22/2003). Shareholders, in general meeting, are also not able to relieve a director from liability.

The Netherlands

Creditors are protected, albeit under tort law, as they can file a claim if, like *in casu*, the directors entered into a contract at a time when it ought to have been clear that the company would not be able to fulfil the obligations. This is also possible with regard to third parties. In the case of bankruptcy, the liquidator or receiver can bring legal proceedings against the board of directors if it can be established that the board performed its duties in an improper manner. This is equally possible for private and public limited liability companies.

Finland

The business judgment rule is applicable in Finland. However, this is not based on a specific article in the companies' legislation but instead is mentioned in the preparatory works to the CA and is based on Finnish legal literature.

The purpose of a company in Finnish law is to make a profit (section 5 of the CA), unless otherwise stated in the articles of association. This creates, at first sight, the impression of a shareholder primacy model. It is, however, stated that directors will be held liable to the company, shareholders or a third party for damage caused deliberately or negligently in violation of the CA or the company's articles of association. This is evidence of a more stakeholder-orientated approach. This goes further stating that a shareholder's consent, to the loan in this case, will not free the director from liability to the creditors for damages. A shareholder might even be found liable for damages to the creditors of the company should he ratify or authorise the transaction (chapter 22, section 2 of the CA).

Poland

The original power of a company is vested in the shareholders in general meeting according to Polish law.

The business judgment rule does not apply; rather there is a presumption in favour of a breach of duty. As such, a director must prove that he or she is not culpable. This is very much evidence of shareholder primacy. The shareholders can, however, 'protect' the directors by authorising their conduct or ratify it *ex ante*. If a 95 per cent shareholder approves of the conduct then it will be highly unlikely that the director will be held liable.

The UK

Under UK law, the management of a company, both private and public, is conducted by a unitary board. The powers of the management are subject to instruction and initiation rights vested in the shareholders. The original decision-making power thus rests with the shareholders but this is delegated to the board of directors. Shareholders are still able to authorise the conduct of the board or ratify it afterwards. In this case, the loan transaction was ratified so the director cannot be sued for breach of duty.

The duty to act with the necessary care, skill and diligence is codified in the UK Companies Act 2006, but there is no business judgment rule. In addition, there is no direct protection available to creditors (only via the liquidator in certain instances). The evidence is thus clearly in line with the shareholder primacy model.

The US

The business judgment rule is applied by the Delaware courts. There are also often clauses in corporate documents protecting directors from personal liability. This is in line with the director primacy claim. Shareholders do not manage the corporation but they are entitled to vote on certain matters such as the removal and appointment of directors. There is no evidence in this case study of any protection, on a direct basis, in favour of creditors.

South Africa

The position in South Africa has changed with the enactment of the Companies Act 2008 as the management of the company is now within the ultimate control of the directors. Shareholder authorisation or ratification is no longer possible. The directors are the ultimate decision-makers (see section 66). The business judgment rule has been codified in the Companies Act 2008 giving additional protection to directors. Various sections in the Companies Act 2008 provide stakeholders with ample protection, such as, for example, section 22 and especially section 218(2). The latter is very wide as it states that any person who contravenes any provision of the Act will be liable to any other person for any loss or damage suffered by that person as a result of the contravention.

Japan

The business judgment rule is applicable in Japan. This has been established through case law and functions analogously to that in US case law. Shareholder authorisation is also possible. If, however, authorisation or ratification occurs informally as in this case rather than at a general meeting, then it will only be possible if all shareholders with voting rights agreed to it. There is evidence of some direct protection to creditors, but in the context of criminal law.

Claim 3: Tables

Table 12.7 Case study 1

Jurisdiction	Evidence of shareholder primacy	Evidence of stakeholder protection	Evidence of director primacy
Latvia			✓
France		✓	✓
Germany			✓
Italy		✓	✓
Spain		✓	✓
The Netherlands		✓	✓
Finland		✓	✓
Poland	✓		
UK	✓		
US	✓		✓
South Africa		✓	✓
Japan	✓		✓

Case study 2: The issues addressed in this case study do not make any useful contribution towards testing the validity of the shareholder primacy claim.

Table 12.8 Case study 3

Jurisdiction	Evidence of shareholder primacy	Evidence of stakeholder protection	Evidence of director primacy
		N/A for this case study	
Latvia			✓
France			✓
Germany	✓		
Italy	✓		
Spain	✓		
The Netherlands	✓		✓
Finland	✓		
Poland			✓
UK	✓		
US			✓
South Africa	✓		
Japan			✓

Table 12.9 Case study 4

Jurisdiction	Evidence of shareholder primacy	Evidence of stakeholder protection	Evidence of director primacy
Latvia	N/A		
France		✓	
Germany		✓	
Italy	✓		
Spain	✓		
The Netherlands		✓	
Finland	✓		
Poland	✓		
UK	✓		
US			✓
South Africa	✓		
Japan			✓

Table 12.10 Case study 5

Jurisdiction	Evidence of shareholder primacy	Evidence of stakeholder protection	Evidence of director primacy
Latvia			No (Based on German law)
France		✓	NO
Germany		✓	NO
Italy		✓	NO
Spain		✓	NO
The Netherlands		✓	NO
Finland		✓	NO
Poland		✓	*No evidence*
UK		✓	NO
US		✓	*No evidence*
South Africa		✓	NO
Japan		✓	NO

Table 12.11 Case study 6

Jurisdiction	Evidence of shareholder primacy	Evidence of stakeholder protection	Evidence of director primacy
			N/A for this case study
Latvia		✓	
France		✓	
Germany		✓	
Italy	✓		
Spain		✓	
The Netherlands		✓	
Finland		✓	
Poland		✓	
UK		✓	
US	✓		
South Africa		✓	
Japan		✓	

Table 12.12 Case study 7

Jurisdiction	Evidence of shareholder primacy	Evidence of stakeholder protection	Evidence of director primacy
		N/A for this case study	
Latvia	✓		✓
France	✓		
Germany	✓		
Italy	✓		
Spain	✓		
The Netherlands	✓		
Finland	✓		
Poland	✓		
UK	✓		
US			✓
South Africa	✓		
Japan	✓		

Table 12.13 Case study 8

Jurisdiction	Evidence of shareholder primacy	Evidence of stakeholder protection	Evidence of director primacy
		N/A for this case study	
Latvia	✓		✓
France	✓		
Germany	✓		
Italy	✓		
Spain	✓		✓
The Netherlands	✓		
Finland	✓		
Poland	✓		
UK	✓		
US			✓
South Africa	✓		
Japan	✓		

Table 12.14 Case study 9

Jurisdiction	Evidence of shareholder primacy	Evidence of stakeholder protection	Evidence of director primacy
		N/A for this case study	
Latvia	✓		
France	✓		
Germany	✓(VERY WEAK)		
Italy	✓(VERY STRONG)		
Spain	✓		
The Netherlands			✓
Finland	✓		
Poland	NO EVIDENCE HERE		
UK	✓		
US	✓		
South Africa	✓		
Japan	✓		

Table 12.15 Case study 10

Jurisdiction	Evidence of shareholder primacy	Evidence of stakeholder protection	Evidence of director primacy
		N/A for this case study	
Latvia	✓		
France	✓		
Germany	✓(WEAK)		
Italy	✓		
Spain	✓		
The Netherlands	✓(STRONG)		
Finland	✓(WEAK)		
Poland	✓		
UK	✓(STRONG)		
US	✓(STRONG)		
South Africa	✓(STRONG)		
Japan	✓(WEAK)		

13

A Quantitative Analysis of Similarities and Differences in Form, Style and Substance

MATHIAS SIEMS

I. Introduction

Quantitative research in comparative company law often starts with an index of variables in order to code legal rules, for example, in order to determine and compare the strength of shareholder protection across countries.[1] In the following, however, a different procedure will be applied. This book did not start with an index of variables: rather it followed a qualitative and legal approach in presenting case scenarios answered by country experts in a narrative text. The idea of this chapter is that the information of this text can be translated into numerical values. Thus, this approach of coding text is a form of content analysis as it is increasingly used in many academic fields, for example, political science, linguistics but also law.[2]

In substance, this chapter aims to contribute to the debate about possible differences and similarities between legal systems in company law, for example, the role of differences between legal families and a possible convergence of legal systems. It addresses these questions at three levels, namely, as it provides an evaluation of the nature and content of the respective legal rules of company law (the 'form'),

[1] The first study in this line of research was R La Porta, F Lopez-de-Silanes, A Shleifer and RW Vishny, 'Law and Finance' (1998) 106 *Journal of Political Economy* 1113. For other research, see M Siems, 'The Leximetric Research on Shareholder Protection' in J Hill and R Thomas (eds), *Research Handbook on Shareholder Power* (Cheltenham, Edward Elgar, 2015) 168–85.

[2] See, eg, J Grimmer and BM Stewart, 'Text as Data: The Promise and Pitfalls of Automatic Content Analysis Methods for Political Texts' (2013) 21 *Political Analysis* 267; R op den Akker, M Bruijnes, R Peters and T Krikke, 'Interpersonal Stance in Police Interviews: Content Analysis' (2013) 3 *Computational Linguistics in the Netherlands Journal* 193; MA Hall and RF Wright, 'Systematic Content Analysis of Judicial Opinions' (2008) 96 *California Law Review* 63.

the sources of those rules (the 'style') and the results reached on the application of such rules (the 'substance'). For this purpose, two topics from each of the ten cases (thus, 20 components in total) have been coded in terms of legal rules, the underlying legal sources and the actual results.

The chapter is structured as follows. Section II outlines previous taxonomic research, referring to the literature on comparative law, company law and corporate governance. Section III explains the coding of the components and presents the main findings of form, style and substance. Section IV concludes.

II. Previous Taxonomic Research

In the comparative law literature, it is sometimes said that legal families, in particular common and civil law, fundamentally differ in their legal rules and mentalities. Similarly, in the company law and corporate governance literature, it is not infrequently claimed that the protection of shareholders varies across countries and that convergence is unlikely to happen – while others suggest that legal differences have become less pronounced. This section explains this line of research[3] in order to provide the basis for the subsequent quantitative results.

A. Comparative Law and Legal Families

The core idea of legal families is that the diversity of legal systems around the world is not random but that groups of countries share common features in terms of legal history, legal thinking and positive rules. Particular relevance is attributed to the distinction between common and civil law countries as common law and civil law are said to 'constitute the basic building blocks of the legal order', with this distinction seen as the 'most fundamental and most discussed issue in comparative law'.[4]

In particular, common law and civil law are said to differ in their relevant sources of law and legal methods. In the civil law, the main source of law is statute law, underpinned by academic writings. The main pieces of legislation are 'codes', which provide a logical, systematic and coherent set of rules, enabling judges to apply these rules in a deductive and legalistic way. The common law, by contrast, is at its core case law: judges reason inductively from case to case, paying close attention to the

---

[3] It is based on my previous research on this topic, in particular: M Siems, *Comparative Law* (2nd edn, Cambridge, Cambridge University Press 2018); M Siems, 'Taxonomies and Leximetrics' in J Gordon and W-G Ringe (eds), *The Oxford Handbook of Corporate Law and Governance* (Oxford, Oxford University Press, 2018); M Siems, *Convergence in Shareholder Law* (Cambridge, Cambridge University Press, 2008). For an alternative taxonomy, see M Siems, 'Varieties of Legal Systems: Towards a New Global Taxonomy' (2016) 12 *Journal of Institutional Economics* 579.

[4] VV Palmer, 'Mixed Jurisdictions' in JM Smits (ed), *Elgar Encyclopaedia of Comparative Law* (2nd edn, Cheltenham, Edward Elgar, 2012) 590–99 at 591; U Mattei, *Comparative Law and Economics* (Ann Arbor, University of Michigan Press, 1997) 70.

facts and being aware that such reasoning is not strictly logical but is also based on common sense.[5]

Thus, in the common law, judges not only aim to solve an individual dispute, but their decisions are a means of developing the law 'from below', with previous judgments acting as binding precedents. Common law judges are also prepared to display judicial creativity and are praised for being 'market-wise', for instance, in guaranteeing the freedom of contract.[6] Meanwhile, judges in civil law countries are said to reason very differently. They have more discretion in interpreting statutory law, but once this is completed, they are mere 'law-appliers', following a strict legal syllogism: first, they identify the legal rule and how it should be interpreted; second, they subsume the facts within these legal rules; and, third, they apply the consequences of the legal rules.[7] Since court decisions are only binding between the parties to the dispute, case law is typically not regarded as a source of law.[8]

It is also often said that the role of legal scholarship harnesses a civil law and common law divide. The civil law tradition is associated with the concept of 'learned law'. In particular, law professors have had a strong influence on the character of German law, in contrast to the importance of the judiciary in England and the legislature in France.[9] For example, legal scholars perform a key role in the statutory interpretation of legislation. They produce detailed multi-volume annotated guides on the main codes, and monographs, textbooks and journals also deal extensively with the interpretation of statutory law. Often, then, what emerges is a predominant view (*herrschende Lehre* in Germany, *la doctrine* in France) which is as treated as being as authoritative as the positive law itself.[10]

To be sure, this crude binary distinction between common law and civil law is not without its problems. Often it is regarded as too simplistic. For example, with respect to legislation, drawing a distinction between countries on the basis of whether they have (or do not have) a code is said to have lost its relevance. In civil law countries, codes are no longer seen to be the most significant sources of law, and common law countries are said to have reached the 'age of statutes'.[11] Turning to the courts, the main criticism is that the common law/civil law divide mischaracterises the way in which the judiciary works in today's civil law countries. For example, according to Martin Shapiro, it is 'fundamentally incorrect' to assume that the civil law judge simply applies a set of complete and self-explanatory rules in a mechanical way.[12]

---

[5] For an overview, see JM Smits, *The Making of European Private Law: Towards a Ius Commune Europaeum as a Mixed Legal System* (Antwerp, Intersentia, 2002) 73–94.

[6] B Arruñada and V Andonova, 'Common Law and Civil Law as Pro-Market Adaptations' (2008) 26 *Washington University Journal of Law and Policy* 81.

[7] JR Maxeiner, G Lee, A Weber and H Weber, *Practical Global Civil Procedure: United States-Germany-Korea* (Durham, NC, Carolina Academic Press, 2010) 33, 241.

[8] However, this has changed over time: see MN Marchenko, 'Convergence of Romano-Germanic and Anglo-Saxon Law' (2010) 5 *Journal of Comparative Law* 211 at 223–25.

[9] RC van Caenegem, *Legislators, Judges, Professors* (Cambridge, Cambridge University Press, 1987).

[10] See U Mattei, T Ruskola and A Gidi, *Schlesinger's Comparative Law* (7th edn, New York, Foundation Press, 2009) 442.

[11] For a critical analysis of the latter, see G Calabresi, *A Common Law for the Age of Statutes* (Cambridge, MA, Harvard University Press, 1985).

[12] M Shapiro, *Courts: A Comparative and Political Analysis* (Chicago, Chicago University Press, 1981) 126–56.

Moreover, when trying to classify countries, it becomes clear that the distinction between common and civil law is not always helpful. Starting in continental Europe, it has been said that the 'differences between French and German law may be as great, or even greater, than those between French and English, or German and English law'.[13] Thus, most classifications distinguish between a Romanist and a Germanic model of continental civil law;[14] yet, often civil law countries are something of a mixture between these two categories: for example, Italy, Spain and Poland may usually be regarded as being part of the Romanist civil law, but there have also been significant German influences. There is also uncertainty as regards the Scandinavian countries: they have some distinct features, such as the absence of comprehensive codes, but they have also been influenced by German civil law, and recently they have shifted towards Anglo-Saxon law.[15]

Japan poses a similar problem: there is some German influence by virtue of legal transplants, more recent American influence, but also distinct 'Asian' features, such as reliance on informal mechanisms of dispute resolution.[16] South Africa is often seen as a mixed legal system[17] but there are also different dynamics in different areas of law – with company and commercial law mainly based on English law. Finally, with respect to England and the US, one also encounters assertions to the effect that in 'in many respects US law represents a deliberate rejection of common law principles, with preference being given to more affirmative ideas clearly derived from civil law',[18] whilst 'English law [may be] gradually becoming less English'.[19] Thus, overall, it is not implausible to say that all legal systems may be regarded as mixed legal systems.

B. Categories in Corporate Governance and Company Law

Corporate governance and company law can be seen as two overlapping circles. Starting with corporate governance, one of its key research questions is whether firms based in the same country are run in a similar way. Thus, one has to explore the historical, political, legal, cultural and economic characteristics that underpin corporate governance in a particular jurisdiction, with company law being one of the sub-categories. As regards company law, most company statutes deal with a variety of topics, such as how to incorporate a company, how to raise capital, how a company is run and how it deals with conflicts between shareholders, directors and other constituencies. Here, then, corporate governance is a sub-category of company law because its main interest

---

[13] R Zimmermann, *Roman Law, Contemporary Law, European Law: The Civilian Tradition Today* (Oxford, Oxford University Press, 2001) 113.

[14] See eg K Zweigert and H Kötz, *An Introduction to Comparative Law* (3rd edn, Oxford, Clarendon Press, 1998).

[15] See, eg, J Husa, K Nuotio and H Pihlajamäki (eds), *Nordic Law—Between Tradition and Dynamism* (Antwerp and Oxford, Intersentia, 2008).

[16] Zweigert and Kötz, *An Introduction to Comparative Law* (n 14) 282–83.

[17] See, eg, R Zimmermann and D Visser (eds), *Southern Cross: Civil Law and Common Law in South Africa* (Oxford, Clarendon 1996).

[18] HP Glenn, *Legal Traditions of the World* (4th edn, Oxford, Oxford University Press, 2014) 262.

[19] R Cooke, 'The Road Ahead for the Common Law' (2004) 53 *International and Comparative Law Quarterly* 273.

is the law related to the management of the company, as distinguished, for instance, from questions of corporate finance law.

Both the literature on corporate governance and company law tend to use categories similar to the general division into legal families. On one side, one finds the Anglo-Saxon common law model. This is seen as pursuing a market-based approach, where the shareholder's individual interests are to the fore. Moreover, in these countries, capital markets are seen as more developed, so that interest in shares is broader and shareholder ownership is often dispersed.[20] In civil law countries, by contrast, it is claimed that concentrated ownership structures mostly prevail in public companies.[21] Since management cooperates with the dominant shareholders, what counts more are relations within the company than control through the markets. This 'insider model' is to be explained by the fact that banks and employees hold a strong position. The firm is accordingly run not primarily in the interests of shareholders, but of all stakeholders in the undertaking. In these countries too, state influence has a large part to play, so that political views are brought to bear inside the companies.

Further distinctions are frequently made. For instance, since the category of non-Anglo-Saxon countries is very broad, it is suggested that one must distinguish between a Germanic, Latin and Japanese (or Asian) model of corporate governance. Here, for example, it is said that only in the Germanic model does there tend to be a division between a management and supervisory board, that the Latin and Japanese models are more network-oriented than the Germanic, and that stock markets are more important in the Germanic and Japanese model than in the Latin model.[22] Another distinction is between the company law and corporate governance systems of developed, developing and transition economies. In particular, the transition economies of Eastern Europe and Asia have received close attention since it was viewed as an interesting test case whether in the 1990s they could successfully switch from socialism to a system of privately owned companies.[23]

A number of studies by financial economists have suggested that countries of English legal origin (ie common law countries) provide better business law than countries with French or German legal origin (ie civil law countries) and, as a result, more developed financial markets. The first of these studies was that conducted by Rafael La Porta and colleagues on 'Law and Finance'.[24] This study used a quantitative methodology in order to examine the differences in shareholder protection in 49 countries

---

[20] K Hopt, 'Comparative Corporate Governance: The State of the Art and International Regulation' (2011) 59 *American Journal of Comparative Law* 1, 9.

[21] See, eg, M Becht and C Mayer, 'Introduction' in F Barca and M Becht (eds), *The Control of Corporate Europe* (Oxford, Oxford University Press, 2001); M Faccio and LHP Lang, 'The Ultimate Ownership of Western European Corporations' (2002) 65 *Journal of Financial Economics* 365; S Claessens, S Djankov and LHP Lang, 'The Separation of Ownership and Control in East Asian Corporations' (2000) 58 *Journal of Financial Economics* 81.

[22] J Keenan and M Aggestam, 'Corporate Governance and Intellectual Capital: Some Conceptualisations' (2001) 9 *Corporate Governance* 259; J Weimer and J Pape, 'A Taxonomy of Systems of Corporate Governance' (1999) 7 *Corporate Governance* 152.

[23] See, eg, B Black, R Kraakman and A Tarassova, 'Russian Privatization and Corporate Governance: What Went Wrong?' (2000) 52 *Stanford Law Review* 1731 K Pistor, 'Patterns of Legal Change: Shareholder and Creditor Rights in Transition Economies' (2000) *European Business Organization Law Review* 59.

[24] La Porta et al, 'Law and Finance' (n 1).

and its impact on financial development. For the purposes of measuring the law, eight variables were used as proxies for shareholder protection ('one share one vote', 'proxy by mail allowed', 'shares not blocked before the meeting', 'cumulative voting', 'oppressed minorities mechanism', 'pre-emptive rights to new issues', 'share capital required to call an extraordinary shareholder meeting' and 'mandatory dividend'), and in each case a country was graded either '1' where shareholder protection was present or '0' where it was not. Other studies have applied this approach to measuring law to many other areas of law, and have mostly confirmed the alleged supremacy of common law countries.[25]

These studies have been highly influential.[26] The problem is, however, that the findings by La Porta et al have been shown to be inaccurate. Subsequent research has identified many coding errors,[27] and the limited number of variables employed by La Porta et al hardly provides a meaningful picture of the legal protection of shareholders.[28] A number of additional problems have been found as regards both the legal and the econometric elements of these studies.[29] It is also not self-evident that similarities and differences between legal systems can be explained by the distinction between countries with English, French and German legal origin. Since countries of the same legal origin are often neighbouring countries with a similar culture, La Porta et al's results may simply show that geographic vicinity and a common culture make it likely that the laws of two countries influence each other. Moreover, as the following section will address, historical linkages between countries may have become weaker as a consequence of the convergence of legal and economic systems.

C. Convergence, Europeanisation and Americanisation

It is sometimes thought that in the modern world, legal differences, in particular the distinction between civil and common law countries, have become less marked.[30] The company and corporate governance literature has also identified various types of convergence, distinguishing between formal, functional, contractual, hybrid, normative

---

[25] R La Porta, F Lopez-de-Silanes and A Shleifer, 'The Economic Consequences of Legal Origins' (2008) 46 *Journal of Economic Literature* 285. See also M Siems and S Deakin, 'Comparative Law and Finance: Past, Present and Future Research' (2010) 166 *Journal of Institutional and Theoretical Economics* 120.

[26] See B Durisin and F Puzone, 'Maturation of Corporate Governance Research, 1993–2007: An Assessment' (2009) 17 *Corporate Governance* 266.

[27] H Spamann, 'The 'Antidirector Rights Index' Revisited' (2010) 23 *Review of Financial Studies* 468.

[28] For the use of alternative indices, see P Lele and M Siems, 'Shareholder Protection—A Leximetric Approach' (2007) 7 *Journal of Corporate Law Studies* 17; D Katelouzou and M Siems, 'Disappearing Paradigms in Shareholder Protection: Leximetric Evidence for 30 Countries, 1990–2013' (2015) 15 *Journal of Corporate Law Studies* 127.

[29] See, eg, CJ Milhaupt and K Pistor, *Law & Capitalism: What Corporate Crises Reveal about Legal Systems and Economic Development around the World* (Chicago, Chicago University Press, 2008) 27–44; LA Bebchuk and A Hamdani, 'The Elusive Quest for Global Governance Standards' (2009) 157 *University of Pennsylvania Law Review* 1263, 1313–16.

[30] See, eg, BS Markesinis (ed), *The Gradual Convergence: Foreign Ideas, Foreign Influences, and English law on the Eve of the 21st Century* (Oxford, Clarendon Press, 1994); M Siems, 'Legal Origins: Reconciling Law and Finance and Comparative Law' (2007) 52 *McGill Law Journal* 55.

and institutional convergence. Ron Gilson and John Coffee assume that functional convergence is likelier than formal convergence.[31] 'Functional' in this context means that a comparable result is produced with, say, bad managers being dismissed, but along different statutory paths. Alternatively, according to Gilson, there may be contractual convergence, where the formal differences may be functionally relevant, but equivalent effects can also be reached through contractual arrangements.[32] Furthermore, the dualism between formal and functional convergence is supplemented by Paul Rose with the concept of hybrid convergence. This concerns the situation where a firm 'escapes' domestic law by shifting its registered seat to another country.[33] Outside the legal sphere, one may, with Curtis Milhaupt, raise the question of 'normative convergence'.[34] Here, 'normative' means that the notion of convergence is applied to extra-legal norms.[35] Further, David Charny employs the term 'institutional convergence', where de facto the structures in firms become more similar.[36]

A research monograph by the author of this chapter has examined the convergence of the company laws of the UK, the US, France, Germany, Japan and China.[37] In this book, it was shown that in all of these legal systems, various mechanisms of good corporate governance interpenetrate. This can be illustrated by the theoretical distinction between the shareholder as 'owner', 'parliamentarian' and 'investor'. In favour of the 'ownership analogy', for instance, is the fact that in all countries, shareholders can in principle freely sell their shares and are entitled to special rights. In the sense of the 'parliamentarian model', however, there are also mechanisms intended to enable the company to have a self-governing organisation. This also fits in with the fact that alongside the powers of the general meeting, the interests of the overall organisation and a division of powers and checks on power within the company are constructed. In view of the company's ability to attract capital, finally, the 'shareholder as investor' enters into the equation, because finance or disclosure-related provisions of company and securities law are aimed primarily at them.

Convergence has remained a controversial topic. Some scholars object that path dependencies still play an important role. As regards the law, this may be the result of fundamentally different legal mentalities between common and civil law countries,[38] and in terms of corporate governance, historical and cultural differences may

---

[31] RJ Gilson, 'Globalizing Corporate Governance: Convergence of Form or Function' (2001) 49 *American Journal of Comparative Law* 329, 337–45; JC Coffee, 'The Future as History: The Prospects for Global Convergence in Corporate Governance and its Implications' (1999) 93 *Northwestern University Law Review* 641, 679–80.

[32] Gilson, 'Globalizing Corporate Governance' (n 31) 346–50.

[33] P Rose, 'EU Company Law Convergence Possibilities After Centros' (2001) 11 *Transnational Law and Contemporary Problems* 121, 134–35.

[34] CJ Milhaupt, 'Creative Norm Destruction: The Evolution of Nonlegal Rules in Japanese Corporate Governance' (2001) 149 *University of Pennsylvania Law Review* 2083, 2125–28.

[35] Ibid.

[36] D Charny, 'The German Corporate Governance System' (1998) *Columbia Business Law Review* 145, 165.

[37] Siems, *Convergence in Shareholder Law* (n 3).

[38] eg, P Legrand, 'European Legal Systems are not Converging' (1996) 45 *International and Comparative Law Quarterly* 52.

persist, reflecting different types of market economies.[39] More nuanced positions are also possible. For instance, it could be said that today's legal systems do not primarily differ because of different legal families, but instead because of their belonging to a particular regional group. In particular, this may be the case in Europe since the EU has harmonised some aspects of company law and the Europeanisation of economic and legal thinking may also have led to convergence on other topics.

Alternatively, it may be said that there is no actual convergence of legal systems but one-sided Americanisation. There is some general literature on how the US has influenced the positive law and legal culture of other countries since the mid-twentieth century.[40] More specifically, Henry Hansmann and Reinier Kraakman, borrowing from Francis Fukuyama,[41] postulated under the title 'The End of History for Corporate Law', that the historical differences in company law and corporate governance would fade in favour of approximation to the US model.[42] Indeed, it can be shown that the legal systems of continental Europe and Asia have copied some investor-related provisions from US law, without there being a converse feedback into US law. Thus, law-makers in other countries are keen to improve the potential of their companies to attract capital, because of intensified international competition. US law is particularly influential here as big foreign companies are often listed on US markets, US institutional investors have special weight and the US as a world power can exert political pressure.[43]

However, one may also adduce factors which militate against one-sided Americanisation in company law. One indication here comes from the G20/OECD Corporate Governance Principles. While it has been said that they have an underlying Anglo-American tendency, so that their influence is less beneficial for other legal cultures,[44] against this is the fact that, for instance, German company law also largely corresponds to these principles. In the provisions that address the role of stakeholder interests, it can also be seen that the G20/OECD Principles very much show a compromise nature.[45] Moreover, at the country level, it has not been exclusively US concepts that have been 'imported': for example, Japan and China have engaged in a sort of 'cherry-picking', with different elements of various legal systems having been adopted.[46]

---

[39] eg, DM Branson, 'The Very Uncertain Prospect of 'Global' Convergence in Corporate Governance' (2001) 34 *Cornell International Law Journal* 321. See also JN Gordon and MJ Roe (eds), *Convergence and Persistence in Corporate Governance* (Cambridge, Cambridge University Press, 2004).

[40] eg, W Wiegand, 'Die Amerikanisierung des Rechts, insbesondere des Bank- und Wirtschaftsrechts' in T Baums, KJ Hopt and N Horn (eds), *Corporations, Capital Markets and Business in the Law (Liber Amicorum Buxbaum)* (The Hague, Kluwer, 2000) 601; J Wiener, *Globalization and the Harmonization of Law* (London, Pinter, 1999) 197.

[41] F Fukuyama, *The End of History and the Last Man* (London, Penguin, 1992).

[42] H Hansmann and R Kraakman, 'The End of History for Corporate Law' (2001) 89 *Georgetown Law Journal* 439.

[43] Siems, *Convergence in Shareholder Law* (n 3) 226–27.

[44] G McCormack, 'Company Law and the New Millennium: Some Cautionary Tales from the Past' (2000) 21 *Company Lawyer* 57 at 58.

[45] See M Siems and O Alvarez-Macotela, 'The G20/OECD Principles of Corporate Governance 2015: A Critical Assessment of their Operation and Impact' (2017) *Journal of Business Law* 310.

[46] See Siems, *Convergence in Shareholder Law* (n 3) 227.

III. Coding and Quantitative Analysis

The quantitative analysis of this chapter is based on the coding of 20 components of the ten case studies. This section explains the approach to coding the legal rules, the underlying legal sources and the results of these components. Subsequently, it analyses the three datasets under the perspective of similarities and differences between the company laws of the 12 countries of this study.

A. Coding of Components

The ten case studies deal with a variety of legal topics. For the purposes of the following analysis, two key topics from each of the cases, ie 20 components in total, have been identified. Subsequently, these components were coded at three levels, namely the similarities and differences in terms of the legal rules, the underlying legal sources, and the actual results. The full codings are available in the Annex to this chapter. Table 13.1 illustrates how one of the components was coded.

Table 13.1 Coding example for 'veil piercing' (Case 6, first component)[47]

	FRA	GER	ITA	SPA	NL	FIN	POL	LAT	UK	US	RSA	JP
Legal rules	A	B	B	B	B	B	C	C	B	B	B	B
	Explanation: concept of fictitious company (A); concept of piercing the corporate veil (B); no such concepts (C)											
Sources of law	C	C	L,A	C	A	C,A	N	N	C	C	L,C,A	C
	Explanation: legislation (L); courts (C); academics (A) (if cited as a quasi-source of law, instead of a further reference); (N) problem unknown (ie, no law).											
Results	C	S	S	S	S	S	S	S	S	S	S	S
	Explanation: result favouring shareholders (S); creditors (C).											

With respect to the category 'legal rules', the coding was influenced by two conflicting considerations. On the one hand, for the purposes of the subsequent analysis, it would have been pointless to consider each of the 12 legal systems as unique. On the other hand, it would have been equally uninteresting to say that at their core, all legal systems tend to be similar. Thus, it was aimed at identifying between two and four categories for each of the 20 components,[48] such as three (A, B, C) in Table 13.1.

---

[47] In the tables of this chapter the countries are abbreviated as follows: FRA (France), GER (Germany), ITA (Italy), SPA (Spain), NL (The Netherlands), FIN (Finland), POL (Poland), LAT (Latvia), UK (United Kingdom), US (United States), RSA (South Africa) and JP (Japan).
[48] See Annex, Tables A1 and A2, below.

The coding of 'sources of law' was understood in a functional way. For instance, case law and academic writings have been included notwithstanding that they are not regarded as a source of law in a technical sense in all jurisdictions. In addition to the categories shown in Table 13.1, in some of the 20 components the legal responses were based on self-regulation (such as corporate governance codes) or left to the discretion of the company (eg, its articles of association). The final category codes the results of the 20 components. In the example of Table 13.1, there were only two options, namely that this particular component of the case protects the interests of either the shareholders or the creditors. Some of the other cases coded the conflict between the interests of shareholders and directors, on the one hand, and minority and majority shareholders, on the other. In some instances, a country was also coded as not providing a clear answer as to the result of the component in question.

Based on this approach, the subsequent analysis entails an evaluation of the nature and content of the respective legal rules of company law, the sources of those rules, and the results reached on the application of such rules. This approach enables quantification of similarities and differences, going beyond anecdotal examples. To be sure, this does not mean that this approach can be entirely objective: the data reflect the selection of the cases and other local lawyers from the same jurisdictions may not have provided exactly the same answers. However, the design of the project[49] also took measures to reduce the degree of subjectivity: the assignment of each national reporter to draft one of the cases aimed to achieve a good mix of cases; the organisers of the project coordinated the drafting of the cases so as to strike a balance between cases addressing core topics of company law; and to mitigate against idiosyncrasy in the answers, national reporters were asked to clarify whether their legal solutions were likely to be shared by other lawyers from their countries, in circumstances where there was a degree of doubt as to that solution.

B. Comparison of Legal Rules

The coding of the legal rules according to the 20 components[50] offered the opportunity to assess the similarities and differences between the 12 countries in their black letter law. For this purpose, the coded attributes needed to be converted into relations showing the differences between each pair of countries. This is achieved by ascertaining whether each variable in the law of a particular country corresponds to that of any of the other 11 countries, whereby each observation of difference was coded as '1'. Subsequently, the absolute values of these differences are added together.[51] For example, the

---

[49] See ch 1, above.

[50] See Annex, Tables A1 and A2, below.

[51] This approach of turning attributes into relations is accepted in network analysis: see, eg, R Hanneman and M Riddle, *Introduction to Social Network Methods* (2005) ch 6, available at http://faculty.ucr.edu/~hanneman/nettext/; D Knoke and S Yang, *Social Network Analysis* (2nd edn, Beverly Hills, CA, Sage 2008) at 7. For its application to company law, see M Siems, 'The Web of Creditor and Shareholder Protection in 25 Countries: A Comparative Legal Network Analysis' (2010) 27 *Arizona Journal of International and Comparative Law* 747. For legal families, see Siems, 'Varieties of Legal Systems' (n 3).

coding in Table 13.1 shows that France and Germany have different rules that govern the topic of veil piercing (the first component of Case 6). Thus, for this component, the difference between France and Germany is '1'. A corresponding procedure was applied to all 20 components. Adding all of those numbers together led to the result that, for example, in 13 out of 20 components, France and Germany have different legal rules. The outcome of this process for all country pairs is the matrix of differences in Table 13.2.

Table 13.2 Matrix on differences in legal rules (max 20, min 0)

	FRA	GER	ITA	SPA	NL	FIN	POL	LAT	UK	US	RSA	JP	Mean
FRA		13	7	12	8	14	10	13	12	13	11	13	11.45
GER	13		9	9	10	11	8	10	13	16	13	12	11.27
ITA	7	9		8	8	12	9	10	12	10	10	12	9.73
SPA	12	9	8		11	10	10	7	10	10	10	12	9.91
NL	8	10	8	11		9	7	11	13	13	11	11	10.18
FIN	14	11	12	10	9		10	12	10	15	10	14	11.55
POL	10	8	9	10	7	10		6	14	15	14	13	10.55
LAT	13	10	10	7	11	12	6		13	13	15	13	11.18
UK	12	13	12	10	13	10	14	13		11	3	10	11.00
US	13	16	10	10	13	15	15	13	11		11	10	12.45
RSA	11	13	10	10	11	10	14	15	3	11		11	10.82
JP	13	12	12	12	11	14	13	13	10	10	11		11.91

First, Table 13.2 reveals which countries are most similar to and different from the other eleven. The result is that Japan and the US are the most 'eccentric' and Spain and Italy are the most 'mainstream' (see the final column). This may reflect the fact that Japan and the US are, together with South Africa, the only non-EU countries involved in this study. Though it has sometimes been said that EU harmonisation is trivial in company law,[52] a number of the case solutions referred to the EU Directives, for instance, as far as takeovers are concerned, on questions of capital maintenance and the right of shareholders to ask questions in the general meeting.[53] The 'mainstream-ness' of Spain and Italy also makes sense since the company laws of these countries have been influenced by both the French and the German legal traditions. However, overall, even the most similar countries have different legal rules in close to ten of the

---

[52] L Enriques, 'EC Company Law Directives and Regulations: How Trivial Are They?' (2006) 27 *University of Pennsylvania Journal of International Economic Law* 1. For more recent assessments, see L Enriques, 'A Harmonized European Company Law: Are We There Already?' (2017) 66 *International and Comparative Law Quarterly* 763; M Gelter, 'EU Company Law Harmonization Between Convergence and Varieties of Capitalism' in H Wells (ed), *Research Handbook on the History of Corporation and Company Law* (Cheltenham, Edward Elgar, 2018) 323.

[53] See chs 4 and 5 (on takeovers), ch 7 (on capital maintenance) and ch 9 (on shareholder rights), above.

20 components, thus showing that the convergence of company laws has not led to identical rules.

Second, it is interesting to see whether certain intuitive expectations about similarities are confirmed or refuted. The most similar pairs in Table 13.2 are the UK and South Africa, Latvia and Poland, Italy and France, Latvia and Spain, and Poland and the Netherlands. These results may show certain similarities between common law countries on the one hand, and between civil law countries on the other, as one would expect. On the other hand, with respect to the US and both the UK and South Africa, the difference between them is considerable, and at least as high as some of the differences which arise between them and civil law countries. For example, this can be seen in the case studies on takeovers, as well as those on shareholder rights and litigation.[54] Similarly, the literature frequently points towards differences between UK and US company law, in terms of both the legal rules and the law in action.[55] There is also no evidence of an 'Americanisation' of continental European company law, since the US is not particularly close to any of them. Finally, Table 13.2 shows that Japanese company law is closer to that of the United States, as well as to that of the UK, than it is to the law of any of the civil law countries, thus confirming the Japanese shift towards the US system, at least as far as the positive rules are concerned.[56] For instance, the lack of general pre-emption rights and the availability of derivative actions are features of Japanese law that are shared with the US, and make it different from most continental European countries.[57]

The relative proximity of the jurisdictions to one another can also be presented as a network.[58] For this purpose, the information about each of the pairs was entered into a network analysis program (UCINET): it enables to represent the closest 'ties' (ie, relationships between countries), and the more similar the country pair the bolder the tie in Figure 13.1. In addition, using the technique of spring embedding, the network analysis program has shifted the position of nodes according to the strength of their relationships, so that countries whose laws are relatively similar are moved closer together.

---

[54] See chs 4, 5, 9 and 10, above.

[55] See, eg, CM Bruner, *Corporate Governance in the Common-Law World The Political Foundations of Shareholder Power* (Cambridge, Cambridge University Press, 2013); MT Moore, *Corporate Governance in the Shadow of the State* (Oxford, Hart Publishing, 2013); J Armour, B Black, B Cheffins and R Nolan, 'Private Enforcement of Corporate Law: An Empirical Comparison of the United Kingdom and the United States' (2009) 6 *Journal of Empirical Legal Studies* 687; RA Aguilera, CA Williams, JM Conley and DE Rupp, 'Corporate Governance and Social Responsibility: A Comparative Analysis of the UK and the US' (2006) 14 *Corporate Governance* 147; S Toms and M Wright, 'Divergence and Convergence within Anglo-American Corporate Governance Systems: Evidence from the US and UK, 1950–2000' (2005) 46 *Business History* 267.

[56] For this shift since the mid-20th century, see Siems, *Convergence in Shareholder Law* (n 3) 20–22.

[57] See chs 5 and 10, above.

[58] The approach of this chapter is similar to the previous analysis of D Cabrelli and M Siems, 'Convergence, Legal Origins and Transplants in Comparative Corporate Law: A Case-Based and Quantitative Analysis' (2015) 63 *American Journal of Comparative Law* 109. Conversely, the previous edition of this book displayed 'neighbour networks'.

Figure 13.1 Network based on similarity of legal rules (with three clusters)

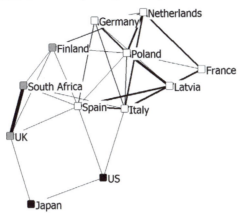

As Figure 13.1 illustrates, the UK and South Africa are connected with a strong link. There is also a close network between most of the continental European countries. This group is then more loosely connected with South Africa and the UK. Finally, the US and in particular Japan are relatively distant from the other countries.

Network analysis also provides tools to identify community structures, such as clusters.[59] A division into three clusters is particularly revealing as it leads to a US-Japan cluster, a UK-South-Africa-Finland cluster, as well as a cluster of the Romanist and Germanic European civil law countries (see the shades of the nodes in Figure 13.1).[60] This result reflects that civilian systems of company law share core similarities, regardless of whether they belong to the German and French branches of the civil law. Finland, as the only country of the Nordic legal family, has, however, been allocated to a cluster with the UK and South Africa – possibly, indicating a hybridity of civil and common law influences. Finally, the remote US and Japan cluster substantiates the point articulated above that the company laws of these two countries are most different from the other countries of the study.

C. Comparison of Underlying Sources of Law

Comparative lawyers often highlight differences in the prevalent sources of law. It is often asserted that case law is more important in common law jurisdictions, whereas in civil law countries, the codes and academic writings play a stronger role.[61] In addition, the company law and corporate governance literature claims that company law rules

---

[59] See, eg, Knoke and Yang, *Social Network Analysis* (n 51) 77–91; Hanneman and Riddle, *Introduction to Social Network Methods* (n 51) chs 11 and 13. For a definition of (optimisation) clusters, see www.analytictech.com/ucinet/help/2cvtid.htm (a formal method that optimises a cost function which measures the total distance or similarity within classes for a proximity matrix); note that this does not depend on the cut-off point used for the purposes of Figure 13.1.

[60] The R^2 of this division into 3 clusters is 0.422.

[61] See II A, above.

are frequently mandatory in continental European legal systems, which can be contrasted with Anglo-Saxon firms who are said to enjoy a greater degree of flexibility:[62] thus, there may also be differences in the extent to which questions are left to self-regulation and the articles of association. But this view of a big divide is not without controversy, as stated previously:

> All the same, in the countries studied here [France, Germany, Japan, China, the US and the UK] convergence in shareholder law has come about. This can be seen, first, in the relevant legal bases ... there are similar basic patterns, with codifications of company and securities law being supplemented by case law, articles of association, shareholder agreements and corporate governance codes. Moreover, market forces play an important part, without a legal system necessarily on that account giving up statutory control mechanisms.[63]

The evidence from non-quantitative statements of the current project is mixed. For example, two of the conclusions show that civilian systems of company law may be more inflexible than their common law counterparts inasmuch as the former are more likely to prohibit or restrict the ability of companies to (i) include provisions in their articles which prevent the heir of a deceased shareholder from inheriting the latter's shares[64] or (ii) issue debt securities convertible into equity.[65] This can be contrasted with two other conclusions which confirm that both civilian and common law jurisdictions recognise (i) the highly flexible informal unanimous consent rule or a functional equivalent in their company laws[66] and (ii) the validity of pre-emption provisions in the articles of their companies, with or without restrictions.[67]

Table 13.3 Prevalence of sources of law (max 20, three highest values highlighted)

	FRA	GER	ITA	SPA	NL	FIN	POL	LAT	UK	US	RSA	JP
Legislation	17	17	19	18	18	18	16	17	15	8	16	18
Case law	11	13	5	4	12	2	2	1	15	15	9	10
Academic	1	11	7	9	6	3	6	2	0	0	3	2
Self-regulation	0	0	0	1	0	2	0	0	4	0	2	0
Discretion	0	0	0	0	0	0	0	0	0	2	0	0
None	0	0	1	0	0	1	3	3	0	2	0	1

The quantitative coding of sources of law for the purposes of this chapter[68] leads to the following general results, as reported in Table 13.3. First, it can be seen that legislation is the most relevant source for at least 75 per cent of the components (ie 15) in all legal systems except the US. The difference between the UK and the US may be surprising, but it is not wholly implausible. The frequent reforms of UK company law have expanded the scope and detail of the Companies Act. For example, in the UK

---

[62] See II B, above.
[63] See, eg, Siems, *Convergence in Shareholder Law* (n 3) 225, also 59.
[64] See ch 11 at III G, above.
[65] See ch 3 at III B, above
[66] See ch 10 at III B (ii), above.
[67] See ch 11 at III B, above.
[68] See A, above, and Annex, Table A3, below.

Companies Act 2006, topics such as directors' duties have now been partly codified, whereas even in civil law countries such as France and Germany, these are still largely based on case law.[69]

Second, the data show that case law is not only important in the UK and the US but also in Germany, the Netherlands, France and Japan. It plays less of a role, however, in the jurisdictions with a smaller pool of case law, possibly because they have relatively new company laws (Poland, Latvia) or because they are relatively small jurisdictions (Finland, Latvia). It is also worth pointing out that to say that case law plays a role in both civil and common law countries does not mean that their actual mode of operation is identical in practice; for instance, there may still be differences in terms of the prevalent judicial approach, such as whether to adopt legal reasoning based on ideas of justice or efficiency.[70]

Third, academic research plays a significant role in many of the case solutions from Germany, Spain and Italy, whereas it was not decisive for the UK and the US. This could be viewed as confirming the difference between civil and common law – and the slightly higher values for South Africa and Japan may therefore reflect elements of their partly civilian heritage despite. Yet, there is also considerable variation within the civil law family, noting the low numbers for France, Finland and Latvia. For this category in particular, it is also worth restating the caveat[71] that personal preferences of the contributors may have influenced the frequency of references to academic writings.

Although the final three categories were only relevant for few of the countries, the results can be seen as plausible. (i) Self-regulation plays a relatively important role in UK company law, for instance with respect to takeovers.[72] (ii) In the US, there are a few instances where there is simply no law at all or the decision is left to the discretion of the company; this is to be explained by the 'light approach' in regulating the internal affairs of companies[73] that has been adopted by Delaware, the corporate seat of almost half of the listed companies in the US. (iii) Finally, Poland and Latvia have only relatively recently promulgated a set of company laws. Therefore, it is perhaps unsurprising that in a few instances a response was received to the effect that a particular legal problem or solution was not yet known.

---

[69] UK Companies Act, 2006, ss 171–178. For comparative overviews, see C Gerner-Beuerle, P Paech and E Schuster, *Study on Directors' Duties and Liability* (London, LSE Enterprise 2013), available at http://eprints.lse.ac.uk/50438/; B Black, B Cheffins, M Gelter, H-J Kim, R Nolan and M Siems, 'Legal Liability of Directors and Company Officials Part 1: Substantive Grounds for Liability' (2007) *Columbia Business Law Review* 614. See also chs 2 and 3, above.

[70] See II A, above.

[71] See A, above.

[72] See, eg, J Armour and D Skeel, 'Who Writes the Rules for Hostile Takeovers, and Why? The Peculiar Divergence of US and UK Takeover Regulation' (2007) 95 *Georgetown Law Journal* 1727. See also chs 4 and 5, above.

[73] Critics call this a 'race to the bottom'; see WL Cary, 'Federalism and Corporate Law: Reflections Upon Delaware' (1974) 83 *Yale Law Journal* 663. Conversely, others emphasise its efficiency; see R Romano, *The Genius of American Corporate Law* (Washington DC, AEI Press, 1993) 14. See also D, below.

Table 13.4 Prevalence of sources of law

	Total (ie all 10 cases)	Cases on private companies	Cases on public companies
Legislation	82.08%	85.42%	79.86%
Case law	41.25%	38.54%	43.06%
Academic	20.83%	25.00%	18.06%
Self-regulation	3.75%	0.00%	6.25%
Discretion	0.83%	1.04%	0.69%
None	4.58%	3.13%	5.56%

Does the preference for a particular source of law vary between private companies (such as the 'Ltd' in the UK and the 'GmbH' in Germany) and public companies (such as the UK's 'plc' and the German 'AG')? As the scenarios of this book always specified the type of company in question,[74] it was possible to calculate the prevalence of the sources of law for private and public companies: Table 13.4 shows that there are only small differences. This is also a reflection of the scope of the project as its main focus was on topics of company law. Of course, if one were to consider rules specifically applicable to companies admitted to a stock exchange, listing rules and other forms of secondary regulation would play a decisive role for public companies.

Table 13.5 Matrix on differences in sources of law (max 20, min 0)

	FRA	GER	ITA	SPA	NL	FIN	POL	LAT	UK	US	RSA	JP	Mean
FRA		7.84	7.51	6.84	7.17	8.67	9.17	9.00	6.84	12.34	5.84	6.17	7.94
GER	7.84		8.17	7.17	8.18	10.00	9.84	11.50	8.84	12.33	10.00	8.67	9.32
ITA	7.51	8.17		7.17	8.34	4.50	9.50	5.17	10.67	12.33	7.67	7.34	8.03
SPA	6.84	7.17	7.17		8.01	7.50	8.17	7.84	10.17	13.00	9.67	7.51	8.46
NL	7.17	8.18	8.34	8.01		8.01	7.50	8.17	7.84	10.17	13.00	9.67	8.73
FIN	8.67	10.00	4.50	7.50	8.01		9.17	3.84	10.00	13.00	9.67	7.34	8.33
POL	9.17	9.84	9.50	8.17	7.50	9.17		6.33	11.84	15.50	12.33	10.66	10.00
LAT	9.00	11.50	5.17	7.84	8.17	3.84	6.33		11.84	13.67	10.00	8.50	8.71
UK	6.84	8.84	10.67	10.17	7.84	10.00	11.84	11.84		8.00	7.00	8.34	9.21
US	12.34	12.33	12.33	13.00	10.17	13.00	15.50	13.67	8.00		7.00	8.67	11.45
RSA	5.84	10.00	7.67	9.67	13.00	9.67	12.33	10.00	7.00	7.00		8.67	9.17
JP	6.17	8.67	7.34	7.51	9.67	7.34	10.66	8.50	8.34	8.67	8.67		8.32

---

[74] The cases in chs 2–3, 7, 10 deal with private companies and those in chs 4–7, 9, 11 with public companies. See also ch 1 at II B, above.

Figure 13.2 Network based on similarity of sources of law (with three clusters)

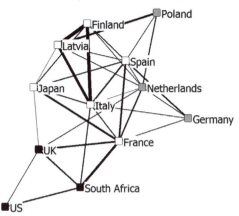

As in the previous section, the data can be transformed into a matrix showing the differences between country pairs which can then be used to produce a network picture with a division into three clusters.[75] The resulting Table 13.5 and Figure 13.2 can then be explained as follows (also drawing on the information from Table 13.3, above): Latvia, Finland and Italy are fairly close since in all three countries legislation is by far the most important source of law. The other civil law countries – here, in contrast to Figure 13.1, including Japan – are also connected with this group. Yet, some differences can also be observed: for example, the fact that Germany, the Netherlands and Poland are allocated into a separate cluster may be due to the significant role of the academic literature. France is close the UK and South Africa, possibly, due to the high influence of case law and the low influence of academic writing. Finally, the UK, the US and South Africa are connected to each other and form their own common law cluster. Overall, it is also worth noting that the US is most different, in particular since it relies much less on legislation in company law than do the other countries of this study.

D. Comparison of Results

As explained at the beginning of this book,[76] the ten case scenarios have been selected in order to cover topics of directors' duties, creditor and shareholder protection. Thus, it was possible to examine whether legal systems tend to favour the interests of directors, shareholders or creditors. In addition, in companies with a dominant shareholder, the main conflict is often between minority and majority/controlling shareholders. All of this was reflected in the coding of the results for the 20 components.[77] Table 13.6 aggregates those data. Since not all potential interests are addressed in each of those components, it also indicates the maximum that can be achieved in each of the categories.

---

[75] The R2 of this division into 3 clusters is 0.378.
[76] See ch 1 at III, above.
[77] See Annex, Table A4, below.

Table 13.6 Preference for interests of directors, shareholders and creditors (highest values highlighted)

	FRA	GER	ITA	SPA	NL	FIN	POL	LAT	UK	US	RSA	JP
Directors (max. 11)	6	5	6	6	6	3	3	6	6	9	3	4
Shareholders (max. 11)	4	3	5	3	5	6	4	3	5	3	4	4
Creditors (max. 3)	2	2	1	2	1	1	2	2	1	1	3	2
Majority shareholders (max. 8)	2	2	1	2	2	3	4	3	7	4	4	6
Minority shareholders (max. 8)	4	5	4	2	4	4	4	4	1	0	2	1
Unclear (max. 20)	2	3	3	5	2	3	3	2	0	3	4	3

Starting with positions of directors and shareholders, Table 13.6 points towards US exceptionalism since the US tends to favour directors more often than all of the other countries. This is in line with other studies that stress the predominance of the 'director primacy' model in US corporate law,[78] while disaffirming the view expressed by Hansmann and Kraakman that modern US law leads the way in having adopted a shareholder-oriented model.[79] Some scholars have argued that the director primacy approach of US law has worked very well,[80] though others have suggested that existing rights must be made more effective and that the power of shareholders to modify the company's charter ought to be improved.[81]

The low aggregate level of shareholder protection in US law raises doubts about the legal origins 'story', namely the argument that the comparatively robust shareholder protection of common law countries has led to more dispersed shareholder ownership and more developed capital markets.[82] This does not deny that US law has some elements that may be particularly favourable towards shareholders. For example, the combination of contingency fees and the 'American cost rule' creates strong incentives

---

[78] Note that this specifically refers to US corporate law, while in securities law, the US may be more effective in the protection of investors, eg through advanced disclosure requirements and a well-funded regulator; see HE Jackson and MJ Roe, 'Public and Private Enforcement of Securities Laws: Resource-Based Evidence' (2009) 93 *Journal of Financial Economics* 207.

[79] See II C, above.

[80] eg, SM Bainbridge, *Corporate Governance After the Financial Crisis* (Oxford, Oxford University Press, 2012) 233–55; I Anabtawi, 'Some Skepticism About Increasing Shareholder Power' (2006) 53 *UCLA Law Review* 561.

[81] eg, LA Bebchuk, 'The Myth that Insulating Boards Serves Long-Term Value' (2013) 113 *Columbia Law Review* 1637; J Velasco, 'Taking Shareholder Rights Seriously' (2007) 41 *UC Davis Law Review* 605; LA Bebchuk, 'Letting Shareholders Set the Rules' (2006) 119 *Harvard Law Review* 1784.

[82] See II B, above.

to enforce breaches of directors' duties.[83] This can be contrasted with the more stringent preconditions applied in the context of a derivative action in Spain and Finland, where a shareholder must hold a minimum of 5 and 10 per cent of the shares of the company respectively; it is likewise more stringent in the UK, where the courts apply statutory pre-hearing criteria in a manner which is generally hostile to the continuation of derivative litigation.[84] Conversely, in other situations, the UK provides better shareholder protection and heightened accountability of directors than the US, for example, as it applies a strict duty of board neutrality in takeover law.[85]

The data on the protection of majority or minority shareholders show that here in particular there is a civil-common law divide since the countries with a company law influenced by the common law model (UK, US, South Africa but also Japan) have lower levels of minority shareholder protection than the civil law countries. This can be explained by the relatively concentrated ownership structures of continental European companies, leading to the risk that the dominant shareholder exploits the minority. In the UK and the US, shareholder ownership is more dispersed and therefore there may be less need to interfere with the principle of majority rule.[86] Hence, there is indeed some evidence for the proposition that civil law systems may prioritise the eradication or minimisation of horizontal agency costs more than common law jurisdictions by placing greater emphasis on duties owed by controlling shareholders to minority shareholders.[87]

The remaining two categories of Table 13.6 have to be interpreted cautiously as they include few observations. Creditor protection seems to be stronger in most civil law countries than in the UK and the US, which may reflect that in the former countries, bank finance is more important than market finance. Indeed, the findings from the case on 'veil piercing' and related topics suggest that French and Japanese law are the most pro-creditor and the US the least.[88] However, since this category is based only on three variables, the results should not be overinterpreted. Finally, it is difficult to adduce why in a particular jurisdiction there were more 'unclear' results indicated by the national reporters than in others; however, it may make sense that in UK company law there are no unclear results, reflecting its long history of codification and case law.

Table 13.7 Matrix on differences in results (max 20, min 0)

	FRA	GER	ITA	SPA	NL	FIN	POL	LAT	UK	US	RSA	JP	Mean
FRA		12	7	10	13	9	9	10	12	12	13	14	11.00
GER	12		9	9	12	11	7	6	12	15	14	14	11.00
ITA	7	9		4	10	10	10	7	13	9	12	12	9.36

(continued)

---

[83] See M Siems, 'Private Enforcement of Directors' Duties: Derivative Actions as a Global Phenomenon' in S Wrbka, S Van Uytsel and M Siems (eds), *Collective Actions: Enhancing Access to Justice and Reconciling Multilayer Interests?* (Cambridge, Cambridge University Press, 2012) 93–116.

[84] For further details, see ch 10, above.

[85] See ch 4 at III B, above.

[86] For the latter, see ch 8, above.

[87] See also II B, above. For a similar finding see Lele and Siems, 'Shareholder Protection—A Leximetric Approach' (n 28).

[88] See ch 6 at III C, above.

Table 13.7 *(Continued)*

	FRA	GER	ITA	SPA	NL	FIN	POL	LAT	UK	US	RSA	JP	Mean
SPA	10	9	4		10	9	9	7	11	8	10	11	8.91
NL	13	12	10	10		13	10	9	13	12	11	14	11.55
FIN	9	11	10	9	13		8	10	11	13	12	15	11.00
POL	9	7	10	9	10	8		5	11	16	11	16	10.18
LAT	10	6	7	7	9	10	5		11	12	12	14	9.36
UK	12	12	13	11	13	11	11	11		10	8	9	11.00
US	12	15	9	8	12	13	16	12	10		10	7	11.27
RSA	13	14	12	10	11	12	11	12	8	10		10	11.18
JP	14	14	12	11	14	15	16	14	9	7	10		12.36

Figure 13.3 Network based on similarity of results (with three clusters)

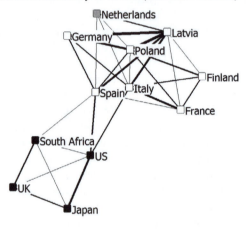

As in the previous sections, the data can be transformed into a matrix showing the differences between country pairs which can be used to produce a network picture with a division into three clusters.[89] In Table 13.7 and Figure 13.3 then, the continental European civil law countries are shown to be relatively similar in the results, almost all of them belonging to the same cluster. Italy and Spain are particularly close, as well as Germany, Poland and Latvia as they all have slightly lower shareholder protection but score well in creditor protection (see Table 13.6). The network analysis program has allocated the Netherlands to a different cluster: in the aggregate score, it does not seem to be very different from the other European countries; yet, in the difference matrix this is the case (see Tables 13.6 and 13.7). The explanation is that Dutch law deviates from some of the mainstream tools of shareholder protection, for example in not providing derivative claims, as also found in other quantitative research.[90]

---

[89] The R2 of this division into 3 clusters is 0.513.
[90] See Katelouzou and Siems, 'Disappearing Paradigms in Shareholder Protection' (n 28).

Finally, the remaining four countries – the US, the UK, South Africa and Japan – are relatively different from this continental group. As already explained, this is due to the relatively low levels of shareholder or minority shareholder protection; yet, there is some diversity within this group, for example, due to the director primacy of US law, higher levels of creditor protection in South Africa and Japan, and the lack of any unclear results in the UK (see Table 13.6).

E. Relationship between Legal Rules, Sources of Law and Results

Since the three 'difference matrices' and corresponding network pictures use the same measure (namely, how different each of the countries is from the others), they are useful tools for a combined analysis of legal rules, sources of law and results. This section will provide different ways of implementing such an analysis.

First, one can simply sum up the data and identify which pairs of countries are most similar. When the pairs are ranked, the three most similar pairs are Latvia and Poland, the UK and South Africa, and Italy and Spain (difference of 17.33, 18.00 and 19.17 out of 60). It is then also possible to aggregate all of the pairs for each country: this shows that Italy, Spain and Latvia are the 'most mainstream' countries (difference of 27.12, 27.28 and 29.26), while the US is the 'most eccentric' one (differences of 35.18). The same can also be seen in Figures 13.1–13.3, above, where Italy and Spain are always at the centre of the networks while the US at the fringes.

It may be a surprise to learn that none of the 'origin countries' of legal families (England [ie here the UK], France or Germany) is at the centre of the networks. Yet this outcome is not implausible since it is other countries, such as Italy, Spain and Latvia, which have been influenced by multiple origin countries, thus explaining their relative similarity. It also confirms another quantitative study, which found that, with respect to creditor and shareholder protection in 25 countries, transplant countries were typically the countries most similar to the other 24.[91]

Table 13.8 Comparison of clusters in three fields of analysis

Legal rules	US			JP		SPA ITA LAT FRA GER POL NL			
		RSA UK			FIN				
Sources of law	US RSA UK		JP FIN SPA ITA LAT FRA			GER POL NL			
Results	US RSA UK JP		FIN SPA ITA LAT FRA GER POL			NL			

Second, Table 13.8 compares the three clusters of the respective networks. It can be seen that there are some common patters but also some variations. On the one hand, the US, UK and South Africa are always in one of the common law clusters, while Spain, Italy, Latvia, France, Germany, Poland and the Netherlands are always in one of the civil law clusters. On the other hand, Japan and Finland have less consistent positions. They can be explained as follows: as far as legal rules are concerned it is

---

[91] Siems, 'The Web of Creditor and Shareholder Protection in 25 Countries' (n 51).

fairly easy to adopt rules from other countries; thus, it is not implausible that Japan and Finland join some of the common law countries here despite their (mainly) civil law nature.[92]

Third, it is interesting to examine the relationship between legal rules, sources of law and results more formally. The correlation between the sources of law and the other two categories is positive yet relatively modest (0.38 for legal rules and 0.26 for results), but there is a strong positive correlation between legal rules and results (0.64). Of course, correlation does not imply causation. Thus, it was also calculated the extent to which the differences in results are determined by the differences in legal rules and/or the sources of law: the resulting regression output shows that the legal rules are strongly significant but the sources of law are not.[93]

This regularity does not mean, however, that the content of the legal rules is automatically reflected in the results. For example, on the one hand, the positive law may be similar but applied differently, for instance because a legal transplant does not work as well as it does in the origin country ('transplant effect').[94] On the other hand, it may be suggested that even where the positive law is different, the results may be similar since different legal rules can be functional equivalents.[95]

Fourth, therefore, in order to assess this point, one may compare the mean differences of the three categories. These are 55 per cent for legal rules, 45 per cent for sources of law and 53 per cent for the results. Thus, considering the 2 per cent gap between rules and results, it may follow that there are some formal differences which functionally lead to the same result. However, a problem with this reasoning is that in the dataset, the category results usually only had three options per component (eg, protecting shareholders, protecting directors, or 'unclear'), whereas sometimes there were more options in the legal rules category.[96] Thus, it cannot be excluded that this feature of the dataset may be the main reason why there appear to be more differences in terms of legal rules.

Fifth, a suitable method for establishing the relationship between rules and results is to examine selected pairs of countries. This has been done in Table 13.9, scaling the three categories from −1 to 1 (based on the most similar and different country pairs in each of the categories). Thus, for example, the positive number of 0.08 in the GER–LAT column indicates that Germany and Latvia are slightly more different than average in terms of legal rules, while the number −0.67 means that with respect to the results, Germany and Latvia are relatively similar, as compared to the average.

---

[92] See II A, above.

[93] Legal rules: standardised coefficient 0. 639748; significance 0.000. Sources of law: standardised coefficient 0.017865; significance 0.449; R[2]: 0.418. This uses the regression method for network data, called 'QAP via full partialling', see Hanneman and Riddle (n 51) ch 18.

[94] For the latter point, see, eg, D Berkowitz, K Pistor and J-F Richard, 'The Transplant Effect' (2003) 51 *American Journal of Comparative Law* 163; TT Arvind, 'The 'Transplant Effect' in Harmonization' (2010) 59 *International and Comparative Law Quarterly* 65.

[95] This is a frequent claim of comparative lawyers; see, eg, B Markesinis, 'The Destructive and Constructive Role of the Comparative Lawyer' (1993) 57 *Rabels Zeitschrift für ausländisches und internationales Privatrecht* 438 at 443 ('we must try to overcome obstacles of terminology and classification in order to show that foreign law is not very different from ours but only appears to be so').

[96] See Annex, Table A1, below.

Table 13.9 Differences from mean for selected pairs of countries (with similarities highlighted)

	GER-LAT	US-JP	UK-RSA	UK-FRA	NL-RSA	UK-US
Legal rules	0.08	0.08	−1.00	0.38	0.23	0.23
Sources of law	0.31	−0.17	−0.46	−0.49	0.57	−0.29
Results	−0.67	−0.50	−0.33	0.33	0.17	0.00

One might expect that Germany and Latvia, the US and Japan, and the UK and South Africa have relatively similar legal rules since the latter countries borrowed rules from some of the former ones. But perhaps these legal transplants did not come to function in the same way as in their original jurisdictions, as they became shaped by the socio-economic, political and cultural context of the host jurisdictions. Table 13.8, however, only confirms this point for the UK-South Africa relationship; by contrast, the country pairs of Germany–Latvia and the US–Japan are closer in their results than in their legal rules. This sounds like a negative finding; however, it may also be put in a more positive light, namely that there is no support for the proposition that transplanted laws cannot work as well as non-transplanted ones.[97]

With respect to the next three examples of Table 13.8, there are also some interesting findings in terms of sources of law. For the UK–France relationship the similarity in this regard may be surprising while for the Netherlands–South Africa relationship the difference may be surprising as far as one may expect some residual influence of civilian thinking in South Africa. Finally, the US and the UK are only relatively close in their sources of law; thus, in this regard it shows some commonality of the common law which largely seems to have disappeared as far as legal rules and results are concerned.

Sixth, it can be examined as to whether case law generates different results than other sources of law, in particular statute law. Thus, the mean differences of the three categories were recalculated, focusing on the solutions that refer to case law. Here, the difference between legal rules is 43 per cent – compared to 55 per cent for all sources of law; and between the actual results it is 56 per cent – compared to 53 per cent for all sources of law. This can be explained as follows: topics where case law is important, such as directors' duties, have legal rules that are fairly similar across countries today; however, differences in the results may be more pronounced since courts are keen to apply these rules to the specific socio-economic context of the country in question.

In addition, a recalculation was performed to determine whether courts have a greater tendency than legislatures to protect shareholders. The background to this question is that some have argued that the common law countries are better at protecting shareholders since their courts are more alive to the protection of property rights, whereas legislatures more often pursue other aims, such as the redistribution of resources.[98] However, the data show virtually no difference, with 41 per cent of both

---

[97] It may even be possible that sometimes they work better than in the country of origin. See M Siems, 'The Curious Case of Overfitting Legal Transplants' in M Adams and D Heirbaut (eds) *The Method and Culture of Comparative Law: Essays in Honour of Mark Van Hoecke* (Oxford, Hart Publishing, 2014) 133–45.

[98] See, eg, T Beck and R Levine, 'Legal Institutions and Financial Development' in C Menard and MM Shirley (eds), *Handbook of New Institutional Economics* (Dordrecht, Springer, 2005) 251–78.

'all solutions' and 'solutions with case law' favouring shareholder protection. Thus, according to the data, case law does not have a greater tendency to protect shareholders than other sources of law.

IV. Conclusion

This chapter has provided a quantitative analysis of the ten case studies. The main aim was to inform the understanding of the extent to which the legal systems explored have fundamentally similar company law rules and sources of company law, as well as the nature of the results reached on the application of such rules. Though not all results point in a clear direction, a number of concluding observations can be made:

The first is that it is not possible to confirm a global convergence, in particular a general Americanisation, of company laws. There is some evidence of legal transplants, for example as regards the relationship of Japanese to US company law. Yet, overall, in all three categories – legal rules, sources of law and results – the US is the outlier. Hence, there is no evidence for Hansmann and Kraakman's view of 'an end of history for corporate law' with the modern US model of company law having won the day.[99] Moreover, both the US and Japan are relatively different from the European countries of the study, thus raising some doubts about a global convergence of company laws.

Secondly, the question of Europeanisation of company law is more difficult to answer. There is some evidence that EU law has led to some convergence of company laws. Still, the UK system of company law is a bit of an outlier in terms of the nature of the rules, the sources of those rules, and the outcome reached when such rules are applied. Moreover, it is remarkable that even the continental European countries differ considerably. For instance, while the two Eastern European countries of the study (Latvia and Poland) have transplanted some rules from other legal systems, there are still notable differences in the underlying sources of law, in particular in the role played by case law. There are also differences remaining in the protection of shareholders, even within continental Europe, with Spain providing less protection than the other civil law countries. Thus, while there is some evidence for convergence, even in a relatively homogeneous region such as the EU, there is clearly no 'end of history for company law'.

Thirdly, it is sometimes argued that convergence only leads to formal similarities and fails to respond to the need for functionally equivalent legal rules. The results, however, do not confirm such scepticism. It was not possible to confirm functional similarity with formal dissimilarity (or formal similarity with function dissimilarity) which also means that it was not possible to find a 'transplant effect' in countries that have been influenced by foreign legal rules. It was also established that there is a strong positive correlation between the content of legal rules and the actual results: thus, formal convergence can work insofar as law-makers possess a willingness to achieve common standards, for instance in the protection of shareholders or creditors.

---

[99] See II C, above.

Fourthly, legal families have only been found to play a limited role. Some of the most similar country pairs can be related to legal families, for example the very similar legal rules in the UK and South Africa. There are also some similarities between the UK and the US in terms of sources of law, yet case law also plays an important role in Germany, France and Japan. One of the findings shows that, possibly due to their more concentrated ownership structures, the civil law countries of continental Europe provide stronger protection for minority shareholders against the majority than do the UK and the US. But, more generally, many of the similarities and differences in legal rules and actual results do not align with the categories of legal families. More specifically, the findings do not confirm the hypothesis that the case law of common law countries is a crucial determinant for their high levels of shareholder protection.[100]

Annex

Table A1 Topics and coding of legal rules

Chapter and topic		Topics with coding in brackets
2	Directors' duties	Legal system has both duties of loyalty and care (A); otherwise (B)
	Shareholder approval	Ratification of breach of duties does not have effect on substantive law (A); ratification has such an effect (B); *ex ante* waiver of liability possible (C)
3	Promissory note	Possible (A); possible under certain restriction (B); possible only for public companies (C)
	Interested directors	Vote of interested director does not invalidate resolution if majority of disinterested directors (A); resolution is invalid or at least voidable (B)
4	Sale of assets	No approval by general meeting needed for sale of substantial assets, eg 30 per cent of all assets (A); approval needed (B); more information needed (C)
	Board neutrality (1)	No strict board neutrality rule (A); board neutrality rule even before official offer (B); board neutrality only after offer (C); board neutrality only if opt in by company (D)
5	Pre-emption rights	Company law requires pre-emption rights (A); no pre-emption rights (B)
	Board neutrality (2)	As chapter 4, second topic
6	Veil piercing	Concept of fictitious company (A); concept of piercing the corporate veil (B); no such concepts (C)
	Directors' duties to creditors	Creditor interests may need to be considered even before insolvency (A); ditto, but this can also be enforced by creditors (B); just general directors' duties but may be enforced by creditors (C); no special rules of creditor protection (D)

(continued)

---

[100] See II B, above.

Table A1 *(Continued)*

7	Challenge dividends	Dividends determined by accounting-based models (A); solvency-based models (B)
	Challenge payment	Prohibition of disguised distributions (A); other forms of restrictions (B); no such restrictions (C)
8	Non- payment of dividends	No general right to dividends (A); right that decision on dividend distribution is taken (B); right to dividends (C)
	Interested shareholder	Interested shareholder is allowed to vote (A); some exceptions (B); entire fairness standard (C); other solution (D)
9	Q&As at shareholders' meeting	Right to ask question and demand answer at shareholders' meeting (A); subsequent answer possible (B); no such rights (C)
	Challenge resolution	Merger resolution cannot be challenged (A); substantive assessment possible (B); injunction needed to stop merger (C); other solution (D)
10	Implicit shareholders' meeting	Unanimous consent rule (A); consent of all shareholders only assumed under additional requirements (B); not possible (C)
	Derivative action	Derivative action in principle possible (A); not possible (B)
11	Pre-emptive offer	Possible to require pre-emptive offer for sale of shares (A); limited possibility (B); not possible (C)
	Inheriting shares	Possible to restrict succession of shares (A); limited possibility (B); not possible (C)

Table A2 Similarities of legal rules (based on coding template of Table A1)

Chapter and topic		FRA	GER	ITA	SPA	NL	FIN	POL	LAT	UK	US	RSA	JP
2	Directors' duties	A	A	A	A	A	A	A	A	A	A	A	A
	Shareholder approval	A	A	A	A	A	A	A	B	B	C	A	B
3	Promissory note	A	C	C	C	B	B	C	C	A	A	A	B
	Interested directors	B	A	A	A	B	B	B	A	A	A	A	A
4	Sale of assets	A	C	A	A	A	C	A	B	A	B	C	
	Board neutrality (1)	D	D	D	C	D	B	D	C	B	A	B	A
5	Pre-emption rights	A	A	A	A	A	A	A	A	A	B	A	B
	Board neutrality (2)	D	D	D	C	D	B	D	C	B	A	B	A
6	Veil piercing	A	B	B	B	B	B	C	C	B	B	B	B
	Directors' duties to creditors	A	C	D	C	D	D	D	D	A	D	B	B
7	Challenge dividends	A	A	A	A	A	B	A	A	B	A	B	A
	Challenge payment	B	A	B	A	B	A	A	A	A	C	B	A

(continued)

Table A2 *(Continued)*

Chapter and topic		FRA	GER	ITA	SPA	NL	FIN	POL	LAT	UK	US	RSA	JP
8	Non-payment of dividends	A	B	A	A	C	C	A	A	A	A	A	B
	Interested shareholder	A	B	D	B	A	B	A	A	B	C	B	A
9	Q&As at shareholders' meeting	A	A	A	B	A	B	B	B	A	C	A	A
	Challenge resolution	A	D	C	C	B	B	B	D	B	C	B	B
10	Implicit shareholders' meeting	C	B	C	B	B	B	B	B	A	A	A	C
	Derivative action	A	B	A	A	B	A	B	B	A	A	A	A
11	Pre-emptive offer	A	B	A	A	A	B	A	A	A	A	A	A
	Inheriting shares	C	B	B	A	A	B	B	B	A	A	A	A

Table A3 Sources of law

Chapter and topic		FRA	GER	ITA	SPA	NL	FIN	POL	LAT	UK	US	RSA	JP
2	Directors' duties	L,C	L,C,A	L,C,A	L,C	L,C,A	L,A	L	L,C,A	L,C	C	L,C,A	L,C,A
	Shareholder approval	L	C,A	L,A	L	L	L	N	L	L,C	C,F	L	L,A
3	Promissory note	L	L	L	L	L	L	L	L	L	L	L	L
	Interested directors	C	L,C,A	L,A	L,C,A	L,A	L,A	L,A	L,A	L,C	L,C	L,C	L,C
4	Sale of assets	L	L,C	N	L,S	L,C	N	L	N	S	N	S	L
	Board neutrality (1)	L	L,A	L	L	L,C	L,S	L	L	L,S	C	L	L,C
5	Pre-emption rights	L	L	L	L	L,C	L	L	L	L,C	C	S	L,C
	Board neutrality (2)	L	L,A	L	L	L,C	L,S	L	L	L,S	L,C	L	L,C
6	Veil piercing	C	C	L,A	C	A	C,A	N	N	C	C	L,C,A	C
	Directors' duties to creditors	L,C	L,A	L	L,A	L,C	L	L	L	L,C	C	L,C	L,C
7	Challenge dividends	L,C	L,A	L,A	L	L,C	L	L	L	L,C	L,C	L,C	L
	Challenge payment	L,C	L,C,A	L	A	C,A	L	L,C,A	L	L,C	N	L	N
8	Non-payment of dividends	L,C	L,C	L,C,A	L,C,A	L,C	L	L	L	L,C	C	L,C	L,C
	Interested shareholder	L	L,A	L,A	L,A	L,C	L,A	N	N	C	C	L	L

(continued)

Table A3 *(Continued)*

Chapter and topic		FRA	GER	ITA	SPA	NL	FIN	POL	LAT	UK	US	RSA	JP
9	Q&As at shareholders' meeting	L,C	L,C	L,C	L,A	L,C	L	L,A	L	L,S	F	C	L
	Challenge resolution	L	L,C	L	L	L,A	L	L,C	L	C	C	L,A	L
10	Implicit shareholders' meeting	C	L,C,A	L	L	L,C	L	A	L	C	L	C	L
	Derivative action	L	C,A	L	L,A	L	L	L	L	L,C	L,C	L,C	L
11	Pre-emptive offer	L,C	L,C,A	L,C	L,A	L,A	L,C	L,A	L	L,C	L,C	L,C	L,C
	Inheriting shares	L,C,A	L,C,A	L,C	L,A	L,A	L	L,A	L	L,C	L,C	L,C	L,C

Notes: legislation (L); courts (C); academics (A) (if cited as a quasi-source of law, instead of a further reference); discretion of firm (F) (going beyond simply filling in the content); self-regulation (S) (stock exchange rules, takeover codes, corporate governance codes, etc); (N) problem unknown (ie no law).

Table A4 Results of cases in terms of interests

Chapter and topic		FRA	GER	ITA	SPA	NL	FIN	POL	LAT	UK	US	RSA	JP
2	Directors' duties	D	S	D	D	S	D	S	S	D	D	S	D
	Shareholder approval	MIS	MIS	MIS	MIS	MIS	MIS	MIS	MAS	MAS	MAS	MIS	MAS
3	Promissory note	D	X	S	S	S	S	S	S	D	D	D	D
	Interested directors	S	D	D	D	S	S	S	D	D	D	D	D
4	Sale of assets	D	MAS	D	D	D	D	MAS	D	MAS	D	X	MAS
	Board neutrality (1)	D	D	D	D	D	S	X	D	S	D	S	D
5	Pre-emption rights	MIS	MIS	MIS	MIS	MIS	MIS	MIS	MIS	MAS	D	MAS	MAS
	Board neutrality (2)	D	D	D	D	D	X	D	D	D	X	X	X
6	Veil piercing	C	S	S	S	S	S	S	S	S	S	S	S
	Directors' duties to creditors	D	D	D	D	C	D	D	D	D	D	C	C
7	Challenge dividends	C	C	C	C	S	S	C	C	S	C	C	C
	Challenge payment	S	C	S	C	X	C	C	C	C	S	C	X

(continued)

Table A4 *(Continued)*

Chapter and topic		FRA	GER	ITA	SPA	NL	FIN	POL	LAT	UK	US	RSA	JP
8	Non-payment of dividends	MIS	X	X	X	MIS	MAS	MIS	MIS	MIS	MAS	MIS	MAS
	Interested shareholder	MAS	MAS	X	X	X	MAS	MAS	MAS	MAS	X	X	MIS
9	Q&As at shareholders' meeting	X	S	X	X	D	X	X	X	S	D	X	S
	Challenge resolution	MAS	MIS	MIS	X	MIS	MAS	MAS	MIS	MAS	X	MAS	X
10	Implicit shareholders' meeting	S	X	S	X	D	X	X	X	D	D	D	S
	Derivative action	S	D	S	S	D	S	D	D	S	S	S	S
11	Pre-emptive offer	X	MIS	MAS	MAS	MAS	MIS	MAS	MAS	MAS	MAS	MAS	MAS
	Inheriting shares	MIS	MIS	MIS	MAS	MAS	MIS	MIS	MIS	MAS	MAS	MAS	MAS

Notes: directors (D); all shareholders (S); minority shareholders (MIS); majority shareholders (MAS);[101] creditors (C); intermediate or unclear results (X).

---

[101] This includes rules that release directors from liability if approved by a shareholder majority.

Index